MIXED LEGAL SYSTEMS, EAST AND WEST

Juris Diversitas

Rooted in comparative law, the *Juris Diversitas* series focuses on the interdisciplinary study of legal and normative mixtures and movements. Our interest is in comparison broadly conceived, extending beyond law narrowly understood to related fields. Titles might be geographical or temporal comparisons. They could focus on theory and methodology, substantive law, or legal cultures. They could investigate official or unofficial 'legalities', past and present and around the world. And, to effectively cross spatial, temporal, and normative boundaries, inter- and multi-disciplinary research is particularly welcome.

Forthcoming title in the series

Of Doubt and Proof
Ritual and Legal Practices of Judgment
Edited by Daniela Berti, Anthony Good and Gilles Tarabout
ISBN 978 1 4724 3451 7

Mixed Legal Systems, East and West

Edited by

VERNON VALENTINE PALMER
Tulane University, USA

MOHAMED Y. MATTAR
Johns Hopkins University, USA

and

ANNA KOPPEL
Johns Hopkins University, USA

Routledge
Taylor & Francis Group
LONDON AND NEW YORK

First published 2015 by Ashgate Publishing

Published 2016 by Routledge
2 Park Square, Milton Park, Abingdon, Oxfordshire OX14 4RN
711 Third Avenue, New York, NY 10017, USA

First issued in paperback 2016

Routledge is an imprint of the Taylor & Francis Group, an informa business

British Library Cataloguing in Publication Data
A catalogue record for this book is available from the British Library

Library of Congress Cataloging-in-Publication Data
Mixed legal systems, east and west / by Vernon Valentine Palmer, Mohamed Y. Mattar and Anna Koppel
pages cm. — (Juris diversitas)
Includes bibliographical references and index.
ISBN 978-1-4724-3106-6 (hardback : alk. paper)
1. Legal polycentricity. I. Palmer, Vernon V., editor. II. Matar, Muhammad Yahya, editor. III. Koppel, Anna, editor.
K236.M59 2014
340.5—dc23

2014019261

ISBN 13: 978-1-138-63903-4 (pbk)
ISBN 13: 978-1-4724-3106-6 (hbk)

Contents

Part IV The Islamic Legal System and Western Legal Traditions

Part V Patterns of Mixing in Specialized Areas of the Law

List of Figures

Notes on Contributors

Pacifico Agabin is professor of law and chairman of the Constitutional Law Department of the Philippine Judicial Academy, which is a unit of the Philippine Supreme Court. At the academy, he lectures before judges on developments in constitutional law. He is also currently a member of the Executive Committee of the Philippine Mediation Center and of the Alternative Dispute Resolution Department of the Philippine Judicial Academy. In addition, he is a practicing lawyer and partner at the Agabin, Verzola & Layaoen Law Offices, where he specializes in appellate litigation. He is general counsel of the Integrated Bar of the Philippines and a professorial lecturer on constitutional law, legal history, and the legal method at the University of the Philippines College of Law. Previously, he was dean and professor of constitutional law at the College of Law, Lyceum of the Philippines University, and dean and professor of law at the College of Law, University of the Philippines. Among other academic and legal positions, he served as external counsel to the Senate of the Philippines, handling cases for the Senate involving constitutional issues. He has published and edited a number of books, including *Mestizo: The Story of the Philippine Legal System* (University of the Philippines College of Law, 2011) and *The Political Supreme Court* (University of the Philippines Press, 2012). Agabin received his LLB from the University of the Philippines and his SJD from Yale Law School with a specialization in constitutional law.

Biagio Andò is lecturer in comparative law at the Faculty of Political Science of the University of Catania, Italy. He was a visiting researcher at the Max Planck Institute for Comparative and International Private Law in Hamburg, Germany, in 2010 and 2012. In December 2011, he was one of the two promoters and a speaker at the conference "Costituzione, Globalizzazione e Tradizione Giuridica Europea", at the Kore University of Enna, Italy. In June 2011, he spoke on "Methodology and Innovation in Mixed Legal Systems" at the Third International Congress of the World Society of Mixed Jurisdiction Jurists, which took place at the Hebrew University of Jerusalem. During 2009 and 2011, he gave a series of lectures in a postgraduate course, "Customers' Care and Consumers' Protection", at the University of Catania. From 2002 to 2008, he lectured on commercial law at the Faculty of Political Science of the University of Catania, and in 2005, he lectured on English law at the London School of Economics and Political Science. Andò is author of a number of books and articles, including *Il Problema della Responsabilità delle Autorità di Vigilanza sui Mercati Finanziari* (Giuffre, 2008). In 1996, Andó received his law degree (cum laude), with a dissertation on private law titled "Unfair Terms in Consumer Contracts", and in 2003, he obtained his PhD in law and economics in international systems, with a thesis on liability in tort for financial false information, at the Sapienza University of Rome.

Kevin Aquilina is the dean of the Faculty of Laws at the University of Malta. He has served as chief executive of the Malta Broadcasting Authority and as chairman of Malta's Planning Appeals Board and the Press Ethics Commission. Aquilina lectures in administrative law and on the Maltese legal system. He holds a doctorate of philosophy in law from the London School of Economics and Political Science, an LLD from the University of Malta, and a master's degree in international maritime law from the International Maritime Law Institute, Malta.

Luis Muñiz Argüelles, a member of the International Academy of Comparative Law and of the World Society of Mixed Jurisdiction Jurists, holds a doctorate from the University of Paris II; a JD from the University of Puerto Rico; an MA from the Columbia University School of Journalism, New York; and a BA from Cornell University, Ithaca, New York. Since 1979, he has been professor at the University of Puerto Rico School of Law, where he has taught courses in property, obligations, secured transactions, comparative law, and conflicts of law and judicial administration, among others. He has also taught or lectured at universities in Argentina, Brazil, Canada, Lithuania, Spain, the United States, and Uruguay. He is author of several books on legal research, negotiation and mediation, and conflicts of laws and obligations and has written some 60 law review articles in Spanish, English, and French on topics including civil law, language law, and judicial administration. He has worked extensively with civil code revision.

Seyed Mostafa Mirmohammadi Azizi is a faculty member of the Department of Law at Mofid University in Qom, Iran, and the director of the Center for Comparative Legal Studies of Mofid University. He holds a PhD in international law from the University of Allameh Tabatabaei in Tehran, Iran. He has studied the Islamic sciences in Qom since 1981 and is the author of five books and more than 20 articles. Azizi served as the director of the Research Cooperation Office of Mofid University from 2001 to 2004 and is currently editor in chief of the Mofid University law journal. His areas of research and teaching interests include Islamic law, international law, comparative law, human rights law, humanitarian law, and children's rights.

Ignazio Castellucci is professor of Asian legal traditions and Chinese law at the University of Trento in Trento, Italy, and professor of comparative legal systems at the University of Macau, China. He is also a practicing lawyer admitted before the Italian Supreme Court and a fellow at the Chartered Institute of Arbitrators of London in the United Kingdom. Since 2001, he has served as senior editor of the UNILEX online database of world case law on UNIDROIT (International Institute for the Unification of Private Law) Principles and the United Nations Convention on Contracts for the International Sale of Goods. He has also served as associate to the Institute for Theory and Technique of Legal Information of the Italian National Research Council. He has previously served as assistant to the chairs of comparative law (Rome), civil law (Trento), and African law and institutions (Trento) and as lecturer on private law and family law at the University of Asmara, Eritrea. He founded and developed the University of Macau's master's program in European, international, and comparative law. He authored a research book on the Latin American legal system, wrote a student handbook on Asian legal systems, and edited a book on the Macau legal system (forthcoming). He also authored several articles published in different jurisdictions (China, Macau, Belgium, Italy, Switzerland, and the United States) on Chinese Law, Hong Kong and Macau issues, general comparative law and methodology, mixed jurisdictions, Roman law and legal history, African law, international commercial arbitration and legal reforms, transnational legal issues, and environmental law. Castellucci received his LLB from the University of Rome ("La Sapienza") magna cum laude, his LLM from the University of Rome ("La Sapienza") magna, and his PhD from the University of Trento.

Anton Cooray is professor of law at the City Law School, City University of London. He was formerly professor and associate dean of law at City University of Hong Kong. Prior to that, he was head of law and dean of law at the University of Colombo, Sri Lanka. Cooray graduated in law from the University of Colombo and received a PhD from the University of London as a commonwealth scholar. Later he returned to the University of London as a commonwealth academic fellow. His research publications cover diverse areas such as constitutional law, trusts law, and planning and environmental law. He has a special interest in comparative aspects of private and public law. He has published several journal articles on Sri Lanka's pluralist legal system, including "Comparative Law in a Small State: The Mixing of Indigenous Laws in Sri Lanka" in the *Interdisciplinary Studies of Comparative and Private International Law* (2011). His first contribution on the Sri Lanka's mixed legal system was "Asian Customary Laws through Western Eyes: A Comparison of Sri Lankan and Hong Kong Colonial Experience", in *Law, Society, and the State: Essays in Modern Legal History*, edited by Louis A. Knalfa and Susan W.S. Binnie (University of Toronto Press, 1995). Cooray has contributed chapters in books on mixed and mixing legal systems, especially books edited by Esin Örücü, and generally adopts a comparative approach in his research publications. He recently stepped down as editor of *Asia Pacific Law Review* (LexisNexis), which he edited for almost 20 years, and has launched a new journal, the *Journal of International and Comparative Law*, for Westlaw/Sweet & Maxwell.

Seán Patrick Donlan teaches in the School of Law of the University of Limerick, in Ireland. His teaching and research focus on comparative law, legal history, and legal theory. Donlan is particularly interested in mixed traditions and in legal (normative) pluralism. In addition to numerous articles, he coedited and contributed to *Comparative Law and Hybrid Legal Traditions* (Swiss Institute of Comparative Law, 2010). As president of Juris Diversitas, Donlan co-organized a conference in Malta in 2010 that resulted in a special issue of the

Journal of Civil Law Studies (2011). He also manages a project on Mediterranean hybridity, addressing the complexity of both its state laws and its nonstate norms. Donlan is secretary-general of both the World Society of Mixed Jurisdiction Jurists and the European Society for Comparative Legal History and is a member of the International Academy of Comparative Law. He was recently chosen to be the chief editor of the journal *Comparative Legal History*.

Sue Farran received her university education in South Africa and at Cambridge, UK, studying English and social anthropology before taking up law. Her academic career started at the University of Natal in Pietermaritizburg, South Africa, and has included posts at the University of the West of England, Bristol; the University of the South Pacific, Fiji and Vanuatu; and the University of Dundee, Scotland. She has also taught at the University of Angers, France; Jean Moulin University Lyons III, France; and Stamford College, Kuala Lumpur. She is currently a professor of laws at Northumbria University, Newcastle, UK, and an adjunct professor at the University of the South Pacific, Vanuatu. Farran's research interests are inspired by the island countries of the South Pacific and focus on issues of human rights, particularly as they pertain to the areas of land and its related resources, the family (especially women and children), and intellectual property rights. Case studies from the region inform and are informed by much larger themes and concerns such as legal pluralism and legal hybridity, development and sustainability, globalization, and legal colonialism. As a comparativist, Farran is interested in the interface between legal systems and normative frameworks within states and between states and the relationships among national, regional, and international players in shaping and developing legal responses to contemporary issues.

Charles Manga Fombad is a professor of law and head of the department of public law at the Faculty of Law, University of Pretoria, South Africa. He is also the head of the constitutional law unit of the Institute for International and Comparative Law in Africa, based at the Faculty of Law of the University of Pretoria. He holds a law degree from the University of Yaoundé, Cameroon; an LLM and PhD from the University of London; and a diploma in conflict resolution from Uppsala University, Sweden. He has taught at the University of Botswana, Gaborone (1997–2009) and the University of Yaoundé II (1988–1997) and was visiting professor at the Universities of Dschang and Buea in Cameroon. From 2003 to 2007, he was also a professor *extraordinarius* of the Department of Jurisprudence, School of Law at the University of South Africa, Pretoria. Fombad has written or edited eight books and has authored more than 60 articles in local and international peer-reviewed journals, more than a dozen chapters in books, numerous other publications and conference papers. In 2003, he received the Bobbert Association Prize for the best first article in the *Journal for Juridical Science* and was awarded the Wedderburn Prize for a paper that appeared in the *Modern Law Review*. Fombad received a special commendation award from the University of Botswana Research Awards Committee for research excellence in 2004, 2005, and 2007. Fombad is a member of the editorial board of several international journals and is founding editor in chief of the *University of Botswana Law Journal*, serving from 2005 to 2009. He is also a member of numerous professional associations. His research interests are in comparative constitutional law, delict (tort law), media law, international law, and legal history – especially issues of legal harmonization.

Naser Ghorbannia is faculty member and dean of the Department of Law at Mofid University in Qom, Iran. He holds a PhD in international law from Tehran University and has studied the Islamic sciences for more than 25 years in Qom. He served as the research deputy at Mofid University from 2004 to 2010 and was the editor in chief of the *Mofid University Law Journal* from 2008 to 2011. He was secretary of the scientific committee of the International Conference on Human Rights and Dialogue of Civilizations, which took place in Tehran in 2011. He is the author of six books and more than 50 research articles. His areas of teaching and research interests include Islamic law, international law, human rights law, humanitarian law, children's rights, women's rights, and bioethics.

Nikitas E. Hatzimihail obtained his law degree with first-class honors from the University of Athens (1995). He completed his graduate and doctoral studies at Harvard Law School (LLM 1997, SJD 2002), receiving fellowships from Fulbright Program in Greece, the Onassis Foundation, the Leventis Foundation, and the

Harvard Law School Byse and Lewis funds. At Harvard, he twice received the Addison-Brown commencement prize for written work on private international law. Prior to his appointment as assistant professor at the University of Cyprus (2006), Hatzimihail served as research fellow and then senior research fellow at the Université Libre de Bruxelles (2002–2006). He also taught graduate courses at the University of Athens Law Faculty (2005–2008). He has taught courses and seminars at Harvard Law School (Byse fellow, 2000); the University of Oklahoma College of Law (Crowe & Dunlevy visiting associate professor, 2001); and the Law Faculty of the Vietnam National University at Hanoi (short-term visiting professor, 2005). Hatzimihail has been a member of the Athens Bar since 1998, with practical experience principally in international commercial arbitration and business transactions. He also worked as adviser on legal and institutional affairs to the Greek minister on the Aegean and Island Policy (2005–2006). Hatzimihail is editor-in-chief of the Cypriot law review *Lysias*, published twice annually by the Nicosia Bar (in Greek). His research interests include private law, with an emphasis on contract law, European private law, and the theory and history of private law; private international law, including international civil litigation, commercial arbitration, and business and trade law; comparative law, with an emphasis on the Western legal tradition, mixed legal systems, and US law; and legal theory, with an emphasis on legal sociology and intellectual legal history. Selected publications include *Preclassical Conflicts of Laws* (forthcoming, Cambridge University Press); "The Many Lives – and Faces – of *Lex Mercatoria*: History as Genealogy in International Business Law", *Law and Contemporary Problems* (2008); *International Litigation in Intellectual Property and Information Technology* (Kluwer, 2008, as coeditor with Arnaud Nuyts and Katarzyna Szychowska); "Bartolus and the Conflict of Laws", *Revue Hellénique de Droit International* (2007); "Pages of History: Friedrich Juenger and the Historical Consciousness of Modern Private International Law", in *Tradition and Innovation of Private International Law at the Beginning of the Third Millennium* (Juris Publishing, 2006).

Nir Kedar is an associate professor (senior lecturer) of law and legal history at the Bar Ilan University Faculty of Law in Ramat Gan, Israel. Kedar has an LLB and a BA in history from Tel-Aviv University and an SJD from Harvard Law School. He clerked for the Honorable President of the Israeli Supreme Court Aharon Barak. His main fields of interest are Israeli, American, and modern European legal history, comparative law, and legal and political theory. In these fields, Kedar has published numerous articles and three books. His book *Mamlakhtiyut: David Ben-Gurion's Civic Thought* (Yad Ben-Zvi & Ben-Gurion University Press, 2009) won the Shapiro Prize for best book on Israel for 2009 from the International Association for Israel Studies. His second book, *Israeli Republicanism*, written with Avi Bareli, appeared in 2010 (Israel Democracy Institute). His third book, *Ben-Gurion and the Constitution: On Constitutionalism, Democracy, and Law in David Ben-Gurion's Policy* was set to be published in 2012.

Anna Koppel is director of research and development at The Protection Project at Johns Hopkins University School of Advanced International Studies. Ms. Koppel has more than 10 years of experience designing and carrying out research and training programs in the areas of international human rights law, comparative law, and the rule of law, especially in the Middle East region. She has worked extensively to facilitate international academic exchange in these fields and has organized numerous seminars bringing together scholars from all regions of the world. She has managed and continues to manage a number of multiyear international research and capacity-building projects related to the fields above and has edited and contributed to many of The Protection Project's academic publications. Ms. Koppel received her BS in psychology from the University of Maryland and her MA in international relations from The Johns Hopkins University School of Advanced International Studies. She is currently an MSt in international human rights law candidate at the University of Oxford.

Mohamed Y. Mattar is a senior research professor of international law and executive director of The Protection Project at The Johns Hopkins University, School of Advanced International Studies (SAIS), Washington, DC. He is also a non-resident distinguished professor of law at Alexandria University College of Law in Alexandria, Egypt. His professional expertise is in comparative and international law, especially international human rights and trafficking in persons. For over 15 years, Mattar has worked in more than 50 countries to promote state compliance with international human rights standards and has advised governments on drafting and implementing human rights legislation. He teaches courses on corporate social responsibility, international business and human rights, international trafficking in persons, Islamic law, and international contract law. His latest publication is "Article 43 of the Arab Charter on Human Rights: Reconciling National, Regional, and International Standards," *Harvard Human Rights Journal*, Volume 26, Spring 2013. He received his SJD and LLM from Tulane University in New Orleans, his MCL from the University of Miami, and his LLB from Alexandria University, Egypt.

David McQuoid-Mason, BComm (Natal), LLB (Natal), LLM (London), and PhD (Natal), is professor of law at the Centre for Socio-Legal Studies at the University of KwaZulu-Natal, Durban, South Africa. He is an advocate of the High Court of South Africa, founder of the South African Street Law program, and cofounder of the Democracy for All program. He is a fellow of the University of KwaZulu-Natal and was dean of the Howard College Law School, University of Natal, for 13 years. He began teaching law in 1971 and specializes in privacy law, medical law, access to justice, and legal education. He is chair of the Institute for Professional Legal Training and Street Law South Africa and chair and acting director of the Centre for Socio-Legal Studies at the University of KwaZulu-Natal. He established the first law clinic at the University of KwaZulu-Natal in 1973 and the first street law program in South Africa in 1986. He has been a member of the International Bar Association's continuing legal education panel for developing countries and has taught negotiation and mediation skills to law teachers, legal practitioners, and paralegals. He has facilitated training, curriculum, and materials development workshops on street law, human rights, and democracy in more than 100 countries and has helped draft legal aid legislation, advised on setting up and improving legal aid schemes, trained paralegals, helped develop paralegal advice offices and materials, provided professional legal training and clinical legal education training, and conducted medical law workshops. McQuoid-Mason has published more than 130 articles in law and medical journals, contributed more than 50 chapters to books, and authored or coauthored several books. He co-edits the *Journal for Juridical Science* and the *South African Journal of Bioethics and Law* and serves on the editorial boards of several other journals. In 2004, he was awarded a special mention by the United Nations Educational, Scientific, and Cultural Organization for his work in human rights education; in 2008, he was awarded a DCL (honoris causa) by the University of Windsor, Ontario, for his international work on access to justice; and in 2009, he received the Advocate of the Year Award by Street Law Inc. for his work in establishing street law legal literacy programs.

Daniel R. Mekonnen obtained his primary legal education in Eritrea where he served as, among other things, judge of the Zoba Maekel Provincial Court in Asmara. He obtained his LLM from the University of Stellenbosch, South Africa, in 2003 and his LLD from the University of the Free State, Bloemfontein, South Africa, in 2008. He has worked in a number of European universities as a postdoctoral researcher and lecturer. Recently, he was a Bank of Ireland Fellow at the Irish Centre for Human Rights at the National University of Ireland, Galway, where he taught a graduate course on international security law. Currently, a Georg Forster Postdoctoral Fellow, he is based at the Felsberg Institute for Education and Academic Research in Germany. His areas of teaching and research include comparative law, human rights, international criminal law, and transitional justice. During his stay in Felsberg, Mekonnen will be involved mainly in a research project "Blue Berets in Vain: A Critical Appraisal of the UN Peacekeeping Mission in Eritrea and Ethiopia".

Esin Örücü completed her LLB at Istanbul University in 1965. From 1968 to 1969, she studied at the London School of Economics and Political Science as a research student. In 1969, she received her PhD from Istanbul University, and in 1975, she became associate professor there. Between 1986 and 1999, she was honorary guest professor at Leiden University Faculty of Social Sciences and Faculty of Law in the Netherlands. Since 1976, she has taught jurisprudence and comparative law at Glasgow University School of Law in Scotland – as a lecturer between 1976 and 1983, as a senior lecturer between 1983 and 1992, and as a professor since 1992. She is professor emerita of comparative law at the University of Glasgow School of Law; honorary senior research fellow, University of Glasgow School of Law; emeritus professor of comparative law at Erasmus University Rotterdam, Faculty of Law; honorary professor of Turkish law at the University of Utrecht Faculty of Law; visiting professor of Turkish family law, Amsterdam Free University; visiting professor of comparative law, Okan University, Istanbul; and visiting professor of comparative law, Yeditepe University, Istanbul. Örücü is a member of the International Academy of Comparative Law and the World Society of Mixed Jurisdictions Jurists (former vice president), member of the advisory board of Juris Diversitas, and vice chair of the Scottish Association of Comparative Law. She was the first convener of the comparative law subject section of the Society of Legal Scholars (1998–2006) and is a member of the editorial advisory board of the *Journal of Comparative Law*. Örücü occasionally teaches comparative law theory at the European Academy of Legal Theory in Brussels. Her research interests include comparative law methodology; transmigration of laws; changing paradigms in the new world order; mixed jurisdictions; systems in transition, legal systems and legal cultures, and convergence and divergence between legal systems and cultures; problems of the recipient systems in legal export–import, transpositions; core of rights; comparative jurisprudence; and Turkish law, culture, and language. Örücü holds an honorary degree from the University of Uppsala, Sweden, granted in 2009; a BA from the American College for Girls, Istanbul, 1961; an LLB from the Faculty of Law, University of Istanbul, 1965; a PhD from the Faculty of Law, University of Istanbul, 1970; and a Doçent Degree (higher PhD) from the Faculty of Law, University of Istanbul, 1975.

Vernon Valentine Palmer is the Thomas Pickles Professor of Law and Codirector of the Eason Weinmann Center for International and Comparative Law at Tulane University in New Orleans. He is best known for his work in the field of comparative law. He is a titular life member of the International Academy of Comparative Law, and his scholarly work now includes more than 12 books and 50 articles, much of it emphasizing the value of comparative law as a means of understanding the interaction between common law and civil law in world legal systems. Dr. Palmer is the founder of the World Society of Mixed Jurisdiction Jurists. He has held faculty appointments at universities around the world, including La Sorbonne in Paris and universities in Barcelona, Spain; Fribourg, Geneva, and Lausanne, Switzerland; Hamburg, Germany; Martinique; Trento, Italy; and Strasbourg, France. In 2012, he paid a research visit to Tokyo. Palmer graduated from the Tulane Law School with law review honors, received an MA in law from Yale Law School, a DPhil from Pembroke College of Oxford University, and a doctorate *honoris causa* from Paris Dauphine University.

Christa Rautenbach was in the employ of the South African Department of Justice as a prosecutor before she became a professor at the faculty of law, North-West University (Potchefstroom Campus), South Africa. Her qualifications include BJuris, LLB, LLM, and LLD. She is also a part-time practicing advocate of the High Court of South Africa. Currently, she teaches legal pluralism and law of succession to undergraduate and postgraduate students and is actively involved in researching issues pertaining to African customary law, religious legal systems, legal pluralism, and cultural diversity. She has published extensively on these subjects in national and international journals and also has made numerous presentations at national and international conferences. She is an Alexander von Humboldt alumna and undertook several research visits to the Max Planck Institute for Comparative Public Law and International Law in Heidelberg, Germany. Other research visits include the Van Vollenhoven Institute, Leiden, the Netherlands; Melbourne University, Australia; Tilburg University, the Netherlands; and the School of Oriental and African Studies, London. She is coeditor or coauthor of a number of textbooks or chapters in textbooks, including "Customary Law of Succession and Inheritance", in *Law of South Africa* (LexisNexis, 2009); *Introduction to Legal Pluralism in South Africa* (LexisNexis, 2010); and *Law of Succession in South Africa* (Oxford University Press, 2009). She is also coeditor of customary law for the *Potchefstroom Electronic Law Journal*.

Hossein Mir Mohammad Sadeghi is professor of law at the Faculty of Law of Shahid Beheshti University in Tehran, Iran. He also serves as the director of the Department of Criminal Law and Criminology at the Faculty of Law of Shahid Beheshti University, as well as director of the Education and Research Institute of Iran's Chamber of Commerce, Industries, and Mines. He is former dean of Iran's judiciary faculty of Judicial Sciences (1994–2006) and former deputy head of the Iranian Judiciary's Education and Research (2002–2004). He is author of numerous books and articles on criminal law, comparative law, and contract law. He holds a PhD from the University of Liverpool, an MPhil from the University of London, and an LLM from the University of London.

Mohamed Ahmed Serag is professor of Islamic studies at the Department of Arab and Islamic Studies at the American University in Cairo. He has also served as professor of Arabic Studies at the Department of Arab and Islamic Civilization at the American University in Cairo; professor and head of the Islamic Law Department at the Alexandria University Faculty of Law, Egypt; visiting professor at Sana'a University in Yemen; chair of the Department of Islamic Law at Cairo University; assistant and associate professor of law at the International Islamic University in Islamabad; and associate professor of Islamic Studies at Cairo University. He has authored, translated, and co-edited numerous books on Islamic law, including books on the Islamic law of trusts; Islamic legal theory and practice; Islamic laws of contract, inheritance, and bequests; the Islamic banking system; and torts in Islam.

Mathilda Twomey is a native of Seychelles and has been a resident of Ireland since 1995. She graduated from the University of Kent at Canterbury, United Kingdom, with a BA in English and French law in 1986 and a law degree from the Université de Paris-Sud in 1985. She was admitted to the Bar of England and Wales in 1987 and practiced in Seychelles as a barrister. She subsequently has had eclectic legal practice and training. She was a member of the Seychelles Constitutional Commission in 1993, which was charged with drafting the third constitution of Seychelles. She worked and campaigned in the disability law sector in Ireland. She graduated with an LLM in public law from the National University of Ireland, Galway. She has written and advised about the maritime piracy difficulties currently being faced by Seychelles. She has tutored in tort and contract and is currently undertaking a PhD in the area of comparative law. The working title of her PhD thesis is "Legal Métissage: The Mixing of Common Law and Civil Law in Seychelles". She was appointed judge on the Seychelles Court of Appeal in 2011.

Mohd Zakhiri Md Nor underwent his legal studies and worked extensively as an advocate and solicitor at Messrs. Idris Zaidel & Partners, specializing in Islamic banking and finance. He was an in-house counsel for the Felda Group of Companies, managing the group's day-to-day legal affairs, including corporate, industrial relations, and company secretarial matters. He was also admitted as a Syar'e lawyer of the federal territory of Kuala Lumpur. Currently, he is on leave for three years studying for his PhD at the International Centre for Education in Islamic Finance (INCEIF). His PhD research focuses on the interaction between *fatawa*, Shari'a rulings, resolutions, and conventional laws in the contemporary Islamic finance and is under the supervision of Zainal Azam Abd Rahman and Ashraf Md Hashim. He was a research assistant at the International Shari'ah Research Academy for Islamic Finance. Zakhiri is currently a law lecturer (Islamic banking and finance) at the College of Law, Government, and International Studies at Universiti Utara Malaysia and recently was appointed as a Shari'a committee member at a local development bank in Malaysia. At many colleges, he has lectured on business law, company and employment law, Islamic finance, and *Fiqh al-Mu'amalat*. He graduated from the International Islamic University, receiving both an LLB and LLB (Shari'a) with honors and earned a master of comparative laws and CIFP from INCEIF. He has presented many papers locally and abroad and is fluent in English and Arabic.

Preface

Vernon Valentine Palmer and Mohamed Y. Mattar

The essays in this book represent the attempt of numerous scholars to stretch the goals and the bounds of comparative law and to bring it into closer contact with the rapidly mixing globalized environment of the twenty-first century.

In our view, traditional comparative law is rightly criticized for being too Western-centric and preoccupied only with civil law and common law differences. It is also rightly criticized for usually focusing on a few large countries or the so-called seminal systems, such as those found in Germany, France, and the United Kingdom, while ignoring the fascinating pluralism of the smaller systems of the world. And comparative law is rightly criticized for almost entirely neglecting the non-Western indigenous and religious law that makes up such a large part of our legal universe.

This book's rich collection of essays offsets some of these deficiencies and takes us far beyond not only the usual focus of comparative law but beyond the *locus* of traditional mixed jurisdictions. Merely scanning the table of contents is sufficient to see it is an outreach to small mixed systems such as Malta, Seychelles, Cyprus, Vanuatu, Cameroon, and Eritrea. In some cases, legal developments within these countries are completely unknown to Western lawyers, and these accounts may be some of the first available in English. But this collection is far more than that.

It also opens a window on the world of Islamic law as it coexists or competes with other religious systems and customary laws. The interesting value added for the reader is that these chapters look at unfamiliar *non-Western* laws, the laws that govern the vast majority of these countries' inhabitants. Similarly, another chapter sheds light on the least known and most under-researched facet of the world's largest mixed jurisdiction—the customary laws of the indigenous Philippine peoples.

Finally, a number of these chapters focus directly on the Middle East and the particular role of Islamic law in Egypt, Iran, and Turkey. We have noticed that, in the past, scholars dealing with the Middle East have not collaborated with or drawn on the scholarship of their colleagues studying mixed jurisdictions, and mixed jurisdiction scholars have equally ignored the work of specialists on the Middle East. This omission is, of course, a mutual mistake, for we do not believe that the study of mixed jurisdictions and the study of mixed systems should be entirely separate. We hope that the present book may serve as a template for more dialogue and cross-pollination, not only between Western specialists, but also between comparative law colleagues in the East and the West.

We take this opportunity to thank Anna Koppel of the Protection Project and Johns Hopkins University for her great skills and dedication in organizing our 2012 Malta conference, which brought colleagues together and gave rise to these chapters. We also thank her for all her additional work in readying the conference papers for publication. Special thanks are also due to the Protection Project for its generous financial support of the conference and the Eason Weinmann Center for International and Comparative Law, Tulane University, and the European Mediterranean University (EMUNI) and Joseph Mifsud, its president from November 2008 through April 2013, for co-sponsoring the event. We wish to also thank Seán Donlan, general secretary of the World Society of Mixed Jurisdiction Jurists, who was very kind in suggesting and contacting our publisher. Finally, as a personal note, Vernon Palmer would like to thank his colleague and coeditor, Dr. Mohamed Mattar, for everything he has done to promote this unique comparative law venture.

October 1, 2014
New Orleans and Washington D.C.

List of Abbreviations

BMA	British Military Administration
CCJA	Common Court of Justice and Arbitration
CSBDS	Committee for the Settlement of Banking Disputes of SAMA (Saudi Arabia)
CSNID	Committee for the Settlement of Negotiable Instrument Disputes (Saudi Arabia)
EPLF	Eritrean People's Liberation Front
EU	European Union
FMB	Financial Mediation Bureau (Malaysia)
ICC	Indigenous cultural community
ICJ	International Court of Justice
IP	Indigenous people
KLRCA	Kuala Lumpur Regional Centre for Arbitration
OHADA	Organisation pour l'Harmonisation en Afrique du Droit des Affaires, or Organization for the Harmonization of Business Law in Africa
PFDJ	People's Front for Democracy and Justice (Eritrea)
SAMA	Saudi Authority Monetary Agency
UN	United Nations
YÖK	Yükseköğretim Kurulu, or Council of Higher Education (Turkey)

Part I
The Contemporary Nature of Mixed Legal Systems

Chapter 1
"As Slippery as an Eel"? Comparative Law and Polyjural Systems

Biagio Andò

This chapter's focus is on *polyjural* systems—that is, systems that are built on several different legal traditions whose contribution to the recipient legal system is individually discernible—and on the gauntlets such systems throw down to those comparative law scholars who try to understand how they work in practice.[1]

In this chapter, I will use some general concepts that recur in comparative analysis of legal systems (such as the concept of legal tradition or legal culture). Because of their wide use and consequent high degree of vagueness, I will explain briefly, for the ease of the reader, the way in which the key concepts will be used throughout this chapter.[2]

The expression *legal system* will be used when the aim is to emphasize the importance of formal written provisions. *Legal tradition*,[3] which will be discussed in more detail later in the chapter, highlights conceptual units that are wider or narrower than national legal systems. *Legal culture*[4] refers to the style of thought and the patterns of reasoning within and about the law pursued by jurists of the recipient system[5] and thus affecting the reconstruction of the set of meanings of written rules (Cotterell 2006).

1 I prefer the word *polyjural* to the term *mixed*, although the latter is more often used. In my opinion, polyjural expresses better the variety of disparate elements that can be traced back to different legal traditions and legal cultures. Although I use a different word to indicate these systems, I accept the good definition used for mixed systems by Palmer (2008: 24): as "political entities where two … systems apply cumulatively or interactively, but also entities where there is a juxtaposition of systems as a result of more or less clearly defined fields of application."

2 However, for ease of understanding, the reader may find that, instead of paying attention to definitions, whose importance is relative, a better strategy may be to focus on the different perceptions of law that lie beneath the words.

3 See Glenn (2010), whose ideas will be discussed in further detail later in the chapter.

4 In this work, legal culture is seen as a constituent of legal tradition. Merryman and Peréz-Perdomo (2007: 1) understand legal tradition and legal culture as aspects of the same phenomenon, consisting in "a set of deeply rooted, historically conditioned attitudes about the nature and role of law in society, the proper organization and operation of the legal system, the way law is or should be made, applied, studied, perfected and taught; the legal culture or tradition relating the legal system to the culture of which it is a partial expression." A different view of these phenomena will be introduced later in this chapter.

5 On this point, reference can be made, among many others, to Nelken (2007: 109–11), who observes that "taken generally, the terms 'law' and 'culture' when brought together cover a large range of possible permutations of law in culture or culture in law: … These meanings can include law seen as a cultural artefact … ; law as it becomes present in every-day life experience or as filtered through the media …, or even the significance of law in accommodating cultural defences or protecting cultural treasures.… In one common use (outside of English-language jurisdictions) the term signifies the aspiration towards the 'culture of legality.'" Ewald (1995a) advocates the need to make recourse to "comparative jurisprudence" to understand foreign legal systems. Ewald (1995a: 1948–49) explains his conception of comparative law in these terms: "[T]his conception of comparative law rests, as it must, on a philosophical view about what law is. That view needs to be spelled out in detail; but for the present it can be said that, for the purposes of comparative law, law is best viewed not as a collection of rules, nor as a device for maximizing the wealth of the society, nor as the commands of sovereign, nor as a reflection of timeless truths about the universe, but as a kind of conscious mental activity, and above all as the record of the attempts, by jurists, in light of their conception of law, to arrive at the correct answers to legal questions." This effort would be useful—according to Ewald—not only to achieve a deeper theoretical understanding of law, but also, at an operational level, to satisfy practical needs of society.

This topic not only implies a profound awareness of some comparative law key concepts, but also deals with some complex issues relevant at the level of comparative law methodology. The links between these latter and the field of inquiry are two-way: on the one hand, a grasp of the general issues, such as admissibility of legal transplants and patterns of development of European private law, is necessary to deal with this theme; on the other hand, the specific topic discussed in these pages provides a deeper comprehension of those general issues.

As to the first aspect, the theme of polyjural systems may give an insight into the patterns through which legal transplants may occur.[6] Polyjurality is the effect of the interaction or mutual influence of autochthonous law and foreign law in a sociolegal context that is other than the one the foreign law comes from. It is a consequence of a massive reception of foreign law occurring in two alternative ways: either through spontaneous reception or through imposition by a colonial power.

Spontaneous reception is the by-product of several factors, such as the role that is played by the autochthonous legal culture during the reception of these materials and which lies behind *that* change.[7] Studying how this reception occurred may help us understand whether the reception of legal materials may be deemed a response to societal needs, so that a symmetrical relationship between law and society may be depicted (as so-called mirror theories suggest),[8] or whether law evolves in a rather independent and dysfunctional way,[9] as the result of the initiative of minorities or elites.[10]

Arguably the mind-set of jurists has a primary role in polyjural systems, greatly affecting the ways in which rules coming from different traditions were combined and accommodated within the same system.[11] Therefore, to seize the ways in which the legal culture produced the set of meanings necessary to assimilate

6 With respect to the issue of voluntary reception, the question is whether grafting legal materials into a different soil from that of origin leaves them unchanged and whether the autochthonous legal culture does not play any effective role or the local factors play an active role in this regard. Thus, the word *transplant* would be nothing but an oversimplified metaphor hiding a far more complex interaction between *exporters* and *recipients*. Transplants are metaphors, according to Nelken (2002). Twining (2005: 204) points out the characteristics of a "naive model of diffusion" in two main characteristics: (a) a "direct one-way transfer" of legal rules involving formal enactment or adoption without major change and (b) a transfer occurring from an "advanced system" to a "less developed" system to satisfy a need of modernization. Twining defines this model as "naive" because it would not be able to explain why a transplant is successful, contenting itself with the easy justification that if a transplant occurs successfully, it works in the reception context. This model, defined "the country and western tradition of comparative law," is marked by "an almost exclusive focus on municipal law of major … legal systems, and an over-simple model of diffusion" (Twining 2005: 213). Örücü (2002b: 206) shows a critical attitude toward the concept of legal transplants, stating that "the legal transplant theory [is] in need of refinement." Law to Örücü is "a series of transposition and tuning."

7 The issue of legal transplants is part of the wider one of the relationship between society and legal change. This relationship is a matter of interest not only for comparative law scholars, but also for sociologists of law, legal theoreticians, and comparative law scholars. These issues are closely linked questions in Alan Watson's works (see, for example, Watson 1993; 2001). All these aspects are gathered under the expression *diffusion of law*. On diffusion of law, see Twining (2004; 2006; 2007).

8 Mirror theories are understood not as a single theory, but "rather as a *class* of theories," according to Ewald (1995b: 493), who summarizes them in the following way: "Nothing in the law is autonomous; rather, law is a mirror of X, and every aspect of the law is molded by X. In other words, this class of theories varies according to the choice of X; and … different (non-legal!) values: geography, religion, the Weltgeist, market economics, power-relations, the interest of the dominant class, or whatever."

9 This idea is the core of Alan Watson's position.

10 Legal history may help us understand the interaction of law and society when attention is focused on specific experiences (Donlan 2011b).

11 As to the possible strategies used by a legal culture to cope with "others," see Monateri (2001: 6–7), who identifies the strategy of "insulation" and the opposite one of "unification," which is pursued by searching for a common core among different experiences. According to Berman (2010: 11–12), "legal pluralists have long charted this process of negotiation, noting, for example, that colonial legal systems did not eradicate indigenous systems (even when they tried to). Instead, there was a layering and intermingling of systems. And, just as important, actors strategically used the variety of fora to gain leverage and make their voices heard."

the legal foreign materials and to enable them to be enforced,[12] one must pay attention to the sociolegal context in which rules are bound to work.[13]

From a more specifically European viewpoint, the study of polyjural systems may be assessed—and some years ago a scholar attempted to make such an assessment (Smits 2001; 2002; see also Kötz 2003)—as a useful paradigm to understand how the development of a common European private law may occur despite the clear and huge differences existing among national legal systems.

In the following pages, I will not attempt to propose either a new approach or new definitions. My aim is more modest. I will try to frame the topic, moving from the methods and definitions suggested by some scholars whose approach to the subject seems to me particularly significant. I will try to highlight their conceptual and theoretical apparatus (and also their practical goals). The definition of *mixed systems* or *mixed jurisdictions* is widely used by those involved in the study of these complex entities.[14] I will attempt to clarify this term for those making recourse to it.

---

12 For the assumption of the lack of a systematic theory of diffusion of law, see Twining (2005: 204–205), according to whom the most widespread model of diffusion is the "naive" one, involving a "bipolar relationship between two countries involving a direct one-way transfer of legal rules or institutions through the agency of governments involving formal enactment or adoption at a particular moment of time (a reception date) without major change." Monateri (2001: 3) argues against the mechanical conception reducing the "import and export of legal models" to a process of commodification of legal rules. Monateri's thesis rests on three basic arguments. First, law, being a complex phenomenon not reducible to written legal rules, has to be understood as a "narrative," through a process of communication used by a culture to define itself. Second, this narrative is made by elites. Third, those elites govern the process of borrowing. Monateri acknowledges his debt to Watson's (1993) theory of transplants and Sacco's (1991) theory on formants. From Watson, Monateri takes the idea that the borrowing is due to the initiative of some elites. From Sacco, he takes the idea that law, a wider phenomenon than that of written legal rules, is a social activity that is the result of the combined influence of diverse social groups. Sacco (1991: 21) strongly challenges the principle of unity of legal systems, consisting in the idea "that in a given country at a given moment the rule contained in the constitution or in legislation, the rule formulated by scholars, the rule declared by courts, and the rule actually enforced by courts, have an identical content and are therefore the same. Within a given legal system, the jurists assume this unity. Their main goal is to discover 'the legal rule' of their system." According to Sacco (1991: 22), this assumption would be an unrealistic view of how the system works, because "even the jurist who seeks a single legal rule, indeed who proceeds from the axiom that there can be only one rule in force, recognizes implicitly that living law contains many different elements such as statutory rules, the formulations of scholars, and the decisions of judges—elements that he keeps separate in his own thinking. In this essay, we will call them, borrowing from phonetics, the 'legal formants.'" Monateri's (2001: 6–7) conclusion is that "the meaning of the borrowed institutions will depend only on the struggle among the formants of the receiving system, which almost always will produce something different from the original." The ideology of the receiving system is not the result of local factors, but the effect of contaminants coming from outside.

13 Marini challenges the validity for comparative law of the traditional dichotomy between legal rules and socioeconomic context. Marini (2010: 2) writes that "la dicotomia è stata rimessa in discussione dall'ormai acquisita consapevolezza che molte delle osservazioni che entrano a dar corpo al dato culturale non possono essere ignorate da nessun metodo che si proponga di realizzare una seria comparazione" (this dichotomy is challenged because remarks grounded on culture cannot be disregarded in a comparative law survey). See also Wise (1990: 21), who conceives of "law as a system of meaning by which human experience is shaped and represented—a peculiarly important system, not just a language game played by lawyers for their own profit and amusement. Law cuts across all social life, creating and maintaining ideas of right and wrong and modes of visualizing and describing human relationships. It is so closely woven into the texture of society that no neat dichotomy is possible between legal and extra-legal or 'social reality.' The two are inextricably intertwined: specialised legal discourse is both a prototype and dialect of social speech."

14 On the issue of the meaning of 'mixed systems,' see Palmer (2008) and Örücü (2010: 19ff). In his essay, Palmer (2008:6, 13) conceives of mixed systems as "a group of systems whose private law was a western hybrid, characterized by a core of common law and civil law elements" and based on subjective opinion and a pluralist conception, whose "principal criterion" is "simply the presence or interaction of two or more kinds of laws or legal traditions within the same system or 'social field.'" This perspective is picked up again in Palmer (2012b).

Two Significant Attempts to Explain the Phenomenon of Polyjural Systems: The Approaches of Palmer and Örücü

Terms currently used in comparative law scholarship (such as *mixed jurisdictions*) are the by-product of theorizing efforts; they are not part of the language of a given lawmaker. There is no uniform approach to mixed jurisdictions, nor is there a common methodology to identify the main characteristics of such jurisdictions. I will therefore deal with two specific approaches, those by Palmer and Örücü, and I will do so in two stages. First, I will sketch a neutral (insofar as it is possible) description of the two approaches, and then I will attempt a critical appraisal.

Regarding the first point, some implicit premises are common to both Palmer and Örücü:

1. Both authors believe that mixed systems cannot be considered as exceptions or anomalies today. They are no longer considered isolated entities.[15]
2. Both authors feel the need for a classificatory grid, and thus they restrain the scope of their survey (even if they do so in different ways).
3. Both approaches agree that, to avoid a superficial comprehension of those jurisdictions, a survey cannot be bound to the analysis of legal rules. Law has to be put in context. Both Örücü and Palmer (though in different ways) call for the need to go beyond formal law.

However, there are also some important differences in their approaches:

- The object of their analysis is different. Whereas in Palmer's work the key concept is jurisdiction, in Örücü's work it is "system" (a notion that is used in some examples with a meaning different from that of state legal order).
- Palmer's approach is much more specific than Örücü's. It focuses on those entities dominated by polyjurality, especially jurisdictions that rest on civil and common law foundations.

To better explain the differences between these two approaches, I will consider them in turn.

The Cultural Roots and the Corollaries of Palmer's Approach

Palmer's approach is at the same time traditional and new.[16] It is traditional because Palmer's reasoning is grounded on the concept of *legal families*,[17] a deeply rooted idea in comparative legal systemology.[18] However, here the concept of legal family is used to group legal systems that are dissimilar from those usually considered in that they show peculiar traits and do not exhibit the unity and coherence of "pure" jurisdictions that form traditional legal families.

15 The way of looking at mixed legal experiences was rooted in the dichotomy rule: pure systems versus exceptions (mixed systems). Glenn (1996: 1) reconstructs the process of creation of the mixed system concept: "[T]he concept of a mixed legal system appears to have been a creation of nineteenth- and twentieth-century doctrine, which was largely transfixed by the idea of law as a pure and national product, capable of construction in the form of autonomous systems. Where this intellectual construction became too obviously strained in its application to a particular country or jurisdiction, resort was had to the scientific tradition of the anomaly—the unexplainable though marginal case, which remained for the time being outside the explanatory power of general scientific theory."

16 A thorough description of Palmer's theories can be found in Palmer (2012a). In this work, nine mixed jurisdictions are examined in as many reports. See also Du Plessis (2006), whose survey is largely indebted to Palmer's survey.

17 On the concept of families of law, see among others Krislov (1985) and Podgorecki (1985).

18 With the neologism *systemology*, I mean that particular branch of comparative law devoted to macrocomparison—that is, the branch involved in the study of legal systems.

Legal systems were usually conceived as coherent orders with distinct, clear-cut constitutive elements.[19] Systems showing features that made them hybrid[20] were not considered influential experiences, because they did not disclose common patterns or resemblances among themselves.[21] This anomaly condemned them to what has been aptly defined by Du Plessis (2006: 480) as a "classificatory limbo."

Today the position assessing polyjural systems as entities in isolation has to be considered a relic of the past.[22] Scholars living in these jurisdictions have recently started an enhanced dialogue to encourage mutual intelligibility between their systems. These systems are now considered to be a relevant ground for a comparative law survey. A change in perspective has occurred.

This change was fostered by the pioneering inquiries of Walton (1899), Lee (1915), and Amos (1937). These studies shed light on systems that could not be classified under either the civil law or the common law label because their ingredients did not fit well into either. Walton (1899) remarked that some systems—such as Quebec, Louisiana, and Scotland—were a kind of hybrid occupying a position midway between common law and civil law, because they had features that were amenable to both.

Lee's (1915) contribution was twofold. On the one hand, on the ground of terminology, he coined the word *mixed* to define those systems whose peculiar features made them not suitable to fit into the traditional categories in which the world's legal systems were mapped. On the other hand, he widened the scope of the survey in comparison with that made by Walton and extended it to more systems. Lee attempted to show how civil tradition managed to resist the ever-increasing invasion of common law into areas that were traditionally civil realms. Later, an important figure in this field of study was Smith (1965: 4), who often used the expression *mixed jurisdictions* for those entities, "basically … civilian," "that had been under pressure from the Anglo-American common law and … in part … overlaid by that rival system of jurisprudence."

Smith's most significant contribution to the growth and development of this area of studies was the idea that identifying the specific relationship between the common law and the civil law constituents was essential to define the identity of those systems. He noted that the identity of each of those legal systems was not unique. Conversely, Smith (1965) observed that these experiences were worthy of study, because they could be useful for their "neighbours in law" (that is, for the other mixed jurisdictions). Mixed jurisdictions came out of isolation and became a useful ground of comparison by studying those legal issues that they held in

---

19 In this group, leading authors include David and Jauffret Spinosi (2004) and Zweigert and Kötz (1998).

20 By *hybrid systems*, I mean those that cannot be clearly classified in any of the accepted legal families and are not based on the dual foundations of common law and civil law traditions.

21 David's approach rests on a state-centric (because of a Eurocentric) conception of legal systems. The result is a lack of care for systems that were expressions of other cultures. I agree with the remark made by Monateri (2001: 5) that the act of dividing "the legal world into legal families, through the tracing back of common roots," is a creation of "genealogies to explain the present. Genealogies serve to define who we think we are, or would like to think we are. They define an 'us' and 'them,' and they are an essential mechanism of how identities are constructed. The 'tracing back of the roots' is a work of representation." This last statement can be understood if linked to the passage dedicated by Monateri (2001: 6) to the meaning that has to be attributed to comparative law as a discipline: "[W]e can see how much it has been an attempt to meet different audiences, and their expectations. Which is to say that comparative law has not normally been 'transnational' at all, but rather it has grown within the frameworks of different legal traditions, responding to the inner needs of legal élites." Within the concept of legal family, hybridity is of little importance. As Donlan remarks in Chapter 2, "hybridity challenges … the dissection of plural and dynamic traditions into discrete, closed families or systems. More critically, hybridity undermines commonly held and conjoined beliefs in legal nationalism and positivism, legal centralism and monism."

22 The idea of isolation as a clue used in the past to understand the phenomenon of mixed jurisdictions is developed in a passage by Reid (2003: 7): "A striking characteristic of mixed jurisdictions, viewed historically, is their mutual isolation. Partly this was a matter of geography. Mixed jurisdictions were often the products of failed colonialism.… But isolation is also in part an attitude of mind. That mixed jurisdictions form a coherent grouping, a 'third legal family' even, is a modern idea, and some would say a forced one. But if 'family' is the correct term, it is a family in which the members were, for many years, estranged and often hardly aware of each other's existence. There is no developed body of mixed jurisdictions law, nor even a literature articulating shared ideas and concerns. For the most part lawyers in mixed jurisdictions have been ignorant of, or indifferent to, the law of other mixed jurisdictions."

common (Smith 1965).[23] Smith's interest—far from being merely scientific—was rather practical. Because Smith was strongly oriented toward the civil law tradition, his survey was aimed at understanding if in those systems the civil law tradition could resist attacks by common law.

Palmer's position did not, therefore, blossom like a flower in a desert. He walked on the path paved by the aforementioned scholars and refined their theories on mixed jurisdictions. In Palmer's (2012b: 373) view, the taxonomy *mixed jurisdictions* encompasses those systems that, despite "the indisputable diversity of peoples, cultures, languages, climates, religions, economies, and indigenous laws existing among them," share some characteristics, which this chapter will discuss further.

The first feature Palmer singles out is the specificity of the mixture, because those systems have their roots in civil law and in common law. These two traditions affect distinct areas of the legal system, playing the role of building blocks: the civil law tradition molds the field of private law, whereas the common law tradition shapes the fields of procedural, constitutional, and commercial law.[24] Second, Palmer notes that this coexistence of different roots is accepted and considered obvious by those who live and work within those legal systems.[25]

The third important characteristic is that of "mentality," a factor that encompasses the ways in which scholars who are insiders in mixed systems conceive of law. Palmer singles out three kinds of scholars at work in mixed jurisdictions: the *purists*, who have been educated according to civil legal culture and resist the interferences of common law;[26] the *pragmatists*, who are open to contamination by civil and common law; and the *pollutionists*, who are in favor of Anglo-American law because they believe in its superiority.

A Different Perspective on Mixed Systems: Örücü's Approach

Örücü's approach has a wider scope than Palmer's. Palmer's approach aims at putting together specific systems sharing some features, and therefore Palmer's focus is on the criteria ascertaining *what* a mixed system is. Nonetheless, Örücü's effort seems aimed at formulating a theory able to explain the phenomenon of mixes that results from the interaction of laws of a different type or source. Therefore, Örücü's focus is on *how* a system may be mixed.

The differences between Palmer's and Örücü's approaches concern the taxonomies used to describe their object of analysis: Palmer's focus is on mixed jurisdictions, whereas Örücü (1996) refers to mixed legal systems. Palmer looks at a set of institutions, principles, and rules enacted in a given territory, whereas Örücü's analysis goes beyond the scale of state. Her approach looks at all kind of mixes at the state, intrastate, and supranational levels. Although Palmer's approach is grounded on exclusion (as the entities examined are restricted to a specific group sharing some basic features), the keyword that best summarizes Örücü's approach is the opposite of exclusion—expansion (Örücü 2008).

23 As Reid (2003: 12) remarked, "the focus of Smith's attention was not the intricate interplay of common law and civil law nor the idea of mixed systems as a laboratory of comparative law. Nor was he much interested in those systems where common law had gained the upper hand. But in the more robust of the mixed jurisdictions—in South Africa, and in … Quebec and Louisiana … —Smith saw both an example for Scotland and a source of practical help."

24 To avoid the risk of a too simplistic statement, Palmer (2012a: 10) warns that "the content of these respective spheres is never *purely* civil nor *purely* common, but it will be *predominantly* of one kind rather than the other." According to Cashin Ritaine (2010: 146), the technique of classification that is based on building blocks and is focused on legal sources and legal techniques is "an attempt at adopting a DNA approach to law."

25 This characteristic is the quantitative and psychological element. It is defined as quantitative in the sense that a quantitative threshold has to be overcome before the presence of polyjurality will be perceived as obvious.

26 A clear example of a purist scholar is Smith (1975), who thinks that the bulk of mixed jurisdictions is caught in the fact that "mixed systems have been basically civilian, but subsequently were penetrated or overlaid by common law influences." According to Smith, the influence of English law is a distortion of the civil nature of the Scottish system and particularly of its coherence and systematic nature. The penetration of common law was due to "new" legal issues that were dealt with by common law on the assumption that the common law principles were found to correspond to judicial common sense.

What is disclosed by Palmer would be but one specific kind of mixing (resulting from the encounter of civil and common law traditions, defined by Örücü as simple), whereas other elements could affect the blend of mixed systems, such as the chthonic, religious, and customary ones interacting with one of the two main legal traditions and thus giving rise to other kinds of mixes. This approach is not restricted to Europe or to the Western world; it applies also to other contemporary mixed systems and to systems in transition. The resulting mix would depend on the degree of closeness or similarity among the factors forming the blend, according to the greater or lesser points of contact among the legal and social cultures of the blended traditions. The mixes could be accommodated on a spectrum (Örücü 2008: 12). At one end are those mixes that form a compound of elements from different legal traditions that lost their identity in the mixed system and, because of their strong affinity on sociocultural and legal-cultural grounds, are indistinguishable within the new entity. At the other end are the dysfunctional mixes—those that are not able to work correctly because of the huge differences in their traditions. In the middle, the systems in which the different elements coming from the diverse traditions are recognizable, because the degree of similarity of the systems giving rise to the mixed one is less evident.[27]

Örücü's approach is developed through the intermingling of two theories borrowed from linguistics: the family trees approach[28] and the wave theory. The first rests on the extension to legal systems of the theory disclosing the parentage of languages. This theory, Örücü (2008: 9) writes is "initially deconstructive, disintegrative, and critical," is apt to unveil the ramifications and divergences among systems that come from the same root; however, it is not apt to explain similarities among systems that do not share the same roots, such as the convergences coming from horizontal transfers. Örücü pursues this aim through the wave theory, which explains common traits among diverse legal systems on the basis of the diffusion of the same institutions.

Örücü's overt purpose is to reach an all-embracing theory of mixedness through which to explain all the different kinds of mixing and therefore draw "a more reliable map of the legal systems of the world" (Örücü 2008: 9). The phenomenon of mobility of law would make it possible to discover the ingredients and historical antecedents of each legal system together with their present blends through the mechanisms of pollination, cross-fertilization, and so forth.

Some elements of Örücü's (1987) theory of mixedness are outlined in brief in one of her earlier articles devoted to legal systems. Mixedness would be the result of the crossing of elements belonging to three basic systems—civil law, common law, and socialist law.[29] The internal logic of these systems would be coherent,[30] resulting from the typical logical unfolding of the necessary elements,[31] historically conditioned by "the attitudes about the nature and the role of law in society, the proper organization and operation of the

27 Örücü (1995) uses gastronomic metaphors, such as those of English salad and Italian salad, to the extent that the ingredients of the legal system keep or do not keep the identity they had before the mix. According to Örücü (1995: 6), the maintenance of their previous identity depends on the degree of cultural affinity, which may be seized at a sociocultural and legal-cultural level: "[V]arious combinations occur when legal institutions migrate from legal system to legal system. Such movements can take place between legal systems of cultural affinity and between systems of cultural diversity. In the first case … when elements from systems of cultural affinity move together and come into contact, there are two possible levels of combination. When there is both legal cultural affinity and socio-cultural affinity, the elements unite to form a new compound.… However, when the movement occurs between systems of socio-cultural affinity but legal cultural diversity, then the elements do indeed mix but still retain their separate identity. Here the metaphor used is a 'mixing bowl.' … The system is hybrid. In the second case … where systems are culturally diverse both in legal culture and socio-culture we can talk of dual or plural law."

28 On the family trees approach, see Örücü (2004: 359), according to whom legal systems "would be classified according to their parentage, their constituents elements, and the resulting blend and then grouped on the principle of predominance."

29 According to Örücü (1987: 311), mixed systems would result from the "crossing between the columns, disrupting the existing vertical internal logic." This event would be "responsible for the creation of most mixed jurisdictions."

30 Örücü (1987: 317) writes, "[E]ach step is a logical necessity, an essential element in the unfolding."

31 According to Örücü (1987), those permanent characteristics cannot arise out of substantive rules of law but must be related to the structural and philosophical roots of legal families. Each step in the unfolding is the sine qua non of the other and results from the relationship between legal systems and legal cultures.

legal system, the way law is or should be made, applied, studied, perfected, and taught; the legal culture or tradition relating to the legal system to the culture of which it is a partial expression" (Örücü 1987: 311). The idea of internal logic implies their pure nature. This logic is subverted when a system mixes basic elements of those three systems. Thus, mixed systems would be the by-product of the mobility of law. A system that at a given point may be considered part of a legal family may go out from it and float "on the periphery, poised on the verges of two, and sometimes three traditions" (Örücü 2002a: 133).

Whereas Palmer's approach seems to have a practical aim—that is, to foster a dialogue among the systems that make up the mixed jurisdictions family to deal with legal issues that arise in daily legal practice—Örücü's approach seems to have a more theoretical aim.

Recently, a different viewpoint on those systems has been supported by Seán Donlan, who emphasizes the idea of hybridity—an idea that straddles legal theory, legal history, anthropology, sociology, and comparative law (Donlan 2011a; 2011b; see also Chapter 2 of this volume). Whereas Palmer focuses on a certain kind of mix and Örücü aims to expand comparative analysis to other kinds of mixes (such as those found in Turkey), Donlan's concept of hybridity paves the way for a different assessment of the complexity of the normative phenomenon. Hybridity is one of many ways in which normativity can be expressed containing state norms and nonstate norms. Nonstate norms are significant despite their lack of a legally binding character.[32] The crucial difference between the two kinds of norms is the latter's lack of institutional form.

Hybridity is able, more than other concepts, to explain the complexity of legal systems. As Donlan states in Chapter 2 of this volume, it "does not emphasize, as … in most discussions of mixed legal systems, the marriage of two relatively discrete and self-contained sections, but the deeper complexity shot through every aspect of legal and normative orders." Donlan has applied that approach to the Mediterranean region as the fittest one so to have a grasp on its "complex history of conquest, colonization, and social and legal diffusion across shifting and porous political boundaries" (Donlan 2011a: 357). This complexity can be understood only by taking into account both legal[33] and normative hybridity and by going beyond the level of state law, which is but one type of law that came later than nonstate or prestate law (Donlan 2011a: 360). As Donlan states in Chapter 2, legal and normative hybridity would be able to "cover the fluid complexity of both laws and norms at the levels of both principle and practice," the word *practice* covering the aspects of interpretation and application of written law. Donlan's analysis has to be carefully considered because it sheds light on the multifarious meanings normativity may have.

A different way of seizing normative complexity may be pursued through the recourse to the concept of legal tradition. In the next section, a specific viewpoint on tradition will be discussed, that of Patrick Glenn.

Legal Tradition and Polyjural Systems

At first sight, the category of legal tradition seems to disclose a point of view that is at variance with formal conceptions that are based on the equation of state law with law *tout court* and that affect the concept of the legal system and jurisdiction. Whereas law implied within the well-established conception of the legal system is identified with state legislation, legal tradition seems not to rely on formalistic and conceptual views of law and goes beyond the idea that the state enjoys a monopoly in law production.

This approach is not formalistic, and it stresses the value of time as a key factor to understand law instead of the value of space, which is closely linked to the idea of the state as the only possible lawmaker. More than other concepts, tradition would be able to highlight the role played by society in shaping its legal system. The premise, according to which legal tradition would be expression of a nonformalistic approach to law, is widely agreed on.[34]

32 The separation of two spheres of state norms and nonstate norms is artificial (Berman 2010).

33 This legal hybridity would result from the coexistence of the Anglo-British, canonical, continental, Islamic, Ottoman socialist, and Talmudic traditions as well as various customary and transterritorial legal traditions.

34 On this aspect, see Somma (2004). The use of the concept of legal tradition comes from a common law environment; in those experiences, there has not been the gap between *ius commune* and codification in civil law systems. According to Somma (2004: 171), "le costruzioni prodotte in area di common law fanno

I focus now on Glenn's theories for a more comprehensive approach to tradition. Glenn points out that the concept of legal family has, as its basis, the idea of law as something that can be ascertained on an objective footing and that preexists (and is not created from) the conceptual tools used by a comparative law scholar to carry out a survey.[35] He advocates a dynamic version of tradition, a view clearly different from the well-entrenched view of tradition as a static form of social order.

The concept of tradition highlights that law is a by-product of legal culture, thus reflecting specific values and ways of thinking. Tradition would be the result of an account—that is, the selection of some elements as constituents of legal systems. Tradition would be made legitimate by the past. Its features would not be stable; they would evolve and, at the same time, be a symbol of continuity and of innovation. Hence, the character of this concept is intrinsically dynamic.

According to Glenn, tradition is a set of (normative) ongoing information captured and transmitted within a specific social context, thereby linking past and present. Its existence depends on processes not only developing inside the systems, but also resulting from the exchange with other traditions.

The definition of tradition as a set of information allows Glenn to draw a distinction between three aspects of tradition that shape its identity—aspects that have to be kept distinct because they imply a different amount of information.[36] The first expresses the overall identity of tradition, one that contains the whole of information and includes contrasting or dissenting elements; the second is the leading or primary version of tradition, "which, at any given time, appears accepted as its truest version"; and the third is the underlying or basic element of the tradition, without which other elements of the tradition could not stand (Glenn 2010: 39–40).

The coincidence between state law and law *tout court*—implying the disappearance or the insignificance of other identities preexisting to the state—would be nothing but the clear result of a specific version of tradition, which may be assessed as the leading version in the civil law culture.[37] This state-centric tradition is a by-product of a systematic view of law. This idea of system has a twofold set of consequences: on the one hand, it posits physical boundaries, and on the other hand, it rests of necessity on the principle of state sources of law. This wide concept of tradition not only would overcome the dichotomy between state law and the other legal layers that do not depend on the decision of a state lawmaker, but also would be a bridge between different legal cultures.

---

cioé istintivamente riferimento al diritto come parte di una vicenda intellettuale, valutata prevalentemente dal punto di vista del suo sviluppo nel tempo, piuttosto che nello spazio" (common law legal concepts are rooted on a view of law as intellectual construction, in which time, more than space, is significant).

35 See Glenn (2006: 422), who writes, "The notion of an existing family … was a product of its times and appeared to accept and even reinforce the idea of autonomous national legal systems." Glenn notes that among the concepts of legal families and legal traditions there is no relation of opposition. The former concept represents a subset of the second. Glenn (2006: 426) observes that "the idea of legal families would represent a particular legal tradition the influence of which is now in decline, leaving the older and more general idea of legal traditions to play a more obvious role."

36 Glenn's concept of tradition is presumably influenced by his Quebec origin. In a work on Quebec, Glenn (1996) distinguishes between structured and unstructured *mixité*, which have characterized Quebec in different periods of its history. The hybridity of the system would not have fixed characteristics; therefore Quebec would be a good example of a conceptual bran tub, the metaphor Glenn chooses to describe tradition. The premise on which Palmer's approach is based—the distinct influence displayed by civil and common law on mixed systems (defined by Glenn as *conceptual mixité*)—is challenged by Quebec experience. Glenn remarks that this feature of distinct influence is losing importance to the extent that common law principles are penetrating the field of private law and civil law principles are penetrating the field of public law. The general traits underlying Glenn's (1996: 15) concept of tradition are taken from Quebec experience: "The Quebec experience thus indicates that law is tolerant of high levels of complexity; that the various types of mixité which may exist are capable of co-existence and mutual re-inforcement; that mixité is capable of extension across any structural boundaries which may be sought to be imposed; and that mixité may be not only broad and of multiple types, but extended through time. Ongoing mixité implies preservation, however, of the sources of mixité. It implies limits to law-making activity." This passage clearly expounds the view of tradition as phenomenon marked from multiplicity.

37 According to Glenn (2010: 54), "the state may be explained by the ascendance, in the west, of a tradition of individualized, constructive rationality.… [A] state (or national legal 'system') is only an institutionalized recognition of the ascendancy of a particular tradition at a particular time, which is unlikely to have obliterated other, competing traditions even within its territory."

In fact, the idea of tradition as information is more apt than other definitions to provide a refined paradigm to illustrate the mechanisms of diffusion of law,[38] which result in the spread and communication of legal materials able to produce the development of plurijural systems. The same concept of tradition rebuts the idea of purity and postulates a *mélange* that is possible because the differences between legal traditions are not insurmountable, in that

> there are no fundamentally different, totally irreconcilable social identities in the world. Each is constituted by tradition and all traditions contain elements of the others. The "West" ... contains the "East." The French expression "mixité" thus best describes the common condition of humanity, and notions of societal ... purity of the nineteenth or early twentieth century are no longer sustainable (Glenn 2010: 39).

The main reason that this concept of tradition is appealing is its flexibility,[39] or the fact that it is a concept that admits openness and is at variance with what is implied by the idea of system—a closed entity. Tradition is able to express better than other conceptual tools some of the features that seem to be characteristic of the global law of the twenty-first century, such as its mutability, dynamism, and porosity.[40]

The question, however, is whether this concept can be usefully employed to deal with practical issues concerning polyjural systems. And how can it be employed? Readers should not take positive answers for granted.

Conclusion

This chapter dealt with various approaches which might be considered appropriate to understand how polyjural systems work in practice. It is self-evident that people cannot grasp these systems if only written rules are considered.[41]

38 According to Twining (2005: 215–16), diffusion would be a "pervasive continuing phenomenon rather than a series of isolated, exceptional events."

39 Marini (2010: 4) highlights as "un ... interessante novità ... l'emersione ... dell'idea di tradizione giuridica che affianca e talvolta sostituisce del tutto nei discorsi del *mainstream* le più classiche ricostruzioni in termini di famiglie e sistemi giuridici" (something new, the idea of legal tradition; this latter goes with and sometimes replaces the taxonomies "legal families" and "legal systems"). The appeal of this concept is explained in this way: "la tradizione giuridica ... pare meglio attrezzata rispetto ai suoi predecessori per accogliere al suo interno il fenomeno di una molteplicità di diritti, compreso quello *soft*, e di una graduazione della loro forza che si può applicare in un dato spazio giuridico reso evidente dal declino dello stato nazionale e dall'affermazione di altre entità giuridiche che con esso concorrono" (legal tradition, more effectively than other concepts used in the past, catches the manifold acceptations of law, among which that of "soft law" emerged following the decline of the nation-state and the parallel achievement of other legal entities in competition with this latter).

40 Glenn draws the conclusion that tradition (understood not only in the specific meaning of legal tradition) is the largest conceptual unit that structures social identity. Glenn (2010: 39) remarks that "the conclusion that tradition is the controlling element in determining social identity means that there are no fundamentally different, totally irreconcilable social identities in the world." On the reasons for the success of the concept of legal tradition, see Marini (2011: 182–83): "L'idea di tradizione giuridica appare oggi—nell'era della globalizzazione—uno strumento più idoneo a svolgere un'indagine di tipo comparativo. E ciò non solo perché l'idea di tradizione giuridica sembra meglio attrezzata per cogliere ed esprimere certe caratteristiche come la mutevolezza, la dinamicità e la porosità che oggi tendono a comparire all'interno delle più classiche unità di analisi; e non solo perché le tradizioni riescono meglio ad inquadrare il fenomeno di una molteplicità di diritti che si intrecciano, compreso quello soft, e di una graduazione della loro forza che si può verificare in un dato spazio giuridico. Le tradizioni riescono anche a dare meglio conto del contesto in cui la comparazione si svolge." (Nowadays—in the era of globalization—the idea of legal tradition seems to be a device fit for comparative law research. This is not only because it catches better some features of present law, such as mutability, dynamism, and porosity, but also because traditions express better the conceptual frame work of comparative law surveys.)

41 In general, this point is more for all legal systems. For similar remarks, see Moccia (2012), one of many in the Italian legal literature. See Ewald (1995a; 1995b). Ewald's emphasis on comparative law

In the previous pages, I analyzed and discussed some approaches to the topic. I think that grouping mixed systems into the same family on the grounds of alleged similarities offers the advantage of giving a fixed point; however, the analysis of these systems has to go beyond that point.[42] We need to focus attention on the sociocultural context, which has great importance in shaping the general identity of the system. In this way, we mitigate the risk that the recourse to the didactic device of the legal family may turn into a straitjacket and may be a hurdle to a deeper understanding of these systems; conversely, we can more easily assess the high complexity and mutability of these systems.[43] What those systems are nowadays depends mostly on how they became polyjural.

Might this issue be better appraised through the concept of legal tradition? The main advantage of legal tradition is its flexibility, because it goes beyond state law and is well suited to cope with the trait of diversity, which is the DNA of polyjural systems. The concept of legal tradition is, by nature, relative; what it shows is the lack of universality of the concept of law. Heterogeneity and mutability are its constituents.

Legal tradition has to be handled with care; its many possible versions make it hardly manageable, thus giving birth to uncertain results.[44] To be sure, the concept of tradition is certainly fit to express the complexity of legal systems: it is well suited to express the idea of multiplicity within a unitary context, thereby broadening the field of facts that are relevant to understanding the different levels of normativity. However, whether and to what extent the concept of tradition may help in practice is open to doubt.

Basically, tradition depends on the subjective choices of those who claim its existence. An effort has to be made to understand what lies *behind* a certain version of tradition—for example, which interests urge that version of tradition.

A possible field of application might be that of gaps in law or of cases in which law in force is inadequate and thus unable to deal effectively with societal needs. The recourse to legal tradition may be useful to disclose the basic elements of the context in which courts act and decide, showing the fundamental structures of the system—that is, those elements that could not be modified without producing a change of the same tradition.

Interest for polyjural systems has arisen nowadays in comparative law studies. The interest may be explained by the fact that the systems express—better than other experiences—the idea that diversity among disparate sources of law does not necessarily produce conflict. The diversity may coexist in the same context. An Italian scholar recently advocated that those who delve into comparative law studies have the task to build bridges between worlds that are distant, thereby pleading the need to support a view of law based on an inclusive distinction.[45] Polyjural systems may be an interesting field of application in this regard.

---

understood as comparative jurisprudence highlights the necessity of being aware of the importance of the role played by jurists' thoughts to have a thorough understanding of what the law actually is in a given legal system.

42 See also Levasseur (2010: 35), who finds for the necessity of going "beyond th[e] purely 'photographic,' 'instamatic,' 'still' stage and [focusing the] inquiry more deeply into the great variety of social elements and creative forces, of all sorts, which influence the structure, the substance, the scheme of law-making."

43 See Glenn (2006: 422, 427), who writes, "The concept of legal families ... distorts or impoverishes our understanding of the legal world.... Legal families would thus conceal more than they reveal and are not justifiable as a means of understanding.... [T]he concept of legal families is inherently static by fixing, at least temporarily, the objects of classification for purposes of their classification."

44 Marini (2010: 32) stresses that traditions have a complex structure resulting from "certe particolari condizioni locali, e non d[a] una logica interna" (certain peculiar local conditions, and not from an internal logic). For this reason, Marini (2010: 33) advocates the necessity of researching their genealogy: "ricostruire la genealogia ... permette ... di mettere in luce che la strada della [loro] costruzione è segnata dalla storia, dal conflitto e dalla contingenza" (reconstructing their genealogy ... highlights the fact that their conceptualization is characterized from historical events and social conflict). In this way, "la comparazione si rivela anche una vera e propria teoria critica (della società)" (comparative approach is also a critical theory of society).

45 See Moccia (2011), who advocates a globalized view of law—a view that is able to go beyond differences linked to the element of territory.

References

Amos, M.S. 1937. The common law and the civil law in the British Commonwealth of nations. *Harvard Law Review*, 50(8), 1249–74.

Berman, P.S. 2010. Towards a jurisprudence of hybridity. *Utah Law Review*, 1, 11–29.

Cashin Ritaine, E. 2010. Mixed and hybrid jurisdictions: Comparative and methodological considerations, in *Comparative Law and Hybrid Legal Traditions*, edited by E. Cashin Ritaine, S.P. Donlan, and M. Sychold. Basel, Switzerland: Schulthess, 141–60.

Cotterell, R. 2006. Comparative law and legal culture, in *The Oxford Handbook of Comparative Law*, edited by M. Reimann and R. Zimmermann. Oxford, UK: Oxford University Press, 710–37.

David, R., and Jauffret Spinosi, C. 2004. *I Grandi Sistemi Giuridici Contemporanei*. Padova, Italy: Cedam.

Donlan, S.P. 2011a. The Mediterranean hybridity project at the boundaries of law and culture. *Journal of Civil Law Studies*, 4, 355–96.

Donlan, S.P. 2011b. Remembering: Legal hybridity and legal history. *Comparative Law Review*, 2(1), 1–35.

Du Plessis, J. 2006. Comparative law and the study of mixed legal systems, in *The Oxford Handbook of Comparative Law*, edited by M. Reimann and R. Zimmermann. Oxford, UK: Oxford University Press, 477–512.

Ewald, W. 1995a. Comparative jurisprudence (I): What was it like to try a rat? *University of Pennsylvania Law Review* 143(6), 1889–2149.

Ewald, W. 1995b. Comparative jurisprudence (II): The logic of legal transplants. *American Journal of Comparative Law* 43(4), 489–510.

Glenn, H.P. 1996. Quebec: Mixité and monism, in *Studies in Legal Systems: Mixed and Mixing*, edited by E. Örücü, E. Attwooll, and S. Coyle. The Hague: Kluwer, 1–15.

Glenn, H.P. 2006. Comparative legal families and comparative legal traditions, in *The Oxford Handbook of Comparative Law*, edited by M. Reimann and R. Zimmermann. Oxford, UK: Oxford University Press, 422–40.

Glenn, H.P. 2010. *Legal Traditions of the World: Sustainable Diversity in Law*. 4th ed. Oxford, UK: Oxford University Press.

Kötz, H. 2003. The value of mixed jurisdictions. *Tulane Law Review*, 78(1–2), 435–39.

Krislov, S. 1985. The concept of families of law, in *Legal Systems and Social Systems*, edited by A. Podgorecki, C.J. Whelan, and D. Khosla. Dover, MA: Croom Helm, 25–38.

Lee, R.W. 1915. The civil law and the common law: A world survey. *Michigan Law Review*, 14(2), 89–101.

Levasseur, A. 2010. Two hundred (200) years of civil law in English: Louisiana's lonely destiny, in *Comparative Law and Hybrid Legal Traditions*, edited by E. Cashin Ritaine, S.P. Donlan, and M. Sychold. Basel, Switzerland: Schulthess, 35–54.

Marini, G. 2010. La costruzione delle tradizioni giuridiche nell'epoca della globalizzazione. Working paper, Comparazione e Diritto Civile, Salemo, Italy. Available at: http://www.comparazionedirittocivile.it/prova/files/urb_marini.pdf [accessed: November 5, 2013].

Marini, G. 2011. La costruzione delle tradizioni giuridiche ed il diritto latinoamericano. *Rivista Critica di Diritto Privato*, 2, 163–93.

Merryman, J., and Peréz-Perdomo, R. 2007. *The Civil Law Tradition: An Introduction to the Legal Systems of Europe and Latin America*. 3rd ed. Stanford, CA: Stanford University Press.

Moccia, L. 2011. Comparazione giuridica, diritto e giurista europeo: Un punto di vista globale. *Rivista Trimestrale di Diritto Procedura Civile*, 3, 770–71.

Moccia, L. 2012. Riflessioni sparse (e qualche involontario aforisma) su interpretazione e diritto. *Rivista Trimestrale di Diritto Procedura Civile*, 3, 915–29.

Monateri, P.G. 2001. The "weak law": Contaminations and legal culture. *Global Jurist Advances*, 1(3), 1–7.

Nelken, D. 2002. Legal transplants and beyond: Of disciplines and metaphors, in *Comparative Law in the 21st Century*, edited by A. Harding and E. Örücü. London: Kluwer, 29–34.

Nelken, D. 2007. Defining and using the concept of legal culture, in *Comparative Law: A Handbook*, edited by E. Örücü and D. Nelken. Portland, OR: Hart, 109–32.

Örücü, E. 1987. An exercise on the internal logic of legal systems. *Legal Studies*, 7(3), 310–18.

Örücü, E. 1995. A theoretical framework for transfrontier mobility of law, in *Transfrontier Mobility of Law*, edited by R. Jagtenberg, E. Örücü, and A.J. De Roo. The Hague: Kluwer Law International, 1–15.

Örücü, E. 1996. Mixed and mixing systems: A conceptual search, in *Studies in Legal Systems: Mixed and Mixing*, edited by E. Örücü, E. Attwooll, and S. Coyle. The Hague: Kluwer, 335–52.

Örücü, E. 2002a. Approaching public law as a "mixed system." *Juridical Review*, 2(3), 131–42.

Örücü, E. 2002b. Law as transposition. *International and Comparative Law Quarterly*, 51(2), 205–23.

Örücü, E. 2004. Family trees for legal systems: Towards a contemporary approach, in *Epistemology and Methodology of Comparative Law*, edited by M. Van Hoecke. Oxford, UK: Hart, 359–75.

Örücü, E. 2008. What is a mixed legal system: Exclusion or expansion. *Electronic Journal of Comparative Law* [Online], 12(1), 1–18. Available at: http://www.ejcl.org/121/art121-15.pdf [accessed: November 5, 2013].

Örücü, E. (ed.). 2010. *Mixed Legal Systems at New Frontiers*. London: Wildy, Simmonds & Hill.

Palmer, V.V. 2008. Two rival theories of mixed legal systems. *Electronic Journal of Comparative Law* [Online], 12(1), 1–28. Available at: http://www.ejcl.org/121/art121-16.pdf [accessed: November 5, 2013].

Palmer, V.V. 2012a. Introduction to the mixed jurisdictions, in *Mixed Jurisdictions Worldwide: The Third Legal Family*, edited by V.V. Palmer. Cambridge, UK: Cambridge University Press, 1–93.

Palmer, V.V. 2012b. Mixed legal systems, in *The Cambridge Companion to Comparative Law*, edited by M. Bussani and U. Mattei. Cambridge, UK: Cambridge University Press, 368–83.

Podgorecki, A. 1985. Social systems and legal systems: Criteria for classification, in *Legal Systems and Social Systems*, edited by A. Podgorecki, C.J. Whelan, and D. Khosla. Dover, MA: Croom Helm, 1–24.

Reid, K.G.C. 2003. The idea of mixed legal systems. *Tulane Law Review*, 78(1–2), 5–40.

Sacco, R. 1991. Legal formants: A dynamic approach to comparative law. *American Journal of Comparative Law*, 39(1), 1–34.

Smith, T.B. 1965. The preservation of the civilian tradition in "mixed jurisdictions," in *Civil Law in the Modern World*, edited by A.N. Yiannopoulos. Baton Rouge: Louisiana State University Press, 3–26.

Smith, T.B. 1975. Mixed jurisdictions, in *International Encyclopedia of Comparative Law: Property and Trust*. Vol.6. Tübingen, Germany: Mohr, 115.

Smits, J.M. 2001. The Contribution of Mixed Legal Systems to European Private Law. Antwerp, Belgium: Intersentia.

Smits, J.M. 2002. The Making of European Private Law: Toward a Ius Commune Europaeum as a Mixed Legal System. Antwerp, Belgium: Intersentia.

Somma, A. 2004. Giochi senza frontiere: Diritto comparato e tradizione giuridica. Boletín Mexicano de Derecho Comparado, 37(109), 169–205.

Twining, W. 2004. Diffusion of law: A global perspective. Journal of Legal Pluralism, 49(1), 1–45.

Twining, W. 2005. Social science and diffusion of law. Journal of Law and Society, 32(2), 203–40.

Twining, W. 2006. Diffusion and globalization discourse. Harvard International Law Journal, 47(2), 507–15.

Twining, W. 2007. Globalisation and comparative law, in *Comparative Law: A Handbook*, edited by E. Örücü and D. Nelken. Portland, OR: Hart, 69–91.

Walton, F.P. 1899. The civil law and the common law in Canada. *Juridical Review*, 11(4), 282–301.

Watson, A. 1993. *Legal Transplants: An Approach to Comparative Law*. 2nded. Athens: University of Georgia Press.

Watson, A. 2001. *Society and Legal Change*. 2nd ed. Philadelphia: Temple University Press.

Wise, E.M. 1990. The transplant of legal patterns. *American Journal of Comparative Law* 38, 1–22.

Zweigert, K., and Kötz, H. 1998. *Introduzione al Diritto Comparato*. Milan, Italy: Giuffrè.

Chapter 2

To Hybridity and Beyond: Reflections on Legal and Normative Complexity

Seán Patrick Donlan[1]

> There are … no *pure* individuals, no *pure* cultures, no *pure* genres. All things are of necessity *hybrid*. Of course we can construct them to be relatively *pure*, and in fact we do so, which is precisely how we manage to get (new) hybrids from purebreds that are (former) hybrids.
>
> —Brian Stross (1999: 266–67)

I have referred to my recent research on legal and normative complexity as the study of *hybridity and diffusion*, the modest investigation of the mixtures and movements of laws and norms, past and present and around the globe (see, for example, Donlan 2010b). I have argued that such research must be comparative across both space and time, involving comparative law and legal history, as well as the social sciences—especially anthropology and sociology—and legal philosophy. I suggest that my approach might prove a useful perspective from which to better understand the role that laws and norms play in the daily lives of ordinary people around the world (compare, for example, with Shahar 2008). This chapter attempts to briefly lay out the broad outlines of this approach and to encourage similar research through interdisciplinary and transdisciplinary collaboration.[2] The chapter also takes a brief detour to discuss the Western folk concept of law. My intention is not to erect a new terminology or taxonomy but to sketch a rough conceptual map that allows scholars to better understand both legal and normative practices. I want to create a type of descriptive, critical, and constructive *deep focus*, analogous to the way in which that term is used in photography and cinema, wherein clarity in depth is achieved through significant light and sustained focus.

As I define it, *hybridity* relates to two related axes of investigation. The first is a distinction, whether seen as practical or philosophical, between normativity and legality. Although making a practical distinction rooted in contemporary convention dividing state law from nonstate norms may be a prudent approach to legal-normative scholarship, a deeper investigation shows that an earlier, more well-established convention separates laws and norms on the basis, in significant part, of institutional form. The result is that a meaningful definition of nonstate laws is available without applying law to all forms of normative ordering. The second axis divides the examination of normative and legal orders of various types on the basis of their respective titular principles and actual practice. This approach is far from revolutionary, but the investigation of both principles and practice must obviously go hand in hand if the subject of investigation is to be fully understood. For me, this approach has already proved useful in research on the present and the past. I have written, for example, on legal hybridity in Malta and proposed a wider project on legal and normative hybridity in the Mediterranean (Donlan 2011a; Donlan, Andò, and Zammit 2012). I have proposed the generation of histories of hybridity, "histories that take as their focus the plurality of past laws" informed by comparative analysis and the social sciences (Donlan 2010c: 22). I have written on eighteenth-century Britain and Ireland and the wider movement of Western legal history, from hybridity to comparative unity (Brown and Donlan 2011b; Donlan 2010a; 2011b). Recent research applies this approach to early nineteenth-century Spanish West Florida and

1 Although this chapter is closely related to the themes of *Juris Diversitas* (http://jurisdiversitas.blogspot.com [accessed: February 13, 2014]), it represents only my opinion. Earlier versions were delivered at the conferences on New Frontiers of Comparative Law (Macau, November 11, 2011) and on Mixed Legal Systems, East and West (Malta, May 14–15, 2012).

2 These themes are explored in greater detail in Donlan (2011a).

to a wider project on jurisdictional complexity in Western legal history (circa 1600–1900).[3] Hybridity and diffusion point toward a historical, comparative, and institutional theory that explores normative complexity by setting research on legality within the wider matrix of normativity.

As this introduction suggests, comparative and historical scholarship is important to my approach.[4] Hybridity is not merely an element of the contemporary, formally colonized global East or South. Throughout Western history, a unified system of national state common laws is the historical exception rather than the rule. Before the rise of the state, laws, largely defined in institutional terms, already existed and competed both with rival legal regimes as well as with other forms of normativity. When such a system arose, the law of the state was parasitic on an established, conventional concept of law as well as, more importantly in practice, preexisting legal institutions.[5] Recognizing this background has real benefits. Indeed, I have argued that "remembering" the hybridity of our own past "better [prepares us] to understand and address the pluralism of the present" (Donlan 2011b: 3). It does so, as António Manuel Hespanha (2004: 45) wrote in relation to legal history and legal education, by "deep[ening] the sense of complexity."[6] Indeed,

> the mission of legal history is to render problematic the implicit assumptions of dogmatics, namely, the rational, necessary, ultimate nature of our law. Legal history accomplishes this mission [by] stressing the fact that law is necessarily bound to a cultural (in the deepest sense of the word) environment and, furthermore, that legal knowledge is also a "local knowledge" … whose categories are deeply rooted in historical *epistemes*. (Hespanha 2004: 41).

Acknowledging complexity has consequences not only for comparative law and legal history, but also for legal philosophy and the meaning of *law*. Hybridity challenges, for example, the dissection of plural and dynamic traditions into discrete, closed families or systems. More critically, hybridity undermines commonly held and conjoined beliefs in legal nationalism and positivism, legal centralism and monism. It points, in fact, toward a more plural jurisprudence.[7]

In sum, I suggest that jurists must take general normativity, beyond legality, seriously.[8] But social scientists must also respect legality's unique normative position. Both jurists and social scientists have much to gain from each other and from active collaboration. As the anthropologist Baudouin Dupret (1999: 31) has written in a different context, "Law must be stripped of its conceptual status and returned to the fold of general normativity." Legality, which is inherently conventional, must be set within normativity. Nonstate normativity must be understood not as a minor add-on to provide context for state law, but as fundamental to the lives of people around the world, both in the West and beyond. And the scholarly ability to generate an accurate, if static, image of normative and legal traditions remains insufficient without attention to the degree to which its principles are implemented in practice and alter over time (see Halpérin 2011). I am not interested merely in legal and normative *fixité*, but in the complex and ongoing process of *mixité* (Drummond 2008: 169; see also Drummond 2005). In this sense, the diffusion or movement of laws and norms that generate different legal-normative mixes over time is an essential aspect of the study of hybridity (Donlan 2011a: 10–12).

---

3 See Donlan (forthcoming b). The project, organized with Dirk Heirbaut, is funded by the Gerda Henkel Foundation in Germany. A collection will be published with the German publisher Duncker & Humblot in its Comparative Studies in Continental and Anglo-American Legal History Series.

4 Compare the mission statement of *Comparative Legal History: An International and Comparative Review of Law and History* at http://www.hartjournals.co.uk/clh/.

5 *Juris Diversitas*, with the Swiss Institute of Comparative Law, held a conference in October 2011 on the Concept of "Law" in Context: Comparative Law, Legal Philosophy, and the Social Sciences. A collection of essays developed from that conference is forthcoming in the Juris Diversitas Book Series (Ashgate).

6 As Samuel (1990: 21) noted, the complexities of "[h]istorical jurisprudence can show, in other words, that there are no right answers in law as such."

7 Compare the efforts of Roughan (2011).

8 This idea has been recognized by some juriprudes, including Brian Tamanaha (2001) and William Twining (2009a) in their respective approaches to general jurisprudence.

Hybridity and Diffusion

In its origins, *hybrid* had a very narrow meaning. The Latin *hibrida* was "the offspring of a (female) domestic sow and a (male) wild boar" (Stross 1999: 254). In fact, a hybrid is still commonly seen as a complex individual entity, a singularity, from two parents. More recently, however, the word has become far broader in application. Indeed, the word in its current usage is arguably, "a slippery, ambiguous term, at once literal and metaphorical, descriptive and explanatory" (Burke 2009: 54). This more elastic meaning is, however, occasionally productive. In postcolonial studies, for example, hybridity serves as a critique of binary, reified thinking about cultures and their members. Instead, it emphasizes a very deep and dynamic complexity, "the ambivalent in-between space created by the interaction of the colonizers and the colonized" (Roy 2008: 340). Until the past few years, however, hybridity was only rarely used in legal and normative scholarship. When used by comparatists, hybridity is largely synonymous with *mixity*, the coexistence of diverse, discrete state legal traditions within a jurisdiction. It is a common but minor usage, often little more than a rhetorical relief from *mixed* (see, for example, Anthony 1992: 217). Less commonly, *legal hybridity* has been used in a manner equivalent to *legal pluralism* (see, for example, Holbrook 2010). *Hybridization* is almost unheard of.[9] And when *hybrid* and its variants appear, there is little precision in their use.[10] In recent years, I have tried to suggest how we might use *hybridity* as a term of art, in more constructive, nuanced ways to cover the fluid complexity of both laws and norms at the levels of both principle and practice.

My use of *hybridity* is related, in this general sense, to postcolonial scholarship. Although the focus of that work has been on individual identities, the same sense of hybridity can meaningfully be applied to the complexity of legal and normative institutions. This is especially true as both are deeply marked by colonial encounters and the diffusion of Western laws and norms. In descriptive terms, this use of *hybridity* is also closely linked to the scholarship of radical, critical, or postmodern legal pluralists (see, for example, de Sousa Santos 2002, Kleinhans and Macdonald 1997, Vanderlinden 1989). In different ways, these scholars argue, in a critique of the reification of laws or norms into discrete and closed systems, that law and plurality are best seen as products of individuals rather than institutions. This argument is, as Jacques Vanderlinden (1989: 152) phrased it, "not centered upon a given legal system but upon the *sujet de droit* ... who can be subjected to many legal orders as a member of many networks." Individuals are the constant, if incremental, creators of laws in a complex and fluid normative web. And although he could have been writing about the Western past as much as the present, Boaventura de Sousa Santos has noted, "We live in a time of porous legality or of legal porosity, multiple networks of legal orders forcing us to constant transitions and trespassing. Our legal life is constituted by an intersection of different legal orders, that is, by *interlegality*" (de Sousa Santos 2002: 437). If this statement neatly captures the dynamism and ubiquity of normativity, he adopts, along with many moderate legal pluralists, an overbroad, unconventional use of the word *legality*.[11] And even if we accept the descriptive account of postmodern legal pluralists, we must be careful not to exaggerate the liberating potential of recognizing legal-normative hybridity. We must be careful, that is, to attend to the larger forces that drive subjects in their choices. Individuals may be the nexus of normative activity, but they do not generate norms *ex nihilo*. They may be little more than flotsam and jetsam in a hurricane (see Donlan 2012a). Hybridity, as defined here, may be seen as a *jurisprudence rooted in normativity*; it is not, however, intended to be a normative jurisprudence with prescriptive lessons for social life (Berman 2010). As de Sousa Santos (2002) states, "[T]here is nothing inherently good, progressive, or emancipatory about *legal pluralism*."

Similar to the approach of these theorists of radical normative hybridity, my approach stresses that laws and norms always exist in a complex and fluid web that can only roughly be captured in the language of

9 But compare the more limited use in Delmas-Marty (2009).

10 Following Iza Hussin (2007), Salvatore Mancuso (2013) uses the term *legal hybridity* for the power relationships that affect the practices of legal pluralism. While Hussin's emphasis on power is also important here, her use of *hybridity* and *mixed legal system* (as synonymous with legal pluralism) is unusual. Of course, so is my use of *hybridity*.

11 Given the *iura* and *legis* distinction, with the latter linked to formally enacted law of an authority, *jurality* might be a better choice. Compare the "multiple sites of legal normativity (polyjuralism)" discussed in Macdonald and MacLean (2005: 727n14). See also Macdonald and MacLean (2005: 732n32). Jean Carbonnier (1977) also uses the term *internormativity*.

pan-national legal and normative movements. Hybridity does not emphasize the marriage of two relatively discrete and self-contained sections, as in most discussions of mixed legal systems, but the deeper complexity shot through every aspect of legal and normative orders. Assigning labels to the different fragments of an order, no less than to the order itself, is always an approximation that will fail to capture the nuances of actual practice. Orders, including more institutionalized legal regimes and state legal systems, are never closed, never static. Norms, whether legal or nonlegal, are always in flux, stabilized only—though profoundly, in fact—by the weight and inertia of convention, of traditions, and of practices. Still, the aggregative normativity and legality of corporate communities and their institutions must be taken seriously. This is, of course, the natural concentration of much legal and social science. Accepted as working generalizations, as useful shorthand that allows us to get work done, this communal or institutional focus need not involve reification, deny individual possibility, or ignore complexity. It offers, however, a manageable viewpoint from which to understand legal-normative creation and negotiation. Indeed, an individual focus can blind us to these wider patterns of normative influence.

Finally, note that hybridity, understood in this way, has gone hand in hand with *diffusion*, the movements that generate legal-normative complexity.[12] The discussion of diffusion is, in fact, common among comparatists, in a bewildering and occasionally enlightening vocabulary of receptions, transplants, transfers, contaminations, irritants, migrations, and transfrontier mobility of law.[13] Michele Graziadei (2006) has even suggested, reflecting a rich vein of Italian comparative scholarship that explores law in context, that we can see "[c]omparative law as the study of transplants and receptions." And the study of diffusion by jurist William Twining extends this vocabulary beyond the law. In what deserves to be quoted at length, Twining (2004: 34–35) suggests how complex these processes are:

> (i) Relations between exporters and importers are not necessarily bipolar, involving only one exporter and one importer. The sources of a reception are often diverse.
>
> (ii) Diffusion may take place between many kinds of legal orders at and across different geographical levels, not just horizontally between municipal legal systems.
>
> (iii) The pathways of diffusion may be complex and indirect and influences may be reciprocal.
>
> (iv) Diffusion may take place through informal interaction without involving formal adoption or enactment.
>
> (v) Legal rules and concepts are not the only or even the main objects of diffusion.
>
> (vi) Governments are not the only, and may not be the main, agents of diffusion.
>
> (vii) Do not assume one or more specific reception dates. Diffusion often involves a long drawn out process, which, even if there were some critical moments, cannot be understood without reference to events prior and subsequent to such moments.
>
> (viii) Diffusion of law often involves movement from an imperial or other powerful centre to a colonial, dependent, or less developed periphery. But there are also other patterns.
>
> (ix) The idea that transplants retain their identity without significant change is widely recognized to be outmoded.
>
> (x) Imported law rarely fills a vacuum or wholly replaces prior local law.

---

12 Compare J.M. Blaut (1993), in which *diffusion* marks the spread of purportedly more advanced Western forms around the world.

13 For additional citations, see Donlan (2011a: 368–70).

(xi) Diffusion of law is often assumed to be instrumental, technological, and modernising. But there is a constant tension between technological, contextual-expressive, and ideological perspectives on law.

(xii) There is a tendency in the diffusion literature to talk of receptions "working" or "failing." Only recently have attempts been made to evaluate and measure impact empirically. Many of the instruments that have been developed are suspect, but this is an area that needs serious academic attention.

Normative diffusion is obviously still more complex, but Twining's sophisticated understanding of its complex relation to law (see Twining 2005; 2006; 2007) parallels similar discussions within the social sciences and suggests how we might better understand the processes that give us "(new) hybrids from purebreds that are (former) hybrids" (Stross 1999: 267).

Normativity and Legality

The first axis of hybridity, at least as understood here, is a distinction between normativity and legality. This division may be seen as merely practical, allowing us to get on with research on various normative forms by accepting modern conventional distinctions between nonstate norms and state laws. At a deeper philosophical and conceptual level, however, social norms (norms) and legal norms (laws) should be seen as conceptually distinct, though without any necessary reference to the state, a very late and specific institutional normative form. According to the *Oxford English Dictionary*, which effectively records the cumulative, conventional usage of terms and the concepts to which they are assigned in practice, a *norm* "is a model or a pattern; a type, a standard."[14] This usage is long established, but it originally grew out of the Latin *norma*, a craftsman's tool used to create right angles. Such norms—and related normative communities of various sorts—appear to be a universal aspect of human existence. We are normative animals, expressing evaluative judgments of appropriate claims and conduct. Normativity is thus universal. Legality is not. Laws, as defined by centuries of Western convention, are points on a normative continuum and always rest within the wider matrix of less institutionalized normativity. Legal norms are a subset of social norms. But if laws and norms may be distinguished in this way, they cannot be divorced. For this reason, jurists must take general normativity seriously, and social scientists must respect legality's unique normative position.

As I suggested, the state may be used, for convenience, to mark the border between the legal and the nonlegal. This approach largely reflects juristic practice and more general modern understandings of nonjurists across the West for much of the past two centuries. In this sense, such a distinction is meaningful, defensible, and accepted in practice by jurists, many social scientists, and the public. And state laws are distinct, at least in practice, from other norms. For much, though admittedly not all, of the world, the modern state and state legal systems play a critical role that should not be ignored (Roberts 2005). This simple law–norm division, largely accepting a central defining role for the state, is the approach taken in the Mediterranean Hybridity Project.[15] An initiative of *Juris Diversitas*, that project is developing a collaborative transdisciplinary network of experts to produce national reports and cross-cultural analyses of the legal and normative complexity of the region. The project marries conceptual and empirical models from the legal and social sciences to investigate the principles and practices of (a) diverse state laws (including those of customary and religious origin) and (b) lived nonstate norms (especially nonstate justice systems).[16] This information will assist the work of academics, practitioners, policy makers, and civil society organizations, as well as the wider community. But the choice, in effect, of state ratification as establishing the law–nonlaw boundary is merely a practical maneuver. Accepting this simple—perhaps simplistic—division is an attempt to bracket or set aside deeper,

14 The *Oxford English Dictionary* is available online at www.oed.com/.

15 See especially Donlan (2011a: 364–67). As noted previously, *juralities* might be a better choice.

16 On nonstate justice systems, see Forsyth (2009), chapter 7, "A typology of relationships between state and non-state justice systems."

passionate philosophical debates in the interests of generating useful data.[17] Indeed, this definitional fiat has not limited the range of our study. If minor nonstate norms, such as the rules and principles of etiquette (although even social mores may extend to significant taboos), are not included, others—especially so-called nonstate justice systems—may be quite significant in practice. Although we may find that norms are encircled and hemmed in by the state, we may also find that laws act in the shadow of very meaningful nonstate norms (compare Coorter, Marks, and Mnookin 1982).

Defined in this manner, legal hybridity obviously includes the study of mixed legal systems, Western or non-Western, where the diverse origins of state laws lie in reasonably visible and frequently discrete, identifiable sections.[18] This category is already quite large, including my native Louisiana, as well as Malta, Turkey, and much of the world.[19] These mixed systems, including some quite exotic hybrids, were often the result of Western political expansionism and the diffusion of its laws. Especially through colonialism, Western laws came into contact with numerous other legal and normative traditions: Asian, Hindu, Islamic, a wider variety of customary traditions, and so on. Some of these traditions were already complex hybrids, but the addition of Western laws—either by imposition or through borrowing under Western hegemony—further complicated the normative spaces of much of the world. The global result was a number of coherent, if not closed, legal traditions that are both national and meaningfully pan-national. Far-flung jurisdictions, including many postcolonial states, continue to look to the mother traditions for guidance. But context is everything. Although simplistic taxonomic classifications may be necessary for pedagogical and professional purpose, it is mistaken and deeply Eurocentric to assume, for example, that India is best classified as an Anglo-American system or that China is best classified as belonging to the continental legal traditions, without recognizing the practical importance of the different contexts (for example, Chelsea and Kolkata) and the presence of additional, competing traditions, Western and non-Western, within law and without (see, for example, Castellucci 2012).

Indeed, if one draws deeply on comparative legal history and the extensive comparative literature on the processes of diffusion, the recognition of legal hybridity extends much further. Legal hybridity is, as Vernon Palmer (2007: 1210) notes, "a universal fact." All state laws are examples of what social scientists call *state or weak legal pluralism*. The legal system remains, at least in theory, unified. Jurisdictional conflict is handled, either formally or informally, by state institutions, whose recognition or ratification, if it comes, effectively converts the rules and decisions of other orders (including state-sanctioned customary orders) into state laws. This conversion need not happen explicitly; the complex and varied ingredients of a legal tradition may lie hidden below the state law's superficial surface. This process applies even to England: "Europe's multifarious legal traditions were forever in motion towards new permutations and equilibria. If the triumphalist dominance of its *common law* often obscures English legal hybridity and diffusions, this kaleidoscopic motion was, and is, no less true of the Anglo-American legal traditions" (Donlan 2010a: 290–91).

Indeed, in an article that is especially important to the approach taken here, Esin Örücü (2004: 363; see also Örücü 2007) has proposed a "family trees" approach that "regards all legal systems as mixed and overlapping, overtly or covertly, and groups them according to the proportionate mixture of the ingredients." This genealogical method combines both top-down and bottom-up perspectives, the formal codes and informal contexts of the law, to explore the "various degrees of hybridity" found around the globe (Örücü 2004: 367). Although these ancestors may have little continuing control over their progeny, the recognition of historical hybridity alerts us to the complexity of even the most ordinary and apparently autochthonous

17 Although it is something of a fudge, referring to laws and other norms collectively as *legalities* or some similar neologism can usefully underline their similarities without ignoring their differences (Donlan 2011a: 366–67). See also Brown and Donlan (2011a).

18 I have explored the conventional terminology of what I call *legal hybridity*—that is, mixed systems, mixed jurisdictions, classical mixed jurisdictions, and the third legal family—in several articles. See, for example, Donlan (2011a: 374–83).

19 Compare the rough count and classification by the University of Ottawa, including 98 "civil law monosystems," 47 "common law monosystems," and 95 "mixed systems." Available at: http://www.juriglobe.ca/eng/sys-juri/class-poli/sys-mixtes.php [accessed: November 20, 2013].

system.[20] Indeed, as Örücü (1996) stressed in an earlier article, change is necessarily change over time: we must take both "mixed and mixing systems" seriously.

What is just as important is that neither the state nor those laws that preceded the state have ever had normative exclusivity. There has been—and is now—no unified and pure legal or normative space, controlled respectively by either an all-embracing state or an all-embracing society. Instead, laws and norms always rest within the wider web of *strong or deep legal pluralism*—the totality of normative orders and more diffuse normative influences. What I call *normative hybridity* is often referred to in contemporary social science as *legal* or, more recently, *normative pluralism*, usually in reference to the interaction of state laws and semiautonomous nonstate normative orders that lack the sanction of the state (see generally Donlan 2011a: 383–95; see especially Twining 2010). Indeed, the focus of such analysis is still typically on nonstate norms beyond the West, often in the shadow of a failed and imported state. The lessons of normative hybridity are also obviously relevant in the West. For example, in a well-known study, Julio L. Ruffini (1976) wrote about norms and practices among Sardinian shepherds that, although an alternative to the state, were meaningful to those within it. With the laudable aim of insisting on value parity between Western and non-Western forms, legal pluralists have attacked the jurist's narrow focus on the state and the politics of colonialism and hegemony they saw linked to it. This practice has often succeeded in making scholars sensitive to similarities between law and norms, but the blurring of these categories has also often confused jurists, arguably dissuading many from engagement.[21] Against an "ideology of legal centralism," the sociologist John Griffiths (1986: 1) argued that state law was but one type of law and that legal pluralism was "the presence in a social field of more than one legal order."[22] But the suggestion that *any* normative order is a legal order is overbroad, indiscriminate, and ultimately unhelpful. Or so I suggest. The language of legal pluralists and their allies—*everyday law*, *living law*, *implicit law*, *unofficial law*, *ubiquitous law*, and even *law in brief encounters*—seems to jumble enlightening metaphors with established meanings.[23] This jumbling undermines—along with an occasional, totalitizing cultural essentialism—pluralist insights.

A Folk Concept of Law

Adopting the contemporary convention of dividing laws and norms by their relationship to the state and bracketing wider debates about the concept of law are reasonable, practically productive moves. This approach fits very well, too, with my sense of hybridity and diffusion. I also slip easily, if often accidentally, into that vocabulary myself. But if questions are asked about law's meaning, this *entente cordiale* is insufficient. A general theory of normativity, or even legality, cannot center on the state and its laws. Even in the West, state law is a relatively recent normative form, though one that is particularly colonizing and domineering. Indeed, in most contemporary conceptions of law, state law is seen, explicitly or implicitly, as the yardstick by which others are measured. Such concepts, which reflect the government forms with which we are most familiar, have impoverished our professional discourse for much of the past two centuries. They have also distracted us from a deeper, more public past convention that might be more useful for the present and, indeed, for the future. I suggest—and it is not surprising that a historian would make such a proposal—that if our sense of law is not to be a mere neologism for what we find interesting in the fleeting present, then the etymology of law must be taken far more seriously. Too often, jurisprudes have concocted concepts to be applied to reality rather

20 Such descriptions must also be clearly distinguished from more prescriptive purposes. Some scholarship on mixed jurisdictions, especially as related to the prospect of a *novum ius commune Europaeum*, has been influenced by wider political and cultural purposes. Compare the aggressive and entertaining critique of Douglas J. Osler (2007: 185), which emphasizes *ius diversum*.

21 Understandably, perhaps, jurists are often more interested in legal norms than in social norms. In fact, both comparative lawyers and legal historians, reflecting their disciplinary training and a more general conventional use of law, use *legal pluralism* as a synonym for what I call *legal hybridity*.

22 But Griffiths later recanted, switching to *normative legal pluralism*. See Griffiths (2005).

23 See, respectively, Macdonald (2002), Ehrlich ([1936] 2002), Fuller (1968), Chiba (1998), Melissaris (2009), and Reisman (1999). I am aware that, at least in some cases, these usages reflect a translation from a more nuanced word—for example, *ius*—to the English law.

than looking to existing public meanings. If a look at our conventional use of law will lack philosophical precision, or preciosity, it is meaningful exactly because identification of different forms of normativity is not a matter of a priori necessity but of rough, a posteriori classification and abstraction. It is, to use an idiom, complicated.

The relationship between words and the world around us is always bridged by concepts rooted in convention, the product of specific experiences, times, and places. This is no less true for law. *Law* has no fixed, perennial meaning or essence, a lesson that comparative analysis, in either time or space, can provide without the need for jurisprudential scrutiny. But because law has no essence, convention matters. Law is not a scientific concept, but a necessarily parochial and shifting folk concept rooted in our experiences in the West, the *communis opinio* of both legal literati and laypeople, though similar forms were and are known around the globe.[24] Although the term should not be seen to be univocal, *law* and its cognate forms were applied to norms of specific institutions structured in specific ways in specific times and places.[25] The wider linguistic practice over the *longue durée* of Western history has defined law, generally speaking, as an institutional normative order, subject to some minimally accepted authority and external substantive metrics (distinguishing laws from the rules and sanctions of, for example, banditti).[26] I repeat, the state is not part of this definition. It cannot be. Laws and legal institutions preceded the state. This nonstate or prestate institutional form is arguably law's focal meaning, distinguishing it both from later state law as well as from other, less organized—but no less valuable—instances of social normativity.[27] Law, as defined here, is not superior to other normative orderings; a place without law simply manages its norms differently. And, of course, the meaning of law can be consciously changed. If our individual invention is collectively embraced, it may become the new convention. But then law will have been transformed, and we will no longer be discussing the same concept.

A rough and revisable genealogy of law, rooted in historical and comparative research, requires us to sketch a basic typology of normative institutionalization. As will be clear, the focus throughout is not on the state, a late and particularly abstract and artificial community, but on normative communities more generally as well as the individuals who populate them. If we grossly simplify a complex past, a spectrum of more or less institutionalized normative forms in the West might be characterized as:

1. *Normative practices and orders*, such as social customs; the moral economy; natural law (*ius naturale*); informal mediation (priests, neighbors, the *pater familias*); and so on.
2. *Normative regimes*, such as moderately institutionalized custom (chthonic customs), the internal jurisdiction of nonstate corporate bodies (such as guilds), some arbitration, perhaps dueling, and so on.
3. *Legal regimes*, such as overlapping customary laws, canon law, royal law, urban law, and so on.
4. *State legal regimes*, such as the early modern Western state.
5. *State legal systems*, such as the modern Western state.

Although this spectrum represents, in general, a movement in time, it need not be seen as progressive or unidirectional.[28] The pattern is not universal, but analogous forms and developments occurred beyond the West both before and after European colonialism and hegemony. Even as the later forms arise, the older ones

24 As a historical fact, state legal regimes and systems have often been diffused through Western colonialism and hegemony. Compare Halpérin (2009). On the internal colonization or diffusion of Mediterranean law throughout Europe, see Whitman (2009).

25 Noninstitutionalized norms were also recognized and analyzed. The lawyer's distinction, from scholarship on custom, might be that between norms *intra* or *praeter legem* (within or consistent with the enacted law) and *contra legem* (against the enacted law).

26 For a modern Anglophone institutional theory, see MacCormick (2006). But compare Twining (2009b: 18), which, among other things, criticizes the presentist bias of MacCormick's institutional theory).

27 On focal meaning, see Finnis (1980: 276–81).

28 Similarly, the mere provision of a mediator or adjudicator (whether lay or law trained) with the sanction of a legal regime or system (with or without a discrete body of substantive norms) in summary and discretionary jurisdictions can effectively allow a normative regime to bootstrap on the recognized parent regime or system. Compare, for example, the discretionary jurisdictions of Anglo-American justices of the peace, who are often laypeople.

persist and may thrive. These types represent the fact that social norms may be rationalized through language to general principles or more specific rules. These principles or rules are further instantiated in tradition, from a large variety of implicit and noninstitutionalized *normative practices and orders* (an interrelated assemblage of norms) to ever-more institutionalized forms.[29] All are dedicated to channeling or clarifying certain ends. At least in the origins of these orders, the ends will determine the institution's aims; over time, the institution will usually develop some autonomy and alter the ends accordingly.[30] And while a clear rule cannot be established, the creation of a *normative regime* can be seen as the inclusion of a minimal level of specialization—perhaps largely in personnel—in normative creation, consciously or inadvertently, or in decision making, whatever its content. The further shift to a *legal regime* is obviously significant. The formalities that historically led to recognition as law included additional specialization in personnel, training, and language, assisted by the introduction of writing and archives, which permit an institutional memory of authorized or authentic norms to be maintained over time and space.[31] As a practical matter, these normative and legal regimes will, if they are to survive, perform basic jobs.[32] Although this practice might provide some sense of social order, was often backed by more or less positive incentives or negative sanctions, and generally sought resolutions or settlements in fact, none of these are—at least according to this wider convention—essential elements.[33]

We might simplify and say that Western legal history since the fall of Rome is a movement from *ius* (a sense of rightness, closely associated to the meaning of *norm,* often with respect to social mores) to *lex* (the posited rule of an authority), though the latter is often created to ensure the former and has frequently operated behind the veil of custom. But until relatively recently, law required no claim to dominance. Legality, like normativity, took plural forms. In the period after the fall of the Roman Empire, for example, multiple contemporaneous normative and legal regimes coexisted and overlapped in the same geographic space and at the same time, although often affecting different individuals. They included multifarious folk laws, local and particular *iura propria*, the Romano-canonical learned laws or *ius commune*, and other transterritorial *iura communia* (including feudal law and, perhaps, the *lex mercatoria*). To these regimes must be added numerous summary and discretionary jurisdictions of low justice, arbitration of different sorts, the internal jurisdiction of nonstate corporate bodies such as guilds, and a wide variety of alternative methods of dispute resolution. These arguably affected more people more of the time than did royal or common laws. Normative and legal ordering was multicentric, with disparate competing centers of power and persuasion. Legal regimes only rarely sought—and still less often expected—to govern their rivals. The ability to legislate or adjudicate authoritatively was contested for centuries. One searches in vain for a *Grundnorm*, though practicalities could determine the dominance of different institutions at different times and in different places. When they finally developed late in Western history, states were more formally institutionalized. *State legal regimes* make the novel claim to sovereign dominance or exclusivity. Other normative orders and regimes were seen, at least in

29 What may appear to be an isolated or floating norm will typically turn out to be part of a wider normative order. Holding a door open or tipping a hat, for example, may be necessary for a gentleman.

30 Evaluating these developments, I suggest that the order's reference to justice is only relative. Compare von Daniels (2010: 99) and Donovan (2008: 251) on law as fairness. That is, justice may be best seen as *aretaic*, as largely an order-specific belief rather than a meaningful universal claim. Indeed, this approach allows a differentiation of institutionalized laws and norms from etiquette and morality. The latter two are the residual aspiration of normative ordering—minor and more significant, respectively—left outside the order. This leaves us with a soft legal-normative relativism that emphasizes the conventional nature of justice itself. Rightness, and perhaps even justice, might best be seen as a system-specific sense of excellence—as acting according to ends instantiated in the particular normative tradition. Although some minimal human goods may exist across time and space on the basis of generally common human inclinations, these values are so extraordinarily plastic and so profoundly altered in different normative contexts that nominally common elements are invariably thin. They include law, although its institutionalization results in a greater level of autonomy vis-à-vis both other norms and the order from which the legal regime developed. I will develop this argument in a future publication.

31 See Mariano Croce's (2011: 42) more nuanced understanding of the distinctiveness of law. See also Croce (2012).

32 Compare Karl N. Llewellyn's (1940) law-jobs theory. Note, however, that the element of supremacy Llewellyn suggests for legal authorities is inconsistent with the historical record.

33 The concept offered here does not "characterize law in terms of social order, … state law, [or] in terms of justice and right" (Tamanaha 2009: 6).

increasingly important theories of state sovereignty, as reliant on the sufferance of the state. Finally, the modern Western *state legal systems* of the nineteenth century make these claims meaningful while also threading together the diverse legal regimes into a single common law, though still without displacing its rivals. Earlier ideas and institutions might, of course, continue to exist within reformed structures.[34] Although the past half-century has brought many changes and the future promises more, this modern legal world persists.[35]

Because law has no essence, various conceptions are possible, and different concepts may prove useful in diverse contexts. Although it is unnecessary to my approach to hybridity and diffusion to accept this conventional definition, there are strong reasons to employ it. This Western concept of law as an institutionalized normative order can serve as an ideal type, a working model or metric, for analysis. Not only is this conception is less arbitrary than its rivals; it also provides a meaningful *via media* between the jurist's equation of law with the state and the novel use of law among legal pluralists.[36] This institutional definition separates the legal regimes—or regimes of law—that meet its conditions, including state legal regimes, from nonsystematic norms and other normative orders. This concept provides a meaningful nonstate law. It does so on the basis of established, if sometimes forgotten, conceptual characteristics. Like any such conception, it is an admittedly limited, operational concept. It is rebuttable and revisable. Like any such model, some bias and evaluation are inevitable in my description. But there is no neutral vantage point. Like any such theory, it is a generalization from practice, leaving a gap, however small, between its general terms and actual multifarious uses. But by being rooted in the practice of centuries, this sense of nonstate law may allow us to clearly and honestly engage in conversations from within our own unavoidably conventional conceptual language with those immersed in alternative forms of normativity.[37] It, as well as the spectrum of normative forms around it, also provides rich conceptual resources for the study of other normative orderings, past and present. We can abandon the search for a singular concept of law without giving up on meaningful debates rooted in established understandings of law and while remaining alert to both new usages and new challenges (Halpin 2011: 519).

Principle and Practice

To return to my central theme, all contemporary normative and legal traditions are hybrid creations, an ongoing gumbo of nominally native elements and new, often borrowed features. But in addition to this division of laws and norms, hybridity also involves another crucial distinction. The second axis of hybridity previously mentioned divides the examination of normative and legal orders of various types on the basis of their titular principles and actual practice.[38] That is, discussions of hybridity often focus on the origins and organization of the rules and principles of an order, regime, or system. In this sense, the image presented will often appear static and coherent. Complexity will seem to be an aspect of the order's past and, however unintentional, an impression of unity will be suggested. But hybridity also involves—indeed is still more concerned with—the varying interpretations and applications of such rules and principles and their effects on these standards over time. It reveals that these approximations, or reifications, are never the whole story. With

34 Even as different laws are swallowed by the unitary institutions of the state, they may not be entirely digested and can continue to exist semi-independently. Equity, for example, is still a unique substantive part of English law—now common law—although distinct structures no longer exist since the fusion of law and equity in the nineteenth century.

35 This type of historical analysis can generate many of the same conclusions as contemporary social science. But as our own comparative legal history, it may have more purchase in conceptual debates and in legal education. See Donlan (forthcoming a). Indeed, legal pluralist literature, so often premised in fact on a state-nonstate distinction, often neglects normative and legal hybridity without a state.

36 Concern that the adoption of a Western concept by scholars inevitably creates real-world repression is unconvincing (see Tamanaha 2011).

37 My defense of a single convention as an ideal type differs from Tamanaha's (2000: 313) suggestion that "*[l]aw is whatever people identify and treat through their social practices as 'law' (or recht, or droit, and so on)*" (italics in original). In addition, Tamanaha's analysis of Western law is ironically limited to legal theorists rather than to people more generally.

38 Compare Eberle's (2007: 97–99) use of internal law.

respect to both normative and legal orders, there may be a significant divide between its overt understanding or self-understanding and the often covert, unarticulated realities of its practice. That being said, one cannot deny that principle and practice influence each other in dialectical form. The "feedback loop" between formal doctrine and actual outcomes, which David Ibbetson (2012: 140) referred to with respect to comparative legal history, is no less relevant here.

But this analysis of legal and normative practice should not focus only on internal considerations and professional activities. Internal decision making is increasingly affected by all manner of global norms, a fact that legal theory is struggling to come to grips with (Halpin and Roeben 2009: 275). And these norms are external both to national state laws and to law itself. The public interpretation and application, or obstruction to application, are critical to my approach. *Legal consciousness* (that is, "the understandings and meanings of law circulating in social relations") and *normative consciousness* are as important as codes or case law (Silbey 2008: 695; see also Ewick and Silbey 1998). Indeed, because the influences on adjudication and legal consciousness go beyond considerations merely internal to an order, it is necessary to include still more diffuse normative and practical influences. Dominant political, economic, and ideological forces inevitably affect legal and normative practices of norm generation and interpretation. Although these influences may be seen as external, they are "secreted in the interstices" of internal practices.[39] The explicit recognition of these forces, of "power relationships between actors in the law and between legal [normative] orders," is essential in providing a deep focus on the normative whole (Hussin 2007: 759). Indeed, it is often better to see hybridity less as involving questions of governing (including legislating, adjudicating, and administering) than as regarding questions of Michel Foucault's "governmentality," wherein social regulation is not centered in the state—or, presumably, its normative proxies—but is rooted in the practical play of power (Rose, O'Malley, and Valverde 2006). This power can be both local and global. Diffusion occurs, for example, not on the basis of rational choice but under the influence of cultural prejudice and political, economic, and ideological hegemony (see, for example, Mattei 2003).

This focus on practice is obviously able to draw on numerous well-established approaches to law that underline the complexity of the most ordinary law and legal system. Roscoe Pound (1910: 15) famously formulated the gap between the *law in books* and the *law in action*, "between the rules that purport to govern the relations of man and man and those that in fact govern them."[40] As part of a critique of legal formalism begun over a century ago on both sides of the Atlantic, similar statements can be found in other American realists (for example, Frank 1930, Llewellyn 1930). If this is now a standard—indeed tired—bromide in legal scholarship, it should be remembered that if *law in action* is not merely meant to be a vulgar behaviorism, it must actually concern itself with what William Ewald (1995) called the "*law in minds*" (see also Ewald 1998; Valcke 2004). Similarly, Rodolfo Sacco's (1991a; 1991b) theory of *legal formants* goes beyond the inevitable slippage of legal interpretation. Instead, Sacco underscores the considerable diversity in the interpretation of state laws, a complexity frequently rooted in practical, professional differences among those interpreting the law (especially judges, jurists, and legislators).[41] There is, contrary to appearances, no single legal norm in a coherent and neatly hierarchical system, not even in the most apparently monolithic tradition. Numerous other modern schools of legal philosophy—perhaps especially postmodern legal theory, critical legal studies, and different schools of hermeneutics—provide many of the same conclusions. In each of these instances, the insistence on context significantly problematizes the concept of closed and discrete systems of rules.

These theories are primarily rooted in law and legal practice. They understandably focus their attention on the role of legal actors expounding on doctrine or interpreting enacted laws and the jurisprudence (case law) produced in adjudication. Indeed, law reports, whatever their formal status as sources of law, are central to this scholarship, functioning as (unscientific) case studies of normative application. The analysis of texts

39 Maine (1883: 389) wrote that "[s]o great is the ascendancy of the Law of Actions [i.e., writs] in the infancy of Courts of Justice, that substantive law has at first the look of being gradually secreted in the interstices of procedure."

40 *Law in action* and *living law* are frequently confused. But *law in action* is the law as applied, in contrast to the *law in books*, whereas the *living law* includes social norms in contrast to legal norms (Nelken 1984; see also Hertogh 2004).

41 Similarly, the study of legal polycentricity stresses legal diversity within or internal to state law, especially with regard to sources (Hirvonen 1998; Petersen and Zahle 1995).

is a large part of this type of legal study, although it is not the whole part of it. But the complexities of interpretation and application are often less obvious in normative traditions that are more oral than written. Failing to redact these norms may disguise the variable content, or indeed vacuity, of a normative order. And where it is appropriate to talk of sustained development in any direction, this conversation occurs *sub silentio*, without individual intention or explicit acknowledgment. The absence of texts and often the multiplication of applicable languages and cultures significantly complicate an understanding of the tradition. On the one hand, all of these considerations are relevant for much of Western legal history.[42] On the other hand, the process of writing down norms, whether social or legal, has often significantly altered their meaning and application. This was true both in the European past as well as in Europe's colonial encounters with other legal and normative traditions. And, in both cases, redaction has often had the effect of placing elites—both juristic and legislative redactors and adjudicators—in a more powerful position. All of these points are vital to my approach to hybridity. But actual public practices and legal and normative consciousness are still more important. Elaborating on his own praxiological perspective, Dupret (2007) has similarly underscored the importance of replacing grand theory with "the close investigation of actual data reflecting the ways (methods) in which people (the members of any social group) make sense of, orient to, and practice their daily world." Although the challenges here—historiographical, comparative, and social scientific—are significant, a "close investigation" of normativities in action and in the minds is at the heart of hybridity and diffusion.[43]

Conclusion

Hybridity and diffusion is a promising method for examining legal and nonlegal normative complexity by a deep, descriptive focus on lived normativity in all its forms. It can achieve this by taking seriously both general normativity and legality and by recognizing the gap between the principles of an order and its actual practice. *Hybridity* may be characterized as providing a blurry snapshot of this complexity or perhaps a short sequence of frames that attempt to record normative movement. *Diffusion* relates to larger movements, to the ongoing creation and revision of normative practices more generally. Both may concentrate on the individual, but as a practical matter, they typically do so by recognizing individual actions as instantiations of wider, porous, and overlapping institutions. Understood in this way, the method of hybridity and diffusion joins the social and legal sciences, not least legal history and legal philosophy. It is complicated. It is perhaps too complicated for an ordinary jurist like myself. But collaborative interdisciplinary and transdisciplinary research could make hybridity and diffusion invaluable to investigating the intersections and interplay, the complex interjurality, of East and West, North and South, and past and present.

References

Anthony, K.D. 1992. The identification and classification of mixed systems of law, in Commonwealth Caribbean Legal Studies: A Volume of Essays to Commemorate the 21st Anniversary of the Faculty of Law of the University of the West Indies, edited by G. Kodilinye and P.K. Menon. London: Butterworths: 179–218.

Berman, P.S. 2010. Towards a jurisprudence of hybridity. Utah Law Review, 1, 11–29.

Blaut, J.M. 1993. *The Colonizer's Model of the World: Geographical Diffusionism and Eurocentric History*. New York: Guilford.

Brown, M., and Donlan, S.P. 2011a. *The Laws and Other Legalities of Ireland, 1689–1850*. Farnham, UK: Ashgate.

42 In the context of eighteenth-century Ireland, see Donlan (2012b: 157–58).

43 Such an investigation was the focus of a meeting of historians, jurists, and social scientists at the conference on Doing Justice: Official and Unofficial "Legalities" in Practice, held in Rabat, Morocco, on June 18–19, 2012.

Brown, M., and Donlan, S.P. 2011b. The laws in Ireland, 1689–1850: A brief introduction, in *The Laws and Other Legalities of Ireland, 1689–1850*. Farnham, UK: Ashgate, 1–31. Available at: http://www.ashgate.com/pdf/SamplePages/Laws_and_Other_Legalities_of_Ireland_1689_1850_Intro.pdf [accessed: November 18, 2013].

Burke, P. 2009. *Cultural Hybridity*. Cambridge, UK: Polity.

Carbonnier, J. 1977. Les phénomènes d'internormativité. *European Yearbook in Law and Sociology*, 1, 42–52.

Castellucci, I. 2012. Legal hybridity in Hong Kong and Macau. *McGill Law Journal/Revue de Droit de McGill*, 57(4), 665–720.

Chiba, M. 1998. Other phases of legal pluralism in the contemporary world. *Ratio Juris*, 11(3), 228–45.

Coorter, R., Marks, S., and Mnookin, R. 1982. Bargaining in the shadow of the law: A testable model of strategic behavior. *Journal of Legal Studies*, 11(2), 225–51.

Croce, M. 2011. Is there a place for legal theory today? The distinctiveness of law in the age of pluralism, in *Law's Environment: Critical Legal Perspectives*, edited by U. de Vries and L. Francot. The Hague: Eleven International Publishing, 19–44.

Croce, M. 2012. *Self-Sufficiency of Law: A Critical–Institutional Theory of Social Order*. New York: Springer.

Delmas-Marty, M. 2009. *Ordering Pluralism: A Conceptual Framework for Understanding the Transnational Legal World*. Portland, OR: Hart.

de Sousa Santos, B. 2002. *Towards a New Legal Common Sense: Law, Globalization, and Emancipation*. 2nd ed. London: Butterworths.

Donlan, S.P. 2010a. "All this together make up our common law": Legal hybridity in England and Ireland, 1704–1804, in *Mixed Legal Systems at New Frontiers*, edited by E. Örücü. London: Wildy, Simmonds & Hill, 265–302.

Donlan, S.P. 2010b. Comparative law and hybrid legal traditions: An introduction, in *Comparative Law and Hybrid Legal Traditions*, edited by E. Cashin-Ritaine, S.P. Donlan, and M. Sychold. Zurich: Schulthess, 1–10.

Donlan, S.P. 2010c. Histories of hybridity: A problem, a primer, a plea, and a plan (of sorts), in *Comparative Law and Hybrid Legal Traditions*, edited by E. Cashin-Ritaine, S.P. Donlan, and M. Sychold. Zurich: Schulthess, 21–34.

Donlan, S.P. 2011a. The Mediterranean Hybridity Project at the boundaries of law and culture. *Journal of Civil Law Studies*, 4, 355–96.

Donlan, S.P. 2011b. Remembering: Legal hybridity and legal history. *Comparative Law Review*, 2(1), 1–35.

Donlan, S.P. 2012a. Book review: Ubiquitous law: legal theory and the space for legal pluralism (2009) by Emmanuel Melissaris. *Canadian Journal of Law and Jurisprudence*, 25(1), 177–82.

Donlan, S.P. 2012b. "They put to the torture all the ancient monuments": Glib reflections on making eighteenth-century Irish legal history and the proceedings of some writers on Ireland relative to that subject, in *Making Legal History: Approaches and Methodologies*, edited by A. Musson and C. Stebbings. Cambridge, UK: Cambridge University Press, 146–63.

Donlan, S.P. Forthcoming a. Everything old is new again: Stateless law, the state of the law, and comparative legal history, in *Stateless Law: Evolving Boundaries of a Discipline*, edited by S. van Praagh and H. Dedek Farnham, UK: Ashgate.

Donlan, S.P. Forthcoming b. Entangle up in red, white, and blue: Spanish West Florida and the American Territory of Orleans, c.1803–1810, in *Entanglements in Legal History: Conceptual Approaches*, edited by T. Duve. Frankfurt am Main, Germany: Max Planck.

Donlan, S.P., Andò, B., and Zammit, D. 2012. "A happy union": Malta's legal hybridity. *Tulane European and Civil Law Forum*, 27(1), 165–208.

Donovan, J.M. 2008. *Legal Anthropology: An Introduction*. Plymouth, UK: AltaMira.

Drummond, S. 2005. Prolegomenon to a pedestrian cartography of mixed legal jurisdictions: The case of Israel/Palestine. *McGill Law Journal*, 50(4), 899–949.

Drummond, S. 2008. Dishing up Israel: Rethinking the potential of legal mixité. *Windsor Yearbook of Access to Justice*, 26(1), 163–202.

Dupret, B. 1999. Legal pluralism, normative plurality, and the Arab world, in *Legal Pluralism in the Arab World*, edited by B. Dupret, M. Berger, and L. al-Awaini. The Hague: Kluwer, 29–40.

Dupret, B. 2007. Legal pluralism, plurality of laws, and legal practices: theories, critiques, and praxiological re-specification. *European Journal of Legal Studies* [Online], 1(1). Available at: http://www.ejls.eu/1/14UK.pdf [accessed: November 18, 2013].

Eberle, E.J. 2007. Comparative law. *Annual Survey of International and Comparative Law*, 13(1), 93–102.

Ehrlich, E. [1936] 2002. *Fundamental Principles of the Sociology of Law*. New Brunswick: NJ: Transaction.

Ewald, W. 1995. Comparative jurisprudence (I): What was it like to try a rat? *University of Pennsylvania Law Review*, 143(6), 1889–2149.

Ewald, W. 1998. The jurisprudential approach to comparative law: A field guide to "rats." *American Journal of Comparative Law*, 46(4), 701–707.

Ewick, P., and Silbey, S. 1998. *The Common Place of Law: Stories from Everyday Life*. Chicago: University of Chicago Press.

Finnis, J. 1980. *Natural Law and Natural Rights*. Oxford, UK: Oxford University Press.

Forsyth, M. 2009. *A Bird That Flies with Two Wings: Kastom and State Justice Systems in Vanuatu*. Canberra: ANU E Press.

Frank, J. 1930. *Law and the Modern Mind*. New Brunswick, NJ: Transaction.

Fuller, L. 1968. *The Anatomy of Law*. New York: Praeger.

Graziadei, M. 2006. Comparative law as the study of transplants and receptions, in *The Oxford Handbook of Comparative Law*, edited by M. Reimann and R. Zimmermann. Oxford, UK: Oxford University Press, 441–76.

Griffiths, J. 1986. What is legal pluralism? *Journal of Legal Pluralism*, 24, 1–55.

Griffiths, J. 2005. The idea of sociology of law and its relation to law and society, in *Law and Sociology: Current Legal Issues*, edited by M. Freeman. Oxford, UK: Oxford University Press, 49–68.

Halpérin, J.-L. 2009. The concept of law: A Western transplant? *Theoretical Inquiries in Law*, 10(2), 333–54.

Halpérin, J.-L. 2011. Law in books and law in action: The problem of legal change. *Maine Law Review*, 64(1), 46–76.

Halpin, A. 2011. Conceptual collisions. *Jurisprudence*, 2, 507–19.

Halpin, A., and Roeben, V. 2009. Concluding reflections, in *Theorising the Global Legal Order*, edited by A. Halpin and V. Roeben. Oxford, UK: Hart, 273–78.

Hertogh, M. 2004. A "European" conception of a legal consciousness: Rediscovering Eugen Ehrlich. *Journal of Law and Society*, 31(4), 457–81.

Hespanha, A.M. 2004. Legal history and legal education. *Rechtsgeschichte*, 4, 41–56.

Hirvonen, A. (ed). 1998. *Polycentricity: The Multiple Scenes of Law*. London: Pluto.

Holbrook, J. 2010. Legal hybridity in the Philippines: Lessons in legal pluralism from Mindanao and the Sulu Archipelago. *Tulane Journal of International and Comparative Law*, 18(2), 403–50.

Hussin, I. 2007. The pursuit of the Perak Regalia: Islam, law, and the politics of authority in the colonial state. *Law and Social Inquiry*, 32(3), 759–88.

Ibbetson, D. 2012. Comparative legal history: A methodology, in *Making Legal History: Approaches and Methodologies*, edited by A. Musson and C. Stebbings. Cambridge, UK: Cambridge University Press, 131–45

Kleinhans, M.-M., and Macdonald, R. 1997. What is a critical legal pluralism? *Canadian Journal of Law and Society*, 12, 25–46.

Llewellyn, K.N. 1930. *The Bramble Bush: On Our Law and Its Study*. New York: Oceana.

Llewellyn, K.N. 1940. The normative, the legal, and the law-jobs: The problem of juristic method. *Yale Law Journal*, 49(8), 1355–400.

MacCormick, N. 2006. *Institutions of Law: An Essay in Legal Theory*. Oxford, UK: Oxford University Press.

Macdonald, R. 2002. *Lessons of Everyday Law/Le Droit du Quotidien*. Montreal: Queens University School of Policy.

Macdonald, R.A., and MacLean, J. 2005. No toilets in park. *McGill Law Journal*, 50, 721–87.

Maine, H.S. 1883. *Dissertations on Early Law and Custom*. London: John Murray.

Mancuso, S. 2013. Creating mixed jurisdictions: Legal integration in the Southern African Development Community (SADC) region. *Journal of Comparative Law*, 6(1), 146–60.

Mattei, U. 2003. A theory of imperial law: A study on U.S. hegemony and the Latin resistance. *Indiana Journal of Global Legal Studies*, 10(1), 383–448.

Melissaris, E. 2009. *Ubiquitous Law: Legal Theory and the Space for Legal Pluralism*. Farnham, UK: Ashgate.

Nelken, D. 1984. Law in action or living law? Back to the beginning in sociology of law. Legal Studies, 4(2), 157–74.

Örücü, E. 1996. Mixed and mixing systems: A conceptual search, in *Studies in Legal Systems: Mixed and Mixing*, edited by E. Örücü, E. Attwooll, and S. Coyle. The Hague: Kluwer, 335–52.

Örücü, E. 2004. *Family trees for legal systems: Towards a contemporary approach, in Epistemology and Methodology of Comparative Law*, edited by M. Van Hoecke. Oxford, UK: Hart, 359–75.

Örücü, E. 2007. A general view of *legal families* and of *mixed systems*' in *Comparative Law: A Handbook*, edited by D. Nelken and E. Örücü, 169–87.

Osler, D.J. 2007. The fantasy men. *Rechtsgeschichte*, 10, 169–92.

Palmer, V.V. 2007. Mixed legal systems … and the myth of pure laws. *Louisiana Law Review*, 67, 1205–18.

Petersen, H., and Zahle, H. 1995. *Legal Polycentricity: Consequences of Pluralism in Law*. Brookfield, VT: Dartmouth.

Pound, R. 1910. Law in books and law in action. *American Law Review*, 44, 12–36.

Reisman, W.M. 1999. *Law in Brief Encounters*. New Haven, CT: Yale University.

Roberts, S. 2005. After government? On representing law without the state. *Modern Law Review*, 68(1), 1–24.

Rose, N., O'Malley, P., and Valverde, M. 2006. Governmentality. *Annual Review of Law and Social Science*, 2, 83–104.

Roughan, N. 2011. The relative authority of law: A contribution to "pluralist jurisprudence," in *New Waves in Philosophy of Law*, edited by M. del Mar. Basingstoke,UK: Palgrave Macmillan.

Roy, A. 2008. Postcolonial theory and law: A critical introduction. *Adelaide Law Review*, 29(2), 315–58.

Ruffini, J.L. 1976. Disputing over livestock in Sardinia, in *The Disputing Process: Law in Ten Societies*. New York: Columbia University Press, 209–46.

Sacco, R. 1991a. Legal formants: A dynamic approach to comparative law (I). *American Journal of Comparative Law*, 39(1), 1–34.

Sacco, R. 1991b. Legal formants: A dynamic approach to comparative law (II). *American Journal of Comparative Law*, 39(2), 343–401.

Samuel, G. 1990. Science, law and history: Historical jurisprudence and modern legal theory. *Northern Ireland Legal Quarterly*, 41, 1–21.

Shahar, I. 2008. State, Society and the Relations between Them: Implications for the Study of Legal Pluralism. *Theoretical Inquiries in Law* 9(2), 417–41.

Silbey, S. 2008. Legal consciousness, in *The New Oxford Companion to Law*, edited by P. Cane and J. Conaghan. Oxford, UK: Oxford University Press, 695.

Stross, B. 1999. The hybrid metaphor: From biology to culture. *Journal of American Folklore*, 112(445), 254–67.

Tamanaha, B. 2000. A non-essentialist version of legal pluralism. *Journal of Law and Society*, 27(2), 296–321.

Tamanaha, B. 2001. *A General Jurisprudence of Law and Society*. Oxford, UK: Oxford University Press.

Tamanaha, B. 2009. Law. Oxford International Encyclopedia of Legal History, edited by S.N. Katz.

Tamanaha, B. 2011.What is "general" jurisprudence? A critique of universalistic claims by philosophical concepts of law. *Transnational Legal Theory*, 2(3), 287–308.

Twining, W. 2004. Diffusion of law: A global perspective. *Journal of Legal Pluralism*, 49(1), 1–45.

Twining, W. 2005. Social science and diffusion of law. *Journal of Law and Society*, 32(2), 203–40.

Twining, W. 2006. Diffusion and globalization discourse. *Harvard International Law Journal* 47(2), 507–15.

Twining, W. 2007. Globalisation and comparative law, in *Comparative Law: A Handbook*, edited by E. Örücü and D. Nelken. Portland, OR: Hart, 69–91.

Twining, W. 2009a. *General Jurisprudence: Understanding Law from a Global Perspective*. Cambridge, UK: Cambridge University Press.

Twining, W. 2009b. Institutions of law from a global perspective: Standpoint, pluralism and non-state law, in *Law as Institutional Normative Order*, edited by M. del Mar and Z. Bankowski. Farnham, UK: Ashgate, 17–34.

Twining, W. 2010. Normative and legal pluralism: A global perspective. *Duke Journal of Comparative and International Law*, 20, 473–517.

Valcke, C. 2004. Comparative law as comparative jurisprudence: The comparability of legal systems. *American Journal of Comparative Law*, 52(3), 713–40.

Vanderlinden, J. 1989. Return to legal pluralism: Twenty years later. *Journal of Legal Pluralism*, 28, 149–57.

von Daniels, D. 2010. *The Concept of Law from a Transnational Perspective*. Farnham, UK: Ashgate.

Whitman, J.Q. 2009. Western legal imperialism: Thinking about the deep historical roots. *Theoretical Inquiries in Law*, 10(2), 305–32.

Chapter 3
Mixed Jurisdictions: The Roads Ahead

Luis Muñiz Argüelles

Professor Vernon Palmer's (2012) introduction to *Mixed Jurisdictions*, now in its second edition, provides an outstanding analysis of the origins and characteristics of mixed jurisdictions in many Western countries. Often as the result of conquest and at times by choice, these countries have learned to live and also to love, if I may say so, a legal system based on continental European and Anglo-American concepts.

It is time, however, to look at the roads ahead. We may have very little quarrel with the analysis offered in *Mixed Jurisdictions*, but most of us may wonder what the future holds from the perspective of non-Western countries or jurisdictions. Those of us from countries with mixed Western legal systems seek not to have a temporary niche carved out for us as a mere marker in the paths we have traveled, a marker that legal anthropologists may use in the future to describe what existed in the past. We feel there is something unique about our legal systems and would like to continue our journey along new paths that will lead us to new quarries, where we can find materials from which to build not another niche, but a stronger edifice. The question we have to ask ourselves is whether these quarries exist mainly in our Western world or whether we can legitimately search for them elsewhere.

The systems analyzed in both the first and second editions of the book are "exclusively western, drawn as it is from Romano-Germanic and Anglo-American legal materials" (Palmer 2012: 8). It may be a personal feeling, but here in Malta those of us from the Americas are not only physically but also emotionally closer to systems that draw from sources other than traditional European ones. Having listened to scholars coming from primarily Islamic law countries, I have come to wonder about the roots and the nature of our particular legal systems. Now that we have identified what is common between us, contrasting these findings with what exists elsewhere will, I believe, help us learn more about the essential nature of our mixed jurisdictions, better understand ourselves, enrich our traditions, and share with others those facts that we have gathered. The third legal family "is also conceived for purposes of convenience, utility, and explanatory power, and basically it deserves to be used only if it provides better insights than comparative analysis has provided in the past" (Palmer 2012: 16).

My goal in this chapter is to pose some questions that may help us gain some of these insights. I choose to ask more than to answer, as experience has taught me not to try to provide solutions before surveying the ground on which I am being asked to build. And so I ask the following questions:

- First, how is it that existing Western-based mixed legal systems have come about?
- Second, how have some of the conditions that helped forge our systems been reaffirmed, and why do they survive?
- Third, how might these conditions be replicated elsewhere, thereby allowing us to see beyond the cultural limits of our world to other jurisdictions where we may find (a) that this third legal family is common or (b) that there are other systems—a fourth and fifth legal family, new or traditional—with a legitimate claim to be counted as part of something else?

Sociopolitical Foundations of Our Legal Systems

Mixed legal systems, as they have been identified, are generally the result of colonialism and impositions by the conquering power. It is true that we find exceptions, Israel being one of the latest and Scotland one of the earliest, but even in those cases, it was colonialism that led the British to Palestine, and it was cultural and economic expansion, if not expansion in other forms, that made British presence ever more meaningful in and around Edinburgh.

But colonialism is not now and has never been an exclusively British trademark. It has been around for ages, as we can ascertain from reading about the Greek origins of Cleopatra in Egypt or those of Julius Caesar and Marc Antony, her two Roman "sentimental partners," as we would call them in today's politically correct parlance. These latter two led an empire where law was an important building block. Colonialism as we define it today was also present in the expansion of the various Islamic caliphates and the multiple Chinese conquests, to add just two non-European examples.

In more modern times, we have had far-reaching, legally ruled empires centered in France, in Castile, in Lisbon, in Brussels, and in Rome, to name but some of the Western centers. At one time, the kings of Spain ruled over an empire on which, as was later said of its British counterpart, "the sun never sets." The Spanish territory comprised as much, if not more land, than did the British Empire.

Why then, when we speak of mixed jurisdictions, do we speak mainly of countries that were conquered by English-speaking armies and not of those colonized by the French, the Spaniards, or others in many other parts of the world? The answer, I propose, lies in time, in politics, in demography, and in self-perception and not in philosophy or in law itself.

The Time Element

The answer lies in time because the political hegemony of other Western empires is today a thing of the past, and the influences the colonial powers left are either forgotten or taken for granted, accepted as "natural" in the same countries where they were first felt. The merchants who in Roman times met in the Palmyra Oasis in what is now Syria often communicated in Greek, some say, so as to show their resistance to Roman conquest and impositions, but this history is too far in the past to be noted in modern-day legal classifications. Some legal impositions are not part of today's political reality.

The last of the great Western empires was British. London was last to deal with conquered peoples—especially conquered Western peoples, for culture has a lot to do with the fact that most mixed jurisdictions identified in Palmer (2012) are in place in countries where the former power was also Western and not in those where Western systems were superimposed as a whole, with little or no respect for entrenched values.

Spain lost most of its empire almost two centuries ago, in the early 1800s, when the American republics shed their political links with Madrid. The controlling elites, however, were very much in tune with the cultural mold of the old metropolis and chose to keep the many cultural traits they valued. They did not experiment with mixed legal systems because as leaders of new Western nations, struggling for recognition from what was then the center of the economic and intellectual world, they never thought of incorporating legal rules from nonmodern, which then meant non-Western, local ethnic groups. It was only in the late twentieth century that the descendants of native populations achieved some sort of cultural recognition, mainly in language rights (Muñiz Argüelles 2001).

It is not that some of the Spanish cultural or political leaders neglected to value and fight for the rights of the conquered. The Spaniard Fray Bartolomé de las Casas was one of the first in the modern era to stand out as a champion of those rights. The Jesuits in Paraguay also set up missions to aid local populations, albeit while keeping administrative control of the missions. However, the protection they afforded was not for local legal autonomy, but rather against outright exploitation and cultural genocide. Arguments for the rules of marriage and procedure, as important as they may be to us now, pale in the light of the struggle for mere survival as a people and a culture. Mixed jurisdictions were not in the minds of those who valued and defended other ethnic groups.

The French, who lost much of their Western empire to the British from the late eighteenth century to mid-nineteenth century, did attempt to deal with local cultures in their North African and sub-Saharan colonies, which were conquered primarily in the mid-nineteenth century during what some have called "the scramble for Africa." Much has been said of the French colonial policy of *assimilation*,[1] which meant that, in theory, all conquered peoples could aspire to become as much *citoyens et citoyennes* as those born in the Hexagon. It should be added, however, that assimilation did mean different things at different times and in different places. French policies were not so uniform as often portrayed.

In the late nineteenth century, Paris adopted, for some of its colonies, the Code de l'Indigénant, which recognized a separate legal system for some of the conquered. In theory at least, the institution resembled the so-called British indirect rule system. It is true that, when applied to non-Western peoples, the code came, at least for a time, with forced labor, multiple taxes, and forced conscription, which made it somewhat less appealing than the conquering nation would have thought. In addition, in areas of large French population, legal matters were solved in French-styled courts, and when local courts or legal rules were used, they applied only to the non-French, as can be seen not only in legal studies but also in writings such as Albert Camus's *L'Étranger*. The mixed legal systems described in Palmer (2012) apply all rules to all groups, be they the conquerors or the conquered.

British rule over conquered non-Western peoples was not altogether gentle or respectful of their local values, which casts some doubt on why it is now at times portrayed as more accommodating and more acceptable than the other imperial systems.

Recent studies have argued that British policies were often similar to those of France, whether because Paris did not fully practice assimilation or because Britain did not always, to say the least, actually put in place its system of local autonomy through indirect rule.[2] Obviously, there was little of local rule in the submission of China between 1839 and 1860 to further the opium trade, in the submission of local peoples who had faced off with the British in Burma, or in the suppression of others in places where there was a sparse population not needed for economic development, regardless of whether indirect rule was later recognized in some of these places. For the moment, it is sufficient to say that the impact of English-speaking conquests is more recent and thus more present than that of other countries, which were able to "transculturize," if that word exists, or which were never able to impose their legal systems on others. The details of Spanish colonial policies in the Americas from the sixteenth to the early nineteenth centuries are somewhat distant, unlike those of nineteenth- and twentieth-century Anglo-American policies.

Political and Demographic Elements

The reason that the legal systems we currently identify as mixed combine Anglo constitutional and procedural rules and continental European substantive private rules lies partly, I believe, in politics. Two factors contribute to this outcome. The first is the character of British imperialism vis-à-vis the imperialism of France and Spain. The second is the desire of modern Western mixed jurisdictions to hold on to a cherished though sometimes idealized past, a topic I will briefly discuss later in the chapter.

Britain, unlike other imperialist nations, has recently (that is, in the past century or two) ruled over an enormously diverse empire. In Britain's case, it was hard to devise a uniform system for a vast array of different cultures, some Western, some African, some Middle Eastern, some from the Indian subcontinent, and some from the Far East. Britain's interest, like that of France's or Spain's, was exploitation of the colonies for the benefit of the metropolis, but to do so it needed peace. It devised solutions that were not always coherent with its past or with its expressed goals, which is not surprising given that history is often somewhat messy, but it did come up with solutions that served its purpose for a time.

1 Literature on colonialism in general and on English and French colonialism in particular is vast. Two central French works that in different ways favor the colonial policies, since highly questioned, are Sarrault (1923), which claimed that colonial policies could benefit both the conquered and the conqueror, and Girault (1943).

2 See, for example, Bleich (2005: 190), who states, "The historical record shows that the assumptions central to this argument—that France's colonial policies and integration structures have been assimilationist and direct, and that Britain's have been differentialist and indirect—are not as true as they first appear." See also Beer (1933; 2010); Deflem (1994); Lawrence (1997); Roberts (1929); and Woodberry (2004), who questions if the transfer of political culture was a result of altruism or of British democracy, which, he points out, also existed at home in other colonial powers.

All conquerors, if not all peoples, feel somewhat superior to others. In largely empty territories, where local populations were sparse and lacked the technological means to oppose the British, the British not only conquered but also populated the land. Perhaps the most obvious examples are Australia, Canada, and much of the United States. In these places, there was not only a lack of recognition of local customs but also a simple substitution of the population.

In other, more populated and advanced cultures, cultural transformation, either through the imposition of the colonizer's language, culture, or laws, was a means of conquest, but if transformation was not complete, the goal of gaining economic wealth was achieved by changing the superstructure, all while forgoing or postponing cultural transformation of the conquered peoples. One of the few times the British expressly admitted this economic motive was in the Declaratory Act of 1766, in which it asserted, ironically regarding a culturally Western territory—that is, French North America—that its empire existed to serve the economic interests of the mother country (see, for example, Evans 2006).

Where the British faced a dense, highly organized local population, they eventually chose to control and not transform it, for transformation was an impossible feat in this situation. India, one of the world's most densely populated regions, with a recorded history dating back further than that of Europe, is perhaps a prime example. Indirect rule, which recognized some local values, even though at times marked by repression and excesses, was necessary to allow for control without outright resistance and to regulate the main source of revenue for the British Empire.

Obviously, there were other factors, and they played out differently in various regions. New France, although populated by a fair number of people at the time of its conquest by France, also proved militarily strategic, given what was even then the almost foreseeable uprising in the British colonies to the south. Initial assimilation attempts were set aside to guarantee the allegiance of the ancestors of today's Quebecers, an allegiance that proved to be warranted when two centuries ago that province, together with British troops, fought back American attempts to incorporate Canada during the second war between Britain and the United States—what in North America is called the War of 1812. That allegiance was rooted in what can be called concessions to the French-speaking settlers in the 1774 Quebec Act, which among other things guaranteed respect for the colony's legal tradition, French language, and Catholic faith. That legal tradition, accessible through a common language with the old French metropolis, allowed the Quebecers to adopt, in 1865, a greatly modified but still identifiable version of the French Civil Code, the Civil Code of Lower Canada.

Further to the South, in Louisiana, Americans also recognized local culture by allowing the continuance of legal traditions. The result was the 1808 Louisiana Civil Code, which was also inspired by the *Code Napoléon*. There, too, the English-speaking newcomers to the Louisiana Territory arrived in an even more densely populated area—that of New Orleans and its surroundings—with strong cultural ties to a known and admired, though rival, European country. The sparse population of most of the Louisiana Territory, where technologically less developed, non-Western peoples lived, allowed for the rapid cultural transformation of the region, but Louisiana itself retained its legal tradition.

In the case of Puerto Rico, the fact that the United States was far more interested in securing naval coaling stations in the Caribbean than in expanding its culture or even its commerce with the island (where businesses, in any case, relied more on contraband American products than on Spanish goods) allowed Puerto Rico, which also had a known European culture, to retain much of its private law. American Secretary of War Elihu Root expressly said so in his 1899 report to Congress, citing the Quebec and Louisiana precedents to back his argument. The goal of the new conquering power was not to incorporate and thus culturally transform the island but to politically control it, thereby securing control of the Caribbean Sea and the Panama Canal, which was then being built. The transformation of private law would have meant unrest and economic chaos, said Root, and was not necessary to achieve the political goals of the conquering power. The US Supreme Court ruled shortly thereafter that Puerto Rico, the Philippines,[3] and Guam—all three wrested from Spain

3 The case of the Philippines differs from that of Puerto Rico in that early on a decision was made to grant them independence, a decision that was put off until after World War II. Puerto Rico was the subject of more debate, and outright attempts were subsequently made to convert the island into a culturally American territory. Teacher strikes, legislative pronouncements, and some violent resistance finally led to the recognition that Puerto Rico was culturally Spanish speaking, although its final political status is still the subject of an immense debate around which all political parties are organized. Racial differences also played a role, and Root noted in his 1899 report that the ruling elite in Puerto Rico, contrary to that in the Philippines, was of European origin, as was that of the United States.

in the 1898 Treaty of Paris, which put a formal end to the Spanish-American War—were not incorporated territories.[4] Thus, there need not be a blueprint for their becoming American states, which allowed the United States to control them but not transform their cultures or legal foundations.[5]

For diverse reasons, therefore, the British and Americans chose to respect local private law and concentrate their legal imperialism on public law—that is, on constitutional and administrative law and on judicial organization and procedure, the arenas where political battles of control were to be fought. Private law in the colonized territories was, after all, not too different in its content than that in the conquering powers. It is interesting to note that the colonizers chose to transform public law in places where known and respected—though sometimes criticized—Western cultures were in place. Secretary of War Root stated this explicitly in his 1899 report to Congress.

French and Spanish conquerors acted differently with regard to non-Western cultures, as did the British with regard to some their conquered non-Western colonies. I acknowledge that the French or Spanish colonies were at one time formally seen by the metropolis as parts of the European nation, but I question whether deep down these colonies or the local population felt that they really were part of that metropolis. True, Martinique, Guadeloupe, French Guiana, Réunion, and Mayotte are *départements d'outre mer*, and Algeria was, for a time, said to be an integral part of France. When push came to shove, however, Algeria, the largest and closest of these territories, was granted independence in 1962, just 16 years after its incorporation into France in the 1946 constitution, which set up the Fourth Republic. The writings of Aimé Césaire and Frantz Fanon also suggest that conquered peoples do not always share the thoughts of their conquerors. Even in formal terms, the French *départements d'outre mer* and other overseas territories may today, with exceptions, mold their law to their needs and not follow Paris completely.[6]

While recognizing the Latin American local elite as descendants, the Spanish did not grant them the same status as people from the Iberian Peninsula, who were called the *peninsulares*. This failure to recognize the status of local elite was one of the causes of the Wars of Independence in South America. The colonies were there, as are colonies everywhere (Wehler 1980: 291ff), for the benefit of the metropolis (Bonilla 1991). In this sense, the goals of the Spanish were not too different from those of the British, but political, demographic, and technological realities led the Spanish to practice policies that the British did not always implement.

I believe this difference in colonial policies was not the result of the British or Americans adhering to the doctrine of separation of powers—one of the few disagreements I have with Palmer (2012: 9)—but of the other socioeconomic realities I have mentioned. The doctrine of separation of powers is as much a part of the continental European tradition as of Anglo-American culture, even when it manifests itself in somewhat different ways.

The Local Political Factor: A State of Mind

Mixed systems, as I said earlier, have existed for ages, but only now are they being recognized as such. I hold that this change is also the result of politics—happy politics, for a change.

We who are part of Western mixed legal jurisdictions are proud of what we have and thus defend it. The old Spanish procedural law, which was not modernized until the late twentieth century, originated in the early

4 See *De Lima v. Bidwell*, 182 U.S. 1 (1901); *Goetze v. United States*, 182 U.S. 221 (1901); *Dooley v. United States*, 182 U.S. 222 (1901); *Armstrong v. United States*, 182 U.S. 243 (1901); *Downes v. Bidwell*, 182 U.S. 244 (1901); *Huus v. New York and Puerto Rico Steamship Co.*, 182 U.S. 392 (1901); *Dooley v. United States*, 183 U.S. 151 (1901); and *Fourteen Diamond Rings v. United States*, 183 U.S. 176 (1901).

5 Some exceptions must be noted. Divorce was introduced in Puerto Rico from the start, through Military Order 19 of March 17, 1899. The same exception was made in Quebec, where local autonomy as to private law does not include divorce, which the English-speaking power felt was crucial. Thus, today the Code Civil du Québec does not have its divorce articles in force.

6 See, for example, the website of the French Legal and Administrative Directorate at http://www.vie-publique.fr/decouverte-institutions/institutions/collectivites-territoriales/outre-mer/comment-dom-rom-peuvent-ils-adapter-lois-ou-fixer-regles-leur-territoire.html [accessed: November 21, 2013]. The latest revision of local prerogatives dates from the law of February 21, 2007.

nineteenth century and was based on pre–French Revolutionary procedure, which is politically repugnant to today's societies. Thus, in Puerto Rico, we cherish modern procedure, which was brought to us not by the Spanish monarchy but by the United States, albeit through imposition, but revered nonetheless. We have adopted useful constitutional structures, also through imposition, but also now cherished.

We could go back to the Spanish, French, or other models, which are probably as useful as the ones we have in place today, but the cost and toil of doing so does not seem to warrant the effort. We learned the legal rules now in place through years of hard studies in our universities, and our professors will probably continue to teach what they best know, even when they can also learn that the rules in force are not the only valid model. Conversely, regarding the substantive private law rules that we have maintained from the prior continental European systems, their replacement by Anglo rules, substantively not too different from those in place, would imply the rejection of a familiar language that has served us well and that keeps the legal rules current; this rejection also is a cost that seems too high.

We are not happy with all we have, and we complain that the imperial background of our systems often means that some odious rules remain in place. However, we know that most of these rules—like the ones that force Puerto Ricans to pay American import tariffs and use American ships in transporting goods to and from the United States—are not matters of legal culture but of pure politics. These discrepancies are perceived as raw political conflicts, not matters that will sway us as to the merits or demerits of our mixed legal system. And some of the rules that once seemed odious, such as divorce in Quebec and Puerto Rico, are today accepted in those legal systems as they were in the old metropolitan centers, and it would be unthinkable to live without them. We have thus adapted and learned to live with and love what we have, even when we want to change some of the details.

Western mixed jurisdictions are mixed because the people in those countries do not see much conflict in the rules that came from the original Western centers. Such cultures value what they have and do not want to do away with it. As Palmer (2012: 8) states, there are many "quantitative and psychological factors" that explain why we wish to keep what we have. We do not want to reject what we have just because it was not part of the law before our conquest, any more than the British want to do away with many of their contract rules simply because the Law Merchant was largely the result of their need to do business with France, when France was the center of the European world.

The question we must ask ourselves is whether countries that have adopted Western molds—codes, case laws, and procedures—but not substantive Western legal rules will identify with Western mixed jurisdictions that adopted these molds or structures but retained their Western values. Others may feel that the molds—codes, case laws, and procedures—are useful but the substance of the law, because it is different or derives from another source, is sufficient to reject the *mixed system* nomenclature. To ask the question more directly, are some Islamic countries mixed because they have both private law codes and public case law, or are these structures just molds that do not change the fact that they are mainly or essentially Islamic law jurisdictions? Are Western mixed jurisdictions seen as a third legal family only in the West because they have managed to work with two Western molds while retaining their own essentially Western legal values, a factor that would make the category less appealing to other cultures that see their identity not in the molds but in the essence?

The Roads Ahead

I began this chapter with the question of what we are to do in the future. Are we to study ourselves further to identify other characteristics that we will add to so that our legal niche, which marks us as distinct from the systems of the former or current metropolitan cultures, becomes a comfortable dwelling place and not a roadside shelter that will soon decay and disappear? Are we to build on our system with rocks from our own quarries, because they are the ones that best fit in with the blocks we have so far used to identify and defend our systems in ways that past cultures never did? Or are we to look beyond our borders, to see if experiences in other cultures offer other building materials that we can incorporate into our edifice and to trade some of our own building blocks with those cultures so that they too can join us in this third legal family, or rather legitimately claim to be part of a fourth or fifth one?

I believe we are at a crossroads, and as legal architects or perhaps as professors of legal architecture, we should travel not one but many roads in search of the materials that will help us better build on what we have.

Some may look deeper into the changes that have taken place in Scotland and Israel, where colonialism played a different role than in Quebec, Louisiana, or Puerto Rico (the three legal cultures I know best), to examine what took place there and why. I suggest that language had a lot to do with the degree of change in those countries but that language may be a factor that weighs less today, thanks to the number of translations available and to the number of lawyers and law professors who are learning to master languages other than their own.

Some may look further into the changes that have taken place or that loom near in those systems where ties with the Anglo-American community are not only economic but also political, to see whether the political will exists to keep what has in the past served well. If the political will exists, those systems will continue to be kept in the future.

Some may look beyond our borders, to the Islamic countries, for instance, which are far better known to us than other parts of the world, for Islamic Toledo was for centuries the main European center of learning and, let us not forget, of tolerance toward other cultures, mainly our own Western one.

Some may look further, to Africa and the Far East, to see if the adoption of some Western models provides us with answers on what makes for a healthy mixed system, so that our growth may be more coherent and fruitful.

Some may even look at the more traditional European and American models, to see if the adoption of legal rules and practices (such as constitutional review,[7] precedents,[8] trusts,[9] anticipatory breach of contract,[10] "floating" securities,[11] or the modern procedural rules of the partly American-inspired Model Civil Procedure Code for Iberian America), which once seemed foreign, does not signal a negative change in these systems, but rather a healthy development, even though these Western countries do not see themselves as "mixed." We should remember that legal transplants occur constantly, and that American lawyers did not feel terribly less like common law lawyers after New York adopted the Field Code of Civil Procedure or after a host of states adopted the European-inspired Uniform Commercial Code proposed by Karl Llewellyn.

Mixed jurisdictions involve a host of factors. We look at our past and hope to have found many of the answers, but a look at others from the outside can also shed light on other questions. We need to be open to the world, linguistically and culturally, knowing why certain institutions were transplanted and how they can help us to improve our own law. To do so, we have to be able to examine ourselves and others in their own playing fields, with their own languages, and through their own prisms.

We should continue to meet, but also to form a network from which to better understand an evermore pleasant and useful structure. As Palmer (2012: 65) explained, "Without consultation, judicial minds in all these systems have conceived a similar set of passports for the common law." I propose that with consultation the process may be far more efficient. Much has been achieved, and much more can be done.

References

Beer, G.L. 1933. *The Old Colonial System, 1600–1754.* New York: Peter Smith.

Beer, G.L. 2010. *A Short History of British Colonial Policy.* New York: Cambridge University Press.

7 Constitutional review existed in most American nations from the time of their independence and was adopted in Europe in more recent times.

8 The French case of *Jand'heur v. Les Galeries Belfortaises* (Ch. Réunies) of February 13, 1930, is a prime example. Civil law jurisdictions make use of precedent almost as much as do common law jurisdictions, as is evidenced by the economic success of publishers, who print out or electronically distribute a host of boring and hard-to-read cases for lawyers who must read and cite them. The doctrines of *jurisprudence constante* and *doctrina legal* in France and Spain, as elsewhere, are based on the binding nature of case law.

9 Trusts were adopted in Puerto Rico from a Panamanian (that is, a traditionally civil law) jurisdiction. See Vilella Sánchez (1976).

10 This provision was incorporated into proposals for common contract rules in Europe, including the Principles of European Law in its article 9.201(2).

11 This provision was adapted from the common law system of secured transactions in article 2715 of the new Quebec Civil Code.

Bleich, E. 2005. The legacies of history? Colonization and immigrant integration in Britain and France. *Theory and Society*, 34(2), 171–95.

Bonilla, H. 1991. *El sistema colonial en la América española*. Barcelona: Editorial Crítica.

Deflem, M. 1994. Law enforcement in British Colonial Africa. *Policy Studies*, 17(1), 45–68.

Evans, S. 2006. Language policy in British colonial education: Evidence from nineteenth-century Hong Kong. *Journal of Educational Administration and History*, 38(3), 293–312.

Girault, A. 1943. *Les Colonies Français avant et depuis 1815*. Paris: Sirey.

Lawrence, J. 1997. *The Rise and Fall of the British Empire*. New York: St. Martin's Griffin.

Muñiz Argüelles, L. 2001. Les politiques linguistiques des pays latino-américains: Commission des États généraux sur la situation et l´avenir de la langue française au Québec. Presented as part of the International Colloquium at the Université Laval, Quebec, March 24.

Palmer, V.V. 2012. *Mixed Jurisdictions Worldwide: The Third Legal Family*. 2nd ed. Cambridge, UK: Cambridge University Press.

Roberts, S.H. 1929. *History of French Colonial Policy, 1870–1925*. London: P.S. King & Son.

Sarrault, A. 1923. *La Mise en Valeur des Colonies Françaises*. Paris: Payot.

Vilella Sánchez, L.F. 1976. Desviaciones fundamentales y accidentales en la ley de fideicomisos respecto del derecho Angloamericano sobre trusts. *Revista del Colegio de Abogados de Puerto Rico*, 37(3), 417–52.

Wehler, H.-U. 1980. El imperialismo alemán, in *El Imperialismo: La Controversia Robinson-Gallagher*, edited by W.R. Louis. Mexico City: Nueva Imagen.

Woodberry, R.D. 2004. The shadow of empire: Christian missions, colonial policy, and democracy in postcolonial societies. PhD dissertation, University of North Carolina, Chapel Hill.

Part II
Patterns of Common and Civil Law Hybridities

Chapter 4

Do Pronouncements of the Constitutional Court Bind *Erga Omnes*? The Common Law Doctrine of *Stare Decisis* versus the Civil Law Doctrine of Nonbinding Case Law within a Maltese Law Context

Kevin Aquilina

The Maltese legal system is a mixed legal system comprising the legal families of civil law and common law, as well as European Union law since European Union accession in 2004. These three legal traditions are superimposed onto autochthonous native law. In this chapter, I pose the following question: Do the pronouncements of the Constitutional Court—the highest court in the land—bind *erga omnes*, or do they exclude third parties? This is a fundamental question for the Maltese legal system because of the discord that accompanies its answer. Such disagreement emerges not only in case law but also in doctrine. I will first discuss the binding nature of judgments by referring to case law, doctrine, and the jurisprudential debate that has ensued. This chapter considers these antagonistic viewpoints, discusses the contribution of the Select Committee of the House of Representatives on the Recodification and Consolidation of Laws and the Commission for the Holistic Reform of the Justice Sector, and concludes by presenting its own solution to this *vexata quaestio*.

A Divided Case Law

Case law is not unequivocal concerning the supremacy of the Constitution. Notwithstanding the fact that the defendant is always the Maltese government in those judicial proceedings that question the validity of a law, the Maltese courts are not unanimous in holding that a lawsuit against the government should always apply *erga omnes* (that is, against the government with regard to everyone). On the contrary, the Constitutional Court has consistently decided that a lawsuit requesting the declaration of an ordinary law is in breach of the Maltese constitution and is, therefore, void. A lawsuit instituted against the government binds only the person instituting that lawsuit (the applicant) and the government (the respondent). In other words, such a judgment does not bind third parties, even if the same legal principle applies both in the case of the applicant and in the case of the third party. The salient points arising from the convoluted case law of the Maltese courts on the supremacy of the constitution are discussed in this chapter.

In *Vincent Cilia v. Prime Minister et*,[1] the Civil Court held that the Constitutional Court had already declared on November 30, 2001, that paragraph (c) of subarticle 4 of the Sixth Schedule of the Value Added Tax Act of 1994 was in breach of both the Maltese constitution and the European Convention of Human Rights and Fundamental Freedoms. The Civil Court further maintained that it was bound by the declaration of the Constitutional Court that the provisions of the 1994 enactment were a breach of human rights. The Civil Court, First Hall, then declared these same provisions as a breach of the Maltese constitution and of the European Convention of Human Rights and Fundamental Freedoms. On appeal, the Constitutional Court,[2] in

1 The case was decided by the Civil Court, First Hall, sitting in its constitutional competence, per Justice Gino Camilleri, on June 20, 2003.
2 *Vincent Cilia v. Prime Minister et* was decided by the Constitutional Court on January 28, 2005.

the case of *Anthony Frendo v. Attorney General* on November 30, 2001, agreed that it had already declared paragraph (c) of subarticle 4 of the Sixth Schedule of the Value Added Tax Act of 1994 to be in breach of article 39(2) of the constitution and article 6(1) of the European Convention of Human Rights. The court held that this decision bound only the parties to that suit and did not bind *erga omnes*. However, the court noted that its decision did not negate the ability of the Constitutional Court or the Civil Court, First Hall, sitting in its constitutional competence, to declare a particular provision of the law in conflict with the rights of a citizen in one case and then to make the same declaration regarding another person in a similar case.

Note that the Constitutional Court, in recognizing that a provision of a law runs counter to the constitution when challenged by a particular person, fails to extrapolate that finding to others who end up in the same fate as that person. Because Malta does not subscribe to the doctrine of precedent, the Constitutional Court could declare a provision of ordinary law to be in breach of the constitution in one lawsuit and then come to the opposite conclusion regarding the same provision in another lawsuit. This observation is neither a conjecture nor a hypothetical scenario, for there have indeed been instances in which the Constitutional Court has successfully managed to contradict itself, sometimes within in a very short span of time. A case in point relates to the institute of arbitration.[3]

In *John Buhagiar et v. Registrar of Courts et*,[4] the Civil Court, First Hall, had to decide, among other issues, whether to declare that a judgment delivered by the Rent Regulation Board on January 19, 1993, in *Josephine Mangion pro et noe v. Mary Louise Camilleri et* did or did not bind the parties to the suit before the Civil Court. The court noted that after it had examined its records of the proceedings, the file of the Rent Regulation Board, and the warrant of ejectment from immovable property that was referred to in the writ of summons, it came to the conclusion that the plaintiffs to the case—John Buhagiar and his spouse, Maryanne Buhagiar—were not parties to the proceedings before the Rent Regulation Board in the case *Josephine Mangion pro et noe v. Mary Louise Camilleri et*. John and Maryanne Buhagiar were not cited as parties in the proceedings before the Rent Regulation Board and were not part of the acts of the proceedings of the warrant of ejectment. The court thus concluded that the proceedings before the Rent Regulation Board did not bind John and Maryanne Buhagiar, and the court accepted the plaintiffs' request on the basis of article 237 of the Code of Organization and Civil Procedure. The provision reads as follows: "A judgment shall not operate to the prejudice of any person who neither personally nor through the person under whom he claims nor through his lawful agent was party to the cause determined by such judgment." This provision is based on the Roman Law maxim of *res inter alios acta vel judicata aliis nec nocere nec prodesse potest* (translated as "things done between strangers ought not to injure those who are not parties thereto"). The court also held that the warrant of ejectment cannot be executed against a third party. This principle was enunciated by the Court of Appeal, sitting in its commercial competence in *Gulab Chatlani v. George Grixti* (Malta Courts 1991: 605), in which the court decided that a warrant of ejectment issued against a tenant could not be enforced against a subtenant who was not indicated by name in the warrant and who was consequently a third party to those proceedings. Note that the Civil Court, First Hall, applied article 237 of the Code of Organization and Civil Procedure within a civil—as opposed to a constitutional—setting. In this sense, the court's judgment was correct, and the application of article 237 sound.

In *Mario Galea Testaferrata et v. Prime Minister et*, the Constitutional Court heard an appeal of a judgment delivered by the Civil Court, First Hall, sitting in its constitutional competence. The Constitutional Court pointed out in its partial judgment on January 10, 2005, that the final judgment in this case would, in accordance with article 237 of the Code of Organization and Civil Procedure, bind only the applicants (Mario Testaferrata et), on one side, and the respondents (Prime Minister et), on the other. In my view, the Constitutional Court wrongly applied the law of civil procedure within a constitutional procedure context. Indeed, what might be proper and correct within the context of a civil procedure might not be just and fair within the context of a constitutional procedure.

3 For a discussion of contradictory judgments of the Constitutional Court on arbitration, see Attard (2012: 207–10).

4 The case was decided by the Civil Court, First Hall, per Justice Noel Cuschieri, on June 4, 2004.

In *Maria Azzopardi et v. Saver Sciortino et*,[5] the court referred to the *Mario Testaferrata* judgment of the Civil Court, First Hall, on October 3, 2000. In the latter case, the court had declared articles 12(4) and (5) of the Housing (Decontrol) Ordinance, chapter 158 of the Laws of Malta, to be in breach of article 37 of the constitution. Nevertheless, the court did examine whether articles 12(4) and (6) of chapter 158 applied to plaintiff Maria Azzopardi. Although the Civil Court, First Hall, was bold enough declare to the nullity of a law by the same court, though in a previous judgment, it did not go far enough to apply that judgment to the case at hand. Instead it decided to consider the legal issue of the case at hand afresh, even though the legal issue had already been determined in the previous case.

In *Mary Anne Busuttil v. Medical Doctor John Cassar et*,[6] the court referred to article 237 of the Code of Organization and Civil Procedure and commented that although it was correct that the provision unreservedly stated that a judgment may not prejudice a third party, nothing in that provision stated that a judgment may benefit or assist a third party in his or her claim to a right. This observation applied to any case in which a court must decide whether a law is valid or invalid or—as in the current case before the court—whether a provision of a law is in line with the constitution. The court further noted that the applicants were not challenging the provisions of articles 12(4) and (5) of chapter 158 but that their application gave rise to a breach of article 37 of the constitution dealing with protection from deprivation of property without compensation and to a breach of article 1 of the First Protocol to the European Convention for the Protection of Human Rights and Fundamental Freedoms dealing with the right to property. Note that the Civil Court, First Hall, attempted to circumvent the provisions of article 237 of the Code of Organization and Civil Procedure by arguing that article 237 did not expressly or impliedly prohibit a third party from benefiting from a previous judicial interpretation. In this case, the declaration of nullity was of assistance to a third party and could be used to his or her benefit.

In *Paola sive Pawlina Vassallo v. Marija Dalli*,[7] the court was requested to decide a plea that once articles 12(4) and (5) of chapter 158 were declared null and void in the *Mario Galea Testaferrata et v. Prime Minister et* judgment insofar as they ran counter to the constitution of Malta, these provisions of chapter 158 were not operative at law and could no longer be applied. The judgment, therefore, would apply *erga omnes*, notwithstanding that the provisions still formed part of the Maltese statute book. However, the court noted the defendants' submission that the *Mario Galea Testaferrata et* judgment was *res inter alios acta* because it applied to the parties to those proceedings but not to the parties to the present proceedings; therefore, in accordance with article 237 of the Code of Organization and Civil Procedure, the judgment did not bind third parties. In fact, the court noted that the plaintiffs were not requesting the declaration of articles 12(4) and (5) of chapter 158 to be in violation of the constitution and therefore null and void at law, pursuant to the previous declaration by the Constitutional Court in the *Mario Galea Testaferrata et* case. Instead, the plaintiffs were requesting the court to apply the *Mario Galea Testaferrata et* case to the current proceedings insofar as the latter judgment had already found articles 12(4) and (5) of chapter 158 to run counter to the constitution and that this judgment was *res judicata*. The court noted that, notwithstanding the *Mario Galea Testaferrata et* case, articles 12(4) and (5) of chapter 158 still remained operative in the statute book and that the Maltese parliament had not taken any action to have the articles amended or revoked.

The court then examined article 6 of the constitution[8] and consequently stated that it had to inquire whether the *res judicata* judgment bound *erga omnes*. The court referred to the Constitutional Court's judgment of *Vincent Cilia* in which the latter court had answered this question by stating that its own judgments bound the parties thereto but not *erga omnes*. The Civil Court, First Hall, reexamined the whole issue and did not rest on the previous declaration of unconstitutionality. The court thus concluded that in light of the case law of the Constitutional Court, it was bound to reexamine the merits once the judgments of the Constitutional Court

---

5 Decided by the Civil Court, First Hall, sitting in its constitutional competence, per Justice Raymond C. Pace, on January 31, 2007.

6 The case was decided by the Civil Court, First Hall, sitting in its constitutional competence, per Justice Joseph R. Micallef, on September 18, 2008.

7 The case was decided by the Civil Court, First Hall, sitting in its constitutional competence, per Justice Raymond C. Pace, on October 30, 2008.

8 Article 6 states that "if any other law is inconsistent with this Constitution, this Constitution shall prevail and the other law shall, to the extent of the inconsistency, be void."

bound only the parties thereto. Conversely, the court argued that once article 6 is applied and a law or provision thereof is declared unconstitutional, that provision should not be enforced. The court thus concluded that once the provision under examination was declared null and void and the judgment became *res judicata*, the court could not then apply the provision that had already been declared unconstitutional. That is, since article 6 provided that the constitution is supreme law, the unconstitutional provision was therefore null and void even though the Maltese parliament had not repealed or amended it. When a law is declared null and void, it is no longer enforceable, and its illegitimate status is *erga omnes* according to article 6 of the constitution. There should be no situation in which one law applies for some persons but not for others; one law should apply to everyone. Note that the Civil Court, First Hall, applied article 237 of the Code of Organization and Civil Procedure and took the same line of thought as the Constitutional Court did in the *Mario Galea Testaferrata* partial judgment of January 10, 2005. However, the court distinguished between an application for nullity of a law—which was not the case in the current proceedings—and an application of a judgment declaring a law null, as in the current case. However, it followed the *Vincent Cilia* judgment of the Constitutional Court to the letter, only adding that once a provision had already been declared null by the Constitutional Court, the court was not bound at law to apply the provision because the law in question would not be applied uniformly to one and all. This interesting judgment tries to reconcile article 237 of the Code of Organization and Civil Procedure with article 6 of the constitution.

In *Mario Galea Testaferrata et v. Prime Minister et*,[9] the court referred to article 6 of the constitution and held that articles 12(4) and (5) of chapter 158 were in breach of article 37 of the constitution and were thus null and void. The appeal was declared abandoned by the Constitutional Court on October 16, 2006, and, therefore, the judgment of the Civil Court, First Hall, became *res judicata*.

In *Josephine Bugeja v. Attorney General et*,[10] the court held that the *Mario Galea Testaferrata* judgment on October 3, 2000, bound only the parties thereto and did not bind *erga omnes*. The *Bugeja* judgment was, however, revoked by the Constitutional Court in its judgment on December 7, 2009.

In *Ruth Debono Sultana et v. Department for Social Welfare Standards et*,[11] the court held that article 114(2) of the Civil Code was discriminatory and in breach of article 14 of the European Convention of Human Rights. The court went on to order that in each adoption procedure, article 114(2) should be read in a way that was not discriminatory. Austin Bencini (2011: 393) holds that this case came "closest to a declaration of invalidity *erga omnes*.... Uniquely the court decided to amend the law in a virtual manner, by filling in the gap it created itself through its declaration of inconsistency, whenever such an inconsistency faces any application made by the applicants." The Constitutional Court, in its judgment on April 3, 2009, confirmed this judgment *in toto*, offering its own wording regarding how article 112(2) should be construed in the future. In this respect, the court has adopted a legislative approach in the interpretation and amendment of article 114(2) of the Civil Code in light of article 14 of the European Convention of Human Rights.

In *Conrad Axisa v. Attorney General et*,[12] the court concluded that the right that the attorney general enjoyed in terms of articles 575A(2) and (3) of the Criminal Code to appeal a magistrate's bail decision to the Criminal Court was in breach of the equality of arms principle if the accused did not enjoy the same remedy that the attorney general did. The court ordered the government to move a bill before the House of Representatives to guarantee the equality of arms by either replacing articles 575A(2) and (3) of the Criminal Code or extending that right to the accused. Amendment had to be affected within three months from the date of the court's judgment. If the House of Representatives took no action within those three months, the court ordered that articles 575A(2) and (3) had to be construed as giving to the accused *mutatis mutandis* the same

9 The case was decided by the Civil Court, First Hall, sitting in its constitutional competence, per Justice Raymond C. Pace, on October 3, 2010.

10 The case was decided by the Civil Court, First Hall, sitting in its constitutional competence, per Justice Tonio Mallia, on October 3, 2008.

11 The case was decided by the Civil Court, First Hall, sitting in its constitutional competence, per Justice Giannino Caruana Demajo, on October 14, 2008.

12 The case was decided by the Civil Court, First Hall, sitting in its constitutional competence, per Justice Tonio Mallia, on April 20, 2012. For a critical study of this judgment from the perspective of a European Court of Human Rights, see Bonello (2012b) and Debono (2012a). For a contrasting view, see Debono (2012b, 2012c).

right enjoyed by the attorney general. Note that the Civil Court, First Hall, was very proactive in this case, establishing a procedure that would be followed if the House of Representatives took no action to comply with the court's decision. Rather than having a situation of contempt of court result from the House's inactivity, the court came up with its own enforcement mechanism to ensure that its judgment would be enforced despite inaction by the House of Representatives.

In *H. Vassallo & Sons Limited v. Attorney General et*,[13] the Constitutional Court concluded that if a cause is not instituted under article 116 of the constitution (the popular action), the applicant must prove juridical interest.[14] As this case was not instituted under article 116, the court had to consider the case within the limits of juridical interest. Note that the constitution distinguishes between actions that require juridical interest and actions that do not require juridical interest. In the case of a popular action under article 116 of the constitution, the person exercising that action does not have to prove that he or she has a juridical interest in that case.

Taking Stock of the Emerging Jurisprudential Debate

From this discussion and commentary on the activity of the Maltese Courts from a jurisprudential angle, two schools of thought emerge:

- On the one hand, the view of the Constitutional Court is that, when it declares a law unconstitutional, that declaration binds only the parties to that judgment.
- On the other hand, some of the judges of the Civil Court, First Hall, sitting in its constitutional competence, are prepared to consider a judgment of the Constitutional Court or of the Civil Court as being binding *erga omnes*, provided that no appeal has been lodged to the Constitutional Court or that the Civil Court's judgment has become *res judicata*.

Unfortunately, there is little certainty in this field. Considering that Malta does not accept the doctrine of precedent, the judgments of the Constitutional Court—though highly authoritative—are not binding either to itself or to inferior courts. This unusual feature occurs because the Maltese legal system follows the civil law legal system, which allows inferior courts to dissent from the judgments of superior courts. Interestingly, although the Maltese constitution is derived from British public law (hence from the common law legal system), the procedure to enforce the provisions of the constitution vests with the law of civil procedure, which derives from the civil law legal system. Unfortunately, this dichotomy within the Maltese legal system creates more tensions than it solves.

A Divided Doctrine

On this point, Austin Bencini, head of the Department of Public Law at the Faculty of Laws of the University of Malta and eminent constitutionalist, states that an analysis of Maltese judgments indicates that the judges of the Civil Court, First Hall, "have attempted to affirm the *erga omnes* interpretation, while the Constitutional Court seems quite determined to resist such an interpretation even though allowance needs be made to a few chinks in the appellate court armour" (Bencini 2011: 382).

Judge Giovanni Bonello takes a very critical approach to the case law of the Constitutional Court. He argues:

13 The case was decided by the Constitutional Court on October 8, 2012.

14 Juridical interest is an institute of the law of civil procedure. For an action to be instituted in court, a person must possess juridical interest. Without such interest, the courts of civil jurisdiction will throw out an applicant's case unless it is the law itself (as in the case of article 116 of the constitution) that exempts the applicant from proving that he or she has an interest in those court proceedings.

> Parliament has been allowed to arrogate unto itself the final say as to whether those laws declared void by the Constitutional Court, should still remain valid and binding, or should be repealed.... The Constitutional Court has, by default, waved the supremacy of the Constitution goodbye.... The Constitutional Court, after solemnly declaring a provision of law to be null and void and anti-constitutional will, in a subsequent case, still consider that provision it has determined to be anti-constitutional and null, to be perfectly valid and legally binding—because ... Parliament has done nothing to repeal it." (Bonello 2013a: 4)

Judge Bonello further criticizes the two doctrines that the Constitutional Court has embraced—"that determinations of invalidity of laws only affect the parties to that particular law suit, and that a declaration of nullity of a law has no effect on that law unless Parliament repeals it" (Bonello 2013a: 7; see also Bonello 2012a). Bonello's incisive criticism of the workings of the Constitutional Court hits the nail on its head!

Chief Justice Emeritus Professor Giuseppe Mifsud Bonnici (2012a; 2012b; 2012c) takes the side of the Constitutional Court judgments cited previously when he distinguishes between the concept of validity and that of consistency. He argues that these two concepts are not synonymous. Bonnici (2012a: 8) writes:

> The Constitution does not authorise any Constitutional Court to declare null any law—whether old or new. Nor does it authorise any Constitutional Court to declare "invalid" any law, whether pre-1964 or [post-]1964. What the Constitution does is that it enables the competent courts to declare a law as being "inconsistent with or in contravention of" any one of the articles that list the fundamental rights.

It is then up to parliament to take the necessary legislative corrective measures.[15]

The 2013 Doctrinal Debate: Chief Justice Silvio Camilleri versus Austin Bencini

The contribution of Chief Justice Silvio Camilleri (2013a: 25), "The Constitutional Court and the Invalidity of Laws," sets a historical precedent. Camilleri published the article in a leading weekly newspaper under his name, thereby entering into the fray of interpreting the constitutional provision outside a judicial setting. In the article, Camilleri holds that

> neither in the English text nor in the Maltese text do we find the use of the word "null." In the English text, the word used is "void" while in the Maltese text what is used is the phrase "tkun bla effect."[16] I do not consider it appropriate here to enter into the possible implications that this wording may have (and possible implications do exist, especially when combined with the fundamental notion of "personal juridical interest" endorsed by our legal system, as indeed it is by many other jurisdictions).

The chief justice gives special weight to this distinction and, without spelling out quite clearly its constitutional implications (as "what could be added is not for me to add on account of the position I occupy" (Camilleri 2013a: 25)), he hints at the possibility that a law declared unconstitutional by the Constitutional Court is void or without effect, but not null. He also states that *null*, on the one hand, and *void* or *without effect*, on the other, are not identical in meaning and that different consequences can therefore be drawn from a law that is pronounced null and a law that is pronounced void or without effect.

On the other hand, Austin Bencini takes to task the sitting chief justice's distinction between the terms *without effect* and *null*. Bencini (2013: 21) asks:

---

15 For a criticism of this view, see Aquilina (2012); Bencini (2012); and Bonello (2012c, 2012d, 2012e, 2013b).

16 The translation of *tkun bla* reads "is without."

> Should constitutional supremacy depend on this semantic disquisition between "without effect" and "null"? According to the Oxford dictionary "null" means "having no legal or binding force—invalid." So, wouldn't an unconstitutional law being "without effect" also mean having "no binding force"? The Constitution proclaims it shall "prevail" over any inconsistent law. The dictionary defines "prevails" as "to prove more powerful or superior." Therefore, the Constitution is more powerful or superior than "any other law." How is this? By itself rendering that other law "without effect," in the sense of having "no binding force." Perfect! The English version of the Constitution refers to an unconstitutional law as "void." The Oxford dictionary defines void as "not valid or legally binding," and the example is "a contract is not legally binding" and therefore void. Clear isn't it?

In yet another unprecedented move by the head of the judiciary in Malta, the incumbent chief justice entered into a controversial doctrinal dispute with Bencini that cut across the principle of neutrality of the judiciary. The chief justice wrote a letter to the editor of *The Sunday Times of Malta* to criticize Dr. Bencini's argument (Camilleri 2013b: 26):

> The position taken by the Constitutional Court is in no way in contradiction with the principle of the supremacy of the Constitution. When the Constitutional Court interprets the Constitution and gives application to that interpretation it does no more and no less than give effect to the supremacy of the Constitution. One may agree or disagree with the Constitutional Court's interpretation but the Constitutional Court would be betraying the Constitution if it did not give effect to that interpretation which it has determined to be the right one—and this is true whether the supremacy principle needs to be expressly stated or is necessarily implicit.

Reflections on Case Law and Doctrine

The text of article 6 of the Maltese constitution is "if any other law is inconsistent with this Constitution, this Constitution shall prevail and the other law shall, to the extent of the inconsistency, be void." Several principles emerge from a study of this provision.

First, article 6 of the constitution does not restrict itself only to inconsistency with any provision of chapter 4 of the constitution dealing with human rights and fundamental freedoms. Article 6 goes beyond that and subjects all laws (other than the constitution itself) to consistency with all the provisions of the constitution except for those contained in articles 47(7) and (9) and article 66. *Law* is defined in the constitution as "any instrument having the force of law and any unwritten law." Therefore, law includes subsidiary legislation (regulations, rules, orders, bylaws, schemes, warrants, and so on) and customary law such as usages of trade or constitutional conventions.

Second, once the competent constitutional courts—the Constitutional Court and the Civil Court, First Hall, sitting in their constitutional competence—come to the conclusion that another law is inconsistent with the *Grundnorm*—the constitution—such courts are bound, in terms of article 6, to note that the other law is void. I say *note*, not *declare*, because it is not the court's judgment that renders void the inconsistent law; it is the Constitution in article 6 that does so. The marginal note to article 6 reads: "Constitution to be supreme law." Although in law, marginal notes are not normally used for interpretation (see *Chandler v D.P.P.*[17]), there is no doubt that the marginal note in question is an apt and faithful synopsis of the provision under examination.

Third, the concept of a *void* law has to be contrasted with that of an *invalid* law. Article 116 of the constitution allows a "right of action for a declaration that any law is invalid on any grounds other than inconsistency with the provisions of articles 33 to 45 of this Constitution." A similar provision is found in article 95(2)(e). Invalidity, to have effect, requires an express declaration in a court judgment. However, this is not the case with a void law because the inconsistent law is void *ab initio* and *ipso jure*. The constitution establishes a hierarchy of nullity of laws—the most superior being void laws followed by invalid laws. Void

17 *Chandler v. D.P.P.* [1964] AC 763, [1962] 3 All ER 142.

laws and invalid laws therefore produce different effects at law. *Void* is retroactive, and its effects date back to the date of its enactment. *Null* is prospective and applies from the date it is so declared onward.

The constitution uses three terms: *inconsistency*, *void*, and *invalid*. The term *nullity* is not used (although the term *annulled* is used with regard to elections). *Void*, in law, has more serious consequences than *invalid* because, in the case of article 6, the inconsistent law is *ex lege* void without necessarily requiring a pronouncement by a competent constitutional court declaring the inconsistent law to be void. The inconsistent law is inherently void by its very own nature. Although the law remains on the statute book, once it is inconsistent with the constitution, even if no court has taken note of such a state of affairs, it has *ipso jure* no legal effect: it is unenforceable and is a dead letter. Therefore, such a law has no binding effect and no one (courts, government, public administration, any person) should follow its command. Hence, it is "without effect," as the Maltese version of *void* in article 6 of the constitution puts it. *Void* implies that the provision is by its very own essence or being an absolute nullity. Once a law is void, it binds no one and does not require a court declaration to that effect. If there is a court judgment noting that such an inconsistent law is void, that court judgment obviously binds the parties thereto in terms of article 237 of the Code of Organization and Civil Procedure. The same judgment also binds third parties, not by virtue of article 237 but insofar as third parties are bound by operation of article 6 of the constitution. In law, a distinction is made between *void* and *voidable*. The latter term means that a provision is valid until it is annulled. Although *voidable* requires a pronouncement by a court, what is inherently void requires no court pronouncement other than the word of the law to that effect.

In this respect, an inconsistent law is void *ab initio* and *ipso jure* and not when it is so declared by the competent constitutional court. The court's pronouncement that an inconsistent law is void is an indication, an observation, a certification, or an attestation of the legal status of that inconsistent law. Indeed, the court's judgment does not make the provision void even though it has practical relevance because through the court's authoritative pronouncement the community is informed that an inconsistent law is void. The court's decision simply notes a situation of fact when the judgment is delivered. However, the court's judgment is retroactive in effect when it recognizes that the inconsistent law was void not at the time of the delivery of the judgment but at the time the inconsistent law was enacted. This treatment is but a manifestation of the constitution's supremacy over parliament. The constitution uses its inbuilt defensive mechanism to strike down any ordinary law enacted by parliament that is inconsistent with the constitution without needing to have recourse to the judicial organ of the state to declare the inconsistent law void. Hence, the other law can be both inconsistent and void. These are two different concepts, but they are very much interlinked from a constitutional point of view. Inconsistency with the constitution makes a law void—the inconsistency has to do with the juridical nature of the norm—whereas a void law concerns the effects of the inconsistency of the norm. The supremacy of the constitution over parliament is further manifested through the court's declaration of invalidity of a law in terms of articles 116 and 95(2)(e) of the constitution.

Fourth, foreign courts and authors have adopted similar interpretations in their own legal systems. The German Federal Constitutional Court has held that an unconstitutional law is "inconsistent with the Basic Law and therefore invalid" (Schlaich 1994: 220–21). Klaus Schlaich (1994: 220–21) states that an "unconstitutional law is from its inception (*ex tunc*) and without need for any further act (*ipso iure*) inoperative.... The German view is that the Federal Constitutional Court does not annul a statute, [the court] does not invalidate: it merely establishes the invalidity [in a declaratory way]." The South African Constitutional Court has declared that "laws are objectively valid or invalid depending on whether they are or are not inconsistent with the Constitution. The fact that a dispute concerning inconsistency may only be decided years afterwards, does not affect the objective nature of the invalidity" (Schlaich 1994: 220–21).

Commission for the Holistic Reform of the Justice Sector's Proposal

In the *Second Consultation Document* published by the Commission for the Holistic Reform of the Justice Sector (2013: 75),[18] the commission referred to article 237 of the Code of Organization and Civil Procedure and

18 The Commission for the Holistic Reform of the Justice Sector is composed of Chairman Judge Emeritus Giovanni Bonello and the following members: Judge Emeritus Philip Sciberras, Professor Kevin Aquilina, and Dr. Ramona Frendo.

noted that what was not being recognized by the courts of constitutional jurisdiction (that is, the Constitutional Court and the Civil Court, First Hall, sitting in its constitutional competence) was that the government is always the defendant in constitutional cases. Therefore, the government is also bound by the judgment of such courts when they declare a law as running counter to the constitution and the European Convention on Human Rights and Fundamental Freedoms. Although the Commission for the Holistic Reform of the Justice Sector recognized the validity of article 237 insofar as civil proceedings were concerned, the same could not be said of article 6 of the constitution and article 3(2) of the European Convention Act because these two provisions hold that they are superior to any ordinary law. The commission maintained that where judgments of a constitutional and conventional nature are concerned, the principle that has to be followed is that these judgments should apply *erga omnes* and not be limited to the parties to the suit, because the state is always the defendant. Furthermore, insofar as the state is concerned, such judgments bind the state irrespective of the opposing party to the suit. The commission thus advocated the adoption of the procedure set out in the Bill for an Administrative Code,[19] whereby the law commissioner appointed in terms of the Statute Law Revision Act of 1980 would be empowered. This procedure would follow a final judgment in which a legal provision would be declared in violation of the constitution or the European Convention on Human Rights and Fundamental Freedoms. The legal provision would then have to succumb to annotation in the Laws of Malta to the effect that such a provision or law would no longer be in force or binding, even if such a law still formed part of the Laws of Malta and even if parliament had not abrogated it.

A Solution to This Legal Quandary

In my opinion, the Constitutional Court's judgment declaring a law or a provision void is final, including the provisions of article 6 of the constitution read in conjunction with articles 95(2)(c) and (d). In terms of the latter provision, the Constitutional Court within the Maltese legal system has the final word "as to the interpretation of this Constitution" whereas the Constitutional Court has the last say on "questions as to the validity of laws" in terms of article 95(2)(d). Therefore, once the Constitutional Court declares a law invalid, that judgment binds *erga omnes* irrespective of the parties to the suit, the merits of the case in question, or the law or provision that is declared void. Once the Constitutional Court has declared a law or a provision invalid, it continues to be invalid and should no longer be applied by the public administration, even if parliament does not abrogate that law or provision. It is the responsibility of the attorney general to issue guidance to the public administration to consider such a law or provision as a dead letter that is no longer applicable to any case. Forgoing such responsibility would open the public administration to an action for damages because the department in question would be acting in bad faith. Furthermore, the law or provision is invalid in terms of article 6 of the constitution *ab initio* and *ipso jure*; strictly speaking, the Constitutional Court's judgment declares a law or a provision to be inconsistent with the constitution even if that law or provision is still in the statute book.

The remedy is the empowerment of the law commissioner by law through an amendment to the Statute Law Revision Act to enter an annotation to the Laws of Malta through a footnote that states that the law or provision in question has been struck down by a Constitutional Court judgment. However, a difficulty arises in that striking down a law or a provision may not be enough. In such a case, parliament should intervene and update the law or provision to bring it in line with the Constitutional Court's judgment. Moreover, article 237 of the Code of Organization and Civil Procedure should be subjected by an express amendment of the law to article 6 of the constitution, not out of necessity but because some members of the judiciary give precedence to

19 The Bill for an Administrative Code was drawn up by the Select Committee of House of Representatives for the Recodification and Consolidation of Laws. It is available at http://www.parlament.mt/sc-codification [accessed: December 30, 2013]. The Select Committee was composed of Chairman Franco Debono and the following members: Francis Zammit Dimech and José Herrera. Before parliament was dissolved on January 7, 2013, the code was still pending a consultation process by the Select Committee, and it had not been adopted by the Select Committee or tabled in the House of Representatives. When parliament was opened on April 6, 2013, the Select Committee for the Recodification and Consolidation of Laws was not reconstituted, and the bill for an Administrative Code has been kept in abeyance.

ordinary law—the Code of Organization and Civil Procedure in this case—over the fundamental law of Malta. Finally, a time limit of one month should be established by law for the House of Representatives to discuss a bill that the law commissioner should prepare to bring the invalid law up to date with the Constitutional Court's judgment.

In this respect, I agree with Judge Emeritus Giovanni Bonello's argument that when the Constitutional Court continues to apply a dead law that has previously been declared void, it is itself in breach of the constitution. Therefore, the time is ripe for the Constitutional Court to bring its house in order by affirming the supremacy of the constitution over ordinary law—namely, article 237 of the Code of Organization and Civil Procedure—and the doctrine of juridical interest driven by case law.

Conclusion

The chief justice and all judges sitting in the Constitutional Court and in the Civil Court, First Hall, sitting in its constitutional competence, should interpret the constitution not through the application of rules of civil procedure but through the provisions of constitutional procedure as set out in the constitution itself. Juridical interest, declaring that judgments proclaiming invalid laws apply only to the parties to the action in question, and other provisions of civil procedure do not necessarily make sense from the perspective of constitutional procedure. That being said, the judiciary should not be blamed for such an interpretation because the fault lies primarily with the legislator who has not drawn up proper rules of procedure for constitutional proceedings but allows the courts to rely on the application of civil procedure rules to constitutional proceedings. Nonetheless, the judiciary is not quite blameless, because the constitution does bestow on it the power to give precedence to the constitution over the law of civil procedure and to uphold the supremacy of the constitution over ordinary law.

In addition, there is a rift in the judicial organ of the state, with the judges sitting in the court of first instance being more willing to uphold the supremacy of the constitution over ordinary law than their brethren sitting in the Constitutional Court. The incumbent chief justice's distinction between *null* and *void* or *without effect* is relevant; *void* implies that the law is *ab initio* and *ipso jure*, inoperative though enacted, whereas the nullity of a whole statute or a provision comes into operation from the moment it is so declared by the competent court of constitutional competence. It is not clear what the chief justice intended by this distinction because he did not elaborate, leaving his reader unaware of the finesse of such a distinction. I trust and hope that this chapter has set out correctly the divergent case law and doctrine on the subject of constitutional supremacy and nullity of laws and that the proposals for change will clarify this legal complexity. In future judgments, the Constitutional Court should change its current course and walk the path outlined, thereby affirming once and for all constitutional supremacy over ordinary law.

References

Aquilina, K. 2012. The constitution is supreme. *Times of Malta*, June 13.
Attard, D.J. 2012. *The Maltese Legal System*. Volume 1. Msida: Malta University Press.
Bencini, A. 2011. The supremacy of the constitution of Malta. PhD dissertation, Faculty of Laws, University of Malta, Msida.
Bencini, A. 2012. Upholding the constitution's values. *Times of Malta*, June 23.
Bencini, A. 2013. Constitutional supremacy is self-evident. *Sunday Times of Malta*, May 26.
Bonello, G. 2012a. Bad law? Worse remedy. *Times of Malta*, May 2.
Bonello, G. 2012b. Bailing out human rights. *Times of Malta*, April 27.
Bonello, G. 2012c. Constitutional law obfuscation. *Times of Malta*, June 6.
Bonello, G. 2012d. True and faithful allegiance. *Times of Malta*, June 20.
Bonello, G. 2012e. Constitution: A stretcher case. *Times of Malta*, July 4.

Bonello, G. 2013a. The supremacy delusion: Unconstitutional laws and neo-colonial nostalgias. Presented at the President's Forum at the Palace at Valletta, April 25. Available at: http://president.gov.mt/forum_president_it-tieni_edizzjoni?l=1 [accessed: November 25, 2013].
Bonello, G. 2013b. The Constitutional Court and the supremacy of the constitution. *Sunday Times of Malta*, May 19.
Bonnici, G.M. 2012a. The supremacy of parliaments. *Times of Malta*, June 2.
Bonnici, G.M. 2012b. Supremacy of parliament. *Times of Malta*, June 16.
Bonnici, G.M. 2012c. Supremacy: "What is" against "what should be." *Times of Malta*, June 28.
Camilleri, S. 2013a. The constitutional court and the invalidity of laws. *Sunday Times of Malta*, May 12.
Camilleri, S. 2013b. Quoting the constitution correctly. *Sunday Times of Malta*, June 2.
Commission for the Holistic Reform of the Justice Sector. 2013. *Second Consultation Document*. Valletta: Parliamentary Secretariat for Justice, Office of the Prime Minister.
Debono, F. 2012a. Illegal arrest and bail. *Times of Malta*, May 16.
Debono, F. 2012b. Legal apples and turnips. *Times of Malta*, May 8.
Debono, F. 2012c. No violation in Strasbourg: Violation in Malta. *Times of Malta*, May 11.
Malta Courts. 1991. *Collection of the Decisions of the Superior Courts of Malta*. Vol. LXXV, II. Valletta: Malta Courts.
Schlaich, K. 1994. *Das Bundesverfassungsgericht*. 3rd ed. Munich, Germany: C.H. Beck.

Chapter 5
The Parts That Make a Whole? The Mixity of the Laws of Seychelles

Mathilda Twomey[1]

More than a decade ago, George Gretton (1999: 164) noted of Scots property law that "one can live and work in a system and still massively fail to understand it in context." Such peripheral blindness may be common across a number of legal traditions and systems. It is certainly found in the mixed, microjurisdiction of the small island republic of Seychelles. This investigation marks the beginning of comparative research on Seychellois law and legal institutions in the hope of bringing them into greater focus.

In particular, this chapter will consider Seychellois law in light of the traits, trends, and tendencies characteristic of the "third legal family," as defined by Palmer (2012) in *Mixed Jurisdictions Worldwide*. For Palmer, the third legal family includes those systems that experienced double colonization, thereby combining in one jurisdiction both continental (civil law) private law and "common law" public law with judicial institutions and procedural and evidential law reflecting significant assimilation of Anglo-American legal mechanisms.

To determine the traits of the Seychellois legal system, we must examine its sources of law, substantive and procedural rules, legal infrastructure, and institutions. To analyze its trends, we need to describe its legal methodology and style. To examine its tendencies, we need to look at the values, traditions, and language underpinning the legal system.[2] Finally, we must be aware that recent developments in Seychelles suggest the sustainability of its legal *métissage*. These developments include the establishment of a law school at the University of Seychelles and the assistance of international legal experts to modernize and equip Seychelles for economic competition.

Finally, we will attempt to determine the taxonomic context of Seychellois law. Classifying this legal system is at best tentative, especially in view of the polemic surrounding legal taxonomy and the lack of a universally accepted legal classification system (Donlan 2010a). Moreover, whether the existing Seychellois legal system will be hardy enough to remain viable is questionable.[3]

Geography of Seychelles

The Republic of Seychelles is an archipelago of 115 islands scattered in the West Indian Ocean between 4 and 10 degrees south and 46 to 56 degrees east and about one thousand miles east of Mombasa, Kenya, "a spot in a world of waters!" (Edwards 1893: 7). The biggest island is Mahé, 17 miles long and 5 miles at its widest. The

---

1 This article draws on my PhD research, which is being supervised by Marie McGonagle of the National University of Ireland in Galway and Seán Patrick Donlan of the University of Limerick, Ireland. I am especially grateful to Dr. Donlan, who offered his comments and suggestions on the material contained herein.

2 See Palmer (2012: xiii). In explaining the aim of his study of the third legal family, Palmer refers to the experience as "a broad evolutionary one that may reveal the salient traits, trends, tendencies within such systems." See also Anthony (1992: 190), who outlines the constituent elements of a mixed legal system as institutional foundations; substantive rules and their sources; and the accompanying legal methodology, legal style, and values underpinning the system.

3 See Örücü (2004: 365). Örücü uses the expression "hardy" in her comparative analysis of legal systems and plants.

town of Victoria, the capital of Seychelles, is on Mahé, and it is the seat of government. The only other islands of importance are Praslin and La Digue. Together with Mahé and another 40 islands, they make up a unique geological feature—the only mid-oceanic islands of granite in the world. The remainder of the islands—the Aldabra, Alphonse, Amirante, Coëtivy, and Farquhar groups—are all coralline.

The population of Seychelles is 89,700,[4] a well-integrated mix of European, African, and Asian peoples. They are the descendants of the early French settlers and African slaves brought to Seychelles in the eighteenth century, of Chinese who arrived as traders in the nineteenth century, and of Indians in the early twentieth century. About 75 percent of Seychellois live on Mahé. Most others live on Praslin and La Digue; the remaining smaller islands are either sparsely populated or uninhabited.

The climate is often described as tropical but healthy. The southeast trade winds blow from May to October. The northwest monsoon winds bring heavy squalls of rain between November and April. January is the wettest month; July and August are the driest. The temperature remains constant throughout the year, at 24–31°C with humidity at around 80 percent. Onshore breezes make for a pleasant environment. The country is outside the cyclone belt.

Seychellois culture is a mixture of French and African influences. Creole is the native language;[5] however, English and French are commonly used. English remains the language of government and commerce. The constitution of Seychelles in article 4 states: "The national languages of Seychelles shall be Creole, English, and French." Since independence in 1976, Seychelles has been a member of the Commonwealth of Nations and is also a member of the Organisation Internationale de la Francophonie. It is also a member of the Organisation of African Unity and the Southern African Development Community.

The per capita gross domestic product (GDP) is US$10,727.50,[6] and the public debt in early 2012 is 70 percent of GDP (Government of Seychelles 2012). The International Monetary Fund intervened in October 2008 to bail out Seychelles, whose financial crisis was exacerbated by Somali marine piracy, which today continues to negatively affect the two stalwarts of the country's service-based economy: tourism and fisheries.

Historical and Legal Perspective

There is no record of the ancient history of Seychelles (originally named *Séchelles*). Navigators visited, made observations, and charted some of the 115 islands of the archipelago, which they marked as uninhabited.

Discovery and Settlement

The Cantino World Map of 1502 does show Seychelles, but the first authentic records are charts made by Pedro de Mascarenhas in 1544 and the celebrated Vasco de Gama. In their charts, Mahé (the main island) and the adjacent islands were called *as sete irmãs* (the seven sisters), and they were known under that name until 1742 (Bradley 1940: 1). There is a record of a landing in 1609 by the crew of an English East India Company vessel, the *Ascension*, but no settlement by the English (Jourdain 1905: 349). There is no doubt, however, that the islands were a pirate retreat. The conditions were ideal: the islands were uninhabited and had good water, plentiful trees for masts, numerous creeks where ships could be repaired, plenty of food, and no men-of-war to interrupt the nefarious activities. Indeed, during the administration of General Charles Decaen in Mauritius (1803–1810) and the battle for the supremacy of the Indian Ocean, corsairs (pirates) were encouraged to operate and were furnished with ships and arms (Bradley 1940: 8).

The history of Seychelles is closely associated with that of Mauritius. Mauritius had been discovered by the Portuguese, but it was not settled; the Dutch settled the island in 1638 and gave it its name (after Prince Maurice of Orange), but they abandoned it in 1712. The French took possession of Mauritius in 1715 and renamed it Isle de France. It was administered by the Compagnie des Indes (French East India Company) from 1722. In 1742, after Mauritius was ceded to France, the island's governor-general, Bertrand-François Mahé

4 This statistic is for 2011 and was provided by the Seychelles National Bureau of Statistics.
5 The Seychelles Creole language is French based. See Fleischmann (2008).
6 This statistic is for 2011 and was provided by the Seychelles National Bureau of Statistics.

de Labourdonnais, who was concerned about English ambitions in the Indian Ocean, decided to prevent any attempt by the English to colonize other uninhabited islands in the area and dispatched Captain Lazare Picault on a voyage of discovery (Lionnet 1972: 57). In 1742, "on Thursday 22 November at 4, they approached the shores of an unknown island, lowered their boats and made a reconnaissance of the shores" (Bradley 1940: 10).

Picault named the island Isle d'Abondance. Another journey was made to the island in 1743, and it was renamed Mahé after the governor-general. As the French then turned their attention to India, there was a hiatus in the history of Seychelles. The break lasted until 1756, when René Magon, then administering Mauritius on behalf of the French, learned that the English were sending ships to discover any uninhabited islands in the Indian Ocean. To forestall his enemies, he sent an Irish sailor, Captain Cornelius Nicolas Morphey, to take formal possession of the islands for the French king. The islands were renamed Séchelles, perhaps after Jean Moreau de Séchelles, the French controller-general of finances (Bradley 1940: 10).

The French did not establish a settlement on the islands, however, until 1770 (Scarr 2000: 2). Poor white families and landowners with slaves took up *habitations*, planting maize, rice, bananas, coffee, cotton, and spices such as nutmeg, pepper, and cinnamon. On November 5, 1788, during the administration of Louis Jean-Baptiste Philogène of Malavois, the first law of Seychelles was decreed, putting an end to the freebooting life of the settlers (Bradley 1940: 34–35).[7]

French Rule: Transplantation of Civil Law

Seychelles was a dependency of Mauritius, administered locally by appointed administrators. News of the French Revolution changed this arrangement temporarily. The settlers, in the spirit of the revolution, set up their own colonial assembly, drafted a constitution without reference to Mauritius or France, invested the assembly with both criminal and civil judicial powers, and declared Seychelles a separate colony from Mauritius. Two attempts to reject this self-assertion, to modify the self-imposed constitution, and to bring Seychelles back under the control of Mauritius failed (Lionnet 1996: 191). Commandant Armand Esnouf of the Pondicherry regiment, who had been sent to retake control, was snubbed, more than likely because he tried to enforce the abolition of the Code Noir, a move that found little support among the colonists, the visiting corsairs, and slavers.

Only the arrival of Commandant Jean-Baptiste Quéau de Quinssy in Seychelles in 1793 reestablished formal control by Mauritius (Fauvel 1909: 189).[8] The beginning of the governorship of Decaen, who was then captain-general of the French settlements beyond the Cape of Good Hope, put an end to the Seychelles Colonial Assembly (Fauvel 1909: 324–25). De Quinssy's administration saw the flourishing of the colony but also a series of capitulations to the British (in 1794, 1801, 1804, 1805, 1806, and 1807), with the French flag rehoisted as soon as the British had sailed (earning de Quinssy the nickname of the "Talleyrand of the Indian Ocean"). The terms of these capitulations, however ephemeral their duration, ensured that French laws would remain in force even after the final capitulation of 1804:

> [The inhabitants] will, during the period of capitulation, observe strict neutrality and will govern themselves during said period with respect to civil matters according to French law, no amendments to it being permitted. (Article 3, Capitulation of Seychelles, November 22, 1804)

In summary, the laws of Seychelles during French rule had four distinct periods: (a) the laws of the French East India Company from 1722 to 1766,[9] (b) the royal decrees promulgated by the king of France from 1766

7 The decree, a list of dos and don'ts for the taking of tortoises, firewood, coconuts, and land concessions, represents a first constitution of Seychelles. The document was kept in the Museum of Caen until October 28, 2013, when it was officially handed over to Seychelles National Archives.

8 De Quinssy was also from the Pondicherry regiment and a page to Louis XV in his youth (Scarr 2000: 22).

9 There was little legislation apart from that relating to slavery. The laws that did exist, in any case, ceased to have effect after 1788 (Glover 2011).

to 1790 including the Code Noir, (c) the edicts published by the Colonial Assembly of Mauritius from 1790 to 1803, and (d) the laws of Decaen from 1803 to 1815 (Glover 2011).

A Code Pénal was published October 15, 1791, and adopted by the Colonial Assembly of Mauritius in 1793. The Code Civil was promulgated in Mauritius on September 25, 1805. A new edition of the civil code, under the title of Code Napoléon, was promulgated there on September 3, 1807. Decaen published the French Code de Procédure Civile on July 20, 1807; the Code de Commerce on October 1, 1809, after several modifications; and the new Code Pénal in 1810. Some of the provisions of these codes remain in force to this day. During Decaen's administration, litigants in Seychelles had the right of appeal to the Supreme Court in Mauritius. That court was composed of a president, vice president, three judges, four clerks, and a government commissioner with a clerk and the clerk to the court. There was no jury. Seychelles was allowed a justice of the peace, a clerk to the justice, and a clerk to the court. Criminal affairs were judged by French laws of 1670 until those laws were repealed in the revolution of 1793 (Bradley 1940: 122–23). Two notaries from Mauritius were appointed to Seychelles. Even today, in cases of land disputes and ownership of properties, deeds of these former notaries continue to be consulted.

By 1806, however, the Union Jack had been firmly planted on the soil of Seychelles, and the ever-pragmatic de Quinssy flew the capitulation flag on all ships traveling from Seychelles (Guébourg 2004). Thus, the protected ships passed without interference to the blockaded port of Port Louis in Mauritius. This passage ensured not only that trade would continue but also that Seychelles would be prosperous even during the worst hostilities (Guébourg 2004).

By July 1810, de Quinssy had received a copy of the proclamation of Sir Robert Farquhar, the first governor of the nearby Isle de Bourbon (now known as Réunion), which had been captured from the French. The proclamation invited Mauritius to surrender to British rule. On December 3 of the same year, after a short battle, Mauritius finally fell to the British, and because of its dependency on its mother colony, so did Seychelles. The terms of the Mauritian capitulation again ensured that existing laws would continue. Specifically article VIII of the 1810 Capitulation of Mauritius stated, "que les habitants conserveront leur religion, leurs lois et coutumes" (the inhabitants will retain their religion, their laws, and customs).

In 1814, when nations were negotiating the Treaty of Paris, the question of returning the islands to France was discussed. England was prepared to exchange them for its remaining French possessions in India, but France refused this proposal. The Isle de Bourbon was returned to France and, to this day, remains a French *département d'outre-mer* (overseas department). Seychelles, a dependency of Mauritius, stayed with the British. These three countries, cheek by jowl in the Indian Ocean, today share the same gene pool and speak very similar Creole languages, and yet they have different legal regimes.

Unlike the Canadian province of Quebec and the island country of St. Lucia, where the legal customs of Paris were still in force on cession to the British, the Napoleonic Codes had already been promulgated and applied when Mauritius and Seychelles formally passed to the British in 1814.

British Rule: Infusion of Common Law

After the capitulation, the first English governor was Sir Robert Townsend Farquhar. Despite the appointment of Lieutenant Bartholomew Sullivan of the Royal Marines as British civil agent in Seychelles, de Quinssy remained as the *juge de paix*, or the police court magistrate, until 1815. French laws continued to be applied unchanged (Scarr 2000: 39).

The Effects of Capitulation

The capitulation was formalized by proclamation on December 5, 1810 (Farquhar 1822). But at the Treaty of Paris in 1814, no allusion was made either to the terms of the Seychellois and Mauritian capitulations preserving French law or to the fact that the islands were ceded to Great Britain "in full right and sovereignty" (Renton 1909a: 105). Renton, in this context, argues that because the treaty was never confirmed by any imperial statute, the maintenance of French law depended solely on the capitulation and proclamation and the rule in *Campbell v. Hall.*[10] Hence, in his estimation, the laws preserved were those enacted up to 1787 (the Code Delaleu),[11] those passed between 1787 and 1803, and the Code Decaen containing the French civil and commercial codes and the Code of Civil Procedure, but not the Napoleonic Penal Code or the Criminal Procedure Code, which had never been promulgated. Consequently, until 1831, the old French Criminal Ordinance of 1671 was still observed, and the French Penal Law of 1791 was observed until 1838 (Renton 1909a: 106).

The laws enacted from 1810 to 1840 are collectively referred to as the Code Farquhar. In this respect, French law continued to operate, but in an English context. Both the English language and English law were introduced tentatively. During those first 30 years of British colonial rule, local ordinances, the governor's proclamations, and other public acts or notices of the executive government were usually promulgated in both English and French, and both versions were deemed authoritative.[12] After 1841, all laws, including those that amended the French codes, had to be written in English.[13] However, in the case of *R. v. Ramjan Mirza*, in considering the English and French versions of the Penal Code, the Supreme Court of Mauritius stated that the accused was entitled to benefit from a contradiction or a difference between the two texts, where any existed.[14] Unlike Seychelles, later legislation in Mauritius reversed this restriction, authorizing the Mauritian legislature to use the French language for amendments to codes that were drafted in French or in English and French.[15] Today in Seychelles, where French provisions have survived, section 21 of the Interpretation and General Provisions Act, Cap 103 of the Laws of Seychelles stipulates:

> (1) Where in an Act terms or expressions of French Law are used, they shall be interpreted in accordance with French Law.
>
> (2) Where in an Act English words are followed by terms or expressions of French Law in parenthesis, subsection (1) applies to those terms and expressions and English words shall be treated as being the equivalent only of those terms or expressions.

As for the retention of French law, in the case of *Lang & Co. v. Reid & Co.*,[16] the Privy Council accepted that French law was preserved on the islands by the capitulations. More emphatically, in 1902, the Supreme Court of Mauritius unanimously held in the case of *Colonial Government v. Widow Laborde* that[17]

> [t]he provisions in the Capitulation of 1810, ceding Mauritius to England, that the religion, laws, and customs of the inhabitants should be preserved was not abrogated by the Treaty of Paris 1814, either because the treaty was silent as to it, or because the treaty ceded the colony to England in full right and sovereignty.

But academic disputes about the effects of capitulations in international law have continued (Bridge 1997). In 1952, when the bill for the new penal code of Seychelles was first moved in the legislative assembly, Gustave de Comarmond, the member representing Praslin and la Digue, objected strenuously on the grounds that the bill contravened the terms of capitulation. The new code was eventually adopted on the recommendation of a committee of lawyers who had received the advice of Sir Sydney Abrahams, a member

10 *Campbell v. Hall* [1558–1774], All ER 252 at 255: "The articles of capitulation on which the country is surrendered, and the articles of peace by which it is ceded, are sacred and inviolable according to their true intent and meaning."

11 The Code Delaleu (Delaleu 1777), also known as the Code Jaune, regulated the regime under which slaves were kept in Réunion, Mauritius, and Seychelles.

12 Whether the English or French version would be regarded as the original and authentic version had been a subject of difficulty.

13 This mandate was pursuant to Order in Council, February 25, 1841.

14 *R. v. Ramjan Mirza* (1891) MR 9.

15 Order in Council, January 25, 1962.

16 *Lang & Co. v. Reid & Co.* (1858) 12 Moo. PCC 72, 88.

17 *Colonial Government v. Widow Laborde and Others* (1902) MR 19.

of the Privy Council (Lionnet 1972: 122–23). In contrast, in 1961, Sir Rampersad Neerunjun, the chief justice of Mauritius, went as far as to state that the Napoleonic Code had survived through an erroneous interpretation of the treaty (d'Unienville 1969). In 1997, the Privy Council in the case of *Matadeen v. M.G.C. Pointu*[18] had to consider whether La Déclaration de Droit de l'Homme et du Citoyen (The Declaration of the Rights of Man and of the Citizen)—more specifically the concept of *égalité* (equality) contained therein—which was adopted in 1793 by the Colonial Assembly of Mauritius, had survived capitulation. The council found that it had, but that the provisions of the declaration could not curtail the application of the provisions of the constitution of Mauritius, which was supreme law.

Initial Mixing of Common Law and Civil Law

In a recent article, d'Unienville (2012) argues that the personal efforts of Farquhar, who was sympathetic to the plight of the settlers, led to the maintenance of French laws in the colony. Farquhar traveled from Mauritius to London and for two years negotiated with Lord Henry Bathurst, the colonial secretary; his undersecretary, Henry Goulburn; and the astute legal adviser James Stephen to persuade them not to impose English law on the colony and its dependencies.

A letter from Bathurst dated March 28, 1820, certainly confirms the retention of French laws and infuses in the mix the first English legal doctrines (Clark 1834: 586). This letter is confirmed by an Order in Council of 1831, namely, that the Civil, Commercial, and Civil Procedure Codes would be preserved except where modification was necessary and that English criminal law would henceforth be applied. A jury would be impaneled for criminal cases; civil courts would be presided over by a judge and two assistants; the Court of Appeal would be reduced to four judges, two of whom would be English and would be invested with the powers of the court of equity as well as that of a court of law; and civil commissioners would be invested with the powers of justices of the peace.

Seychelles continued to be administered by civil agents and commissioners under the direct orders of the governor of Mauritius and under Mauritian law applicable by implication. Although an Order in Council of 1888 created both a Legislative Council and a Supreme Court in Seychelles, the order reserved legislative power to Mauritius, and the Supreme Court of Seychelles was subordinate to the Supreme Court of Mauritius.

Edwards (1893: 7) made the following observations:

> The islands are but English in name: indeed they are as much French as they were a hundred years ago. The language, manners, customs are emphatically French; French is spoken in the Law Courts, where French law is also pre-eminent.

And of the law in action,[19] Edwards (1893: 18–19) notes:

> Judicial work in Seychelles, during the last nine years has been administered by Mr. Justice Brown, and it is generally conceded that he has proved an upright and painstaking-individual, always acting—up to the light that is within him. He has certainly upheld the dignity of the bench in a Nebuchadnezzarian manner, and his court is a pattern of order, cleanliness, and sobriety. He seldom commits himself to an impromptu judgment, rather than that there should be any miscarriage of Justice, to take time to consider. True, the time often extends over a long period, yet judgment when given, is exhaustive, if not always lucid.

By 1900, there was still only one court in Seychelles that had jurisdiction over both civil and criminal matters not necessitating a jury. In cases of appeal and serious criminal offenses, recourse was made to the Supreme Court of Mauritius (Murat 1900: 14).

The digest of decisions of the Court of Appeal from 1870 to 1902 shows that the judicial style of decision writing had already changed from the French style to that of English reasoned judgments (Bourke 1934).

---

18 *Matadeen v. Pointu* [1998] UKPC 9.

19 See Pound (1910). The use of the phrase "law in action" here serves only to illustrate the actual practice of law in Seychelles toward the end of the nineteenth century.

Vigorous Mixing in the Twentieth Century

Only in 1903 did Seychelles become a fully fledged colony detached from all control by Mauritius.[20] The laws in force were preserved except where they were incompatible with legislation passed by Seychelles.[21] But it is also at this juncture that the erosion of French law began. The mixing with English law accelerated more rapidly than in the case of Mauritius, whose laws developed separately from those of Seychelles from that point forward.

The following examples illustrate the potent mixing that took place and the various problems that were encountered.

Section 21 of the 1903 Order in Council (preserved by section 12 of the current Evidence Act, chapter 74 of the Laws of Seychelles) states that "except where it is otherwise provided in this Act or by special laws now in force in Seychelles or hereafter enacted, the English law of evidence for the time being shall prevail."

In the fraud case of *Paul Gardette v. R.*,[22] the Court of Appeal for East Africa, in an appeal from Seychelles on whether oral evidence could be admitted despite the prohibition in article 1341 of the Napoleonic Code (as the principle had been extended to criminal trials in France), stated that the English law of evidence applied, at least in criminal trials. In 1969, in the case of *Kim Koon & Co. Ltd. v. R.*,[23] the question arose as to whether section 12 of the Evidence Act meant the English law of evidence from time to time or as in force on the date of enactment of section 12. The court held that it meant the law as it stood only at the time of the enactment of the Evidence Act. Sauzier suggests that this limitation applies only to statute law and not to courts interpreting common law.[24] A question does arise, however (and this question has not been decided), regarding whether this limitation would include new concepts of the common law (Sauzier, Angelo, and Klauser 2011: 2).

In civil cases, the English law of evidence prevails except where special laws exist, and such special laws are numerous in terms of the provisions of the Civil Code. They can sometimes go not only to proof but also to the validity of transactions, as in the case of gifts, wills, leases, and mortgages (Sauzier, Angelo, and Klauser 2011: 5).

Another example of mixing is the 1904 Penal Code. This code was, in effect, a patchwork of the previous French code with some importations from the British Indian Penal Code (Scarr 2000: 149). It remained in force until 1955, when it was replaced by a new penal code, this time based on the Penal Code of East Africa, which was itself derived from English law.[25] In deciding criminal cases to this day in Seychelles, Mauritian, Indian, East African, and English precedents are referred to. Lately, cases from the British Commonwealth have also been relied on (Angelo 2010).

The Seychelles Code of Criminal Procedure and the Seychelles Code of Civil Procedure were promulgated, respectively, in 1919 and 1920. In the case of the latter, again because of the retention of the Napoleonic Code, several provisions of the original French Civil Procedure Code were also saved. One provision includes the quaint but useful French procedure of *interrogatoire sur faits et articles* (interrogatory on facts and acts pertinent to the case), contained in sections 169–170 of the code (sections 162–67 of the present Seychelles Code of Civil Procedure). In such circumstances, the party called to testify does not do so on oath and is treated as an adverse witness for the purpose of obtaining an admission or statement prejudicial to the testifying party's cause or to substantiate the opponent's case. The procedure is most commonly used to obtain an *aveu judiciaire* (judicial admission) or to get around the rule against oral evidence in article 1341 of the Civil Code of Seychelles, where a party to a suit is unable to provide adequate proof of the averments in the pleadings.

Section 327 of the present Seychelles Code of Civil Procedure expresses the status quo for French provisions that have survived and for those that are obsolete by stating, "Articles of the French Code of Civil Procedure repealed by any law which is repealed by this Code shall remain repealed."

---

20 Letters Patent, August 31, 1903.

21 Seychelles Legislature in Council 1903.

22 *Gardette v. R.* (1959) SLR, Vol. 2, 191.

23 *Kim Koon & Co. Ltd. v. R.* (1969) SCAR 60.

24 André Sauzier is a former attorney general, Supreme Court judge, and Court of Appeal judge of Seychelles. He is also an author and an expert on the laws of Seychelles.

25 See *Gardette v. R.* (1959) SLR Vol 2 184.

Finally, some Napoleonic Code provisions, notably in relation to the law on domicile[26] and the law of defamation[27] were also amended with the introduction of English law concepts.

Independence: Pragmatism and a Hybrid Legal System

In the years preceding the independence of Seychelles from Great Britain, the colony was groomed for the event. It was determined that several aspects of its legal system had to be modified or tweaked if it was to meet the challenges of nationhood. In addition, the construction of new shipping facilities and the Seychelles International Airport in 1971 awakened the islands to the economic realities of the twentieth century. Sauzier (2010) summarizes the position thus:

> This event had the same effect as the kiss of Prince Charming on Sleeping Beauty. Seychelles opened up to the world and experienced an immediate economic boom. This change required an updating of the law, especially the Civil and Commercial Codes, in order to bring them in line with the economic reality of Seychelles.

Recodification

To modernize and equip Seychelles with the requisite economic and legal tools to meet the new challenges of a young nation, it was necessary to redraft the Seychelles Code of Commerce. The work was undertaken by the English expert, Robert Pennington, who had done similar work for Trinidad and Tobago. The Code of Commerce was largely replaced by the Companies Ordinance 1972, which was based on English company law. Few provisions of the French code of commerce promulgated in 1809 survived the revision but the original numbering is preserved although the provisions are translated into English. The most important provisions that remain are those regulating commercial books, pledges, the sale of goods, and arbitration.

The most dramatic change to the legal landscape came in the work of A.G. Chloros, who was charged not only with the revision of what remained of the code of commerce after the promulgation of Pennington's new company law but, more important, with the Napoleonic Code. Chloros preserved the shell of the Napoleonic Civil Code, which had been introduced in 1808, thereby maintaining the 2,281 articles, although not all the 2,281 articles remained in existence (Chloros 1977: 7). Some interesting parallels with other jurisdictions may be made. Article 1, largely borrowed from the Louisiana code,[28] states: "Law is a solemn and public expression of legislative will" (Chloros 1977: 7; see also Bogdan 1989: 44–46).

Other innovations concern judicial appointment of guardianships.[29] In changing the law substantively on this issue, Chloros (1977: 52) argued that neither the English nor the French notions of guardianship were applicable in Seychelles because they were far too sophisticated "for the very different society of an African country" and because "substantial injustices were done in the name of the very persons whom the law intended to protect."[30] This argument has drawn sharp criticism from legal practitioners in Seychelles, who, not surprisingly, have found those comments condescending and unfounded and the new provisions problematic in practice.[31]

26 Domicile Act 1948, Laws of Seychelles, chapter 66.

27 Defamation Ordinance 1948, repealed and replaced by article 1383(3) of the Civil Code of Seychelles.

28 Article 1 of the Civil Code of Louisiana refers to the 1870 Revised Civil Code of Louisiana. This provision was substantially changed in the revision of 1987. See Yiannopoulos (2008).

29 Civil Code of Seychelles, articles 402–22, 429–37.

30 Chloros (1977) states, "The administration and the control of a minor were very complicated indeed. These features are still retained in France. However, it is doubtful at the very least, tradition apart, they are suitable for the very society of an African country."

31 See, for example, Judge Hodoul, in *Louise v. Barbier* (2005) SCA 14, unreported.

Another innovation to the law is the concept of trusts partially introduced in cases of co-ownership of property.[32] Whereas Chloros claims to have acknowledged that the concept of trusts did not exist in Seychelles and borrowed from Scots law for this provision, he introduces the concept of a fiduciary.[33] A fiduciary is a person (whose duties seem similar to that of a trustee) through whom only co-owners may act, but the redacted provision seems to do away with co-ownership altogether: "When a property … is transferred to two or more persons, the right of co-ownership shall be converted into a claim to a like share in the proceeds of sale of any such property."[34] This understanding is not helped by article 817(2), which seems to be an afterthought and does nothing to solidify either the notion of trusteeship or co-ownership: "Paragraph 1 of this article regulates the exercise of the right of co-ownership. It does not affect the rights of co-ownership itself." There have been several court challenges, but it now appears to be established that the fiduciary provision affects only the *exercise* of the right of co-ownership and not the *transfer* of the right.[35]

Chloros is also much criticized for his translation of *titre* to "instrument of title."[36] The word *titre* in French law has a variety of meanings, including an authentic deed or a right. However, Chloros limits the application of the concept in the law of property of Seychelles and leaves no room for interpretation when he translates the word into "instrument of title," especially because section 5 of the Civil Code of Seychelles provides that "[t]he text of the Civil Code of Seychelles as in this Act contained shall be deemed for all purposes to be an original text, and shall not be construed or interpreted as a translated text."

Another innovation of the code concerns the provisions relating to floating charges,[37] a concept hitherto unknown in Seychelles or in France.

Although there is no introduction of the doctrine of "consideration" in the law of contracts, the notion of "cause" was changed. The provisions relating to cause[38] were retitled "Public Policy" (formerly *De la Cause*). In *Corgat v. Maree*,[39] the first case relating to cause after the promulgation of the new code and a case involving a promissory note, Sauzier held that *cause* had meant consideration under the old articles. Although cause was no longer a doctrine in the new code, he said, "there must be a reason for making an agreement to make the agreement valid though the reason need not be stated." This interpretation stemmed from the fact that the document tendered as a basis for the agreement was deemed a promissory note under the Bill of Exchange Ordinance (a very English legal instrument). Section 27 of the ordinance provides that "valuable consideration" for a bill may be constituted by any "consideration" sufficient to support a contract. In the subsequent case of *Jacobs & anor v. Devoud* (1978),[40] Sauzier expanded on the doctrine of cause. He maintained that although cause was omitted from the Civil Code of Seychelles, it could not be ignored altogether because if it were contrary to the law or against public policy, the obligation would be invalid.[41] This view still obtains and seems to be an approximation of cause with consideration.

Jurisprudence (Precedent)

There is an altogether curious approach combining both civil law and common law methods in the practice of civil law in Seychelles. Article 5 of the Civil Code of Seychelles states, "Judicial decisions shall not be

32 Article 818 of the Civil Code of Seychelles states: "If the property subject to ownership is immovable, the rights of the co-owners shall be held on their behalf by a fiduciary through whom only they may act."

33 Civil Code of Seychelles, articles 824–35. See also Chloros (1974: 839).

34 Civil Code of Seychelles, article 817(1).

35 *Michel v. Vidot* (1977) SLR 214 and *Legras v. Legras* (1983–1987) SCAR 356.

36 Civil Code of Seychelles, article 690. See Sauzier (2010), who writes that "the translation has resulted in some cases in a complete betrayal: sometimes even a total change of the ambit and application of the original text. For example, the word "titre" was translated by the expression "instrument of title" which effectively means a written document whereas we do know that in French Law the expression "titre" carries with it a much wider meaning."

37 Civil Code of Seychelles, article 2091.

38 Ibid., articles 1131–33.

39 *Corgat v. Maree* (1976) SLR 109.

40 *Jacobs & anor v. Devoud* (1978) SLR 164.

41 Civil Code of Seychelles, article 1108.

absolutely binding upon a court but shall enjoy a high persuasive authority from which a Court shall only depart for good reason." Furthermore, section 5(2) of the code provides, "Nothing in this Act shall invalidate any principle of jurisprudence of civil law or inhibit the application thereof in Seychelles except to the extent that it is inconsistent with the Civil Code of Seychelles." Additionally, section 9 of the same act makes it clear that the Interpretation and General Provisions Act—specifically section 2(1), which states that where terms or expressions of French law are used, they shall only be interpreted in accordance with French law—does not apply to the Civil Code. In practice, legal practitioners have applied the same principles of precedent as are used in criminal cases in Seychelles, insofar as previous decisions of the Supreme Court and Court of Appeal are treated as binding on lower courts. In addition, French and Mauritian cases and scholarly works, such as the Encyclopédie Dalloz, Sirey, Ripert, Planiol, Mazeaud, Carbonnier, and Capitant, are also heavily relied on and have persuasive value.

In the case of *Attorney General v. Olia*,[42] the Supreme Court held that French jurisprudence (scholarly works and decided cases) applied when the terms or provisions in Seychellois law were based on French law. Similarly, in *Desaubin v. Concrete Products*,[43] the provisions of the Civil Code of Seychelles limited the concept of *faute*, or fault, in article 1382 as compared to that in the French Civil Code. Despite this limitation, the court found that because both notions required an element of imprudence, negligence, or an intention to cause harm, it would be appropriate to rely on French jurisprudence.

By contrast, the application of section 5(2) has meant that French jurisprudence does not apply in cases of motor vehicle accidents.[44] The reason given was that the interpretation of the Cour de Cassation[45] went further in such cases than the confines of the provision.[46] The interpretation imposed the theory of risk in all cases of motor vehicle accidents, thus voiding the application of *faute* as contained in articles 1382 and 1383. The presumption of fault introduced in article 1383(2) of the Civil Code of Seychelles has changed this position. In Mauritius, an amendment to the country's civil code in 1983 to take into account the French position has now accepted that the *gardien* of a motor vehicle involved in an accident is responsible for damage caused by the vehicle. The *gardien* can only evade such responsibility if he or she can prove that the damage was the result of *force majeure* or the *faute exclusive* of the victim.[47] However, the principle that a text based on French law must be interpreted or applied in accordance with French jurisprudence except where the solutions offered by French jurisprudence contradicts the actual working of the provision still applies.

Hence, the vertical binding effect of judgments is strictly adhered to in Seychelles, and there have been no instances in which the Supreme Court has had to chide a lower court for failure to disregard the rule. The only exception is the rule stated in *Ilias Durdunis v. the Owners of the Ship "Maria"*—namely, that a decision of a court made per incuriam might not bind later courts.[48] However, in terms of horizontal binding, there have been many instances in which courts have not considered themselves bound by past decisions. Recently, in the case of *Lucas v. R.*,[49] the Court of Appeal unanimously held that corroboration in some sexual cases was not always required if the witness was reliable, thus overturning a long list of its own cases and indeed settled law on the matter. The same principle applies to civil cases.

As far as English rules of equity are concerned, there have been some ingenuous attempts in Seychellois case law to introduce equitable concepts with limited success (Bogdan 1989: 49). Section 6 of the Courts Act, promulgated in 1964, contains the following provision:

> [T]he Supreme Court shall continue to be a Court of Equity and is hereby invested with powers, authority, and jurisdiction to administer justice and to do all acts for the due execution of such

42 *Attorney General v. Olia* (1964) SLR 142.

43 *Desaubin v. United Concrete Products* (1977) SLR 164.

44 Civil Code of Seychelles Act 1976, section 5(2).

45 The Cour de Cassation is France's court of last resort.

46 *Mangroo v. Dahal* (1937) MR 43. Although *Mangroo* is a Mauritian case, the same position was adopted in Seychelles. See, for example, *Coopoosamy v. Delhomme* (1964) SLR 82.

47 *Rose Belle SE Board v. Chateauneuf* (1990) MR 9.

48 *Ilias Durdunis v. The Owners of The Ship "Maria"* (1994) SCA 24/1994, unreported.

49 *Lucas v. R.* (2011) SLR 303.

> equitable jurisdiction in all cases where no sufficient legal remedy is provided by the law of Seychelles.[50]

In *Teemooljee v. Pardiwalla*,[51] it was argued that both legal and equitable estoppel was part of the law of Seychelles. The Court of Appeal found that because those doctrines were in conflict with the provisions of the Civil Code (which contained its own forms of estoppel), the operation of section 12 of the Evidence Act would limit their application. Using mixed metaphors, the Court of Appeal held that the Evidence Act and the Courts Act had the effect of permitting "the reception of grafts but not transplants" and that their purpose was

> to insert into the stock of [the Seychellois] law of evidence buds that may grow in harmony with it, not to introduce into the body of substantive law an organ of proof which has been severed from a foreign body of law and which can only live and properly function in that body.[52]

However, in the recent case of *Atkinson and Others v. Government of Seychelles*,[53] the Court of Appeal found that equitable estoppel could be relied on where a party had entered into a contract on the representation of certain facts by the other party.

In *Hallock v. d'Offay*,[54] regarding a property settlement after a lengthy cohabitation by an unmarried couple, the dissenting judgment of Sauzier found that equity could be used to grant a share in the property. This approach has great merit in a country where a large proportion of couples live in *concubinage* as opposed to marriage, but it has generally not been followed, and parties in similar circumstances have resorted to basing their claim in unjust enrichment.[55]

Equitable doctrines are however generally used, for example, "equity defeats delay" *(Attorney General v. Ray Voysey and Others)*.[56] The Courts Act has also resulted in the introduction of equitable concepts such as specific performance and injunctions.[57]

Three Republics and Three Constitutions

Since achieving independence from Great Britain on the June 29, 1976, Seychelles has known three constitutions and three republics.

The 1976 Constitution

The first constitution lasted almost as long as the time necessary to draft it. It succeeded an almost identical and unpopular interim colonial constitution that was imposed to see Seychelles through independence. The interim constitution, dubbed the Deverell constitution after the constitutional adviser Sir Colville Deverell (Scarr 2000: 175), was insensitive to local needs. The subsequent Constitutional Conference at Marlborough House in London adopted most of the Deverell constitution's provisions. Midway through negotiations, however, the basis of the constitution changed dramatically from a government to be headed by a governor-general with the queen to a republic with a president and a prime minister.

50 Laws of Seychelles, chapter 52.
51 *Teemooljee v. Pardiwalla* (1975) SLR 39.
52 *Teemooljee v. Pardiwalla* (n 94) 55.
53 *Atkinson and Others v. Government of Seychelles* (2003) SCA 20/2002, unreported.
54 *Hallock v. d'Offay* (1986) SCAR 295.
55 Civil Code of Seychelles, article 1381(1).
56 *Attorney General v. Ray Voysey and Others* (1996) SCA 1/3/1996, unreported.
57 See sections 3–6 of the Courts Act, Laws of Seychelles, chapter 52.

The Socialist Republic of Seychelles

Less than a year later, the prime minister had overthrown the coalition government. The constitution of 1979, decreed after the coup, turned Seychelles into a one-party state with political activity conducted only under the auspices of the Seychelles People's Progressive Front. Seychelles was declared a sovereign socialist republic. The constitution was deemed the supreme law, and any law inconsistent with it invalid and ineffective. The Supreme Court was expanded to include the chief justice and an additional puisne judge, making a total of three judges. The composition of the Court of Appeal remained unchanged, with its jurisdiction exercised by a bench of at least three members.

The era saw the passing of some interesting socialist laws, sometimes potentially in conflict with provisions of the Civil Code. One of these was the Tenant's Rights Act 1981,[58] the purpose of which is described in its section 4:

> [T]o assist in enabling every Seychellois family to own its own home by giving security of tenure to Seychellois who own and occupy a home on another person's land or who are residential tenants, and by enabling those Seychellois to purchase the land or premises and, in the administration of this Act, regard shall be had to that object.

Other laws in the same vein include the People's Housing Mortgages Act 1981[59] and the Lands Acquisition Act 1977.[60] Some actions arising from the application of these acts make for interesting reading. In the case of *Nageon de l'Estang v. Government of Seychelles*,[61] in which the valuation for compensation arising from an acquisition was challenged, the Supreme Court had to decide whether the method of valuation of the land and building were contrary to the "fair compensation" provision of the Civil Code, and indeed the court did find that to be the case.

In summary, the Civil Code has emerged unscathed and unamended from the socialist era, with many of the socialist laws repealed or substantially amended after a new constitution came into effect in 1993.

The Democratic Republic of Seychelles

The 1993 constitution provides for a democratic multiparty sovereign republic with the president as head of the executive branch, the legislative power vested in the unicameral assembly, and the judiciary comprising the Court of Appeal, the Supreme Court, the Constitutional Court, and subordinate courts and tribunals. The constitution contains and entrenches the Seychelles Charter of Fundamental Rights and Freedoms.[62] This charter is, in effect, a bill of rights borrowing heavily from the European Convention on Human Rights. It has, however, also included provisions relating to bail in article 18 (the right to liberty). Similarly, article 19 (the right to a fair hearing) has explicit provisions on the presumption of innocence and rights during trial and appeal. This bill of rights has made for a busy Constitutional Court and has also resulted in numerous appeals to the Court of Appeal.

Judicial Structure

The biggest difference to the judicial structure has been the institution of the Constitutional Court, which has jurisdiction and powers "in respect of matters relating to the application, contravention, enforcement or interpretation of the Constitution."[63]

The Supreme Court has both original jurisdiction and supervisory jurisdiction over subordinate courts, tribunals, and adjudicating authorities. The word *supreme* is now an anomaly; the Supreme Court is not supreme in the sense of being a court of final resort. Historically, it was supreme in Seychelles, because

58 Laws of Seychelles, chapter 235, repealed by the Tenants' Rights (Repeal) Act 1992.
59 Laws of Seychelles, chapter 164.
60 Ibid., chapter 104, repealed.
61 *Nageon de l'Estang v. Government of Seychelles* (1986) SLR 50.
62 Constitution of the Republic of Seychelles 1993, chapter III, part I.
63 Ibid., article 129(1).

appeals from it in civil matters were heard in Mauritius until independence in 1976, and in the case of criminal matters, appeals were heard in East Africa until 1954 and then were made to the Privy Council until 1976. Unlike the Supreme Court of Mauritius, which in some respects has more similarities with French courts, the jurisdiction of the Supreme Court of Seychelles is exercised in practice by a single judge, although article 125(4) does provide that a bench of more than one judge can exercise the jurisdiction of the court. When it sits as a constitutional court, its jurisdiction and powers have to be exercised by at least two judges.[64] The Supreme Court has unlimited jurisdiction at first instance. It has all the powers, privileges, and jurisdiction of the High Court of Justice of England and is also a court of equity having power to do justice when there is no remedy at law.[65] It hears the more important civil and criminal cases, and in cases of murder or treason, it sits with a jury of nine.[66] The death penalty was abolished in Seychelles in 1993 by virtue of article 15(2) of the constitution.

The Court of Appeal of Seychelles consists of a president, two or more justices of appeal, and other judges who are ex-officio members of the court (drawn from the Supreme Court in certain circumstances).[67] Decisions of the Supreme Court in civil and criminal matters given at first instance or on appeal are subject to appeal to the Court of Appeal as are the decisions of the Constitutional Court.[68]

The Magistrates Court is a subordinate court established by the Courts Act.[69] Its jurisdiction in both civil and criminal proceedings is exercised by a bench of one magistrate sitting alone. Its civil jurisdiction is limited both in subject matter and the value of the claim: the senior magistrate may entertain civil claims of up to SR 350,000 in value (approximately US$25,000); the limit for other magistrates is SR 250,000 (approximately US$18,000). Its criminal jurisdiction is limited to less serious crimes. Senior magistrates have the power to sentence a convict to a maximum of ten years' imprisonment; other magistrates can convict up to seven years. Magistrates are fully qualified lawyers.

Other courts include juvenile courts, tribunals, and public authorities that exercise quasi-judicial functions, such as the Employment Tribunal, the Family Tribunal, and the Rent Control Board.

Judges in Seychelles are appointed by the president from nominees recommended by the Constitutional Appointments Authority,[70] which comprises a presidential appointee, an appointee of the leader of the opposition party, and a chairman elected by the two members of the authority.[71]

The biggest criticism relating to the appointment of judges has been the practice of appointing judges who are not Seychellois and who have little knowledge of the political, economic, and cultural traditions or the intricacies of the mixed legal system of Seychelles. The constitution provides that a Seychellois judge may remain in office until the age of 70,[72] but a non-Seychellois judge may remain up to a term of seven years except in "exceptional circumstances."[73] This provision led Philippe Boullé, a practicing senior barrister, to comment "while Seychellois aspired to become Judges even before independence, today it is the Judges who aspire to be Seychellois" (Boullé 2003). Indeed, there have been two cases of non-Seychellois judges obtaining Seychellois nationality through naturalization during their first term of office. One still remains on the bench of the Supreme Court; the other has retired as a judge but is now the law reform commissioner.

Language

The 1993 constitution provided that the national languages of Seychelles are Creole,[74] English, and French, but laws may provide for the use of any one or more of these languages for any specific purpose.[75] Court language, laws, and official documents are all in English. Interpreters are used in court to translate Creole

---

64 Ibid.
65 See sections 4–6 of the Courts Act, Laws of Seychelles, chapter 52.
66 Criminal Procedure Code, section 225.
67 Constitution of the Republic of Seychelles 1993, article 121.
68 Ibid., article 120.
69 Courts Act, Laws of Seychelles, chapter 52, section 27.
70 Constitution of the Republic of Seychelles 1993, articles 123 and 127.
71 Ibid., article 140(1).
72 Ibid., article 131(1)(d).
73 Ibid., article 131(4).
74 Creole in Seychelles, also known as *Kreol*, is the lingua franca as well as being an official language with English and French. Creole in Seychelles may also denote its people, customs, traditions, or cuisine.
75 Constitution of the Republic of Seychelles 1993, article 4.

testimony into English, both for the advantage of non-Seychellois judges and for the court record.[76] Language had been the source of bitter feuds before independence between old landed families descended from the first French settlers (*grands blancs*), the English colonizers, and the Creoles (those of mixed race who are the progeny of the colonized and the colonizer and also their descendants) (Scarr 2000: 178). Those feuds no longer exist because of the intermarriage and harmonious mix of members from all backgrounds. Whereas the French language had been the exclusive medium of education until the turn of the twentieth century, when it was replaced increasingly by English,[77] in 1981 the socialist government decided to make Creole the first language taught in schools, with English taking over subsequently and with French taught later as a foreign language (Ammon 2006). The use of written and spoken French has since declined considerably. Creole is spoken by 99 percent of the population (Purvis 2004). The present educational policy provides that Creole is the medium of education in preschools and the first two years of primary school, with English being the language of instruction from the third year of primary school. In the fourth year of primary school, all three languages are taught (Campling, Confiance, and Purvis 2011).

The influence of the national language of Creole on Seychellois law is important. Although one cannot liken its influence to the criterion of language as used by Arminjon, Nolde, and Wolff (1951) in determining a distinctive legal family, one can take a tentative approach in understanding the development of Seychellois law since Creole's official status. In a parallel Irish context, Brown and Donlan (2011: 2) argue that although the origins of the laws in Ireland mattered little, what was important was "the ability of the greater part of the Irish nation to have some sense of possession over the process of law-making" (Brown and Donlan 2011: 29). The Irish law itself acted as "the crucial frontier between the people and polity" (Brown and Donlan 2011: 30). In Seychelles, the enactment of Creole as a national language coupled with the independence of Seychelles created both national pride and national identity. This national identity acted as a catalyst for the creation of distinctive legal provisions peculiar to Seychelles and is shaping the course of its historical and legal development.

Challenges to the Seychellois Legal System

Seychelles began experiencing serious financial difficulties more than a decade ago and defaulted on its foreign debt repayment in 2008. All pillars of government were publicly scrutinized. The donors and the financiers who bailed the country out had the privilege to raise questions not only about governance but also about the structures that had led to the economic collapse. This scrutiny included an inquiry into the competence and viability of the Seychellois legal system.

The aid that trickled in, though temporarily solving the national debt crisis, brought its own neocolonial threats in the form of international capital regulations and of experts reproducing homogeneous Anglo-American legal instruments to deal with the crisis. Economic survival in the twenty-first century, it would seem, depends on a country's willingness to adopt the laws and legal tools of its trading partners.

Some proposed amendments to the law in Seychelles, such as the new Companies Bill[78] and the Trusts Bill,[79] have produced a frisson among some legal practitioners who perceive the interventions as a serious threat to the distinctive Seychellois legal framework and as leading to the inevitable erosion of the mixed legal system. In this respect, Seychelles is not alone. In a more serious development, for example, Rwanda's

76 The Constitution (Use of Official Language) Regulations, preserved by article 4(2) of the Constitution of the Republic of Seychelles 1993.

77 The Education Ordinance of 1944 provided that English be the medium of education.

78 The Company Bill 2011 encroaches on provisions of the Civil Code of Seychelles, especially in relation to pledges and incapacity. See the reaction of the Bar Association of Seychelles at http://robingroom.blogspot.com/2011/02/bar-association-of-seychelles-speaks.html [accessed: November 27, 2013].

79 The Trusts Bill 2011 proposes to introduce a concept of trust that is inconsistent with the existing provisions of the Seychelles Civil Code, especially in relation to property rights. The existing International Trusts Act 1994 introduced trusts for the first time but established a regime only for international trusts and not for domestic trusts. The trust property cannot include property situated in Seychelles or shares, debentures, or any interests in a body incorporated in Seychelles.

rich mixed legal system (of Belgian and German influences and customary Gacaca courts) and even one of its official languages face serious threats. These threats come from Tutsi leaders who in exile lived in Kenya, Tanzania, and Uganda and grew accustomed to an Anglo-American legal system and the English language. The Tutsi leaders are supported by the United Nations and Western nongovernmental organizations in their endeavor to introduce English as the medium of education and a common law system to replace French and the existing civil law system, respectively (International Crisis Group 1999; see also McGreal 2009).

Today it is almost impossible for countries to remain insular even when situated in remote geographic locations. The advent of technology and the involuntary rapprochement resulting from the World Wide Web percolate and penetrate all systems. For the legal community in Seychelles, it is time to begin an examination of conscience and to query the pertinence of Seychellois law and legal structures in the twenty-first century. For law and legal traditions to be meaningful, purposeful, and viable, their application must be context sensitive and not just text sensitive. At this, the crossroads of the Seychellois legal system, when a third wave of colonialism is being experienced, it is imperative to look at the "judicial personality" (Antoine 2008: 59) of the legal system, to examine its purpose, and to determine whether it continues to serve Seychelles.

In this context, Palmer's (2012) discussion in which he defines *purists*, *pollutionists*, and *pragmatists* is extremely useful in understanding the development of law in Seychelles. Purists, Palmer (2012: 40) says, are "those who seek to keep the civil law coherent, unsullied by encroachment and true to its sources." Palmer (2012: 41) defines pollutionists as Anglo-Americans (or English-speaking nationals) who may "have only common law training" and "favor reception of common law rules or even the overthrow of civil law." And pragmatists, according to Palmer (2012: 41), are those who "may regard interaction of the two laws and their institutions as an inevitable process that permits the judge or legislator to blend the best features of both worlds and to create better rules than either system could offer on its own."

For example, in 2010, the University of Seychelles opened its doors to law students. Before then, students had been sent for training either to Mauritius or to the United Kingdom. The advantages of Mauritius, which is affiliated with the University of Kent (United Kingdom) and the University of Aix-Marseilles (France), was that its syllabus had components of both English and French law with the degree taught in both languages. This duality seems to have ensured the viability of its legal system. Conversely, the Seychellois syllabus, perhaps because of accreditation solely with the University of London, treats only English law components through the English language and poses substantial threats to Seychellois mixity.

Graduates of the law school still have to pass the Seychelles Bar exams, which require an extensive knowledge of the Civil Code and Seychellois law. The first cohort of graduates from the University of Seychelles will begin the optional Seychelles bar exams course in 2014. However, the University of Seychelles has so far missed the opportunity to impart specialist knowledge and training for the mixed jurisdiction of Seychelles. More important, it may have put into motion forces that will erode the unique mixed legal system.

The other concern continues to be the influence of largely Anglo-American legal instruments on Seychellois law. Indeed, this influence is part of a larger global development in which Anglo-American law is seen to be both more just and more market friendly than other traditions, including the continental traditions (La Porta, López-de-Silanes, and Shleifer 2008). Seychellois tax laws are inspired by Australian provisions; the anti-money-laundering provisions are Irish inspired; and the offshore banking and investment provisions, including those governing international commercial trusts, are also copied from largely Anglo-American legal instruments.

One could argue that there is absolutely nothing intrinsically wrong with this approach and that economic survival clearly dictates the adoption of such instruments. The purist's uneasiness stems from the fact that civil law influences are progressively being eroded and may completely be eradicated without so much as a debate on the subject. What is also clear is that the introduction of the new style of laws in the past decade is not the result of conscious deliberation on the part of any authority but rather is evidence of the piecemeal approach of dealing with situations and crises as they arise and of taking expert advice proffered by aid countries and organizations.[80]

These are challenges exacerbated by the fact that Seychelles is a microjurisdiction and has to engage with other huge and influential legal systems. Given those demands, it is possible that the Seychellois hybrid

80 See, for example, in this context Mattei and Monti (1998).

legal system, unlike its Mauritian counterpart, may morph into a common law system. Conversely, the recent trend in the appointment of Seychellois judges sensitive to the rich mixed legal system may counteract the imbalance of the new common law influences.

In any case, the Seychellois legal tradition is continually evolving. Like its language, Seychelles has adopted and adapted features from other traditions and continues to do so as often as its national assembly sits to legislate. The broad brushstrokes earlier portray a multilayered legal system that is in a state of flux, but that seems true of all legal systems, as has been so well articulated by Ugo Mattei (1997: 14), who states that "legal systems never are, they always become." Seychellois law cannot be said to fall exclusively under any distinctive legal tradition. The only certainty is that it is a hybrid legal system[81] and will remain so as long as the civil law and common law traditions subsist and the balance is not tipped in favor of either system.

Currently, the Seychelles legal system does seem to fit the mold of the third legal family (Palmer 2012). It exhibits the traits, trends, and tendencies of other mixed civil law and common law jurisdictions. There is certainly a close sense of legal affinity with mixed jurisdictions of those countries that have experienced double colonization by France and Great Britain or have influences from the French and Anglo-American legal systems, such as the Canadian province of Quebec, the US state of Louisiana, and the countries of Mauritius and St. Lucia.

However, viewed from the wider perspective of the classic macrocomparative legal classification, identifying the exact family or grouping under which the legal system of Seychelles can best be classified is difficult.[82] The polemic of one comprehensive classification system that has persisted over the past century with concepts of legal families (David and Jauffret-Spinosi 2002; Zweigert and Kötz 1998) and legal traditions (Glenn 2010; Merryman and Pérez-Peroma 2007) has greatly aided the comparative process and general understanding of legal systems. However, this polemic has not assisted in understanding either the nature or the trajectory of mixed legal systems. Lack of understanding is especially problematic for microjurisdictions such as that of Seychelles. The more recent approaches to taxonomy, such as patterns of law (Mattei 1997), family trees (Örücü 2004), legal cultural families (Van Hoecke and Warrington 1998; 2004), and hybridity (Donlan 2010a),[83] are more useful and practical in that they illustrate the complexity of legal systems and acknowledge both legal and normative rules in the makeup of a legal tradition. In this context the *métissage* of Seychellois law, both in its civil law and common law *mixité* and also in its *creolité*,[84] finds resonances. Ugo Mattei (1997: 6) states that taxonomy is important in transferring knowledge from one area of law to another. Microjurisdictions struggle in their choice of knowledge from competing jurisdictions and remain at the mercy of economic superpowers and globalization. However, Seychelles does have the possibility of showcasing a happy cohabitation of rules from two great legal systems. It must, in this respect, boldly devise and negotiate its own policies and laws, while remaining skeptical of legal origins theorists (La Porta, López-de-Silanes, and Shleifer 2008) and resisting the imposition of homogeneous Anglo-American legal instruments. As Charles Fombad (2005: 24) has pointed out in the context of Botswana (also a mixed jurisdiction), a rule is not good or bad because of its pedigree, nor is there any value in preserving it because of its common law or civil law ancestry. Rather,

> Borrowing from other legal systems, although inveterate and unavoidable, must be pursued with careful planning and alertness to the omnipresent dangers of inconsistencies, contradictions and ambiguities. These difficulties are not lessened by the hasty but simplistic attempts of trying to eliminate one of the two legal traditions. A better approach is to assume the challenge of getting

81 Hybridity in this context refers to only legal hybridity. See Donlan (2010a).

82 See, for example, Donlan (2010a) and Husa (2009) on the near impossibility of devising an ideal system of classification for law.

83 Of special interest is the assertion by Donlan (2010a) that the study of hybridity must include both legal and nonstate norms. See also Donlan (2010b).

84 At the United Nations World Conference of Ministers for Youth, Patrick Pillay, who was then the Seychelles minister for youth and culture, defined *créolité* as "a special blend of European, African, and Asian influences that were central to [Seychellois] identity. Créolité was a unified social and cultural consciousness that embraced the country's diversities and established a common set of human, social and cultural values." See United Nations World Conference of Ministers for Youth (1998).

> the best out of the two inherited legal traditions whilst being alert to the need to maintain internal coherence and harmony within the mix. (Fombad 2005: 24)

The same applies to Seychelles.

Concluding Remarks

Seychelles stands at a crossroads of its legal structure. It has journeyed under the aegis of first an exclusive civil law tradition followed by the coexistence of the civil law and common law traditions. In the twenty-first century, as it struggles to survive the world recession and exploitation by foreign donors and creditors, it also faces the challenge of adapting its existing legal tradition to meet demands, mainly from the Anglo-American hegemony.

The main changes to its legal framework also emanate from the requirements of its offshore industry. If it wants this business to grow, international credibility seems to demand the accommodation of Anglo-American legal norms, including the concept of trusts that is incompatible with its Civil Code. In trying to meet its international financial commitments, Seychelles has to borrow and adapt rules from many different sources. It may see this task as a quest for a distinctive and unique body of laws appropriate to its needs, but ultimately the same exercise may also undermine the fundamental legal regime that has molded its very structure, values, beliefs, traditions, and culture. In other words, this exercise may be either the legal, political, economic, and cultural undoing of Seychelles or its survival.

The challenge for Seychelles in trying to achieve economic and legal viability is to walk the tightrope between neocolonialist influences and its unique legal tradition and identity. If the country succeeds, it may be a model for the successful cohabitation of two legal systems and the adaptation of rules from different systems in forging a new distinctive tradition.

References

Ammon, U. 2006. *An International Handbook of the Science of Language and Society*. 2nd ed. Boston: Walter de Gruyter.

Angelo, A. 2010. *Leading Cases of Seychelles 1988–2010*. Wellington: Law Publications.

Anthony, K. 1992. The identification and classification of mixed systems of law, in *Commonwealth Caribbean Legal Studies*, edited by G. Kodinliye and P.K. Menon. London: Butterworths, 179.

Antoine, R.-M.B. 2008. *Commonwealth Caribbean Law and Legal Systems*. 2nd ed. London: Routledge.

Arminjon, P., Nolde, B., and Wolff, M. 1951. *Traité de Droit Comparé, Tome III*. Paris: Librairie Générale de Droit et de Jurisprudence.

Bogdan, M. 1989. *The Law of Mauritius and Seychelles*. Stockholm: Juristförlaget.

Boullé, P. 2003. The evolution of the legal system of Seychelles. Address delivered at the Conference on Understanding Legacies and Facing Future Challenges at the National Institute of Education, Mont Fleuri, Seychelles, March 22, 2003.

Bourke, P. 1934. *A Digest of the Ruling Decisions of the Supreme Court of Seychelles from 1903 to 1933 and the Reported Cases on Appeal therefrom to His Majesty's Privy Council from 1870 to 1902*. Victoria, Seychelles: Government Press.

Bradley, J. 1940. *The History of Seychelles*. Victoria, Seychelles: Clarion Press.

Bridge, J.W. 1997. Judicial review in Mauritius and the continuing influence of English law. *International and Comparative Law Quarterly*, 46(4), 787–811.

Brown, M. and Donlan, S.P. 2011. The laws in Ireland, 1689–1850: A brief introduction, in *The Laws and Other Legalities of Ireland, 1689–1850*, edited by M. Brown and S.P. Donlan. Farnham, UK: Ashgate, 1–32.

Campling, L., Confiance, H., and Purvis, M.-T. 2011. *Social Policies in Seychelles*. London: Commonwealth Secretariat.

Chloros, A.G. 1974. The projected reform of the civil law of the Seychelles: An experiment in Franco/British codification. *Tulane Law Review*, 48, 815–45.

Chloros, A.G. 1977. *Codification in a Mixed Jurisdiction: The Civil and Commercial Law of Seychelles.* Amsterdam: North-Holland.

Clark, C. 1834. *A Summary of Colonial Law, the Practice of the Court of Appeals from the Plantations, and of the Laws and Their Administration in All the Colonies.* London: Sweet, Maxwell, and Stevens.

David, R., and Jauffret-Spinosi, C. 2002. *Les Grands Systèmes de Droit Contemporains.* 11th ed. Paris: Dalloz.

Delaleu, M. 1777. *Code des Isles de France et de Bourbon.* Paris: L'Imprimerie Royale.

Donlan, S.P. 2010a. Comparative law and hybrid legal traditions: An introduction, in *Comparative Law and Hybrid Legal Traditions*, edited by E. Cashin Ritaine, S.P. Donlan, and M. Sychold. Lausanne: Swiss Institute of Comparative Law.

Donlan, S.P. 2010b. Histories of hybridity: A problem, a primer, a plea, and a plan (of sorts), in *Comparative Law and Hybrid Legal Traditions*, edited by E. Cashin-Ritaine, S.P. Donlan, and M. Sychold. Lausanne: Swiss Institute of Comparative Law, 21–34.

d'Unienville, R.M. 1969. L'Évolution du droit civil Mauricien. PhD dissertation, La Faculté de Droit d'Aix-en-Provence, Marseille, France.

d'Unienville, R.M. 2012. Capitulation revisited: Ce que nous devons a Farquhar. *Mauritius Law Review*, 17.

Edwards, A. 1893. The Seychelles archipelago. Foreign and Commonwealth Office Collection, London.

Farquhar, R.T. 1822. *Code Régissant la Législation aux Seychelles.* Victoria, Seychelles: Government Press.

Fauvel, A.A. 1909. *Unpublished documents on the history of the Seychelles Islands anterior to 1810.* Mahé, Seychelles: Government Printing Office.

Fleischmann, C.T. 2008. *Pour Mwan Mon Lalang Maternel i Al avek Mwan Partou: A Sociolinguistic Study on Attitudes towards Seychellois Creole.* Bern, Switzerland: Peter Lang.

Fombad, C.M. 2005. Botswana and the dynamics of legal modernisation within a dual English common law/Roman-Dutch law legal heritage. *African Journal of International and Comparative Law*, 13(1), 7–24.

Glenn, P. 2010. *Legal Traditions of the World: Sustainable Diversity in Law.* Oxford, UK: Oxford University Press.

Glover, V. 2011. Legislative drafting in Mauritius: A developing discipline. *Loophole: Journal of the Commonwealth Association of Legislative Counsel* [Online], 3, 20–25. Available at: http://www.opc.gov.au/calc/docs/Loophole_papers/Glover_Aug2011.pdf [accessed: November 27, 2013].

Government of Seychelles. 2012. Debt management strategy for the years 2010–2012. Victoria: Government of Seychelles.

Gretton, G. 1999. Scots law in a golden age, in *Now and Then: A Celebration of Sweet & Maxwell's Bicentenary*, edited by A. Kinahan. London: Sweet & Maxwell, 163–72.

Guébourg, J.-L. 2004. *Les Seychelles.* Paris: Karthala.

Husa, J. 2009. Legal families, in *Elgar Encyclopedia of Comparative Law*, edited by J.M. Smits. Cheltenham, UK: Edward Elgar, 382–93. Available at: http://papers.ssrn.com/sol3/papers.cfm?abstract_id=1529574 [accessed: November 27, 2013].

International Crisis Group. 1999. Five years after the genocide in Rwanda: Justice in question. Africa Report 1, International Crisis Group, Brussels. Available at: http://www.crisisgroup.org/en/regions/africa/central-africa/rwanda/001-five-years-after-the-genocide-in-rwanda-justice-in-question.aspx [accessed: November 27, 2013].

Jourdain, J. 1905. *The Journal of John Jourdain, 1608–1617.* Cambridge, UK: Cambridge University Press.

La Porta, R., López-de-Silanes, F., and Shleifer, A. 2008. The economic consequences of legal origins. *Journal of Economic Literature*, 46(2), 285.

Lionnet, G. 1972. *The Seychelles.* Devon, UK: David and Charles Publishers.

Lionnet, G. 1996. Les effets de la Révolution Française aux Seychelles, in *Révolution Francaise et Océan Indien: Prémices, Paroxysmes, Héritages et Déviances*, edited by C. Wanquet and B. Jullien. Paris: L'Harmattan, 187–94.

Mattei, U. 1997. Three patterns of law: Taxonomy and change in the world's legal system. *American Journal of Comparative Law*, 45(1), 5–44.

Mattei, U., and Monti, A. 1998. *Comparative Law and Economics.* Ann Arbor: University of Michigan Press.

McGreal, C. 2009. Why Rwanda said adieu to French. *Guardian Weekly*, January 15. Available at: http://www.guardian.co.uk/education/2009/jan/16/rwanda-english-genocide [accessed: November 27, 2013].

Merryman, J.H., and Pérez-Peroma, R. 2007. *The Civil Law Tradition: An Introduction to the Legal Systems of Europe and Latin America*. 3rd ed. Redwood City, CA: Stanford University Press.

Murat, M. 1900. *Gordon's Eden: or The Seychelles Archipelago*. Port Louis: Central Printing. Available at: http://www.jstor.org/discover/10.2307/60231890?uid=3739256&uid=2&uid=4&sid=21102908911797 [accessed: November 27, 2013].

Örücü, E. 2004. Family trees for legal systems: Towards a contemporary approach, in *Epistemology and Methodology of Comparative Law*, edited by M. Van Hoecke. Oxford, UK: Hart, 359–75.

Palmer, V.V. 2012. *Mixed Jurisdictions Worldwide: The Third Legal Family*. 2nd ed. Cambridge, UK: Cambridge University Press.

Pound, R. 1910. Law in books and law in action. *American Law Review*, 44, 12–36.

Purvis, M.-T. 2004. Education in Seychelles: An overview. *Seychelles Medical and Dental Journal*, 7(1), 46–51.

Renton, W. 1909a. French law within the British Empire: I. Historical introduction. *Journal of the Society for Comparative Legislation*, 10(1), 93–119.

Renton, W. 1909b. French law within the British Empire: III. Points of departure. *Journal of the Society for Comparative Legislation*, 10(2), 250–60.

Sauzier, A. 2010. The influence of the French judicial model on the Seychelles. *Bar Association of the Seychelles Law Journal* [Online], August 19. Available at: http://www.bas.sc/law-journal-1/theinfluenceofthefrenchjudicialmodelontheseychelles [accessed: November 27, 2013].

Sauzier, A., Angelo, A.H., and Klauser, V. 2011. *Sauzier on Evidence*. 2nd ed. Wellington: Law Publications.

Scarr, D. 2000. *Seychelles since 1770: History of a Slave and Post-slavery Society*. London: Hurst.

United Nations World Conference of Ministers for Youth. 1998. Effects of armed conflict, youth participation in economic development, media influence discussed at Lisbon conference. Press release, August 10. Available at: http://www.un.org/events/youth98/pressrel/youth8.htm [accessed: November 27, 2013].

Van Hoecke, M., and Warrington, M. 1998. Legal cultures and legal paradigm: Towards a new model for comparative law. *International and Comparative Law Quarterly*, 47(3), 495–536.

Van Hoecke, M., and Warrington, M. 2004. *Epistemology and Methodology of Comparative Law*. Oxford, UK: Hart.

Yiannopoulos, A.N. 2008. The civil codes of Louisiana. *Civil Law Commentaries* 1(1), 1–23. Available at: http://www.law.tulane.edu/uploadedFiles/Institutes_and_Centers/Eason_Weinmann/v01i01-Yiannopoulos(1).pdf [accessed: November 27, 2013].

Zweigert, K., and Kötz, H. 1998. *An Introduction to Comparative Law*. 3rd ed. Oxford, UK: Clarendon Press.

Chapter 6
Reconstructing Mixity: Sources of Law and Legal Method in Cyprus

Nikitas E. Hatzimihail

Aptly described as a "colorful plurilegal mosaic" (Symeonides 2003: 442), Cyprus law constitutes a mixed legal system in the traditional sense of the word. Like the better-known members of Vernon Palmer's (2001b: 7–9) "third legal family," Cyprus law is built on the twin foundations of common law and continental law, each in control of different legal subjects.[1] It is, however, pretty much a unique mixed legal system in which private law (in most subjects) and criminal law follow the English common law, and public law has a continental orientation. Procedural law is purely common law—a major factor in the mutation of the more continental elements of the legal system.

Like all major mixed legal systems, the bijurality of Cyprus law was founded on a transfer of sovereignty from British colonial rule (1878–1960) to independence.[2] The bijurality of the legal system has been strengthened—and challenged—by the bilingualism of the system and the power politics of the legal elites.[3] The constitution did not acknowledge English as an official language, and all new legislation to this day has been in Greek, but English remained in use in the courts until 1990, and the translation of colonial legislation into Greek was completed only in the mid-1990s. The legal profession has, moreover, been divided between continental- and English-educated lawyers, a split with a generational or even a class dimension and repercussions as to subject matter. All these factors contribute to a complex picture of a unique legal system, which has seldom been studied properly from either the inside or the outside.

This chapter examines an important aspect of the legal system: its sources of law. The chapter forms part of a broader project on Cyprus as a mixed legal system from a comparative law point of view, which includes general studies of the legal profession and legal education in Cyprus and of the structure of the legal subject matter. This project makes use of modern theories of comparative law—notably with regard to mixed jurisdictions, legal influences, and hybridity—in accounting for the complexities of Cyprus law. This chapter, however, represents an early stage in the project and is less ambitious in its goals.

It is structured in five parts. The next part serves as a more detailed introduction to the legal system as a whole. The two following parts discuss written law, encompassing statutory law and sources superior to legislation, and the penultimate part discusses case law and interpretive methods. The final part consists of four case studies, regarding contract, family, and procedural law, that illustrate certain dimensions of the system.

---

1 In a legal system classified as *mixed* under Palmer's (2001b: 8) definition, "[t]he presence of these dual elements will be obvious to an ordinary observer," a condition that probably requires "a quantitative threshold" (a condition met, for example, by Louisiana but not by Texas and California, despite their civilian roots). Palmer (2001b: 8–9) also emphasizes the structural allocation of content. Of course, in Palmer's ideal type of mixed jurisdiction, civil law is dominant but "cordoned off within the field of private law."

2 On the importance of such "defining moments" in the "foundation" of a mixed jurisdiction, see Palmer (2001a: 17–31).

3 See Palmer (2001a), 41–44 and 31–40, on the importance of the linguistic factor and the roles of local jurists in maintaining mixity.

Prelude: Cyprus Law in Context

A Historical Introduction

I begin with the shortest of historical introductions.[4] Cyprus is the largest island in the eastern Mediterranean. Since the second millennium B.C., a significant majority of its population has identified itself as ethnic Greek. For the past 800 years, however, it has been ruled successively by the Lusignan kings of Jerusalem, the Republic of Venice, the Ottoman Empire, and the British Empire. When the British took over the island in 1878, the legal environment mixed Byzantine Roman law, as administered by the institutions of the Greek Orthodox Church, and Islamic law with Western-styled secular Ottoman legislation. Initially, British procedural law was added to this mix. When Cyprus formally became a British colony in 1925, English substantive law began its conquest of the land. By the time of independence in 1960, Cyprus would be regarded as a small but definite member of the common law tradition.

On its face, independence should have led Cyprus away from the common law tradition: after all, it empowered a people—or peoples—attached to motherlands and languages falling firmly within the continental legal tradition. In effect, however, independence was imposed on the vast majority of Cypriots. Greek Cypriots, who had fought for union with Greece, were instead called to share power—in a manner viewed by most as disproportionate to ethnic and social demographics—with the ethnic Turkish minority (whose leadership flirted with the idea of the island's partition between Greece and Turkey). In any event, the institutional arrangements put in place at independence would disallow significant law reform. The constitution established a presidential system of two separate communities, Greek and Turkish.[5] For each Greek Cypriot in a constitutionally prescribed government office, a Turkish Cypriot deputy with veto power was appointed.[6] The House of Representatives effectively consisted of two caucuses, with separate majorities needed for matters such as taxation, electoral reform, and city government.[7] Relative parity was provided in the two supreme courts of the land and quotas in the civil service. Separate municipal structures—both mayors and city councils—were elected in the five major cities.[8]

The political conditions soon deteriorated into a state of emergency in 1963–1964, culminating in a bombardment by Turkey, the departure of the Turkish Cypriot leaders from their government posts, and the segregation of Turkish Cypriots into autonomous enclaves. The republic continued to operate on the fiction that Turkish Cypriots would return to their positions, although amendments were made in the function of certain institutions under the so-called necessity doctrine. The fiction persisted even after the two-stage Turkish invasion in 1974 effectively divided the island. Today, the Republic of Cyprus controls a little less than two-thirds of its actual territory; its institutions remain bicommunal, but the vast majority of Turkish Cypriot residents of the island live in the northern territory controlled by Turkey. Turkish Cypriots are citizens of the republic and can travel freely in its territory and the rest of the European Union (EU), but they do not participate in the political institutions of the republic pending solution to the "Cyprus problem."

Law in Present-Day Cyprus

Cyprus is that unique combination of a European and a postcolonial country. Much of the legislation and the legal institutions still in place have a distinctively colonial or postcolonial flavor; however, Cyprus has always

4 For more details, see notably Hatzimihail (2013: 42–54) and Symeonides (2003: 443–53).

5 Constitution of the Republic of Cyprus (1960), article 2. The constitution acknowledges three non–Greek Orthodox religious groups (Armenian, Maronite Catholic, and Latin Catholic). These three groups elected in 1960 to join the Greek community pursuant to article 2(3).

6 See the Constitution of the Republic of Cyprus, article 1 (President and Vice-President of the Republic) and article 72(1) (Speaker and Deputy Speaker of the House of Representatives). With regard to the independent officers of the republic, see articles 112(1) (Attorney General and Assistant Attorney General), 115(1) (Auditor General and Assistant Auditor General), 118(1) (Governor and Deputy Governor of the Central Bank), 126(1) (Accountant General and Deputy Accountant General).

7 Ibid., articles 62 and 78(2).

8 Ibid., article 173.

identified with Europe and, especially since accession to the EU in 2004, the country and its professional elites have been active participants in European law and institutions. Moreover, the complicated political situation has led to a combination of a traditionalist mentality with the sense of perpetual temporariness.

To this day, the common law has maintained its hold on Cyprus law. The court structure certainly looks like a common law judiciary, with a unitary court system consisting of one trial and one appellate instance. Procedural law has been a tool for the continued dominance of the common law. Contrary to classic mixed jurisdictions, the heart of private law—namely, the law of obligations—is a stronghold of English common law in Cyprus. Criminal law is another privileged domain of the common law.

However, pockets of resistance to the common law have been expanded or created. Let us consider, for example, family law. By the end of British colonial rule, only divorce was left to ecclesiastical jurisdiction; the family law reform in the early 1990s, however, not only transplanted secularized Greek family law across the legal field but also extended its effective application to all Cyprus domiciliaries. But the principal example of resistance against the common law concerns public law. Greek administrative law (itself developed by case law in the spirit of the French administrative legal tradition) became the principal source of the new administrative law of Cyprus. Today, the general principles of Cyprus administrative law are codified in statute, and the case law of the Greek Council of State is held in high esteem.

Mutation might in fact be the key word in describing the present-day Cyprus legal system. On the one hand, legal fields inspired by the continental legal tradition have been mutated through the use of common law procedure and a common law mentality among the judiciary. On the other hand, the legal profession has also mutated away from common law ideal types: the bar is a massive, unitary body (consisting of *advocates*: the distinction between barristers and solicitors was never adopted); the politics and daily function of the Cyprus bar are, in fact, more similar to those of Athens than those of London. As to the judiciary, the system of promotions and transfers—with the Supreme Court justices acting as the Supreme Judicial Council—has established a hierarchical, even bureaucratic system. The Supreme Court itself is not just a common law court of last resort; absent an intermediate jurisdiction, the Supreme Court has to sit on all civil and criminal appeals. Moreover, it acts as a two-instance administrative jurisdiction and a constitutional court.

Sources Superior to Statutory Law

Cyprus law follows a clear hierarchy of sources, with a rigid written constitution at the top and a prominent place granted to international law and especially EU law. The existential challenges that the republic has faced from its very beginning have made the constitution the paramount factor in Cyprus politics as well as law.[9] International law and European law are also frequently invoked in the legal and political discourse, as might be expected of a republic that stakes its continued existence and any hopes of restoring its territorial integrity on international legality and European integration.

The Constitution

The Republic of Cyprus was established by an international treaty between the United Kingdom, Greece, and Turkey. The Constitution of the Republic came into legal existence as an annex to the Zurich-London treaty agreements. It is an extremely rigid instrument. Many provisions have been characterized as "fundamental" and may never be amended: 15 articles have been declared fundamental in their entirety, along with provisions from 33 more,[10] to the point that some question whether the principle of popular sovereignty is actually enshrined in the constitution. For other provisions, a two-thirds vote by the representatives of each community, Greek and Turkish, is required for any amendment.[11]

9 See, for example, Kourtellos (2000), Papasavvas (1998), and Polyviou (2013). Among literature in Greek, most notable is the treatise by Loizou (2001), designed as an article-by-article commentary, and the generalist monographs of Emilianides (2006) and Nicolaou (2000).

10 Constitution of the Republic of Cyprus, article 182(1), referring to annex III.

11 Ibid., article 182(3).

In fact, the 1963–1964 breakdown of the bicommunal system of governance established by the constitution led to corrective legislation under the so-called doctrine of necessity, which was aimed at allowing state institutions to continue to function.[12] The role of the Supreme Court of Cyprus (created from the merger of the High Court and Supreme Constitutional Court) as the final arbiter of constitutional questions became especially significant (Papasavvas 1998).

The constitution is the supreme law of the land.[13] It contains a comparatively modern bill of rights, which is modeled after and has been largely interpreted in light of the European Convention of Human Rights. The importance traditionally granted to the office of the attorney general (which has so far acted as legal counsel to both the executive and the legislative branches of government) has translated into an effective (usually, but not always) mechanism of a priori control of the constitutionality of executive decrees and bills discussed by the legislature. Constitutional review a posteriori is an important—and more visible—mechanism of the legal system. Any litigant may raise the issue of constitutionality before any court or tribunal of the republic, which must refer the issue to the Supreme Court.[14] The president of the Republic may, moreover, refer to the court the question of constitutionality of any legislation passed by the House of Representatives.[15] Last but not least, courts are explicitly tasked with interpreting legislation—especially colonial legislation maintained in force after independence—in conformity with the constitution.[16] Given how much colonial legislation (often dating from the nineteenth century or representing more repressive attitudes) remained in place after independence, this constitutional control became an important tool for step-by-step law reform.[17] More recently, the Supreme Court acknowledged the right of individuals to make use of constitutional provisions in civil litigation.[18]

European Union Law

Cyprus formally acceded to the European Union on May 1, 2004. EU law has been challenging and transforming institutions in every field of law.[19] The question of the hierarchical relationship between the national constitution and EU law was solved early on by an amendment to the constitution, which acknowledged the supremacy of EU law in its entirety over the constitution.[20] The constitution ought, moreover, to be interpreted in conformity to EU law.

International Law

International law is also an important source of Cyprus law—as well as political discourse.[21] In terms of legal sources, we must distinguish between treaty and customary law. As to the former, the constitution explicitly

---

12 See especially the landmark case of *Attorney-General v. Ibrahim* (1964) CLR 195. For the practical application of this doctrine, see, for example, *Mesaritou v. Cyprus Broadcasting Corporation* (1972) 3 CLR 100 and *Ioannides v. The Police* (1973) 2 CLR 125. In dealing with the 1974 Turkish invasion and the dramatic situation on the ground, the doctrine was taken further in *Ambrosia Oils Margarine Industry Ltd. v. Bank of Cyprus Ltd.* (1983) 1 CLR 55. The issue of whether it would be possible to affect amendments of certain constitutional provisions was discussed inconclusively in *Nicolaou v. Nicolaou* (1992) 1 CLR 1338 and finally resolved in affirmation in *Koulountis v. House of Representatives* (1997) 1 CLR 1026. For a discussion see Polyviou (2013: 26–63).

13 Constitution of the Republic of Cyprus, article 179. See also article 188(2).

14 Ibid., article 144.

15 Ibid., article 137.

16 Ibid., article 188(4).

17 See, for example, *Pelides v. The Republic* 3 RSCC 12; *Djirkalli v. The Republic* 1 RSCC 36.

18 *Giallouros v. Nicolaou* (2001) 1 CLR 558.

19 On European law, see Kombos (2010a; 2010b).

20 Constitution of the Republic of Cyprus, article 1A (amendment made by Law 127(I)2006).

21 On the role of international law in Cyprus appellate cases, see the cases reported and commented on by Aristoteles Constantinides in the *Oxford Reports on International Law in Domestic Courts* database, available at http://www.oxfordlawreports.com [accessed: January 17, 2014]. Among literature involving international law, usually with regard to the "Cyprus problem," see, for example, Chrysostomides (2000) and Tornaritis (1983).

provides that treaty law supersedes any legislative provision to the contrary.[22] Statutory provisions should be given, if possible, an interpretation conforming to international treaties.[23] As to customary international law, however, we can infer its status only from the occasional obiter dicta of Supreme Court justices and comparative legal reasoning (Constantinides 2011). The approach followed by common law jurisdictions is to treat customary law as incorporated into the common law without any legislative or judicial interference. The approach followed by many continental countries, including Greece, is to apply the constitutional provision on treaty law by analogy. The Supreme Court might well go either way when the time comes to decide.

Statutory Law

From a constitutional point of view, the statutory law of Cyprus consists of (a) legislation enacted during the colonial era and maintained under article 188(1) of the constitution[24] and (b) legislation enacted subsequent to independence by the House of Representatives in accordance with articles 61 et seq. of the constitution.[25] The former group of laws was originally written in English and translated only in the past quarter-century. It is organized by subject as "chapters" in the six-volume Statute Laws of Cyprus and is commonly referred to by chapter (cap.) number. The latter, written in Greek, are published in the *Official Journal of the Republic* and are referred to by their short title and year of publication or by the statute's number and year.[26]

The few elements of religious law that survive in present-day Cyprus law—notably, the rules on the inalienable religious endowments known as *Vakf*—constitute a third source. These institutions constitute an expression of the constitutional recognition of the political and cultural autonomy of the communities and religious groups of Cyprus; as such, they can be reformed or eliminated by the initiative of the respective community. From a legal positivist perspective, they continue to exist by virtue of their incorporation into statutory law.[27]

A more fruitful distinction would be to divide existing legislation in accordance with the principal stages of Cyprus legal history. The colonial period could thus be subdivided into three stages: the first from 1878 until the official establishment of a colony of the Crown in 1925; the second from 1925 to World War II; and the third covering the postwar colonial period, during which the long-term status of the island was put in question. The postindependence period could, in its turn, be subdivided into the first decades of independence and the period of preparation for and actual accession to the European Union.

Identifying these five *stromata* of legislation allows us to better understand the evolutionary process that led to the present-day mixed or hybrid legal system and perhaps even to predict its development (Hatzimihail 2013: 72). A more pertinent reason for the purposes of this chapter, however, is that the origins (and age) of legislative texts play an important role in determining the methods used in their interpretation. Thus, legislation seen as a statement or restatement of English common law principles is handled differently by courts and the legal profession than legislation that is indigenous in origin or is derived from the continental legal tradition.

22 Constitution of the Republic of Cyprus, article 169(3).

23 See *Larkos v. Attorney General* (1995) 1 CLR 510, at 515, and *Aristidou v. The Republic* (1967) 2 CLR 43.

24 Courts of Justice Law 1960, article 29(1)(b), in combination with article 188 of the constitution.

25 Courts of Justice Law 1960, article 29(1)(a), in combination with articles 78 and 179 of the constitution.

26 Statutory legislation may be found in online legal databases—namely, the commercial database Leginet and the open-access CyLaw (http://www.cylaw.org [accessed: January 17, 2014]). Statutory collections are a recent phenomenon; see, notably, Neocleous and Hatzimihail (2013).

27 See the Evcaf and Vaqfs Law (cap. 337) enacted by Law 32/55. As to divorce, modern statutory law provides a special statutory regime for members of the three religious groups recognized in the constitution (Armenian, Maronite, and Latin) that incorporates, by reference, the grounds provided in the respective religious laws but also lists a number of mandatory grounds. See article 11 of the Family Tribunals (Religious Groups) Law 1994 (enacted as Law 87(I)/1994) and annex I thereto. Religious ceremony under the rules of the respective denomination constitutes a valid form of marriage with no need for the involvement of a civil authority. See article 9(2) of the Marriage Law 2003 (Law 104(I)/2003).

Procedural Law Reform: The Early Colonial Period

The first half-century of British colonial rule did not see much legislative reform of substantive law. The administration of the justice system was redrawn from early on, with colonial courts replacing Ottoman tribunals and chipping away at ecclesiastical jurisdiction over succession and marital property. However, Ottoman law (much of it in Westernized form, following the *Tanzimat* law reforms of the mid-nineteenth century) survived as the residual legal system until the official introduction of the common law by the 1935 Courts of Justice Law. The strong control of the courts of justice by British colonial lawyers of course mitigated this regime from the very beginning.[28]

Many of the procedural law reforms of this period were significant, but most instruments were replaced by the interwar efforts to create a proper common law regime. However, much of the legislation on enforcement matters has survived, with little change, since 1885: the so-called Civil Procedure Law (cap. 6), concerning precisely the enforcement of local judgments, is the principal example.[29] Specific performance of land contracts provided the other until 2011.[30]

Codifying the Common Law: The Interwar Period

Substantive law reform began in earnest only once Cyprus became a colony of the Crown in 1925. In 1935, "the common law and the doctrines of equity" were finally made the residual system of norms—and yet they were to apply as in force on November 8, 1914 (the day Cyprus was annexed to the Crown following the declaration of war between the British and the Ottomans). An interesting specimen of the conservative attitudes of British colonial lawmaking from this period concerns the Evidence Law (cap. 9): the colony's evidence rules were reformed into a consolidated statute in 1946, but Cyprus's courts were nonetheless to apply "in any civil or criminal proceeding ... so far as circumstances permit, the law the statutes in question and rules of evidence as in force in England on the 5th day of November, 1914."[31] The fact that this provision is still in place (even though the Evidence Law was amended a few years ago) also indicates the traditionalist mentality of the country's legal elites to this day.

The interwar era's lasting contribution has been the transplantation, mostly from other colonies, of important legislation on the basic fields of substantive law. Commercial law statutes dating from that period and still in force today are the Bills of Exchange Law (cap. 262),[32] the Carriage of Goods by Sea Law (cap. 263),[33] the Partnerships Law (cap. 116),[34] and the Bankruptcy Law (cap. 5).[35] But the most notable interwar statutes, in terms of both practical application and contribution to comparative law and legal history, are the three "codes" of Cyprus: the Criminal Code (cap. 154),[36] the Contract Law (cap. 149),[37] and the Civil Wrongs Law (cap. 148).[38] Such legislation constituted an effective codification of common law principles in their respective fields, and the statutes in question are still in force today, often with little modification.

The lineage of these codes is worth a separate study. The Criminal Code and the Contract Law are generally accepted as effective transplantations of the respective nineteenth-century Indian statutes, whereas

---

28 See, for example, *Ismail v. Attorney-General* (1929) 16 CLR 9, at 12 ("the rule of English law as to the binding nature of the decisions of appellate tribunals" must be followed "in the absence of a clear rule of Ottoman law in the subject").

29 Enacted as Law 10/1885.

30 Sale of Land (Specific Performance) Law (cap. 232) (enacted as Law 11/1885 and replaced by its namesake, Law 81(I)/2011).

31 Evidence Law, article 3. The full title of L. 14/46 was "A law to amend and consolidate certain provisions relating to the law of Evidence."

32 Enacted as Law 20/28. The law was identical to the English Bills of Exchange Act 1882. Its provisions on checks were reformed in 1997.

33 Enacted as Law 8/27.

34 Enacted as Law 18/28.

35 Enacted as Law 8/30.

36 Enacted in 1928 by an order in council.

37 Enacted as Law 24/30.

38 Enacted as Law 35/32.

the provenance of the Civil Wrongs Law is more of a mystery. However, the full lineage of colonial statutes is more complicated. It has, for example, been documented that the Cyprus Criminal Code traces its immediate ancestry to the Nigerian code, which in turn is a descendant of the Queensland Code.[39] As to the Civil Wrongs Law, the 1932 Cyprus statute appears to follow the 1927 draft of a Civil Wrongs Ordinance for Palestine, which in turn was based on the Civil Wrongs Bill prepared for India by Frederick Pollock.[40]

Be that as it may, what does transplantation mean in this case? Let us use the example of the Contract Law, which appears to be almost a copy of the Indian Contract Act of 1872.[41] The primary differences between the two texts are technical. Certain explanations of the Indian legislator have been moved into the main text, and the illustrations have been removed; the chapter on the sale of goods came last in the original Cyprus statute and was subsequently abolished. Moreover, specific performance is provided for—in a single provision—in the Cyprus statute.[42] The principal substantive difference is that the Cyprus statute provides explicitly that it be interpreted in accordance with English law[43]—even though on at least one occasion (namely, the rule on past consideration) Cyprus courts, unlike Indian courts, have read the same text as deviating from the common law.[44]

The sole substantive deviation of the Cyprus statute from the Indian prototype concerns the capacity of minors. Until 1970, English common law considered minors ("infants") all persons not having attained 21 years of age; capacity of minors was—and still is—governed by a series of intricate rules (see, for example, Beatson, Burrows, and Cartwright 2010: 232–46).[45] The Indian Contract Act espoused a clear-cut rule: capacity to contract depended on the person reaching the age of majority according to his or her personal law ("the law to which he is subject").[46] The Cyprus Contract Law followed the Indian rule as to the noncapacity of minors but avoided a similar reference to personal laws, simply fixing the age of majority at 18.[47] In 1955, following a case in which incapacity was used as a defense by a minor against an action for breach of a promise to marry,[48] article 11 was amended to include a reference to the English rules on capacity.[49]

The merits of the new rule have been debatable: it may be superior in fairness of result in individual cases and weaker in predictability. Even the claim of fairness would have been debatable were the provision not to deviate from the general rule in Cyprus that English common law is followed but not British legislation enacted subsequent to 1960, but at least the provision as it stands has allowed Cyprus courts to take into account the British statutory reform of the common law regime under the Minors Contract Act 1987. The Cyprus regime on minors' contracts certainly perplexes law students, but then the whole issue of minors'

---

39 The Cyprus Criminal Code provided the original for the Palestinian Criminal Code Ordinance. See Abrams (1972: 26–28), with a discussion of the origins of the Cyprus Criminal Code at 28–31.

40 On Pollock's influence, see Friedmann (1975: 342n104). The Mandatory Civil Wrongs Ordinance finally enacted in 1944 "reflects independent thinking and in many important points differs from both the Cyprus Ordinance and English law."

41 On the history of the Indian Contract Act, see Tofaris (2010). The principal reference work on the act (occasionally cited in Cyprus appellate cases to this day) is Pollock and Mulla (2006).

42 Article 76(1) of the Contract Law states, "A contract shall be capable of being specifically enforced by the Court if (a) it is not a void contract under this or any other Law; and (b) it is expressed in writing; and (c) it is signed at the end thereof by the party to be charged herewith; and (d) the Court considers, having regard to all circumstances, that the enforcement of specific performance of the contract would not be unreasonable or otherwise inequitable or impracticable." An older, separate law (cap. 232), promulgated in 1885, governs specific performance over the sale of land. In contrast, specific performance in India is now governed by the Specific Relief Act 1963.

43 Contract Law, article 2(1).

44 See the case study on past consideration later in this chapter.

45 The age was lowered as of January 1, 1970, with the Family Law Reform Act 1969, section 1.

46 Indian Contract Act, article 11.

47 Contract Law, article 11(2).

48 See *Myrianthousis v. Petrou* (1956) 21 CLR 32.

49 Article 11(2) of the Contract Law (cap. 149), as amended by Law 7/56 reads as follows: "The law in force in England for the time being relating to contracts to which an infant is a party shall apply to contracts in which a person who has not attained the age of eighteen years of age is a party." The second sentence of article 11(2), conferring capacity to contract on a married person who has not yet attained the age of 18 years, was maintained.

contracts has lost most of its significance in the real world. However, the story is indicative of the strong orientation of late colonial (and even postcolonial) Cyprus toward the English common law and its rules. It might also serve as a cautionary tale with regard to the pitfalls in haphazard legislative intervention in core subject codes.

In the Shadow of English Law: The Postwar Period

In the years following World War II and leading up to independence, the colonial government sought to consolidate the British position in Cyprus and to promote law reform in subjects that had previously been left to the status quo ante. Legislation on the administration of justice was thoroughly reformed; the new Courts of Justice Law made applicable in Cyprus the common law (and equity) as currently in force; last but not least, much legislation was imported from England and Wales directly or via other colonies. Leaving aside labor and administrative reform, one finds that the main area of such legislative activity was business and commercial law. The principal examples of statutes surviving from this period are the Companies Law (cap. 113)[50] and the Trustee Law (cap. 193).[51] To these we must add the Trade Marks Law (cap. 268) of 1951, which replaced an earlier statute dating from 1910.[52] A new Sale of Goods Law (cap. 267) was enacted in 1953,[53] modeled after the English Sale of Goods Act 1893 and repealing the Contract Law chapter on the sale of goods (modeled after the Indian Contract Act). That statute has been itself recently repealed, just like most colonial era legislation on intellectual property.[54]

The increased participation of Greek and Turkish Cypriot lawyers in the colonial justice system also allowed, to a limited degree, the preservation or incorporation of continental legal institutions into Cyprus law: intestate succession follows the Roman-Byzantine norms nurtured by the Greek Orthodox ecclesiastical jurisdiction,[55] whereas Turkish Cypriots are governed by the secular family law of Turkey, which has been transplanted in replacement of Islamic legal institutions of personal law.[56]

A Postcolonial Legal System: First Decades of Independence

Following the consolidation of the republic and under the reign of the doctrine of necessity, the House of Representatives pushed "indigenous" legislation seeking to deal with local concerns and political issues. A second wave of such indigenous legislation followed as the country sought to recover from the 1974 invasions and their socioeconomic consequences. The needs of a modern bureaucratic state have also led to a lot of normative administrative acts derivative of statutory legislation.

Transplantation of English and Greek law also took place to a considerable degree. English legal transplants notably dominated commercial and business law reform in this period. In 1963, shipping legislation (which

50 Enacted by Law 7/1951.

51 Enacted as Law 46/1955, as a transplantation of the English Trustee Act 1925.

52 Enacted as Law 2/51. The law was subjected to several, relatively small, amendments since 1962; it was seriously revised more recently, especially by Law 176(I)/2000 and 121(I)/2006, in the process of implementation of the EU directives on intellectual property. The Appellation (Cyprus Wines) Protection Law (cap. 127; enacted by Law 2/50) still remains in force.

53 Law 25/1953.

54 See notably the Copyright Law (cap. 264), which was repealed in 1976. Enacted by an ordinance of April 25, 1919, it arranged for the application in Cyprus of the (Imperial) Copyright Act 1911. See also the Merchandise Marks Law (cap. 265; enacted as Law 35/58), which was repealed in 1987, and the Patents Law (cap. 266; enacted as Law 40/1957), which was repealed in 1998.

55 See the Wills and Succession Law (cap. 195; enacted by Law 25/1945 and modified between 1951 and 1955). The law was subjected to minor amendments by Law 75/70 and Law 100/89 regarding forced heirship rules.

56 See the Turkish Family (Marriage and Divorce) Law (cap. 339; enacted as Law 4/1951, amended by Law 63/54) and the Turkish Family Courts Law (cap. 338; enacted by Law 43/1954 in replacement of Law 3/51).

had been left unreformed under British rule) was adopted in the mold of English law.[57] Other transplants eventually replaced (or actually updated) previous English transplants: the Sale of Goods Act 1994 has effectively copied the English Sale of Goods Act 1979;[58] the Trade Descriptions Law 1987 replicates its 1968 English namesake;[59] and the Copyright Law 1979 is inspired by the English Copyright Act 1956.[60] Other jurisdictions were used as models in matters of offshore finance. For example, the International Trusts Law 1992 reproduces much of the wording and concepts found in Caribbean common law jurisdictions.[61]

Greek law claims a strong influence in public law and in noncommercial civil matters. As to the former, the General Principles of Administrative Law 1999, which was meant to codify the case law of the Supreme Court of Cyprus (itself strongly influenced by Greek academic writings and case law), relied heavily on Greek doctrinal works.[62] With regard to private law, two examples from different moments might give an idea of both influence and mutation. One example is the Associations and Foundations Law 1972, which governs many, but by no means all, nonprofit institutions, because it coexists with colonial legislation on charitable companies, trusts, and clubs.[63] The law effectively reprised articles 61–120 of the Greek Civil Code with one key difference, which indicates the strong role of the civil service in Cyprus: in Greece, registration is a matter for district courts, whereas in Cyprus it is dealt with by a specialized governmental official (the registrar, or Έφορος).

But the primary field of Greek influence over private law has been family law. Originally, the law of marriage and divorce had been left to the personal law of Cypriots. In the 1990s, following the establishment of state-run family courts, the family law of Cyprus was rewritten in a series of statutes modeled after the 1982–1983 reform of Greek family law. Application of the new family law was gradually extended to all Cyprus residents. Greek law was the direct influence for the law of marriage, divorce (including marital property), children, and parenthood.[64] The principal exception concerned adoption, which had traditionally been dealt with in accordance with English law.[65] The primary reason was that the reform of adoption law in Greece was still not completed at the time, but another reason may well have been the orientation of the committee member who was entrusted with producing a draft statute. (The strong role in adoption matters of administrative services under the Ministry of Labor and Social Welfare may have also played a part.) Another exception concerns the protection of adults, which has been left outside family jurisdiction (Hatzimihail, forthcoming).

A European Legal System: Accession to the EU

In 2004, after 15 years of internal debates and international negotiations, Cyprus became a member of the European Union. Cyprus did not adopt the practice of some other EU member states, where framework legislation authorizes the executive power to implement EU directives by presidential decrees. As a result, the implementation of European secondary law has come to constitute the principal task of the House of

57 Law 45/63, known as the Merchant Shipping (Registration of Ships, Sales and Mortgages) Law 1963, relied on the English Merchant Shipping Act 1894.

58 Law 10(I)/94, replacing cap. 267.

59 Law 2/87, as subsequently amended between 1987 and 2002.

60 Law 59/76 (as subsequently amended), replacing cap. 264.

61 Law 69(I)/92, as amended by Law 20(I)/2012. An English translation of the original statute (prior to its 2012 amendment) with notes is found on the website of the Central Bank of Cyprus, http://www.centralbank.gov.cy/media/pdf/ITLWE_ITCSLAW.pdf [accessed: January 20, 2014].

62 Law 158(I)/1999. Its full name reads, "Law codifying the general principles of administrative law that ought to govern the actions of the civil service." The treatises of Athens professor Prodromos Dagtoglou on administrative law and procedure supposedly provided most of the definitions used.

63 Law 57/72.

64 The following statutes (as amended) constitute the corpus of Cyprus family law: the Family Courts Law 1990 (Law 23/90), the Relations between Parents and Children Law 1990 (Law 216/90), the Pecuniary Relations between Spouses Law 1990 (Law 232/91), Children (Relation and Legal Status) Law 1996 (Law 187/96), and the recast Marriage Law 2003 (Law 104(I)/2003). A draft law on personal relations between spouses, again modeled after Greek law, died in parliamentary committee. See also Nicolaou (1998).

65 Law 19(I)/95.

Representatives. Moreover, a constellation of independent regulatory authorities (commissioners) was established in Cyprus. The effect of these commissioners is being felt rather slowly, but surely.[66]

Most legislation adopted since the mid-1990s—and especially the early 2000s—appears to have been oriented toward preparing the country for European integration and implementing the community *acquis*. For example, the Law on Unfair Terms in Consumer Contracts 1996 constituted an early implementation—at the time, perhaps more of a transplantation—of Directive 93/13/EEC.[67]

The accession in 2004 by Cyprus to the Vienna Convention on the International Sale of Goods can also be seen in light of European integration.[68] The United Kingdom has not to this day adopted the convention, so by implication much of the sale of goods in Cyprus has been separated from English law. The fact that Cyprus adopted as official text the translation prepared by Greece a few years prior has led to some degree of mutation of what had up to that point been a purely common law subject. Moreover, Cyprus law may now claim, in several cases, two words in Greek for the same concept of the law of sales.

Cyprus's implementation of legislation has tended to follow prototypes from Greece and the United Kingdom. On certain occasions, however, implementation legislation has asserted a distinctive local touch.[69] The most common practice, however, has been to transpose the text of the directive into statute with little attempt to consolidate EU derivative law. Consumer sale of goods is thus treated in a statute distinct from the Sale of Goods Law 1994;[70] two separate laws were enacted on the same day to implement the directives on contracts negotiated away from business premises and on distance contracts.[71]

Case Law

If written law provides the Cyprus legal system its foundations and building structures, it owes its actual shape to case law. The influence of English common law in Cyprus is such that the country is frequently regarded as a common law jurisdiction. Local case law is important in all legal fields, especially those inspired by continental substantive law, and the EU courts have been increasingly influential across the board.

A distinction should, in principle, be drawn between those legal fields that are regarded as falling under the English common law—notably procedural law, as well as most private law and criminal law—and those fields in which English common law is not regarded as applicable, granting its place to local case law and other authorities. The Supreme Court, however, has extended the doctrines on judicial precedent even with regard to the latter.[72]

Legal and Political Foundations of Judicial Precedent in Cyprus

According to the Supreme Court, rule by judicial precedent is grounded on the principle of judicial hierarchy and the need for predictability.[73] Nevertheless, one can search the constitution in vain for an express legal basis for a case law system, or even for the maintenance of English common law—in contrast to the explicit constitutional provisions regarding the transitional maintenance in force of colonial statutes[74] and the continued use of prerogative writs as a remedy granted by the High Court.[75] The colonial status quo was

66 For a list of independent authorities and a brief discussion of regulatory tensions, see Hatzimihail (2013: 81).

67 Law 93(I)/96.

68 Law 55(III)/2004.

69 For a case study on the implementation process, see Iliopoulos (2006).

70 Law 7(I)/2000.

71 Law 13(I)/2000 in implementation of Directive 85/EEC and Law 14(I)/2000 in implementation of Directive 97/7/EC, respectively.

72 See notably *Republic of Cyprus v. Demetriades* (1977) 3 CLR 213; *Elefetheriou-Kanga v. The Republic* (1989) 3 CLR 262.

73 See *Republic of Cyprus v. Demetriades* (1977) 3 CLR 213.

74 Constitution of the Republic of Cyprus, article 188(1).

75 Ibid., article 155(4).

instead confirmed by the new Courts of Justice Law 1960,[76] which repeated most of the provisions of the colonial Court of Justice Law (cap. 8) enacted in 1953.[77] Article 29 the 1960 law has reprised article 33 of 1953 law in stating the "law to be applied" by "every Court in the exercise of its civil or criminal jurisdiction." According to article 29(1)(c), such law includes "common law and the principles of equity save in so far as other provision has been or shall be made by any Law and so far as not inconsistent with the Constitution." With the exception of the reference to the new constitution that was added, the new provision simply translates article 33(1)(c) of the 1953 law. Admittedly, the original wording, "doctrines of equity," has been translated into Greek as "principles of equity," but this change was less a conscious mutation than a result of the absence of an exact word.[78]

The provision has been vividly criticized: in the words of Symeon Symeonides (2003: 450), it "went much further than the letter and spirit of the Constitution, and sought to tie the legal system of Cyprus surreptitiously and permanently to the English common law." No temporal limitation applied, meaning that "a post-1960 decision of the House of Lords would be binding on the courts of Cyprus, and—what is more—even if a subsequent statute of the British Parliament had superseded that decision" (Symeonides 2003: 450).

Symeonides (2003: 450) notes that the whole statute was "drafted by a well-known former servant of Her Majesty's government" and promulgated by an "inexperienced House of Representatives." In their defense, the representatives took the easy way out in repeating the preexisting provision. The republic began its life in an uneasy truce between realities and aspirations; its constituent communities were locked in an opposition that soon came to hinder the state's very operation. Moreover, the various social groups, including the newly formed legal and political elites, were still trying to find their footing in the postcolonial era. One could argue that neither a consensus nor the massive intellectual power needed to engage in large-scale law reform existed in 1960; on the contrary, maintaining the status quo would leave all options open for the future—and the status quo was a common law regime, with the probable exception of administrative law. Even though the right of appeal to the Privy Council was abolished on independence, the new High Court was but the continuation of the colonial Supreme Court in law and in spirit: its foreign president had to be a Commonwealth national, and its Cypriot members boasted of long service in the colonial judiciary.

Symeonides is nonetheless correct in pointing to personal biases as well as what was to become a key conflict within the Greek Cyprus bar. For the past 30 years of British colonial rule, membership in the Cyprus bar had been effectively preserved for people trained in England as barristers (many without a law degree).[79] Following independence, bar membership began expanding significantly. An increasing number of new lawyers came from nonlegal families, and the vast majority of new entrants to the profession held university degrees from the Greek law schools (aided by scholarship policies, entrance exams, and especially the lack of university tuition). This situation resulted in a generational as well as a class conflict whose traces are still visible today. Maintenance of the English common law thus became a vehicle for the domination of the established group of colonial advocates—and their children—in the emerging legal profession of Cyprus. The absorption of the Supreme Constitutional Court, after only three years of existence, by the High Court affirmed the long-term continuation of a monolithically common law judiciary. But this internal conflict is best illustrated in the use of the English language. After independence, the legal system took three decades to complete the transition from English to the republic's official languages. The basic colonial statutes were translated only in the 1990s. To this day, no official translation has been done of the principal instrument of

76 Law 14/1960.

77 Law 40/53.

78 Note that the numbering of section (1)(c) has been maintained by a conscious effort: the colonial provision named "the Laws of the Colony"; the Ottoman laws still in force (namely, the law on *Vakfs* and the Maritime Code); common law and equity; and the "Statutes of Her Imperial Parliament, and Orders of Her Majesty in Council, applicable either to the colonies generally or to the Colony save in so far as the same may validly be modified or other provision made by any Law of the Colony." The new provision, postindependence, names first the constitution and laws produced by the republic, second the colonial legislation maintained under article 188 of the constitution, third common law and equity, fourth the laws and principles on *Vakf* (*ahkamul evkhaf*), and fifth British laws applicable in Cyprus immediately before independence.

79 See the original (1955) article 3 of the Advocates Law (cap. 2), which states that admission to practice as an advocate was reserved to those "entitled to practice" as a barrister-at-law or "admitted to practice" as a solicitor in England or Northern Ireland, or as an advocate in Scotland.

civil litigation, the Civil Procedure Rules.[80] It is perhaps not mere coincidence that it took a little more than three decades after independence for the first Cypriot graduates of a Greek law school to reach the appellate bench.

The Common Law in Practice

Case law might rule Cyprus law in its entirety, but the sources used and the extent of discretion allowed to judges depends on the subject at hand.

Cyprus Rules of Precedent

The Supreme Court has adopted the English rules of *stare decisis*, as contrasted to the more liberal U.S. approach.[81] It has, moreover, reserved its right to reverse its own judgments—a judicial policy grounded on English judgments and dicta, but asserted more vigorously in Cyprus.[82] The district courts, family courts, and specialized tribunals are bound by Supreme Court judgments, although district judges are known to have held contrary to Supreme Court rulings by invoking English authorities when applicable. A single Supreme Court justice sitting at first instance is on the contrary not considered as an "inferior court" but is nonetheless bound by the decisions of an appeals bench.[83] The full bench, however, may reverse its own case law. An appellate panel should accordingly be able to explicitly reject (or reverse) the rule created by another appellate panel. Consistency is usually sought after, but a line of precedent has been disregarded in some cases, leading to a contrary line of precedent coexisting with the established one.[84]

English Law as Binding Authority

English common law may be regarded as binding, in accordance with article 29(1) of the Court of Justice Law, subject to a contrary statutory provision. At the same time, this statement has practical limits. Cyprus long ago abolished any overseas appellate control (namely, by the Privy Council), and the last foreign judge trained in the common law left Cyprus 50 years ago. The Supreme Court of Cyprus is the court of last resort in all legal questions (except, of course, EU law and European human rights law), which means that Cyprus courts may conceivably deviate from the English common law with no means for correction, especially given that the persistence of British influence on Cyprus and respect for English law seldom translates into an emotional or metropolitan bond. The fact that another language, Greek, is now the language of the courts, government, parliament, and population at large has driven a further wedge between law in books and law in action. One not infrequently hears or even reads allegations that the English common law constitutes "persuasive" authority even in fields where this is clearly not so. At the same time, the Supreme Court has to act as an intermediate court of appeals, in panels, with no right to restrict appeals. The sheer mass of cases determined by appellate panels and the lack of a superior appellate court of "last resort" judging only cases of importance have undermined any effort to develop a consistent Cyprus case law distinct from the English one.

The abundance of statutory provisions, especially colonial statutes, seen as having codified the common law in the respective subject, further complicates matters. Such provisions and the broader legal regimes they create are generally accepted to be interpreted in accordance with present-day English common law.[85]

---

80 The official rules are available online at http://www.cylaw.org/cpr.html [accessed: January 20, 2014]. All amendments since 1960 have been in the official languages (notably Greek), but the main body of the rules has remained unchanged (and untranslated) since the British era. Legal practitioners use unofficial translations, notably by a former registrar, in atrocious Greek.

81 See, for example, *Republic v. Demetriades* (1977) 3 CLR 213 at 259–64 (Loizou, J.), and especially 296–320 (Triantafyllides, P.).

82 See an early case, *Papageorgiou v. Komodromou* (1963) 2 CLR 221. See also *Mavrogenis v. House of Representatives* (1996) 1 CLR 315.

83 *Republic v. Demetriades* (1977) 3 CLR 213, at 320. See also *KEO Ltd. v. The Republic* (1998) 4 CLR 1023.

84 For example, see the below section entitled "Competing Lines of Precedent," pp. 55–8.

85 See, for example, *Stylianou v. The Police* (1962) 2 CLR 152, notably Josephides, J., at 171: "[I] am of the view that, as a general rule, our Court should as a matter of judicial comity follow decisions of the English Courts of Appeal on the construction of a statute, unless we are convinced that those decisions are wrong."

Occasionally, the statutory provision is seen as simply the starting point for a discussion of more modern English authorities. Moreover, such legislation is certainly not without gaps. Lacunae are directly filled by the common law. For example, a number of common law torts today coexist with those expressly sanctioned in the Civil Wrongs Law.[86] There are also instances in which gaps have been read into legislation aimed at abolishing common law regimes to bring common law institutions back into play.[87] At the same time, we can witness the contrary case, where the letter of a law normally seen as codifying the common law is applied in a manner to invent derogation from the common law.[88]

The Common Law Tradition as Persuasive Authority

British legislation enacted after 1960 is regarded as not having any authority in Cyprus. Coupled with the reluctance of lawyers and legislators to reform basic laws, this really means that English common law rules superseded by statute in the United Kingdom are still valid in Cyprus; an example that comes to mind concerns the common law doctrine of privity of contract and third-party rights. However, one might be able to "cheat" the court, using reference works and subsequent case law, into accepting that English law as modified by statute in effect constitutes English common law (Vasilakakis and Papsavvas 2002: 50).

The common law case law of other Commonwealth jurisdictions (notably Australia, New Zealand, and Canada), and at times the United States, has persuasive authority.[89] Especially in the early life of the republic, U.S. case law was invoked in constitutional law matters.[90] Given that Privy Council jurisdiction was abolished on independence, Cyprus law should arguably follow the English approach, which regards decisions issued by the Judicial Committee ("Board") of the Privy Council as of persuasive—and not of binding—authority.[91] "Authoritative" textbooks and other works on English law also have persuasive authority.[92]

Precedent into Continental Law?

Contrary to traditional stereotypes and despite pronouncements to the contrary, case law does form a source of law throughout the Western legal tradition, especially when actual legal practice is concerned. One might, in fact, speak of a neoformalist streak in present-day continental legal tradition, where legal writers are reluctant to deviate from or criticize established case law solutions. The case law of the European Court of Justice is especially authoritative; the anonymous long reasoning of its judgments is quoted as if stating the law, with little regard to fine concepts such as *obiter dicta* and distinguishing precedents. If common law judgments were meant to produce legal norms *auctoritate rationis*, continental case law produces norms *ratione auctoritatis*. The case law of superior courts is binding because of the hierarchical control they exercise over lower courts. Superior courts tend to affirm their own rules out of respect for legal certainty, but especially to economize judicial time.

---

86 See, for example, *Universal Adver. and Publ'g Agency v. Vouros* (1952) 19 CLR 87 (the Civil Wrongs Law does not preclude an action for the passing-off of a business); *I.C.P. (Cyprus) Ltd. v. Times Newspapers Ltd.* (1972) 4 JSC 455 (likewise for innocent dissemination).

87 See the case study of constructive trusts involving spouses later in this chapter.

88 See the case study of past consideration later in this chapter.

89 See, for example, *Republic v. Alan Ford et al.* (1995) 2 CLR 232 (referring to "Canadian and American cases" regarding criminal procedure); *Jirkotis & Achilleos Co. Ltd. v. Paneuropean Ins. Co. Ltd.* (2000) 1 CLR 537, citing *The Esmeralda I* (1988) 1 Ll.R. 206 (Aus.), as well as English treatises (among ordinary civil appeals [three-justice panel]); and *Standard Fruit Co. (Berm.) Ltd. v. Gold Seal Shipping Co. Ltd.* (1997) 1 CLR 464 (citing US and Canadian cases).

90 See, for example, *Khadar v. The Republic* (1978) 2 CLR 130, at 230–33 (discussing *Furman v. Georgia*, 33 L.Ed.2d 349).

91 See, for example, *R v. Blastland* (1986) AC 41, 58 (Privy Council decision in *Ratten*'s case, All ER 801 [1971]) ("Not technically binding" but "of the highest persuasive authority" in view of the Board's "constitution"). See also Whittaker (2006: 721).

92 See *Standard Fruit Co. (Berm.) Ltd. v. Gold Seal Shipping Co. Ltd.* (1997) 1 CLR 464. The court, in this admiralty case, uses English treatises on international trade and carriage of goods as primary authority, excerpting at length from Carver and Colinvaux (1971) and Schmitthoff and Adams (1990). Publication dates are not mentioned in the decision; cases are cited in only an incidental fashion.

The administrative law of Cyprus is a case in point. British colonial rule left behind a well-functioning civil service, at least in certain areas, and a lot of ad hoc legislation. With the exception of prerogative writs, however, it left little in terms of either judicial review of administrative action or, more generally, administrative law doctrine. This lack can be easily explained in light of the delayed development of administrative law in the United Kingdom. Only in 1958 did British administrative tribunals begin to be regarded as judicial ("external") rather than administrative ("internal") bodies, and only in 1959 was a theory of judicial review of administrative acts elaborated as a doctrine, with the appearance first of S.A. De Smith's (1959) and then William Wade's (1961) books.

The constitution had provided for a separate Supreme Constitutional Court with jurisdiction to hear, apart from constitutional cases, petitions for the annulment of administrative acts.[93] In the meantime, all traditional, "common law" subjects were left with the High Court. As a result, the Supreme Constitutional Court, finding itself more and more drawn toward administrative litigation, soon oriented itself, under the leadership of German professor Ernst Forsthoff, toward the "continental administrative system" and the "principles enunciated" in continental administrative courts.[94] The tenure of Forsthoff, whose judicial writings bear an unmistakably German touch, was short-lived. In 1964, the Supreme Constitutional Court was merged with the High Court. The continental legacy of Cyprus administrative law continued, however, albeit with a decisive turn toward Greek administrative law. At the time, Greek administrative law was modeled after French administrative law and was essentially judge-made, with the Council of State elaborating "general principles" of administrative law (see Spiliotopoulos 2004).[95] The case law of the Greek Council of State thus became the predominant authority in the early years of the republic, supported by Greek academic writings.

The Supreme Court still makes frequent reference to the Council of State case law (and, occasionally, guiding cases from the Greek administrative appeals courts). Over time, however, it has developed its own corpus of landmark cases that decide many important questions. Under Greek administrative law, the basis for treating such case law as a source of law would be to consider the case law as embodying "general principles" of administrative law; moreover, the values of legal certainty and predictability and especially the principle of judicial hierarchy constitute convincing arguments in favor of adherence to precedent.[96] The Supreme Court has repeatedly held that the *stare decisis* principle does apply to administrative law cases, precisely on the basis of the principle of judicial hierarchy and predictability.[97]

Where does this lead us? The decisions of the five-member Supreme Court panels sitting on administrative litigation appeals (erroneously called "plenary benches" in colloquial legal jargon) are clearly binding on individual Supreme Court judges sitting on first instance.[98] The same rule certainly applies to judgments by the entire Supreme Court (which sits in full bench on cases involving constitutional questions, as well as on cases deemed of fundamental importance). The full bench, however, may reverse its own case law. An appellate panel should accordingly be able to explicitly reject (or reverse) the rule created by another appellate panel, which has often led to contrary lines of precedent coexisting.[99] Moreover, it is not always easy for practitioners and judges alike to draw a sharp distinction as to the binding authority of Supreme

93 Constitution of the Republic of Cyprus, article 146.

94 *Ioannides v. The Republic* (1979) 3 CLR 295.

95 Under the 1975 constitution, German influence over Greek administrative law has expanded, even though the French influence remains stronger to this day. Since 1977, two "trial" instances of regular administrative courts were created (replacing specialized jurisdictions such as tax courts), supervised by the Council of State, which, however, still retains much of its first instance jurisdiction. After decades of rule by case law, the Code of Administrative Process (along with the Code of Administrative Litigation Procedure) was enacted in 1999.

96 *Amanuel v. Alexandros Shipping Co. Ltd.* (1986) 1 All E.R. 278, 282.

97 *Demetriades v. The Republic* (1977) 3 CLR 213, notably at 320. See also *Elefetheriou-Kanga v. The Republic* (1989) 3 CLR 262.

98 *Elefetheriou-Kanga v. The Republic* (1989) 3 CLR 262. See, for example, *KEO Ltd. v. The Republic* (1998) 4 CLR 1023, in which Nikitas, J., sitting at first instance, holding "the stare decisis principle" made "absolutely binding" on him an appellate ruling on the point in question, citing *Republic v. Costas Tymvios Ltd.* (1994) 3 CLR 553. In the case cited as authority, the appellate panel reversed the first instance judgment of Nikitas, J.

99 See, for example, a note by Laris Vrahimis in 1 *Lysias* 56 (2008), on the conflicting case law regarding the possibility of changing the legal ground on which applications may be filed under Order 48 of the Civil Procedure Rules.

Court judgments in administrative first instance and appeals judgments. For example, in holding that the Advocates' Pension Fund constituted a private law rather than a public law entity, a civil appeals panel led by the chief justice referred to Supreme Court judgments in administrative first instance as settling the issue.[100] The practical result has a direct effect on the workload of Supreme Court judges. In a civil case, the district court would have first instance jurisdiction, with a three-judge panel on appeal, whereas in an administrative case, six judges would have been employed, one on first instance and five on appeal. The eventual creation of separate administrative courts to take over the Supreme Court's first instance jurisdiction in administrative cases, which is being seriously discussed as this chapter is heading into press, may stabilize this system, although this outcome will depend on the degree of the appointees' acquaintance with administrative law and possibly the level of their judicial ambition.

Statutory Interpretation and Interpretive Fusion

Statutory interpretation reflects the key characteristics of the legal system. Were we to give a one-sentence summary, we could say that legislation of common law origin is interpreted in accordance with common law cases and authorities, whereas when legislation of continental provenance is interpreted, continental authorities—usually Greek—will be used. But things are more complicated in practice. My research so far indicates that the terms, concepts, and authorities used will to a considerable extent vary depending on the individual case and the actors involved—both counsel and judges. In a contract case, for example, counsel may or may not present helpful English (or Indian) authorities. The judge sitting on the case will certainly take note of authorities mentioned by counsel. On occasion, the judge will do further research on his or her own, but we can hardly expect this to happen very often. On the whole, however, the principles on which the legal system has been grounded hold reasonably well.

We must nonetheless consider the factors that influence judicial—and legal—reasoning. Undoubtedly, the common law nature of Cyprus court procedure and the common law mentality of most judges, as well as many legal practitioners, constitute a very important factor—perhaps the primary one. The system of the adversarial process helps maintain the common law attitude, even in fields of continental influence, such as family litigation. We must not underestimate, however, the impact of the quantity—and quality—of the caseload. An important factor has to do with numbers. On the one hand, the lack of variety in factual patterns within a small jurisdiction means fewer complex issues for judicial decision making; as a result, local authorities are very few compared with what is readily available from abroad. On the other hand, the lack of an intermediate appellate jurisdiction, which would act as a filter of cases on appeal and thus allow Supreme Court judges more time for reasoning in depth, affects both mode and quality of judicial reasoning. Unlike many of their brethren at the English High Court, few, if any, judges of the district courts had a specialist legal practice prior to joining the judiciary, and they are certainly unable to specialize once on the bench. In their turn, Supreme Court judges, who spend a considerable amount of their time judging administrative cases at first instance, have effectively learned administrative law while on the Supreme Court bench. In short, Cypriot appellate judges deal with too many "easy" cases and too few guiding or landmark ones.

We must then consider the language factor: English was the original language of the system—in fact, until recently it was the principal language. English terms and materials are still used—translated or not—in everyday practice. In certain legal proceedings, counsel appear not even to have read the statute, working instead straight out of the textbook used in their British law school studies. For example, in discussing the formation of contracts, the Contract Law speaks of *proposal* and *acceptance*. The term *proposal* is regarded in Indian law as the equivalent of *offer*; it has been officially translated into Greek as *πρόταση*—a word that is both the exact linguistic equivalent of *proposal* and the established term used in Greek for *offer* (Stathopoulos 1995). The word *προσφορά*, used in colloquial Greek as the equivalent of *offer*, is also used in correspondence

100 *Raphael v. Advocates' Pension Fund* (2008) 1 CLR 300, [2008] *Lysias* 95: Artemides, P., cited as previous authority *Raphael and Hadjiprodromou v. Advocates Pension Fund* (2000) 4 CLR 1212 (Kronides, J.), which cited *Koumas v. Advocates Pension Fund* (2000) 4 CLR 1167, where Artemides, J., referred to *Nicolaou v. The Republic* (2000) 3 CLR 221. That final case actually concerned the government-controlled Surplus Personnel Fund, which dealt with redundant private sector employees, citing Greek authorities more than two decades old.

to terms such as *tender* or even *bargain*. All this has never been a matter of contention in Cyprus. Nonetheless, every once in a while an appellate judgment makes reference to *προσφορά* (*offer*) as the statutory term.[101]

At the same time, for the past three or four decades, the majority of practitioners have been educated in Greece. Greek terms, concepts, and authorities have also made their way into judicial reasoning. Modern Greek legal thinking has insisted on looking for the purpose and meaning of the statute: *teleological interpretation* often prevails over *grammatical interpretation*. In Cyprus, lawyers and judges are much fonder of invoking the letter of the law, which has the additional advantage of not having to rely on external authorities. In fact, they appear more likely to consult and cite a dictionary of modern Greek than their brethren in Greece.[102] But Cypriot judges also frequently use the teleological method—certainly more than their English brethren traditionally have.[103] This observation does not hold as true, of course, when dealing with statutory provisions seen as stating a common law rule: such provisions are usually interpreted in light of English cases and legal literature. Even there, however, we observe interesting examples of mutation, such as Cyprus contract cases where teleological interpretation is invoked as the method of interpretation of a contract,[104] even though the term—certainly not used in the applicable English common law—is not really used in Greek law either with regard to contract interpretation.

Case Studies

In this section, I examine four Supreme Court of Cyprus cases of interpretive fusion of Cyprus written (statutory) law with English case law and doctrine. In the first case, the Supreme Court of Cyprus, in a consistent line of cases, appears to have discovered (effectively to have carved out) a statutory exception with regard to past consideration to the common law of contracts (which is generally accepted—and explicitly recognized—as applicable to Cyprus). In the second case, Supreme Court panels adopted divergent approaches about whether the statutory transplantation of continental marital property law left a window for the concurrent application of common law institutions such as constructive trusts. In the third case, the Supreme Court had to interpret, with regard to freezing orders and the territorial scope of their effect, a procedural provision originally taken from English civil procedural law, considering the extent to which its evolving interpretation by English courts should bind Cyprus courts, local conditions notwithstanding. The final case offers another example of mutation in the law of civil procedure, with competing lines of authority from Supreme Court panels in light of or in spite of the amendment of the written rule.

Carving Statutory Exceptions to the Common Law: Past Consideration in Cyprus Contract Law

In 1998, a three-judge panel of the Supreme Court of Cyprus sitting on a civil appeal split over whether Cyprus law deviated from the English common law with regard to past consideration.[105] It is well known that, in the English law of contracts, "past consideration is not good consideration."[106] This rule is not, however,

---

101 See, for example, *Georgiou v. Cyprus Airways* (1998) 1 CLR 1794; *Aresti v. LOEL* (2008) 1 CLR 1305, [2010] 3 *Lysias* 47 (with a critical note by N. Hatzimihail, at 48–50).

102 See, for example, *Pericleous v. Latsia Municipality* (2002) 2 CLR 459 (looking into two dictionaries for the "common and natural meaning" of the word *store* in a criminal appeal). A quick search at the CyLaw legal database reveals (as of December 13, 2013) a total of 75 Supreme Court judgments in the past 14 years with judge or counsel citing Bambiniotis (1998) or subsequent editions.

103 English law has somewhat moved toward purposive interpretation since *Pepper v. Hart* AC 593 (1993).

104 *Club "Anorthosis" of Famagusta v. Apollon Athletic Football Club of Limassol* (2002) 1 CLR 518, at 525.

105 *Etaireia Diatheseon Tsimentou Vasilikou Apollon Ltd. v. Kathidjioti* (1998) 1 CLR 687.

106 See e.g. McKendrick (2012: 199: "The general rule is that past consideration is not good consideration"); Treitel (2007: 84: "... where there has been an interval of time between an act and the promise said to have been given in return for it, the alleged consideration is ... said to be 'past consideration' and therefore bad").

absolute: exceptions can be traced to 1615.[107] The principal exceptions to the rule were restated by the Privy Council in 1979,[108] but the notion can be traced to 1615 and was never in doubt.

Yet on the matter of past consideration, Cyprus law appears to have made a break: in Cyprus, past consideration *is* good consideration across the board.[109] The rule has been grounded, first and foremost, on the letter of Cyprus statutory law: the definition of consideration in article 2 of the Contract Law makes use of the past tense.[110] The special provisions on what constitutes consideration for guarantees and bills of exchange appear worded likewise.[111] The other ground for this holding was an apparent line of precedent created by Supreme Court decisions so interpreting these provisions, dating to 1971.

Both these grounds appear shaky on closer inspection. The very same wording has been used to define *consideration* in the Indian Contract Act, and the prevailing opinion has been that the past tense simply refers to "the exception to the general rule laid down in *Lampleigh v. Brathwaite*" (Pollock and Mulla 2006: 84). The same holds true of article 85 on consideration for guarantees.[112] As to the provision of the Bills of Exchange Law, it is but the exact copy of article 27(1)(b) of the English Bills of Exchange Act 1882, which holds an "antecedent debt or liability" is valid consideration for a bill of exchange. Courts had already held that consideration in this case consists in the fact that the creditor forbears from suing for the debt or treats the bill as conditional payment.[113] With regard to the line of precedent, the 1971 case simply contains an *obiter dictum* to the effect that "past consideration may well be good consideration sufficient to support a valid contract under our law."[114] The 1991 case actually dealt with a bill of exchange but also referred to the Contract Law provision as if it explicitly stated that past consideration is good consideration and to the 1971 decision as having affirmed this interpretation.[115] The majority opinion in the 1998 case was written by the same judge as the 1991 case; unsurprisingly, he regarded his 1991 statement as containing all that needed to be said on the matter and did not respond to the arguments of the dissenting judge.

Reading Common Law Institutions into Non-English Statutory Law: Constructive Trusts in Marital Property Law

In 1991, the legislative reform of Cyprus family law, inaugurated with the amendment, in 1989, of article 111 of the constitution and the creation of family courts in 1990, was extended to marital property issues. Up to that moment, even though jurisdiction over marriage and divorce was vested with the ecclesiastical courts, marital property issues were dealt with by the regular courts, which applied English common law.

---

107 *Lampleigh v. Braithwait* [1615] EWHC KB J 17.

108 *Pao On v. Lau Yiu Long* [1979] UKPC 2, [1980] AC 614: "An act done before the giving of a promise to make a payment or to confer some other benefit can sometimes be consideration for the promise. The act must have been done at the promisors' request: the parties must have understood that the act was to be remunerated either by a payment or the conferment of some other benefit: and payment, or the conferment of a benefit, must have been legally enforceable had it been promised in advance."

109 The rule is thus perceived by Koudounari (2000: 377), with no reference to *Etaireia Diatheseon Tsimentou Vasilikou Apollon Ltd. v. Kathidjioti* (1998) 1 CLR 687.

110 Article 2(2)(d) of the Contract Law (cap. 149) states, "When, at the desire of the promisor, the promisee or any other person has done or abstained from doing, or does or abstains from doing, or promises to do or to abstain from doing, something, such Act or abstinence or promise is called a consideration for the promise."

111 Article 85 of the Contract Law (cap. 149) states, "Anything done, or any promise made, for the benefit of the principal debtor, may be a sufficient consideration to the surety for giving the guarantee." Article 27(1)(b) of the Bills of Exchange Law (cap. 262) states, "Valuable consideration for a bill may be constituted by … (b) an antecedent debt or liability. Such a debt or liability is deemed valuable consideration whether the bill is payable on demand or at a future time."

112 On the equivalent section 127 of the Indian Contract Act, see Pollock and Mulla (2006: 1795), which states, "Mere past benefit to the principal-debtor is not a good consideration."

113 *Currie v. Misa* (1875) LR 10 Ex 153, *affirmed sub nom Misa v. Currie* (1876) 1 AC 554.

114 *Raif v. Dervish* (1971) CLR 178.

115 *Romanos v. Chrysanthou* (1991) 1 CLR 991, 995.

The legislative reform sent these issues to the new family courts.[116] Appeals from the family courts would be adjudicated by the Family Court of Second Instance, composed of a rotating panel of Supreme Court judges.[117]

The Regulation of Patrimonial Relations between Spouses Law 1991[118] effectively transplanted much of the legal regime established in Greece by the 1983 reform of Book 4 of the Civil Code. As in Greece, Cyprus marital property law espouses the general principle of separate properties between spouses.[119] Whereas the Greek Civil Code grants spouses the (rarely used) option of selecting a community property regime, no such provision exists in Cyprus law. Spouses are allowed, however, to present claims for the recovery of their contribution to the amount by which their spouse's property was augmented during their marriage.[120] As in the Greek Civil Code, the law grants a rebuttable presumption that such contribution may be estimated to be one-third of the augmentation.[121]

Before the 1991 law was enacted, marital property issues were resolved on the basis of the equity doctrine of implied or constructive trusts. Constructive trusts, in fact, continue to provide legal relief for unmarried cohabitants, given that Cyprus family law has so far made no provisions for any relationship but marriage.

This background brings us to the following question: Are constructive trusts still an existing regime for Cyprus marital property law?

In 1998, a Supreme Court panel, presided by the president of the Supreme Court, George Pikis, sat on an appeal from a district court judgment that used references to the law of equity as an interpretive aid to the construction of article 14.[122] Pikis, who had studied law and trained as a barrister in London in the 1950s and was defending the common law as late as the mid-1980s, had by the early 1990s undergone a Paulian conversion that led him to support the legislative reforms abolishing the use of English in Cyprus court proceedings and to make substantial use of Greek-educated law clerks, especially in administrative litigation. In *Orphanides*, Pikis argued that article 14 not only does not constitute a codification of the principles of equity, but on the contrary sets out provisions that cover the matter exhaustively and in a manner significantly different from that of English law.[123] Pikis listed three principal differences between the new regime and the old (English) regime: (a) article 14 grounds claims on the criterion of an actual contribution to the augmentation of property, regardless of the existence or not of any agreement, tacit or explicit, which is the decisive factor in English law; (b) claims under article 14 regard the augmentation of property value rather than the asset itself; and (c) in the case that the precise amount of contribution cannot be ascertained with clarity, article 14 establishes a formal presumption of one-third, as opposed to the equity maxim "equality is equity."[124] Moreover, the *Orphanides* court held, "Article 14 establishes a self-sufficient and comprehensive code regarding the division of property between the spouses, so that it leaves no scope for supplementation by or auxiliary application of the principles of English law."[125]

The *Orphanides* rule was endorsed in other Supreme Court decisions. In *Christophorou*, which involved a constructive trust over sold real estate, the court reiterated the rule that article 29(1)(c) makes the principles of equity applicable in Cyprus in their entirety, absent a different statutory provision, pointing to article 14 of the Patrimonial Relations Law as an example of such a different provision.[126] More interestingly, the reasoning in *Orphanides* was endorsed, two years later, by the full bench of the Supreme Court sitting as constitutional court.[127] That case, *Papaioannou*, involved the possible interference with the right to property of the marital property provisions—especially the ones providing intrusive procedural remedies for asset disclosure—insofar as they would regulate "retroactively" existing property arrangements. Of the court's 13 members, 10 joined the opinion written by Judge Ioannis Constantinides (the first Athens law graduate to

116 Family Courts Law 1990, articles 11(1) and 11(2)(e).
117 Constitution of the Republic of Cyprus, article 111(4).
118 Law 232/1991.
119 Patrimonial Relations Law 1991, article 13.
120 Ibid., article 14(1).
121 Ibid., article 14(2).
122 *Orphanides v. Orphanides* (1998) 1 CLR 179.
123 Ibid., 186.
124 Ibid., 187.
125 Ibid.
126 *Christophorou v. Christophorou* (1998) 1 CLR 1551, 1562.
127 *Papaioannou v. Papaioannou* (2000) 1 CLR 656.

ascend to the appellate bench), which insisted on the *Orphanides* reasoning about article 14 establishing a new, comprehensive legal regime and made extensive use of Greek legal literature on family and constitutional law to make the point that the new regime created claims that were based on the law of obligations rather than property and *in personam* rather than *in rem*.[128] A minority of three, including President Pikis, dissented on the basis precisely of the new regime's novelty.[129]

The matter would not be settled that easily, however. At about the same time as *Papaioannou*, another Supreme Court panel sat on an appeal from a family court decision regarding a claim on a car allegedly held by the defendant spouse as trustee of her claimant spouse.[130] The Limassol District Court had transferred the case to the Limassol Family Court, which in its turn held that it lacked jurisdiction to hear a claim not based on the Patrimonial Relations Law. The appellate court held that the Family Courts Law 1990 had endowed family courts with all powers exercised by the district courts under the Courts of Justice Law 1960, including remedies based on the law of equity under article 31 of that law.[131] A similar conclusion was reached by a five-judge panel a year later.[132] The matter was discussed in more detail in 2003 in a case involving the claim of a spouse that he was the beneficiary of a 50 percent share on a piece of land held in trust by his wife.[133] The panel split. Two judges, both members of the *Michael* panel, endorsed *Longinos* and affirmed that family courts had jurisdiction in all matters involving patrimonial relations between spouses, even when the legal basis is supported not by the Patrimonial Relations Law but by the law of equity.[134] President Pikis wrote a dissenting opinion, in which he dismissed arguments in *Longinos* and subsequent opinions, seeking to reconcile them with *Orphanides* on the basis of minor legislative amendments defining in more clear terms the subject matter jurisdiction of family courts and the term *patrimonial relations*.[135] For Pikis, the case at hand did not form part of patrimonial relations between spouses but constituted instead a case of breach of the trustee's fiduciary duties against the beneficiary and should accordingly be seen as falling under the general jurisdiction of district courts.[136]

This situation has led to a confusing state of affairs. Cyprus publications on family law tend to acknowledge a diversity of opinion between the different lines of authority represented by *Orphanides* and *Longinos*. Given that such publications tend to come from family law judges and practitioners, it should come as no surprise that most of them avoid taking a position on the matter that could be viewed as critical of the Supreme Court—or that would possibly prejudice their own position in a future case. Among the publications that take a position, however, the prevalent opinion is to present *Longinos* as an erroneous deviation from *Orphanides* and thus to deny the doctrinal validity of remedies based on constructive trusts with regard to the marital property between spouses.[137] At the same time, denying such as remedy would be extremely awkward, if requested. A case decided recently illustrates the complex equilibrium reached.[138] The case involved a husband's claim against both his wife and a company, owned by her father, which according to the plaintiff has held in trust assets belonging to his wife. On the one hand, this judgment affirms the role of constructive trusts in a marital property case. On the other hand, it is not a case about marital property claims being decided on a basis other than article 14, but rather a case in which the law of trusts came to the aid of family law and prevented asset dissipation.

---

128 Ibid., Constantinides, J. (joined by other eight judges), as well as Artemides, J., concurring.

129 Ibid. (Hadjihambis, J.).

130 *Longinos v. Longinos* (2000) 1 CLR 1347.

131 Ibid. (Kallis, J.).

132 *Michael v. Yiangou* (2001) 1 CLR 1643. The panel sat on an appeal from a writ of prohibition issued in 1999 by another Supreme Court judge against an order by a president of district court asserting district court jurisdiction. See *In re Yiangos* (1999) 1 CLR 703 (Nicolaides, J.). Judge Nicolaides was a member of the *Longinos* panel.

133 *Filippou v. Filippou* (2003) 1 CLR 1343.

134 Ibid. (Gavrielides, J., joined by Hadjihambis, J.).

135 Ibid. (Pikis, P.).

136 Ibid.

137 See, for example, Serghides (2010). The president of the Nicosia-Kerynia Family Court, Serghides is the senior family judge in Cyprus (in fact, the senior trial judge in Cyprus).

138 *Pericleous v. Englezou* (2011) 1 CLR.

This misunderstanding illustrates both the virtues and vices of Cyprus law today. First, we must accept that the Patrimonial Relations Law has introduced a comprehensive, continental-style regime with regard to marital property; this regime clearly governs claims to another spouse's property under the contribution rule of article 14.[139] The power of this regime is buttressed by another development: today, litigation between spouses—including asset-related claims—is a matter for family courts. The vast majority of both judges and practitioners before family courts have been educated in Greece and are therefore more comfortable with article 14 than with the law of constructive trusts. Family courts have developed their own practices and local case law on the identification and—effectively—allocation of assets and claims between spouses. In Cyprus family law today, the principal common law influence concerns (mutated) elements of court procedure and evidence law. At the same time, none could simply dismiss a claim for equitable relief that is based on constructive trusts doctrine.

In fact, even though the contrast between constructive trusts and article 14 can be taken as an opposition between Greek- and English-educated Cypriot lawyers, the opposition is not absolute. Thus, judges educated at the University of Athens proved more tolerant of a role for constructive trusts than the London-educated Pikis. On closer inspection of the facts and precise reasoning of each case, a more important motivation emerges: on the one hand, the policy of reducing the load of district courts by shifting all family-related cases to the family courts;[140] on the other hand, the desire to provide effective relief on the individual case. The frequent references to publications by both academics and practitioners from Greece, as well as to the local legal literature, did not aim—or at least succeed—at providing a comprehensive doctrinal system with answers to every question and every case occupying Cyprus legal practice. Faced with difficulties, practitioners and courts find the traditional, easy-to-use remedy easier to invoke, whether it is doctrinally justified or not.

Taking Stock of Developments in English Case Law? Worldwide Mareva Injunctions

In 2007, the full bench of the Supreme Court was called to revoke the granting of a worldwide freezing order against a Cypriot businessman accused of securities fraud by a U.S. liquidating trust. The order was also addressed against companies controlled by him and business partners seen as providing cover for him.[141] On the basis of article 32(1) of the Courts of Justice Law 1960 and the most recent English case law on *Mareva* injunctions, the district judge had granted the interim orders requested by the trustees. Article 32(1) provided that

> every Court, in the exercise of its civil jurisdiction may, by order, grant a mandamus or injunction (interlocutory, perpetual or mandatory) or appoint a receiver in all cases in which it appears to the Court just or convenient so to do, notwithstanding that no compensation or other relief is claimed or granted together therewith. Provided that an interlocutory injunction shall not be granted unless the Court is satisfied that there is a serious question to be tried at the hearing, that there is a probability that the plaintiff is entitled to relief and that unless an interlocutory injunction is granted it shall be difficult or impossible to do complete justice at a later stage.

The provision had been translated verbatim from article 37(1) of the colonial Courts of Justice Law (cap. 8). In all likelihood, the original scope of such provisions was more modest.[142] By 1975, however, English

139 See, for example, *Malaos v. Malaou* (2005) 1 CLR 1191.

140 Thus *Pericleous v. Englezou*, with references to Supreme Court case law expanding Family Court jurisdiction, both *ratione personae* and *materiae*, including *Dadakaridis v. Dadakaridou* (1990) 1 CLR 566; *Christodoulidou v. Toumain* (2007) CLR 1024; *Toumain v. Christodoulidou* (2009) 1 CLR 881; and *Sioukrou v. Ulrich* (2011) 1 CLR. This last case endorsed Hatzimihail's "from tribunal to court" narrative—that is, the idea that family courts, although tracing their ancestry to the ecclesiastical tribunals of the Greek Orthodox community, have become superior courts of specialized jurisdiction over all family-related cases.

141 *Seamark Consultancy Services Ltd. v. Lasalle* (2007) 1 CLR 162.

142 See *Polish Ocean Lines v. Spyropoullos* (1955) 20 CLR 73, holding that the power to make interlocutory injunctions is confined to orders affecting the subject matter of the proceedings.

courts had asserted the power of issuing interlocutory injunctions restraining the disposition of defendant's assets within the jurisdiction, the so-called freezing or *Mareva* orders.[143] Cyprus courts soon followed.[144]

Thirty years later, the question regarded the granting of injunctions addressed to assets outside the court's jurisdiction. Such a "worldwide" injunction would require a reversal of the existing case law of the Cyprus Supreme Court. In 1987, an appellate panel declined to issue a *Mareva* injunction with regard to a ship located off jurisdiction.[145] Judge Pikis, having noted that article 32 was "modeled on the provisions" of section 45(1) and thus tracing the roots of the provision to the nineteenth-century fusion of common law and equity courts, noted:

> While I agree that the language of a Cyprus statute should be the principal guide to its interpretation, it is perfectly legitimate to consult English case law on the interpretation of a similar statute where, as in this case our legislature intended to reproduce an English enactment in our law for the achievement of similar objectives."[146]

Pikis also found it "legitimate to interpret [the law] in the light of the history of the evolution of the remedy."[147] The *Mareva* injunction was thus

> regarded as a powerful addition to the armoury of the law, warranted by vast technological changes in transport and the mobility associated therewith of persons and goods. The discretion of the Court to make a Mareva injunction must be exercised with great circumspection and always with due regard with the specific aims of the law, notably an aid to the process of execution designed to forestall action likely to undermine the efficacy of the judicial process.[148]

At the time, however, English case law had still not espoused the idea of worldwide effect of *Mareva* judgments, although things were already beginning to change.[149] In 1987, however, Pikis could still draw on English cases warning that "the extra territorial extension of Mareva Injunctions ... would not only be oppressive to the defendant but difficult to enforce as well."[150]

A few years later, another panel adopted a somehow different perspective in declining once more to grant an injunction with worldwide effect.[151] Judge Christos Artemides characterized article 32 as "identical" or "verbally identical" to section 45.[152] The second term is used to showcase the difference: even if it was called a "modification of practice," the fact is that English case law, faced with the rapid technological evolution that has led to near-instant communication and money transfers, has made a dramatic change, "one of the most serious law reforms, by means of case law."[153] Even so, the problems created by *Mareva* injunction led, at the instigation of the English judiciary, to legislative intervention (the Supreme Court Act 1981), a solution that was not reprised in Cyprus.[154]

---

143 *Nippon Yusen Kaisha v. Karagiorghis* [1975] 1 WLR 1093, and especially *Mareva Compania Naviera SA v. International Bulkcarriers SA (The Mareva)* [1975] Lloyd's Rep. 509, [1980] 1 All ER 213.

144 *Nemitsas Industries Ltd. v. S. & S. Maritime Lines Ltd.* (1976) 1 CLR 302. See also *Linmare Shipping Co. v. Roustani* (1979) 1 CLR 37 and *Misirlis v. Jaber* (1978) 2 JSC. 304. All three were trial cases, the first two coming from the admiralty jurisdiction of the Supreme Court.

145 *Pastella Marine v. Iranian Tanker* (1987) 1 CLR 583.

146 Ibid., 598.

147 Ibid., 600.

148 Ibid., 602.

149 See, for example, *Babanaft International Co. v. Bassatne* (1989) 1 All ER 433. See also *Derby & Co. Ltd. v. Weldon* (1989) 1 All ER 1002 and *Gidrxslme Shipping Co. Ltd. v. Tantomar Transportes Maritimos Ltd. (The Naftilos)* [1994] 4 All ER 507.

150 (1987) 1 CLR 602.

151 *ABP Holdings Ltd. v. Kittalides* (1994) 1 CLR 694.

152 Ibid., 700, 701.

153 Ibid., 700.

154 Ibid., 700–701.

Artemides is accordingly reluctant to take the next step: "We are not going to translate Greek into English in order to be bound by English case law. The Courts apply the laws of our country, after interpreting them in accordance with the known rules of interpretation."[155] In this process, legislative intent "as expressed in the law's text" is paramount, along with "the thought that laws were instituted in order to be applied in our land, which has its own morals, habits and way of life."[156] Moreover, Cyprus, being the destination of so many tourists who are transiting or staying for limited time, has to beware of the prospect of their transactions ending in its own courts.[157]

Thirteen years later, the full bench in *Seamark* instead went all the way in adopting the English case law on *Mareva* injunctions.[158] The district court had already declined to follow *ABP Holdings*, relying instead on the most recent English cases.[159] The Supreme Court affirmed. Writing for a unanimous bench (with Artemides as president), Judge Myronas Nikolatos summarized the evolution in the position of English case law on the matter and quoted approvingly minor points in *ABP Holdings*, such as article 32 being identical to section 45 and evolving technologies challenging court authority, to bring forward his conclusion that the "modern rhythms of life" necessitate the reshaping of the framework of court powers to allow interlocutory orders to remain effective until the final resolution of the dispute.[160]

Competing Lines of Precedent

In that same year, 2007, a Supreme Court panel was called to rule on an application for the reinstatement of an appeal.[161] Counsel for the would-be appellants had forgotten to submit their appellate brief (apparently because of having misplaced the documents of the case while moving their office's premises). Alas, their negligence did not stop there: the legal bases stated in their application for reinstatement were wholly irrelevant to the remedy requested.[162] Before considering the application on its merits,[163] the appellate court had to consider whether the lack of a correct legal basis should prove fatal to an interim application.[164]

In the case at hand, the court dismissed the application as legally inadmissible. The court relied on a 1990 case, *Machlouzarides*, where Judge Pikis had held that the lack of a correct legal basis makes the interim application void *ab initio*. That case was subsequently, if summarily, affirmed by another panel in 1992 and by yet another panel in 2001.[165] As has been pointed out, however, the 1990 case involved a final application, and its reasoning should thus be characterized as *obiter dicta*, rather than as setting a rule. Judge Pikis had

---

155 Ibid., 701–702.

156 Ibid., 702.

157 Ibid.

158 *Seamark Consultancy Services Ltd. v. Lasala* (2007) 1 CLR 162.

159 A 2006 judgment by District Court President Nathanael.

160 *Seamark Consultancy Services Ltd. v. Lasala* (2007) 1 CLR 162.

161 *Flourenzou v. Cashgrove Betting Ltd.* (2007) 1 CLR 393, [2008] *Lysias* 54 (with a note by L. Vrachimis, 56–57).

162 In fact, instead of relying on the Appeals Regulations 1996, the appellants had invoked provisions from the Civil Procedure Rules.

163 The court did, in fact, summarily consider the application on its merits, suggesting that it would fail. Consistent case law has held that negligence or omissions by counsel may not constitute an excuse for extending deadlines.

164 Applications are governed by Order 48 of the Civil Procedure Rules. Effects of noncompliance are governed by Order 64. The rules (full title, "Rules of Court made under the Civil Procedure Law, Cap. 7, the Mandamus Law, Cap. 23, the Dealings between Merchants and Farmers Law, Cap. 196, the Civil Wrongs Law, Cap. 9, the Cyprus Courts of Justice Orders and Laws 1927 to (No. 2) 1935, and Sections 37 and 40 of the Courts of Justice (Supplementary Provisions) Law, Cap. 12") were codified in the British colonial era by the colonial Supreme Court and constitute the backbone of Cyprus civil procedure. No official translation of the rules has yet taken place, although in practice, an unofficial translation by a former registrar is commonly used. Amendments made since 1960 are in Greek. The authoritative text of the rules can be found online at http://www.cylaw.org/cpr.html [accessed: January 20, 2014].

165 *Savva v. Cyprus Airways* (1992) 1 CLR 1146 and *Christophorou v. Oikodomikes Epicheiriseis Iordanous Ltd.* (2001) 1 CLR 743, respectively.

also disregarded previous cases, which had held that such irregularity could be corrected under Order 64 as it then stood.[166]

Be that as it may, in 1995, Order 64 was replaced by a more liberal article, apparently in line with developments in English civil procedure. The concept of void proceedings was notably abolished, leaving only the notion of irregularity. The court maintained considerable discretion, in the interest of justice, but could set aside proceedings only in limited circumstances. In 1999, a Supreme Court panel (which included President Pikis, the author of *Machlouzarides*) unanimously held in *Wunderlich v. Panayiotou* that the noninclusion of the correct legal basis in an interim application did not make the application void, but rather constituted an irregularity that could be subsequently cured.[167] The panel had expressly discussed *Machlouzarides* and held that the new rule prompted a different treatment of such cases. Developments in English law, which allegedly prompted the amendment of Order 64, were also discussed.[168] The new rule was subsequently endorsed by other appellate panels.[169]

The *Wunderlich* rule has better appeal to both fairness and doctrine. Today, most judges would probably adhere to it. At the same time, it is remarkable that a dissenting line of authority has persisted for almost two decades and can still not be written off.

Conclusions

Sources of law help illustrate as well as reconstruct the hybrid nature of Cyprus law. They confirm both the persistent, strong influence of English common law and the centrifugal tendencies of a system where the English language is still influential but no longer the language of the law, let alone the people.

First, Cyprus law adheres to a clear hierarchy of sources to a degree not usually associated with the English common law tradition. The constitution is the cornerstone of both legal and political discourse—and extremely hard to amend—whereas international law has long had significance of an existential nature for the republic. EU law is gradually becoming the firmament of the entire legal system. Accession to the European Union has further increased the significance of written, notably statutory, law to the Cyprus legal system. But ever since Cyprus gained its independence, statutory law has been the foundation of every legal subject in Cyprus law, including the traditional fields in which English common law still dominates. In contract, tort, commercial, and procedural law, among other fields, English and Cyprus case law are used, along with legal literature, to interpret statutory provisions and fill legal gaps. This simple statement masks the relative confusion in the field in determining what constitutes binding rather than persuasive authority (let alone the role of modern English legislation modifying the common law rules).

Second, Cyprus is a relatively small legal system that cannot afford self-sufficiency. The strong common law influence may have meant that Cyprus courts can find it easier to chart an independent course in fields dominated by continental transplants than in English-dominated ones. More generally, even though local case law has developed a mostly adequate body of rules in some fields, in other fields a constant need exists to look to London, especially (and Athens, sometimes, for administrative law) for new developments. Regardless of its desirability (or nondesirability), self-sufficiency is certainly not helped by the workload of the appellate bench. Over the past half-century, the (now) 13 judges of the ubiquitous Supreme Court of Cyprus have spent more and more of their time adjudicating administrative law cases (on first instance as well as on appeal).

166 See notably *In re Hadjisoteriou* (1986) 1 CLR 429 and *In re Williams and Glyn's Bank plc* (1987) 1 CLR 85. Order 64, rule 1 (as it stood prior to the thorough amendment of Order 64 in 1995), reads: "Non-compliance with any of these Rules, or with any Rule of practice for the time being in force, shall not render any proceedings void unless the Court or Judge shall so direct, but such proceedings may be set aside either wholly or in part as irregular, or amended, or otherwise dealt with in such manner and upon such terms as the Court or Judge shall think fit."

167 *Wunderlich v. Panayiotou* (1999) 1 CLR 366 (Kallis, J.).

168 Ibid., with reference to *Metroinvest Anstalt v. Commercial Union Assurance* [1985] 2 All ER 318 and Order 2, rule 2 of the Civil Procedure Rules as standing at the time.

169 *Demetriou v. Gabriel* (2001) 1 CLR 16. See also *Merkis v. Intertobacco (Cyprus) Ltd.* (2006) 1 CLR 788.

The lack of an intermediate jurisdiction (appeal being a guaranteed right) not only means the judges have no discretion over which cases to review but also leads to appellate review by ad hoc panels—a system that sometimes creates precedent too easily and sometimes sows confusion.

Not unlike Cyprus itself, Cyprus law thrives on paradoxes. The border between influence and authority is often hard to delimit. Judicial gravitas often masks the power of advocates to shape legal arguments. Traditionalism is a force to be reckoned with but also a vehicle for juristic innovation. From legal borrowings, transplants, and enclaves, Cyprus law is gradually, slowly transforming into something unique.

References

Abrams, N. 1972. Interpreting the Criminal Code Ordinance, 1936: The untapped well. *Israel Law Review*, 7(1), 25–64.

Bambiniotis, G. 1998. *Dictionary of Modern Greek*. Athens: Lexicology Centre.

Beatson, Jack, Andrew Burrows, and John Cartwright. 2010. *Anson's Law of Contract*. 29th ed. Oxford, UK: Oxford University Press.

Carver, T.G., and Colinvaux, R.P. 1971. *Carriage by Sea*. 12th ed. London: Stevens & Sons.

Chrysostomides, K. 2000. *The Republic of Cyprus: A Study in International Law*. The Hague: Martinus Nijhoff.

Constantinides, A. 2011. International law in the Supreme Court of Cyprus. Unpublished paper on file with author.

De Smith, S.A. 1959. *Judicial Review of Administrative Action*. London: Stevens & Sons.

Emilianides, A. 2006. *Beyond the Cyprus Constitution* [in Greek]. Thessaloniki, Greece: Sakkoulas.

Friedmann, D. 1975. Infusion of the common law into the legal system of Israel. *Israel Law Review*, 10(3), 324–77.

Hatzimihail, N.E. 2013. Cyprus as a mixed legal system. *Journal of Civil Law Studies*, 6(1), 37–96.

Hatzimihail, N.E. Forthcoming. Cyprus, in *International Protection of Adults*.

Iliopoulos, C.P. 2006. *The EU-Membership of the Republic of Cyprus: The Harmonization of the Company Law and the Law of Intellectual Property* [in Greek]. Athens: Sakkoulas.

Kombos, C. 2010a. Cyprus: The Supreme Court of Cyprus' approach to standing for judicial review and to the preliminary reference procedure. *European Public Law*, 16(3), 327–55.

Kombos, C. 2010b. Cyprus: The Supreme Court of Cyprus' approach to standing for judicial review and to the preliminary reference procedure, in *Studies in European Public Law: Thematic, National and Post-National Perspectives*, edited by C. Kombos. Thessaloniki, Greece: Sakkoulas, 101–13.

Koudounari, E. 2000. Law of contract, in *Introduction to Cyprus Law*, edited by D. Campbell. Limassol, Cyprus: Neocleous, 373–419.

Kourtellos, P.N. 2000. Constitutional law, in *Introduction to Cyprus Law*, edited by D. Campbell. Limassol, Cyprus: Neocleous, 15–43.

Loizou, A. 2001. *The Constitution of Cyprus* [in Greek]. Nicosia: Kaila.

Neocleous, A., and Hatzimihail, N.E. 2013. *Compendium of Cyprus Laws*. 2nd ed. Athens: Nomiki Vivliothiki.

Nicolaou, E. 2000. *Constitutional Review and Allocation of Competences between State Organs in Cyprus* [in Greek]. Athens: Sakkoulas.

Nicolaou, E. 1998. Recent developments in family law in Cyprus, in *International Survey of Family Law*, edited by A. Bainham. The Hague: Martinus Nijhoff, 121–34.

Palmer, V.V. 2001a. A descriptive and comparative overview, in *Mixed Jurisdictions Worldwide: The Third Legal Family*, edited by V.V. Palmer. Cambridge, UK: Cambridge University Press, 17–80.

Palmer, V.V. 2001b. Introduction, in *Mixed Jurisdictions Worldwide: The Third Legal Family*, edited by V.V. Palmer. Cambridge, UK: Cambridge University Press, 3–16.

Papasavvas, S. 1998. *La Justice Constitutionnelle à Chypre* [in French]. Paris: Economica.

Pollock, F., and Mulla, D. 2006. *Indian Contract and Specific Relief Acts*. 13th ed. New Delhi: LexisNexis Butterworths.

Polyviou, P.G. 2013. *Cyprus on the Edge: A Study in Constitutional Survival*. Nicosia, 2013.

Schmitthoff, C.M., and Adams, J. 1990. *Schmitthoff's Export Trade: The Law and Practice of International Trade*. 9th ed. London: Stevens & Sons.
Serghides, G.A. 2010. Patrimonial relations between spouses under Cyprus law [in Greek], in *Pecuniary Relations of Spouses and Cohabitants*, edited by G. Serghides. Nicosia: Leukosia, 3–23.
Spiliotopoulos, E. 2004. *Greek Administrative Law*. Athens: Sakkoulas.
Stathopoulos, M. 1995. *Contract Law in Hellas*. Athens: Sakkoulas.
Symeonides, S.S. 2003. The mixed legal system of the Republic of Cyprus. *Tulane Law Review*, 78(1–2), 441–56.
Tofaris, S. 2010. A historical study of the Indian Contract Act 1872. PhD thesis, Cambridge University, Cambridge, UK
Tornaritis, C. 1983. The operation of the European Convention for the Protection of Human Rights in the Republic of Cyprus. *Cyprus Law Review*, 3, 455–64.
Vasilakakis, E., and Papasavvas, S. 2002. *Elements of Cyprus Law* [in Greek]. Athens: Sakkoulas.
Wade, H.W.R. 1961. *Administrative Law*. Oxford, UK: Clarendon Press.
Whittaker, S. 2006. Precedent in English law: A view from the citadel. *European Review of Private Law*, 14(5–6), 705–46.

Chapter 7

Managing Legal Diversity: Cameroonian Bijuralism at a Critical Crossroads

Charles Manga Fombad

Until fairly recently, comparatists and legal historians had shown little interest in one of the fairly unique mixed—or to be more precise, bijural—legal systems in the world: the Cameroonian bijural system. Yet the Cameroonian system provides "a fascinating example of a comparative law melting pot with peculiar and multifaceted problems" (Fombad 1999: 22). Although quite young in comparison with most mixed systems, it has long exemplified some of the intricate issues that may arise when two modern competing but often divergent European legal systems—the English common law and the French civil law—coexist within a developing country. Cameroon is in the process of modernizing its legal system by developing homegrown uniform national laws. Most existing literature on the country's legal system examines some of the laws that have been harmonized in the legal modernization process since the 1970s and also considers some of the challenges that the country has grappled with in the process (see Anyangwe 1987; Clarence-Smith 1968; Fombad 1991; 1997; 1999; Munzu 1989; Parant, Gilg, and Clarence-Smith 1967; Tumnde 2010). None of these studies have attempted to provide a substantive overview of the nature and scope of the emerging harmonized national laws and their effect on the bijural legal framework. In 1993, along with 13 other mostly francophone West and Central African countries, Cameroon signed a treaty establishing the Organization for the Harmonization of Business Law in Africa (generally referred to by its French acronym, OHADA).[1] When it came into effect by Decree 96/177 of September 5, 1996,[2] the treaty immediately subjected the whole country to the OHADA Uniforms Acts and, in doing so, raised complex questions about the prospects for sustaining the bijural system at a time when the English law element of the mix appeared to be fast disappearing.

Much can be said for more research into the Cameroonian problematic. As in most African countries, economic development and trade have been stifled by the continuous reliance on antiquated laws inherited from the colonial period. The numerous challenges that Cameroon has faced in modernizing its legal system while respecting its sensitive inherited bijural legacy offer many interesting lessons for other countries faced with similar problems. Law, it must be said, is much more than a body of rules that can simply be imposed on others by those who dominate the formal processes of lawmaking.

This chapter will start with a brief look at the historical origin and the theoretical context of the Cameroonian bijural system. It will then turn to an overview of legal developments in public law, private law, procedural law, and the system of administrative justice since the introduction of the bijural system in Cameroon. The chapter will show that the process of legal reforms has led to an overwhelming predominance in style, form, content, and formulation of civil law over common law in what can be perceived only as a one-sided invasion and assimilation of the former by the latter. Because bijuralism in Cameroon is not only a historical fact but also a daily reality that cannot be ignored or wished away, this chapter will examine ways of correcting the bijural deficit. It will argue that adopting a diversity-conscious approach to legal reforms in Cameroon or, in fact, any country facing such a dilemma is the best way to sustain bijuralism in the country. In conclusion, the

1 OHADA stands for the Organisation pour l'Harmonisation en Afrique du Droit des Affaires. OHADA was created by treaty in Port Louis, Mauritius, on October 17, 1993, and now comprises 16 African states: Benin, Burkina Faso, Cameroon, Central African Republic, Chad, the Comoros, the Democratic Republic of Congo, Côte d'Ivoire, Equatorial Guinea, Gabon, Guinea-Bissau, Mali, Niger, the Republic of Congo, Senegal, and Togo.

2 The Cameroon parliament, by Law 94/4 of August 4, 1994, authorized the president of the republic to ratify the OHADA treaty.

chapter notes that the coexistence of legal traditions is both a practical reality and a practical necessity in an increasingly plurality-conscious world where dynamic equity rather than flattening equality prevails.

Historical Origins and Theoretical Context

This section briefly explains how the bijural system came about and some of the complex issues that are associated with it. It then situates this system in the broader family of mixed legal systems in the world. Any legal developments in Cameroon must be understood against this historical background.

Historical Origins

The modern Cameroon is largely a German creation, although the Portuguese were first to arrive at its coast in the 1500s.[3] Malaria prevented the Portuguese from penetrating the interior. Before the Berlin Congress of 1884–1885, the British had showed an interest in the territory. But it was the Germans who established a colony in Cameroon in July 1884 (see generally Ardener 1968; Rudin 1938). The country went through two main colonial experiences: the German period from 1884 to 1916 and the combined British and French period from 1916 to 1961.

During the German period, all the diverse ethnic groups in the country were united into a single cohesive modern polity. A law passed in the Reichstag in 1886 that conferred powers on the Kaiser to legislate by decree for order and good government in Cameroon. To maintain peace and tranquility, the legislation established two systems of courts: one for Europeans and the other for Cameroonians. On this basis, two laws—the Consular Jurisdiction Law of April 7, 1900, and the Colonial Law of September 10, 1900—rendered German law applicable in the European courts, while the Cameroonian courts, which dealt with all disputes involving non-Europeans, applied customary law. The Germans were thus the first to introduce legal dualism into the country, with the coexistence of German law applicable to whites and customary law applicable to Cameroonians. However, the two legal orders did not exist on an equal basis. Like the other colonial powers, the Germans made the validity of customary law to be subject to German law. However, the German period was short—merely 32 years—and it is no surprise that there is hardly any relic of the German presence in the Cameroonian legal system today.

The German period in Cameroon came to an abrupt end during the First World War, when the last remnants of German troops in the country were defeated by a combined British and French expeditionary force in Mora in February 1916. An Anglo-French declaration of July 10, 1919, signed in Paris, partitioned the conquered territory between the two victors. The British settled for two small and narrow noncontiguous parts of the country in the West, while the French took the rest, about four-fifths of the territory. The British motives for this division have never been clear. However, some have speculated that the British feared incurring further financial responsibilities in taking on another colonial territory and desired to take on nothing more than what was absolutely necessary to consolidate their Nigerian colony. Under article 119 of the Treaty of Versailles, the Germans renounced all their rights to their overseas territories in favor of the allied powers. The Anglo-French arrangement over Cameroon was formally recognized in articles 22 and 23 of the League of Nations Covenant, which conferred mandates over the territory to both powers. Under article 2 of the Mandate Agreements, both countries had responsibility for maintaining "peace, order and good government of the territory and moral well-being and social progress of its inhabitants." Article 9 explicitly gave the two countries "full powers of administration and legislation" and the "liberty to apply [their] ... laws to the territory under mandate subject to the modifications required by local conditions." This provision was the basis for the almost wholesale exportation of the English common law and the French civil law to Cameroon.

3 In 1472, the Portuguese sailor Fernando Poo came to the island that today bears his name. His caravels anchored in the River Wouri. The large number of shrimp in the waters of this river so astonished the sailors that they decided to name the river *Rio dos Camarões*—that is, Shrimp River. This name was later changed to *Camarones* by the Spanish, *Kamerun* by the Germans, *Cameroun* by the French, and *Cameroons* by the British. Initially, the name was also given to Douala. When the Germans signed a protectorate agreement with the local chiefs, it became the name of the whole country.

The British administered their portion of the territory as an integral part of their Nigerian colony. The southern area of the territory was known as Southern Cameroons, and the northern area was known as Northern Cameroons. Although Southern Cameroons was joined to Southern Nigeria and Northern Cameroons was joined to Northern Nigeria, no fusion or incorporation resulted. Nevertheless, the two territories were, for all practical purposes, administered from Nigeria. The extent of direct administration from the Nigerian provinces lessened with time. Nevertheless, many of the laws introduced by the British into Nigeria were simply extended to Cameroon. But the general basis for the application of English law and the extent of its application in Southern Cameroons is specified in section 11 of the Southern Cameroons High Court Law 1955, which states the following:

> Subject to the provisions of any written law and in particular of this section … (a) the common law; (b) the doctrines of equity; and (c) the statutes of general application which were in force in England on the 1st day of January, 1900, shall insofar as the legislature of the Southern Cameroons is for the time being competent to make law, be in force within the jurisdiction of the court.[4]

The interpretation of this vague provision, like that of similarly worded provisions on the reception of English law in many former British colonies, has provoked a lot of controversy and debate over the years.[5] It suffices to say that on the basis of this statute, numerous English statutes, as well as Nigerian laws and ordinances, were made applicable to Southern Cameroons and continue to apply in the two anglophone regions of the country today. The British, like the Germans and French, also operated two parallel systems of courts, but unlike the German and French systems, the British system was not separated on racial lines. One structure was for the traditional sector of the population, mainly Cameroonians, and the other was for the modern sector, mainly Europeans or Cameroonians who opted to use it. However, Native Courts Ordinance 5 of 1918 (a Nigerian piece of legislation), which recognized and established the customary court system, made it clear that the decisions of these customary courts were subject to review by local administrative officers. This ordinance was subsequently replaced by the Southern Cameroons Customary Court Law of 1956, which limited the jurisdiction of customary courts to specified matters. According to section 18(1) of the Customary Courts Law, customary law was only valid and enforceable to the extent that it was neither repugnant to natural justice, equity, and good conscience nor incompatible, either directly or by natural implication, with any written law in force at the time. This so-called repugnancy test could be used to invalidate a rule of customary law. More generally, however, administrative officials had the last word as to what was customary law during this period. In essence, customary law was given an inferior status.

Before this chapter turns to a brief discussion of the reception of French civil law in the francophone regions of Cameroon, note that in February 1961, the United Nations organized plebiscites in Northern and Southern Cameroons to determine whether they wished to become independent by joining either Nigeria or French Cameroon, both of which had been granted independence in 1960. Although Northern Cameroons opted to join Nigeria and has been part of Nigeria ever since, Southern Cameroons decided to reunite with French Cameroon. The bijural system resulted from this reunion of Southern Cameroons and French Cameroon, which had lived separately from each other since 1916.

Regarding French Cameroon, the French did not attempt to incorporate the territory into their existing colonies as the British had done. The introduction of French civil law into the francophone regions of Cameroon was based on a French decree of May 22, 1922, which extended to French Cameroon all laws and decrees promulgated in France for French Equatorial Africa. Two parallel system of courts—one administering the *justice de droit Française* for the whites, and the other being *justice de droit indigène* for the ordinary Cameroonians—were introduced. Because of the French colonial policy of assimilation, the *justice de droit Française* was reserved not only to the whites but also to assimilated Cameroonians.[6] The customary courts,

4 This provision was enacted under powers granted by the Foreign Jurisdiction Act 1890.

5 For more on this debate, see, in particular, Allott (1970: 13–21), Park (1963: 14–42), and Roberts-Wray (1960: 66, 70–71). With respect to the debate in Cameroon, see Fombad (1991).

6 The French grouped Cameroonians into two categories: those who had been granted the status of *citoyen* (assimilated French person) and the rest of the population, which was classified as *sujet* or *indigène*. The status of assimilated French person was reserved to a few dozen Cameroonians who were considered to have evolved from the status of natives by attaining an acceptable level of French civilization and culture. For further details of French policy of assimilation in Cameroon, see Gardinier (1963: 10–24).

which dealt with disputes involving ordinary Cameroonians, had jurisdiction in civil and commercial matters. French administrators presided over the customary courts and used the local chiefs and notables merely as assistants or assessors. A particularly striking and unsettling feature of the reception of French civil law in francophone Cameroon was a rule that laws, decrees, and regulations in force in France could be rendered executory in Cameroon merely by a decree of the French head of state.[7] French legislative policy during this period appeared to work by trial and error because enacted laws were often quickly amended, repealed, reenacted, or simply replaced (Anyangwe 1987: 97).

Yet when the anglophone and francophone parts of the country were formally reunited in 1961, the new federal constitution provided for the continuous application of the laws received in the two legal districts of the country, unless such law had been expressly or implicitly repealed in subsequent national legislation. The uncertainty over the exact quantum of foreign laws that had been received and were still applicable, especially given the vague limitation date of 1900 in the reception clause in the Southern Cameroons High Court Law 1955, made it inevitable that legal reform was going to be a priority issue after the reunification of the two territories. Reunification was never going to be easy in a country that one writer described as "two different countries in one" (Azevedo 1984: 5). Another writer went even further to assert that reunification was far from being the reunion of two prodigal sons who had been unjustly separated at birth and was more like a loveless arranged marriage courtesy of the United Nations between two people who hardly knew each other (Susungi 1991).

Besides having two divergent and potentially antagonistic legal systems, each with strong colonial cultural baggage, identification, and loyalty, the country has a wide diversity of ethnic groups, cultures, and languages. With a population estimated at 20,129,878 (July 2012),[8] Cameroon has an extraordinary multiplicity of about 250 tribes that speak more than 280 indigenous languages. It is doubtful whether there is any other country of comparable size that has as many ethnic groups and languages. Superimposed over this complex mix is the anglophone-francophone divide. Anglophones live in two of the 10 political regions of the country and make up 20 percent of the population, whereas francophones live in eight regions and make up 80 percent of the population. The population imbalance between the two groups has had a considerable effect on the operation of the bijural system and has completely overshadowed other potentially divisive factors such as ethnic origin. There is also religious diversity: about 40 percent of the people are Christian (of whom about half are Roman Catholic), 20 percent are Muslim, and about 40 percent practice a wide variety of indigenous beliefs. The overwhelming majority of Muslims live in the northern part of the country, but others live in a small area in the west (see Fombad 2010). With this background in mind, one can see exactly how the Cameroonian legal system fits within the general legal family of mixed systems.

The Cameroonian System in the Family of Mixed Jurisdictions

As pointed out earlier, in the family of mixed jurisdictions, the Cameroonian system is probably one of the youngest and least researched. It dates to the reunification of the former British Southern Cameroons and the former French Cameroon in 1961, 45 years after they were separated. Although repeated often enough to become trite, this fact remains important: almost all modern legal systems of any sophistication or complexity are mixed (see, for example, Church, Schulze, and Strydom 2007: 47; Glenn 1996: 1–3; Palmer 2001). Most of these mixes are a result of direct or indirect borrowing by lawmakers or judges when they use or cite foreign law. The Cameroonian legal system is mixed in its own unique way, which is fairly different from that of most classical or conventional mixes. It is therefore not surprising that the Cameroon system has missed the critical attention of most comparatists. But to what extent is it different from other mixed systems or jurisdictions?

Comparatists almost all agree that there is no comprehensive and generally accepted definition of a mixed system or even criteria for determining what constitutes one. The complex nature and wide diversity of mixed jurisdictions, as well as their dynamic nature and questions about the structure and degree of mix required, account for this difficulty. For example, in her analysis of mixes, Esin Örücü (2008: 11) distinguishes between

7 See articles 1 and 2 of the Decree of April 16, 1924.

8 See Index Mundi's 2013 demographics profile for Cameroon, available at: http://www.indexmundi.com/cameroon/demographics_profile.html [accessed: December 2, 2013].

overt and covert, structured and unstructured, complex and simple, and blended and unblended mixes. The diverse and sometimes confusing and contradictory classifications of mixed systems underscore the challenges of finding an acceptable definition (JuriGlobe 2013; Örücü 1996; 2008). For example, the JuriGlobe World Legal Systems Research Group argues that the term mixed should not be construed narrowly and suggests that "this category includes political entities where two or more systems apply cumulatively or interactively ... [as well as] entities where there is a juxtaposition of systems as result of more or less clearly defined fields of application" (JuriGlobe 2013). On this basis, JuriGlobe places Cameroon in a group of "mixed systems of civil law, common law and customary law," along with Zimbabwe and Lesotho. Suffice to say that there are many anomalies in this classification, particularly the suggestion that there is no customary law in countries such as South Africa, Botswana, Namibia, and Mauritius.[9] Even a more elaborate and complex classification provided by Esin Örücü (2008: 16–18) is not free of contradictions.[10]

Nevertheless, the numerous definitions that have been suggested can be described as either broad or narrow in their approaches. On the one hand, the broad approach defines a mixed system as one that is made up of at least two diverse components derived from two or more systems generally recognized as independent of each other (Church, Schulze, and Strydom 2007: 49; McKnight 1977: 177). Some of these broad definitions, according to Esin Örücü (2008: 11), use the term *mixed* to refer to a "combination of various legal sources"; a "combination of more than one body of law within one nation, restricted to an area or to a culture"; "the existence of different bodies of law applicable within the whole territory of a country"; and "legal systems that have never had a single dominant culture." Although the JuriGlobe definition referred to earlier falls into this category, it is rather too broad and vague. On the other hand, those who adopt the narrow approach define a mixed system as one in which the common law and civil law interact within the same jurisdiction (see, for example, Smith 2005; Smits 2008: 7). A proponent of this narrow approach, Vernon Palmer (2001: 7) states that a mixed jurisdiction should have at least "three abstract characteristics that set them apart from others." The first characteristic is the specificity of the mixture, which requires that it be built on the dual foundations of common law and civil law materials. In other words, the expression is limited to mixtures from the Romano-Germanic and Anglo–American systems. The second characteristic is a quantitative and psychological feature that requires the dual elements to be obvious to an ordinary observer. Palmer (2001: 8) argues that an occasional transplant or even a series of them from one tradition to another is not enough: there must be a large number of principles and rules of a distinguishable pedigree to create a "distinctive bijurality." The third characteristic is structural and involves a structural allocation of content in which civil law will deal mainly with private law matters and the Anglo-American element will regulate public law matters.

Cameroon may be classified as a mixed jurisdiction under the broad definition, yet the two legal systems that operate within the country to a large extent coexist rather than interact. This situation is certainly changing, but by constitutional design, the intention was to allow these two systems to operate side by side. Conversely, if the narrow definition is applied, the same reasons militate even more strongly against considering the Cameroonian system as mixed. However, even if the Cameroonian system is not mixed in the strict sense of either the narrow or the broad definition of the term, it can still be considered to be mixed and mixing in a sense that brings it somewhere between the two definitions. In this respect, it is mixed in that two distinct legal systems operate within the same jurisdiction, and it is mixing, as we shall soon see, in that there has been extensive interaction between the two systems by legal harmonization to bring about uniform laws.

Another factor that makes the Cameroonian system complicated is that it also displays features of legal dualism. Such legal dualism is based on customary law, variously referred to at some stage or in some jurisdictions as "native law" (in the colonial days), traditional law, indigenous law, or African law. Nevertheless, the idea of legal dualism based on the operation of customary law is more of a historical fact than a practical reality today. For a long time during the colonial period, the customary law courts were the only method of resolving disputes available to Cameroonians, and these courts operated alongside the modern courts, which were reserved for the whites. However, as noted earlier, although they appeared to coexist, they

9 See the classifications of these countries in JuriGlobe (2013).

10 For example, there is no rational reason why in her analysis, South Africa and Lesotho—but not Botswana, Swaziland, and Zimbabwe—should appear in complex mixes.

were not equal because the recognition and enforcement of customary law was subject to standards set under the received laws.

Their jurisdiction was also progressively reduced, and colonial administrators had the powers to review decisions made by these customary courts. By the time of independence, the essentially symbolic legal dualism had virtually ended as a single court structure was set up with customary courts placed at the bottom of the hierarchy of courts. Customary courts continued to administer exclusively customary law, but appeals from these courts were heard by the modern courts. The subservient role reserved for customary courts during the colonial period has continued not only because the recognition and enforcement of customary law has continued to depend on the repugnancy test or similar tests set up during the colonial period but also because their subject-matter jurisdiction has been progressively reduced. For instance, they no longer have any jurisdiction in criminal matters. Cameroon is one of the many African countries today where customary courts play very little role in the settlement of disputes.[11] The only exception is the northern part of the country, where Muslim law and Shari'a courts still play a large part in regulating the lives of the rural people.[12] The interpretation part of section 27(1) of the Southern Cameroons High Court Law 1955 defined "native law and custom," which is what we now refer to today as customary law, to include "Muslim law." This inclusion was rather odd and inaccurate because Muslim law is not indigenous to Cameroon. Like English and French law, it came from abroad. It was imposed on parts of the northern Cameroon in the early nineteenth century through trade contacts and religious wars of conversion known as *jihad* (see Fombad 2010). When considered along with the other influences, particularly customary ones, on the overall legal system, the element of religious law in the northern part of Cameroon suggests a degree of legal pluralism. However, the concept of legal pluralism has also been the subject of diverse and often conflicting definitions over the years (Griffiths 1986; Menski 2006: 82–128; Örücü 1996: 350). For the purposes of this chapter, it will suffice to describe *legal pluralism* as referring to a situation in which two or more legal systems or legal orders coexist in the same social setting and operate within different cultural or religious groups. Thus, legal pluralism in the Cameroonian context emphasizes the aspect of both customary law and Muslim law in the legal system.

Nevertheless, it would not be accurate to describe the Cameroonian system simply as mixed, and Vernon Palmer's (2001) narrow definition of the expression makes more sense. If the broader definition were adopted, there would hardly be any justification for not describing all legal systems in Africa—or even in the world—as mixed. Neither would it be accurate to describe the Cameroonian legal system merely as dualistic or pluralistic. Although it manifests features of both traits, those features are not the dominant aspects of the system. The Cameroonian legal system is more accurately described as bijural, because the two distinct and dominant legal systems in the country coexist in two separate legal districts. The closest example of such bijuralism is that in Canada between the civil law system in the province of Quebec and the common law system in the rest of Canada. Inevitably any two systems operating within a country will interact and enable the overall legal system to develop in a harmonious manner. In the case of Cameroon, a high degree of mixing of the two laws has occurred, resulting in the enactment of uniform laws applicable to the two legal districts. This situation has raised questions about whether the bijural system is giving way to a mixed system or a hybrid system that is uniquely Cameroonian. The next section examines how the system has developed in the past half-century.

A Balance Sheet of Cameroonian Bijuralism

From the very nature of the reunification of the English-speaking and French-speaking parts of Cameroon, one could fairly assume that there was an intention to maintain the bijural legal heritage. On the basis of this assumption, the next section will try to develop some principles that should guide future legal harmonization of laws in the country.

11 Their role contrasts very markedly with the role of customary courts in countries such as Botswana (see Fombad 2004).

12 According to the 30-Days Prayer Network (2013), "Several Muslim groups are encouraging the installation of Islamic law (sharia) in the northern part of Cameroon."

First, however, a brief review of the constitutional basis of the bijural system is necessary. As pointed out earlier, on reunification of the British and French Cameroons in 1961, the constitution provided for the continuous application of the preexisting laws in both parts of the country. This position has been repeated in all subsequent constitutions. On this issue, article 68 of the 1996 amendment to the 1972 constitution (usually referred to as the 1996 constitution) states the following:

> The legislation applicable in the Federal State of Cameroon and in the Federated states on the date of entry into force of this constitution shall remain in force insofar as it is not repugnant to this constitution, and as long as it is not amended by subsequent laws and regulations.

This provision is usually taken as the basis of the bijural system. It is supposed to be reinforced by article 1(3), which states, "The official languages of the Republic of Cameroon shall be English and French, both languages having the same status. The State shall guarantee the promotion of bilingualism throughout the country." One could rely on article 1(3) and several other provisions—such as those in the preamble stating that "all persons shall have equal rights and obligations," and "the state shall ensure the protection of minorities"—to argue that the two dominant inherited legal cultures were to operate on a basis of equality. However, no law has ever been enacted to implement any of these constitutional provisions. Also, as we shall soon see, no mechanism ensures that these constitutional provisions are not violated. Furthermore, no mechanism ensures that if they are violated, actions are taken to correct the illegality. Hence, bijuralism and bilingualism depend on these bare constitutional provisions.

Another problem with the constitutional basis of the bijural system is that it assumes that there is certainty with respect to what the constitution refers to as the "legislation applicable in the Federal State of Cameroon and in the Federated states," which the constitution declares must apply until replaced by a new law. In practice, this provision means that, in all matters not regulated by new Cameroonian legislation, the received English and French laws continue to apply. This interpretation seems simple, but in reality, the exact scope and quantum of these received laws as they apply to certain issues have never been certain. For example, as pointed out earlier, in the anglophone legal district, the reception clause—which was worded much like similar English law reception clauses in anglophone African countries—has often given rise to debate and diverse interpretations (see further Fombad 1991: 450–53). When the clause limits the application of English law to legislation that was in force on January 1, 1900 (an arbitrary date by all standards because the British period started in Cameroon only in 1916), does this date apply only to statutes of general application, or does it also extend to the common law and doctrines of equity? If the latter is true, clearly Cameroonian law will be frozen in time. And if the former is true, Cameroon will simply blindly follow laws adopted abroad in Britain that hardly reflect the local conditions.

Probably because of the establishment of the bijural system, the adoption of uniform national laws became a priority quite early after the two Cameroons reunited. Two federal law reform commissions were set up as early as February 1964: the Federal Commission for Penal Legislation and the Federal Commission for Civil and Customary Legislation.[13] The only uniform law drafted by these commissions was the Penal Code of 1967. Although there have been other codes—such as the Labor Code, Land Tenure Laws, and Civil Status Registration Ordinance—most of these codes were adopted through the normal parliamentary lawmaking processes. The perceived bias in the law reform process, which has seen the adoption of uniform laws that are essentially based on French civil law, has been widely commented on (see, in particular, Fombad 1991; 1997; 1999; Munzu 1989). The most recent uniform law is the Criminal Procedure Code, which was brought into force by Law 2005/007 of July 25, 2005, and came into effect on January 1, 2007, thus concluding a process that started 30 years earlier. But the most extensive and probably most profound change in the legal landscape was brought about when Cameroon became a party to the OHADA treaty. In a single move, not only was the country's commercial law updated but also all English commercial law principles that previously applied in the anglophone legal district were replaced by civil law principles.[14] It is therefore appropriate after a half

---

13 See Decree 64/DF/84 of February 29, 1964.

14 By virtue of article 10 of the OHADA treaty, the Uniform Acts, which cover the whole field of commercial law, have automatically replaced and directly repealed all existing legislation on the matter.

century of bijuralism in the country to see what effect legal reforms have had on the system. This overview will look at developments in public law, private law, procedural law, and the system of administration of justice.

Public Law: Symbolic Bijuralism from the Start

In the public law area, the influence of English law in reunified Cameroon was short-lived. English law was very quickly replaced by civil law, a development that had a profound effect on how the legal system has evolved.

In 1960, after the leaders of Southern Cameroons voted in favor of reuniting with French Cameroon, they tried to negotiate a new constitutional arrangement with the president of the Republic of Cameroon, Ahmadou Ahidjo, that would have provided a relatively loose and decentralized federation. However, since they were then fully committed to reunification with an already independent Republic of Cameroon,[15] the Southern Cameroonian representatives held a negotiating position that was quite weak. Ahidjo was under no pressure to make anything more than token concessions and felt obliged to amend the 1960 constitution of the now independent French Cameroon only by an annexure called "transitional and special dispositions." What then became the federal constitution of the Federal Republic of Cameroon was nothing more than a law revising the independence constitution of French Cameroon of March 4, 1960, which was essentially based on the Gaullist French Fifth Republic constitution of 1958. This so-called federal constitution provided for a two-state federation consisting of West Cameroon, made up of the former British Cameroons, and East Cameroon, corresponding to the former French Cameroon. Although this constitution reflected an uneasy compromise between the centralizing impulses of President Ahidjo and the desire of Southern Cameroons politicians to retain as much political identity as possible, the federation turned out to be more symbolic than real. The unitary and highly centralized features of the 1960 French Cameroon constitution were carried over wholesale into the new federation. On the crucial issue of the distribution of powers between the federal government and the two federated states of West Cameroon and East Cameroon, the former was totally dominant. In the final analysis, the federated states were allowed to act only in matters that the federal government did not wish to act on. Article 4 of the constitution defined the federal authority as inhering in the president and the Federal National Assembly. But the president was given wide-ranging powers that enabled him to control and dominate all national institutions, effectively making the federal structure a sham *ab initio*.

On May 20, 1972, a referendum was held to replace the federal state with a unitary state, and on June 2, 1972, the Federal Republic of Cameroon was replaced by what was officially known as the United Republic of Cameroon. This date marked the end of a highly centralized federal system of government that bore a resemblance to a federation only in name. The new constitution formally eliminated the already largely nominal positions of prime minister in the two federated states as well as the state legislatures. The powers of the president under the new constitution were considerably enhanced. When, in 1984, President Paul Biya, by Law 84/001, abolished the appellation "United Republic of Cameroon" and replaced it with "Republic of Cameroon," this act was seen by many as removing one of the last symbolic vestiges of the 1961 reunification. What is currently in force is supposedly only an amendment to the constitution of June 2, 1972, and is officially referred to as Law 06 of January 18, 1996, to amend the Constitution of June 2, 1972. However, for more than a decade, most of the new structures contemplated by this new constitution were not established (see Fombad 2008).

The Cameroonian constitution exhibits all the weaknesses and limitations of a Gaullist constitution. The 1996 amendments merely reinforce a highly centralized autocratic state system in which the president has extensive powers at the expense of a considerably weak and ineffective legislature and judiciary. For example, without consulting anybody, the president can name and dismiss cabinet members, judges, generals, regional governors, prefects, and the heads of the numerous parastatals. The president can approve or veto newly enacted laws, declare a state of emergency, and authorize public expenditure. The president also has extensive powers to legislate and can rule by decree.

15 It became independent from France on January 1, 1960.

Although the 1996 constitution professes to institute for the first time what it terms *judicial power*, judicial independence is effectively compromised by the president's unlimited power to appoint and dismiss judges. The constitution does not have the force of a supreme, overriding law, and consequently no guarantee exists for respect of the rule of law. Only the president and a few specified political elites can challenge the constitutionality of any law before the Constitutional Council (one of the key innovations of the amendment, which, like most of the others, is yet to be established), a body composed essentially of the president's nominees. Given that these political elites are usually the persons who make laws that violate the constitution, it is absurd to expect them to challenge the constitutionality of such laws. There is thus no effective judicial review.

Although retaining the centralized state structure, the constitution provides for the possibility of some deconcentration of powers through the creation of regional and local authorities. These provisions are, however, in such dubious, obscure, and circumlocutory language that, for a long time, it was doubtful whether there was ever any serious intention to implement them. Only in 2008 were some timid steps taken to implement the decentralization provisions, but the so-called decentralized structures remain under the control of the central government.

Therefore, clearly, the general constitutional framework was essentially borrowed from the French system. In fact, the entire public law in the country is based on the civil law, with probably very little of the common law system left, even in anglophone regions. The literature has noted that it is rare in a mixed system like this one to find a situation in which the civil law predominates in the public sphere and almost totally excludes the common law (see Palmer 2001: 10). In this respect, Cameroon manifests all the features of Vernon Palmer's "Ruritania."[16]

Private Law: From Bijuralism toward Monojuralism

Until the signing of the OHADA treaty in 1993, the principles of English commercial law applied in the anglophone legal district, while the French Commercial Code applied in the francophone legal district. Since the OHADA treaty came into force in 1996, all business and commercial law matters have been governed by the new regime set up under the treaty. Under the OHADA commercial law regime, nine Uniform Acts deal with commercial matters in Cameroon. These acts govern general commercial law, commercial companies and economic interest groups, securities,[17]simplified recovery procedures and enforcement measures,[18] collective insolvency proceedings,[19] arbitration,[20] accounting,[21] carriage of goods by road,[22] and cooperatives.[23]

The OHADA Uniform Acts are almost entirely based on the French civil law (Kalm 2011; Pougoué and Elongo 2008: 115–17). In fact, one French lawyer observed that "OHADA business laws were often a word-to-word copy of French business laws even to the point of including the same grammar mistakes" (cited by Kalm 2011: 13). OHADA law was controversial in Cameroon not only because it ignored the bijural nature of the country but also because article 42 of the OHADA treaty declared French to be the only working language without due regard to the bilingual nature of Cameroon. Only in 2008 was the treaty amended to add English, Portuguese, and Spanish as working languages. Nevertheless, most of OHADA's official documents are in French, and the few English translations are of poor quality. Another serious incursion on the bijural system by the OHADA regime is article 15 of the treaty, which allows final appeals in commercial disputes to be submitted directly by a party to the proceedings to the Common Court of Justice and Arbitration (CCJA),

16 Ruritania is an imaginary land referred to by Palmer (2001: 10).

17 These first three Uniform Acts were adopted by the Council of Ministers on April 17, 1997, in Cotonou and entered into force on January 1, 1998.

18 Adopted on April 10, 1998, in Libreville, this Uniform Act entered into force on July 10, 1998.

19 Adopted on April 10, 1998, in Libreville, this Uniform Act entered into force on January 1, 1999.

20 Adopted on March 11, 1999, in Ouagadougou, this Uniform Act entered into force on June 11, 1999.

21 Adopted on March 23, 2000, in Yaoundé, the first part of this Uniform Act, relating to companies' individual accounts, entered into force on January 1, 2001. The second part, relating to consolidated and combined accounts, entered into force on January 1, 2002.

22 Adopted on March 22, 2003, in Yaoundé, this Uniform Act entered into force on January 1, 2004.

23 This Uniform Act was adopted on December 15, 2010, at Lomé.

which was created and established under this treaty in Abidjan, or on referral by the Supreme Court. The CCJA is therefore effectively the final court of appeal in all commercial matters and was deliberately created to ensure uniform interpretation of the Uniform Acts. Because no judges have been trained in common law, and because most official OHADA documents are still in French, judges who have trained only in English law now endure considerable pressure to either interpret and apply a series of laws that are based almost exclusively on French civil law as would a civilian judge or risk reversal of their decisions on appeal.

A substantial reform of Cameroon commercial law was long overdue. The received commercial laws were either uncertain or obsolete on many issues and often raised serious questions regarding conflicts of laws between the two legal districts. OHADA provided Cameroon with an opportunity to display its bijural character and take a lead in harmonizing laws that would not only reflect its legal culture but probably also set the pace for harmonizing commercial law in Africa. Unfortunately, this opportunity was lost. The goal of adopting a modern uniform commercial law applicable to both legal districts might well have been achieved. But the challenges of using English common law interpretation techniques to interpret French civil law texts, the bitterness felt when the laws were imposed without discussion or regard to the common law tradition, and the resistance by some judges in the anglophone courts to applying these Uniform Acts weakened the certainty that they were designed to provide.[24]

The OHADA regime illustrates what has happened to private law within the bijural framework and shows how civil law has suddenly displaced common law in the anglophone regions. Developments or lack of developments in procedural law show another dimension of the dynamics of the two legal systems' coexistence.

Procedural Law: The Best of Both Worlds?

For a long while, procedural law in the two legal districts, both civil and criminal, has remained firmly attached to its colonial roots. In many respects, this adherence has not necessarily been helpful. For example, there is the perennial problem of uncertainty, which is particularly acute in the anglophone regions. Reliance on English procedural law actually means relying on English law of uncertain scope and myriad Nigerian pieces of legislation that were extended to the former Southern Cameroons.[25] Moreover, differences in procedural laws have often led to differences in the interpretation of uniform legislation that was designed to ensure uniform and consistent application of the law in both legal districts. For example, differences in procedural matters such as the manner in which witnesses are heard, the role of oral and written evidence, and the standard of proof could affect the outcome of legal proceedings.

One step toward the harmonization of procedural law has been taken by the adoption of the Criminal Procedure Code in 2005. Unlike the case of most of the other pieces of uniform legislation, with the exception of the Penal Code itself,[26] considerable time and effort was taken to include the best elements of the civil and common law systems in this code. In fact, the Penal Code, which was the first piece of unified national law, has in many respects generally been regarded as the most successful piece of harmonized legislation not only because it was drafted by a committee of experts from both legal systems but also because it was inspired by the Swiss, Brazilian, German, and Italian codes. The code was remarkably successful in translating several notions either unknown or with no exact equivalent in the other language or legal system. The experts who drafted the Criminal Procedure Code must have been mindful of this fact, and one commentator speculated

24 For the reaction of anglophone judges, lawyers, and academics, see Tumnde (2010: 127), who states that these acts were seen as "an instrument of French, and Francophone-Cameroonian neo-colonialism, since [they] ignored the bilingual and bijural nature of the country." See also Ekome (2005) and Gwellem (2001). And for examples of cases in which judges refused to apply the acts, see *Achiangan Fombin Sebastian v. Foto Joseph & Others*, HCK/3/96/2000, unreported, and *Meme Lawyers' Association v. Registrar in Chief, High Court and Registrar in Chief, First Instance Court Kumba*, HCK/680S/99/2000, unreported.

25 See, for example, the Evidence Ordinance, chapter 62 of the 1958 Revised Laws of the Federation of Nigeria.

26 For early commentaries on this code, see Clarence-Smith (1968: 651) and Parant, Gilg, and Clarence-Smith (1967).

that this success might explain why the drafting of the code and even its coming into force were delayed after the code was adopted.[27]

Although many of the principles in the Criminal Procedure Code are still from the civil law, a number of significant principles have been borrowed from the common law. The mix of these principles substantially enhances the administration of justice in the country. Some of the common law principles incorporated include the adoption of habeas corpus and the introduction of the accusatory system of justice throughout the country in place of the civil law inquisitorial system. The code provides clear guidelines for arrests and execution of warrants of arrests, treatment of accused persons as well as persons in police custody, rights of clients, attorney-client confidentiality, restrictions on search and seizures, judges' rules, contempt of court, and other protective measures that were completely unknown in the francophone regions. The code nevertheless suffers from a number of serious flaws, some of which were alluded to by the International Bar Association, which was invited to comment on the draft (International Bar Association 2003). Resistance to the numerous restrictions the code tries to place on judicial officers not used to such a regime caused its implementation to be delayed for two years.

Thus, as far as procedural law goes, the only progress has been in the adoption of a Criminal Procedure Code, which appears to incorporate some of the best elements of the civil and common law systems. The same cannot be said of the system of administration of justice, to which we shall now turn.

The Administration of Justice: The Monojural Trap

The effectiveness of any legal system depends not merely on the quality of the laws enacted but also on the judicial system put in place to interpret and enforce those laws. The English and French systems of administration of justice were maintained in the reunified Cameroon for only a short while after 1961. In fact, in 1969, an attempt to unify the two systems was made through a reform project known as l'Avant Projet Comte-Quinn. Reform became easier with the change from a federal system to a unitary system in 1972. Article 42 of the 1972 constitution empowered the president of the republic, for a period of one year, to set up new institutions for the country by ordinances or other statutory instruments. This formed the basis of Ordinance 72/4 of August 26, 1972, or the Judicial Organization Ordinance. It purported to harmonize the system of administration of justice but effectively extended, with slight modifications, the civilian system of administration of justice that was in existence in former East Cameroon to the anglophone legal district. Thus, although the English common law and French civil law coexist and apply in the two legal districts, they are now applied within an essentially civilian-style system of administration of justice. Three main features of this civilian style of administration of justice will be briefly highlighted: the structure of courts, the control of constitutionality of laws, and judicial personnel.[28]

Unlike typical common law systems, the courts in Cameroon fall within three distinct and separate categories: a hierarchy of courts with ordinary jurisdiction, another hierarchy for administrative courts, and a number of courts with special jurisdiction. Courts with ordinary jurisdiction are courts that have jurisdiction to hear and determine actions of every kind, regardless of whether civil or criminal. According to section 3 of the 2006 Judicial Organization Law, these courts consist of the Supreme Court, the courts of appeal, the lower courts for administrative litigation, the lower audit courts, the high courts, the courts of first instance, and the customary law courts. Except for the Supreme Court, which has jurisdiction throughout the country, these courts are highly decentralized. The 1996 constitutional amendment introduced two very significant innovations. The first relates to the decentralization of administrative matters, which until then had been handled exclusively by the Supreme Court. The second deals with provisions providing for the establishment of decentralized "courts" to handle audit matters. The decentralization of the process of handling administrative disputes is provided for but couched in very obscure language in part 5 of the constitution. That provision attempts to introduce the French system of a separate system of administrative courts to handle administrative disputes.

27 See Tande (2007), who wrote, "[A]ttempts to 'cameroonize' the anachronistic systems began in the mid 1970s but the process stalled after Francophone jurists and legal practitioners balked at the preponderance of common law practices in the draft documents that resulted from those initial attempts."

28 For a full discussion of this topic, see Fombad (2003).

The practice in administrative matters from 1972 until 1996 had been for the Supreme Court to exercise both original and appellate jurisdiction in administrative matters. That administrative justice be brought as close to the people as possible was certainly desirable, with the likelihood that it would be cheaper than having to go to Yaoundé (the capital city). Although a law regulating the functioning of these administrative courts was enacted more than a decade later, these courts have yet to see the light of day. However, courts with special jurisdiction deal either with specific matters that are provided for by law or for a particular class of persons. The main courts with special jurisdiction are the Court of Impeachment, the military tribunals, the State Security Court, and in some respects, the Constitutional Council.

In looking at judicial personnel, this chapter will concentrate only on judges, their appointment, and their status. All modern states generally recognize as sacrosanct that judges be assured of an optimum degree of independence and freedom from extrajudicial pressures so that they can function properly. The Cameroon constitution, as noted previously, purports to transform the judiciary into a so-called judicial power, but follows the Gaullist approach. Unlike the practice in anglophone Cameroon before 1972, judges begin their professional careers as judges. They qualify to enter judicial service after obtaining a law degree and undergoing practical training at the National School of Administration and Magistracy (better known by its French acronym ENAM, which stands for the *École Nationale d'Administration et de Magistrature*) in Yaoundé. On graduation, they can be appointed as either judges or state prosecutors.

Apparently to ensure the independence of judges, article 37(2) of the constitution declares that, "judicial power shall be independent of the executive and legislative powers." Then, quite paradoxically, and as if the president of the republic is no longer a member of the executive, it declares further in article 37(3) that, "the President of the Republic shall guarantee the independence of the judicial power." The president is supposed to do so through appointing, promoting, and disciplining judges and is assisted in this task by the Higher Judicial Council, which shall "give him its opinion on" all these matters. Although it is clear that the president is bound to consult the Higher Judicial Council, the president is not bound to follow any advice received from this body. It is in fact significant that this body is not specifically required to make proposals but just to "assist" by expressing its "opinion" on measures that the president considers taking.

One final peculiarity about the Cameroonian system that impinges on the independence of the judiciary is that a person who is a judge can at any moment be appointed as a prosecutor or to a senior position in the Ministry of Justice. This feature clouds the distinction between judicial office and functions that must be performed by a judge on the one hand and the prosecutorial functions that usually fall under the control of the executive on the other hand. In essence, the critical elements of judicial independence are missing in the Cameroonian system. Also worth noting is an emerging tendency to appoint to or transfer into either the francophone region or the anglophone region persons who have undergone studies entirely in either English or French law and who in ENAM were trained to practice in either the anglophone region or the francophone region.

One last point about the Cameroonian system of administration of justice, and in fact the basis for suggesting that it is caught in a monojural trap, is the absence of an effective mechanism for checking any violations of the constitution. Cameroon, in its 1996 constitution, inexplicably reintroduced the French Constitutional Council model of constitutional review in its pure and undeveloped form with all its defects and weaknesses. The constitution reserves exclusive powers to control the constitutionality of laws to the Constitutional Council, a quasi-administrative body, rather than a judicial body, composed of persons who are not necessarily judges and are appointed almost exclusively by politicians, who are also the only persons who have the power to trigger the Council's review. If the manner of choosing the members of this body, which has been referred to as the "original sin" and "congenital defect" of this model, compromises the chances of an efficient review, the nature of the control itself, essentially by way of abstract prepromulgation review of legislation, makes the whole system irrelevant and unreal (Fombad 1998). Note here three main flaws of this form of control. First, limiting the council's jurisdiction essentially to prepromulgation review of legislation not only prevents it from playing an active role in interpreting constitutional texts, which are often complex open-ended legal documents, and adapting them to the changing realities but also prevents the council from serving as the keeper of the nation's constitutional conscience. Besides, without a real case or controversy, the richness of any potential argument is lost. Second, in anglophone countries, most laws are enacted by parliament, and these laws are subject to judicial review for conformity to the constitution. In contrast, in

Cameroon, as in most francophone countries, a majority of "laws" are made by the executive as part of the so-called residual legislative powers, in the form of decrees, orders, rules, and regulations. All of this legislation escapes any control for conformity to the constitution. Finally, the most serious flaw with the system is that individual citizens, minorities, and other vulnerable groups have no right to challenge the constitutionality of any laws, whether those laws affect them directly or indirectly. Only the politicians themselves—the lawmakers—have been given the exclusive right to challenge the laws.

Hence, there is clearly a steady decline of the common law input and a progressive preponderance of French civil law influence on the evolving Cameroonian legal system. This situation casts serious doubts on the bijurality of the system. What are the prospects for the future?

Toward a Diversity-Conscious Theory of Legal Reforms

Regardless of how it is defined, conceptualized, and applied, law is more than a body of rules or norms that can simply be imposed on others by those who dominate the formal and informal lawmaking processes. Furthermore, laws that ignore the cultural heritage and legitimate aspirations, desires, and fears of a people—particularly in a complex society such as Cameroon, with its rich diversity of cultures and ethnic groups—are bound to be problematic. Nothing is inherently wrong with legal diversity, and after a half-century of reunification, legal diversity cannot be wished away. Diversity is sustainable, and serious efforts to sustain it must be made. With few exceptions, little evidence indicates that a conscious effort has been made to ensure that legal harmonization reflects the bijural culture. This lack of effort has given rise to the perception of a deliberate policy to minimize the influence of English common law on the system and to eventually displace it. Two important things must be done to maintain and sustain a credible bijural system. First, certain myths about legal diversity must be debunked, and second, a diversity-conscious approach to legal reforms and harmonization is imperative.

Debunking Myths about Legal Diversity

A number of myths have misled Cameroonian politicians and others involved in the law reform process. These myths need to be debunked for the process to become rational. The first of these myths perpetuated by politicians is the belief that maintaining legal diversity is incompatible with the goal of promoting national unity and integration. This belief has been transformed into a political issue. For example, in rejecting the "collection and juxtaposition of our diversities," President Paul Biya has pronounced himself as "firmly convinced that we should move on a higher level of unification, which is that of national integration" (cited in Azevedo 1988: 100). There is certainly nothing inherently wrong with resolutely pursuing the goals of national unity and integration. What is problematic is that the Cameroonian political elites, imbued with Gaullist absolutism, have come to regard diversity and the persistence of anglophone particularisms with growing suspicion. Moreover, the dominant majority's continuous and blind obsession with everything French appears to have led to the belief that the French civil law system is the ideal and irreproachable system that must be followed at all cost. The approach adopted seems to be that English law should be retained where indispensable and unavoidable, or sprinklings of it should be accommodated in harmonized national laws to the extent that is absolutely necessary. The continuous influence of the French, as opposed to the British, remains a crucial factor.[29] For example, the French were very instrumental in the adoption of the OHADA regime (Kalm 2011: 10–13). The misplaced bigotry of perceiving the civil law system as the best system often disguises the fact that many francophone jurists are unwilling to learn about a new system late in their careers, at a time when they feel they know everything. Some have even argued that the anglophones voluntarily opted to reunite with the francophones in 1961 and thus implicitly undertook to unconditionally accept and adjust to the legal system operating in the then-independent French part of Cameroon.[30]

29 After sneaking out in 1961, the British have hardly taken much interest in what is happening either in the anglophone regions or in Cameroon.

30 This view is discussed further in Fombad (1997).

A combination of misguided emotional attachment, bigotry, ignorance, arrogance, and political expediency explains why the dominant legal tradition has been used as a basis for modernizing the law. Yet one of Cameroon's great sources of pride is its much vaunted bilingualism and bijuralism. The instances of Scotland in the United Kingdom and Quebec in Canada—two good examples of mixed systems, although to different degrees than that of Cameroon—show quite clearly that the coexistence of different legal traditions is not incompatible with national unity or even legal modernization. There is sometimes fear, especially in African countries, that the recognition and constitutional entrenchment of the rights of minorities may encourage factionalism or separatism and thus undermine national unity and the demands of national development. There is no empirical evidence to sustain this view. For example, the 1960s postindependence myth that suppressing multipartism would eliminate division and factionalism and promote economic development was exploded long ago. The experiences of the past four decades have proven this notion to be a disastrous mistake. There is far more danger in refusing to recognize and protect minority rights and interests through effective and meaningful diversity-conscious reforms. If bijuralism and the imperatives of legal modernization must be pursued, adopting a policy of diversity-consciousness in the legal reform process will be necessary.

Sustaining and Promoting Bijuralism through a Policy of Diversity Consciousness

Arguments for recognizing the inherent plurality of laws are well known in comparative law literature (Menski 2006: 26–36). What have been little discussed and developed are possible ways of sustaining diversity in the classic mixed or mixing jurisdictions or in special varieties like Cameroon's bijural system. The challenges that the Cameroonian system has faced, it is contended, have been due to a lack of a clear strategy of modernizing the laws within a bijural framework in a manner that is conscious of diversity.

Diversity consciousness in the context of legal reforms refers to the permanent disposition to critically review with an open mind all the different legal options that are available, understand them, and see how these can best be reflected in the emerging law.[31] It requires sensitivity to the different legal cultures and traditions as well as the aspirations of those operating within the particular legal culture. Legal reforms that are conscious of diversity while aiming for uniformity through harmonized laws should produce a type of union of harmony whereby all the parts, however opposed they may appear, cooperate for the general good of society—much as dissonances in music cooperate in the production of an overall concord (Montesquieu 1965: 93–94). As Robbie Robertson (2003: 13) rightly points out, "the creation of effective strategies to handle the reality of human diversity is one of humanity's most pressing challenges, as recent wars, ethnic cleansing, genocides, and the restless tides of refugees and displaced persons demonstrate." Several elements are critical in developing and sustaining a diversity-conscious approach to legal reforms. They include striving to find the "best" rules; keeping coherence; and entrenching diversity consciousness in key structures and institutions such as legal education, the courts, the legislature, and law reform commissions.

Finding the "Best" Rules

Choosing the best rules from a plurality of sources is a common problem wherever there is legal diversity. Often wrong choices are made, usually because of bias toward one legal tradition (Smits 2008: 4–5). The Cameroonian lawmaker is not alone in manifesting bias in favor of one system, but the problem in Cameroon has been acute. If the OHADA regime trend is continued, it may soon lead to the relegation of English law in Cameroon into a historical relic. The main lesson from the experience so far is that bias must be avoided at all cost. As the content of the Penal Code and Criminal Procedure Code—the two reasonably successful pieces of harmonized laws—shows, much can be gained from trying to get the best from both legal systems as well as drawing on international best practices.

In the final analysis, recourse and use of either English or French legal sources in formulating Cameroonian law must not be an act of blind faith. A received rule or principle cannot be ignored or copied merely because it does or does not have an English or French law pedigree. Nor is there any intrinsic merit in the survival or preservation of archaic externalities of either common law or civil law ancestry. The dangers of

31 This concept is narrower than the plurality consciousness discussed by Werner Menski (2006: 14–15, 82–84).

judicial parochialism and servility to inherited legal stereotypes are not mitigated by hasty and ill-conceived legislation. Borrowing from other legal systems, although inveterate and unavoidable, must be pursued with careful planning and alertness to the omnipresent dangers of irrational bias. These difficulties are not lessened by hasty but simplistic attempts to eliminate one of the two legal traditions. A better approach is to assume the challenge of getting the best out of the two inherited legal traditions while being alert to the need to maintain internal coherence and harmony within the mix.

Maintaining Coherence

There is always the danger of incoherence in mixed systems such as Cameroon's. This risk results from differences in techniques of legal interpretation of uniform texts as well as differences in sources of law and the weight given to those sources. In fact, the potential for conflict remains enormous despite the hastening pace of uniform laws substantially influenced by civil law (Fombad 1997: 220–28). So far, the tendency has been to play the ostrich game: bury one's head in the sand and pretend there is no problem. It will be necessary to draft a specific law that deals with cases of conflict, ambiguity, and lacuna in the uniform laws.

Some degree of coherence would have been maintained in the anglophone courts through the system of precedents. Unfortunately, there is no organized and regular system of law reporting in Cameroon. No credible system of precedent can operate and contribute to legal development and consistency in the application of the law without an orderly and regular system of law reporting. Some early efforts did not last long. Worse still, although the constitution requires that all laws be published in English and French in the official gazette, such publication seldom occurs. Also, when it is done, the laws are published in French only. It is difficult for any modern legal system to develop where judgments are not published in the dominant language and where laws are only sporadically published in it.

Entrenching a Bijural Conscious Ethos in Key Legal Institutions and Structures

Perhaps one of the greatest weaknesses of the Cameroonian legal system in general and the law reform process is the fact that little has been done to create and sustain a bijural consciousness in critical legal institutions and structures such as law schools, the courts, the legislature, and the law reform commission.

The nature and scope of legal education in Cameroon has not done the cause of bijuralism any favors. For more than two decades after independence, the country's only university until 1993 had a law faculty that taught English law and French law in separate departments. Although students were required to do a number of subjects in both departments, this requirement was usually not enough to instill and cultivate in them an understanding of both systems. In fact, students obtained a degree in either French law or English law with only such superficial knowledge of the other system as was sufficient. In many cases, this technique created in students a long-lasting dislike and mistrust of the other legal system. If future lawyers and judges were not taught to appreciate the basics of the two legal systems at this critical stage of their studies, how then could they be expected to operate in a bijural society? The inadequacy of training is even worse in ENAM. Future anglophone and francophone judges and prosecutors are taught differently following either the English or French system. As pointed out earlier, they are now posted indiscriminately to work in the two legal districts. After 1993, the government created a so-called English-style university in Buea, in the anglophone Southwest Region, and a French-style university in Ngaoundéré, in the Adamawa Region. Both universities have law faculties that teach exclusively either English law, in the case of the former, or French law, in the case of the latter. The weak foundation for a bijural conscious tradition is further aggravated by the failure to teach comparative law courses in any of these universities. The largely Eurocentric orientation of Cameroon's legal education both at the university level and at the professional level in ENAM has created a huge ignorance of local realities and a deep-seated mistrust of one or the other legal culture that has damaged progressive legal developments within the country. It has also played on one major weakness of lawyers: their conservative nature and general inclination to maintain and operate within the status quo.

The importance of comparative legal studies in a bijural country such as Cameroon cannot be denied. Not only does comparative law provide the student with a new and different perspective and the awareness of and familiarity with other legal cultures, but also—most importantly—it helps to counter dogmatism, parochialism, and narrow nationalism. Comparative law creates the disposition to recognize that there are differences and to learn to understand, respect, and appreciate those differences for what they are worth.

Only when there is some familiarity with or understanding of another legal system can a person readily accept adopting or adapting concepts and principles from it without difficulty. Ultimately, it is of the utmost importance that legal education reflects the mixed character of the legal system.

A comparison of the judgments delivered by the anglophone courts in the 1960s and early 1970s with those delivered in the past decade shows a considerable change.[32] Unlike in the past, the recent judgments do not provide detailed facts and are too abstract, containing little legal analysis. This problem is partly because of the poor training at ENAM. Also, it has been aggravated by the appointment to anglophone courts of francophone judges who have little or no training in English common law judicial techniques. Diversity consciousness needs to be embedded in judicial training both at ENAM and in regular in-service training courses and seminars.

Neither the parliamentary committees that debate laws nor the law reform commissions have been constituted to ensure an equitable representation of the two legal cultures. For example, the national commission on the harmonization of commercial law in Africa had 15 members, only one of whom was a common law jurist. The French experts who had prepared the working drafts were always at hand to lead the discussion. It is therefore no surprise that most codes and laws merely replicate French codes and laws, with a few common law principles sprinkled here and there. The bijural system can be sustained only when there is a conscious effort to ensure that the laws adopted reflect the two legal cultures.

The only way in which the perceived decline of the common law influence can be arrested is to strengthen the constitutional foundations of the bijural system. Article 68 of the constitution does not go far enough. Although it implicitly recognizes the continuous application of certain laws, it does not expressly recognize and protect the two legal cultures even in the token way in which the constitution recognizes English and French. A leaf can be borrowed from the Canadian constitution. In 1987, Quebec agreed to sign the 1982 Canadian constitution under the terms of the Meech Lake Accord, which included an amendment to the constitution recognizing, among other things, "that Quebec constitutes within Canada a distinct society." It also recognized "that the existence of French-speaking Canadians ... and English speaking Canadians ... constitute[s] a fundamental characteristic of Canada."[33] Under the accord, at least three of the nine justices of the Canadian Supreme Court are to be appointed from the civil law bar, as opposed to the common law bar (Hannum 1996: 53–68). Another example, closer to home and even more poignant, is the nature and scope of the protection of language rights under section 6 of the 1996 South African constitution and the obligations it imposes on the national and provincial governments. Without being constitutionally recognized and protected in very clear terms, Cameroonian bijuralism may well survive as a rhetorical and pragmatic gesture, but the quality of justice, especially in the anglophone regions, will continue to decline.

Concluding Remarks

This chapter attempts to provide an overall picture of a fairly young but unique mixed jurisdiction: the Cameroonian bijural system. It traces the historical origins of the system to the division of what was previously German Cameroon between the British and the French. Both the British and French colonial powers introduced their legal systems into the parts of the country under their control. When the two parts of the country were reunited under a 1961 federal constitution, the two inherited legal cultures had to coexist within a single country.

From an analysis of the nature of the Cameroonian mix, one can see that it does not easily fit within most conventional classifications of a typical mixed system. While it manifests elements of mixed systems as well as features of legal dualism and legal pluralism, it can be more accurately described as a bijural system. Thus conceived, the two legal systems—English common law and French civil law—coexist and operate more or

32 Some of the early judgments are reported in the *West Cameroon Law Reports* that were published from 1962 to 1968. Others are reported in the *University of Yaoundé Law Reports* that appeared in 1985. Some of the recent judgments are reported in the *Cameroon Common Law Report*.

33 See section 2(1)(b) of the Constitutional Amendment Act 1987.

less independently with limited interaction. Nevertheless, in the natural process of legal modernization, there have been moves to harmonize the law in the country.

This chapter provides an overview of legal developments within the bijural system during the last half-century. Contrary to the case in most mixed jurisdictions, developments in public law in Cameroon have been substantially influenced by French civil law. However, until 1993, private law was based on the received laws in the two legal districts. Since the OHADA treaty came into force in 1996, all business and commercial law matters have been governed by a new uniform regime, substantially based on the French civil law, set up under the treaty. Although procedural law reflects a mix of both systems, the system of administration of justice is entirely based on the French system. Because the legal harmonization process has led to an almost wholesale replacement of English common law principles by most new laws and codes, it has aroused suspicions of a deliberate design to eliminate English law from the system.

Regardless of whether the perception of an agenda to displace English common law is accurate, it is clear that there is bound to be friction in such a delicate process given the historical, ethnic, geographic, and political complexity of the Cameroonian situation. But over and above this issue, the challenges in sustaining the Cameroonian bijural system offer many lessons. They are especially relevant to some African countries that have or might approach mixed systems, such as Rwanda and Burundi. Therefore, much can be said for undertaking a critical review of the Cameroonian bijural system, identifying its challenges, and considering what needs to be done.

Mixed jurisdictions—even ones that are less complicated than Cameroon—are not going to disappear. Instead, the phenomenon of globalization, regionalization, and liberalization and the tendency for it to lead to attempts to adopt uniform harmonized laws have revived interest in how some mixed jurisdictions, such as Cameroon, are dealing with laws from diverse sources. In this way, the advent of the OHADA regime provided a fine opportunity for Cameroon to display its experience in harmonizing laws from different sources. That opportunity was missed, but the fact that OHADA now recognizes that it needs to break out of its civil law trap to appeal to the rest of Africa is a good lesson.

Nevertheless, the main lesson that this chapter draws from the Cameroonian experience is the need for a diversity-conscious approach in any credible effort to make national laws from a diversity of legal systems. In this regard, three main points need to be reiterated. First, when lawmakers adopt a rule, principle, or model into the legal system, their overriding consideration should not be its ancestry but rather whether it will operate for the general good of society. The outcome may not satisfy everybody, but hardly any law can do so. If the law at least strives to achieve Jeremy Bentham's utilitarian principle of the greatest happiness of the largest number of people, it will suffice (Twining 2000: 15–20). Second, adopting, maintaining, and sustaining a bijural or mixed system requires that all those involved in the law or legal process be trained to be diversity conscious and sensitive. It is counterproductive—if not dangerous—to subject the public to lawyers who are trained in only one system of law and who must interpret and apply a different or mixed system. In this regard, the study of comparative law—with emphasis on learning of the fundamentals of the different legal systems in the world—is crucial. Unfortunately, comparative law has been ignored by those educational systems that need it most, such as those of Cameroon. Furthermore, in other countries, such as South Africa, it is fast disappearing from the syllabuses of law schools.[34] Finally, the nature and scope of the obligation to adopt a diversity-conscious approach in law reforms must be entrenched in the constitution in a manner that creates a binding obligation on the three branches of government. In the globalized world of today, a person can hardly succeed as a lawyer without some knowledge—regardless of how superficial—of other legal systems.

Maintaining and sustaining mixed systems generally and bijural systems in particular are a challenge—particularly in countries such as Cameroon, where the legal framework is weak. There is no necessary contradiction between respecting diversity and aiming for uniformity of laws. In any case, the creation of uniform laws is not an effort to achieve some abstract certainty or clarity in law. Its outcome must be laws that people can identify and live with. After a half-century of independence, there is no longer any reason why African countries such as Cameroon cannot develop a homegrown system based on what was received

34 This observation can be confirmed by a quick look at the law programs of the different African law faculties on the Internet.

during the colonial period. The bijural system gives these countries the enormous advantage of gaining from the experiences of two mature legal systems from which they can distill the best elements. A lesson may be learned from the success of Japan in merging both Eastern and Western legal cultural elements into a coherent system while retaining its relative separation (Coyle 1996: 14–15).

References

Allott, A. 1970. *New Essays in African Law.* London: Butterworths.

Anyangwe, C. 1987. *The Cameroonian Judicial System.* Yaoundé: CEPER.

Ardener, S.G. 1968. *Eye-Witnesses to the Annexation of Cameroon, 1883–1887.* Buea, Cameroon: Ministry of Primary Education and West Cameroon Antiquities Commission.

Azevedo, M. (ed.). 1984. *Cameroon and Its National Character.* Clinton, MS: Educators United for Global.

Azevedo, M. (ed). 1988. *Cameroun and Chad in Historical Contemporary Perspectives.* New York: Edwin Mellen Press.

Church, J., Schulze, C., and Strydom, H. 2007. *Human Rights from a Comparative and International Law Perspective.* Pretoria: UNISA Press.

Clarence-Smith, J.A. 1968. The Cameroon Penal Code: Practical comparative law. *International and Comparative Law Quarterly,* 17(3), 651–71.

Coyle, S. 1996. Introduction, in *Studies in Legal Systems: Mixed and Mixing,* edited by E. Örücü, E. Attwooll, and S. Coyle. The Hague: Kluwer, ix–xvii.

Ekome, E. 2005. Reflections on the applicability of OHADA in anglophone Cameroon. *Juridis Périodique,* 61, 75.

Fombad, C.M. 1991. The scope for uniform national laws in Cameroon. *Journal of Modern African Studies,* 29(3), 443–56.

Fombad, C.M. 1997. An experiment in legal pluralism: The Cameroonian bi-jural/uni-jural imbroglio. *University of Tasmania Law Review,* 16(2), 209–34.

Fombad, C.M. 1998. The new Cameroonian Constitutional Council in a comparative perspective: Progress or retrogression? *Journal of African Law,* 42(2), 172–86.

Fombad, C.M. 1999. Cameroonian bi-juralism: Current challenges and future prospects. *Fundamina,* 5, 22–43.

Fombad, C.M. 2003. Cameroon: Constitutional law, in *International Encyclopaedia of Laws: Constitutional Law,* edited by R. Blanpain. The Hague: Kluwer, 33–34.

Fombad, C.M. 2004. Customary courts and traditional justice in Botswana: Present challenges and future perspectives. *Stellenbosch Law Review,* 15(1), 166–92.

Fombad, C.M. 2008. Cameroon's constitutional conundrum: Reconciling unity with diversity, in *Ethnicity, Human Rights and Constitutionalism in Africa,* edited by G.W. Mukundi. Nairobi: Kenyan Section of the International Commission of Jurists, 121–56.

Fombad, C.M. 2010. State and church in Cameroon, in *Encyclopedia of Law and Religion,* edited by G. Robbers. Milan, Italy: International Consortium for Law and Religion Studies.

Gardinier, D.E. 1963. *Cameroon–United Nations Challenge to French Policy.* Oxford, UK: Oxford University Press.

Glenn, H.P. 1996. Quebec: Mixité and monism, in *Studies in Legal Systems: Mixed and Mixing,* edited by E. Örücü, E. Attwooll, and S. Coyle. The Hague: Kluwer, 1–15.

Griffiths, J. 1986. What is legal pluralism? *Journal of Legal Pluralism,* 24, 1–55.

Gwellem, J.F. 2001. Anglophone lawyers say OHADA treaty cannot apply in Cameroon. *Star,* June 18.

Hannum, H. 1996. *Autonomy, Sovereignty and Self-Determination: The Accommodation of Conflicting Rights.* Philadelphia: University of Pennsylvania Press.

International Bar Association. 2003. Review of the draft Criminal Procedure Code of Cameroon. International Bar Association, London. Available at: http://www.ibanet.org/Human_Rights_Institute/HRI_Publications/Country_reports.aspx [accessed: December 3, 2013].

JuriGlobe. 2013. Mixed legal systems. University of Ottawa, Ottawa. Available at: http://www.juriglobe.ca/eng/sys-juri/class-poli/sys-mixtes.php [accessed: December 3, 2013].

Kalm, G. 2011. Building legal certainty through international law: OHADA in Cameroon. Working Paper 11-005, Buffett Center for International and Comparative Studies, Northwestern University, Evanston, IL. Available at: http://www.cics.northwestern.edu/documents/workingpapers/Buffett_11-005_Kalm.pdf [accessed: December 3, 2013].

McKnight, J. 1977. Some historical observations on mixed systems of law. *Juridical Review*, 22, 177–86.

Menski, W. 2006. *Comparative Law in a Global Context: The Legal Systems of Asia and Africa*. Cambridge, UK: Cambridge University Press.

Montesquieu, Baron de. 1965. *Considerations on the Causes of the Greatness of the Romans and Their Decline*, translated by D. Lowenthal. Ithaca, NY: Cornell University Press.

Munzu, S. 1989. Cameroon's search for a uniform legal system: The example of criminal justice. *African Journal of International and Comparative Law*, 1(1), 46–68.

Örücü, E. 1996. Mixed and mixed systems: A conceptual search, in *Studies in Legal Systems: Mixed and Mixing*, edited by E. Örücü, E. Attwooll, and S. Coyle. The Hague: Kluwer, 335–52.

Örücü, E. 2008. What is a mixed legal system: Exclusion or expansion? *Electronic Journal of Comparative Law*, 12(1): 1–18. Available at: http://www.ejcl.org/121/art121-15.pdf [accessed: December 3, 2013].

Palmer, V.V. (ed.). 2001. *Mixed Jurisdictions Worldwide: The Third Legal Family*. Cambridge, UK: Cambridge University Press.

Parant, P., Gilg, R., and Clarence-Smith, J.A. 1967. Le Code pénal camerounais: Code africain et Franco-Anglais. *Revue de Science Criminelle et de Droit Pénal Comparé*, 2, 339–84.

Park, A.E.W. 1963. *The Sources of Nigerian Law*. London: Sweet & Maxwell.

Pougoué, P.-G., and Elongo, K. 2008. *Introduction Critique à l'OHADA*. Yaoundé: Presses Universitaires d'Afrique.

Roberts-Wray, K. 1960. The adoption of imported law in Africa. *Journal of African Law*, 4(2), 66–78.

Robertson, R. 2003. *The Three Waves of Globalization: A History of a Developing Global Consciousness*. Hubbards, NS, Canada: Fernwood.

Rudin, H.R. 1938. *The Germans in the Cameroons 1884–1914: A Case Study in Modern Imperialism*. New Haven, CT: Yale University Press.

Smith, T.B. 2005. *A Mixed Legal System in Transition: T.B. Smith and the Progress of Scots Law*. Edinburgh: Edinburgh University Press.

Smits, J.M. 2008. Mixed jurisdictions: Lessons for European harmonisation? *Electronic Journal of Comparative Law*, 12(1): 1–8. Available at: http://www.ejcl.org/121/art121-23.pdf [accessed: December 3, 2013].

Susungi, N. 1991. *The Crisis of Unity and Democracy in Cameroon*. London: N. Susungi.

Tande, D. 2007. Can Cameroon's new Criminal Procedure Code deliver "justice with a human face"? *Scribbles from the Den* (blog). Available at: http://www.dibussi.com/2007/01/can_cameroons_n.html [accessed: December 3, 2013].

30-Days Prayer Network. 2013. Mosques spring up like mushrooms in Maroua, Cameroon. Available at: http://www.30-days.net/muslims/muslims-in/africa-west/cameroon-maroua/ [accessed December 2, 2013].

Tumnde, M. 2010. Harmonization of business law in Cameroon: Issues, challenges and prospects. *Tulane European and Civil Law Forum*, 23, 119–38.

Twining, W. 2000. *Globalisation and Legal Theory*. London: Butterworths.

Part III
Mixed Legal Systems with Indigenous, Customary, and Religious Law

Chapter 8
Pacific Punch: Tropical Flavors of Mixedness in the Island Republic of Vanuatu

Sue Farran

Legal systems are not fixed in time but are continually changing and adapting, if not entirely, then at least partially—a little here, a little there, like a party punch that requires improvisation when the original ingredients start to run low. This process of change, compromise, and modification is particularly notable in "young" systems that are emerging from colonial rule but, rather like a young kangaroo, still very much in the colonial or neocolonial "pocket" or "pouch," with debatable viability if they are cast out too soon or required to face the challenges of the world too fast. At the same time, however, the globalization of ideas offers a tempting "pick and mix" of possible alternatives for legal development once the young state does emerge.

This challenge to the nature and form of mixing is based on an examination of one postcolonial legal system, that of the Republic of Vanuatu in the South Pacific, which, in 2013, celebrated 33 years of independence. It is therefore a relatively young state, which prior to gaining its independence in 1980 was brought under the joint influences of British common law and French civil law. As a country of more than 80 islands, its modest population of around 250,000[1] is predominantly indigenous Melanesian people with a strong sense of tradition and custom, including adherence to customary laws.

It might be thought that a country that was ruled in tandem by Britain and France for nearly 80 years and that to this day retains "the British and French laws in force or applied … immediately before the Day of Independence"[2] would be a classical mixed jurisdiction, particularly because the laws appear in both languages (English and French are two of the three official languages of the country), and English and French are the languages of education.[3] Such, however, is not the case. As this chapter will show, the possibility for a classical mix in Vanuatu has been thwarted and frustrated by various accidents of history. Nevertheless, a mix does emerge, perhaps not of the classical kind, nor of the second-reception kind, but rather a fluid, not quite definable mix, which, in a piecemeal response to pragmatic need, is giving rise to an emerging hybrid.

To understand how the legal system has reached its current cocktail, I have roughly adopted part of the structure of Palmer's questionnaire, which he used to inform his book *Mixed Jurisdictions Worldwide* (Palmer 2001). I have had to depart from this questionnaire at times because Vanuatu does not fit all aspects of Palmer's criteria. Nevertheless, the chapter starts from a presovereign past, taking into account the political forces that shaped Vanuatu's legal system prior to its independence and following this trajectory through to the present day. The justification for this continuum of consideration will, I hope, become evident, because it is pertinent to the questions of whether, when, and how mixing occurred in the past or occurs today and what were—or are—the ingredients.

---

1 The midyear 2011 estimate by the statistics department of the Secretariat of the Pacific Community is 251,784. The Vanuatu national census, last taken in 2009, indicated 234,023.

2 Constitution of the Republic of Vanuatu, article 95(2).

3 Ibid., article 3(1). The national language is Bislama, a form of pidgin Franglais. Most residents speak at least three languages, and many indigenous people speak more. There are more than 100 indigenous languages in the islands.

The Condominium of the New Hebrides

The history of the islands of what is today the Republic of Vanuatu has been one of mixed encounters from the early seventeenth century. The islands were first discovered by the Spanish explorer Pedro Fernández de Queirós, who landed in 1606 on a northern island that he called Espiritu Santo (now known simply as Santo), believing that he had discovered the fabled Terra Australis. The archipelago was later mapped and named by the English explorer Captain James Cook in 1774.[4] He called the islands the New Hebrides. Although an increasing number of traders visited the islands from about 1840 onward,[5] and French Catholic and English Presbyterian missionaries started to arrive in the same period,[6] it was not until the 1860s that the gradual increase in European settlement by English (often by way of Australia) and French (by way of New Caledonia and other French territories in the Pacific) planters resulted in growing competition for the acquisition of land from indigenous owners.[7] This competition, in turn, led to requests from settlers to their respective governments for annexation of the islands.[8] Neither France nor Britain were keen to comply, although both had previously exercised their power over other islands in the region. France had annexed the Marquesas Islands in 1842 and New Caledonia in 1853 and had declared a protectorate over Tahiti in 1842. Britain had acquired Fiji as a crown colony in 1874 and would eventually establish a protectorate over the Solomon Islands in 1893.[9] Such was their reluctance to accede to the settlers' requests that in 1878, an Anglo-French exchange of notes suggested that neither country proposed to interfere with the independence of the islands. Instead they offered naval support and occasional naval protection to their respective settler-citizens.[10] However, as a result of increasing internal violence, competitive land acquisition, agitation from the Australian colonies,[11] Anglo-French suspicion of each other's intentions in the region, and mutual concern over the activities of Germany and the United States in the Pacific, the two countries agreed to a convention in 1887, which, besides other matters, addressed the protection of life and property in the New Hebrides.[12] To achieve this goal, the two powers proposed to establish a joint naval commission that would be charged with the duty of maintaining and protecting the lives and property of British subjects and French citizens in the New Hebrides.[13] The Joint Naval Commission was brought into effect by the 1888 Declaration between Britain and France, for the Constitution of a Joint Naval Commission for the Protection of Life and Property in the New Hebrides.[14] Its inception was not, however, the start of a great classical mixture. Although both the British and the French

4 French mariners had also explored these islands: Louis de Bougainville in 1768, Jean-François de La Perouse in 1788, and Dumont d'Urville in 1789.

5 Sandalwood had been discovered in the islands in 1825, and sandalwood traders were among the first to exploit the islands' natural resources. See Shineberg (1967).

6 Presbyterian missions started to arrive in 1848, followed closely by French Marist missions.

7 "Blackbirding," the forceful recruitment of native laborers for Queensland and Noumea in the mid-1800s, gave rise to legislation on both sides to regulate the recruitment of labor (O'Connell 1968–1969: 72). However, land competition really triggered the need for greater intervention.

8 In fact, early settlers had turned to France with requests for annexation of some of the New Hebridean islands to New Caledonia (O'Connell 1968–1969).

9 Provision had already been made to extend some form of British control over British settlers in the islands by means of the 1872 and 1875 Pacific Islanders Protection Acts. In 1900, France did the same (Loi du 30 Juillet 1900, *Bulletin Officiel du Ministère des Colonies*, 14, 665).

10 The exchange of notes, titled Arrangement between Great Britain and France, Respecting the Independence of the New Hebrides Group, was signed January 18, 1878 (by the French) and February 20, 1878 (by the English). The full text of this document and of others discussed in this chapter is available from the Pacific Islands Treaty Series database at http://www.paclii.org/pits/en/treaty_database/ [accessed: December 3, 2013].

11 The Australian colonies feared the French would establish a penal colony in the islands (Thompson 1980).

12 Titled the Convention between Great Britain and France Respecting Abrogation of the Declaration of the 19th June 1847, Relative to the Islands to the Leeward of Tahiti and for the Protection of Life and Property in the New Hebrides, the agreement was signed in Paris on November 16, 1887.

13 Originally the French had suggested an *entente commune* with joint police surveillance; the British response was to suggest a "Mixed Naval Commission" (O'Connell 1968–1969: 74).

14 This document was signed on January 26, 1888.

agreed that, except in emergencies, the naval representatives of the two powers had to act jointly, in practice the Joint Naval Commission soon proved inadequate to meet the needs of the settler communities. Acting simultaneously but separately, the two countries appointed resident commissioners in 1902. Two years later, in 1904, the two powers signed the Declaration between France and Great Britain concerning Siam, Madagascar and the New Hebrides,[15] indicating an intention to formalize the shared government of the New Hebrides. In 1906, Britain and France agreed a new convention concerning the New Hebrides, confirming the Protocol between Great Britain and France Respecting the New Hebrides and establishing a sphere of joint influence in the islands, under which France and Britain would have parallel jurisdiction over their own subjects.[16] The 1906 protocol, which, in the case of Britain, was made effective in 1907 by the New Hebrides Order in Council of November 2, 1907, replaced the 1887 convention, retaining only the provisions for the Joint Naval Commission. Under it, neither France nor Britain exercised joint or separate jurisdictional competence over all the occupants of the islands for all purposes, and each regarded its relationship with the islands somewhat differently. From the French perspective, shared influence over the New Hebrides meant that it was regarded under the Constitution of the Fourth Republic as a French Pacific possession rather than as an overseas territory of metropolitan France. From the British perspective, the New Hebrides was a protectorate under the British Crown rather than a colony or dominion.

Framed with the purpose of ensuring absolute equality between the two powers, the stated purpose of the 1906 protocol, as set out in its preamble, was "to secure the exercise of their [the governments of Britain and France] paramount rights in the New Hebrides," or, as stated in the French version, "en vue d'assurer l'exercise de leurs droits de souveraineté." Both powers appointed absentee high commissioners: the French high commissioner for the New Hebrides was the governor of New Caledonia, who was also commissioner-general of France in the Pacific Ocean, and the British counterpart was the high commissioner for the Western Pacific—based in Fiji until 1952 and then in the Solomon Islands. For all practical purposes, France and Britain were represented by their respective resident commissioners. At this stage the term *condominium* was not used to describe the government, and it was unclear what, if any, mixing of jurisdictional powers was envisaged. There was, for example, no provision in either the 1906 protocol or the implementing convention referring to any international law that might apply to the islands or to any procedures to be followed in negotiating or entering into international agreements with respect to the New Hebrides.

Indeed, the term *condominium* seems mainly to have been used in references to administrative areas where cooperation was required—for example, with respect to court personnel,[17] on official documents, and by commentators. This state of affairs continued until 1922, when a new protocol, which had been drawn up in 1914 but was not ratified until after World War I, was implemented.[18] Under the new protocol, greater mixed juridical functions were agreed on, including the administration of a joint court,[19] the making of joint regulations for the order and good governance of the islands,[20] and certain public services to be undertaken in common. From the outset, it was clear that, insofar as French and British residents were concerned, each power retained separate jurisdiction, although the basis for doing so was different. For Britain, the law applied to all persons brought under British jurisdiction; for France, it derived from the sovereignty exercised over

15 This document was signed on April 8, 1904.

16 The protocol was signed in London on October 20, 1906, and is known as the London Convention.

17 See, for example, *Tomarker v. MacKell [Judgment]* Tribunal Mixte des Nouvelles Hébrides [New Hebrides Mixed Tribunal] [1911].

18 Signed on August 6, 1914, the 1914 Protocol Respecting the New Hebrides was ratified on March 15, 1922, and given effect in Britain by the New Hebrides Order in Council on June 20, 1922. Subsequent modifications were agreed on by an exchange of notes between the two powers, which, in the case of Britain, was given effect by Orders in Council (Treadwell 1976).

19 Established under article 10 of the 1922 convention, the Joint Court was to consist of three judges, one of whom was to be president. The king of Spain was asked to nominate a suitable person, but after the 1930s, this practice ceased. Similarly the public prosecutor was not to be French or British. The procedure before the Joint Court was based on an unchallenged equation between French and British courts at all levels (see article 14 of the convention). A native advocate was appointed to represent the interests of indigenous people.

20 See article 7 of the 1922 convention.

the New Hebrides.[21] Moreover, although there was to be a joint court, each power also had its own high court, which was established under the jurisdiction of the respective high commissioners.

The possibility of limited legal collaboration was suggested by article 8(4) of the 1914 protocol, which stated that the condominium administration was to "cause a collection of native laws and customs ... and these where not contrary to the dictates of humanity and maintenance of order shall be utilised for the preparation of a code of native law, both civil and penal." Nothing so extensive, however, was ever achieved. Under the 1914 protocol, the two powers continued to exercise separate jurisdiction over their own subjects, citizens, and optants (that is, other Europeans in the country who chose French or British law). For British subjects and British optants, the laws that applied were any British acts of parliament and subsidiary legislation that were stated to apply to overseas territories and the general principles of common law and equity. The 1973 New Hebrides Order confirmed that the applicable law was that in force at that date (1973) insofar as circumstances permitted, and in 1976, section 3 of Queen's Regulation 2, which established the High Court of the New Hebrides, stated that "statutes of general application in force in England on the 1st day of January 1976" were to apply. Queen's regulations made by the British high commissioner of the Western Pacific and by the British resident commissioner in the New Hebrides also applied. French subjects and optants were governed by those parts of the codes of French law that applied in New Caledonia: the Civil Code, the Commercial Code, the Penal Code, and the Codes of Civil and Criminal Procedure. Laws applicable to the New Hebrides were promulgated in the *Official Journal of New Caledonia*. Hence, there was a filtering process: some laws of metropolitan France applied to New Caledonia, but not all, and some of those laws, or specific different laws, applied to the New Hebrides. The French high commissioner of the Pacific, who was stationed in New Caledonia, also had the power to make regulations for French Pacific territories coming within his jurisdiction, including the New Hebrides.

Thus, for Europeans settled in the New Hebrides, there was no mixing of legal systems even where the courts were administered jointly. Other services that were delivered jointly included posts and telecommunications, public works, native prisons, and public health services. There was also only one set of postage stamps, but both English currency and French currency were legal tender,[22] and only in emergencies did the separate British and French police forces act together.

The two powers did act jointly with respect to the indigenous population, which became subject to its own form of mixed legal system: customary, personal laws, as well as the colonial laws passed by France and Britain as joint regulations, including a Native Criminal Code based on British and French law.[23] One consequence of this system was that different laws applied to the same crime with different consequences. As explained by Chief Justice Vaudin d'Imecourt:

> On the day immediately before the Day of Independence, there were three distinct sets of criminal laws applicable to Vanuatu. The French Penal Code, the English Penal Code made under the Queen's Regulation 9 of 1973 and the Native Criminal Code made under Joint Regulation 12 of 1962, which applied only to the native New Hebrideans. Under Section 8 of the Native Criminal Code Premeditated Homicide (Murder) carried the death penalty, under Article 302 of the French Criminal Code, Murder carried the death penalty, whereas under the British Criminal Code that applied in Vanuatu, Murder carried life imprisonment.[24]

---

21 Article 1 of the French version of the convention stated that the subjects and citizens of the signatory powers would "jouiront des droits égaux de résidence, de protection personnelle et de commerce, chacune des deux Puissances demeurant souveraine à l'égarde de ses nationaux." The English version of article 1 stated that "the subjects and citizens of the two Signatory Powers shall enjoy equal rights of residence, personal protection and trade, each of the two Powers retaining jurisdiction over its subjects or citizens."

22 Initially the currency in the New Hebrides was the French franc and the English pound, but later it was changed to the French-Pacific franc and the Australian dollar.

23 This code was adopted in 1927 and amended in 1962.

24 *Banga v. Waiwo* [1996] VUSC 5. These different criminal laws applied until the year after independence, when the Penal Code was enacted. Similar confusion and pluralism applied to divorce law—also considered in *Banga v. Waiwo*.

Joint regulations were directed primarily at controlling the local population or regulating relations between natives and nonnatives. Natives were unable to acquire the status of subject or citizen of either of the two imperial powers and could not opt to be governed by either French laws or British laws,[25] which meant that there were instances in which no law was found to be applicable to natives.[26] There was, however, some modest recognition of existing indigenous law in the condominium legal system. First, native land rights were recognized indirectly through the provision of dispute settlement mechanisms with respect to land and by acknowledgment that neither of the two powers had proprietorship, either jointly or severally, over all the land in the group. Second, district agents who went out into the field mediated between foreign law and local law. The creation of districts had been provided for in the 1922 New Hebrides Order. Each district was to have two agents, one British and one French. These agents were expected to cooperate in their tours of inspection, and although they dealt with their own nationals and optants separately, both had authority to deal with natives. Under article 8 of the convention, the high commissioners and resident commissioners were required to make codes of native laws, which could then be applied in native courts that were administered by the agents with the assistance of native assessors. Although this process of codification did not happen, some evidence suggests that district agents could work with traditional leadership to enforce law and order.[27] Third, magistrates encountered customary law in their own courts when those accused appeared accompanied by their local chief or elder, who presented evidence that customary fines or payments of compensation had already been paid (Forsyth 2004). In addition, when a matter came before the Joint Court that could not be determined by French law, by British law, or under a joint regulation, the Joint Court could apply customary law. For example, adultery was no longer a crime under either French or British law and was not regulated by a joint regulation. The Joint Court therefore applied customary law, insofar as it could ascertain what the law was, given that no code of customary law existed and customs throughout the islands were not homogeneous (Vurubaravu n.d.).

In the period leading up to independence during the late 1970s, there were some changes. In 1978, Joint Regulation 13/1978 was passed to give effect to a resolution of the new Representative Assembly.[28] The regulation provided for the establishment of joint district courts, which were composed of single judges, except in criminal trials, where the judge was to sit with two other assessors, at least one of whom had to be indigenous. The jurisdiction of the court was largely limited to matters concerning "natives," and the law to be applied was that provided for under joint regulations. If joint regulations did not apply (for example, in civil and commercial matters), the court applied the law under which the contract or act was conducted. If no such law was stipulated, the law applicable to the nonnative plaintiff was used or a decision according to substantial justice was made, taking into account custom wherever possible. The regulation established that two judges would co-preside over the Joint Court, which was to be a court of appeal from the district courts and a court of first instance for certain matters. The judges were to be appointed by the respective high commissioners. Which of the two judges was to act as president in any individual case was to be determined by the nationality of the plaintiff; if the plaintiff was not a native, the laws were applied to the matter by agreement, or if agreement could not be reached, then by lot. The main task of the Joint Court, however, was to determine and register land claims by French and British settlers. In fulfilling this task, the court took different approaches. Under French law, any claim to land by a French citizen was upheld until disproved by the indigenous claimant; under English law, the right of ownership by a British citizen had to be clearly established. In the long term, this approach did not endear the French to customary owners of land.

Thus, on the eve of independence in 1980, a mixed system was indeed practiced in the New Hebrides, but not in a way that might qualify it to be classified as a mixed jurisdiction according to any accepted models.

---

25 Those of mixed race came under the laws of the (male) head of the family—that is, husband or father. A person of mixed race could not be a native.

26 For example, joint regulations prohibited the selling of alcohol to natives by nonnatives. No provision was made that would apply when a native sold alcohol to another native (Vurubaravu n.d.).

27 Forsyth (2004) mentions the work of Larcom in Malekula, which demonstrated that chiefs and the British district agent worked together, with a division of responsibilities. Decisions of chiefs could be appealed to the district agent. The district agent could also enforce the decisions of chiefs. See Larcom (1990: 178).

28 Resolution 93, 1978, provided for judicial reform in the New Hebrides.

French law applied to French citizens and optants (including second-generation, mixed-race citizens);[29] British law applied to British citizens and optants (including second-generation, mixed-race citizens); heterogeneous customary laws applied to indigenous people; and mixed joint regulations applied in various cases to indigenous people only, to nonnatives only, or to all residents of the islands. Indigenous people had also been absorbed into the different colonial administrations, had adopted the different religious faiths proselytized by French and English missionaries, and had been educated in French or English in the schools established first by missionaries and later by the colonial authorities. Islands and peoples were divided.

The movement toward independence also reflected the very different perspectives of France and Britain. During the 1970s, both powers had poured money into the New Hebrides,[30] with minimal returns.[31] Although the British Commonwealth Office was keen to rid itself of the financial burden of the New Hebrides from the 1960s onward, France feared that granting independence to the New Hebrides would trigger demands for independence in magnesium-rich New Caledonia, located to the west of the New Hebrides. In 1974, representatives of the two powers met to discuss the establishment of the Representative Assembly, which came into effect the following year. The possibility of dual nationality for the native population was also considered, as well as the merger of the two administrative services. Plans were drawn up to promote land reform—and thereby meet some of the concerns of indigenous landowners—and to plan for the economic and social development of the country. Differing views over independence were not limited to France and Britain, however. In the 1975 elections, held to choose municipal councils for Vanuatu's two urban areas, Port Vila and Luganville, and to elect representatives for the Representative Assembly, it was clear that the indigenous inhabitants of the country were strongly divided (see Guiart 1983; Plant 1977; Vurubaravu n.d.).

As the scheduled date of independence approached, tensions escalated, not only between the French and English but also between different factions of indigenous people.[32] By 1979, a draft constitution had been drawn up by the Constitutional Committee appointed by the New Hebridean government of national unity. Independence, however, could not be achieved until the two imperial powers revoked the 1914 protocol. On October 23, 1979, by the Exchange of Letters Constituting an Agreement concerning the Granting of Independence to the New Hebrides, the era of joint rule was terminated.[33] But what did this mean for the new country's legal system?

Independence and a New Mixedness

The opening preamble to the 1980 constitution marked what was to be the start of a new mixedness. It states:

> WE, the people of Vanuatu,
> PROUD of our struggle for freedom,
> DETERMINED to safeguard the achievements of this struggle,
> CHERISHING our ethnic, linguistic and cultural diversity,
> MINDFUL at the same time of our common destiny,

---

29 In 1948, more than a third of the 875 French nationals registered with the authorities were of mixed race (Aldrich 1993: 203).

30 Aldrich (1993: 207–8) reports that the combined expenditure of the two powers grew from US$7 million in 1968 to US$14 million in 1972 and increased by over 24 percent in the period from 1972 to 1976, with France providing the greatest proportion of this expenditure.

31 For a time in the 1970s, the New Hebrides had provided much-needed labor to New Caledonia, but as the decade progressed, falling copra and livestock prices adversely affected earnings. Foreigners held all commercial interests, and most of these interests were held by companies registered elsewhere. Although the French predominated in agriculture, the British predominated in commerce.

32 Two secessionist revolts occurred in 1980, both claiming justification in custom and both involving supporters drawn together by a shared opposition to the condominium and to the Anglican, English-speaking, and English-educated political aims of Walter Lini's Vanua'aku Party.

33 This transition was not achieved peacefully. Franco-British troops had to be called in to quell rebellion in Santo, and they remained for several days after independence. They were subsequently replaced by a force from Papua New Guinea under Australian command.

> HEREBY proclaim the establishment of the united and free Republic of Vanuatu founded on traditional Melanesian values, faith in God, and Christian principles,
> AND for this purpose give ourselves this Constitution.

Thus, there was to be diversity and unity in the new government, informed both by principles drawn from a religion brought to the country by the early Catholic and Protestant missionaries and by values based on traditional, indigenous social and political organization. How did this attempt at diversity and unity translate in practice?

Public Law

The classical model of mixed legal systems suggests a common law public law and a civilian private law. The new constitution of Vanuatu and the legal system that it established did not totally conform to this model.

Drawn up by representatives of France, Britain, and local indigenous leaders, the constitution provided a Westminster framework of governance with a continental twist. The New Hebrides became the Republic of Vanuatu, with a prime minister and a president. There was a unicameral, elected legislature: the parliament and an executive Council of Ministers. The National Council of Chiefs was also established; it had advisory powers but no lawmaking power. The court system was essentially based on the common law structure, with the Court of Appeal at its apex, the Supreme Court, and then magistrates' courts at the bottom. Provision was also made for parliament to establish further courts at village and island levels. Under article 91 of the constitution, judges who were in post at the date of independence remained in post. There was no constitutional court, but under article 16(4), the president had the power to refer any legislation passed by parliament that was considered to be unconstitutional to the Supreme Court for a ruling. The new constitution also contained a statement of fundamental rights and obligations: a bill of rights. It therefore offered a new mixedness, incorporating not only elements from French and English public law but also customary law and institutions that had hitherto existed outside the boundaries of official law.

The 1980 constitution, besides declaring that the Republic of Vanuatu was now a sovereign state, also retained all the laws in force until such time as the national parliament made new laws, provided that these existing laws were not incompatible with the new independent status of the country or were not expressly revoked.[34] Hence, the following laws remained applicable: English and French law then in force, joint regulations passed by the condominium government, and resolutions passed by the elected Representative Assembly between 1977 and 1980 that had been approved by the two resident commissioners and enacted as joint regulations. Thus, as far as common law was concerned, the applicable law included legislation either made specifically for the New Hebrides or extended to it; legislation enacted as statutes of "general application," such as Queen's regulations passed for the Western Pacific by the British high commissioner of the Western Pacific, or regulations made by the resident commissioner for the New Hebrides; and the general principles of common law and equity derived from case law. In the case of civil law, such law included French legislation that applied to French territories or legislation made in New Caledonia that was also made applicable to the New Hebrides; regulations made by the French high commissioner of the Pacific; French codes, except for any provision that had been replaced by a joint regulation; and French case law.

34 This provision is found in article 95(2) of the constitution. The French version of this article is distinct from the English, stating: "Sauf décision contraire du Parlement, les loi françaises et britanniques en vigueur aux Nouvelles-Hébrides au jour de l'indépendance constituent à s'appliquer à compter de ce jour tant qu'elles n'auront pas été expressément abrogées et dans la mesure où elles ne sont pas incompatibles avec le statut d'indépendance des Nouvelles-Hébrides et avec la coutume." In contrast, the English version states, "The administration of justice is vested in the judiciary, who are subject only to the Constitution and the law. The function of the judiciary is to resolve proceedings according to law. If there is no rule of law applicable to a matter before it, a court shall determine the matter according to substantial justice and whenever possible in conformity with custom." Hence, the French version suggests a more robust continuing role for French law than that indicated in the English version.

However, two additional sources of law were given constitutional standing. First, under article 74, customary law was to be taken into account wherever possible, and customary law in particular was to be the only law that governed customary land. Second, under article 47, where there appeared to be no applicable law, decisions were to be made according to "substantial justice and whenever possible in conformity with custom."[35] Whether this notion of substantial justice was based on consideration of equitable principles drawn from English law or the fundamental principles that underpin French law was not stated. Nor was it clear whether this constitutional provision ousted customary law or made customary law subject to some vague notion of substantial justice. When independence was granted, it was also unclear whether all citizens of the new state would be governed by all laws or whether there would be a choice of laws, either with respect to all matters or some matters. Eventually the courts would have to make a ruling on this question.

Certainly in the years immediately after independence, French law continued to be applied, either because the matter had been commenced prior to independence or because the litigants were themselves French.[36] However, the question of which law applied to which persons remained confused. In one case,[37] a petitioner seeking a divorce had married first under French law and then under British law. Although the judge held that there were insufficient grounds for divorce under either French or British law (the French lawyer acting for the petitioner argued otherwise), the judge considered that

> the Respondent, having lived here for thirteen years and made his home here, no matter what his status is, is subject to the laws of the State. Having been married under French law, seemingly without any objections, he is bound by French laws relating to that marriage, such laws remaining in force under Article 93(2) of the Constitution.

It appeared that the applicable laws remained to be determined by nationality. In fact, this issue remained unresolved until 16 years after independence. In 1996, in the matrimonial case of *Banga v. Waiwo*, Chief Justice d'Imecourt held as follows:

> [U]nder Article 95 of the Constitution, the French and English Laws that applied on the day before the Day of Independence applied to everyone in Vanuatu, irrespective of Nationality and irrespective as to whether they were Indigenous Ni-Vanuatu or not. They were no longer French or English laws but they became the law of Vanuatu. All those English and French laws that still now apply in Vanuatu … form part of the law of Vanuatu and apply to everyone in Vanuatu irrespective of creed, colour or Nationality. There cannot be a law for the English and another for the French and yet another for the Ni-Vanuatu in the Republic.[38]

Officially this ruling suggested that there was a mix.

The Structure of the Courts

The administration of law from the start of this new sovereignty was based on the common law model of a single hierarchy of courts. There were no separate administrative courts and no constitutional court. The legal profession was fused, with no distinction between barristers and solicitors—as in the common law, or

35 The constitution does not define *custom*, but in the Schedule to the Interpretation Act (chapter 132), it is stated as "the customs and traditional practices of the indigenous peoples of Vanuatu." There is, however, some confusion because the English word *custom*, may not be the same as the Bislama word *kastom*, which is used in the Bislama version of the constitution. This legal and anthropological debate is beyond the scope of this chapter, but for more information, see Rousseau (2008).

36 For example, in *Colardeau v. Mamelin* [1980] VUSC 1, French Civil Code sections 1166 and 815 were applied. See also *Luthier v. Kam* [1980–1994] Van LR 116, *Pentecost Pacific Ltd v. Hnaloane* [1980–1994] 134, and *My v. Société Sariani* [1980–1994] 163.

37 *T v. R* [1980] VUSC 3.

38 *Banga v. Waiwo* [1996] VUSC 5.

between advocates, *notaires*, and *conseil juridique*—as in the civil law. The process was largely adversarial, although the judge was, and remains, more likely to intervene (partly because lawyers are often novices or because the litigant is unrepresented) than might be usual in other common law jurisdictions. There is, however, no trial by jury in criminal trials. The power of the court is backed up by the common law institution of contempt of court[39] and the power to order *habeas corpus*.[40] The rule of precedent is observed, but perhaps more for pragmatic reasons than any other: often there is insufficient case law to wait for the emergence of a *jurisprudence constante*. Indeed, lack of local jurisprudence inclines judges and, indeed, lawyers who argue before the courts to refer to common law cases drawn from elsewhere. Most of these cases are from English law, but increasingly they may be drawn from other common law jurisdictions (Farran 2009). Although the courts are not mandated to anglicize the law, this process of cross-reference to the case law of English courts has led to a second reception of common law. It is very rare nowadays to find reference to the case law of civil law systems.

There are, however, some departures from the common law model. When the court sits as a bench of more than one judge, as in the Supreme Court and in the Court of Appeal, there are no dissenting judgments. Although there is no civil code—other than the continuing relevance of the French Civil Code in force in 1980—the criminal law is codified, and all statute law is consolidated in one collection, the most recent consolidation being in 2006.[41] It is also true that judges bring to the court their own cultural background.[42] In the case of foreign judges, this background is usually the common law, but local magistrates and judges bring knowledge of customary law with them and may draw on that knowledge to inform their judgments, particularly in the lower courts. This practice may not always be approved of if the case goes on appeal, or it may be inappropriate insofar as customary law is not homogeneous. Thus, the individual judge or magistrate will draw on his or her own local customary law, which may or may not apply to the particular litigants, who could be from a different locality. This practice does flavor the mix of law taking place, however.

Procedure and Evidence

The court structure is not unilinear. Although magistrates' courts sit below the Supreme Court and the Court of Appeal, there are also island courts and customary land tribunals, as well as informal meetings of chiefs, village heads, and families that resolve disputes at a local level through mediation and the use of fines and compensation payments. Some of these forums are established under legislation and so might be regarded as state institutions, but others are informally established, although they feed into the formal system. In particular, the island courts and customary land tribunals provide a midpoint "mixing bowl" for indigenous and nonindigenous procedures and practices.

The island courts are provided for under the Islands Courts Act 1983, which confers on the chief justice the power to establish island courts by warrant. Although under section 3(1) each court is to have at least "three justices knowledgeable in custom … at least one of whom shall be a custom chief residing within the territorial jurisdiction of the court"[43] and under section 10 the courts are expected to "administer the customary law prevailing within the territorial jurisdiction of the court so far as the same is not in conflict

39 See the Courts Act, chapter 122, section 23, as applied in *In re Civil Contempt of Court, de Robillard* [1997] VUCA 1. Both civil and criminal contempt of court have been adopted in Vanuatu. See also *Ombudsman v. Leymang* [1997] VUSC 29. Palmer (2001: 35) suggests that this greater autonomy of the court is a feature of courts in mixed jurisdictions, because as a result of common law influence, these institutions have more autonomy than is usually the case in pure civilian systems.

40 Civil Procedure Rules Title 16(2).

41 However, this collection is available only in English.

42 See for example, *Waiwo v. Banga* [1996] VUMC 1 and the contrasting cultural approach in the same case on appeal, *Banga v. Waiwo* [1996] VUSC 1.

43 Prior to colonization of the islands, "chiefs" were not generally a feature of Melanesian social organization, but the colonial authorities found the role useful and promoted it to the degree that it is now an entrenched feature in Vanuatu (Bolton 1998).

with any written law and is not contrary to justice, morality and good order,"[44] these courts are presided over by a magistrate. Through university education, magistrates have become more professional and have become immersed in the common law tradition and in the practices and procedures of the magistrates' courts. As a result, the island courts have been increasingly influenced by state law, rather than customary law.[45] Until 2000, the jurisdiction of island courts, which their warrants limit to minor civil and criminal matters determined by the introduced law, included jurisdiction to determine land matters, thereby bringing customary law—which governs all land held under customary tenure—into the state-established system. Although this jurisdiction was curtailed because of the unmanageably high percentage of cases being appealed to the Supreme Court, island courts continue to hear a backlog of land cases and have been instrumental in the changing articulation of land claims (Farran 2010).

Land jurisdiction was transferred from the island courts to the customary land tribunals under the Customary Land Tribunal Act 2001. This tier of courts, with its own hierarchy of local, custom subareas, custom areas, and island courts, exists separately from the other courts with no cross-reference to the island courts, the magistrates' courts, or the Supreme Court and Court of Appeal except by way of judicial review. The purpose in setting up such courts was not only pragmatic but also purist: "to provide for a system based on custom to resolve disputes about customary land" (section 1). Although various customary practices are incorporated into the Customary Land Tribunal Act, in practice these tribunals have not been a success and have been subject to reviews. It now seems likely that they will be modified under land legislation reforms passed in December 2013. The current system is unwieldy and invites appeals. In some places, no customary land tribunals have been established, and litigants are left without official forums for resolving land disputes. Attempts to constitute tribunal panels with those knowledgeable in local custom and, at the same time, impartial has proved to be very difficult in practice, and efforts to mediate settlements between parties have tended to be short-lived. The structure is also premised on assumptions about localism with respect to custom—namely that all those residing in a particular area subscribe to the same customs. The act also ignores patterns of changing land use.

In the case of land and, indeed, in many areas of daily life, changing values and aspirations prompt new legal needs. In Vanuatu, individuals are mixing tradition and custom with modern and introduced concepts and values. Consequently, there is legal mixing. For example, although customary law regulates customary land tenure and much of family law, there is a crossover with noncustomary law in cases where customary land is leased or where a couple married in custom seek to have their matrimonial property rights decided by a formal court. In these circumstances, the matter moves from the customary forums to the formal courts. The system is not, therefore, entirely parallel or dual. At points it touches.

This factor is important, because different rules of procedure and evidence apply in these different forums. In the case of land disputes for example, litigation involving leases that come before the formal courts—usually the Supreme Court—rely on evidence from documents of contract, registration, mortgage, and so on. If custom is pleaded, it must be proved; it is not accepted as law (see, more generally, Zorn and Care 2002), and indeed it may be necessary to establish that the custom is one that is generally recognized rather than one that is merely local or particular to the plaintiff or defendant.[46] However, disputes that come before the customary land tribunals or even the island courts rely on oral evidence—much of it hearsay, narratives of genealogies and events, and the opinions of witnesses who are prepared to offer views on the truth or falsity of these narratives.[47] Although unrepresented litigants are quite common at all levels of courts, in the customary

44 There are also provisions relating to orders of community work in lieu of fines or imprisonment and the power to order payment of compensation to victims, both of which find some resonance in customary practices. The legislation also provides that "an island court shall not apply technical rules of evidence but shall admit and consider such information as is available" (section 25).

45 For an assessment of the island courts, see Jowitt (1999) and Weisbrot (1989).

46 The decisions of the courts are not consistent on this point; for example, in the case of customary adoption, it appears that different local customs are acceptable. However, fear of the rule of precedent may deter a judge from accepting an argument based on custom. See *Boe and Tage v. Thomas* [1987] VUSC 9.

47 See, for example, *Kalmarie v. Titus* [2011] VUIC 2, in which the court explained, "[T]he claimants must show on probable grounds: 1. That their tribe began on the land. And that there are descendants of the same tribe; going back through generations as far as he/she could. 2. That they are knowledgeable in the past and present cultural practices of the area in dispute; and 3. That they are confident with the boundaries of

land tribunals and island courts, legal representation is forbidden. Despite these official attempts to preserve a distinction, litigants, even if representing themselves, may seek legal advice and choose to present their evidence in a way that is acceptable to courts in the formal system (for example, by presenting genealogies in a linear fashion). Similarly, although the composition of the adjudicating panel in island courts and on land tribunals specifically incorporates custom leaders and those knowledgeable in custom, the procedures established by warrant or under legislation shoehorn customary practices into a formal mold: minutes are taken, written notices are sent, and there are time limits and a clear sequence to the hearing. None of these procedures mirror customary practices, which are usually oral, circuitous, repetitive, lengthy, and often impromptu.[48]

The process of mixing customary law with formal law is challenging, especially if the dominant ingredient is the common law. Like combining oil and water, it could be argued that mixing these two types of law is unlikely to work. However, even in the case of two systems with similar or compatible chemical elements, mixing may still be unsuccessful. In Vanuatu, this analogy appears to reflect the present situation as regards common and civil law.

A Process of Unmixing

There is a moment at which a mixture may begin to separate. Such separation may happen in an instant or rather gradually. In the case of Vanuatu, a number of things occurred that undermined the influence of French civil law. None of them were catastrophic in themselves, and at any moment the process might have been reversed. In combination, however, they have led to a situation in which French law and the civil law system have faded into the shadows.

First, because of political differences surrounding the movement toward independence,[49] many French residents left in 1980, abandoning plantations, leaving businesses, and uprooting themselves. Others were arrested and expelled. Francophone Melanesians who had opposed those now running the government were also arrested and imprisoned.[50] The French legal fraternity withdrew. The last French lawyer, who had long ceased to practice, died in the 1990s, and no new French lawyers appeared until around 2003, when a *notaire* established an office in the capital. Although France maintained some cultural links and a diplomatic presence, French funding dropped off sharply in the decade after independence, thereby affecting scholarships for francophone ni-Vanuatu, who might have attended universities in New Caledonia or metropolitan France. The translation of laws into French was also affected.

Second, the University of the South Pacific, a regional institution that the British founded in Fiji in 1969, started to offer law courses, first at the certificate level for civil servants, magistrates, and police scattered throughout the institution's 12 member countries. Legal education based on the common law and taught in English—the language of education for the university—became increasingly available through distance learning and on-campus provision. Until 1984, those seeking law degrees had to travel further, to Australia, New Zealand, Papua New Guinea, the United States, France, and the United Kingdom. From 1984, however, the University of the South Pacific started to offer law degrees and then vocational training for aspiring lawyers. Consequently, today most lawyers, magistrates, and professionals in the State Law Office and the Public Prosecutor's office have received a common law legal education.

---

the land in dispute.... The court expects to hear evidence of the ORIGINAL TRIBES of the claimants, their custom totems or Naflac" (capitalization in original).

48 See Forsyth (2004) for an account of how chiefly proceedings at village level may proceed.

49 Political affiliation was also along language and religious lines. Thus, for example, Walter Lini, who was to become the first prime minister of the republic, was an Anglican priest, and his pro-independence party was made up of anglophone Protestants. The opposition comprised francophone, French-educated Melanesians, who were largely Catholic and were led by a Catholic priest, Gérard Leymang, and a civil law indigenous lawyer, Vincent Boulékoné (Aldrich 1993: 213).

50 The new government led by Walter Lini refused residence permits to more than 100 French nationals living in the country at the time of independence and had several deported. In total, about 800 French left (Aldrich 1993: 234). Some claim the number was much higher. See Vurubaravu (n.d.), who cites the figure of 2,000 deportees.

Third, until recently, Supreme Court and Court of Appeal judges were drawn from outside the country: from England, Australia, New Zealand, and other Pacific island countries.[51] It is still true that the Court of Appeal is not a permanent court but sits two or three times a year. In addition, much of the fee-earning work of lawyers is generated by nonindigenous litigants, many of whom prefer to either bring in their own lawyers or use nonindigenous lawyers who have a presence in the capital. Even francophone clients have tended to seek legal advice and representation from common law lawyers, partly because of the lack, at least until recently, of available civil law lawyers. A number of common law lawyers are bilingual as a result of being educated in the country or living there.

Fourth, because French law has lacked champions, there has been no debate between the pollutionists and purists in Vanuatu. Although the current chief justice is himself francophone and trained in France, he is an exception. Francophone law students either have to cope with a common law education delivered in English or study common law in French through the services offered by the Agence Universitaire de la Francophonie and through its links to the University of Moncton in Canada and Université Jean Moulin Lyon III in France.[52] For several years, there was a backlog of legislation waiting to be translated into French. Eventually, funding was secured for the translation, but there is still a dearth of French legal material, especially copies of French law that was in force in 1980—such as the Civil Code of that date. The translation process tends to lag in the publication of sessional and subsidiary legislation in English. Virtually no postindependence case law has been translated into French.

Fifth, the gradual process of replacing legislation in force at the time of independence with national legislation involves a slow process of legal reform, much of which depends on foreign aid and expertise. Legal draftspersons or consultants who are brought in, except, perhaps, for the experts from Canada, are not drawn from civil law jurisdictions, and resources for extensive comparative research to inform the law reform process are lacking. The civil law has therefore gradually died from want of oxygen. Legal pragmatism has prevailed.

However, this development does not mean that the legal system in Vanuatu has become singular rather than plural, or refined rather than mixed.

A Different Mixture?

Although today French civil law is rarely referred to, indigenous law has continued to play an important role in the daily lives of ni-Vanuatu, particularly with respect to land and family law. Although some commentators have expressed the view that there has been insufficient mixing of introduced law and customary law (Paterson 1995: 668; Powles 1997: 75; Weisbrot 1989), it might be argued that hybridity is occurring in a more nuanced way.

Critics of failed mixing point to the failure of parliament to meet their constitutional duty to take steps to "provide for the manner of the ascertainment of relevant rules of custom" (article 51) and to develop a national land law (article 76) in order to give effect to the provisions of articles 73–75, which returned the land to indigenous custom owners. They also point to the weak role accorded to the National Council of Chiefs, comprised of elected custom chiefs, which is mandated by article 30(1) of the constitution to "discuss all matters relating to custom and tradition and may make recommendations for the preservation and promotion of ni-Vanuatu culture and languages." Failure to capture customary law in written form has also been highlighted, and indeed the modest attempts to codify or consolidate customary law into a written document have been done only at a local or island level.[53]

---

51 Early reliance on common law can be found in the 1980s in Chief Justice Frederick Cooke's decisions.

52 Although there are now proposals to develop a bachelor's degree in French studies at the University of the South Pacific, it is unclear how far these proposals have advanced and whether the degree will include any modules on civil law.

53 There is, for example, a code of customary law on Tanna, and the Council of Chiefs for the island of Efate has drawn up a code of customary law.

Yet customary law itself represents an intersection between tradition and change, between the state and its people. The constitutional recognition of the "rules of custom" under article 51 and customary law under article 95(3) brought customary law firmly into the mix of laws applicable to Vanuatu. Because the constitution does not indicate which areas of activity (other than land) customary law is to apply to, how it is to be pleaded and proved, or how it is to be judged, the custodians of the law remain the people of Vanuatu. Hence, there is both a state-sanctioned and nonstate arena in which customary law operates.

In the state-sanctioned arena, customary law is recognized in particular in three spheres: family law, land law, and criminal law. In family law, customary marriage, divorce, and adoption are all recognized, and it is clear that property governed by customary rules cannot form the subject matter of allocation by the court in the case of divorce, nor can succession to such property be determined by introduced laws of testacy or intestacy. In land law, customary law governs customary land tenure, and because all land was returned to customary owners at the time of independence, customary law is the main form of legal regulation of perpetual ownership for about 80 percent of Vanuatu's land. In criminal law, custom is recognized in the sentencing of offenders, and if an offender pays the customary compensation, his or her sentence may be reduced (Forsyth 2004; Paterson 2006). In all these areas of public and private law, the inclusion of custom is not under any separate law but integral to the laws that govern these topics. So, for example, the Marriage Act recognizes as valid civil, religious, and customary marriages, provided that they are celebrated by persons authorized to celebrate such marriages, depending on the type of marriage chosen, and provided that the rules relevant to that type of marriage are adhered to. In the case of customary marriages, the formalities are simply that "[e] very custom marriage shall be performed in a place and according to the form laid down by local custom" (section 10). Similarly, the Matrimonial Causes Act (in chapter 192) provides for the dissolution of all forms of marriage and states with respect to customary marriage that such a marriage "may be dissolved, annulled or separation ordered only in accordance with custom" (section 4).

In the case of criminal law, provision can be found in the Penal Code (Amendment) Act 2006 for customary reconciliation and customary compensation payments to the victim or his or her family can be taken into account when the offender is sentenced.[54] Although these specific legal provisions will usually apply where indigenous ni-Vanuatu are involved, they are not specifically limited to such persons, and there have been cases in which it has been held, for example, that customary adoption can apply even though the child is not indigenous and that a valid customary marriage can take place between an indigenous person and a nonindigenous person. Moreover, in principle, customary compensation payments could be made in cases in which the perpetrator of a crime is not indigenous.[55]

In the nonstate arena, customary laws continue to govern the lives of most people, most of the time, especially in rural areas, but interaction in nontraditional areas of life means that people move across boundaries in their legal relationships. For example, under customary land tenure, men acquire stronger rights than women, and on marriage women tend to lose any rights they may have had in their natal land. However, where land translates into money, as where land is used for tourist ventures, new considerations may come into play, such as the establishment of trusts for managing the income and the application of equitable principles for its distribution.[56]

---

54 Section 38 states, "(1) Notwithstanding the provisions in this Act or any other Act, a court may in criminal proceedings, promote reconciliation and encourage and facilitate the settlement according to custom or otherwise, for an offence, on terms of payment of compensation or other terms approved by the court. (2) Nothing in this section limits the court's power to impose a penalty it deems appropriate for the relevant offence." Section 39 states, "When sentencing an offender, the court must, in assessing the penalty to be imposed, take account of any compensation or reparation made or due by the offender under custom and if such has not yet been determined, may, if satisfied that it will not cause undue delay, postpone sentence for such purpose."

55 See, for example, *Jenkinson v. Public Prosecutor* [2000] VUAC 5, in which the perpetrator, a non-indigenous person working for a construction company in Vanuatu, had hit and killed a pedestrian. The court took into account the fact that "when the facts came to his knowledge he was remorseful and has assisted the deceased's family above and beyond that legally required."

56 See *Noel v. Toto* [1995] VUSC 3, in which the unequal distribution of money earned from allowing cruise passengers access to a pristine beach was held to be contrary to the fundamental rights provisions of the constitution regarding protection from discrimination.

There are also areas in which a conscious attempt is made to develop hybrid laws that take account of different normativities derived from different perspectives. An example of such an attempt can be found in recent laws concerning intellectual property.

A Mixing Experiment

The impetus for this development comes from a further ingredient to the general mixture of laws: international treaties and the influence of nonstate agencies such as the World Trade Organization. There are also domestic pressures by a growing middle class to develop a legal system that offers commercial opportunities aligned with development aspirations; however, at the same time, the government must be mindful of the continuing power of traditional leaders and of values derived from the always elusive and changeable traditions of the people.

At the time of independence, Vanuatu inherited a body of intellectual property law derived from Western liberal attitudes toward copyrights, patents, and trademarks. In recent years, however, pressure to reform this law has grown. The pressure comes from two opposing agendas. The first is pressure to conform with the obligations arising under recent World Trade Organization membership.[57] The second is pressure to respond to needs identified internally and externally[58] for legislation to afford better protection to indigenous people against the exploitation of traditional knowledge and expressions of culture and to ensure a more equitable distribution of benefits. In 2000, the Vanuatu parliament passed a number of intellectual property acts that were eventually brought into effect in February 2011. Among these acts is Copyright and Related Rights Act 42 (Farran 2011b). It includes within its scope *expressions of indigenous culture*. This term is defined as meaning any way in which indigenous knowledge may appear or be manifested.[59] *Indigenous knowledge* is stated as meaning any knowledge (a) that is created, acquired, or inspired for traditional economic, spiritual, ritual, narrative, decorative, or recreational purposes; (b) the nature or use of which has been transmitted from generation to generation; and (c) that is regarded as pertaining to a particular indigenous person or people in Vanuatu. The act incorporates the collective rights of customary owners to bring an action against any offending party in circumstances in which (a) the offender is not the recognized customary owner of the expression of indigenous culture or (b) the expression has not been sanctioned or authorized by the appropriate persons or according to the appropriate rules of custom. The right to bring an action is also conferred on the National Cultural Council of the National Council of Chiefs, either at the request of the offended customary owner or independently if the owner cannot be identified.

Although this legislation marks a departure from former legislation and is an innovation in the wider region, it is constrained by the dominant legal system. The rights afforded to indigenous culture are, for example, the standard economic and moral rights associated with copyright and performance rights. The action is premised on assertions of ownership by the customary owner or owners, which implies an exclusivity and certainty that may not be characteristic of the way indigenous people relate to cultural expression (Forsyth 2012). Assumptions are also made about the value system underpinning copyright law, the purpose of which is to exclude and monopolize, whereas the value of much traditional knowledge and cultural expression is that it is part of the common heritage, transmitted from generation to generation.

57 There is also increasing emphasis on developing cultural industries and cultural tourism as a plank in economic development. See, for example, the European Union–funded initiative titled Structuring the Cultural Sector in the Pacific for Improved Human Development (Secretariat of the Pacific Community 2010).

58 For example, such needs were identified by the Pacific Islands Forum Secretariat, a regional organization that published a framework for the protection of traditional knowledge and expressions of culture (Secretariat of the Pacific Community 2002).

59 This term includes all material objects; names, stories, histories, and songs in oral narratives; dances, ceremonies, and ritual performances or practices; and the delineated forms, parts, and details of designs, visual compositions, specialized and technical knowledge and the skills required to implement that knowledge, including knowledge and skills about biological resources use and systems of classification.

It is too early to tell whether this very conscious mixing of legal approaches will be successful or what challenges the resultant hybrid will encounter when put into practice. The attempt, however, demonstrates the fluidity of mixing in response to new demands being faced by emerging legal systems, especially in developing countries, and the possibilities for new hybridities.

The Changing Environment

Although much of the formal legal framework described in this chapter remains of little relevance to people living in rural areas, whose lives continue to be governed largely by customary laws and customary practices, in a country that is faced with the many challenges of rapid social and economic change, the legal mixture is in a constant state of flux. This flux is partly due to a lack of political stability—governments are constantly changing, as are ministerial portfolios—and also because the nature of the mixture depends on who is advocating change. From time to time, for example, there is a purge of foreign legal advisers, a reaction against perceived neocolonial interference, or the emergence of a strong advocate of indigenous rights—and if that person is also a director-general of a government department or a member of the executive, laws may be drafted that strengthen the position of indigenous law or satisfy the demands of a particular lobby group. In a small jurisdiction, individuals can make a significant difference. Were a strong advocate of civil law to come forward in such a young nation, civil law—or at least elements of it—could come out of the shadows to play a more visible role in the Vanuatu legal system.[60]

Conclusion

Although the New Hebrides may have offered an ideal opportunity for a truly mixed legal system, the condominium was a dualist system with the separate parallel lines of French civil law and British common law being intersected only by joint regulations and the occasional need to act together. French and British laws were transplanted for the benefit of French and British citizens and those "nonnatives" who opted to come under one of these two systems. Under the condominium, there was clearly a mixed jurisdiction but not a mixed system. Little cross-fertilization occurred, except insofar as both systems informed joint regulations. Also, limited effort was made to assimilate the indigenous law. Nevertheless, indigenous law survived the colonial era and continued, uncodified, to govern the lives of the majority of indigenous people.

Independence in 1980 marked not only a new political beginning for the Republic of Vanuatu, but also the possible start of a new mixed legal system. The new constitution was promising: its preamble, its provisions as to language, and its provisions regarding existing laws offered equality of importance to the existing civil law and common law, and the new status of customary law suggested the emergence of a less classical mix. However, the early imposition of common law was strengthened by the adoption of further common law elements, leading to a second reception of the common law through judicial intervention, legal drafting, and legal education. The civil law imposed under the condominium remained but was not supported by any second reception and indeed was undermined by that of the common law.

Although it is probable that Vanuatu will continue to favor a predominantly common law approach to new legal developments, law is not the only characteristic of a jurisdiction. Language, culture, education, and outlook are also important. In Vanuatu, French continues to be an official language and the language of education for about 30 percent of the population. French culture—especially music, film, and art—is of contemporary relevance, and the French Embassy and the Alliance Française continue to have a presence and to support various cultural events. Palmer (2001: 31) has suggested that "a mixed jurisdiction is the legal expression of unfinished cultural aspiration," but francophonie by itself will not be enough to ensure the survival of the civil law in Vanuatu. Though many of the elements that could provide a nurturing environment

60 I argued the continuing merits of aspects of French law in Farran (2004).

for the civil law still exist,[61] more is required. In particular, experts and advocates of civil law are needed. Unfortunately, those who are closest at hand to advocate the civil law are in New Caledonia,[62] a country that has not yet escaped colonial control and whose intervention, therefore, may not be well received.[63] The Law Reform Commission, which for many years was dormant, although now revived, does not seem to have expressed any interest in engagement with the civil law and is largely supported by aid from Australia. French influence tends to be restricted to culture and language and not law reform.[64] Arguably, unless comparativists and those from other mixed jurisdictions can engage with lawyers and lawmakers in Vanuatu, the remaining opportunities to build on the civil law may just slip away.

However, a new mix may emerge. Although little has been done to formalize customary law in line with constitutional aspirations, the indigenous law of Vanuatu has held its place in the legal system. True, it has not had much effect in the field of commercial or mercantile law, but in the areas of family law, land, and even in penal law, it has remained significant, and there are examples of pragmatic mixing taking place to address particular needs.[65]

Mixing, however, is not always the best way of ensuring the resilience of laws, because it can lead to a dilution or erosion of the many elements that make up a system. This observation is particularly true of indigenous law, in which the law may be one element of a complex pattern of social, political, and economic organization. In Vanuatu, customary law is just one aspect of *kastom*,[66] much of which sits outside the state system but is not limited merely to the private sphere.[67] Frustration at the failure to formally strengthen the role of customary law may be partly attributable to the cocktail recipe being followed.[68] Trying to integrate indigenous law into Western legal models supposes that law can be sufficiently distinguished from nonlaw—that it can be made captive through codes and rules and rendered certain by judicial reasoning. The challenge is illustrated by the attempt to incorporate traditional knowledge and expressions of indigenous culture within Western intellectual property frameworks. The process is difficult, and the outcome uncertain. Invariably, the weight given to certain ingredients, the receptacle in which the mixing is to take place, and the desired outcome are all determining factors. The danger of mixing informal or unofficial law with formal state law is that the informal law loses its flexibility, becomes frozen in time, and ceases to be an organic element of the wider context in which law operates.

Challenges to the frontiers of mixedness need to consider not only what systems or jurisdictions may or may not be considered mixed but also the form of that mixing (Örücü 2010). The dominant model is that the secondary maps onto, or is accommodated by, the primary. In this process, the characteristics and identity of the secondary may become lost or changed, and the diversity accommodated in a single system is tolerated only as long as that diversity is complementary and not different. These techniques of modification are evident in Vanuatu, where customary law can apply as long as it is not in conflict with "substantial justice" or is in "conformity with law" or not contrary to "justice, morality and good order."[69]

---

61 Such elements include bilingualism, education in French, the publication of laws in both languages, and—if some effort were made—accessibility to the relevant civil law.

62 The same is true of French Polynesia.

63 Vanuatu support for fellow Melanesians seeking greater political autonomy in New Caledonia has from time to time caused political friction with France, and overtures to the University of New Caledonia and the University of the South Pacific Law School, which is based in Vanuatu, have made little progress.

64 Today, the sociocultural divide in Vanuatu is far more evident between non-French expatriates and French ones than among francophone and anglophone ni-Vanuatu. Ni-Vanuatu are moreover united by their adherence to and respect for customary law.

65 For example, in the area of land law, some customary owners of land are securing their tenure by granting family members leases over the land. In other cases, it has been argued that the trust has become a recognized form of customary land tenure. See Farran (2011a).

66 Jolly (1992: 341) has suggested that increasingly *kastom* is "a whole way of life, a culture distinctive of a local group, or a generic indigenous culture opposed to the ways of foreigners."

67 For example, the role of chiefs remains important in securing law, order, and social stability in most communities.

68 Edward (1996) suggests that a similar problem arises with respect to aboriginal law in Australia, because it is not seen as being strictly "legal" from a Western perspective.

69 Constitution of the Republic of Vanuatu section 47(1) 'The administration of justice is vested in the judiciary, who are subject only to the Constitution and the law. The function of the judiciary is to

The example of Vanuatu illustrates the potential for different forms of mixing under colonial and postcolonial influences. The historical moment for a classical mix was perhaps an opportunity lost. The present offers a tentative, ongoing mix of a new kind with potential for developing new hybrid laws and institutions, while there remains a residual potential for incorporating elements of a classical mix.

References

Aldrich, R. 1993. *France and the South Pacific since 1940*. London: Macmillan.

Bolton, L. 1998. Chief Willie Bongmatur Maldo and the role of chiefs in Vanuatu. *Journal of Pacific History*, 33(2), 179–95.

Edward, C. 1996. Australia: Accommodation multi-culturalism in law, in *Studies in Legal Systems: Mixed and Mixing*, edited by E. Örücü, E. Attwooll, and S. Coyle. The Hague: Kluwer, 53–56.

Farran, S. 2004. Family law and French law in Vanuatu: An opportunity missed? *Victoria University of Wellington Law Review*, 35(2), 367–83.

Farran, S. 2009. Palm tree justice? The role of comparative law in the South Pacific. *International and Comparative Law Quarterly*, 58(1), 181–95.

Farran, S. 2010. Law, land, development and narrative: A case-study from the South Pacific. *International Journal of Law in Context*, 6(1), 1–21.

Farran, S. 2011a. Navigating changing land use in Vanuatu. *Pacific Studies*, 33(2–3), 250–268.

Farran, S. 2011b. South Pacific intellectual property law, in *International Encyclopaedia of Laws*, edited by R. Blanpain, Supplement 51. The Hague: Kluwer, 1–96.

Forsyth, M. 2004. Beyond case law: Kastom and courts in Vanuatu. *Victoria University of Wellington Law Review*, 35(2), 427–46.

Forsyth, M. 2012. Lifting the lid on "the community": Who has the right to control access to traditional knowledge and expressions of culture? *International Journal of Cultural Property*, 19(1), 1–31.

Guiart, J. 1983. *La Terre Est le Sang des Morts: La Confrontation entre Blancs et Noirs dans le Pacifique Sud Française*. Paris: Éditions Anthropos.

Jolly, M. 1992. Custom and the way of the land: Past and present in Vanuatu and Fiji. *Oceania*, 62(4), 330–54.

Jowitt, A. 1999. Island courts in Vanuatu. *Journal of South Pacific Law* 3, Working Paper 3(3). Available at: http://www.usp.ac.fj/index.php?id=13150 [accessed: October 3, 2014].

Larcom, J. 1990. Custom by decree: Legitimation crisis in Vanuatu, in *Cultural Identity and Ethnicity in the Pacific*, edited by J. Linnekin and L. Poyer. Honolulu: University of Hawai'i Press, 175–90.

O'Connell, D.P. 1968–1969. The Condominium of the New Hebrides. *British Yearbook of International Law*, 43, 71–145.

Örücü, E. 2010. *Mixed Legal Systems at New Frontiers*. London: Wildy, Simmonds & Hill.

Palmer, V.V. 2001. *Mixed Jurisdictions Worldwide: The Third Legal Family*. Cambridge, UK: Cambridge University Press.

Paterson, D. 1995. South Pacific customary law and common law: Their interrelationship. *Commonwealth Law Bulletin*, 21(2), 660–71.

Paterson, D. 2006. Customary reconciliation in sentencing for sexual offences: A review of *Public Prosecutor v. Ben and Others* and *Public Prosecutor v. Tarilingi and Gamma*. *Journal of South Pacific Law*, 10(1), 39–47. Available at: http://www.paclii.org./journals/fJSPL/vol10/12.shtml [accessed: December 5, 2013].

Plant, C. (ed.) 1977. *New Hebrides: The Road to Independence*. Suva, Fiji: Institute of Pacific Studies, University of the South Pacific.

resolve proceedings according to law. If there is no rule of law applicable to a matter before it, a court shall determine the matter according to substantial justice and whenever possible in conformity with custom.' Read with section 95(2) 'Until otherwise provided by Parliament, the British and French laws in force or applied in Vanuatu immediately before the Day of Independence shall on and after that day continue to apply to the extent that they are not expressly revoked or incompatible with the independent status of Vanuatu and wherever possible taking due account of custom and s95(3) 'Customary law shall continue to have effect as part of the law of the Republic of Vanuatu.'

Powles, G. 1997. Common law at bay? The scope and status of customary law regimes in the Pacific. *Journal of Pacific Studies*, 21(1), 61–82.

Rousseau, B. 2008. "This Is a Court of Law, Not a Court of Morality": *Kastom* and custom in Vanuatu state courts. *Journal of South Pacific Law*, 12(2), 15–27. Available at: http://www.paclii.org/journals/fJSPL/vol12no2/pdf/rousseau.pdf [accessed: December 5, 2013].

Secretariat of the Pacific Community. 2002. Regional framework for the protection of traditional knowledge and expressions of culture. Secretariat of the Pacific Community, Pacific Islands Forum Secretariat, and United Nations Educational, Scientific and Cultural Organization Pacific Regional Office, Noumea, New Caledonia.

Secretariat of the Pacific Community. 2010. EU grants FJD $2m to SPC for cultural programmes. Press release, February 25. Available at: http://www.spc.int/en/our-work/education-training-and-human-development/human-development/news/447-eu-grants-fjd-2m-to-spc-for-culture-programmes.html [accessed: December 5, 2013].

Shineberg, D. 1967. *They Came for Sandalwood: A Study of the Sandalwood Trade in the South-West Pacific 1830–1865*. London: Cambridge University Press.

Thompson, R.C. 1980. *Australian Imperialism in the Pacific: the Expansionist Era 1820–1920*. Melbourne, Australia: Melbourne University Press.

Treadwell, P. 1976. The New Hebrides orders 1922 to 1975 and related provisions.

Vurubaravu, M. n.d. Unrecorded judgments of the Joint Court of the New Hebrides. Available at: http://www.vanuatu.usp.ac.fj/library/Paclaw/Vanuatu/Vurobaravu.pdf [accessed: December 5, 2013].

Weisbrot, D. 1989. Custom, pluralism and realism in Vanuatu: Legal development and the role of customary law. *Pacific Studies*, 13(1), 65–97.

Zorn, J.G., and Care, J.C. 2002. "Barava Tru": Judicial approaches to the pleading and proof of custom in the South Pacific. *International and Comparative Law Quarterly*, 51(3), 611–39.

Chapter 9
"I'm in the East, but My *Law* Is from the West": The East-West Dilemma in the Israeli Mixed Legal System

Nir Kedar

Israel is counted among the "classical mixed jurisdictions" that suits F.P. Walton's definition from the beginning of the twentieth century: "Mixed jurisdictions are legal systems in which the Romano-Germanic tradition has become suffused to some degree by Anglo-American law" (Walton [1907] 1980: 1, as cited in Tetley 1999; see also Walton 1899: 291; Palmer 2001: 7–10, 17ff.). Yet the civil law–common law mixture is only one element in the broader puzzle of Israel's legal identity. Put simply, what makes Israeli law "Israeli"? Even before independence, the Zionists were obsessed with the question of how to fashion the legal order and the law in the future Jewish state, and these concerns continue to bewilder Israelis. This ongoing debate on the "Israeliness" of Israeli law is marked by the tension between East and West. This East-West dilemma does not correspond directly to the Jewish-Arab conflict, nor to the Jewish internal quarrel between Ashkenazi and Sephardi (or Mizrahi) Jews.[1] Instead, it indicates the tension between the universal—Westernlike—character of Israeli law and the wish of many Israelis to express in their laws the identity and culture of the Jewish state located in the Middle East.

This chapter has two aims: the first is to analyze the current debate on the character of Israeli law, demonstrating the dominance of the East-West dilemma in Zionist and Israeli legal discourse from as early as the turn of the twentieth century to the present; the second is to demonstrate the manner in which the Zionist movement and later the State of Israel handled this delicate and complex problem until the 1980s, silencing the quarrel by avoiding as much as possible any political or legal discussion of the issue while paying symbolic tribute to the Jewish East-West dilemma.

The chapter has two parts. The first describes the East-West dilemma, its history, and three of its expressions: the Israeli attitude toward Europe (and Western law in general), the Israeli approach to the East, and the indecision concerning modern Jewish identity. The second part of the chapter analyzes the Zionist and Israeli praxis of cultural silencing and explains the importance of the symbolic presence of Jewish Eastern law within modern Israeli Western law.

The East-West Dilemma in Modern Jewish Culture and Law

The legal tension between East and West is, in fact, rooted in one of the two deepest dilemmas of modern Jewry: the shape of Jewish culture in the modern secularized world. (The other problem is, of course, that of modern anti-Semitism.) The gradual political emancipation during the past 250 years and the ongoing process of secularization forced the Jews—first in Western Europe and later in other parts of the world—to find a way to remain Jewish while abandoning traditional Judaism: both the religious faith and the traditional way of

1 *Ashkenazim* is the common nomenclature for Jews originating from Central and Eastern Europe. (*Ashkenaz* is the medieval Hebrew name of Germany.) *Sephardim* (or *Mizrahim*) is the name for Jews originating in the Mediterranean. It is sometimes used to refer to all non-Ashkenazi Jews (that is, all Jews from the Mediterranean, the Muslim world, and the rest of Asia and Africa).

Jewish life. This question has confounded modern Jewry for 250 years and is still a major source of cultural and political controversy in Israel.[2]

The legal field was one arena in which the cultural dispute took place as many Zionist lawyers strove to mold a legal system that would be both Jewish and progressive (an adjective that they used to describe a Western-oriented system). Their idea, born in the early twentieth century, was to use Jewish law as a major source of the legal system for the Jewish state-in-the-making. For that purpose, a new term was coined: *mishpat ivri* (Hebrew law). The scholars who created this expression did not intend to discuss the law of the ancient Hebrews, but rather to distinguish between the general (religious) Jewish set of commandments and the body of legal norms (themselves part of Jewish law) that seemed fitting for incorporation into the future Jewish state.

The cultural enthusiasm of the early Zionist lawyers should also be understood in light of the legal-intellectual environment of the time, when the historical and nationalist schools of legal thought were still very much à la mode. Developed by jurists such as Friedrich Karl von Savigny in early nineteenth-century Germany, the historical-cultural-nationalist perception of law spread throughout Europe in the course of the next decades and regained new impetus toward the end of the century. The 1892 new edition of Savigny's famous *Vom Beruf unserer Zeit für Gesetzgebung und Rechtswissenschaft* (originally published in 1814) was especially influential in fin-de-siècle Central and Eastern Europe (von Savigny [1814] 1892). As Assaf Likhovski (1998: 341) rightly points out, "Hebrew law was born out of an affair between German Professors and Zionist students."[3]

At an early stage, the enthusiastic Zionist lawyers found that the task of creating modern Hebrew law was not easy, because it entailed cultural and intellectual dilemmas characteristic to processes of legal borrowing.[4] First, they had to decide on their attitude toward Europe and European law. Europe was the place from which most Jews emigrated and the place to which they were affiliated by powerful historical and cultural bonds. Most Israelis saw themselves (and still do) as Europeans and believed that their culture and law should be European based, especially because they perceived European law and culture as superior to other cultures and laws. Thus, most Israelis assumed their laws would have the European shape of constitution and legal codes and the content of the law would be heavily influenced by Western legal principles and norms. Furthermore, Israelis cherished the Western ideas of democracy and the rule of law and saw them not as mere political procedures but as substantial components of their national identity. Israelis love to say that their political community is as democratic as it is Jewish. Thus, the question Israeli lawyers asked themselves was never whether to abandon Western law, replacing it with Jewish or "Israeli" law, but actually which of the two main European legal traditions Israel should embrace: the Anglo-Saxon tradition or one of the continental Romano-Germanic traditions.[5]

2 Among the many books and articles in this subject, see Friedlander, Shavit, and Sagi (2005); Herman (1979); Neher (1977); Rash (1986); Sagi (2002); and Zucker (1999).

3 On the influence of the historical school of law on Hebrew law, see also Edrei (2001: 468–71) and Radzyner (2010: 101–105).

4 On the problems of identity reflected in the work of the "Society of Hebrew Law," see Likhovski (1998: 357–72, 2006: 138–51) and Radzyner (2010).

5 Israel is unique among the classical mixed jurisdictions because it is not a civil law system that was later taken over by common law, but rather a common law jurisdiction that later embraced—and only to a certain degree—civil law. Despite the civil heritage of Ottoman law (which drew heavily on French law), local law in what was then Palestine underwent a massive process of Anglicization during the 30 years of the British Mandate. As a result, to a great extent Israel was established in 1948 as a common law country. Only in the 1960s did Israeli private law move toward the civil tradition, when the Israeli parliament (the Knesset) passed a series of statutes that were deeply influenced by German and other Romano-Germanic private laws. See Goldstein (2001); Palmer (2001: 30–31), and Wasserstein-Fassberg (2003: 155–57). Moreover, no single civil influence on Israeli laws predominates. Although German law was the main source of Israel's new civil-like private law, Israeli law drew on other civil systems, such as French (mainly through Ottoman law), Italian, and Swiss, while at the same time remaining profoundly inspired by English, American, and Canadian laws (Wasserstein-Fassberg 2003: 158). However, unlike the case of other mixed legal systems, this transformation of Israeli law, which took place during the 1960s and 1970s, was not viewed by most Israelis as a fundamental revolution with a deep cultural impact. No cultural or political debates were attached to the legislative processes. If at all, several jurists complained that the new wave of legislation still reflected the Western legal culture, thus paying no heed to the Jewish legal heritage (Kedar 2007b).

Conversely, Europe was also the continent of the Jews' lachrymal past, the place of exile, oppression, and persecution. It was the vale of tears from which they were expelled and where they were almost annihilated during the Holocaust. For these reasons, the new Israelis wanted to turn their back on Europe and create their own culture and law. In 1938, Moshe Silberg, a distinguished Israeli lawyer who would become a justice on the Israeli Supreme Court, rejected the idea of the German or even Swiss civil code as a model for the law of the future Jewish state, because "for us Jews, there is nothing more abominable than the German spirit" (Silberg 1981: 198).

Likewise, the Zionist lawyers had to resolve their rapport with the East. On the one hand, their return to the East was a return not only to the geographical Zion but also to the conceptual Zion—the ideal of creating a model society according to the lofty principles of the biblical prophets. The East was also the cradle of Western civilization. The great civilizations of Egypt and Mesopotamia, and later the great Muslim empires, possessed sophisticated legal systems and gave humanity science and technology, the monotheistic idea, and biblical morality. The East, then, was a veritable treasure house of symbols and laws. Early Zionist jurists believed that the Jewish renaissance would lead the awakening of the East. Consider for example this open letter published in 1910 by the young Samuel Eisenstadt (1910: 208, as cited in Likhovski 2006: 144), who would become a prominent figure in the Hebrew law movement:

> History calls us … [to] look to the shores of the Arab sea and the rivers of India! Great and ancient Eastern nations awake from the slumber of the ages and fight for their liberty. A commotion of revival is heard in the halls of ancient culture, in the halls of the biblical world. A new and enlightened society is being formed on the shores of Asia and in its laws and social customs, the spirit of religion is reflected in its pure Eastern form.... The East longs and yearns for the revelation of a stern and original Eastern law, which sucks and feeds from the sources of Eastern religion. To such and eastern society … we should bring our advanced law, the law of the ancient Semitic nation, the first and foremost of the enlightened nations of western Asia.

As can be seen from this paragraph, young Eisenstadt and his comrades held orientalist views that were both romantic and belittling. They admired the East but at the same time saw it as a backwater, and they conceived of Muslim and Ottoman law as nonrational, chaotic, and generally unsuited to the Jewish state-in-the-making. Eisenstadt wrote his open letter while he was still in Russia. The encounter of these young romantic jurists with the harsh reality of the Jewish-Arab conflict bolstered their suspicion toward the East and Eastern law, thereby strengthening their Western legal and cultural orientation.[6]

But the main problem of the Hebrew law movement was the complex relations between Israel and Judaism. The Zionist movement was, of course, the Jewish national movement, and as such, it emphasized Jewish cultural and collective identity. Zionism—like all national movements—was a revolutionary movement that sought to break with the past and revolutionize all aspects of Jewish public life. Thus, Zionism developed a complicated—not to say schizophrenic—attitude toward Judaism: Zionism was a national movement that wished to remind the Jews of their individual and collective identity, and at the same time, it sought to revitalize Judaism. Israel suffers from the same schizophrenia. It depicts itself (even in its laws) as a Jewish and democratic state. However, it is not clear what Jewishness means here; that is, what does it mean to be Jewish in Israel? Religious Jews claim that to be Jewish means to be a religious Jew, a Jew who believes in the tenets of Judaism and lives according to the commandments of Jewish religion (known as *halakha*). Most Jews, however, in Israel and abroad, do not see themselves as religious people though they identify themselves as Jewish. In the same manner, what Jewish law (or Hebrew law) means in today's Israel is not clear: How is it related to ancient Jewish law or to Jewish culture in general? How will it reflect both Jewish ("Eastern") and modern ("Western") values?

The problem of establishing modern Israeli law on a Jewish legal foundation has two facets: external and internal. The external aspect corresponds to the regular problems of legal borrowing and transplantation, which are similar to the problems that bewildered the Zionists with regard to Western or Eastern law: what

6 Interestingly, however, the encounter with the harsh political reality in Palestine did not weaken Eisenstadt's strong belief in human brotherhood and Jewish-Arab cooperation. See Likhovski (2006: 144–45).

should be borrowed from Jewish law, and how it should be transplanted into the modern legal fabric. The internal aspect refers to Jewish law's special characteristics that hinder the task of turning it into the living law of a modern state.

Borrowing from Jewish law is not an easy task, because Jewish law is a rich and ancient legal tradition composed of many historical and normative layers (compare Kedar 2007a). Judaism, like Islam but unlike Christianity, is an orthopraxy, a "legal religion" in the sense that it is a holistic system composed of countless norms that dictate the life of the believer from the moment he or she wakes until the moment he or she goes to sleep, from birth till death. Jewish law encompasses every aspect of private and public life. It deals with civil, commercial, and public law and even dictates what the Jewish believer may eat, drink, and wear (these are the laws of *kashrut*—the dietary laws concerning kosher food). Jews call their holistic religious legal system *halakha*.

The Torah—the first five books of the Bible—is considered by Jews to be the basic source of *halakha*. But despite the central place of the Bible in Jewish faith and law, *halakha* mainly progressed through a process of "questions and answers" (in Hebrew: *she'elot u'tshuvot*, or *shut*), a process that recalls the Roman institution of *responsa*. People would ask the rabbis for a *halakhic* solution to a particular issue, and the rabbis would base their answer on Jewish law. *Halakha*, therefore, is a set of numerous answers or decisions—a sort of Jewish common law. From time to time, *halakha* was codified. Some of these codes are very old. In addition to the Bible itself, the Mishna and Talmud should be mentioned. The Mishna was the first compilation of Jewish oral *halakha*, codified in the early third century A.D. in Palestine by Rabbi Yehuda Hanassi. The Talmud, which was codified around the fifth century A.D. in Palestine and then recodified in the sixth century in Persia, contained the Mishna and rabbinic commentaries on the Mishna that had been gathered in the centuries following its codification (these commentaries are known as the Gemara). Additional rabbinic codes were codified later, during the Middle Ages and in modern times. The most famous and important of them are perhaps Maimonides's Mishne Tora (completed in 1180) and the Shulkhan Arukh by Rabbi Yossef Karo (published in 1565). The codes (and especially the Talmud) are heavily cited by the rabbis and considered the primary sources of *halakha*, but over the centuries Jewish law clearly progressed mostly through *responsa*—the answers and decisions of the rabbis. Borrowing from Jewish law thus is a complicated process requiring many decisions.

Zionist jurists bickered raucously among themselves over questions such as the following: Which of the legal sources of Jewish law should they apply? Should they prefer the codes or the *responsa*? Is there a preferable line of *responsa*: one of the Ashkenazi legal traditions or a Sephardi one? Should they prefer the Mishna and Talmud that were compiled in Palestine, or would it be better to adopt modern sources? Should they transplant specific Jewish legal norms or institutions, borrow general "Jewish" legal principles, or perhaps embrace the Jewish legal philosophy and way of reasoning while fashioning their own modern laws by themselves? How free were they to change and update the traditional sources? (Likhovski 1998: 357–61, 368–70; Radzyner 2010: 100–110, 124–32).

Jewish law imposed yet another set of problems on the modern Zionist jurists: a set of internal problems that derive from Jewish law's specific character and philosophy. I briefly sketch three of these problems: the scope of Jewish *halakha* and its special form, *halakha* as a holistic religious system, and the authority of the legislators and judges.

The first internal problem that hampers the incorporation of Jewish law into modern state law lies in *halakha* itself or, to be more exact, in the scope and form of *halakha*, which make transforming *halakha* into a modern legal system very difficult. The *halakha* is indeed a holistic system, but in fact the use of Jewish law in many vital areas of living is impossible simply because no reference to them occurs in *halakha* and no central *halakhic* institution can fill this void with legislation. (*Halakha* is silent, for example, on constitutional and administrative law as well as in many modern commercial areas of law.) In addition to *halakha*'s limited scope (by today's standards), its unique form, which is incompatible with the modern state, must be taken into consideration. *Halakha* developed as a decentralized and pluralistic system of *responsa* administered (if this word can be applied to the diffuse evolution of *halakha*) by generations of rabbis. The *responsa* are characterized by frequent disagreements among the rabbis and by *halakhic* questions that remain unresolved. Although the creation of a centralist legislative body of *halakha* is theoretically possible, such a development is very unlikely because it would be a major break from the Jewish legal pluralistic and decentralized tradition.

Hence, codification is almost impossible because we do not know which norm to choose in the numerous cases of contradictory norms or unresolved questions.

The second internal problem that hinders the incorporation of Jewish law into modern state law is the nature of *halakha* as a religious holistic system. This problem can be stated in the following manner: Can *halakha* be applied optionally? If so, which parts of *halakha* should be used? Nonobservant Jews who cherish their rich Jewish heritage will be pleased to incorporate parts of Jewish law into the laws of their modern states, but they will also insist on using only those parts that are appropriate to modern life. They will agree to graft certain rules, principles, or institutions onto modern secular laws, while rejecting other parts of *halakha* that they deem unsuitable for a modern, secular society. From the religious point of view, in contrast, *halakha* cannot be incorporated into any other legal or normative system because it is a unified, eternal, divine system that has precedence over any earthly social legislation. The validity of a *halakhic* norm stems from its being, ipso facto, part of *halakha* and not from the activity of a secular legislator or the decision of a temporal judge. At most, the integration of other norms or institutions into *halakha* may be possible—under certain conditions—but not the other way around. Likewise, from the religious point of view, *halakha* cannot be integrated into a nonreligious system because such an inclusion would profane its holy essence. The very essence of *halakha* as a holistic unified religious system makes its incorporation into modern state law nearly impossible.

The third and most difficult intra-Jewish problem that hampers the integration of Jewish law into modern state law is the problem of authority; that is, who has the authority to legislate or interpret the law? According to Jewish law, only ordained rabbis can decree *halakha*, because according to Jewish belief they are part of a continuous chain that began with Moses, who received the Torah from God. If the law is not enshrined by the rabbis, then it is not part of Jewish law, even if it is based on *halakhic* material. If the state legislates norms that originate in *halakha*, religious believers will obey this law, but only because it is the law of the state and not because they accept it as Jewish law. Naturally, nonreligious Jews or people of other faiths do not accept this religious concept of authority, which is incompatible with modern ideas of democracy and the rule of law. They want their laws to be legislated by a democratic secular parliament and interpreted by independent judges, not by rabbis. These problems hinder the incorporation of Jewish law into modern Israeli law, making the East-West Jewish problem an unresolved living dilemma.

The Place of Jewish Law and Judaism in Contemporary Israeli Law

The term *Hebrew law* was devised by a group of Russian Zionists in Moscow who established the Society of Hebrew Law (*khevrat hamishpat ha'ivri*) in late 1917.[7] Most of the group's members were nonreligious Jews, but all of them—religious and nonreligious alike—believed that the national and cultural renaissance of the Jewish people must be accompanied by a legal resurgence as well and that the growing Zionist community should use its own rich legal heritage as the basis of its laws rather than derive its inspiration solely from modern Western law—"the law of Gentiles." The group invented the term *Hebrew law* to emphasize that it had no desire to force the Jewish religious legal system on the new legal system but rather wanted to take legal norms that had developed in *halakha* and that were judged suitable for modern society and to use them for the law of the future Jewish state. Their idea was to revive legal norms from Jewish *halakha* and to complement or amend them with norms taken from modern nonreligious legal systems so that the new law would satisfy the needs of modern life.

The disagreements among Jews with regard to questions of identity resulted in the foundation of two more societies for Hebrew law: one in Jerusalem and another in London. The anarchy that followed the Bolshevik Revolution forced the Russian Society of Hebrew Law to cease its activity in Moscow. Its members moved to Kiev and then to Odessa, but the society could not operate as well in those cities, and its members decided to recommence their project in Palestine. The majority of them indeed emigrated in the early 1920s. But before most of them arrived in the Holy Land, another company was registered in Jerusalem under the title "A Legal Society for Hebrew Law." Although the Russian society was probably the inspiration

7 On the term *Hebrew law*, see Likhovski (1998: 348–50) and Radzyner (2010: 99–100).

for the Palestinian one, the two companies had rather different characters: the Jerusalem society, like the London branch that was established in 1925,[8] was more conservative and held a more religious conception of Hebrew law than did the Moscow society. When the Muscovites arrived in Palestine, they formally joined the Jerusalem society, but the tensions between the two groups were evident, and many initiatives were carried out independently by former member of the Moscow society despite the Jerusalem society's formal opposition. Thus, for example, members of the society published not one but two different legal journals: the first (edited by Samuel Eisenstadt) represented the progressive secular "Russian line," whereas the second expressed the more conservative and religious "Palestinian line." The Muscovites even organized a world conference on Hebrew law in 1934 and founded the Tel Aviv College for Law and Economics in the same year, two initiatives that were strongly rejected by the Jerusalem society.[9] In addition, the society organized frequent public lectures; financed several independent studies; created bibliographies of Jewish legal sources; translated Roman legal sources, such as Gaius's *Institutions*, into Hebrew; and drew up general plans for the incorporation of Jewish law into the future state. Last but not least, members of the society served as judges or consultants in the Hebrew Peace Courts, an autonomous nonreligious system of Jewish courts of arbitration established in 1909.

Despite the efforts of the Hebrew Law Society, the majority of the Jewish population in Palestine and abroad had little interest in the work of the society's branches. In Palestine, most Jews used British Mandatory law and the Mandatory court system and paid little attention to the issue of Jewish legal autonomy or revival and to the incorporation of Jewish law (be it *halakha* or Hebrew law) into the modern law of the Zionist community. With the lack of active (and paying) members, the society became insolvent in 1938 and closed down its formal activities (Radzyner 2010: 163).

Until 1948, the tension between Jewish law and secular state law was hardly felt because an independent Jewish state did not exist and because the law in Palestine was Ottoman and later British. But as the establishment of the State of Israel approached—and especially after independence—the question of Jewish law and its incorporation into Israeli law burgeoned into a source of legal, political, and cultural controversy.

Once establishing the Jewish independent state in parts of Palestine became a matter of time, Jewish lawyers began to draft laws—many of which were based on *halakha*—for the future state. Between 1938 and 1948 (and especially after 1945), religious and nonreligious lawyers drafted more than ten codes based on Jewish *halakha*. These codes dealt with all aspects of the law—from private law to penal law to constitutional law (Radzyner 2005b: 315n196). Despite the long debates in the months prior to Israel's establishment, the political and legal elite decided that Israel would retain British Mandatory law (Kedar 2007c). Although the decision was intended chiefly to stave off chaos and anarchy in the fledging state, the question of Jewish law and its integration into Israeli law was also one of the factors that influenced the decision to keep British Mandatory law and not embark on the task of legislating a novel, original Israeli law.

As a consequence of this decision, Jewish law plays practically no role in Israeli law today. The law of the State of Israel is completely Westernized (although Israel never translated or copied the laws of another country en bloc as did Turkey, China, and Japan, for example). Israel always drafted its own original laws according to its needs and social purposes, but its inspiration came from Western laws and not Jewish law. Only one enclave of religious law took root in Israeli law: family law, which in the period of Ottoman rule over Palestine was considered part of religious law and not civil law. Ottoman law stated that all matters of family law would be decided according to the religious law of the faith to which a citizen belonged.[10] According to the Ottoman system (called *millet*), Shari'a courts had exclusive jurisdiction over family matters among Muslims, rabbinic courts had parallel jurisdiction over Jews, and the courts of the various Christian churches had a similar domain over their members. When the British conquered Palestine in 1917, they preserved this arrangement. The Israelis did the same in 1948, although Israeli law narrowed the authority of the religious courts to the area of marriage and divorce. All other issues of family law come under the jurisdiction of civil family courts unless the parties wish otherwise.

8 On the London society, see Radzyner (2009).

9 On the Society of Hebrew Law, see Likhovsky (1998), Radzyner (2010), and Shamir (2000: 30–48).

10 In legal terms, we would say that the Ottoman state received by reference the religious law of family. On the reception of religious law by reference, see Englard (1975: 56–77).

Family law notwithstanding, Jewish law as such was omitted from Israeli law. Not a single Israeli law is based in its entirety on Jewish law. Indeed, the Israeli Ministry of Justice has a special department for Jewish law that is supposed to suggest ways of incorporating Jewish law into modern Israeli legislation and to add the perspective of Jewish law to all legislative debates. Although a few academics—Menachem Elon is the most prominent among them—claim that Jewish law has a profound influence on Israeli legislation and jurisprudence (Elon 1994, Elon et al. 1999: 420–22), most Israeli lawyers (both religious and nonreligious) agree that this influence is minimal and that Jewish law is used mostly on the rhetorical level and much less so on the practical level.[11] Even laws that are compatible with principles or norms in Jewish law and that seem to be based on Jewish law are not really so. Israel's laws are generally drafted according to modern Western legal, political, and economic principles, and only in retrospect, after the bill is completely formed, does the Ministry of Justice's Department for Hebrew Law add the "Jewish perspective"—as a kind of symbolic embellishment—to the bill's statement of purpose.

In fact, Israel not only refrained from incorporating Jewish law into its laws, but also made every effort to avoid futile disputes, fancy declarations, and strict formal decisions on matters of culture, religion, and identity in general. Under David Ben-Gurion and Herman Cohn, Israel's attorney general in the 1950s and Ben-Gurion's confidant, a "silencing policy" on religious and cultural issues turned, in practice, into the unofficial position of the Israeli legal system. It was expressed in the sweeping support of the judicial elite in legislating a piecemeal constitution, actually basic laws, instead of a comprehensive formal constitution. This approach was taken in the hope of preventing the rise of ideological and cultural disputes, during the process of formulating and enacting a constitution, over the issue of the state's Jewish character and the Jewishness of its laws (Kedar, forthcoming). The silencing policy was also expressed in the avoidance of any legislation that necessitated a positive clarification of the Israeli Jewish identity and in the almost total avoidance by judges and legal scholars of such discussions, whether in their verdicts or in academic legal publications.[12] Until the 1980s, the Israeli legislature strove to avoid the treatment of religious and cultural issues such as "what is Judaism" and "who is a Jew" and even to avoid inclusion in the laws explicit expressions such as "a Jewish state" or "Jewish heritage."

Some scholars claim that the reason for exclusion of Jewish law—and even of Jewish culture—is historical contingency. In the first years of statehood, there was simply no time to legislate; Israeli lawyers, who were mostly nonreligious, stuck to what they knew best—modern Western law (Harris 2002; Radzyner 2005a: 86–87). This explanation has a lot of truth to it. As noted, the major concern of Israel's emerging political and legal elites was to prevent chaos and anarchy. For this reason, they preserved the law that had been in effect during the British Mandate. The new state's legislators feared that the creation of a novel and original legal system would be too lengthy a process. As mentioned earlier, it is also true that most Israeli lawyers—in the 1950s as today—are nonreligious and have no expertise in Jewish law. As ardent modernists, some of them even conceive of Jewish law as an obsolete system belonging to the distant past and certainly as inappropriate for a modern enlightened state (Radzyner and Friedman 2005). These lawyers are obviously incapable of navigating in the "sea of Talmud" to apply its treasures to the benefit of Israeli law and society.

Yet what looks like sheer expediency and ignorance was really a deliberate position rooted in the Zionist movement's stubborn preference for the creation of a Jewish political-legal framework over the cultural discussion of the Jewish people's nature and identity. Zionism was born in the second half of the nineteenth century out of the belief that without statehood, which would provide Jews with some degree of self-determination, no Jewish culture could flourish over time. Reality in Europe showed that even in places where Jews achieved emancipation and equality, the fruitful existence of Jewish culture and its resistance against the dangers of depletion and assimilation could not be ensured in the long term. Much less could the future of Jewish existence, both physical and cultural, be ensured in places where Jews have been persecuted. The Zionist solution, therefore, was based on the effort to establish an independent state, or at least sovereignty of a lesser degree, under which Jewish modern culture would be able to endure freely over many generations. To this end, from its inception, Zionism focused all its energies and resources on creating statehood for Jews and building a society on that statehood. All factions of the Zionist movement were united against the calls of

11 For a critique of Elon, see Englard (1976).

12 Silencing is a known constitutional tactic. See Holmes (1998) and Sapir (2010: 223–43).

what was known as *spiritual Zionism* to base the Zionist revolution on an internal Jewish cultural debate and on the creation of a modern Jewish culture.

Spiritual Zionism, headed by Ahad Ha'am,[13] evolved at the end of the nineteenth century, seeking to initiate the Zionist revolution from inside—that is, from the shaping of a modern Jewish culture that would preserve the ancient spiritual characteristics of Judaism but adapt them to the modern world, primarily by their secularization (see, for example, Ahad Ha'am [1889] 1946). This position, which attracted many intellectuals and continues to do so to this day, had already been rejected in its entirety by the Zionist majority at the end of the nineteenth century. All Zionist parties—including even the religious Hamizrahi movement[14]—bitterly opposed cultural-spiritual Zionism, and it remained marginal after the establishment of Israel. The Zionist movement regarded spiritual Zionism as hopeless and even dangerous. It was hopeless because cultural shaping alone could not rescue Judaism from its predicament—and certainly not the Jews from theirs. The majority of Zionists believed that there was no future to Jewish culture without the framework of a sovereign state that would allow it to flourish and without an aware and educated civil society that would support and strengthen the national framework. What was the point of debating endlessly the questions of Jewish culture when no institutional, social, and political guarantee would ensure its existence?

Furthermore, Zionist orthodoxy always regarded cultural approaches such as Ahad Ha'am's as dangerous to Zionism. According to most Zionists, the cultural lure of those positions—the belief that it was possible to preserve everything that is good and beautiful in Judaism and to shape a new, modern, and enlightened Judaism to bestow upon the Jewish masses—concealed the fact that this course was a hazardous one with an unclear route and destination. It was not clear what Jewish culture was, what should be preserved and what should be discarded, or what the objective of this cultural contemplation was. Zionist leaders knew that cultural Zionism would draw away precious resources of the Jewish people, lead to culture war, and even threaten the unity of the Zionist movement and its ability to carry out the monumental tasks before it. Therefore, in the course of Zionist history, the potentially dangerous cultural debate was always rejected in favor of the effort to establish an independent state and civil society. The dominant Zionist position was that the culture of the Jewish state would be Jewish by definition, because most of its citizens would be Jewish and because the national framework would express the culture of the Jewish majority and support it.

Thus, the rejection of Hebrew law was in fact the legal expression of Israel's silencing policy, endeavoring to suppress harsh cultural and political disputes. The Zionist, and later the Israeli, elite preferred to adopt English law rather than take the treacherous path of carving out an original "Hebrew" type of law that would express—perhaps—their Jewish culture and identity but was more likely to ignite a *Kulturkampf* and even arouse political unrest.

One should note that the semiformal silencing policy corresponded to the common Jewish modern way of life. Most modern Jews—in Israel and abroad—have "solved" the East-West problem by simply avoiding it. They are secular Jews who consider themselves Jewish. They speak Hebrew, celebrate Jewish holidays, honor Jewish rituals, and revere Jewish symbols, yet they do so without being committed to the Jewish faith or to the principles of *halakha*. Most secular Jews act the way they do without giving much thought to the exact definition of their identity or Jewishness as bridging the East and the West (Katz and Kedar 2012).

Still, Jewish law does have an important cultural function in Israeli law. Although it plays practically no role in Israeli law, Jewish law is retained primarily as a symbol. The will of Israeli society to keep Jewish law as a symbol explains why the Israeli taxpayer is prepared to finance a special department for Jewish law in the Ministry of Justice, even though its influence on the final legislation is basically insignificant. Likewise, the desire to preserve Jewish law as a symbol also explains the tradition of a Hebrew law chair on the Supreme Court. Since Israel's establishment, one of the Supreme Court's justices is an expert in Hebrew law, whose role is to explicate Jewish law's view of the issue before the court. The desire to preserve Jewish law also explains its remarkable presence in the curricula of Israeli law schools: all Israeli law students must take at least one course in Hebrew law. And finally, the significance of Jewish law as an important part of

13 Ahad Ha'am was the pen name of Asher Zvi Hirsch Ginsberg (August 18, 1856–January 2, 1927), a leading prestate Zionist thinker, known as the founder of cultural ("spiritual") Zionism. Ahad Ha'am's secular vision of a Jewish spiritual center in Palestine contrasted with Theodor Herzl's political Zionism.

14 See Don-Yehiyeh (1983), discussing Rabbi Reines and religious Zionism's opposition to Ahad Ha'am.

Israeli culture explains why Israel has bequeathed names taken from Jewish law to many of its laws and legal institutions. For example, the proposed Israeli civil code is not called simply the civil code (*hakodex ha'ezrakhi*) even though the word *codex* is used in Hebrew; instead, it is called *khok diney mamonot—diney mamonot* being the *halakhic* expression for private law. Likewise, the law of rehabilitation and the law of unlawful enrichment also use in their titles expressions from ancient Hebrew, although Hebrew speakers do not use—or often even understand—these archaic idioms today.

Although Jewish law played no role in the creation of the new Israeli civil code, it is still symbolically present in its title. Jewish law was put in symbolic quarantine out of a premeditated silencing policy that endeavored to avoid cultural and political clashes among the different groups within Israeli immigrant society. But thanks to that policy, the East and the West manage to live in relative harmony on the verge of the Israeli volcano.

Conclusions

Since its establishment in 1948, Israel has been engaged in an ongoing debate over its identity, over the ways to create an Israeli Jewish East-West mélange. The legal field did not escape these dilemmas. Israelis were bothered by questions, such as which of the European legal tradition to embrace and to what degree, how to regard Muslim law and other Eastern legal traditions, and to what extent Jewish law should be incorporated into the laws of the nascent state. Familiar with these debates, Israelis are also well aware of their potential harm; academic cultural debates in a classroom, a coffee shop, or an intellectual salon can rapidly deteriorate into a bitter culture war or even into a violent clash. Contrary to the intellectuals' instinct, Israeli society makes every effort to prevent its identity problems from penetrating the political and legal arenas.

In the legal domain, the silencing policy was expressed in the legislation as a "constitution without a preamble" (that is, a series of basic laws instead of a comprehensive formal constitution); in the avoidance of any legislation that necessitated a positive clarification of the Israeli Jewish identity; and in the almost total avoidance by judges and legal scholars of such discussions. Because the "Hebrew Law Project," was potentially harmful, it was practically abandoned as well (although "formal" Israel and the Israeli intelligentsia constantly express their obligation to its execution). Israelis did not solve the (unsolvable) East-West dilemma in their formal laws and constitution, but their everyday life bridges that gap.

References

Ahad Ha'am, [1889] 1946. This is not the path [in Hebrew], in *The Complete Writings of Ahad Ha-Am* [in Hebrew]. Tel Aviv: Dvir, 11–14.

Don-Yehiyeh, E. 1983. Ideology and politics in religious Zionism: The Zionist theory of Rabbi Reines and the politics of the Mizrahi Party under his leadership [in Hebrew]. *Hatzionut*, 8, 103–46.

Edrei, A. 2001. Why teach Jewish law? [in Hebrew]. *Tel Aviv University Law Review*, 25, 467–87.

Eisenstadt, S. 1910. On the history of Hebrew law [in Hebrew], in *The Future: A Literary Collection of Essays on Jews and Judaism* [in Hebrew]. Berlin: Sinai, 194–208.

Elon, M. 1994. *Jewish Law: History, Sources, Principles—Ha-Mishpat Ha-Ivri*. Vol. 4. Philadelphia: Jewish Publication Society.

Elon, M., Auerbach, B., Chazin, D.D., and Sykes, M.J. 1999. *Jewish Law (Mishpat Ivri): Cases and Materials*. New York: Bender.

Englard, I. 1975. *Religious Law in the Israel Legal System*. Jerusalem: Hebrew University Press.

Englard, I. 1976. Research in Jewish law: Its nature and function [in Hebrew]. *Mishpatim*, 7, 34–65.

Friedlander, Y., Shavit, U., and Sagi, A. 2005. *The Old Shall Be Renewed and the New Sanctified: Essays on Judaism, Identity, and Culture* [in Hebrew]. Tel Aviv: Hakibbutz Hameuchad.

Goldstein, S. 2001. Israel, in *Mixed Jurisdictions Worldwide: The Third Legal Family*, edited by V.V. Palmer. Cambridge, UK: Cambridge University Press, 448–68.

Harris, R. 2002. Absent-minded misses and historical opportunities: Jewish law, Israeli law, and the establishment of the state of Israel [in Hebrew], in *On Both Sides of the Bridge: Religion and State in the Early Years of Israel* [in Hebrew], edited by M. Bar-On and Z. Zameret. Jerusalem: Yad Ben-Zvi, 21–54.
Herman, S. 1979. *Jewish Identity: A Social Psychological Perspective* [in Hebrew]. Jerusalem: Hassifriya Haziyonit.
Holmes, S. 1998. Gag rules and the politics of omission, in *Constitutionalism and Democracy*, edited by J. Elster and R. Slagstad. Cambridge, UK: Cambridge University Press, 19–58.
Katz, G., and Kedar, N. 2012. Judaism from the perspective of secular Israeli intellectuals. *Democratic Culture*, 14, 93–152.
Kedar, N. 2007a. Israeli law as a *lieu de mémoire* (*et d'oubli*): Remembering and forgetting Jewish law in modern Israel, in *Erinnern und Vergessen: Remember and Forget*, edited by O. Brupbacher, N. Grotkamp, J. Osterkamp, and T. Roeder. Munich: Meidenbauer Verlag, 196–229.
Kedar, N. 2007b. Law, culture and civil codification in a mixed legal system. *Canadian Journal of Law and Society*, 22(2), 177–95.
Kedar, N. 2007c. New perspectives on the foundation of the Israeli legal system [in Hebrew]. *Israel*, 11, 1–29.
Kedar, N. Forthcoming. *Ben-Gurion and the Constitution*. Ramat Gan, Israel: Bar-Ilan University Press.
Likhovski, A. 1998. The invention of "Hebrew law" in Mandatory Palestine. *American Journal of Comparative Law*, 46(1), 339–73.
Likhovski, A. 2006. *Law and Identity in Mandate Palestine*. Chapel Hill: University of North Carolina University Press.
Neher, A. 1977. *Clef pour le Judaisme*. Paris: Seghers.
Palmer, V.V. 2001. *Mixed Jurisdictions Worldwide: The Third Legal Family*. Cambridge, UK: Cambridge University Press.
Radzyner, A. 2005a. The "Hebrew law" is not *halakhah* (nevertheless it has value). *Akdamot*, 16, 139–67.
Radzyner, A. 2005b. "A scholar who was not properly eulogized": J.S. Zuri and his Jewish law studies on the background of Jewish law research history [in Hebrew]. *Shenaton Hamishpat Ha'ivri*, 23, 253–349.
Radzyner, A. 2009. Jewish law in London: Between two societies." *Jewish Law Annual* 18, 8–12.
Radzyner, A. 2010. "Jewish law" between "national" and "religious": The dilemma of the religious-national movement [in Hebrew]. *Bar-Ilan Law Studies*, 26(1), 91–178.
Radzyner, A., and Friedman, S. 2005. The Israeli legislator and Jewish law: Haim Cohn between tomorrow and yesterday [in Hebrew]. *Tel-Aviv University Law Review*, 29, 167–244.
Rash, Y. (ed.). 1986. Regard and Revere: Renew without Fear—The Secular Jew and His Heritage [in Hebrew]. Tel-Aviv: Hakibbutz Ha'artzi.
Sagi, A. 2002. A Critique of Jewish Identity Discourse [in Hebrew]. Ramat Gan, Israel: Bar-Ilan University.
Sapir, G. 2010. Constitutional Revolution in Israel: Past, Present, and Future [in Hebrew]. Tel Aviv: Miskal.
Shamir, R. 2000. The Colonies of Law: Colonialism, Zionism, and Law in Early Mandate Palestine. Cambridge, UK: Cambridge University Press.
Silberg, M. 1981. The law in the Hebrew state [in Hebrew], in *In Inner Harmony: Essays and Articles* [in Hebrew], edited by Z. Tarlo and M. Hovav. Jerusalem: Magnes, 180–201.
Tetley, W. 1999. Mixed jurisdictions: Common law vs. civil law (codified and uncodified), part I. *Uniform Law Review*, 4(3), 591–619.
von Savigny, F.K. [1814] 1892. *Vom Beruf unserer Zeit für Gesetzgebung und Rechtswissenschaft*. Freiburg, Germany: i.B. Mohr.
Walton, F.P. 1899. The civil law and the common law in Canada. *Juridical Review*, 11, 282–301.
Walton, F.P. [1907] 1980. *The Scope and Interpretation of the Civil Code*. Toronto: Butterworths.
Wasserstein-Fassberg, C. 2003. Language and style in a mixed system. *Tulane Law* Review, 78(1–2), 151–74.
Zucker, D. 1999. *We the Secular Jews: What Is a Secular Jewish Identity?* [in Hebrew]. Tel Aviv: Yedioth Ahronoth.

Chapter 10
Patterns of Legal Mixing in Eritrea: Examining the Impact of Customary Law, Islamic Law, Colonial Law, Socialist Law, and Authoritarian Revolutionary Dogma

Daniel R. Mekonnen

With a history of only 21 years since independence, Eritrea is the second-youngest country in Africa, the youngest country being the newly independent state of South Sudan. The Eritrean legal system derives its influence from more than two legal traditions or legal families. Thus, building on the definition of William Tetley (2003), one can describe Eritrea as a typical example of a country with characteristics of a mixed jurisdiction. In this context, a *mixed jurisdiction* is defined as "a political unit (a country or its political subdivisions) in which a mixed legal system prevails." (Tetley 2003: 181). A *mixed legal system* "is one in which its force is derived from more than one legal tradition or family." (Tetley 2003: 183). And the term *legal system* "refers to the nature and content of the law generally, as well as the structures and methods whereby the law is legislated upon, adjudicated upon, and administered, within a jurisdiction" (Tetley 2003: 181).[1]

In what seems a definitive characterization, Mengesteab Negash (1999) describes Eritrea as a civil law country. This description does not fit well with reality. Eritrea rather portrays significant traces of legal pluralism. Negash's observation holds true only as regards the practice of ordinary Eritrean courts, whose judgments are based primarily on codified laws. These codified laws are the six major codes inherited from Ethiopia in 1991 with some amendments. However, building on Tetley's definition of civil law, it is difficult to characterize Eritrea as a typical example of civil law. According to Tetley (2003: 178), *civil law* is "a legal tradition that has its origin in Roman law, as codified in the *Corpus Juris Civilis* of Justinian (AD 528–534) and as developed subsequently in Continental Europe and around the world." It is true that some, if not all, of the six major Eritrean codes are greatly influenced by the legal traditions in continental Europe. However, *statutory law*, defined as "law found in legislation other than civil codes" (Tetley 2003: 179), is also a very common feature of the Eritrean legal system. Since its independence in 1991, the government in Eritrea has promulgated hundreds of proclamations and legal notices, which make up an unwieldy body of statutory law.[2] According to Tetley (2003: 179), statutory law is a legal characterization common to both the civil and the common law traditions, and its main purpose is "bridging the gap between the civil law and the common law in a mixed legal system."

Moreover, at the center of the Eritrean legal system are Shari'a courts and traditional or customary courts, whose judgments are based neither on modern codified laws nor on statutory law but rather on religious edicts such as Shari'a (in the case of Islamic courts) and written and unwritten indigenous laws (in the case of customary or community courts). As will be seen later in this chapter, in the preindependence era Eritrea also endured considerable influence from socialist law during the reign of the Derg regime from 1974 until 1991. *Socialist law* is defined as a legal system predominately shaped by Marxist-Leninist ideology, and its most

1 For further definitions on relevant terminologies of legal pluralism, see Tetley (2003: 178–91). On mixed jurisdictions, see also generally Palmer (2001).

2 Up to 2004, the Eritrean government issued more than 225 proclamations and legal notices meant to govern diverse societal affairs. What is called an *act* or a *statute* in other jurisdictions is called a *proclamation* in Eritrea. Legislation issued in furtherance of a proclamation is called a *legal notice* and is equivalent to what in other jurisdictions is commonly known as a *regulation* or *subordinate legislation*. See Weldehaimanot and Mekonnen (2009: 180–81).

distinguishing feature is the replacement of private property ownership by state ownership and cooperatives (see generally Quigley 1989). Some of these traits are still common in Eritrea, tracing their origins not from the Derg regime but from the history of the liberation struggle, which at some stage was also strongly influenced by Marxist-Leninist ideology. Eritrea is ruled by what I call (and later explain) *authoritarian revolutionary dogma*. Whether this dogma stands by its own right as a distinct legal system might be subject to controversy. Nonetheless, it is the prevailing politico-legal order in Eritrea. All in all, the Eritrean legal system has significant influences from civil law, socialist law, Islamic law, customary law, colonial law, and authoritarian revolutionary dogma. To a certain extent, the Eritrean legal system may also have some influence from common law. As a result, its legal system has characteristic features of a mixed jurisdiction.

The influence of several legal traditions in Eritrea is linked with at least three major factors: (a) the pluralistic nature of the Eritrean society, (b) the long and successive history of colonialism, and (c) the prevailing repressive political culture in the country. As a home to nine ethnic groups and at least three major religions (African indigenous belief, Christianity, and Islam), the Eritrean legal system heavily draws from religious law and customary law. Eritrea has been ruled in different times by ancient Abyssinian rulers, the Ottoman Turks, the Egyptians, the Italians, the British, and the Ethiopians. Its long and successive colonial history means that the country blends certain elements from each entity that has left its imprint through its colonial legacy. The combined effect is that, with varying degrees of importance, Eritrea retains characteristic features portraying the phenomenon of legal mixing. The legal system also bears tremendous effects from the legacy of the Eritrean liberation struggle, which took place between 1961 and 1991.

Six important stages in the politico-legal history of Eritrea are also essential for our understanding of Eritrea as a pertinent case study of a mixed jurisdiction. These different stages have now become a standard stratification for a serious academic discourse on legal development in Eritrea.[3] The first stage is the precolonial era. The second stage is the colonial era, particularly that of Italian colonialism, which stretched from 1890 to 1941. The third stage is the era of the British administration, which was from 1941 to 1952. The fourth stage is the period stretching from 1952 to 1962, when Eritrea was under a federal arrangement with Ethiopia. The fifth stage is the era of the annexation of Ethiopia from 1962 to 1991, which also coincides with the Eritrean armed struggle for liberation. The sixth and final stage is the postindependence era since 1991.

As previously noted, today Eritrea portrays visible elements from civil law tradition, customary law, Islamic law, and authoritarian revolutionary dogma. The effect of the civil law tradition is noticeable in ordinary Eritrean courts, whose judgments are based mainly on the six codes Eritrea inherited from Ethiopia in 1991. Islamic law applies widely in Eritrean Muslim communities with regard to major social issues such as family, marriage, and inheritance. As a result, the Eritrean legal system accommodates special Islamic courts. With a tailor-made jurisdiction based on Islamic jurisprudence, these courts address disputes arising in Muslim communities. Throughout the country's history, customary law or indigenous legal transition has also enjoyed semiofficial recognition, including in the colonial era, as long as it did not contradict statutory law. Customary law was given more prominence with the establishment in 2003 of a new system of courts, known as *community courts*, which adjudicate on matters by drawing on both customary law and statutory law. The Eritrean legal system also is strongly influenced by the history of the liberation struggle (1961–1991), which gave rise to an authoritarian revolutionary dogma. This dogma affects the protection of fundamental rights and freedoms, and the Eritrean experience has become a major cause for despondency. *Authoritarian revolutionary dogma* refers to the secretive political culture of the Eritrean government, which traces its roots to the liberation struggle ideology characterized by secrecy and excessive centralization of political power.

In different stages of its politico-legal history, Eritrea has endured a number of influences from different legal traditions. Therefore, the Eritrean legal system is one of the best examples for discrediting the ideology of legal centralism, which is defined as a claim that "law is and should be the law of the state, uniform for all persons, exclusive of all other law, and administered by a single set of state institutions" (Griffiths 1986). By examining essential elements of the Eritrean legal system and exploring the interplay of different factors that have shaped legal development in Eritrea, this chapter discusses Eritrea as a pertinent case study of a mixed jurisdiction phenomenon. The objective is to explore the challenges and opportunities of a mixed legal system

3 These stages are thoroughly discussed by, among others, Favali and Pateman (2003) and Gebremedhin (2004).

as experienced in Eritrea with a view to proposing practical recommendations for future improvements, particularly in light of the current politico-legal crisis in the country: authoritarian revolutionary dogma. I also address the extent to which other sources of law, such as Islamic law and customary law have coexisted with statutory law. In the second part, I discuss the role of customary law and its historical background and current status in Eritrea. In the third part, I discuss the legacy of the colonial era, particularly starting from Italian colonialism up to the end of foreign occupation in 1991. In the fourth part, I discuss the postindependence legal development in Eritrea, with more emphasis on the post-2001 politico-legal crisis. This crisis appears to have had the most enduring effect in everyday life of Eritreans, and I have therefore given more discussion space to this particular challenge. I conclude by summarizing the main findings and highlighting essential recommendations for improvement.

Precolonial Era: Eritrea as a Pluralistic State[4]

One of the most important points of departure relating to the theme of legal pluralism in Eritrea is Tesfatsion Medhanie's (1986: 6) characterization of Eritrea as a "poly-ethnic, poly-national state." So what type of legal system applied to the diverse populations of Eritrea? This basic question will help us to understand legal pluralism and legal development in Eritrea. Citing Alan Watson (1985: ix), Yohannes Gebremedhin (2004: 31) notes that an effort to answer the question should begin with an examination of actual historical data. Therefore, a brief discussion of the religious and ethnolinguistic composition of the Eritrean society is in order.

There are nine officially recognized ethnic groups and four officially recognized religious faiths in Eritrea (the Eritrean Orthodox Church, the Evangelical Lutheran Church, Islam, and the Roman Catholic Church). Overall the population is described as evenly divided between Christianity and Islam, except for a small minority whose beliefs are indigenous African. These beliefs also include the veneration of ancestral saints. There are also other less recognized religious groups such as the Beha'i faith. The nine officially recognized ethnic groups, from largest to smallest, are Tigrinya, Tigre, Afar, Saho, Hidarib, Bilen, Nara, Kunama, and Rashaida. Each ethnic group has its own distinct language, which comes from the name of a particular ethnic group. Its members are also called by the same designation. However, there are at least two small communities that have requested official recognition as distinct ethnic groups and whose claim has never been officially acknowledged or denied by the government. These are the two Muslim communities of Jeberti and Tekurir. The Jeberti speak Tigrinya. The Tekurir, who are believed to be recently settled descendants of the Hausa tribe in Nigeria, speak Arabic with an accent (Weldehaimanot 2009).

In the Eritrean context, every ethnic group is addressed as a *biher*, a term that is equivalent to the English term *ethnic group*. The term is usually prefixed before the name of a certain ethnic group, as in the *bihere-Afar* or the *bihere-Hidarib*. David Pool (2001: 11) writes that the most important distinction perceived by Eritreans is that between highlands and lowlands, a distinction that derives not only from climate, ecology, culture, and modes of production associated with such factors but also from religion. Accordingly, most analysts have associated peasantry and the highlands of Eritrea with Christianity and pastoralism and the lowlands of Eritrea with Islam. In reality, the population in the highlands is mostly Christian, and the population in the lowlands is mostly Islamic. The traditional legal systems prevalent in these two major geographic areas are also different, reflecting religion, ecology, and other factors.

In the precolonial era, the Eritrean society was exclusively governed by its own indigenous laws, which are based on deeply held traditional and religious values. For many years, indigenous law was not formally recognized as an official source of law in Eritrea, although it is still followed by the Eritrean society in several aspects. Gebremedhin (2004) notes that because of variations along ethnic and regional lines, uniform application of customary law is also practically impossible in Eritrea. However, through informal incorporation, customary law plays a prominent role in the modern legal system. In most of the individual localities that form modern Eritrea, particular indigenous norms and institutions of customary law govern several aspects of social life. Historical accounts indicate that written records of Eritrean customary laws are

4 This section heavily draws from Mekonnen (2009: 20–24) and Mekonnen (2010).

more than three centuries old. Citing Ludolf's (1681) *Historia Aethiopica*, Gebremedhin (2004: 32) notes that the inhabitants of the highlands of Hamasien elected their own leaders three centuries back and applied their own indigenous laws "like a small republic." He also notes that most of the customary laws of Eritrea were reduced to writing long before the arrival of the Europeans. Gebremedhin (2004: 32–33) continues:

> In the highlands of Eritrea a number of customary laws evolved dating back to the early fifteenth century. According to Ostini, the oldest customary laws are the laws of *Adkeme Mlgha'e*, the edicts of *Habsullus* and the law of *Mehem Mahaza*. Other accounts date the law of *Adkeme Mlgha'e* and other customary laws such as the law of *Loggo Chiwa* and the law of *Adghena Tegheleba* to earlier times.[5]

Muluberhan B. Hagos (2009: 6) notes that the law of *Loggo Chiwa* was established in 1492 during the reign of Emperor Eskender of Abyssinia. The Eritrean highland communities have a long written tradition associated with the Orthodox Church, which had strong ties with ancient Abyssinian rules and remains the most influential church in the highlands. As a result, several customary laws of the highlands were codified before the advent of Italian colonialism. The readily available academic literature mainly focuses on the customary laws of the highland communities, which have a relatively longer written history. In contrast, the pastoral or lowland communities do not have a long written tradition (Abbink 2005). As such, the legal literature on the customary laws of the lowland or pastoral communities is one of the subjects on which there has been a dearth of knowledge and academic writing. Therefore, my discussion focuses on the customary laws of the highlands.

The basis of law in much of rural Eritrea, which constitutes 80 percent of the total population, remains customary law. Eritrean customary laws are greatly influenced by deeply rooted communal values, such as the principles of restorative justice in settling cases of homicide. In the old days, customary laws were made or amended by a village council formed by representatives of the people, who were "elected elders from neighboring villages bound by common heritage convened … under the shade of a sycamore tree found in a secluded common area" (Gebremedhin 2004: 33). The body of representatives or village council, known as *Baito*, is analogous to a modern-day assembly or parliament, denoting the democratic process of lawmaking during the old times.

A unique feature of the Eritrean customary laws of the highland communities, as recognized by Gebremedhin, is that the laws are made up of purposefully formulated rules and standards that determine the reciprocal expectations of conduct in varied circumstances of social interaction. Because these laws are made and amended by elected tribal elders and men of wisdom, the general characterization of customary law by some writers as "any recurring mode of interaction between individuals and groups"[6] does not fit Eritrean customary laws. The laws regulate a wide range of social interaction, "including criminal offences, blood money, torts, marriage, land and public holidays (saint days)" (Gebremedhin 2004: 37). The procedural rules applicable in customary dispute resolution mechanisms were described as "interesting parallels to Roman Law, early Anglo-Saxon, Germanic and the Common Law," by an American scholar, Franklin Russell (1958: 103), who served as attorney general in Eritrea. In elucidating his assertion, Russell particularly mentions one of the earlier court cases[7] decided by the Federal High Court of Eritrea, in which some aspects of Eritrean customary laws were put to the test. The case, known as the *Goat Case*, involved the unlawful seizure and sale of some goats by officials of the government of the day and was possibly decided in the 1950s. Jon Abbink (2005: 346) also describes Eritrean customary laws as "a remarkable corpus, showing the creativity of local communities in settling their disputes and devising corrective mechanisms."

Communality is a major building block in the centuries-old social structure and indigenous dispute resolution mechanisms of the highlands (Longrigg 1945: 65; Trevaskis 1962: 15; Trimingham 1952: 166). The inhabitants of the highlands, the Tigrinya-speaking population, are mainly settled agriculturalists who

5 As examples of these other accounts, Gebremedhin cites Berhane (1969: 15) and Estifanos, Woldemariam, and Ghebremesqel (1990).

6 Gebremedhin (2004: 36) ascribes this kind of general characterization to Roberto Mangabiera Unger (1976: 49).

7 *Deputy Advocate-General v. Fitirauri Hadgu Ghilhabr*, judgment written by Justice G.N. Debbas (date unknown), as cited by Russell (1958: 103).

are organized in village communities that consist of a number of kinship units known as *endas*. The village is the principal social and political unit of the Eritrean highland rural society. From the many sociopolitical inventions of an Eritrean highland village, there are at least two prominent institutions involved in administrative and judicial functions. Local administration is customarily provided by an elected council of elders called *shimagle*.[8] Judicial matters or dispute resolution functions are administered by a *chiqa*, the equivalent of a magistrate in modern judiciaries, and the *nebaros*, a body of God-fearing village elders and wise men. Although the role of the *nebaros* is only advisory to the *chiqa*, notes Gebremedhin, it is very unusual for a *chiqa* or a judge to decide against the opinion of the *nebaros*, who are highly regarded in the community.[9] A pertinent concept from modern legal thought comparable to the *nebaros* would be a trial jury, which represents a group of sworn laypeople convened to assist a court of law on factual and legal findings.[10]

A standard Eritrean highland village has some 800 inhabitants. For example, one study indicates that in Zoba Debub, which is a densely populated administrative area in the Eritrean highlands, 85 percent of the population are agriculturalists and 13 percent are agropastoralists. This administrative area combines considerable parts of the former Akele Guzai, Hamasien, and Seraye provinces. The livelihood system in the highlands depends on rain-fed traditional agriculture combined with livestock rearing (Food and Agriculture Organization of the United Nations 2004: 4–5). As in the case of other agrarian societies, land is a very decisive natural resource in the life of the Eritrean highland community. The following observation by Siegfried Nadel (1946: 1) is illustrative in this regard:

> It has been said of the African that he does not possess his land but is possessed by it. The attitude of the Eritrean peasant towards his land cannot be more aptly described. Indeed, his preoccupation with his landed possessions shows a depth and passion not often paralleled among African races.

Land is not only a fundamental means of livelihood but is also a major indicator of the social status of individuals. One of the major land tenure systems in the Eritrean highlands is known as *risti*. Luca Castellani (2000: 2) defines *risti* as the land held by an extended family (*enda*), in which each head of a nuclear family belonging to the *enda* is entitled to a plot for his or her lifetime. This title is granted only to the original occupants of a village, who are then called *ristegnatat*. They are also known as *deqebat*, meaning original settlers, denoting at the same time a higher social status by reason of their privileged access to land, which is based on the principle of closest proximity to the forefathers. As a result, land law occupies a central place in Eritrean customary laws. At the same time, land law has been subject to considerable alteration since the Italian colonial era, which started in 1890. Indigenous Eritrean laws and traditions recognize two major types of land ownership: individual and communal. For many years, individual and communal land ownership has been the established custom in Eritrea. State ownership of land was introduced to Eritrea by the Italians. With the exception of a brief period during the Ethiopian-Eritrea Federation (1952–1962), land has always been owned by the state, including in the postindependence era. Land tenure is now one of the most controversial issues in Eritrea.

The Colonial Era

As previously noted, what is now known as Eritrea has been ruled successively by ancient Abyssinian rulers, the Ottoman Turks, the Egyptians, the Italians, the British, the Ethiopians, and finally by the Eritreans themselves. However, the modern colonial history of Eritrea, including its creation as a nation-state, starts from the end of the nineteenth century. Like most African countries, Eritrea was created through intricate processes of political and economic conquest by Western colonization. The current political map of Eritrea began to take concrete shape for the first time when Eritrea was officially declared an Italian colony at the end of the nineteenth century. In this regard, Mia Fuller (2011: 3) writes, "Having extended its military presence

---

8 *Shimagle* means elder. *Shimagles* (elders) are also called *shimagle adi*, literally meaning village elders.

9 Compare this statement with article 43 of the customary law of *Adkeme Mlgha'e* and article 95 of the customary law of *Loggo Chiwa*.

10 For the American concept of trial jury, see generally Amar (1998: 81–118).

into the highlands, in 1890 the Italian government declared Eritrea—an area with borders, as well as a name, of its invention—its *colonia primogenita* ('first-born colony')."

Without forgetting the far-reaching negative implications of this particular colonial history (see, for example, Wrong 2005), Italy is credited with laying the foundations of a modern Eritrean state, by establishing Eritrea as a single political entity or unit. Italy also introduced a legal system with a robust bureaucracy and brought about a relatively long period of political stability in the country. Therefore, modern institutions of statehood and formal judicial system were established for the first time by the Italians. In line with its legal history, Italy introduced the major pillars of civil law tradition. In this regard, Tronvoll (2009: 25) observes that "as in other colonies, a juridical distinction was made between Italian colonial officers and settlers, and the native population." Thus, the laws introduced by Italian colonial rulers did not apply uniformly to everyone. For purposes of criminal law, all inhabitants of Eritrea, Italians and Eritreans alike, were subject to the Italian Penal Code. In civil matters, however, the Italian Civil Code applied only if one of the parties was an Italian. The Italians recognized the application of Shari'a in certain matters involving Muslim litigants. Eritrean customary laws applied to disputes involving only Eritreans (Trevaskis 1962: 27). This period marked the beginning of modern litigation in Eritrea.

Italian colonialism in Eritrea lasted 50 years. In 1941, after their defeat in World War II, the Italians were replaced by the British. Eritrea was administered by the British for the next ten years pending an international decision on its future. During this time, the formal name of the occupying foreign power was the British Military Administration (BMA), and its main objective was to be a caretaker administration over an occupied enemy territory. According to Russell (1958: 99), the main important influence of the BMA was that it introduced English criminal procedure and English rules of evidence for the first time in Eritrea. The influence of the BMA on the Eritrean legal system was not that profound when compared to the Italian experience. There are two main reasons for this reduced impact. The first reason has to do with the brevity of the BMA, which lasted only 10 years, compared to the length of the Italian occupation, which lasted five decades. The second reason has to do with the obligations of the occupying force as stated by the Hague Convention of 1907. As noted by Trevaskis (1962: 24), the British "hands were tied by the terms of the Hague Convention of 1907, which denied to an authority occupying enemy territory in war time the right to change existing institutions and laws, except for reasons of military necessity, humanity, and conscience." Thus, the British did not have adequate political space and time to watermark their influence on the legacies of Italian colonialism.

The British are, however, recognized for one major contribution. The British introduced certain things that were never experienced under the Italians. These ideas included educational facilities, political participation, and economic responsibilities, which were important ingredients in forging a politically sensitized population that had not previously existed. This contribution modestly helped to sensitize Eritrean awareness and understanding of fundamental rights. In the words of Trevaskis (1962: 32; see also Ammar 1992: 8), the revolutionary effect of the brief period of BMA is explained as follows:

> A deliberate and indeed cynical, policy of keeping the Eritrean's belly full and his head empty had earned the Italians political tranquility. During the [British] occupation, the process was reversed. Eritrean heads were now filled with new ideas gleaned from lectures and books provided by the English Institute and British Information Office, the weekly Tigrinya newspaper, contact with Indians and Sudanese serving in the British forces, and the liberalism of the British administration. Influences of this kind, married to the economic distress which followed, bred discontent and then political consciousness.

The BMA came to an end in 1952, when Eritrea was federated with Ethiopia under the auspices of the United Nations (UN). The federation was unilaterally abrogated by Emperor Haile Selassie of Ethiopia in 1962, and Eritrea was annexed by Ethiopia and became the fourteenth province of the latter. Henceforth, all laws that were in force in Ethiopia became automatically applicable in Eritrea. The immediate applicability of all major Ethiopian codes in Eritrea took legal pluralism to the next level. Ethiopian law displays strong influences from French and Swiss laws. The Ethiopian Penal Code of 1957, which was drafted by a Swiss jurist, Jean Graven, is a good example. The Ethiopian Codes of Criminal Procedure and Civil Procedure, which Graven also drafted, were applicable in Eritrea as well. The 1960 Ethiopian Civil Code was drafted by a French jurist, René David. All of the above codes, together with the Ethiopian Commercial Code and Maritime Code, were also applicable in Eritrea, introducing a new blending of the French and Swiss legal systems, together with a number of other Ethiopian elements. The Selassie regime was ousted in 1974 by a military junta that came to be known as the Derg regime. The new regime reigned in Ethiopia and Eritrea until 1991.

A characteristic of the Derg regime was that ever since its ascension to political power on September 20, 1974, law was continually used as an effective instrument of repression. Exemplifying the situation, Dadimos Haile particularly discusses legislation that was promulgated between 1974 and 1978, whose only purpose was the consolidation of power and the institutionalization of state repression. The first remarkable legislative development transpired in the form of Proclamation 1/1974 (known as the *Derg Proclamation*).[11] Proclamation 1/1974 established the provisional military government, the Derg. It did so without any formal consent of the Ethiopian people. Article 7 of the law declared all existing laws of the country that did not conform to it null and void. But most important, the proclamation arbitrarily suspended fundamental rights and freedoms, such as the right to freedom of expression and assembly.[12] Another law established a military court authorized to punish individuals who contravened the provisions of the Derg Proclamation.[13] Although article 5(b) of the Derg Proclamation stated that the proclamation would be in effect only until a constitutional government could be established, the envisaged constitutional government did not materialize until the end of the Derg regime in 1991.

In addition to its repressive attributes, the legal system introduced by the Derg regime resonates in several ways with socialist law. The abuse of law as an instrument of repression during the Derg regime is explained by Yakob Haile-Mariam (1999) as a typical characteristic consistent with the Marxist view of the law and the legal process. This observation is noted in light of the formal declaration of Ethiopia by the Derg as a Marxist-Leninist society with the ultimate objective of building a communist society.[14] In keeping with the Marxist-Leninist ideology of the regime, the ultimate objective of the legal system, which was a socialist legal system, was to propagate the principal thesis of communism. This effort called for the withering of the state and law in a gradual societal process, an objective that would be attained with the triumph of communism, which is the apex of socialism (see generally Ludwikowski 1987). As a result, "Marxist interpretation of the law was the only acceptable way to apply, or more correctly 'not [to] apply,' the law" (Haile-Mariam 1999: 676). Haile-Mariam further argues that the Derg regime circumvented the legal process in favor of its narrow political ends, rendering law, "as per Lenin's dictum, 'a political instrument' or politics itself, regarded as an organ for the oppression of one class by another" (Haile-Mariam 1999: 676). In this sense, the revolution and its dogmatic principles were regarded as the highest values against which any action was to be measured. The ultimate end result was that legality became irrelevant insofar as it did not serve as a means of suppression of class elements hostile to the leaders of the revolution. This thinking gave way to one of the biggest state-sponsored campaigns of terror that Africa has ever seen in its postcolonial era. The Derg regime was defeated militarily in 1991, by which time Eritrea became a de facto independent state, thus marking the beginning of the postindependence history of Eritrea.

The Postindependence Era: The Forgotten Promises of Democratization

Eritrea was liberated in May 1991 by the Eritrean People's Liberation Front (EPLF), which changed its name in 1994 to the People's Front for Democracy and Justice (PFDJ). Soon after taking power in 1991, the EPLF established itself as a provisional government and proclaimed legislation that was meant to serve the transitional period before the nation could draft its postindependence constitution and establish a democratic government. Simultaneously, the EPLF also adopted all major codes of Ethiopia with necessary amendments as transitional Eritrean codes. These laws are still operational in Eritrea. Between 1991 and 1993, the transitional

11 As cited in Haile (2000: 12).

12 Derg Proclamation, article 8.

13 Proclamation 7/1974, titled Proclamation for the Establishment of the Special Military Tribunal (cited in Haile 2000: 17).

14 Proclamation 174/1978, as cited in Haile-Mariam (1999: 676).

government was busy preparing the nation for a national referendum that would formally determine the future Eritrea as an independent state. The referendum concluded with an overwhelming vote for independence, and Eritrea was formally recognized by the international community as an independent state in 1993.

Between 1993 and 1997, the provisional government implemented a number of major national projects that were meant, at least in theory, to transform the nation into a democratic constitutional order. From many tasks that were performed in this initial period, two can be mentioned as the most important steps. They are the establishment of a transitional constitutional framework and the drafting of the first postindependence constitution. Pending the drafting and adoption of the postindependence permanent constitution, the government laid the groundwork for a transitional constitutional framework on the basis of several proclamations and legal notices. The transitional constitutional framework, albeit underdeveloped, was based on three basic laws that were promulgated between 1992 and 1994. These laws are Proclamation 23/1992, Proclamation 37/1993, and Proclamation 52/1994. Some writers (for example, Weldehaimanot and Mekonnen 2009: 177) consider these laws as the "interim" or the "transitional" constitutional framework of Eritrea. A number of legal notices were also promulgated in support of these proclamations, and they make up part of the interim or transitional constitutional framework. The laws provided, among other things, for the establishment of a transitional government and its major structures, powers, and functions. The transitional government was meant to last only to 1997. However, the transitional government did not respect this self-imposed deadline, and ever since the country has been ruled by the same transitional government, whose access to power has never been confirmed in free and fair elections. The current government therefore rules without a clearly defined legal mandate or legitimate authority in the conventional sense of the term. In most cases, the government rules by arbitrary executive decrees and draconian military edicts, ignoring several laws or proclamations that provide for the protection of fundamental rights and freedoms. This situation has caused a deep constitutional crisis in the country.

The constitutional crisis exacerbated in the aftermath of the 1998–2000 border conflict with Ethiopia. As is now widely known, Eritrea and Ethiopia fought a devastating border conflict from May 1998 to June 2000. For the past 14 years, Eritrea has been ruled under an undeclared state of emergency, with far-reaching ramifications on fundamental rights and freedoms. One characteristic of the legal system is that Eritrea is now the only country in the world that does not have an operative and formal constitution (Medhanie 2008). The country adopted its postindependence constitution in 1997. However, the constitution has never been implemented, and its provisions have never been enforced by courts of law. The constitution and its drafting and ratification processes have now become one of the major contentious issues, at least within the main circles of exiled opposition groups (Weldehaimanot 2008).

Another problematic area is the lawmaking process of the postindependence era. On paper and in practice, the lawmaking competence of the executive and legislative branches is not clearly demarcated. Legislative powers are nebulously shared between the executive and the legislative branches, resulting in inevitable competing interests between the two. This is true, however, only for the period running from 1993 until February 2002, when Eritrea had a nominal transitional parliament (national assembly). The national assembly was convened for the last time in February 2002, and ever since it has remained in prolonged hibernation. Although it is not formally dissolved, the state president has unilaterally replaced it with an unelected "tripartite body," constituting government ministers, provincial administrators, and senior army commanders. Even during its functional existence, the parliament was used rarely and then as a rubber stamp (Gebremedhin 2004: 136). For the past 10 years, Eritrea has been ruled without a functioning parliament. Even for purposes of window dressing, the country does not have a working parliament. The lawmaking process and governance practice that ensued lack democratic characteristics and defy conventional requirements of accountability, transparency, and good governance. This situation has inexorably contributed to entrenched dictatorship, prolonging the protracted history of unjustified executive dominance in the country. As is now widely reported, with no working constitution, functioning parliament, independent judiciary, free press, bureaucratic accountability, or even an officially published national budget, Eritrea offers a bizarre example of statehood in the modern history of nation-states.[15]

15 I have stated the facts here and in the following paragraphs in a number of my previous works; however, it is difficult to discuss legal development in Eritrea without underscoring these fundamental realities.

Modern litigation characterized by the use and development of case law or precedent is virtually nonexistent in Eritrea. Cases are not well argued in courtrooms; judgments are not well reasoned or articulated. Legal development is further hindered by the complete emasculation of the Eritrean judiciary, particularly since August 2001, when the president of the highest court of the nation was arbitrarily dismissed by the state president after publicly criticizing the interference of the executive branch in judicial processes. Access to laws and official documentation is a critical challenge, because there is no publicly available depository of laws or official documents, making legal research and inquiry extremely difficult. Furthermore, with no official research permits granted to independent researchers, undertaking independent legal research in Eritrea remains difficult (Tronvoll 2009: 16). Despite the deep politico-legal crisis in Eritrea, in 2003 the Eritrean government proclaimed a new law that appeared to have given official recognition to the exigencies of legal pluralism. This law, known as Proclamation 132/2003,[16] provided for the establishment of Eritrean community courts. As a characteristic of legal pluralism, the establishment of the courts and their role in the current human rights crisis will be discussed in the next section.

Eritrean Community Courts

For some obscure reasons, the law establishing community courts does not explain the objective of the courts or why the government decided to establish the courts with particular designation as "community courts." Perhaps this lack of explanation has to do with the haphazard practice and poor record of the Eritrean government on transparency, sound lawmaking process, and good governance. Nonetheless, from the rhetoric of the government, it is not difficult to tell that one of the primary objectives of community courts is to enhance alternative or customary dispute resolution mechanisms, which are deeply rooted practices in the predominantly agrarian and pastoralist society of Eritrea. Citing the Eritrean Ministry of Justice, Senai Andemariam discusses the following as the core objectives of the community courts: (a) enabling the greater participation of the community in the judicial process and making the judicial process accessible to the larger community, particularly the poor, and (b) integrating customary dispute resolution mechanisms in the national legal system and thus alleviating the burden of ordinary courts (Andemariam 2011: 1, 14, 14n33; Elobaid and Andemariam 2007).

Community courts can also be described as pertinent examples of an informal justice system, in that they are intended to resolve disputes primarily on the basis of informal sources of laws—namely, indigenous laws and practices. However, community courts are established by formal law; hence, their description as an example of informal justice system is subject to controversy. To a certain degree, the parameters of Eritrean community courts are flexible enough to allow for inclusion of a hybrid system that combines customary, religious, and statutory norms, thus befittingly falling under the category of parajudicial systems.[17] According to David Bozzini (2007), community courts "lay in between the realms of law and norms, neither deeply founded in customary law, nor closely linked with national law and its reforms." Thus, community courts present a varying mix of customary and administrative authority, including religious norms that are among the main foundations of Eritrean indigenous laws. In effect, this mix has provided for an empirical reality of a plurality of norms and institutions involved in the functioning of the community courts. Thus, the community courts, albeit ineffective in some pertinent matters of the judicial process, are the best examples of the phenomenon of legal pluralism in Eritrea.

Generally, community courts are praised for achieving some of the objectives that prompted their establishment. For example, Andemariam (2011: 1) suggests that community courts are believed to have made, to a certain extent, the judicial process accessible to the larger community, particularly the poor. Undoubtedly, the establishment of community courts has influenced the way justice has been dispensed in postindependent Eritrea. The establishment of community courts has introduced at least two fundamental changes in the Eritrean judicial system. First, as discussed by Andemariam (2011: 5–6), the establishment of community courts abolished two lower court structures: village courts and subregional courts. Second, it

16 The full title of the law is Proclamation to Provide for the Establishment of Community Courts.

17 I borrowed the term *parajudicial* from the Danish Institute for Human Rights (2012).

reversed the effect of article 3347(1) of the Transitional Civil Code of Eritrea, which provided for the repeal of customary law in ordinary courts. Thus, the effect and use of customary law in ordinary courts—or at least in community courts—has been reinstated with the establishment of community courts. Although this change may be recognized as a landmark achievement, the efficacy of community courts in certain important areas—particularly in the promotion of human rights—remains an area that requires more research. Indeed, there is a paucity of literature and research on the role of community courts in this particular aspect.

The most recent academic literature discussing the Eritrean community courts is that of Andemariam (2011). Andemariam discusses community courts as a success story in ensuring access to justice for a large section of the population. However, a notable shortcoming of Andemariam's contribution is that it does not address the role of community courts in promoting human rights. This omission has mainly to do with the fact that the research was authored by a person who resides in Eritrea; thus, it suffers from a lack of academic freedom, which is a requisite factor for an independent and critical inquiry of the subject matter. In keeping with the intolerant political culture of the Eritrean government, Andemariam understandably had to adopt a self-conscious approach to make the contribution compliant with official state ideology, a creed that is very hostile to the concept of human rights. For instance, Andemariam does not mention the term *human rights*, effectively setting aside a very important discussion on the role of community courts, which is to promote human rights. Andemariam also does not discuss the compliance of Eritrean community courts with international standards regarding the protection of fundamental rights and freedoms. By not exploring human rights issues at structural, substantive, and procedural levels, the contribution fails to address the role played by politics and power at local and national levels regarding the functioning of community courts. However, as previously noted, given the current hostile political atmosphere in Eritrea, such limitations on academic freedom are understandable. Eritrea is a country where talking about human rights is "tantamount to treason" (Human Rights Watch 2009: 25). Tronvoll (2009: 16) explains the challenge as follows:

> It is impossible today to undertake independent critical research in Eritrea. No official research permits are granted to independent researchers, and certainly not for the study of human rights and political development. Neither are there any organisations or environments in Eritrea which undertake research or monitoring of human rights in the country. The extensive security and intelligence surveillance in the country prohibits and impedes any clandestine gathering of information on human rights violations which would severely jeopardise the life and wellbeing of any informant.

Given the current politico-legal crisis and the poor record of the government in human rights protection, the role of community courts in promoting human rights remains unreliable. In this regard, Bozzini (2007) notes that the contribution of the community courts is constrained by the government's socialist-oriented form of self-control, which manifests itself in the form of ideology, bureaucracy, and informal agents of the state. This situation has caused, according to Bozzini (2007), "a blurring of the old distinction between customary and state law." In a real sense, community courts have not made any significant contribution to the pervasive problem of human rights in Eritrea. This lack of significant contribution links the debate with the deep human rights crisis in Eritrea, which has taken a different form in the aftermath of the 1998–2000 border conflict with Ethiopia. I will discuss this link in a separate section.

The Prevailing Politico-legal Crisis in Eritrea

The root cause of the current politico-legal crisis is the protracted history of secrecy and authoritarian revolutionary dogma that took shape during the liberation struggle era. Given the exigencies of the liberation struggle and in keeping with the military strategies of a guerrilla war, secrecy and stringent military discipline were the order of the day in the political culture of the EPLF, which is the predecessor organization of the government now in power, the PFDJ. This setting has paved the way for the current authoritarian revolutionary dogma, which does not allow any form of political dissent from official state ideology. Eric Garcetti and Janet Gruber (2002: 213–14, 223) explain this dogma as a postwar policy that draws heavily on the wartime policies of the EPLF. Thus, Eritrea's current crisis is a continuation of ideologies forged over the course of three decades of armed struggle. Understandably, these policies reflect the historical perspectives of wartime experience, which is characterized by controlling every aspect of freedom fighters' lives.

The politico-legal crisis in Eritrea reached an apex in the aftermath of the 1998–2000 border conflict with Ethiopia. The border conflict was officially resolved by two international peace agreements signed by both countries in June and December 2000, respectively. However, a number of residual matters remain unresolved, and in effect the two countries are in a state of "no war, no peace," with a number of sporadic and low level armed conflicts taking place between the two governments even after the official resolution of the border conflict. As a result, since 1998, Eritrea has been ruled under an undeclared state of emergency. In this context, fundamental rights and freedoms have been completely muzzled, thereby creating a deep human rights crisis in the country. There are thousands of victims of detention without trial and of enforced disappearance in Eritrea. Most of them are victims of political and religious persecution. This claim is corroborated by a number of reputable research findings published in the last 10 years.[18] Annie O'Reilly's recent observation is particularly revealing. She confirms the existence of "a prima facie case" that the crimes committed by the Eritrean government in recent years "are sufficiently widespread and systematic to give rise to a presumption that the government is responsible for crimes against humanity" (O'Reilly 2010: 13).

In response to the alarming human rights crisis and related issues such as the conduct of general elections, the Eritrean government repeatedly cites the stalemate with Ethiopia as a "legitimate" excuse to suspend the protection of fundamental rights and indefinitely postpone the conduct of general elections. For example, in a televised interview of December 2011, the Eritrean president stated that for the past 14 years Eritrea had been in a state of war and, as such, important national issues, such as general elections, were suspended. The president stated that although no state of emergency had been officially declared, the country was in effect operating under those controls (Eri TV 2011). However, it is important to remember that despite the government's claim, the situation in Eritrea does not constitute a state of emergency as defined by the relevant provisions of Eritrean laws and international law.[19] Claiming that the issue of general elections was not a priority in Eritrea, the president also reiterated his unwillingness to entertain such questions. He said, "I don't want to involve myself in this kind of argument. We cannot afford to address everything that is been said by mentally unstable individuals. Our situation does not allow this" (Eri TV 2011). Three years before this interview, Al Jazeera asked the president when general elections would take place in Eritrea. The president retorted, "What elections? … We will see what the elections in the US will bring about, and we will wait for about three, four decades until we see genuine natural situations are ripe in Eritrea." He then added that elections might never happen in Eritrea, or it could be decades before elections could take place (Al Jazeera 2008).

Reflecting on the deep politico-legal crisis in Eritrea, Petros Ogbazghi (2011) writes that contemporary Eritrea lacks rudimentary principles of the rule of law and legitimate political institutions. It instead exemplifies personal rule as the main embodiment of the current politico-legal system. This situation is "explained by the political strategy of unleashing sheer coercive force against citizens by the military whose loyalty is bought off by providing its top echelons control over substantial state economic resources" (Ogbazghi 2011: 1). In this context, *personal rule* is defined as "a distinctive type of political system in which the rivalries and struggles of powerful and wilful men, rather than impersonal institutions, ideologies, public policies, or class interest, are fundamental in shaping political life" (Ogbazghi 2011: 3). Ogbazghi (2011: 8) exemplifies the challenge as follows:

> Besides being the President of the State of Eritrea, Isaias Afwerki is head of government, chairman of the National Parliament, Commander in Chief of the army, and Chancellor of the now-closed University of Asmara, the only university in the whole country. He convenes at will and presides

18 This literature includes, among others, Bailliet (2007); Hedru (2003); Hirt (2010); Kibreab (2009); Mekonnen (2010); Ogbazghi (2011); O'Kane and Hepner Redeker (2009); Tronvoll (2009); and Weldehaimanot (2010; 2011).

19 For more on this subject, see Mekonnen (2009).

over all meetings of the party's central council, the National Assembly, the cabinet council, and regional administrators and military council meetings.

The preceding observation has striking resonance with a number of other observations that compare Eritrea either with completely authoritarian states such as North Korea or with failed states like Somalia. Among comparisons of Eritrea with North Korea, the best observations are those of Nathaniel Meyers (2010) of *Foreign Policy*, Shashank Bengali (2009) of the *Christian Science Monitor*, François Soudan (2010) of *Jeune Afrique*, and the editors of *The Guardian* (2009).[20] In what seems to many to be an exaggerated comment, but which seems very balanced in my view, Joel Brinkley (2012), a Pulitzer Prize–winning and former foreign correspondent for the *New York Times* describes Eritrea as "the most repressive nation in the world."[21] With respect to comparisons of Eritrea with Somalia, the following paragraph from a report of UN experts that was compiled for the UN Security Council offers the best observation:

> It would be hard to conceive of two States that offer greater contrasts than Somalia and Eritrea: the former, a collapsed State for over two decades, with no functional national institutions; the latter, possessing the most highly centralized, militarized and authoritarian system of government on the African continent … the two countries present very similar challenges: in both cases, *power is concentrated in the hands of individuals rather than institutions and is exercised through largely informal and often illicit networks of political and financial control* … And both countries—in very different ways—serve as platforms for foreign armed groups that represent a grave and increasingly urgent threat to peace and security in the Horn and East Africa region (UN Security Council 2011: 11, italics added).

The crisis in Eritrea is not limited to the alarming situation of human rights violations inside the country. As suggested by the report of the UN experts, the Eritrean government has also become the leading destabilizing actor in the Horn of Africa, a region that is described by some experts as the most conflicted corner of the world since the end of World War II (Shinn 2010). The Eritrean government is famously known for arming, training, and financing a number of armed groups in the Horn of Africa, of which the most controversial group is the Al-Shabaab of Somalia, an armed group with official links to Al-Qaeda. As a result, Eritrea has been hit by two UN Security resolutions that impose, among other things, stringent sanctions on the political leadership in the country. Such is the paradox of postindependence Eritrea. As noted by Gerard Prunier (2010), a renowned French expert on the Horn of Africa, Eritrea has now become one of "the hardest and worst dictatorships anywhere" and "a hell on Earth." After paying a heavy price to achieve its independence, the country is suffering from an extreme case of authoritarian rule, which has its roots in the revolutionary dogma of the liberation struggle. Authoritarian revolutionary dogma is a major factor in the discussion of legal pluralism in Eritrea.

Concluding Remarks

Eritrea is a postwar nation. From time immemorial to the arrival of the Ottoman Turks in the sixteenth century, local and regional kings who originated from Abyssinia and its neighboring lands have reigned for several centuries in what is now known as Eritrea. After the Ottoman Turks, Eritrea was ruled by the Egyptians in the seventeenth century. The influence of these two foreign rulers on the Eritrean legal system is most noticeable in Islamic law; however, the history of Islam in Eritrea predates the arrival of the Ottoman Turks and the Egyptians. By the end of the nineteenth century, Eritrea had become an Italian colony. The modern history of Eritrea as a nation-state starts from this time. The Italians created modern-day Eritrea and introduced

20 A24Media (2009) produced a documentary titled *Eritrea: A Nation Held Hostage*, which also makes this point.

21 Brinkley laments that despite the unprecedented level of repression in the country, Eritrea still remains far from the attention of mainstream media outlets, which is very problematic.

robust state machinery and formal judicial structures. The civil law legal tradition was formally introduced to Eritrea by the Italians. After Italian colonialism, Eritrea was occupied by the British for a brief period, but the influence of English law in Eritrea is insignificant. Finally, Eritrea was ruled by successive Ethiopian governments until it gained de facto independence in 1991 and de jure independence in 1993.

During these different stages of its politico-legal history, Eritrea has experienced influences from different legal traditions that have left their imprint on the country to this day. The most enduring legal system seems to consist of the customary laws of the Eritrean society, including Islamic law, and these laws are still widely applicable in many local disputes. The Eritrean government tried to revive this old-age legacy of indigenous legal traditional by formally establishing community courts. However, as has been seen before, the process has been fraught by shortcomings, and the contribution of these courts, particularly to human rights protection, remains insignificant. The prevailing authoritarian rule of the PFDJ, the sole political party in the country, also seems to have an enduring effect. As the prevailing politico-legal setting, the current authoritarian rule has far-reaching implications on what will transpire in Eritrea in the future.

One major cause for the politico-legal crisis in Eritrea is the hegemonic-monolithic political culture of the Eritrean government, which traces its roots to the early years of its formation as a liberation movement. Tanja Müller (2005: 219–20) explains the political culture as one that does not envisage the opting out of individuals from the revolution's narrative of progress. Tekle Weldemikael (2009: 15) takes the explanation further when he laments that this type of perverted political culture has finally led to the fetishism of the nation (including the ruling party and its senior leaders) at the expense of all types of individual freedoms. Tricia Hepner Redeker and David O'Kane (2009) also observe that the legacies of the armed struggle have continued to haunt the Eritrean society, by inculcating one of the most repressive systems of governance Eritreans have ever had in their history. Building on the concept of biopolitics, Hepner Redeker and O'Kane (2009: ix–x) characterize the postindependence politico-economic and human rights crisis in Eritrea as an outcome of a violent penetration of state power into the most intimate spaces of human life and consciousness in the name of development, national security, and sovereignty, the end result being excessive perversions of governance and power.[22] According to Bozzini (2011: 104, 110), society imagines the Eritrean state as authoritarian, unaccountable, volatile, and violent, and the political leadership as all powerful and capricious—ready to do whatever it can, at the cost of individual basic freedom, in its uncompromising effort to hold state power intact. The political leadership continues in power despite its large delegitimization and widespread popular disapproval of its policies.[23] Understandably, Eritrea is in dire need of a political transition, whether in the form of revolution or negotiation, that facilitates the establishment of constitutional democratic order. Only then can the challenges of legal pluralism be addressed in a way that ensures the protection of fundamental rights and freedoms.

References

A24Media. 2009. *Eritrea: A Nation Held Hostage*. Available at: http://www.a24media.com/eritrea-a-nation-held-hostage/ [accessed: December 6, 2013].

Abbink, J. 2005. Book review: Blood, land and sex—Legal and political pluralism in Eritrea. *African Affairs*, 104(415), 346–47.

Agamben, G. 1998. *Homo Sacer: Sovereign Power and Bare Life*. Stanford, CA: Stanford University Press.

Al Jazeera. 2008. *Interview with President Isaias Afwerki*. May 22. Available at: http://www.youtube.com/watch?v=UAXKsZ8OsWo&feature=related [accessed: April 27, 2012].

Amar, A.R. 1998. *The Bill of Rights*. New Haven, CT: Yale University Press.

Ammar, W. 1992. *Eritrea: Root Causes of War and Refugees*. Baghdad: Sindbad.

22 Referring to the work of Giorgio Agamben (1998), Hepner Redeker and O'Kane (2009) discuss the concept of biopolitics elsewhere in their work. Their discourse also relies on another contribution that discusses the perversion of government power (Scott 1998).

23 Bozzini (2011) discusses the political crisis in Eritrea in the context of one of the most controversial government policies: the mandatory and indefinite military conscription of virtually every adult member of the society. For further discussion of this topic, see Hirt (2010), Kibreab (2009), and Weldehaimanot (2011).

Andemariam, S.W. 2011. Ensuring access to justice through community courts in Eritrea. Traditional Justice: Practitioners' Perspective Working Paper 3, International Development Law Organization, Rome.

Bailliet, C. 2007. Examining sexual violence in the military within the context of Eritrean asylum claims presented in Norway. *International Journal of Refugee Law*, 19(3), 471–510.

Bengali, S. 2009. Eritrea: Africa's version of North Korea? *Christian Science Monitor*, November 10. Available at: http://www.csmonitor.com/World/Africa/2009/1110/p06s12-woaf.html [accessed: December 6, 2013].

Berhane, Y. 1969. *Delicts and Torts: An Introduction to the Sources of the Law of Civil Wrongs in Contemporary Ethiopia.* Asmara: Il Poligrafico.

Bozzini, D. 2007. Troubled judicial itineraries: The in-between out-of-court cases in Eritrea. Presented at the AEGIS European Conference on African Studies, African Studies Centre, Leiden, Netherlands, July 11–14.

Bozzini, D. 2011. Low-tech surveillance and the despotic state in Eritrea. *Surveillance and Society*, 9(1–2), 93–113.

Brinkley, J. 2012. Eritrea, the most repressive nation on Earth. *San Francisco Chronicle*, April 29. Available at: http://www.sfgate.com/news/article/Eritrea-the-most-repressive-nation-on-Earth-3516449.php [accessed: December 6, 2013].

Castellani, L.G. 2000. Recent developments in land tenure law in Eritrea. Working Paper 37, Land Tenure Center, University of Wisconsin-Madison, Madison.

Danish Institute for Human Rights. 2012. Examining the foundations for programming with informal justice systems. Danish Institute for Human Rights, Copenhagen. [accessed December 6, 2013].

Elobaid, E.A., and Andemariam, S.W. 2007. Eritrea: Capacity building in the justice sector. UNDP Evaluation Report, United Nations Development Programme, Asmara. Available at http://erc.undp.org/evaluationadmin/reports/viewreport.html;jsessionid=3E3C7E107171C88DC7ABB29DCE5B8DF6?docid=1314 [accessed: December 6, 2013].

Eri TV. 2011. *Interview with President Isaias Afwerki*. December 29. Available at: http://www.youtube.com/watch?v=zy3rSMns-VA [accessed December 6, 2013].

Estifanos, Z., Woldemariam, A., and Ghebremesqel, G. (eds.). 1990. *Hghin Sir'atn Nay Meriet Adebo: Codes and Bylaws of Eritrean Regions and Counties.* Germany: n.p.

Favali, L., and Pateman, R. 2003. *Blood, Land and Sex: Legal and Political Pluralism in Eritrea.* Bloomington: Indiana University Press.

Food and Agriculture Organization of the United Nations. 2004. Baseline study on livelihood systems in Eritrea. National Food Information System of Eritrea, Asmara.

Fuller, M. 2011. Italy's colonial futures: Colonial inertia and postcolonial capital in Asmara. *California Italian Studies*, 2(1), 1–17.

Garcetti, E., and Gruber, J. 2002. The post-war nation: Rethinking the triple transition in Eritrea, in *Regeneration of War-Torn Societies*, edited by M. Pugh. New York: Macmillan, 214–37.

Gebremedhin, Y. 2004. *The Challenges of a Society in Transition: Legal Development in Eritrea.* Trenton: Red Sea Press.

Griffiths, J. 1986. What is legal pluralism? *Journal of Legal Pluralism*, 24, 1–55.

Guardian. 2009. Eritrea: The world's biggest prison. *Guardian*, April 16. Available at: http://www.guardian.co.uk/commentisfree/2009/apr/17/eritrea-human-rights [accessed: December 6, 2013].

Hagos, M.B. 2009. *The Laws of the Forefathers in Terms of Modern Standards on Gender Equality.* New Delhi: Aman Printing Press.

Haile, D. 2000. *Accountability for Crimes of the Past and the Challenges of Criminal Prosecution: The Case of Ethiopia.* Leuven, Belgium: Leuven University Press.

Haile-Mariam, Y. 1999. The quest for justice and reconciliation: The International Criminal Tribunal for Rwanda and the Ethiopian High Court. *Hastings International and Comparative Law Review*, 22(4), 668–99.

Hedru, D. 2003. Eritrea: Transition to dictatorship, 1991–2003. *Review of African Political Economy*, 30(97), 435–44.

Hepner Redeker, T., and O'Kane, D. 2009. Introduction, in *Biopolitics, Militarism and Development: Eritrea in the Twenty-First Century,* edited by D. O'Kane and T. Redeker Hepner, New York: Berghahn, ix–xxxvii.

Hirt, N. 2010. "Dreams don't come true in Eritrea": Anomie and family disintegration due to the structural militarization of society. GIGA Working Paper 119, German Institute of Global and Area Studies, Hamburg.

Human Rights Watch. 2009. *Service for Life: State Repression and Indefinite Conscription in Eritrea*. New York: Human Rights Watch.

Kibreab, G. 2009. Forced labour in Eritrea. *Journal of Modern African Studies*, 47(1), 41–72.

Longrigg, S.H. 1945. *A Short History of Eritrea*. Gloucestershire, UK: Clarendon Press.

Ludolf, H. 1681. *Historia Aethiopica* [in Latin]. Frankfurt am Main, Germany: Zunner.

Ludwikowski, R.R. 1987. Socialistic legal theory in the post-Pashukanis era. *Boston College International and Comparative Law Review*, 10(2), 323–42.

Medhanie, T. 1986. *Eritrea: Dynamics of a National Question*. Amsterdam: Grüner.

Medhanie, T. 2008. Constitution-making, legitimacy and regional integration: An approach to Eritrea's predicament and relations with Ethiopia. DIIPER Working Paper 9, Development, Innovation and International Political Economy Research, Aalborg University, Aalborg, Denmark.

Mekonnen, D.R. 2009. *Transitional Justice: Framing a Model for Eritrea*. Saarbrucken, Germany: VDM Publishing.

Mekonnen, D.R. 2010. Indigenous legal tradition as a supplement to African transitional justice initiatives. *African Journal on Conflict Resolution*, 10(3), 101–23.

Meyers, N. 2010. Africa's North Korea: Inside Eritrea's open-air prison. *Foreign Policy*, June 21. Available at: http://www.foreignpolicy.com/articles/2010/06/21/africas_north_korea?page=0,0 [accessed: December 6, 2013].

Müller, T.R. 2005. *The Making of Elite Women: Revolution and Nation Building in Eritrea*. Leiden, Netherlands: Brill.

Nadel, S.F. 1946. Land tenure on the Eritrean plateau. *Africa: Journal of the African International Institute*, 16(1), 1–22.

Negash, M. 1999. Investment laws in Eritrea. *North Carolina Journal of International Law and Commercial Regulation*, 24, 313–79.

Ogbazghi, P.B. 2011. Personal rule in Africa: The case of Eritrea. *African Studies Quarterly*, 12(2), 1–25.

O'Kane, D., and Hepner Redeker, T. (eds.). 2009. *Biopolitics, Militarism and Development: Eritrea in the Twenty-First Century*. New York: Berghahn.

O'Reilly, A. 2010. Eritrea's National Service Program: The human rights–human trafficking perspective. *DePaul Rule of Law Journal* [Online], Fall, 1–22. Available at: http://laworgs.depaul.edu/journals/RuleofLaw/Documents/O%27Reilly%20-%20final.pdf [accessed: December 6, 2013].

Palmer, V.V. 2012, 2nd ed. *Mixed Jurisdictions Worldwide: The Third Legal Family*. Cambridge, UK: Cambridge University Press.

Pool, D. 2001. *From Guerrillas to Governments: The Eritrean People's Liberation Front*. Athens: J. Currey.

Prunier, G. 2010. Eritrea and its discontents. Presented at a conference of the Association for the Study of the Middle East and Africa, Washington, DC, November 5. Available at: http://www.vimeo.com/18716003 [accessed: December 6, 2013].

Quigley, J. 1989. Socialist law and the civil law tradition. *American Journal of Comparative Law*, 37(4), 781–808.

Russell, F. 1958. Eritrean customary law. *Journal of African Law*, 3(2), 99–103.

Scott, J. 1998. *Seeing Like a State: How Certain Schemes to Improve the Human Condition Have Failed*. New Haven, CT: Yale University Press.

Shinn, D.H. 2010. Challenges to peace and stability in the Horn of Africa. Presented at the World Affairs Council of Northern California, San Francisco, March 12.

Soudan, F. 2010. Érythrée: La Corée du Nord de l'Afrique. *Jeune Afrique*, March 17. Available at: http://www.jeuneafrique.com/Articles/Dossier/ARTJAJA2565p022-028.xml0/usa-corruption-islamisme-electionla-coree-du-nord-de-l-afrique.html [accessed: December 6, 2013].

Tetley, W. 2003. Nationalism in a mixed jurisdiction and the importance of language (South Africa, Israel, and Quebec/Canada). *Tulane Law Review*, 78(1–2), 175–218.

Trevaskis, G.K.N. 1962. *Eritrea: A Colony in Transition 1941–1952*. London: Oxford University Press.

Trimingham, J.S. 1952. *Islam in Ethiopia*. London: Oxford University Press.

Tronvoll, K. 2009. *The Lasting Struggle for Freedom in Eritrea: Human Rights and Political Development, 1991–2009.* Oslo: Oslo Center for Human Rights.

Unger, R.M. 1976. *Law in Modern Society: Toward a Social Criticism of Social Theory.* New York: Free Press.

UN Security Council. 2011. *Report of the Monitoring Group on Somalia and Eritrea, Pursuant to UN Security Council Resolutions 751 (1992) and 1907 (2009)*, July 18. Available at: http://www.un.org/ga/search/view_doc.asp?symbol=S/2011/433 [accessed: December 6, 2013].

Watson, A. 1985. *The Evolution of Law*. Baltimore, MD: Johns Hopkins University Press.

Weldehaimanot, S.M. 2008. The status and fate of the Eritrean constitution. *African Human Rights Law Journal*, 8(1), 108–37.

Weldehaimanot, S.M. 2009. Eritrea: Constitutional, legislative and administrative provisions concerning indigenous peoples, in *The Constitutional and Legislative Protection of the Rights of Indigenous Peoples: Country Reports.* Pretoria: International Labour Organization and African Commission on Human and Peoples' Rights, 1–60.

Weldehaimanot, S.M. 2010. African law of coups and the situation in Eritrea: A test for the African Union's commitment to democracy. *Journal of African Law*, 54(2), 232–57.

Weldehaimanot, S.M. 2011. From prisoners to refugees: The right to leave and its ramifications in Eritrea. *East African Journal of Peace and Human Rights*, 17(1), 230–61.

Weldehaimanot, S.M., and Mekonnen, D.R. 2009. The nebulous law-making process in Eritrea. *Journal of African Law*, 53(2), 171–93.

Weldemikael, T.M. 2009. Pitfalls of nationalism in Eritrea, in *Biopolitics, Militarism and Development: Eritrea in the Twenty-First Century*, edited by D. O'Kane and T. Hepner Redeker. New York: Berghahn, 1–16.

Wrong, M. 2005. *I Didn't Do It for You: How the World Betrayed a Small African Nation.* New York: HarperCollins.

Chapter 11

The Influence of Philippine Indigenous Law on the Development of New Concepts of Social Justice

Pacifico Agabin

When the Philippines became a colony of Spain in 1571, the laws of the colonizer were imposed on the colonized. At that time, there were already 130 ethnolinguistic groups in the Philippines.

The earliest inhabitants of the country, according to anthropologist Robert Fox (1959: 29), were the Tabon cave dwellers who must have inhabited the caves in Palawan as early as 50,000 years ago. Under wave migration theory, they would have reached the Philippines when it was still connected by land bridges to Borneo. Other scientists, however, think that the migration of the first wave of settlers came much later. Some scientists theorize that the Aetas or Negritos came during the Stone Age, about 8,000 B.C. (Peterson 1950: 232–33). The Malays came from Malaysia between 1000 B.C. and 500 A.D., during which period the Srivijaya, the great Malay empire based in Sumatra, colonized the Philippines as they founded their capital in Cambodia. The Malays came in boats called *balangay* and settled at river mouths, thus founding a river-based society (Peterson 1950: 233). This settlement pattern, at least, is the wave migration theory held by a number of Western scholars. However, F. Landa Jocano (1975: 30), a Filipino anthropologist, does not agree. He traces the Philippines' earliest ancestors to the Java man, who is thought to have existed on the island of Java two million years ago. Later prehistorians postulate only two movements of people into Southeast Asia: the first movement was that of the Australoid people, exemplified by the Negritos. The second movement was thought to have been made by Southern Mongoloid people some 6,000 years ago (Scott 1994: 11).

The concept of indigenous people has been clarified in highly academic jargon by a recent law passed by the Philippine legislature. According to the law, the term indigenous people

> refers to a group of people or homogenous societies identified by self-ascription and ascription by others, who have continuously lived as organized community on communally bounded and defined territory, and who have, under claim of ownership since time immemorial, occupied, possessed and utilized such territories, sharing common bonds of language, customs, traditions and other distinctive cultural traits, or who have, through resistance to political, social and cultural inroads of colonization, non-indigenous religion and cultures, become historically differentiated from the majority of the Filipinos.[1]

The term also includes

> peoples who are regarded as indigenous on account of their descent from the populations which inhabited the country at the time of conquest or colonization, at the time of inroads of non-indigenous religions and cultures, or the establishment of present state boundaries, who retain some or all of their own social, economic, cultural and political institutions, but who may have been displaced from their traditional domains or who may have resettled outside their ancestral domains."[2]

1 The Indigenous Peoples Rights Act of 1997, RA 8371, section 3(h).
2 Ibid.

The American colonizers were more frank and direct. Calling the nation's ancestor indigenes "non-Christian," they defined this term as "natives of the Philippine Islands of a low grade of civilization living in tribal relationship apart from settled communities."[3]

In short, the indigenous people of the Philippines share distinctive traits that set them apart from the lowland Filipinos: they are non-Christians; they live in less accessible, marginal, and mostly upland areas; they retain a system of self-government that is not dependent on the laws of the central administration; and they follow ways of life and customs that are perceived as different from those of the rest of the population (MacDonald 1995: 345). One scholar properly observes that indigenous peoples of the Philippines do not really fit into a single anthropological category. Some groups have centralized government; some do not. Some are wet-rice agriculturists; some are shifting cultivators. Some have a productive hunting-and-gathering spectrum of activities; some rely on marine products. Some are nearly completely acculturated; some are more resistant to change. However, MacDonald (1995: 347–48) argues that a very clear-cut gap sets them apart from the major social and historical trends in the Philippines and that they are in a very real sense ostracized by the larger society.

When the Spaniards colonized the Philippines, they recognized, in a way, the indigenous tribes. The indigenes were called *indios* by the Spanish conquistadores, who, like Christopher Columbus, thought that they were in India. The Spanish used this term, even though by 1521—the year Ferdinand Magellan stumbled on an island in the Philippine archipelago—people in the West knew that Columbus had not really reached India. Later, when the Spanish succeeded in converting most of the native lowland population to Christianity, they called the rest of the indigenous people *infieles* or *feroces* (pagans). The Spanish colonizers were convinced that the pre-Hispanic indigenous cultures were a "manifestation of the devil" (Schumacher 1979: 265). The Spaniards considered it their sacred duty to convert the natives living "in the obscurity of ignorance" to Christianity and to accord them the moral advantages of community life. Of course, the Spaniards' concept of community was the *reducciones*, the mission towns occupied by forced relocation of indigenous populations.

When the United States took over the Philippines in 1898 as a result of the Treaty of Paris, they called the indigenous people "non-Christian tribes," as opposed to the converted Christians in the lowlands. Explaining the use of the term, the American-dominated Philippine Supreme Court said in 1919 in *Rubi v. Provincial Board of Mindoro* that "the term 'non-Christian tribes' refers not to religious belief, but, in a way, to the geographical area, and, more directly, to natives of the Philippine Islands of a low grade of civilization, usually living in tribal relationship apart from settled communities."[4] This leading case in Philippine jurisprudence shows how the colonizers imposed cultural imperialism on an indigenous tribe called Mangyans. The US colonial administrators compelled the members of the tribe to be resettled in a small area of their ancestral domain, thus treating them in much the same way that the US government treated the Native Americans in the United States. In the Supreme Court case, the members of the Mangyan tribe resisted, not by force of arms, but by using a concept borrowed from the US Bill of Rights, the concept of equal protection, coupled with the tool of the writ of habeas corpus. Denying the petition for habeas corpus, the Philippine Supreme Court held the following:

> Segregation really constitutes protection for the [M]anguianes.
>
> Theoretically, one may assert that all men are created free and equal. Practically, we know that the axiom is not precisely accurate. The Manguianes, for instance, are not free, as civilized men are free, and they are not the equals of their more fortunate brothers. True, indeed, they are citizens, with many but not all the rights which citizenship implies. But just as surely, the Manguianes are citizens of a low degree of intelligence, and Filipinos who are a drag upon the progress of the State.[5]

This ruling illustrates the culture gap between the colonizer and the colonized, and it holds that law is an important aspect of culture.

---

3 *Rubi v. Provincial Board of Mindoro*, 39 Phil. 660 (1919).
4 Ibid.
5 Ibid.

With respect to the development of the Philippine legal system, Spain, as the colonizer, imposed the civil law system, represented by the Code Napoleon, on the Philippines. When the United States took over from Spain, the Americans superimposed the common law system on public law. Consequently, colonial Philippines bred a hybrid legal system—the civilian and the common law—that is alien to the native Filipinos. This hybrid system is the dominant law at present.

Differences in the Philosophical Foundations of Western Law and Indigenous Law

Both the civil law and the common law systems were founded on the philosophy of individualism. The civil law dates to a classical Roman law that puts a premium on the rights of the individual Roman citizen. Likewise, the common law, which reflects the individualist culture of the Teutonic races, became even more individualistic when it was reshaped in the United States in the mold of Puritanism.

In brief, both the civil law and the common law systems were planted on alien soil in the Philippines. The native Filipinos, who earlier fell under the influence of Hindu, Buddhist, and Confucian thought before they were colonized, were steeped in collectivist or communitarian philosophy. They placed social harmony above individual rights, welfare of the community over individual satisfaction, compassion above apathy, sacrifice over self-fulfillment, and spirituality above materialism. They taught that the social life of a person must always be in harmony with the universe. Thus, under such ideology, the indigenes' customary law developed such notions as communal ownership of land, the right to ancestral domain, acquisition of virgin land through family cultivation, concepts of ecological (as distinguished from environmental) justice, and development of methods of resolving disputes by using a go-between or by the use of metaphors instead of logical reasoning.

How does custom become law in a given society? Hoebel (1954) lays down four basic elements of a legal system: (a) norms, (b) regularity of enforcement, (c) judgment mechanisms, and (d) enforcement. P.V. Fernandez (1976: 2) of the University of the Philippines College of Law, Quezon City, suggests two criteria proposed by legal anthropologists: first, there must be a rule of general character prescribing a specific norm of conduct, and second, there must be some form of sanction imposed by the community in case the norm is not observed. People can only speculate now on the basis of what they know from hindsight about which customs became law and which were discarded through the years. Some of the customs that replaced old ones may still exist—such as the custom of offering food to the gods or flowers to dead ancestors—but they have not qualified as law. For the second requirement—regularity of enforcement—consider that primitive society did not codify its laws. Therefore, the test for this requirement was met where a right or privilege was recognized, a duty or liability imposed, or a particular proceeding or other exercise of public authority was authorized (Fernandez 1976: 3). In some instances, the sanctions may have been acknowledged by the ancients to be imposed only by gods or spirits whom they worshipped or feared. For example, Fernandez (1989: 1–2) shows that the religious beliefs of the people of Bontoc, a province in the northern Philippines, are tied up with their justice system, as follows:

(a) It is the main force behind the system of *taboo*, consisting of prohibitions protective of community values.

(b) It is the sanctioning influence behind the sacred oath or pledge exacted of those adjudged guilty of a serious offense, to avoid repetition of the same offense.

(c) It is associated with power for the protection and vindication of the innocent, and for retribution upon the guilty and the unjust. It is the common consciousness of such power, which gives efficacy to the traditional remedies, especially the trial by ordeal as practiced by the Bontocs.

(d) It is the source of the cleansing rituals, by which offenders whose acts have placed them beyond the pale, are reconciled to their brethren, and are restored to the community.

(e) Its belief system invests with the balm of atonement, the harsh or even cruel penalties imposed on violators of Bontoc law, such as the penalty of *mando*.

As Hoebel (1954: 15) observes, sanctions for violation of norms may either be positive or negative. The positive sanctions may range from a pat on the back to posthumous enshrinement; the negative sanctions may range from the raised eyebrow through social ostracism up to execution. However, for such norms to qualify as law, the fundamental requisite is the legitimate use of physical coercion by a socially authorized agent (Hoebel 1954: 26). The word of law must have the sword of force, even if the sword remains in its scabbard.

As customs change and new ones take their place, the replacements may acquire general characteristics if they become acceptable to the populace. The process is both conscious and subconscious—hardly perceptible in one generation yet accepted in the next. Cultures are never static and, in the course of time, may produce results that, if compressed into a short time span, would be unacceptable to the members of a given society, explains Hoebel (1954: 13–14). However, the measure of consistency between basic postulates and between the postulates and the specific behavior patterns will be the measure of integration of the culture. William Henry Scott (1992: 10) cites as an example the custom of headhunting. Scott points out that an Austrian anthropologist, Ferdinand Blumentritt, thought the first wave of Malays that came to the Philippines were headhunters but that the second wave were not. Scott rejects the textbook theory that pre-Hispanic Filipino culture was a kind of formless clay ready to be stamped with patterns introduced from abroad. Rather, he continues, "it suggests a vigorous and mobile population adjusting to every environment in the archipelago, creatively producing local variations in response to resources, opportunities and culture contacts, able to trade and raid, feed and defend themselves" (Scott 1992: 12).

New Concepts of Social Justice Developed through Custom Law

Notwithstanding the fact that indigenous law has had no place at the table in the Philippine legal system and that indigenous people had been ostracized by Christian Filipinos, indigenous law has recently led Filipinos to develop new concepts of justice in four areas of the legal system: (a) social justice in ownership of land by adopting the concept of stewardship,[6] (b) recognition of ancestral domain, (c) development of ecological justice, and (d) the use of alternative modes of dispute resolution that are conciliatory rather than adversarial.

Communal Ownership of Land as Stewardship

The concept of property ownership that the Philippines borrowed from the Code Napoleon is stated in article 428 of the Civil Code, which defines ownership as "the independent and general power of a person over a thing for purposes recognized by law and within the limits established thereby," or "a relation in private law by virtue of which a thing pertaining to one person is completely subjected to his will in everything not prohibited by law or the concurrence with the rights of another" (Tolentino 1983: 45). Ownership of a thing gives the owner *jus utendi* (right of receiving from the thing what it produces), *jus fruendi* (right of enjoying), *jus abutendi* (right of consuming by its use), *jus disponendi* (right of disposing), and *jus vindicandi* (right to exclude third persons from possession).

In contrast to the individual notion of private property that the Spanish colonizers imposed on the Philippines, Philippine indigenous law of property ownership is communal in character. Indigenous law makes a distinction between possession and ownership. Possession is based on usufructuary (use or enjoyment) rights, whereas ownership is common, not individual. This distinction holds true especially for land rights, which evolved out of the culture and environment of the indigenes, who claim identity with their ancestral domains and the bodies of water that sustained their crops.

Before colonization in the Philippines, property was already seen as a bundle of rights. Property rights, such as usufruct, tenancy, and lease, as well as assignment of rights, were widely used before colonization, as the Spanish conquistadores found when they first arrived there. In other words, the Filipinos' primitive ancestors developed what modern jurists call "legal postulates"—that is, generalized statements of the

6 *Social justice* was defined by the Philippine Supreme Court as the "humanization of laws and the equalization of the social and economic forces by the State so that justice in its rational and objectively secular conception may at least be approximated" (*Calalang v. Williams*, 70 Phil. 734 [1940]).

tendencies actually operating and of the presuppositions on which a particular civilization is based (Stone 1946: 337). A chief function of law, says Hoebel (1954: 16), is seen to be one of selecting norms for legal support that accord with the basic postulates of the culture in which the law system is set.

A good example of this selection of norms would be found in the northern Philippines' Ifugao culture, which is based on irrigation of rice terraces carved out of the mountainsides. The Ifugao people evolved a system of water rights, which are perpetual but transferable. Thus, a transfer of rice lands includes rights to water that serves the field. Moreover, sources of water are both common and private property, and water flowing from springs is available to all takers on a priority basis. When ditches are constructed, interest in a ditch may be sold to others. However, the duty of maintaining a ditch belongs to all members. No new construction may impair the previously laid waterworks of others (Hoebel 1954: 108).

Henry Maine (1870: 269–70) believed that private property was chiefly formed by the gradual disentanglement of the separate rights of individuals from the blended rights of the community. For example, the seventeenth-century Spanish chronicler Francisco Ignacio Alcina noted that among the Visayans, a large tribe in central Philippines, when arable land was still readily available, farmers simply drove a stake in the ground or cut some branches off a tree to establish their claim on the crops grown within the boundaries (Scott 1994: 37).

The notion of legal possession, usufruct, or tenancy, became a common practice under a Visayan *datu* (chief) who would assign rights to a member of his clan. And as the population increased, the indigenes began to discover new areas for farming, for setting fish traps, and for breeding animals. If they discovered a new spot for growing crops or for catching fish with the use of nets, they claimed preemptive rights of ownership. The concept of private ownership began to replace communal rights. But the Visayans had a different concept of land ownership. Ownership of land means the right to use the land. Among the indigenes, ownership was tantamount to work; if a person ceased to work, he or she would lose claim to ownership. This concept arose because the indigenous people considered themselves only as "secondary owners," or stewards of the land, which was primarily owned by the spirits guarding the land (Leonen 2009: 200).

This understanding of land ownership probably explains why the early Filipinos worshipped a variety of spirits, deities, and *anitos* (ancestral spirits) called *diwatas*. Of course, this idea is not peculiar to Filipinos. The first Greek speculator in ancient Miletus, Anaximander, noted how "all things are full of gods," meaning that nature is animated by principle. At this stage in the Philippines, all social and cultural activities were religious activities as well, and agriculture certainly had a religious aspect (Toynbee 1972: 48). Worship of spirits is one custom that the indigenes probably borrowed from the Hindu religion because a portion of the country, specifically the Visayan and Sulu islands, was part of the Majapahit empire from 1100 to 1300 (Wigmore 1936: 228). According to Wigmore, in the Philippines at that time, the more advanced tribe used Hindu syllabaries for writing, and the tribe's mythology, folklore, politics, customs, law, and general literature had a distinct Indian cast. The spirits and gods were thought to be generally benevolent beings who could be entreated ritually for good harvest, health, and even fortune, but they also caused calamities and misfortune if not given proper respect.

An English philosopher (Grayling 2009: 444) views this animism as

> the rudimentary and anthropomorphic forms of science and technology, in the sense that they were attempted explanations of natural phenomena such as thunder and wind—this is the science aspect—and attempts to influence the behavior of these natural forces, by petition, sacrifice, and taboo—this is the technology aspect.

This worshipful attitude toward *anitos* hovering over all of the environment provided the necessary sanction to customary law. The other members of the tribe eventually came to recognize claims of ownership for fear of displeasing the gods. A good example would be the Banaue rice terraces. Scott notes that among the Ifugaos, the irrigated fields in the rice terraces on the mountainsides came to be accepted as private property par excellence, like houses, textile, baskets, or pottery (Scott 1994: 261). However, such property and other valuables belonged to the family as a unit and not to any individual, and hence they could not be sold except under dire necessity and only with full approval of the owner's kin (Hoebel 1954: 105). According to Barton

(1919: 39), an American anthropologist who studied the Ifugaos, lands and other articles of value that have been handed down from generation to generation cannot be the property of any person:

> Present holders possess only a transient and fleeting possession, or better, occupation, insignificant in duration in comparison with the decades and perhaps centuries that have usually elapsed since the field or heirloom came into the possession of the family. Their possession is more in the nature of a trust than an absolute ownership—a holding in trust for future generations.

This concept of land ownership as merely stewardship found its way into the constitution of the Philippines. Initially, the 1935 constitution limited itself to motherhood statements and simply provided that "the promotion of social justice to insure the well-being of and economic security of all people should be the concern of the state" (article 2, section 5). The social justice provision was sought to be used by the Philippine government as a justification for breaking up the big landed estates, or *haciendas*, and distributing the land to the landless tenants. However, the program did not work.

At the end of the Second World War, the agrarian unrest in Central Luzon rose to new proportions. Tenants who fought as guerrilla armies during the war did not surrender their arms and refused to be relegated to serfdom again. The predominance of political power in the country at that time continued to reside in the economically privileged. This privileged class thwarted the numerical superiority of the peasants with its economic power by dictating political alternatives to the country. Thus, the tenancy laws of the Philippines continued to reflect the interests of the dominant landowning class.

In 1955, the Philippine Congress finally decided to solve the tenants' problem of tenure. It passed a law that provided that "the sale or alienation of the land do not of themselves extinguish the tenancy relationship" and that "the purchaser or transferee shall assume the rights and obligations of the former landholder in relation to the tenant."[7] When a landowner challenged the constitutionality of this provision, the Supreme Court dismissed the petition. The court held that the state had the power to regulate tenancy contracts in light of the constitutional provision on social justice.[8]

This idea of holding real property in trust for future generations is now embodied in the 1987 Philippine constitution. It provides that "Congress may provide for the applicability of *customary laws* governing property rights or relations in determining ownership and extent of ancestral domain" (article 7, section 5) and recognizes that "the use of property bears a social function" (article 7, section 6). "To this end," the constitution states, "the State shall regulate the acquisition, ownership, use, and disposition of property and its increments" (article 7, section 1).

As for the concept of social justice and agrarian reform, article 7 of the 1987 constitution reads as follows (italics added):

> AGRARIAN AND NATURAL RESOURCES REFORM
>
> *Sec. 4.* The State shall, by law, undertake an agrarian reform program founded on added.the right of farmers and regular farmworkers who are landless, *to own directly or collectively the lands they till* or, in the case of other farmworkers, to receive a just share of the fruits thereof. To this end, the State shall encourage and *undertake the just distribution of all agricultural lands*, subject to such priorities and reasonable retention limits as the Congress may prescribe, *taking into account ecological, developmental, or equity considerations*, and subject to the payment of just compensation. In determining retention limits, the State shall respect the right of small landowners. The State shall further provide incentives for voluntary land-sharing....
>
> *Sec. 6.* The State shall apply the principles of *agrarian reform or stewardship*, whenever applicable in accordance with law, *in the disposition or utilization of other natural resources*, including lands of the public domain under lease or concession suitable to agriculture, subject to prior rights,

7 Tenancy Law of 1955, section 9.
8 *Primero v. CAR*, 101 Phil. 675 [1957].

> homestead rights of small settlers, *and the rights of indigenous communities to their ancestral lands*.

The above provisions of the 1987 constitution show how the program of agrarian reform through distribution of agricultural lands to landless tenant-cultivators is rooted in the stewardship concept of ownership and how ancestral domains have been recognized.

Recognition of Ancestral Domain

The stewardship concept of property is most applicable to land among the Philippine indigenous people. A noted anthropologist, Max Gluckman (1965: 294), sums up the tribals' reverence for land:

> Land is not an individual item which a man owns for himself and by himself. For he secures the rights to land in two ways: Firstly, as a citizen of the tribe he is entitled to some arable land and building land, and to the use of public pasturage, fishing waters, and wild products. Secondly, in all tribes except those who shift their gardens widely and have an abundance of land, he gets rights from membership of a village and a group of kinsfolk. That is, a man's right to land in the tribal home depends upon his accepting membership of a tribe, with all its obligations. The right of every subject, while he is a subject, is jealously safeguarded.

All Philippine tribal societies view land as a gift of their supreme god, and the members of the tribe see themselves only as caretakers of the divine land. Each member sees himself or herself as a steward of the land from which he or she can obtain his or her livelihood; land is communal property with use based only on usufruct. The head of the tribe, or *datu*, distributes land for cultivation to the members, and the members' heirs may inherit the right to cultivate the same parcel of land for generations. Everyone in the village enjoys a common right to the ancestral land, which is natural in a setting of the collective mode of production. The indigenes' worship of ancestral land is best expressed in anguish by a leader of the Kalinga tribe, Macli-ing Dulag, who resisted resettlement to give way for the building of a dam in northern Philippines:

> You asked if we own the land.... How can you own that which will outlive you? Only the race owns the land because only the race lives forever. To claim a piece of land is a birthright of every man. The lowly animals claim their place; how much more man? Man is born to live. Apu Kabunian, lord of us all, gave us life and placed us in the world to live human lives. And where shall we obtain life? From the land. To work [the land] is an obligation, not merely a right. In tilling the land, you possess it. And so land is a grace that must be nurtured. To enrich it and make it fructify is the exhortation of Apu Kabunian to all his children. Land is sacred. Land is beloved. From its womb springs ... life. (Bennagen 1993: 71–72)

The coming of the Spaniards to the Philippines in 1521 turned the life of the aborigines upside down. The indigenous concept of land ownership was turned on its head by the Maura Law, which was introduced by the Spanish colonizers in 1893. The law treated land as an ordinary commodity owned by individuals or as an agricultural asset owned by the state monopolies. This idea was later reinforced by the Torrens title system introduced by the Americans, which made it easy to alienate land as an industrial asset like any other private property. No longer would ownership of land depend on actual use and occupancy; whoever had plenty of the colonizer's currency could get to own land without having to occupy or cultivate it. Land was no longer the source of the cultural and spiritual life of the tribe; it could be the source of money and power for an absentee landlord.

A US scholar who is an ardent advocate of Philippine indigenous law, Owen Lynch (2012), arrives at the rather trenchant and perceptive observation that "the misbegotten nature of the Philippine State, including its twentieth century social contract, is rooted, at least symbolically, in the so-called Regalian doctrine." Under this doctrine, the king, by legal fiction, was regarded as the original proprietor of all lands, the true and only source of title, and from whom all lands are held. The doctrine finds its basis on the papal bull,

Inter caetera, that Pope Alexander VI issued in 1493, which divided the world, like an apple, between Spain and Portugal. (Alexander was the Spanish Pope who fathered the infamous Borgias and who was known to maintain a number of concubines.) On March 31, 1521, Magellan "discovered" the Philippines, considered it *terra nullius* (land belonging to no one), and claimed it in the name of the Spanish king, Philip II. As Lynch (2012: 6) puts it,

> At that same 500-year-old moment, every native in the politically undefined and still unexplored (not to mention unconquered) archipelago became a squatter, bereft of any legal rights to land and to any other natural resources. The only way to reacquire sovereignty was to get it back from the colonial usurpers. The only way to remove the squatter label was by procuring a documented property right from the Spanish regime or its state-successors.

Lynch (2012: 6) concludes that the Regalian doctrine enshrines an arbitrary, mythical, and unjust usurpation of sovereignty and customary property rights and that it is a simple yet perfect tool to marginalize the indigenous people. Yet as early as 1909, the US Supreme Court, in a case originating from the Philippines,[9] recognized the concept of native title claimed by the Igorots, a tribe in the northern Philippines. Justice Oliver Wendell Holmes, in finding for the Igorot applicant on appeal to the US Supreme Court, stated:

> It is true that Spain, in its earlier decrees, embodies the universal feudal theory that all lands were held from the Crown ... [but] it does not follow that ... applicant had lost all rights and was a mere trespasser when the present government seized his land. The argument to that effect seems to amount to a denial of native titles ... for the want of ceremonies which the Spaniards would not have permitted and have not the power to enforce.

The court further emphasized:

> Every presumption is and ought to be against the government.... It might, perhaps, be proper and sufficient to say that when, as far back as testimony or memory goes, the land has been held by individuals under a claim of private ownership. It will be presumed to have been held in the same way from before the Spanish conquest, and never to have been public land.

The 1987 Philippine constitution reverses the Regalian notion of land ownership and adopts the Holmesian view insofar as the ancestral domains of indigenous tribes are concerned. It carves out an exception to the Regalian doctrine in the following provision:

> The State, subject to the provisions of this Constitution and national development policies and programs, shall protect the rights of indigenous cultural communities to their ancestral lands to ensure their economic, social and cultural well-being. The Congress may provide for the applicability of customary laws governing property rights and relations in determining the ownership and extent of ancestral domain.[10]

To give substance to this new constitutional recognition of the rights of indigenous peoples, in 1997 the Philippine Congress passed the Republic Act 8371, known as the Indigenous Peoples' Rights Act, or IPRA. The IPRA recognizes the existence of the indigenous cultural communities (ICCs) or indigenous peoples (IPs) as a distinct sector in Philippine society. It grants them the ownership and possession of their ancestral domains and ancestral lands and defines the extent of these lands and domains. The ownership given is the indigenous concept of ownership under customary law that traces its origin to native title.

Other rights granted to the ICCs and IPs are the following:

9 *Cariño v. Insular Government*, 53 L. Ed. 594 (1909).
10 Constitution of 1987, article 7, section 5.

- The right to develop lands and natural resources
- The right to stay in the territories
- The right in case of displacement
- The right to safe and clean air and water
- The right to right to claim parts of reservations
- The right to resolve conflict
- Rights to ancestral lands, which include (a) the right to transfer land or property to or among members of the same ICCs and IPs, subject to the customary laws and traditions of the community concerned, and (b) the right to redemption for a period not exceeding 15 years from date of transfer, if the transfer is to a nonmember of the ICC or IP and is tainted by vitiated consent of the ICC or IP or if the transfer is for an unconscionable consideration.[11]

Within their ancestral domains and ancestral lands, the ICCs and IPs are given the right to self-governance and empowerment;[12] social justice and human rights;[13] the right to preserve and protect their culture, traditions, institutions, and community intellectual rights; and the right to develop their own sciences and technologies.[14]

A major obstacle to the implementation of the IPRA's provisions is the constitutional provisions adopting the Regalian doctrine. The 1987 constitution states, "All lands of the public domain, waters, minerals, coal, petroleum, and other mineral oils, all forces of potential energy, fisheries, forests or timber, wildlife, flora and fauna, and other natural resources, are owned by the State."[15] When the Congress of the Philippines passed the IPRA, which seeks to give substance to the concept of ancestral domain, it was met with strong opposition from the lawyers, and a case was filed in the Philippine Supreme Court to challenge the validity of the implementing law. The constitutional challenge, posed in the context of a mining claim located in an ancestral domain, was focused on the provision of the IPRA that the members of the tribe within that domain had the right to claim its natural resources.[16] This provision conflicts with the Regalian theory adopted by the constitution, contended the petitioners in that case.

The issue was so controversial that the Philippine Supreme Court divided evenly on the question: 7–7. In brief, seven justices voted to dismiss the petition, whereas the other seven believed that certain provisions of the IPRA law are unconstitutional. Under the constitution, the challenge failed, and the IPRA law was declared to be consonant with the Regalian doctrine adopted by the charter. On the importance of the concept of ancestral domain, one of the seven justices who prevailed wrote:

> Land is the central element of the indigenous peoples' existence. There is no traditional concept of permanent, individual, land ownership. Among the *Igorots*, ownership of land accurately applies to the tribal right to use the land or to territorial control. The people are the secondary owners or stewards of the land and that if a member of the tribe ceases to work, he loses his claim of ownership, and the land belongs or reverts to the beings of the spirit world who are its true and primary owners. Under the concept of "trusteeship," the right to possess the land does not only belong to the present generation but to the future ones as well.[17]

The indigenes' concept of ownership of land was thus recognized in the IPRA, which declares that

11 IPRA of 1997, sections 7–8.
12 Ibid., sections 13–20.
13 Ibid., sections 21–28.
14 Ibid., sections 29–37.
15 Constitution of 1987, article 7, section 2.
16 The IPRA of 1997, section 7(a), provides for "the right to claim ownership over lands, bodies of water traditionally and actually occupied by ICCs/IPs, sacred places, traditional hunting and fishing grounds, and all improvements made by them, at any time within the domains."
17 *Cruz and v. Secretary of Environmental and Natural Resources et al.*, 347 SCRA 128 (2000).

> indigenous concept of ownership sustains the view that ancestral and all resources found therein shall serve as the material bases of [indigenes'] cultural integrity. The indigenous concept of ownership generally holds that ancestral domains are the ICC/IP's private but community property which belongs to all generations and therefore cannot be sold, disposed or destroyed. It likewise covers sustainable traditional resource rights.[18]

The dominant opinion in the *Cruz* case reasoned that the provisions of the IPRA on ancestral domain do not violate the provisions of the constitution incorporating the Regalian doctrine. The court argued that ancestral domains are the private property of indigenous peoples and do not constitute part of the public domain. Furthermore, the right of ownership and possession by the indigenous peoples of their ancestral domains is a limited form of ownership and does not include the right to alienate the same. As for the natural resources within the ancestral domains, the IPRA does not deprive the state of ownership over these. Instead, the constitution allows the state to develop these through the private sector by co-production, joint venture, or production-sharing agreements. The pertinent provision of the IPRA gives the indigenes only the right to manage and conserve natural resources for future generations.

Another provision grants indigenes priority rights in the development and use of natural resources; however, the opinion concluded that these rights do not extend to ownership. The *Cruz* opinion ended with this reflection:

> The struggle of the Filipinos throughout colonial history had been plagued by ethnic and religious differences. These differences were carried over and magnified by the Philippine government through the imposition of a national legal order that is mostly foreign in origin or derivation. Largely unpopulist, the present legal system has resulted in the alienation of a large sector of society, specifically, the indigenous peoples. The histories and cultures of the indigenes are relevant to the evolution of Philippine culture and are vital to the understanding of contemporary problems. It is through the IPRA that an attempt was made by our legislators to understand Filipino society not in terms of myths and biases but through common experiences in the course of history. If the evolution of the Filipino people into a democratic society is to truly proceed democratically, *i.e.*, if the Filipinos as a whole are to participate fully in the task of continuing democratization, it is this Court's duty to acknowledge the presence of indigenous and customary laws in the country and affirm their co-existence with the land laws in our national legal system.[19]

The Concept of Ecological Justice

Contemporary developments in the theory of justice have come up with the concept of ecological justice. This idea has evolved not only from the fact of maldistribution of environmental goods, but also from the status of indigenous people, who have borne the brunt of environmental degradation because they retreated and resettled in the mountains. Environmental activists have now drawn a distinction between environmental justice and ecological justice, the former being seen to neglect the natural world outside human influences. The meaning of *environment* has been too narrowly drawn, and the concept of *justice* has been based on the universalist, singular theory of justice found in the distributional model. In other words, most concepts of environmental justice do not address the issue of doing justice to nature (Schlosberg 2007).

The aspect of justice that indigenous tribes have directly influenced is ecological. They have also contributed much to the concept of environmental justice arising from their experience with injustice (that is, the maldistribution of environmental goods arising from illegal logging; open pit mining; dynamite fishing; and the construction of roads, dams, bridges, and factories in their ancestral lands). But because the indigenous tribes have been rendered invisible and inarticulate by cultural imperialism, they have been unable to significantly contribute to the development of environmental justice until lately. Only recently, when

18 IPRA of 1997, section 5.

19 *Cruz v. Secretary of Environmental and Natural Resources et al.*, 347 SCRA 128 (2000).

environmental activists took up their cause, were the indigenous tribes able to find a voice to participate in the making of decisions about their life and their world.

It is in the development of ecological justice that the direct contribution of the Philippine indigenes can be easily perceived. This perception is not novel in the West, of course. In her book *Silent Spring*, Rachel Carson (1962) pointed out the relationship between the natural world and the animals and plants as well as the concern for human health in the face of increasing industrialization. But long before 1962 and, in fact, long before Magellan, the Philippine ancestors had already conceived the idea of ecological justice. The swidden farmers of old became naturists out of necessity. The Visayan swidden tillers, in fact, became aware of the seasons' changing moods from the appearance of the stars, the shifting direction of the winds, the flowering of plants, and the singing of the birds (Scott 1994: 36). This awareness of the natural world is why they had nature spirits and why they worshipped the sun, the moon, the stars, the winds, the rivers, and the sea (Scott 1994: 78). Even wild animals and huge trees were venerated. Crocodiles were respectfully addressed as "grandfather" by the Visayans and were offered symbolic food by anyone crossing the river. The big balete tree was thought to have sinister powers because of the spirits that dwelled in it, cutting down the balete tree was considered a sacrilege under any circumstances (Scott 1994: 78). Clearly, the Philippine forefathers were the original environmentalists, whose curious customs gave rise to what Western theorists now know as ecological justice.

The extension of the idea of justice to the nonhuman world has now become a part of the worldwide movement for ecological justice. *Ecological justice* is simply defined as "justice to nature"—that is, justice to include the nonhuman natural world, including individual animals, communities, flora, fauna, and the whole of nature (Schlosberg 2007). David Schlosberg, an American environmental theorist, would start by recognizing nature as part of our shared community and include humans and the rest of the natural world in an expanded community of justice. He cites Aldo Leopold's classic "land ethic," which extended the idea of the moral community to include the land we stand on and live with (Schlosberg 2007). This idea is reminiscent of the indigenous people's recognition of the role of land not only in their daily lives but also in their social and political culture. The modern-day theorists in the West and in the East have been able to articulate this way of life through ecological justice: every natural entity is entitled to enjoy the fullness of its own form of life. Nature must have the opportunity to survive, with its integrity intact, in the environment of diversity and autonomy that is characteristic of the biosphere (Schlosberg 2007). The recognition of nature can come out of a more human-centered concern for integrity. This concern for integrity, meaning an integrated, undivided whole, begins with an interest in the integrity of ourselves as organisms; expands to psychological, cognitive, and moral integrity; and provides reasons to respect nonhuman beings and their environments. People are part of nature, and it is in human interests to integrate ecological concerns (Schlosberg 2007). The lack of recognition of nature, the exclusion of nature from theories of justice, and the dismissal of parity of nature have led modernity to a crisis of sustainability. Modernity's social bond, according to recent theorists, is unsustainable without a simultaneous recognition of, and bond with, the rest of the natural world (Schlosberg 2007).

These pretentious sounding theories are actually reminiscent of the simple beliefs of the Philippine indigenes, who worship nature and who believe that the human world and the natural world are one and the same. The early indigenes adored the sun, the moon, the animals, and the birds, and they seemed to consider the objects of nature as something to be respected.[20] This view is not surprising: the birds and animals gave them food, the sun made their crops and trees grow, and the moon conduced fertility—perhaps because it induces romance. In fact, Philippine ancestors practiced animism—that is, worship of animals and other objects of nature. They attributed local spirits to the sun, the moon, the stars, the rivers, the mountains, or even a big tree that guarded their respective domains. These spirits could cause earthquakes, floods, rain, or death if they were displeased (Rasul 2008: 49). When the images of deities took human shape, the early concepts of law and justice applying to human society became linked to the gods. Soon, certain gods were considered specific guardians of law—gods to whom places of jurisdiction were dedicated and gods who were invoked when certain norms were violated (Scott 1994: 46).

20 The Supreme Court justices made this *obiter dictum* in *Cruz v. Secretary of Environmental and Natural Resources et al.*, 347 SCRA 128 (2000).

Today, the Philippines has enacted laws that not only protect the environment but also maintain ecological balance. The country's constitution mandates the state to "protect and advance the right of the people to a balanced and healthful ecology in accord with the rhythm and harmony of nature."[21] The Philippine Supreme Court applied this provision in *Oposa v. Factoran*, where four minors, represented by their parents, asked the high court to cancel all existing timber license agreements, invoking "intergenerational justice" and "intergenerational responsibility."[22] The court affirmed the justiciability of the issue raised by the minors and reversed the trial court's order dismissing the petition, as it recognized the petitioners' right "to a balanced and healthful ecology" and the correlative duty "to refrain from impairing the environment." The Philippine Congress has enacted laws to promote ecological balance, such as the Clean Air Act (1999), the Clean Water Act (2004), the Ecological Solid Waste Management Act (2000), and the National Integrated Protected Areas and Systems Act (1992).

Alternative Dispute Resolution

There are many doors to justice. Until lately, however, the legal systems of the West offered limited access to justice in the form of a singularly defined adversarial procedure and permanent standard: search for truth. The recognition of indigenous law among nations has made the Filipino people realize that claims for justice can be made in different ways and can be articulated in different languages. The Philippines has incorporated various notions of achieving justice into the legal system by adopting the methods of indigenes in resolving their disputes. The Philippines now calls those methods *alternative modes of dispute resolution.* They are alternatives to the primary mode of achieving justice, which is litigation.

Litigation is alien to the indigenous peoples of the Philippines. Instead, they used trial by ordeal or trial by combat. The indigenous peoples evolved the notion of compensation at the same time that the West's legal system invented the concept of damages. Compensation in customary law among one of the Philippine tribes is described by a law professor as follows:

> From the standpoint of Ifugao society, and its concern with the preservation of peace and harmony within the society, the Ifugao system of Justice is an evolved alternative to the harsh conditions engendered by *lex talionis*, including violence, terror, armed strife, and injustice, through a public determination of the truth concerning an alleged wrong participated in by the community, and buying off the vengeance due, in case of a judgment of guilt, by imposition and exaction of sanctions sufficient to make reparation for the wrong done according to custom. (Fernandez n.d.: 5)

This observation is also borne out by the studies of Hoebel (1954) and Barton (1919), who noted that the procedure among the Ifugaos, except in homicide cases calling for direct blood revenge, requires the use of a go-between acting as an adviser or a mediator. The existence of this mediator represents the first step in the development of judicial institutions (Hoebel 1954: 114).

The ancient Filipinos believed that the spirit of a dead ancestor would not rest until after his or her wrongful killing had been avenged by a relative. And so the option of compensation, like bitter medicine, had to be made palatable, usually by means of beliefs acceptable to the primitive mind. Among the Negritos, for example, the concept of compensation had to be given a religious shroud to make it acceptable to the whole tribe. The custom of headhunting for revenge was minimized through the intercession of a go-between who proposed the idea of reconciliation with the relatives of the victim by means of sacrifices to a spirit named Manglobar who soothed angry hearts. The sacrifice would be made in gold or other valuables or with a slave to kill (Scott 1994: 251). This custom is observed even today. Again the Ifugao provide an example:

> Seen in terms of Ifugao religion, the Ifugao system of Justice in its traditional forms is basically the intervention of the gods in the vindication of the innocent and the exposure and condemnation of wrong-doing in breach of the peace, and the purging of sin committed in the latter case, through

21 Constitution of 1987, article 2, section 16.
22 *Oposa v. Factoran*, 224 SCRA 792 (1993).

> repentance by prompt acknowledgement of guilt, atonement through payment of the stipulated reparation, and reconciliation with the brothers wronged through healing rituals. (Fernandez n.d.: 5)

The Kalinga tribe and other ethnic groups in the northern part of the Philippines have perfected the concept of a peace pact, or *bodong*, among themselves. When a conflict arises among the villages, a go-between is chosen to resolve the dispute. If the go-between fails, a tribal war erupts; however, most of the time the go-between succeeds in forging a peace pact among warring tribes.

Filipino forebears had a more sophisticated method of conciliating and mediating between the parties. They followed the folk law of *adat*, which is still practiced among the indigenes as well as the Moros in Mindanao. The adat is an unwritten law on proper conduct, right action, and procedure. It revolves around the issue of what ought to be the law in a given case (Mastura 1986: 44). Its classification of right conduct is not rational but metaphorical, and its contents are formulated in sayings, proverbs, and poems (Koesnoe 1986: 36). Koesnoe (1986: 37) explains this law:

> The starting point in Adat law is the cosmic point of view about human life and the universe. Human life, social and individual, must always be in harmony with the universe. For this end, man has to live in conformity with the teachings of nature symbolized by examples of events governed by nature. The natural events are thereby seen in the Adat as the ultimate, true Adat referred to in folk theory as Adat sabena Adat (literal meaning: the Adat of Adats).

Koesnoe (1986: 37) notes natural events are metaphorical examples for human conduct to follow:

> Everything has to be elaborated in such a way that man may have the benefit of finding forms and ways in controlling their social life in harmony with the universe. This elaboration is human activity and therefore subject to human culture, which is also called Adat. Since this kind of Adat is continuously transferred from and fostered from generation to generation, it is then called the successive Adat (Adat Pusaka Usang).

In 2004, the Philippines enacted different modes of alternative dispute resolution in the Alternative Dispute Resolution Act. The 2004 act covers negotiation, mediation, and arbitration. Also, it provides a different set of rules for court-annexed mediation for the judiciary.

Indeed, the Supreme Court of the Philippines has issued consolidated guidelines to implement the expanded coverage of court-annexed mediation and judicial dispute resolution. The rules are intended to empower the parties to resolve their own disputes and to give practical effect to the state policy expressed in the Alternative Dispute Resolution Act of 2004, which was passed to

> actively promote party autonomy in the resolution of disputes or the freedom of the parties to make their own arrangement to resolve disputes. Towards this end, the State shall encourage and actively promote the use of Alternative Dispute Resolution (ADR) as an important means to achieve speedy and impartial justice and de-clog court dockets.[23]

The first section of the Supreme Court guidelines is a clear recognition of indigenous modes of settlement. It states:

> 1.1 Indigenous [alternative dispute resolution] under [court-annexed mediation]
>
> Such State Policy promoting party autonomy, would necessarily include recognition of indigenous modes of dispute resolution.[24]

23 Alternative Dispute Resolution Act of 2004, section 2.
24 Philippines Supreme Court OCA Circular 51–2011.

Conclusion

Thanks to the influence of the customary law of indigenous peoples, Philippine law has come to recognize more communitarian concepts of property rights, aboriginal title, ecological justice, and even alternative modes of dispute resolution. This trend is, of course, not peculiar to the Philippines. The laws and jurisprudence in other countries that were former colonies of Western countries have likewise followed the trend in recognizing the cultural and social rights of their native population. Even international law has kept in step with domestic laws of the members of the United Nations, as can be seen from the provisions of the United Nations Declaration on the Rights of Indigenous Peoples of 2007.

The Philippine experience is a showcase of the conflict between Western law and the indigenous law of colonized peoples. The legal systems of the West, founded on the ideology of individualism, have emphasized assertion of the rights of the person, self-fulfillment, and development of the individual; preservation and protection of private property; single-minded pursuit of happiness based on material acquisitions; exploitation of natural resources for economic development at the expense of the environment; and even adversarial modes of settling disputes. Conversely, indigenous law based on the collectivist philosophy of primitive man places emphasis on social harmony above the rights of the individual; requires personal sacrifice for the common good; recognizes only community-based property rights; supports recognition of native titles to land; protects forests, trees, water, and other natural resources on which indigenes depend for survival; and adopts modes of dispute resolution that are conciliatory and arbitrative rather than adversarial.

The interface and accommodation of indigenous law with the hybrid legal system of the Philippines that is based on the common law and the civilian system are proof that law is a living thing that quickly adapts to human concerns. In the Philippines, the acknowledgment of customary law reflects the amelioration and resolution through social justice principles of unfair legal arrangements imposed by colonialism.

References

Barton, R. 1919. Ifugao law. *American Archaeology and Ethnology*, 15(1), 1–186.

Bennagen, P.L. 1993. Tribal Filipinos, in *Indigenous View of Land and the Environment*, edited by S.H. Davis. Washington, DC: World Bank, 67–78. Available at: http://www-wds.worldbank.org/servlet/WDSContentServer/WDSP/IB/1993/01/01/000009265_3970311122038/Rendered/PDF/multi_page.pdf [accessed: December 9, 2013].

Carson, R. 1962. *Silent Spring*. Boston: Houghton-Mifflin.

Fernandez, P.V. 1976. *Custom Law in Pre-conquest Philippines*. Quezon City, Philippines: University of the Philippines Law Center.

Fernandez, P.V. 1989. The Bontoc process of law creation. Unpublished manuscript in the University of the Philippines Law Library, College of Law, Quezon City.

Fernandez, P.V. n.d. The process of law creation in Ifugao society. Unpublished manuscript in the University of the Philippines Law Library, College of Law, Quezon City.

Fox, R. 1959. *The Philippines in Pre-historic Times*. Manila: The UNESCO National Commission on the Philippines.

Gluckman, M. 1965. *Politics, Law, and Ritual in Tribal Society*. New Brunswick, NJ: Transaction.

Grayling, A.C. 2009. *Ideas That Matter: A Personal Guide for the 21st Century*. London: Orion.

Hoebel, E.A. 1954. *The Law of Primitive Man: A Study in Comparative Legal Dynamics*. Cambridge, MA: Harvard University Press.

Jocano, F.L. 1975. *Questions and Challenges in Philippine Prehistory*. Quezon City: University of Philippines Press.

Koesnoe, M. 1986. From folk law towards jurists' law. *ASEAN Law and Society*, 1(1), 36–43.

Leonen, M. 2009. Law at its margins: Questions of identity, ancestral domains, indigenous peoples and the diffusion of law. The 6th Metrobank Foundation Professorial Chair Lecture, presented at the University of the Philippines College of Law, Quezon City, October 21.

Lynch, O. 2012. *Colonial Legacies in a Fragile Republic: A History of Philippine Land Law and State Formation with Emphasis on the Early U.S. Regime, 1898–1913*. Quezon City: University of the Philippines College of Law.

MacDonald, C. 1995. Indigenous peoples of the Philippines: Between segregation and integration, in *Indigenous Peoples of Asia*, edited by R. Barnes, A. Grey, and B. Kingsbury. Ann Arbor: Association of Asian Studies, 345–56.

Maine, H.S. 1870. *Ancient Law: Its Connection with the Early History of Society, and Its Relation to Modern Ideas*. London: John Murray.

Mastura, M.O. 1986. Harmonization of adat law vis-à-vis Western law within a single polity: The Philippine experience. *ASEAN Law and Society*, 1(1), 44–51.

Peterson, A. 1950. *The Far East: A Social Geography*. London: Gerald Duckworth.

Rasul, J. 2008. *Philippine History: From Thousand Years before Magellan*. Manila: n.p.

Schlosberg, D. 2007. *Defining Environmental Justice: Theories, Movements and Nature*. Oxford, UK: Oxford University Press.

Schumacher, J.H. 1979. The "propagandists" reconstruction of the Philippine past, in *Perceptions of the Past in Southeast Asia*, edited by A. Reid and D. Marr. London: Heinemann Educational Books, 264–80.

Scott, W.H. 1992. Looking for the pre-Hispanic Filipino: Mistranslations and preconceptions, in *Looking for the Pre-Hispanic Filipino and Other Essays*. Quezon City, Philippines: New Day, 1–14.

Scott, W.H. 1994. *Barangay: Sixteenth-Century Philippine Culture and Society*. Quezon City, Philippines: Ateneo de Manila University Press.

Stone, J. 1946. *The Province and Function of Law*. Sydney: Associated General Publications.

Tolentino, A.M. 1983. *Commentaries and Jurisprudence on the Civil Code of the Philippines*. Vol. 2. Manila: Central Lawbook.

Toynbee, A. 1972. *A Study of History: The First Abridged One-Volume Edition*. New York: Weathervane.

Wigmore, J.H. 1936. *A Panorama of the World's Legal Systems*. Washington, DC: Washington Law Book.

PART IV
The Islamic Legal System and Western Legal Traditions

Chapter 12

Turkey's Synthetic Civilian Tradition in a "Covert" Mix with Islam as Tradition: A Novel Hybrid?

Esin Örücü

Turkey's legal system definitely is not a mix of civil law and common law. Neither is Turkey a mixed jurisdiction in the classic sense, nor does it have an overt mixed legal system. After the collapse of the Ottoman Empire in 1920, legal evolution in the Turkish Republic was instigated through a strong desire to become Western and contemporary, and even today, rapid law reforms are being made to fulfill the requirements of the European Union *acquis communautaire* in the hope of joining it. Legal evolution has occurred through a succession of imports from the civilian world rather than being homegrown and has relied on major translation work. In fact, the legal system of the Turkish Republic has the appearance of belonging to the civil tradition in toto with the ingredients borrowed from Switzerland, Germany, Italy, and France. Yet although the Turkish legal system is not a mixed one in the orthodox sense, it is mixed in two other significant and different senses.

In the first sense, and derived directly from the preceding developments, it is a synthetic and eclectic legal system, legislatively reconstructed, initially between 1926 and 1930, by receiving, adapting, and mixing laws from various foreign Western sources and melting them down in the Turkish pot to form the overlay, the civil legal system. It is interesting to observe how this amalgam, most of whose parts hail from Roman law—a source alien to the endogenous traditions—works.

In the second sense, the legal system is a mix of these diverse laws with the lives of a people, the majority of whose values and demands reflect a different socioculture related to one past element of the legal system, that of the Ottoman Empire. With all of the Ottoman Empire's laws erased by the Turkish Republic, this socioculture is significantly different from the sociocultures represented by the incoming laws. The Ottoman legal system was legally pluralistic, enveloped in Islamic law until 1839; thereafter, until its collapse, it was a legally pluralist mixed legal system with the added ingredient being borrowed from the French system. In its heyday, the Ottoman Empire was an Islamic state with a minority Muslim population ruling a majority of non-Muslims. This unique composite makes it possible to consider the Turkish legal system a "covert mix"—a novel hybrid. And the mix in this sense makes it worthwhile to look for the place of Islam and tradition in this laic civilian legal system (see Örücü 2011).

In a legal system such as the Turkish one, in which the source of law is determined by the formal legal framework and where there is no legal pluralism, custom and tradition become sources of law only when recognized by courts. The Yargıtay[1] (the Court of Last Instance, the Turkish Court of Cassation) was enabled to make adjustments to the law by the flexible rules present in articles 1, 2, and 4, of the 1926 Civil Code (and now the 2002 Civil Code), which correspond verbatim to articles 1, 2, and 4 of the Swiss Civil Code. These are rules on justice and equity, objective good faith, and the principles of the rule of law. The importance of article 1 cannot be overstated for the development of Turkey's law and legal system and the fitting of the frame to the demands of the people, mostly based on Islamic values and tradition. Hence, the covert mix was created:

> The law must be applied in all cases that come within the letter and the spirit of its provisions. If no relevant provision can be found in the statute, the judge must decide in accordance with the

1 For those unfamiliar with the Turkish alphabet, it contains additional letters to the 23 characters of the Latin alphabet: *ç*, *ş*, *ğ*, *ö*, *ü*, and *ı* (undotted *i*) both in the lower case and the upper case (minus *q*, *w*, and *x*).

> customary law and, in its absence, in accordance with the rule that he would lay down, were he the legislator. In so doing, he must be guided by accepted legal doctrine and case law.

Developments as a result of using the referenced articles are extremely important. They met people's needs, because no direct social contact occurred between the models and the recipient, and the culture of the masses, though partially changed, remained, on the whole, unrelated to the models—despite domestic efforts to change the people, their traditions, and their practices. In this chapter, I look at some cases in a number of selected areas where the courts provide innovative solutions, even while considering and developing the so-called source laws (*kaynak kanunlar*). Some Islamic institutions and demands based on them are being accommodated, as long as they are not related to the public law sphere and can be reinterpreted as compatible with the constitution and the legal framework. Turkish judges navigate and try to cater to the needs of people with clashing values—the underlay. This methodology used by the courts through reinterpretation of the framework allows Islam into the legal system, though in the guise of tradition, and justifies the use of the term *covert mix*.[2] A number of such developments and limitations—some of which are supported by the European Court of Human Rights—are analyzed in this chapter.[3]

After briefly touching on the synthetic and eclectic nature of Turkish law, I will assess the position of tradition and Islam today at their convergence with the law, as they progressively become an element in the laic civilian mix.

The Story of the Official Legal System

Directly borrowed from and significantly influenced by foreign models, the legal system of Turkey is eclectic and synthetic. These models are all from continental Europe. None of the models represents an Eastern or religious viewpoint. Legal development involved a total reorientation away from Islamic culture toward Europe. The present legal framework has been synthetically constructed through imposed receptions, voluntary receptions, imitations, adaptations, and adjustments (Örücü 1992, 1996).

The Ottoman Empire went through a number of phases of development: between 1299 and 1839, it was a legally pluralist Islamic state; from 1839 to its fall in 1920, it was a legally pluralist mixed legal system with considerable French influence. Since 1923, the Turkish Republic—heir to the Ottoman Empire but not to its laws—is a centralized, modern, Western, laic, and civilian democracy. Today, as in the past, legal and social evolution takes place through voluntary receptions and at times also through imposed receptions, law being principally regarded in instrumental terms. When, in 1924, the ideological and technological decision was made to move outside the framework of the indigenous system of laws rather than to modernize the existing system, and to use the tool of reception as the sole method of law reform, a commission of 26 members was given the task of translating first the trilingual Swiss Civil Code from its French version. Subsequently, a number of special commissions translated most of the important commentaries on various branches of law into Turkish. During 1926, Turkish legal experts produced three entirely new codes, and more followed. The main aim of this purposive use of law was to demolish the foundations of the old legal system by creating completely new laws and to regulate and legislate people's relationships according to what the Turkish government thought these relationships ought to be: a prime example of optimistic normativism and social engineering through law. The aim was to reduce the public role of Islam and make it solely a basis for personal conviction and morality. The Turkish Republic had a worldview, and its political, legal, and social systems were constructed and geared toward the achievement of this worldview. In discussing legal transplants, Alan Watson (2000) and others referred to the Turkish experience as the most extreme example.[4]

---

2 Note that article 1 of the Civil Code permitted, from the start, resorting to customary law in the absence of codal provisions.

3 I have looked at the Turkish legal system elsewhere in its various aspects. See Örücü (2006, 2008, 2010).

4 See, for example, Zweigert and Kötz (1998: 178). They find this experience remarkable, since "nowhere else in the world can one so well study how in the reception of a foreign law there is a natural interaction between the interpretation of the foreign text and the actual tradition and usages of the country

The various codes were selected from what were seen to be the best in their field for various reasons. The choice was driven at times by the perceived prestige of the model, at other times by efficiency, and sometimes by chance or historical accident. The civil law, the law of obligations, and civil procedure were borrowed from Switzerland; commercial law, maritime law, and criminal procedure from Germany; criminal law from Italy; and administrative law from France—all translated, adapted, and adjusted to solve the social and legal problems of Turkey and to interlock with one another.[5] Later still, significant developments in the fields of democracy, fundamental rights and freedoms, and review of constitutionality found their way into Turkish law, the last by the 1961 constitution, in the preparation of which, wide use was made of the West German and the Italian models. The provisions on economic development were inspired by the 1949 Indian constitution. The 1958 French constitution and the American constitution inspired the present 1982 constitution.

Although interpretation tends to introduce subjective and cultural tonalities and values, foreign law always provides inspiration and stimulus. Laws of European origin, themselves the product of centuries-long interreceptions, displacements, and translocations, had their full influence on Turkey in the past century. This blend gave Turkish law its civil laic character. The goal was to become European—legally, socially, and culturally. This aim has symbolic value in Turkey and has culminated in the desire to be accepted into the European Union as a full member and as a Western European state. The official program was geared to eliminate any kind of personal choice regarded by the formal legal system as undesirable, and to this end cultural and legal pluralism was not acceptable and has never been on the agenda since the collapse of the Ottoman Empire. The reforms in the legal framework were accompanied and complemented by a series of social reform laws aimed at changing people; a most important feature of these far-reaching radical reforms was that their intended effect was to be not just on the legal system, but also on the social system.[6]

A comparatist would have expected the system to become an overt mixed legal system, maybe even similar to that of Algeria: an amalgam of civilian, customary, and Islamic laws. Yet the old institutions were destroyed, and the new ones were erected in their place mainly by legislative enactments (see Örücü 1995: 10).[7] There was no scope for "bottom-up" lawmaking. As would be expected, the discord between the official formal legal system and the existing sociocultural systems was bound to create problems. However, the absence of bottom-up lawmaking in Turkey was—and is—somewhat compensated for by the role allocated to the high courts at the level of civil (Yargıtay), administrative (Danıştay), and constitutional (Anayasa Mahkemesi) matters.

In sum, in Turkey, at the level of law, the success of the import is not questionable; the mixed layers of modern law from various sources have been successfully adapted to the conditions of the recipient. The question, however, is whether the preceding story gives the total picture.

The Reentrance of Islam into the Story as Tradition

At the outset, one factor must be emphasized. Turkish laicism never meant a total separation of religion and state. It can best be described as active neutrality or as assertive laicism, because religion is under the control of the Directorate of Religious Affairs (Diyanet), which was converted in 1963 into a constitutional institution.[8]

---

which adopted it, with the consequent gradual development of a new law of an independent nature." As recently as 2000, Alan Watson (2000: 2) cited the Turkish example to support his views. William Twining (2005: 223–28) also considered this example.

5 See Glenn (1987: 265), who talks of "reception as alliance" and "reception as construction."

6 The social reforms were introduced by the eight reform laws (İnkilap Kanunları), which established secular education and civil marriage, adopted the Latin alphabet and the international numerals, introduced the hat, closed the dervish convents, abolished certain titles, and prohibited the wearing of certain garments. These laws are still protected by the 1982 constitution; their constitutionality cannot be challenged even today, nor can they be amended.

7 In Örücü (1995), trying to build a general theoretical framework, I designated the Turkish legal system as a "purée," in which existing diverse elements were moved into a compound, thereby creating a legal system in the civilian tradition, making the Turkish experience an exception to the rule.

8 This development, together with mandatory religious education in state schools for children deemed to be Sunni Muslims (see the European Court for Human Rights judgment in *Hasan and Eylem*

Because the presidency of this institution keeps an eye on the beliefs, worship, and ethics of Islam; enlightens the public about their Sunni religion; and administers the sacred worshipping venues, paradoxically the laic state has indirectly appropriated religious authority. This development can be assessed as one of the paths contributing to the coming into being of the covert mix.

We should now consider how the legislatively created legal system is coping with cultural, traditional, and religious demands of the people. How far can this laic legal system, born and bred from outside sources and forming the framework and the overlay in this largely conservative and traditional society, accommodate other forces? How do courts tune the received law to meet the needs of society, thus completing the transposition process while at the same time configuring the legal framework to social needs, blending the underlay with the overlay, and in the process providing a door for the entry of Islam—albeit in the guise of tradition—into the laic legal system, thus creating a novel hybrid?

Catering for normative multiplicity without an overarching unitary normative framework does not seem to accord with the idea of the Turkish state. The nation-state was originally built on the idea of an identifiable culture, a cultural unit. In Turkey, we have a monolithic, centralized, territorial, and top-down model of law, which may or may not allow competing sources of law to exist. We know that the technique, the form, and the content of Turkish law and the values reflected therein are all imported. The technique used is codification and the hierarchy of the norms, the accompanying elements—more specifically the civil tradition—deriving from the West. The official content, in many ways foreign to the Turkish way of thinking, reflects values borrowed from the West with some modifications and does not fully reflect the values of the past traditional national spirit. Yet this outcome was intentional because the purpose was to change that mentality. On the one hand, Turkey illustrates that law can be used as a creative tool for bringing about certain desired effects and sometimes even needs in society, rather than rationally and naturally reflecting peoples' needs and desires. On the other hand, though law can act as a harmonizing agent with economic, social, and cultural implications, such a legal system may not escape becoming a covert mixed legal system as the underlay gradually gains access into the realm of law, mostly in the form of unofficial legalities.

It is accepted in Turkey that an assumed similarity of culture exists between the Turkic and Islamic states, alongside an assumed similarity of culture with Europe. A large minority of the population, living mainly in urban areas, is Western in outlook and mentality: the Westernized Turk. For this educated, urbanized elite, a clear affinity of culture and outlook exists with Western Europe and the Western way of life. A much larger part of the Turkish population is rural and has a traditional outlook, which is maintained even when this population moves into the cities. Some of these poorly educated, rural Anatolians have become wealthy and politically effective. In addition, in the cities, the gap between the rich and the poor is wide, and the middle class has shrunk. Moreover, a populace also exists, which, having started with a traditional rural existence, has worked in other countries in Europe for some time and returned. This populace now fits neither into the first category nor the second. Although 98 percent of the population of Turkey is of the Islamic faith, these people are not all of the same sect or school. The inherent problems are not difficult to contemplate, and the courts try to adjust and homogenize the layers of systems within this covert mix.

With the emergence of democratic ideals and principles and of human rights values, standardization becomes more and more difficult to achieve and maintain; therefore, harmony in diversity and further mixedness may have to be accepted. The question is, how far? Because the mores, values, and mentality of the majority of the population are not reflected in the overlay of official law, an underlay of unofficial legalities has grown over the years, some of which have to be given cognizance by the official legal framework. Most of these developments can be seen in family law (religious marriages without a prior civil marriage, the legal status of children born into such unions, inheritance rights, and so on), but they are elsewhere as well.

Zengin v. Turkey, Application 1448/04, dated October 9, 2007), can be interpreted as a de facto violation of the principle of laicism and state neutrality in religious practices by the state, which supports and regulates Sunni religious institutions. Article 136 of the 1982 constitution reads, "The Directorate of Religious Affairs, which is within the general administration, shall exercise its duties prescribed in its laws, in accordance with the principles of laicism, removed from all political views and ideas, and aiming at national solidarity and integrity." For the story of Islam and laicism in the Ottoman Empire and the Turkish Republic and for information on a vast range of topics, including the Directorate of Religious Affairs, see Koçak (2010).

For example, wearing of the headscarf in public places (including universities) has been a major issue of contention for many years.

In the following sections, a number of selected cases[9] are considered where courts face cultural and religious demands contrary to the vision embodied in the official legal framework but still cater for them within the legal framework, though not necessarily in keeping with it. Some aspects of the culture and tradition, such as religious marriage or the wearing of the headscarf in the public sphere, clash with the officially protected vision. These issues are related to laicism protected by the constitution. Therefore, claims based on such issues create major problems for the courts. But even in such cases, solutions have to be found.

The courts can deal with some other aspects of culture by navigating between rules within the legal framework. A number of examples related to bride price, the status of blood brothers for insurance purposes, the special nature of *Hac* (*Hajj*), and the "cow cases" are considered. In all these, we see the blending of the underlay and the overlay, pointing to the developing covert mix of the Turkish legal system and the birth of a novel hybrid.

Religious Marriage

Because laicism manifests itself in the essence of Turkish family law, it follows that only a civil marriage is legally recognized.[10] Marriage has been secularized and is concluded on the oral response of the two parties. For the valid conclusion of a marriage contract, certain conditions have to be fulfilled: the capacity to marry and the absence of certain degrees of consanguinity and affinity, of an already existing marriage, of an adoptive relationship, and of certain diseases.

Mehmet Akif Aydın (2010: 181–82) bemoans the fact that during laicization of marriage, one very important impediment to marriage in Islamic law was left out: fosterage (*süt kardeşliği*, or milk sibling). Fosterage is a relationship between a man and a woman who were breastfed by the same woman during their infancy, which is an impediment to marriage between them in Islamic law and endures in Turkish Islamic tradition. However, it was not mentioned in the 1926 Civil Code as an impediment, nor is it included in the 2002 Civil Code, though most people do adhere to this tradition. There is no legal sanction. This barrier is an unofficial impediment and thus can be considered an unofficial legality.

Following the civil marriage ceremony, a marriage certificate (family record booklet) is given, without which a religious ceremony, *imam nikahı*,[11] cannot take place, and it is a criminal offense to undertake or perform such a ceremony without this certificate. However, in very few cases is a sanction applied, because it is an offense that needs to be brought to the knowledge of the authorities, and when it is, it often results in acquittal.[12]

Empirical research tells us[13] that seven types of traditional marriage exist in Turkey: *berdel* (two families agree, and sons and daughters are exchanged in a double marriage); *beşik kertmesi* (two families agree on the birth of two babies on their future marriage); *başlık paralı evlilik*[14] (marriage takes place on the payment of monies by the prospective husband); *kan bedelli evlilik* (to put an end to blood feuds, one of the daughters of the family whose turn it is to carry out the next killing is given as a wife to the other family); *kuma evliliği* (a woman is married off to a man who already has a wife); *kayın evliliği* (a woman is married off to one of

9 All translations from Turkish are by the author.

10 Exceptions to the rule obviously exist: Islamic family law can penetrate the system either in accordance with international private law rules, which may incorporate Islamic family law, or through the interpretation of secular domestic laws. For instance, foreign marriages concluded abroad are in principle recognized *ex lege* if they meet the requirements of the *lex loci celebrationis*.

11 *İmam nikahı* is a consensual marriage performed by an imam as a religious ceremony.

12 The Fourth Division of the Yargıtay overturned a criminal court ruling, thus acquitting an imam who had performed a religious marriage ceremony without first checking the document proving that a civil marriage had taken place (see Judgments 2000/3127, 2000/4891).

13 The information that follows is from a piece of empirical research that was carried out by the Committee on the Elimination of Discrimination against Women's Committee on Turkey and was cited in Turkish newspapers. The research was conducted in 81 cities and involved interviews with 453 women.

14 For the changes of official attitude to this version, see below.

the brothers of her deceased husband on the decision of the family council); and *akraba evliliği* (a woman is married to a first-degree relative).

Another factual situation also exists, a traditional practice of the fellow-wife in the eastern provinces, whereby a woman lives with a married man. In such a case, if the official wife accepts the fellow-wife, the law cannot intervene; the law will only support her if she asks for a divorce.[15]

Obviously the realities of marriage in Turkey are quite outside the formally regulated one (Yılmaz 2003, 2005). However, none of the preceding types of traditional marriage, apart from *kuma evliliği*, would create a problem if formally concluded as a civil marriage. If the fellow-wife is regarded as a mistress, the law has nothing to do with it. *Kuma evliliği*, however, falls foul of the law, because it would be considered polygamy, which is illegal. Nonetheless, although polygamy is legally banned, one still comes across polygamous unions—though they are rare—in some regions, particularly in rural areas in the southeastern part of the country.[16]

It is a fact that religious conviction, long tradition, remoteness of villages, strict formalities attached to civil marriage, the long time involved in getting documents sorted out, the embarrassment of medical examination, and the like influence the spouses-to-be and their families to opt for religious marriage alone. This type of cohabitation in Turkish society is illegal. Though such informal marriages have no civil legal status in the formal legal order, they are generally justified by certain sections of society through existing tradition.[17] Recently some cognizance has been attributed to this important unofficial legality, as is observed later in this chapter.

Although a religious ceremony is not needed for the marriage to be binding—a rule that is reiterated in the new 2002 Civil Code to indicate the secular nature of marriage in Turkey (article 143)—the fact is that, along with a civil marriage contract, a large number of Muslim couples perform a religious marriage ceremony, a verbal contract of partners in the presence of an imam, in accordance with classic Islamic law. Again, a majority of those who have adhered to religious marriage, even though only subsequent to a civil marriage, would also like to obey the rules of religion on divorce. Marriage in Islamic law can be dissolved by repudiation (*talak*, *talaq*, or the unilateral or bilateral decision of the spouses without going to court): if the spouses pronounce the specific statements, they are considered divorced under Islamic law. However, they are still married according to the laic legal system under which they married in the first place unless they also go to court to obtain a civil divorce. If they do not and they continue to live together, which they are not permitted to do under Islamic law, they would be committing the sin of fornication. Another result would be that any child conceived after the time of the Islamic divorce would be considered illegitimate pursuant to their religious beliefs. Obviously, this situation is not a concern of the official family law, but it has religious consequences for the couple as well as societal consequences for like-minded others (Aydın 2010: 181–82).

In 1998, the constitutionality of article 237/4 of the 1926 Criminal Code, which had been amended in 1936 to criminalize unofficial religious unions (*imam nikahı*) entered into without prior civil marriage and imposed a prison sentence of two to six months on the man and the woman, as well as a prison sentence on persons performing such religious ceremonies without seeing the official certificate of marriage, was challenged as violating several articles of the 1982 constitution: article 2 (the principle of laicism), article 10 (equality), article 12 (the character and the scope of fundamental rights and freedoms), and article 24 (freedom to conduct religious services and ceremonies).

The Anayasa Mahkemesi, in a judgment given in 1999 and published in 2002, stated that article 237 was inserted into the Criminal Code to give support to civil marriage; that without this section, polygamous unions would become possible; and that though such unions have no legal consequence, they pose a threat to the concept of family and are thereby detrimental to the social order. The court opined that if couples enter such illegal unions, women cannot use their rights arising from marriage, children are illegitimate and lose their inheritance rights, and such marriages cannot be invoked against third parties and thus have no legal protection. For those reasons, civil marriage must be strengthened to protect the family and the rights

15 See Çetiner and Bozkurt Yüksel (2008), who discuss this traditional practice and its consequences.

16 See Kağıtcıbaşı (1982: 6). In addition, even though according to the Civil Code men and women have the same inheritance rights, Kağıtcıbaşı (1982: 7) reports that in some traditional and isolated regions, a woman inherits either nothing or one-half of what a man receives, as in Islamic law.

17 For a comparative assessment of such informal unions, see Rutten (2010).

of women and children. The court then added that the law did not violate, as was claimed, the principle of equality between those who live together with no marriage of any kind and those with only a religious "marriage," because members of the first group do not wish their unions to be regarded as marriage, whereas those of the second group consider themselves to be, in fact, married. Equality before the law does not mean that everyone must be treated alike; differentiation based on article 13 on limitation of rights and freedoms is not unconstitutional. The court further pointed out that "the Civil Code is a fundamental building block in the structure of the bridge to a contemporary and laic legal system for the Turkish Republic," and civil marriage, "being in the essence of that block, is also specifically protected by article 174 of the Constitution."[18] The court said that keeping law and religion separate is the most important function of laicism.[19]

Yet, in 2005 the Anayasa Mahkemesi, by annulling article 140/2 of the 2005 Turkish Criminal Code, added a controversy to the debate on religious unions.[20] Article 140/1 states that, upon complaint, a person who enters a sexual relationship with a child of 15, without pressure, threats, or deceit, shall be imprisoned for six months to two years. The annulled article 140/2 stipulated that if the perpetrator were older by five years than the injured, the punishment would be doubled, without seeking the condition of complaint. The court based its decision on the principle of equality before the law. Yet as pointed out in one of the dissenting opinions, this provision did not violate the principle of equality and was not contrary to the principle of protection of the family, the principle of privacy of private life, or proportionality in criminal sanctions. The court should have considered the meaning, the purpose, and the context of the provision. This annulment, on the one hand, could encourage illegal unions entered into without official marriage or, at the very least, send a signal to the traditional and religious sectors of the society that such relationships will be tolerated from now on—a signal to facilitate the upholding of Islamic traditions, the unofficial legality. On the other hand, the decision has created a discrepancy with the new arrangements in the Civil Code, which state that majority is reached at 18 years, which is also the normal age for marriage. Both sexes can get married at 17. The bottom line is a reduction to 16 by the judge for exceptional circumstances.

Quite a different signal was sent, however, through the Law on the Protection of the Family, passed in 1998,[21] pursuant to the amendment to article 41 of the constitution.[22] This law states that when a spouse, a child, or any other member of the family living under the same roof as the violent spouse informs the justice of the peace that she or he has been a subject of domestic violence, the judge can impose any number of sanctions.[23] Though this law uses the word *spouse* throughout, it was passed as affirmation by the legislature that women and children are the ones subjected to violence in this male-dominated society, that society should not tolerate this kind of behavior, and that women and children should have an official power to turn to

18 Article 174 states, "No provision of the Constitution shall be construed or interpreted as rendering unconstitutional the Reform Laws indicated below, which aim to raise Turkish society above the level of contemporary civilization and to safeguard the laic character of the Republic, and which were in force on the date of the adoption by referendum of the Constitution of Turkey: ... 4. The principle of civil marriage according to which the marriage act shall be concluded in the presence of the competent official, adopted by the Turkish Civil Code No: 743 of 17 February 1926, and Article 110 of the same Code."

19 Judgments 1999/27, 1999/42, November 24, 1999; *Resmi Gazete*, 24743, May 2, 2002; *Anayasa Mahkemesi Kararlar Dergisi*, 38 (2003: 160–70). This scene has not changed since the introduction of the New Criminal Code in 2005, which covers this issue in article 230 under the rubric "offenses against the family."

20 Judgments 2005/103, 2005/89, November 23, 2005; *Anayasa Mahkemesi Kararlar Dergisi*, 42 (2006: 437–54).

21 Law 4320, January 14, 1998; *Resmi Gazete*, 23233, January 17, 1998.

22 Article 41 on the protection of the family originally read, "The state shall take the necessary measures and establish the necessary organization to ensure the peace and welfare of the family, the protection of the mother and the children in particular, and for family planning education and practical application." This article gained a first paragraph in 2001, which reads, "The family is the foundation of Turkish society and is based on equality between the spouses."

23 The offending spouse will be cautioned not to behave in such a way as to frighten other members of the family; to leave the family home, which is now allocated to the other spouse and the children, and not return to it; not to visit their place of work; not to damage their belongings; to surrender any firearms to the security forces; and not to come to the family home drunk or having used drugs.

when unprotected.[24] Because the wording used covers *spouse* and *family*, the woman—who may be married off by her family at a very early age to a man through religious marriage alone—or cohabiting partners get no protection whatsoever. This law is in keeping with the laic approach and strengthens civil marriage by introducing measures in addition to the Civil and the Criminal Codes to protect the wife and children, yet it does not cater for the realities of the Turkish families or offer any protection for such "families," which are a persistent social issue in Turkey. All in all, the official attitude is obviously ambiguous, ambivalent, and undecided.

In fact, neither the legal framework nor the Yargıtay (the Court of Cassation) accept the fact that couples living out of wedlock can be regarded as in a relationship to be protected by law. For instance, while the Yargıtay was determining what constitutes an engagement so that it could decide whether gifts beyond the ordinary should be returned on the breaking up of the relationship, it was careful to differentiate between two situations: (a) the breaking up of an engagement (that is, a promise to marry), in which case gifts beyond the ordinary would be returned, and (b) the breaking up of people "living together without a valid marriage act," in which case the gifts need not be returned.[25] In this second instance, the law protects the possessor, because both parties act outside official legality.

It is now worthwhile to consider a recent and significant case brought in the European Court of Human Rights against Turkey, *Şerife Yiğit v. Turkey*, which deals with family life and the prohibition of discrimination (article 8 in conjunction with article 14 of the European Convention on Human Rights).[26] The case is related to a couple with an *imam nikahı* union entered into in 1976. They had six children. The "husband" died in 2002, and the "wife," Şerife Yiğit, asked for registration of their marriage and of the children and requested that she be paid her dead husband's pension and health benefits. Only the registration of the children was accepted; all other claims were refused. She argued that the refusal was a violation of her right to family life. The European Court of Human Rights decided on January 20, 2009, for Turkey.[27] The original chamber's decision was reached by a narrow majority of four to three. According to the European Court of Human Rights, a de facto family life indeed existed, but because Turkey did not recognize other stable relationships alongside civil marriage, Turkey could not be obliged to do so in this case. The court concluded that Turkey's aim was legitimate, that it had an objective and reasonable justification, and that, therefore, the distinction drawn between married and unmarried persons was not a violation in this context. The principle of equality could not be invoked successfully to acquire a legal civil status for a religious union. This judgment implies that the exercise of freedom of religion can be restricted in favor of other rights and interests.

The case was referred to the Grand Chamber on September 14, 2009. On November 2, 2010, the Grand Chamber reached a unanimous decision with two separate concurrent opinions. The Grand Chamber considered the case under article 1 of Protocol 1 in combination with article 14 of the European Convention on Human Rights and under article 8. On the question of whether discrimination existed on the basis of the nature of the marriage, the court accepted that the difference in treatment between civil and noncivil marriages pursued the legitimate aims of protecting public order and the rights and freedoms of women. On the question of proportionality, the court opined that Şerife Yiğit could not argue that she had a legitimate expectation of obtaining a pension and that she was well aware of the fact that she had to regularize her relationship in accordance with the Civil Code. Being religiously married for 26 years, she had ample time to contract a civil marriage. Although Şerife Yiğit argued that "religious marriage was a social reality in Turkey" and that "it

24 A very heated debate took place in parliament while this law was discussed, a very powerful view being that the law has no business interfering with family relationships and family violence, because the father of the family should be able to use his discretion on how to treat and chastise his wife and children. This view was especially upheld by religious right-wing politicians. The day was won by the strong feminist lobby and the progressive camp in parliament.

25 Judgments 1998/10173, 1998/12105, November 24, 1998; *Yargıtay Kararlar Dergisi*, 25 (1999: 170).

26 Application 3976/05, November 2, 2010.

27 A similar decision had already been reached in 1975 in *X v. Germany* (Application 6167/73), where the refusal to register a religious marriage was seen as not violating articles 9 and 12 of the European Convention on Human Rights. For a thorough discussion of a number of such cases, see Rutten (2010).

was a feature of Turkish life,"[28] the court took into account "the importance of the principle of secularism in Turkey" and that "Turkey requires a civil marriage from all its citizens" and concluded that the difference in treatment was proportionate. The court also found no violation of article 8, because the applicant was not prevented from enjoying peaceful family life. The Grand Chamber thus followed the Turkish authorities in its assessment of the legitimate aims. The court was keen to state that "Turkey aimed to put an end to a marriage tradition which places women at a clear disadvantage, not to say in a situation of dependence and inferiority to men."

Judges Christos Rozakis and Anatoly Kovler, however, had misgivings. In his concurring opinion, Judge Rozakis stated the view that religious marriage is actually the backdrop here. He believed that the real issue to be considered should have been a comparison of "long-standing and stable family relationships outside marriage" (that is, cohabitation) and "marriage, as understood by domestic law." He opined that the court should have decided "in view of new social realities which are gradually emerging in today's Europe, manifested in a gradual increase in the number of stable relationships outside marriage, which are replacing the traditional institution of marriage without necessarily undermining the fabric of family life."[29] Judge Kovler, in contrast, believed that the court demonstrated "ideological activism" and "committed a serious error of judgment on the Islamic system of values" and would have liked to see the court take "a more anthropological approach in the position it adopts, by 'not just exploring difference, but exploring it differently.'" Otherwise, he thought that "the Court is in danger of becoming entrenched in 'eurocentric' attitudes."[30]

This case brings to light the fact that the European Court of Human Rights does not support legal pluralism and considers that human rights law cannot be applied in different ways depending on the differing beliefs of the individuals. However, this opinion may be far from resolving the contradictions of modern existence, because legal systems cannot be successful if they are not linked to social values and moral sensibilities, which in their turn are not universal and apolitical.

Nonetheless, interesting developments have occurred here. In its effort to tune the law to the needs of society, and obviously with considerations of doing justice in mind, the Yargıtay, in recent years, has taken a milder position when the claims are based on private law but not on rights arising out of public law. For instance, compensation can be awarded to a woman whose partner in only a religious marriage dies. This compensation could be for pecuniary or nonpecuniary damages (*maddi ve manevi tazminat*) on the basis of articles 43 and 44 of the Code of Obligations,[31] or it could be for lack of financial support following a death (*destekten yoksun kalma tazminatı*) on the basis of article 45 of the Code of Obligations.[32] Hence, courts can award a surviving partner compensation on the general principles of civil liability but can never grant such partners a survivor's pension or social security benefits, which arise from public law, on the basis of the deceased partner's entitlements.[33]

---

28 Application 3976/05, November 2, 2010, para. 65.

29 Ibid., 17–18.

30 Ibid., 19.

31 The Turkish Code of Obligations, annexed to the Civil Code, was translated and received from the Swiss Code of Obligations in 1926.

32 In 1997, the General Assembly of the Danıştay (Supreme Administrative Court) upheld a first-instance judgment, thereby overturning the judgment of its own Tenth Division, on the ground that the four children and the surviving partner from a religious marriage should be awarded compensation after the father and partner was accidentally killed by police bullets. The children and the partner were deprived of his financial support. The court pointed out that although domestic law did not afford protection to or validate such a union, the couple had children together whose births had been recorded under the parents' names in the civil status register, and the deceased had supported the family financially. Judgments 1998/79, 1997/479, October 17, 1997.

33 For instance, in 1990, the Tenth Division of the Yargıtay set aside a first-instance judgment awarding such compensation in a work-related accident because section 23 of the Social Security Act (Law 506) was involved, which guarantees compensation only to the children born of a marriage or a union other than marriage and not to the partner. The court held that in the absence of legislation on the subject, the Social Security Agency (a public body) could require the woman in question to repay the sums wrongly paid to her after her partner's death (Judgments 1990/4010, 1990/6972, September 11, 1990).

In this context, the Yargıtay has extended the right to compensation for death in work-related accidents to the unmarried cohabiting woman (*nikahsız eş*) arising out of private law. For instance, in one case,[34] the childless surviving partner of an *imam nikahı* union asked for material and moral compensation after the death of her partner in a work-related accident. Although the private insurance company objected, the lower court agreed. The Yargıtay supported the lower court but decided on a percentage lower than the one that would be the due of the married wife. In another later case,[35] the insured died in a work-related accident, and the partner, this time referred to by the Yargıtay as the "cohabiting partner," was 18, had a child, and according to the court, had more than a 35 percent chance of remarriage, which is the accepted percentage for an official widow. A telling dissenting opinion by a female judge demanded further recognition of social facts—and a change in the law. She was critical of the differentiation drawn between the two women:

> Here "cohabiting couple" (*nikahsız eş*) refers to a traditional Anatolian relationship where couples live together as husband and wife, with close family ties and children. Therefore, the presence or absence of official wedlock should not be the criterion on which to treat the two women differently. The Social Security Agency will give a pension only to the officially married wife and this for life. This should be the only extra gain for the married woman. An Anatolian village woman is already oppressed and faces the risk of being officially unmarried owing to tradition. She should not be further weakened when facing the law. This situation would only lead to mistrust of justice. The present circumstance is the outcome of the social structure. She should be given equal compensation.[36]

It appears that, progressively, the Yargıtay can accommodate "marriages" not accepted by the official system when the matter at hand is not related to giving effect to the marriage itself but, for instance, to the law of obligations where the court does not have to go into the issue of discussing whether a religious marriage is a marriage in the official sense. Thus, in a case related to the return of jewelry given at such a wedding, the court referred to the female partner as the "unofficial partner" (*gayriresmi eş*) and accepted the claim for compensation because the jewelry was no longer available for return.[37]

Because neither the legal framework nor the courts regard couples living without an official secular marriage as being in a relationship to be protected by law, decisions of courts in this area, converting illegality into legality, are of the utmost importance for such couples. This development is crucial in the assessment of Turkey's legal system as a covert mix in which Islam and tradition play a role.[38]

Children and Paternity

As to the children born into religious marriages with no prior civil marriage, before the passage of the first Amnesty Act of 1933, the Yargıtay attempted to resolve the problem by way of interpretation: when one of the parents died, children of such informal marriages were considered as legitimate by the court through an analogous application of article 249 of the 1926 Civil Code, which said that children of couples who made promises to marry each other but were then unable to marry owing to the death or incapacity of either the man or the woman, could be declared legitimate by a court on the application of the other party or of the child. This approach was one way to accommodate an unofficial legality by interpretation.

34 Judgments 1996/1606, 1996/1661, March 21, 1996; *Yargıtay Kararları Dergisi*, 22 (1996: 1291).

35 Judgments 1997/3331, 1997/4819, July 8, 1997; *Yargıtay Kararları Dergisi*, 23 (1997: 1785).

36 Ibid.

37 Judgments 02/1153, 03/2380, March 6, 2003; *Yargıtay Kararları Dergisi*, 29 (2003: 1044).

38 In 2007, the Yargıtay quashed a first-instance judgment on the ground that a woman married in accordance with religious rites should be paid compensation under articles 43 and 44 of the Code of Obligations following the death of her partner in a work-related accident; 2007/289, 2007/8718, May 28, 2007. This now is the established approach of both the Yargıtay and the Danıştay.

If we consider the passage of the Amnesty Acts previously mentioned, we see that from the very beginning tradition and religious beliefs were once more accommodated indirectly, this time by the legislature.[39] At intervals, the legislature has felt under pressure to legislate on these illicit relationships and the status of children born into them. Where no marriage impediment exists between the parties, these acts, cited as Amnesty Acts or Legitimacy Laws, allow the registration of consensual marriages for those who are without a civil marriage contract, who are living together as husband and wife, and who have a child born into their relationship. Amnesty Acts, the last one in 1991, made the legitimization of thousands of children possible and validated their status. These children are registered as legitimate if they are born to parents living together continuously as husband and wife and not born from a casual relationship. Even the children of fathers who are legally married to women other than the child's mother can be registered as legitimate as long as the mother is not married to another man. Amnesty Acts can be seen as one of state law's means of coping with the nonstate normative order.

As to paternity, article 310 of the 1926 Civil Code stated that, on the demand of a woman, a court can decide on paternity in cases where a man had promised marriage to the woman or where sexual intercourse had constituted an offense or an abuse of position. A lower court brought a case to the Anayasa Mahkemesi, saying, "'Natural fatherhood' in article 297 only gives the right to demand compensation, whereas 'paternity with all its consequences' (article 310) gives the child quite different rights, and from the point of view of the innocent child, this differentiation creates inequality."

The Anayasa Mahkemesi stated, with no dissenting opinion, the following:

> In cases where the conditions of article 310 are not met there can be no decision on "paternity with all its consequences." This provision is for the protection of the family and to discourage other types of cohabitation; this is in the public interest and morality, and the provision does not violate article 10 of the Constitution. This regulation is also in keeping with the necessities of a democratic society and therefore not contrary to articles 12 and 13. Article 41 is for the protection of the child, the woman and the family. The reasoning of this article specifically mentions that the family to be protected and to be established as an institution in society is the family as envisaged by the Civil Code. One of the aims therefore is to prevent free unions and encourage the formation of the family. This provision is not contrary to these aims.[40]

We now see, however, that in the new 2002 Civil Code, no distinction is left between legitimate and illegitimate children or between cases that determine paternity. This intriguing development can be assessed in relation to the attitude toward Islam and an unofficial legality in relation to this subject. On the one hand, this development accords with the values upheld by the European Convention on Human Rights and, on the other, with those of some in Turkey who want to have children born to *imam nikahı* relationships equated to those born in wedlock. Thus, it has a paradoxical consequence, which gives the courts a freer hand to indirectly uphold religious values that clash with one of the values of the official framework: laicism.

Related to this issue is another development that enables a man to acknowledge his children from adulterous relationships. One of the consequences of adultery in the 1926 Civil Code concerned the acknowledgment and inheritance rights of children born into adulterous arrangements. Prior to 1981, the paternity of a child born into an adulterous relationship could not be decided by a court, except as "paternity for financial support only." This provision was found to be unconstitutional by the Constitutional Court in 1981.[41] Thus, a court can declare "paternity with all its consequences" for a child whose father was already married to a woman other than his or her mother at the time of the sexual intercourse. More was to follow. Turkey now adheres to the European principle of "the best interests of the child." Since 1991, a father can acknowledge a child born into an adulterous relationship because the Constitutional Court held in 1991 that the provision of the Civil Code that stated that a married man could not acknowledge his child from an adulterous relationship

39 For more information on this innovation, see Örücü (1988: 228). These acts were introduced in 1933, 1945, 1950, 1965, 1975, 1981, and most recently in 1991.

40 Judgments 1993/37, 1993/56, December 7, 1993; *Resmi Gazete*, 23918, December 26, 1999.

41 ; Judgments E. 1980/29; K. 1981/22, May 21, 1981.

was unconstitutional and that all children should be treated equally, whether born into illicit relationships or not.[42] The Islamists have taken this decision to mean that, in an indirect manner, *imam nikahı* relationships are being condoned, so that a married man (by civil marriage) can acknowledge his children born into his other unions. If this view is given weight, it can be regarded as another instance of the state's laws accommodating an unofficial legality.

Adoption

Because Islamic law had no such institution, adoption as an institution entered Turkish law with the 1926 Civil Code. According to the 1926 Civil Code, however, adoption was only of adults, not small infants, with the added condition that the adopters should have no children of their own. The 2002 Civil Code brought in a fundamental change: the adoption of minors (article 305). This new possibility, in addition to complying with the practices of the European states, addresses a serious social issue in Turkey of people wanting to adopt the children of either their poor or deceased siblings or other family members. Such adoptions are a frequent factual occurrence, especially among the rural population in Turkey. This unofficial legality has now gained legal recognition. Adoption can take place six weeks after birth (article 310). Normally, the conditions for such adoptions are that the adoptive parents must care for and educate the minor for one year, the adoptions must be in the interests of the minor, and the adoption must not adversely affecting the rights of the other children of the adopters.

Spouses can adopt together only (article 306), though article 307 contains some exceptions.[43] Such adopters should be married for at least five years and be 30 years of age. If they are married for two years, however, one spouse, with the condition of being 30 years old, can adopt the child of the other. An unmarried person can also adopt if he or she is 30 years of age (article 307). The possibility of adoption of adults and wards continues as before (article 313), though new conditions have been introduced.[44]

Age of Marriage

Persons gain majority at 18 years of age, and that is the normal age at which individuals should be able to marry. However, article 124 of the 2002 Civil Code states that persons can marry at the age of 17. In addition, with the decision of a judge, couples can marry at 16. Previously, because the principle of equality had not been translated into the 1926 Civil Code, although the age of majority was still 18, boys could marry at 17 and girls at 15. Furthermore, in exceptional circumstances, such as abductions, pregnancy, or terminal illness, these ages could be reduced to 15 for boys and 14 for girls by judicial decision. This arrangement reflected unofficial legalities and social practices. The new article 124 is a fundamental amendment and will have considerable effect on Turkish society. On divorce, both spouses retain the age of the majority acquired through the previous marriage. The 1926 arrangement reflected Turkish realities better, especially among the rural population. It was also considered a measure to combat abductions and elopements at these early ages.

---

42 Anayasa Mahkemesi, 90/15, 91/5, February 28, 1991; *Resmi Gazete*, March 27, 1992. For a discussion of the cases both at the Constitutional Court and the High Court of Appeal, see Örücü (1999).

43 The Anayasa Mahkemesi reiterated that spouses can adopt together only and that this arrangement is not unconstitutional (as it is not in violation of articles 5, 10, 13, and 41). Judgments 2004/38, 2009/108, July 9, 2009; *Resmi Gazete*, 27751, November 6, 2010. This decision pays heed to social values.

44 The adopter's descendants should give overt consent. This clause was amended by the legislature on July 13, 2003, by Law 5399. The clause previously stated that "the adopter should have no descendants." The change came about after the realization by the legislature that this matter was not a condition for adoption of minors; the ward must be in need of help and must have been looked after by the adopter for five years, or must have been looked after for five years as a child. If there are other valid reasons and the adopter and the adoptee have been living together for at least five years, an adult can be adopted. An adoptee who is married can be adopted only with the consent of his or her spouse, as before.

In 2005, the Anayasa Mahkemesi, by annulling article 140/2 of the 2005 Turkish Criminal Code, as discussed previously, added a controversy to the debate on the age of marriage.[45] A person who enters a sexual relationship with a child of 15, without pressure, threats, or deceit, shall be imprisoned from six months to two years, only on complaint (article 140/1). The annulled article 140/2 stipulated that if the perpetrator were older by five years than the injured party, the punishment would be doubled, without seeking the condition of complaint. Now, where there is no complaint, this annulment may encourage illegal unions entered into without official marriage at an early age and creates a discrepancy with the new arrangements in the Civil Code related to the age when persons can marry.

Başlık (Bride Price)

A telling example of the evolution from religion to tradition and, therefore, from illegality and unacceptability to legality and acceptability are the *başlık*[46] (bride price) cases. Once banned, this bride price is now regarded as a traditional gift by the Yargıtay. A number of Yargıtay decisions up to the 1980s regarded money paid by the groom to the father of the girl to be immoral and therefore not to be returned if the engagement dissolved.[47]

First, in 1986 the Yargıtay pronounced that the banning by a local administration of the payment of money by a bridegroom to the bride's father (*başlık parası*) was illegal and that, therefore, not obeying the ban could not be considered an offense. The court said that an administration could not ban a tradition or convert it into an offense. The court stated, "This centuries old tradition is a fact; the practice can only be banned by the legislature if regarded as against public policy."[48] The court added that, in any event, to eradicate such a tradition should be a matter of education and not of law.

The courts now consistently consider money and goods, given under the name of *kalın*, *ağırlık*, or *başlık*, as gifts.[49] Consequently, their return can be demanded, because when an engagement comes to an end, among the gifts to be returned—whether given to the parties, to their families, or to those acting as such—are those whose value is out of the ordinary (that is, things of great value).[50] The practice of these payments continues, especially in rural areas, and is considered to be compensation for the loss of unpaid labor in the household for domestic chores. Official state law did not succeed in eradicating this practice.

In fact, this tradition emanates from religion and is reminiscent of *mahr*, an Islamic custom, whereby the bridegroom has to give a gift to the bride in consideration of the marriage. The gift then becomes the property of the wife. *Mahr* is interpreted by Western courts according to hugely varied legal constructs, such as multiculturalism, fairness, public policy, and gender equality. The Turkish courts appear to have taken very similar attitudes to this once banned practice in the name of "politics of recognition," equality, and "doing justice" and are in fact accommodating an Islamic practice within the laic legal framework by giving it a neutral name: *hediye* (gift).

45 Judgments 2005/103, 2005/89, November 23, 2005; *Anayasa Mahkemesi Kararlar Dergisi*, 42 (2006: 437–54).

46 *Başlık* is money given by the man to the father of the girl to secure the engagement and thereby the marriage.

47 See judgments of the 2nd and 11th Divisions of the Yargıtay: For instance, in judgment 2771/1858, July 7, 1949, the Second Division held that "to give moneys and goods under the name of *başlık* is against public policy and morality. The claim for repayment of such, given to secure an illegal cause cannot be upheld." Again, in the judgment 1980-620/620, February 11, 1980, the 11th Division held that "the moneys and goods taken by the father of the girl, under the name of *başlık*, in order to agree to the engagement, … [are] illegal and therefore any such undertaking is not binding." However, some judgments regarded the repayment of *başlık* as possible, relying on "unjustified enrichment" of the Code of Obligations (article 61).

48 Judgments 1986/2-584, 1986/299, May 26, 1986; *Yargıtay Kararları Dergisi*, 12 (1986: 1689).

49 *Kalın* is money or goods given by the man to the girl to enable her to prepare her dowry. *Ağırlık* is the goods given by the man to the father of the girl to secure the engagement and thereby the marriage.

50 Civil Code of 2002, section 122.

The Headscarf (the Türban Cases)

Claims based on another Islamic practice, wearing the headscarf, remain unacceptable to the official law when the practice involves the public domain—an unofficial legality. For instance, in 1993 the name of a female trainee lawyer was removed from the bar list because she came to court wearing a head cover and refused to remove it. According to the lower administrative court, because she was only a trainee and the matter was solely a moral question, there was no violation of the respect due to the legal profession, though the regulations of the profession do impose certain conditions on appearance. The Danıştay, however, saw no difference between a lawyer and a trainee and regarded the issue as outside "the right to religious freedom," saying, "The behavior of the trainee is contrary to the principles of a laic state governed by the rule of law, is incompatible with the profession of a lawyer and is an obstacle to her becoming and acting as a lawyer."[51]

Headscarf cases have never lost their significance in Turkey and continue to challenge the official legal framework. Indeed, this chronic issue is one that the present government keeps on the agenda. However, the courts are bound by the vision within the official framework. A number of decisions have been given by the Anayasa Mahkemesi, the Yargıtay, and the Danıştay on this issue. More important, the Anayasa Mahkemesi evaluates the headscarf (the *türban*) cases in educational establishments within the context of laicism. The first decision reached on this issue was in 1989, annulling the amendment to the law lifting the ban on the wearing of the *türban* in such institutions.[52] The court opined:

> [T]he fact that wearing of the headscarf, giving the person an appearance of being anachronistic, is gradually spreading, has obvious drawbacks for the Republican reforms and the principle of laicism.... A laic legal order, laic education and laic administration cannot be thought of as separate from one another.... Educational establishments cannot be set up contrary to the requirements of article 42 of the Constitution ... and higher education institutions are no exception. To separate students on religious affiliation, by symbols indicating which belief they support in classes, laboratories, clinics, policlinics and corridors, where students work together to reach the truth by being educated and applying scientific methods in a spirit of friendship and solidarity, would lead to conflict and hinder cooperation.

Later in 1991, in a second case,[53] the Anayasa Mahkemesi decided that the regulation bringing "freedom of attire" to higher education institutions did not apply to "religious dress and covering the neck and hair with a scarf or *türban* due to religious belief" and that this regulation, being unconstitutional, should be annulled. According to the court, any symbol representing religious belief should be kept out of educational institutions, and allowing the wearing of the *türban* in the universities could not accord with a laic scientific environment. The reasoning of the Anayasa Mahkemesi has also been accepted by the European Court of Human Rights, which decided that such a ban on the wearing of the *türban* in public institutions and educational establishments could be regarded as "necessary in a democratic society," and that those who agree to undertake university education are to be deemed as also having agreed to accept the principles of laicism, which is seen as a sine qua non of democracy and one of the fundamental principles of the Turkish state. The European Court of Human Rights decided for Turkey.[54]

Referring to decisions of the Danıştay and the Anayasa Mahkemesi, and after extensive discussion of personality rights and public interest, the Yargıtay held that the headscarf cannot be worn in institutions of higher education, and therefore, the decision by the principal of a university not to allow female students to take exams with their heads covered did not constitute a violation of personality rights and was not a delictual

51 Judgments 92/3342, 93/2611, July 5, 1993.

52 This case is usually referred to in Turkey as the First *Türban* Decision. See Judgments 1989/1, 1989/12, March 7, 1989; *Resmi Gazete*, 20216, July 5, 1989. The appellant was the president of the Republic.

53 This case is referred to in Turkey as the Second *Türban* Decision. See Judgments 1990/36, 1991/8, April 9, 1991; *Resmi Gazete*, 20946, July 31, 1991. The appellant was the Sosyal Demokrat Halkçı Parti (Social Democratic Populist Party), the main opposition party at the time.

54 *Leyla Şahin v. Turkey*, Application 44774/98, judgments of June 29, 2004 and November 10, 2005.

act, as claimed.[55] In interpreting section 17 of the Law 2547 of 1990 on Higher Education, the court held that "freedom of dress" was to be understood as "within what was allowed by law," and although no provisions in any legislation banned the wearing of the headscarf, decisions by the Anayasa Mahkemesi and the *Danıştay* did, and the courts have the duty to interpret the law, law being a whole.

Furthermore, in 2008, as the protector of the system, and in view of the immutable concept of laicism in article 2 of the constitution, the Anayasa Mahkemesi invalidated a constitutional amendment to articles 10 and 42 of the constitution by rejecting the addition by the parliament of the clause "in the utilization of all public services" to article 10 on equality and of the sentence "no one shall be deprived of his/her right to higher education unless expressly prohibited by law" to article 42 on education. Both were introduced with the purpose of abolishing the ban on wearing headscarves for female university students. The court stated:

> Covering for the sake of religious belief and the freedom to wear clothing symbolizing one's religion may cause conflict in society by the use of pressure on individuals whom they understand do not share the same belief as themselves. This may induce them to perform preventive and harmful acts against one another's freedom of religion and belief and even to exclude those who are not of their own belief.[56]

Nevertheless, the position has been changing slowly but surely in an intriguing manner. Although neither the legislation nor the court decisions have changed, first, Yusuf Ziya Özcan, the head of the Council of Higher Education (Yükseköğretim Kurulu, or YÖK), held a press conference in 2010, and from then on, universities started allowing students with headscarves into the campuses. Then, in March 2010, following a complaint, YÖK sent an instruction to the administration of the Istanbul University stating that "if a student is already in class with a headscarf on, she cannot be asked to leave; the lecturer continues with the lecture, and if need be, informs the office of the dean of the incident." Consequently, at the beginning of the 2011/12 academic year, the condition stating "the head should not be covered" was removed from the application information booklet. Thus, legally, the ban still exists, and some lecturers declare that they would not allow headscarves to be worn in their classes. Nevertheless, female students with headscarves abound in the universities, both private and public. This development shows that, although the legal norms do not change, when the implementers change, the implementation also changes to reflect tradition and religious belief. An unofficial legality is accommodated in the name of doing justice, presenting more food for the developing covert mix and novel hybrid![57]

Blood Brother's Rights

In one case, a life insurance policy was taken out for the benefit of a "blood brother." The insurance company refused to pay. The official law makes no reference to this customary relationship. The status of blood brother exists only as an unofficial legality. However, the Yargıtay said that, according to Turkish folklore and customs, this institution is valued, that it is a private pact that creates a relationship like brotherhood or bosom friendship, and that since the blood brother should be considered to have a moral interest in the continuation of the life of the other, he therefore should be accepted as the beneficiary.[58] Here we see tradition being upheld in the absence of legal norms.

55 Judgments 99/2625, 99/4428, May 14, 1999; *Yargıtay Kararları Dergisi*, 25 (1999: 1656).

56 Judgments 2008/16, 2008/116, June 5, 2008; *Resmi Gazete* 27032, October 22, 2008. This decision has been assessed as "usurpation of power" by the court. See Özbudun (2009).

57 Since October and November 2013, as part of the "democratization package," the official situation has also changed in that, to date, there are three female members of parliament who entered parliament with headscarves for the first time in its history. Female students and civil servants can also wear the headscarf.

58 Judgments 95/3856, 95/4829, June 9, 1995; *Yargıtay Kararları Dergisi*, 21 (1995: 1412, at 1414).

Special Nature of Hac (Hajj)

Some religious and traditional values are given additional weight by the Yargıtay. For instance, when baggage—gifts brought back from the *Hac* (*Hajj*)[59]—was lost in transit, though article 22 of the Montreal Protocol amending the Warsaw Protocol to the Hague Convention was to be applied, the Yargıtay stated, "When the special nature of this journey and the spiritual value of the gifts to be given to relatives and friends are taken into account, it emerges that the claimant should be given 'moral' compensation and not solely 'material' compensation."[60]

The Cow Cases

A most remarkable case serves as an example of the interlocking of the social, religious, and legal cultures and of the official and unofficial legalities, through the innovative dexterity of the Yargıtay. This decision, reached in 1979,[61] is a perfect illustration of the inherent covert mixed nature of this legal system and of how Islam can be subsumed under the guise of custom and tradition. The case concerned the sexual involvement of an underage village boy with a neighbor's cow. The owner of the cow, rather than suing for bestiality under the Criminal Code, sued to recover damages from the father of the boy under the Civil Code. He claimed that according to religious sources, which he cited, his cow had become untouchable and could not be sold or its meat and milk consumed. The case was dismissed by the lower court for lack of legal ground, because religious law is not a recognized source of Turkish law. The owner of the cow appealed. The Yargıtay overturned the decision of the lower court, saying:

> Although religious rules or sentiments could not form the basis of any claim, if the complainant could prove, by expert evidence, that there were local religious or moral beliefs or customs to the effect that the meat and the milk of such an animal could not be consumed, then the animal would be considered to have lost its market value, in which case, by the application of the *noxal* rule of Roman law, the cow should be given to the father of the boy and the claimant should be given the market value of the cow by the father.[62]

A second, very similar case occurred in 1998, where the lower court decided that the pursuer had no case because there was no "medical objection" to the use of the meat and the milk of such an animal. The Yargıtay overturned the decision, declaring that when no codal provision is applicable to a matter, then according to the previously referenced article 1 of the Civil Code, tradition and custom are to be resorted to:

> Since facts are not in dispute in this case, tradition and custom have to be investigated in line with the claim, and if custom, tradition, religious and moral beliefs and conceptions are in line with the claim, then the existence of damages cannot be questioned. The pursuer should be asked whether he wishes to surrender the animal to the defendant in return for the market price, and if not, then reasonable compensation must be decided upon.[63]

---

59 *Hac* (*Hajj*) is the religious pilgrimage to Mecca.

60 Judgments 01/5985, 01/8861, February 12, 2003; *Yargıtay Kararları Dergisi*, 29 (2003: 43).

61 Judgments 79/1644, 79/14383, December 21, 1979. I have used this example on many occasions in my work.

62 What is worth noting here is that, in the use of the Roman law principle, the Yargıtay seems to have inverted it to fit the situation. The principle has been crystallized by a local evaluation of legal concerns. Understood and applied in its original form, it should have been the boy who, as the offending object, was returned to the owner of the cow and not the cow to the boy's father!

63 Judgments 98/2632, 98/3249, March 24, 1998; *Yargıtay Kararları Dergisi*, 24 (1998: 834). These are the only two cases I have come upon on this subject!

The formula is a fine example of how the Yargıtay resolves disputes within the formal legal system without openly facing an unofficial legality, which, in this case, is based on religious belief. The case shows how the layers of systems, official and unofficial, may be interlocked.

Concluding Remarks

The cases considered in this chapter show that in Turkey, though the official legal framework does not permit competition between the rules of the legal system and the rules of nonstate normative orders, the courts try to create such harmony. In the Turkish experience, the concepts and values introduced in the early years of the republic were to a large extent incompatible with those of the endogenous system, and the deeper values and purposes of the two were not commensurable. One way out was to establish a global purpose and hope that a bridge could be built between traditional culture and Western-style expression of the norms and standards by the courts. Over the years, however, we see that, on the one hand, the Western link is strengthened through the state law, for instance, with the amendments to the constitution and to family law in the 2002 Civil Code; on the other hand, by treating religious claims as traditional or customary ones, the courts are trying to meet the demands of the people, which may have stemmed from their religious beliefs and yet can be fit within the official framework by state organs recognizing the nonstate normative orders. Considerations of the equality principle, freedom of religion, prohibition of discrimination, and protection of family life are being balanced by the legislature and the judiciary in the name of doing justice.

Yet we have seen that the messages sent are mixed. One might be forgiven for thinking that the present situation is ambivalent and suffers from conceptual incoherence. The gap between what is in law and what is in fact is as wide as ever. When the social deficit widens, it affects the distance between official and unofficial legalities in Turkish practice. The formal legal system in Turkey performs a balancing act, sometimes trying to maintain a firm stance and at other times allowing the traditionalist views to be heard. This modus vivendi and the complex relationship between the state and nonstate legalities contribute to the emergence and development of the covert mixed legal system. With more space allocated to Islam and tradition, this mixity is strengthening today.

As noted, the modern layer of the Turkish legal system is the ultimate and predominant one, reflecting the civil and laic nature of the law and embodying the mixing layers of the system. This modern layer is synthetic and eclectic, and this mixed nature of the modern layer has been kept alive. In fact, one can talk of the mixed modern layer, or modern layers, rather than of the modern layer of law. The interaction between the modern layers is of utmost importance for the functioning of the legal system, but so is the interaction between the modern layers and the underlying layers, such as the traditional and religious layers.

What is the proper place for Islam and tradition in laic Turkish law? Should they be accommodated, tolerated, or reconciled? Will the outcome be a novel hybrid with a more pronounced role for indigenous culture and Islam and, thus, more than a weak legal pluralism enveloped in the monolithic legal system? How can law and society cope with the social deficit? Will we see more rules emerging representing these other normative orders? Is the answer for Turkey to effectively promote modernization and yet reach out to more traditional and Islamic elements in the society, since we see that in Turkey, traditional values override claims to modernity? Can a good synthesis be achieved between the positive aspects of traditional cultures and Islam and the demands of laicism, modernity, and democracy?

Whatever the future developments and the shape of the mixture, both the legal and the sociocultural systems will remain in a relationship that is mixed, maybe with more space created for Islam, albeit in the guise of tradition, and the rules of nonstate normative orders. The future lies in a covert mixed legal system: a novel hybrid.

References

Aydın, M.A. 2010. Family law in Turkey: The journey from Islamic law to secular law, in *Familj, religion, ratt*, edited by A. Singer, M. Jantera-Jareborg, and A. Schlytter. Uppsala, Sweden: Justus Förlag, 163–84.

Çetiner, S., and Bozkurt Yüksel, A.E. 2008. "Fellow-wife" and the law, in *The International Survey of Family Law 2008*, edited by B. Atkin. Bristol, UK: Jordan, 475–80.

Glenn, P. 1987. Persuasive authority. *McGill Law Journal*, 32(2), 261–98.

Kağıtcıbaşı, Ç. 1982. Introduction, in *Sex Roles, Family and Community in Turkey*, edited by Ç. Kağıtcıbaşı. Bloomington: Indiana University, 1–32.

Koçak, M. 2010. Islam and national law in Turkey, in *Sharia Incorporated: A Comparative Overview of the Legal Systems of Twelve Muslim Countries in Past and Present*, edited by J.M. Otto. Leiden, Netherlands: Leiden University Press, 231–72.

Örücü, E. 1988. Turkey: Reconciling traditional society and secular demands. *Journal of Family Law*, 26(1), 221–36.

Örücü, E. 1992. The impact of European law on the Ottoman Empire and Turkey, in *European Expansion and Law: The Encounter of European and Indigenous Law in 19th and 20th Century Africa and Asia*, edited by W.J. Mommsen and J.A. de Moor. London: Berg, 39–58.

Örücü, E. 1995. A theoretical framework for transfrontier mobility of law, in *Transfrontier Mobility of Law*, edited by R. Jagtenberg, E. Örücü, and A. de Roo. The Hague: Kluwer, 5–18.

Örücü, E. 1996. Turkey: Change under pressure, in *Studies in Legal Systems: Mixed and Mixing*, edited by E. Örücü, E. Attwooll, and S. Coyle. The Hague: Kluwer, 89–113.

Örücü, E. 1999. Improving the lot of women and children, in *The International Survey of Family Law 1997*, edited by A. Bainham. The Hague: Kluwer, 465–83.

Örücü, E. 2006. A synthetic and hyphenated legal system: The Turkish experience. *Journal of Comparative Law*, 1(2), 27–47.

Örücü, E. 2008. Judicial navigation as official law meets culture in Turkey. *International Journal of Law in Context*, 4(1), 35–61.

Örücü, E. 2010. Turkey's synthetic legal system and her indigenous socio-culture(s) in a "covert mix," in *Mixed Legal Systems at New Frontiers*, edited by E. Örücü. London: Wildy, Simmonds & Hill, 150–203.

Örücü, E. 2011. How far can religion be accommodated in laic Turkish family law, in *The Place of Religion in Family Law: A Comparative Search*, edited by J. Mair and E. Örücü. Antwerp, Belgium: Intersentia, 117–58.

Özbudun, E. 2009. Judicial review of constitutional amendments in Turkey. *European Public Law*, 15(4), 533–38.

Rutten, S. 2010. Protection of spouses in informal marriages by human rights. *Utrecht Law Review*, 6(2), 7–92.

Twining, W. 2005. Social science and diffusion of law. *Journal of Law and Society*, 32(2), 203–40.

Watson, A. 2000. Legal transplants and European private law. *Electronic Journal of Comparative Law* [Online], 4(4). Available at: http://www.ejcl.org/44/art44-2.html [accessed December 10, 2013].

Yılmaz, İ. 2003. Non-recognition of post-modern Turkish socio-legal reality and the predicament of women. *British Journal of Middle Eastern Studies*, 30(1), 25–41.

Yılmaz, İ. 2005. *Muslim Laws, Politics and Society in Modern Nation States: Dynamic Legal Pluralism in England, Turkey and Pakistan*. Aldershot, UK: Ashgate.

Zweigert, K., and Kötz, H. 1998. *An Introduction to Comparative Law*. 3rd ed. Oxford, UK: Oxford University.

Chapter 13
Integration of Islamic Law in the Fabric of Legal Thought in Egypt

Mohamed Ahmed Serag

My research starts from observing the hybrid nature of the present Egyptian legal system that fuses together, in its fabric, two different legal sources with two different frames of reference. The first source is Islamic Shari'a, which was confined in 1883 to only the area of personal status. The second source, which constitutes the bulk of Egyptian laws and refers to other areas, draws from Western authorities and was introduced at the same time. The collision that took place between these two systems when they were brought together was substantial, and a great deal of time and effort was required to reconcile the tension between these two rival components and to facilitate the smooth administration of Egyptian justice. In this chapter, I will endeavor to shed light on these efforts and the methodologies adopted in fusing, to a working extent, the two essential components of the Egyptian legal system. I will briefly analyze the dramatic story of the sudden collision between these two systems and the gradual alleviation of the natural tension that resulted.

It is noteworthy, perhaps, from a historical perspective, to state that Islamic law was the only legal system applied in Egypt (as was the case with other Muslim countries) until its occupation by imperial powers in the modern age. The colonial powers, during or slightly before the last quarter of the nineteenth century, reshaped the legal system in these countries and managed to enforce laws of Western origin in all legal fields apart from family law. A type of hybrid legal system emerged then, when Islamic law was confined to family matters, while other areas were assigned to nationally codified laws taken from Western legal sources and were applied by different court systems. Thus, legal education necessarily had to endure a dramatic transformation. The occupation authorities had to launch a campaign, in cooperation with loyal authorities and elites, to produce an acceptable image for the new system under the banner of progress and modernization, in an effort to justify the prompt enforcement of this hybrid legal system instead of the reformation of the traditional system. Claims were voiced that the newly introduced laws did not contradict the conventional system. One piece of evidence for these claims comes from the requirement in Egyptian criminal law, dating from 1883, that in death penalty sentences the Grand Mufti's approval must be sought prior to the announcement of the court's decision. In this vein, it was also assumed, as referred to by Abdel Razzaq al Sanhuri, the great Egyptian jurist, that the conventional system of Shari'a was still the law of the land and continued to apply where the promulgated laws were silent. According to this assumption, these new Western laws were the exceptions, and Shari'a remained the rule.

Whatever it may have become, the amalgamated legal system in Egypt seemed, particularly by the end of the nineteenth century, to be lacking in philosophical and authoritative unity. Thus, Egyptians reacted differently in view of the limited options available to them under the British occupation. Shocked by the dramatic shift to a foreign system and the replacement of the conventional one, many jurists and reformers declared hostile attitudes—which are still favored by many political forces today, such as the Muslim Brotherhood and Salafis—toward copying these foreign laws and preferred the other option of modernizing and reforming the old system that suits most of Egypt's customs and prevailing culture.

This attitude found its earliest expression in the comparative research conducted by a group of Egyptian lawyers and jurists during the late nineteenth and early twentieth century. These early studies comparing the Islamic system and French law, which constituted the main source for the newly introduced law in the country, aimed at identifying prevailing similarities and explaining the relatively few differences between the two systems. This comparative approach, with its focus on prevailing similarities, perhaps unintentionally helped to build bridges between both the concepts and terms of the two poles of this hybrid system. The great Egyptian reformer Rifa'a Rafi' al Tahtawi made this early comparative approach possible by producing his own translation of French civil law into Arabic during the 1870s, under the auspices of Khedive Isma'il. Three major comparative works must be recognized in this chapter: that of Justice Makhluf al Miniawi; that of Egyptian Minister of Justice Mohammad Qadri Basha, who died in 1886; and that of the lawyer Abdullah Hussein al Taydi, who left his prosperous work as a lawyer at the Sorbonne Law School to return to Egypt and produce his massive work comparing the French Civil Code and its Islamic counterpart. Was Islamic law seeking recognition through these comparative works? This possibility should be investigated.

Many other strategies that perhaps evolved from modern legal education have emerged over time to prove its effectiveness in building the necessary bridges between the two pillars of Egyptian law. The Khedival School of Law was actively engaged in comparative research since its inception and, more importantly, created a common ground for exchanging views and methodologies between its two distinct groups of faculty members. The first group of faculty members, in keeping with their traditional background, taught Shari'a courses, and the other group of faculty members, who had modern qualifications, taught legal topics. The writings of these two groups reflected their efforts to fill the gaps and inspiring approximation between the different systems in both origin sources. The traditionalists abandoned the long-followed mode of writing commentaries on recognized authoritative texts and focused instead on presenting the main concepts and theories of Islamic law. This newly adopted approach must have helped in the aching process of integration. Modernists also participated in this process through their enthusiastic engagement in a more systematic and comprehensive approach to the comparative study of Islamic and Western legal systems. These comparative endeavors quickly led to the extremely significant call for the reform (*tanqih*) of the old Egyptian civil law, as was anxiously reflected in the prolific writings of al Sanhuri. It could be said without any exaggeration that the new Civil Code of 1949 was the zenith of the old and new waves of comparative strategy.

I must also point out that Egyptian judges also participated in this complex integration process by interpreting the new legal provisions in accordance with their own customs, culture, and values. The course of legal integration in Egypt was invigorated by the promulgation of new Arabic civil laws between 1949 and 1976, to which comprehensive compendia were attached. These compendia link the sections of the law, modeled on the Egyptian pattern, with Islamic legal concepts and authorities. The Civil Law of Jordan of 1976 and that of the United Arab Emirates of 1985 illustrate this approach, which successfully brings together concepts of both Islamic law and laws of Western origin. This type of amalgamation and hybridism is socially and culturally justified and improves the image of the legal system in the eyes of the public. However, much work is needed to minimize the present tension between the two rival pillars of Egyptian law and to bring harmony and unity to the composition of the applicable system.

If this work is to succeed, Egypt's lawyers and jurists will have to tirelessly exhaust the available strategies for amalgamation, which include comparative research of Islamic and Western legal systems, along with improved methodologies for the study of Islamic law. The recognition of the judges' contribution to this effort will also be essential. Moreover, the attachment of extended compendia to new laws, which are modeled on the Jordanian pattern, will secure acceptability of the hybrid legal system in Egyptian society and will bring to it more harmony and integration.

I will now briefly discuss the effectiveness of these strategies in shaping the prevailing hybrid legal system, which draws from both modern Western and traditional Islamic sources.

Islamic Law's Interactions with Other Systems

The thesis of this chapter is that Islamic legal philosophy permits change and adaptability by employing principles of social interest, custom, and equitable preference, and it does not constitute an impediment to modern society's search for progress. Note that in its long history, Islamic law played an essential role in Muslim societies, and its principles greatly accommodated many different cultures and communities. Various interpretations and attitudes in Islamic law facilitate the adoption and assimilation of alien sources into its fabric. The resemblance of Islamic law to universal legal systems smooths its interaction with these systems. British judges in colonial India were entrusted with the task of applying Islamic law from traditional sources for more than a century and half, integrating its principles with their own legal background. As a consequence, a hybrid system called *Anglo-Muhammadan law* emerged. This term was used to signify a mixed body of

Islamic law as interpreted by British judges trained in their own legal traditions. The same thing happened in North African Muslim countries, which witnessed the emergence of another mixed legal system called *Muhammadan-French law*, as a result of the application of Islamic law by French judges. Even before modern times, mutual influences between Islamic law and Western legal systems were noticeable. Certain Islamic legal terms, such as *aval*, *chèques*, and *diwan* became known in European languages. Interactions in the modern era became more aggressive, and Islamic law has largely been shaped by a wide range of processes imposed either by colonial powers or by external pressures. From the eighteenth century to the mid nineteenth century, the British authority in India gradually enforced common law principles before it legislated comprehensive codes in all fields, apart from family law, in the latter half of the nineteenth century. Within the same period, the Western powers pressured the Ottomans to adopt laws of mostly civil origins into the fabric of Islamic law, which witnessed partial codification of the Ottoman Mejelle in civil, procedural, and judicial spheres.

Egypt, in its turn, was not immune to these pressures and in 1876 had to apply the Napoleonic Code through the newly introduced system of mixed courts. This institution was designed to bring harmony to the capitulatory different European laws then applicable to Egypt as a part of the Ottoman state. The intended harmony was attained by introducing one single code that was based on the French system and agreed by European states to be applicable to all disputes involving any of their citizens. The mixed court system in Egypt was felt to have been against the national legal integrity and therefore was abolished in 1948. Codified laws modeled on the French system were enforced in the country in 1883, immediately following its occupation by the British. With the introduction of the civil law elements, which caused a great shock, the two camps of traditionalists and modernists were completely divided for some time, though both groups soon realized that this division was not necessary and that they should instead work hand-in-hand to bring about the unification of their differing elements. The symbolic abolishment of Shari'a courts and religious councils entertaining family matters in 1956 was an important step toward this goal. This achievement was not possible without exploring and rigorously employing all of the aforementioned tools, which I will briefly discuss in the remainder of this chapter. I will also briefly examine the obstacles to the ongoing process of legal integration in Egypt in an effort to offer a more balanced picture.

Legal Education and the Establishment of Khedival School of Law

Traditional legal education prevailed over the centuries in religious schools, where students studied Islamic jurisprudence and its principles, syllogism, Qur'anic interpretation, the Hadith, and the Arabic language. The graduates of al Azhar University, in particular, were appointed in courts to administer justice in Egypt until the late nineteenth century. However, because of political and legal changes in Egypt, including the restriction of Islamic law to personal matters and the imposition of Western laws by the British in 1883 to regulate other areas, it was thought necessary to change legal education through the two connected strategies of establishing a modern law school and modernizing traditional legal education. The former was carried out through the establishment of both Madrasat Dar al Ulum in 1872, and the Shar'i Judiciary School (*Madrasat al Qada' al Shar'i*) in 1907. These two schools originated as a result of the activities of two influential reformists, Ali Mubarak and Mohammad Abdu. Both schools advanced the study of Islamic law, as is evident from fact that their graduates were recruited to teach at the Khedival School of Law from the time of its inception. Many renowned scholars such as Ahmad Ibrahim, Abdel Wahhab Khallaf, Mohammad Zaid al Ibiani, Mohammad Salama, and Mohammad Abu Zahra felt a sense of responsibility to meet societal expectations and brought fresh air into the study of Islamic legal theories and principles. Their methods of presenting Islamic legal concepts influenced their students as well as their colleagues, perhaps because of the general commonalities in terminology and abstract ideas that they were able to share. Their efforts shifted the writing of legal texts from the traditional distorted issues method, which is based on listing somehow disconnected factual cases or precedents (*mas'alas*) to the modern principled approach to legal writing.

The modernization of legal education, in contrast, began within the School of Languages (*Madrasat al Alson*), which had generally been at the forefront of enlightenment in Egypt since its inception in 1835. One of the essential components of this modernization is that the Administrative Department was redesigned to offer courses on Islamic, Roman, and commercial law. To expand on these offerings, this department was, in 1882, separated from the School of Languages and became a full-fledged school in its own right. Shortly afterward, in July 1886, it became the Khedival School of Law, which has since proved to be a vital instrument in leading the fight for political and legal independence and modernization, not only for Egyptians but for all Arabs. Its graduates were recognized by the state to have been trained in both Islamic and French law and thus came to occupy key positions in the Egyptian government and judicial system. The French language was the sole teaching medium at the school until 1889, when an English option was added. Later, in 1916, English became the only teaching language. The school was also affiliated with the Ministry of Education until 1912. It then became associated with the Ministry of Justice and, in 1925, was joined to the Egyptian University, now known as Cairo University.

Cairo University soon became a universal seat of legal learning, actively engaged in the two strategies I have previously mentioned, the development of comparative studies between Eastern and Occidental laws and the modernization of Islamic law. These two connected strategies shaped the transformation of Arab laws from the traditional conservative framework to the present hybrid legal system, which comprises Western legal principles and a modernized form of Islamic legal thinking. The hybridity of the system was achieved through an extremely complex process that engaged various specific methods and instruments. A brief discussion of these methods and instruments follows.

Early Comparative Approaches and Works

In the 1870s, practical needs induced the Egyptian administration to start examining the similarities and dissimilarities between the Napoleonic Code and the Islamic legal system—particularly the Malikite and Hanafite schools—with the intention of adapting Islamic law to the requirements of modernization. Khedive Isma'il commissioned Rifa'a Rafi' al Tahtawi, the renowned Egyptian reformer, to translate French civil law and later instructed Makhluf al Miniawi, a judge from al Menia in Upper Egypt, to conduct a comparative study of this code. The learned judge carried out this official responsibility from the Malikite perspective in his work *al Muqaranat al Tashri'iyya*, or *Legal Comparisons*. The approach adopted in this work was to simply quote the French section of the code, followed by relevant opinions and principles from the Malikite sources. Al Miniawi's conclusions typically came at the end of each section, usually emphasizing the similarity between the two systems. In contrast, Mohammad Qadri Basha, the Egyptian minister of justice, conducted a similar comparative study from the Hanafite perspective, but he emphasized in his conclusions the differences between the two systems. In the 1930s, Abdullah Hussein al Taydi conducted a more comprehensive comparison, emphasizing the prevailing agreements between the French and Islamic legal systems and arguing for the superiority of Islamic principles in cases of exceptional differences. These early comparative works conducted by traditional scholars established a methodology that prevailed among renowned law students and scholars in all legal fields up to modern times.

A Later, More Systematic Comparison

A comparative methodology of studying Islamic and Western legal systems was developed in the twentieth century by the graduates and faculty members of the Khedival School of Law. Their comparative works were highly advanced studies covering specific private and public legal areas such as the abuse of rights, obligations, torts, constitutional law, and administrative law. This comparative approach accelerated the modernization of Islamic law and helped smooth its integration with Western legal principles. This smooth integration was clearly evinced in the synthesizing strategies adopted in drafting the new Egyptian Civil Law of 1949.

Abdel Razzaq al Sanhuri exemplified these strategies in his voluminous work on Islamic law, *Masadir al Haqq*. Heading directly toward his objective of integration, Sanhuri adopted in this work a revealing approach that is based on juxtaposing principles and theories of Islamic law with their Western counterparts. In *al Wasit*, he highlighted similarities between selected trends in Islamic law and their equals in European systems. In cases of differences between Islamic and Western legal thinking, he clearly expressed in both *al Wasit* and

Masadir al Haqq his conviction that Islamic law has been a step forward in the evolution of legal development and can be complemented by availing itself of the progress made by European legal thinking.

In contrast to the earlier comparatists, Sanhuri adopted a more practically acceptable approach. Although Makhluf al Miniawi focused, for seemingly theoretical purposes, on similarities between the Napoleonic Code and the Malikite jurisprudence, Qadri Basha attempted, for similar reasons, to highlight the differences between the Napoleonic Code and Hanafite jurisprudence. Abdullah Hussein al Taydi, conversely, was more interested in establishing the general accord of the Napoleonic Code with Islamic jurisprudence, without missing the exceptional differences between them both. Al Taydi repeatedly emphasized that Islamic law precedes the Napoleonic or European code and corresponds to the aspirations of modern peoples of his society. According to al Taydi, in cases of exceptional difference, Islamic precepts represent an ethically superior attitude, at least from the perspective of Muslim society.

Both the earlier and later comparative scholars, however, felt the need to expand their vision through comparative examination of Islamic legal principles, so as to accommodate them to European laws. Although Sanhuri emphasized the position of Western law as the latest step in legal development, the earlier comparative authors declared their unlimited support for the attitudes adopted within Islamic jurisprudence as it nearly reached the final conclusion. (Unlike Sanhuri, these earlier comparatists did not think of enforcing the concept of development in their legal analysis, and they seemed to have thought of Islamic law as a static system.) Comparative scholars are still divided along these two lines, although both approaches have contributed to the modernization of Arab laws.

Theorization

Because of the influence of Khedival Law School, Islamic legal writings shifted from the traditional approach of commenting on and abridging celebrated texts by offering definitions, decisions of distorted cases, and argumentation into the articulation of legal theories and topics, following the same pattern used by Western legal authors. As a result, a flood of works started to appear on topics of Islamic law, such as contracts, ownership, partnership, documentation of debts, and abuse of rights. It is not surprising that the offerings of the Khedival School of Law and its comparative research strategies invigorated these works, which were written by its graduates, who received higher education in French institutions, and its faculty members, who were trained in the traditional and quasi-traditional institutions of al Azhar, al Qada' al Shar'i, and Dar al Ulum. Its leading scholars include Ahmad Ibrahim, Mohamed Zeid al Ibiany, Ali al Khafif, Abdel Wahhab Khallaf, and Mohamed Abu Zahra. Certainly, their use of common legal language and jargon must have contributed to building bridges with legal experts and must have advanced the integration of Islamic jurisprudence into the fabric of applicable Egyptian law.

Codification

Codified laws in both Egypt and Jordan included certain important provisions from Islamic law and jurisprudence. This is also the case in many other Arab countries, such as Iraq, the United Arab Emirates, and Kuwait. Juxtaposing Islamic and Western legal elements in the same code would certainly facilitate the integration process of the two systems. Moriondo, an Italian judge in the mixed courts, and Qadri Basha, who was an expert in Islamic law, drafted the old Egyptian Civil Code of 1883. The new Civil Code of 1949 refers to Islamic jurisprudence in so many concepts and principles that the master architect of the code, Abdel Razzaq al Sanhuri, declared it on many occasions to be a successful blend of Islamic jurisprudence and Western laws, proving this point in both of his major works, *al Wasit* and *Masadir al Haqq*. The explanatory memorandum of the Jordanian civil law, which is squarely based on the Egyptian civil law, refers to provisions of Islamic jurisprudence in nearly every section. Mejellet al Ahkam al Adliyya and Murshid al Hayran, Qadri Basha's two codifications of Hanafite law, are very often quoted. This blending brings about a sort of accommodation between Islamic law and the elements of Western origin. The breadth of Islamic legal literature and the variety of attitudes included in its manuals over the long centuries of its implementation in different circumstances provide a wide pool for selecting solutions acceptable in modern societies. I must emphasize that producing comprehensive compendia and allowing public consultation at the drafting stage of a new code will secure public support and acceptability. The Jordanian and United Arab Emirate civil laws provide a good illustration of this point.

Court Decisions

Egyptian judges are influenced by their training in Islamic law in law schools, as well as by their cultural and religious backgrounds, in their interpretation of legal provisions or when they need to establish new principles in cases where the law is silent. The judges' contribution was taken into consideration in the call for amending the old Egyptian Civil Code. One illustration comes from the celebrated case of *Hisham Mustafa*. In that case, the appellate court replaced the sentence of execution handed down by the primary court (and justified by the Egyptian Criminal Law of 1937) with a lesser punishment of 15 years. The court of first instance rightly followed Criminal Law provisions in awarding the death penalty for the culprit's participation in the murder of a female singer, Suzan Tamim. The appellate court altered this decision after reaching a settlement between the culprit and the father of the victim, though reconciliation is not envisaged in Egyptian criminal law and is recognized only in financial matters. The appellate court must have followed the traditions of Islamic law in considering reconciliation as sufficient ground for awarding the lesser punishment. Egyptian judges are currently implementing the principle of interpreting legal statutes evolved from within Islamic jurisprudence. This exemplifies the role of judges in the integration process.

Constitutional Instruments

Article 2 of the Egyptian constitution and the decisions of the Egyptian Constitutional Court cannot be ignored in the integration process. Article 2 states that Islamic Shari'a is the basic source for legislation, and one of the major functions of the Supreme Constitutional Court is to examine the constitutionality of any given legal provision and to annul any provision contradicting the principles of Islamic Shari'a. This court is presumed to play a significant role in the integration of Islamic legal principles within the fabric of the present legal system.

In conclusion, the development of the modern legal system in Egypt was not simply an issue of blind application of Western jurisprudence but was rather subjected to decades of academic work based particularly on comparison, practice through the courts, and legal processes. Additionally, the efforts of this legal experiment fundamentally changed the way legal texts were approached, with both perspectives altered to bring Islamic and Western legal systems closer together. In the future, the concerted use of all of these strategies will bring more harmonization and unity between the two essential components of the Egyptian legal system: Islamic Shari'a and Western law.

Chapter 14
The Influence of Religion on Law in the Iranian Legal System

Naser Ghorbannia

The relationship between religion and law is complex, and the influence of religious ideas on legal traditions is undeniable. This chapter aims to explain the influence of Islam as a religion, and especially Islamic jurisprudence, as an important part of the Iranian legal system. It is important to point out at the outset the philosophical foundations for this phenomenon. Religious beliefs constitute central elements of the values that shape the rules, principles, rights, obligations, and institutions governing societies. Religious morals and law are indistinguishably mixed together. Many consider religion and law to be inseparable concepts and deem them to be one and the same. Conversely, according to most legal philosophers, any legislation should be based on social values. Religions provide an ethical system that is widely viewed as benefiting us all.

The law and social norms of societies have deep ties to the various religions of the world. Without their religious foundations, it would be difficult to claim that we could still view legal systems—especially criminal law systems—in the same light, except in the sphere of *lex naturalis*, or natural law.

The laws against murder are legislated to protect human beings. Even if there were no religions, murder would still be prohibited under the law, because it is a part of our human nature to abhor murder. This prohibition is rational, eternal, and universal. All human beings can understand it by the nature of their very reason, which has been considered intrinsic to the Prophet Mohammed in the Islamic tradition. But this proscription against murder is also the most fundamental part of divine books. For example, we read in the Bible, "You shall not murder," and the Holy Qur'an emphasizes that killing one person is the same as killing all human beings: it destroys all of humanity.

Likewise, we are all socialized to know that it is wrong to steal, to commit fraud, and to commit perjury. Also, Almighty God commanded that we should not steal, commit fraud, or tell lies under oath.

In addition, one can understand by reason that it is obligatory to honor one's contract. God commanded us to observe the natural rule *pacta sunt servanda* (all agreements must be kept), but it is evident that all legal rules are not natural. Emile Durkheim (1961: 475) credits religion with maintaining social order. According to Durkheim, religion plays an important role in legitimizing and reinforcing society's values and norms.

In his book *Law and Religion*, Gad Barzilai (2007: 650) writes that different Muslim cultures have interpreted religious rituals in a variety of ways. He has demonstrated that contemporary legal systems derive nourishment from the religions and religious values of their respective societies.

It is not difficult to show how discrete religious traditions contribute to evolving legal traditions. Religious ideas have influenced criminal law and family law not only in Islamic societies but in non-Islamic societies as well. The French legal philosopher Georges Ripert has shown that many fundamental principles and rules of the French Civil Code, even those in the Law of Obligations, have been derived from Christian ethics. In his book *La Règle Morale dans les Obligations Civiles* (*Moral Rules in Civil Obligations*), he criticized René Demogue, a French law professor, because he interpreted the French Civil Code without paying attention to Christian morals (Ripert 1949). Even according to Hans Kelsen ([1967] 2005), who strongly defends "pure theory of law," legal provisions cannot totally be separated from ideological considerations.

It is important to point out that even in the sphere of international law and relations, a large and uncontested body of ethical rules would provide an ideal guarantee for the respect of international law (Tomuschat 1995: 129).

An important and interesting question is currently being discussed by philosophers of public and criminal law: whether the states have the right or obligation to protect morals and religious values. Although two theories—perfectionism and moral neutrality—oppose each other on this issue, both perfectionists and moral neutralists believe that some moral and religious values should be protected by states, and some of these scholars insist that even criminal protection is permitted.

Now I will provide an overview of the Islamic character of the Iranian legal system. In Iran, not only after the Islamic Revolution of 1979, but also in the era before the Islamic Republic was founded, Islamic values had a strong influence on all aspects of Iranian life. The majority of Muslims consider Islam to be a comprehensive way of life, whose teachings directly or indirectly cover every possible human relationship.

Although the legal and judicial aspects of the era before the Islamic Republic were centered on non-Islamic values and principles, and although the state tried to legislate on the basis of secularism, it could not totally change the legal system to a secular judicial form. And for this reason, although the Iranian criminal law in place before the Islamic Revolution (the Public Criminal Code) was based on secular law and was influenced by European law, the Iranian Civil Code, which constitutes the most important part of the legal system, had an Islamic foundation.[1] It is significant that the Iranian monarchy, three years before the Islamic Revolution, ratified the International Covenant on Civil and Political Rights, which committed the monarchy to change national laws and regulations that were contrary to the covenant. However, changing those laws proved politically and religiously impossible.

After the Islamic Revolution, Iran's political and legal system became completely Islamic. The preamble to the constitution of the Islamic Republic of Iran describes the basic element of the Islamic Revolution that distinguished it from other movements that have taken place in Iran during the past hundred years: its ideological nature.[2]

According to the constitution, the state's legitimacy is derived first from its Islamic nature, and the will of the people is a secondary source of legitimacy. Article 56 of the constitution provides that absolute sovereignty over the universe and human beings belongs to God and that it is God who has made human beings master of their social destiny. According to article 4 of the constitution, all laws and regulations, including civil, criminal, financial, economic, administrative, cultural, military, and political measures, must conform with Islamic criteria. Although the constitution under the Iranian monarchy had a similar provision, it was ignored. So today the ultimate source of law in the Islamic Republic of Iran is Islamic law or Shari'a. Certain aspects of Iranian law are derived from Islamic jurisprudence, and even though the parliament has the right to legislate, its freedom of choice is restricted by religious rules and criteria, and Islamic jurists (*fuqaha*) of the Guardian Council are judges in this matter.

Shari'a influences the legal system in most Muslim countries. Shari'a may apply either directly as a common law of the state, where there is no fully developed legal system, or indirectly through the application of statutory law based fully or partly on Islamic law or as a source of law to fill legislative gaps. In Iran, Shari'a does not apply directly. Article 167 of the Iranian constitution states: "The judge is bound to endeavor to judge each case on the basis of the codified law. In case of the absence of any such law, he has to deliver his judgment on the basis of authoritative Islamic sources and authentic *fatwas*." The article states that a judge may not, "on the pretext of the silence of or deficiency in the law, or its brevity or contradictory nature, … refrain from admitting or examining cases and delivering a judgment."

Parliament has the right and duty to legislate, but all legislation passed by the parliament must be confirmed by the Guardian Council. When an act is incompatible with Islamic law or with the constitution, it will fail to become law.

In addition, Islamic law is considered as a source of law to fill legislative gaps. Article 167 provides that if a necessary provision is absent, if there is contradiction between articles of code, or in cases of ambiguity or obscurity, a judge is not permitted to deny justice. The judge has the duty to decide according to valid Islamic sources and authentic doctrines. Shari'a is also applied as a source of interpretation of legal regulations. Thus, Shari'a has three functions in the Iranian legal system: first, as an important source for the development of legislation; second, as a supplementary source to fill legislative gaps; and third, as a historically significant foundation of Iranian law and, therefore, as an interpretative source for legal rules and provisions.

---

1 The full text of the Iranian Civil Code is available online at http://www.wipo.int/wipolex/en/text.jsp?file_id=197898 [accessed: December 28, 2013].

2 The full text of the constitution is available online at http://faculty.unlv.edu/pwerth/Const-Iran%28abridge%29.pdf [accessed: December 28, 2013].

Most significantly, the question arises as to which exactly is the legitimate version of Islamic law. Not only may Islamic jurists' interpretation of the Holy Qur'an (which is the all-encompassing source) differ, but also their tradition of interpretation. Moderate interpretation is more flexible on issues of morality and norms of social behavior, as compared to the more radical orthodox interpretation. Proponents of the more radical forms of interpretation fear that any degree of moderation will cause Western influence to enter society and threaten Islamic culture and values.

When we examine the 34 years since the Islamic Revolution, we can infer that the Islamic Republic of Iran has adopted a moderate policy for the interpretation of Islamic law and has implemented this policy in its legislation. For example, most Islamic jurists believe that a woman who has been bound to a man through a marriage contract must not leave the house without the husband's permission, must surrender herself for any pleasure that he wants, and must not prevent him from having intercourse with her without a religious excuse. A woman is completely at the service of her husband, and her social activities are conditional on her husband's permission. But the Iranian Republic does not have such a regulation in its Civil Code. Furthermore, according to Shari'a, men can obtain a unilateral divorce from their wife or wives, the marriage age for a female may be as low as nine, and the age of criminal responsibility is likewise nine for females. However, in today's Iran, provisions and regulations passed by the parliament and confirmed by the Guardian Council differ from these precepts.

Marriage regulations are defined by Islamic laws, but the Iranian government endeavors to legislate that interpretation of Islam to improve the situation of the family, especially by providing rights for women and children. For instance, even though polygamy is permitted in Shari'a, the Iranian parliament has attempted to discourage polygamy through legal restrictions. For example, the permission of the first wife is required before the court will allow a second marriage to proceed.

Likewise, the age of marriage has been increased to 13 for girls and 15 for boys, and child custody regulations have been changed in favor of mothers. Today, no Iranian man can obtain a unilateral divorce from his wife.

As we know, contractual freedom is restricted in the field of family law in all legal systems, because the provisions of that branch of law are strongly related to public morals. Even though freedom of choice is more restricted under Islamic and Iranian family law, the stipulation of condition is considered as a key principle to solve some problems. In any case, at the time of the marriage contract, the wife can stipulate conditions in that contract. For example, the wife can stipulate that the husband should not take a second wife or that the wife will have the right to obtain a divorce, and so on. These conditions are legally valid, and Muslims are bound by their conditions. Almighty God has ordered them, as stated in the Qur'an: "O you who believe, honor your contracts and fulfill your obligations."

It should be emphasized that these changes to Iranian law should not be interpreted as deviations from Islamic jurisprudence or Shari'a, because, as has been stated, interpretations of Islamic legal sources can differ. By invoking a moderate attitude toward the interpretation of Shari'a, the Islamic government can make important progress on some fundamental issues affecting Iranian society.

My final point is that some branches of Iranian law have not been derived directly or indirectly from Islamic jurisprudence, but are derived from or influenced by European law (especially French or Swiss law). These areas include trade law, administrative law, maritime law, private international law, and some elements of procedural law. As far as the Iranian legal system is concerned, these kinds of laws and regulations should not be incompatible with Islamic criteria, and jurists of the Guardian Council are to be the judges in this matter. Obviously, when there is an ambiguity in these areas, the parliament or judges will rely on the original source for its interpretation. For this reason, the constitution of the Islamic Republic of Iran has established the criteria for compatibility of laws and regulations with Islamic jurisprudence. Therefore, we can say that a kind of hybridity and mixture has been accepted by the Iranian legal system.

References

Barzilai, G. 2007. *Law and Religion.* Aldershot, UK: Ashgate.

Durkheim, E. 1961. *The Elementary Forms of Religious Life*. Oxford, UK: Oxford University Press.

Kelsen, H. [1967] 2005. *Pure Theory of Law*. Clark, NJ: Lawbook Exchange.
Ripert, G. 1949. *La Règle Morale dans les Obligations Civiles* [*Moral Rules in Civil Obligations*]. Paris: Librairie Générale de Droit et de Jurisprudence.
Tomuschat, C. 1995. Ethos, Ethics and Morality in International Relations, in *Encyclopedia of Public International Law*. Vol. 9. Amsterdam: North-Holland, 126–29.

Chapter 15

The Reception of Islamic Law in Sri Lanka and Its Interplay with Western Legal Traditions

Anton Cooray

Thus described at the turn of the nineteenth century, Sri Lanka has an irresistible charm not only to lovers of nature but also, equally, to the comparativist. Sri Lanka's attraction to the comparativist is its rich mix of legal traditions influenced by oriental and occidental cultures as well as a wide range of religions. With its original settlers from India, Sri Lanka came under the influence of Hindu law and Buddhism. With Arab traders, came Islam. With the Western powers—the Portuguese, the Dutch, and the British—came the modernizing influence of Christianity.

The Oriental and Occidental Mix of Sri Lankan Law

The Sri Lankan legal system is commonly described as a mix of oriental and occidental legal traditions (Cooray 1996). The Roman-Dutch law and English law make up the occidental component, whereas Kandyan law, Thesawalamai, and Muslim law form the oriental component.

The laws of the Sinhalese constitute the first known legal system of Sri Lanka. The Sinhalese are the descendants of the earliest settlers from India, principally northern India, who arrived in the fifth century BC. They gradually developed their own language, culture, and legal system, which is uniquely Sri Lankan. Still, the origin of the Sinhalese language, culture and law can be traced to India. The Sinhalese also came under the benevolent influence of Buddhism, but their laws are not to any appreciable extent based on religion. Sinhalese laws and customs flourished in the Kandyan Kingdom (the central parts of Sri Lanka with Kandy as the seat of the Sinhalese kings) and came to be administered in a hierarchy of local tribunals and courts. These laws are collectively known as Kandyan law.

During the time of Sinhalese kings, Kandyan law applied as territorial law to all inhabitants of the Kandyan provinces, who happened to be almost exclusively Sinhalese. This situation continued unchanged. However, in the maritime provinces, which were under Western domination for 450 years (by the Portuguese from 1504 to 1656, the Dutch from 1656 to 1796, and the British from 1796 to 1948), the Sinhalese gradually came to be governed by the laws of the conquerors. The Kandyan Kingdom resisted Western military advances until 1815, when it fell to the British. A convention between the British colonial administration and the Kandyan aristocracy guaranteed the continuation of the administration of justice to all classes of people in the Kandyan provinces "according to the laws, institutions and customs established and in force among them."[1] It appears that in the early years of British rule in the Kandyan provinces, Kandyan law continued to be applied as a territorial law. Later, when the influx of Europeans became sizable, the judiciary and the administration decided that the laws peculiar to native Sinhalese could not be applied to all residents. After a number of judicial decisions and legislative enactments, Kandyan law came to be regarded as a personal law applicable only to Sinhalese who were domiciled in the Kandyan provinces.

A second wave of settlers from southern India arrived in the third century BC, by which time the Sinhalese nation had been well established. These Indians settled in Jaffna province, which is today the Northern province plus certain adjoining areas. Traditionally, their descendants, called Jaffna Tamils, have constituted an almost exclusive population in that area. Because of their close connection with southern India, they preserved the Tamil language received from there and continued to be influenced by Hindu law as well as

1 Convention of 1815, clause 4.

southern Indian customs and practices. Their laws—collectively known as *Thesawalamai*, meaning local law—applied as personal laws to Tamil inhabitants of the Jaffna province.

Both Thesawalamai and Kandyan law are based on local customs and practices. During the Dutch administration of Sri Lanka (1654–1796), the laws of the Jaffna Tamils were codified, and this codification gained the seal of approval of the British, who translated and promulgated the Dutch code in consultation with the Jaffna Tamil community leaders. Thesawalamai, thus, has a statutory starting point, although unwritten custom and case law are equally valuable sources of law. The British did not manage to create a code of the customs and usages of the Kandyan Sinhalese, but several statutes were passed to clarify and state some parts of Kandyan law. Legislation has played an important part in clarifying, modifying, or replacing Thesawalamai and Kandyan law.

Muslim law, the third personal law of Sri Lanka, differs from Thesawalamai and Kandyan law at least in two aspects. First, the application of Muslim law depends on neither belief in Islam nor any racial consideration. The vast majority of Muslims are descendants of Muslims from the Middle East, Malaysia, and coastal areas of southern India, and it is believed that they intermarried with natives (mostly Tamils). Muslim law has no territorial element. Thus, whereas the Jaffna Tamils or Kandyan Sinhalese will cease to be governed by their personal law if they lose their Jaffna or Kandyan domicile, respectively,[2] Muslim law follows a Muslim wherever he or she moves in Sri Lanka.[3]

Second, Muslim law, being inextricably linked to the religion of Islam, may rightly be regarded as a received legal system. As distinguished from Kandyan law and Thesawalamai, Muslim law is indigenous only to the limited extent that Muslims of Sri Lanka have developed customary practices that are unrelated to the general principles of Islamic law. To the extent that general jurisprudence of Islamic law governs the Muslims of Sri Lanka, Muslim law can be recognized more as a received system than as an indigenous law.

Roman-Dutch law and English law are described as received legal systems first because they were introduced by foreign rulers of the island and second as a way to highlight how they differ from the three laws that are native—native in the sense that they had long been established in Sri Lanka at the start of Western domination.

Muslim Law in a Secular State

The purpose of this chapter is to examine how, and how much of, Islamic law was received in Sri Lanka and the extent to which local customs and the general law of the land have made inroads into it. The chapter will also examine the role played by the legislature in developing and reforming it. An examination of case law also indicates much deference to Islamic law, though the judges were not unmindful of modernizing law. I will first give a broad-brush view of the place of Muslim law in the legal system of Sri Lanka and then examine two specific areas that illustrate the interaction between common law and Muslim law. These areas are the custody of minor children and the law of gifts.

The application of Muslim law concerning the custody of minor children highlights how judges trained in English law and Roman-Dutch law interpreted what appeared to be rigid principles in a way to reach a result that would, at least to an appreciable extent, be consistent with the common law. In these cases, there is no blatant citation of English cases facilitating modification of the Muslim principles. Evident instead is a show of great respect to Muslim jurisprudence, while confidence is instilled in the community that solutions reached by judges are just and fair. Any modification of Muslim law was nonconfrontational and wholly defensible.

---

2 In *Spencer v. Rajaratnam* (1913), 16 *Ceylon New Law Reports* 414, a Jaffna Tamil—who had left Jaffna when he was very young, settled in Colombo, and married a Colombo Tamil woman—was held not to be governed by Thesawalamai. There is no case law on this point in relation to Kandyan law, but it is well settled that once a Kandyan Sinhalese ceases to be domiciled or resident in the Kandyan provinces, he or she is no longer subject to Kandyan law. See Tambiah (1968: 84).

3 "[M]uhammadan law is based on religion, and is applicable to all followers of Islam," per *Khan v. Marikar* (1913), 16 *Ceylon New Law Reports* 425, 427. See also *Ramupillai v. Minister of Public Administration* (1991), 1 *Sri Lanka Law Reports* 11.

The next area of law concerns the inroads that common law made into Muslim law, not by judicial activism, but by engineering from the Muslim community itself. What one sees is the adoption by the Muslims of land transaction devices. Although the devices were unknown to Muslim law, the Muslim community saw their usefulness and consequently adopted them. The role of the courts was to provide a legal foundation for the coexistence of such elements of common law with traditional Muslim law.

Muslim Law in Sri Lanka: An Introduction

Well before the time of the Prophet Mohammed, Persians and Arabs knew Sri Lanka as an important trading place. Islam found a receptive audience in the small Persian and Arab population in Sri Lanka. In later years, waves of Indian Muslims came to Sri Lanka, swelling the Islamic community. Many of these Muslims married Tamil women, and some others married Sinhalese women. Because of the deep religious consciousness of the Muslims, these women, who would otherwise have been governed by their native law or the general law of the land, became Muslims and subject to Muslim law. The Muslim community grew as a distinct ethnic community—on religious lines and not racial lines—and continued to be governed by religious law, except where Muslims voluntarily adopted elements from the general law or a native law and where legislation, and to a limited extent judicial decisions, replaced Muslim law.

The religion of Islam came to Sri Lanka, bringing with it rules from the traditional sources of Islamic law. The Dutch courts recognized the application of Muslim law to the Sri Lankan Muslim community. Muslim law in Sri Lanka, just as Muslim law in India, consisted of Islamic jurisprudence as adapted to the local circumstances and added to by local customs of the Muslim community. When the Dutch prepared a code of Muslim law, it contained an outline of the main legal principles that the Sri Lankan Muslim community considered to be binding on them. In the early years of the British period, this code was translated into English, and in 1806, it was adopted by the governor in council. Before its adoption, the translated code was put to the local Muslim leaders for confirmation that it was a true reflection of their laws and customs. The code was not a comprehensive statement of Muslim law and continued to be supplemented by local customs and by reference to general Muslim jurisprudence.[4] However, courts did not go so far as to say that the whole body of Muslim jurisprudence was applicable in Sri Lanka to supplement the code. Reference to general principles of Muslim law was permissible only when there was evidence that such principles had been adopted by local custom or when reference to general Muslim jurisprudence was needed to elucidate the meaning of a legislative provision.[5] The application of Muslim law was in the hands of the ordinary courts of law in the early years of British administration, but in the early twentieth century, the British administration gave effect to a prevailing practice among Muslims to have their disputes settled by a Muslim priest or judge called the *quazi*. Legislative provision was made for the creation of *quazi* courts, and certain matrimonial matters were left exclusively in the hands of these Muslim judges. Space does not permit an examination of these tribunals; note that these tribunals followed insofar as possible judicial practices, including the adherence to precedent, in resolving disputes (see Cooray 2012).

For a better understanding of the interaction of common law and Muslim law, I will now examine two areas that are not within the exclusive jurisdiction of the *quazi* courts.

4 See *Narayanen v. Saree Umma* (1920), 21 *Ceylon New Law Reports* 439, 440, where Justice De Sampayo said, "The local Muhammadans Code of 1806, it is true, provides only for such matters as [inheritance and matrimonial affairs].... By a long course of judicial practice, which cannot be questioned, the original sources of Muhammadan law and the recognized commentaries thereon have always been referred to as authorities on any points not provided for in the Muhammadan Code of 1806, which, though called a Code, is not, and does not profess to be, a complete embodiment of the laws applicable to Muhammadans."

5 See *Abdul Rahiman v. Ussan Umma* (1916), 19 *Ceylon New Law Reports* 174, 185.

Custody of Minor Children: Muslim Law in a Common Law Wrapping?

Custody of minor children is an area that illustrates how Muslim law operates in a secular state. Without any statute codifying the Muslim law principles relating to custody, and without vesting of jurisdiction in custody matters in the Muslim *quazi* courts, the ordinary courts of Sri Lanka were given the opportunity to understand, evaluate, and apply Muslim jurisprudence to custodial disputes in the context of the general law of the land on the subject. The response of the judges of ordinary courts of law, who had been trained in the English legal tradition, to Muslim law of custody has ranged from bemusement to respect.

To understand how judges of ordinary courts of law dealt with custody disputes among Muslims, one must appreciate the differences between Muslim law on the one hand and Sri Lanka's common law—an amalgam of the Roman-Dutch law and English law—on the other hand.[6]

Muslim law is based on the idea that the father has overall responsibility for the welfare of, and authority over, the child. However, children of tender years do benefit from maternal love and care. Thus, Muslim law draws a distinction between guardianship and custody. The father has guardianship of the child, and after the death of the father, or when he is unfit to be guardian, his power devolves on an appropriate male relative of his. The mother has no powers over the child, and her responsibility is to provide loving care to her minor children. When a family is divided, the custody of children of tender years belongs to the mother, and when she is dead or is unfit to the task, it passes on to her female relatives. The father retains guardianship and parental control over the child. Thus, the father makes all important decisions regarding the minor child, such as decisions related to education. His parental power comes with responsibilities, mainly the duty of support.

In Muslim law, the end to a marriage is not simply a dispute between the father and mother. If the mother is disqualified for purposes of custody, custody does not automatically pass to the father. The right to custody remains in the family of the mother, and her mother or sister is regarded as the appropriate person to care for the child. Custody is awarded to the father only if circumstances compel the judge to disregard the preferential right of the mother and her relatives.

The Roman-Dutch law position is that, in a divided family, the father has a preferential right to custody, and in a dispute between a natural parent and a third party, the natural parent has a preferential right. Thus, the father has both custody and guardianship over minor children. However, if the court grants custody to the mother, she also gets the powers of guardianship of the child, with the father remaining responsible for maintenance of the child. The preferential right of the father may be replaced if strong evidence is shown that it would be greatly detrimental to the interests of the child to remain with the father.[7] It is because of the English influence that the welfare and interests of the child are the paramount consideration in all custody disputes.[8]

To an English-educated judge, the Muslim law of custody would seem unacceptable, especially in relation to a dispute between female maternal relatives of the child and the natural father. Although English and Roman-Dutch law would prefer the father as custodian, the Muslim law favors female maternal relatives.

6 The courts of Sri Lanka have repeatedly asserted that the general law in relation to custody of minor children was Roman-Dutch law and not English law, although there were similarities between the Roman-Dutch law and the English law on the subject. Justice H.N.G. Fernando said in *Ivaldy v. Ivaldy* (1956), 57 *Ceylon New Law Reports* 568, that although there were many judicial decisions in Sri Lanka that settled custody disputes with reference to English law, "which, by reason of the essential similarity of the English and Roman-Dutch principles, will in all probability be found to conform with the latter," courts should have direct resort to the Roman-Dutch law. In *Kamalawathie v. de Silva* (1961), 64 *Ceylon New Law Reports* 252, Justice Tambiah took a more sympathetic view of the English influence and said that the courts of Ceylon had relied on English decisions and sometimes on Roman-Dutch law to support the principle that the father's preferential right may be denied in the best interests of the child, observing that "law, like race, is not a pure blooded creature."

7 See *Ivaldy v. Ivaldy* (1956), 57 *Ceylon New Law Reports* 568; *Kamalawathie v. de Silva* (1961), 64 *Ceylon New Law Reports* 252; *Fernando v. Fernando* (1968), 70 *Ceylon New Law Reports* 534; and *Karunawathie v. Wijesuriya* (1980) 2 *Sri Lanka Law Reports* 14.

8 As Justice Weeramantry said in *Fernando v. Fernando* (1968), 70 *Ceylon New Law Reports* 534, 537, "There can be no doubt that in all questions of custody, the interests of the child stands paramount, a principle on which English and modern Roman-Dutch law are agreed."

This judicial dilemma is clearly illustrated by an early decision of the Supreme Court in *re Sego Meera Lebbe Ahamado Lebbe Marikar*,[9] where the father sought to recover the custody of his young son from the maternal grandmother with whom the child had been living since his mother's death. Both judges who heard the case were bemused that in a dispute between a natural parent and another person, preference is to be given to the other person. Justice Clarence said, "The father's right is certainly the most consonant with justice and convenience: and in my opinion we should uphold the father's right, unless it clearly appears that there is law to the contrary, and of that I am not satisfied."[10] Justice Dias said, "[T]he rule, or the alleged rule, of Mohammedan Law now put forward on behalf of the grandmother is opposed to all modern ideas of the relative position of parent and child. But if there is such a law, we are bound to carry it out."[11]

In *re Sego Meera Lebbe Ahamado Lebbe Marikar*,[12] the Supreme Court justices not only expressed their dissatisfaction with the Muslim law that subjugates the father's right to that of a maternal relative, but also found a way not to apply it, even though the parties were Muslims who were to be governed by Muslim law and not the common law of the land. The justices did so by holding that the Muslim law relating to custody disputes was not part of the Muslim law of Sri Lanka. In their view, that part of the Muslim law relating to custody of minor children had not been introduced by legislation or received by local custom. As the Supreme Court had said in a 1916 case, only those parts of Muslim law that have been received and followed in Sri Lanka have force of law:

> What is the Muhammadan law which prevails in Ceylon? It cannot for one moment be pretended that the whole body of Muhammadan jurisprudence obtains currency here, for the obvious reason that all law must derive its sanction by virtue of legislation or custom or judicial decisions. [The whole body of] Muhammadan law stands devoid of any sanction here, because Muhammed had no right to impose his laws on the inhabitants of any British territory.[13]

The Supreme Court held that because there was no specific provision in the 1806 code of Muslim law on custody of minor children, and because there was no convincing evidence that Muslims of the country had adopted the general Muslim law on the subject, the general law of the land should be applied.[14]

The *re Sego Meera Lebbe Ahamado Lebbe Marikar* case was followed only in one case, *Mohamadu Cassim v. Cassie Lebbe* (1927).[15] Having stated that the *Sego Meera* case upheld the father's preferential right, the Supreme Court nonetheless preferred the custody rights of a maternal aunt of the child, taking all the circumstances of the case into account. In two previous cases, the Supreme Court had refused to follow the ruling in the *Sego Meera* case because the ruling was inconsistent with the general judicial view that Muslims were governed by Muslim law with respect to questions of custody of minor children.

Thus, the long-established judicial view in Sri Lanka is that custody disputes among Muslims are governed by Muslim law. The right of the mother is founded on the natural bond between a mother and her child: "The spittle of the mother is better for thy child than honey, O Omar."[16] It is the importance of a loving woman's warmth to a child that ensures custody to maternal relatives in the absence of its mother. If, after consideration by the court of all circumstances and the best interests of the child, custody is to be granted to

9 *Re Sego Meera Lebbe Ahamado Lebbe Marikar* (1890), 9 *Supreme Court Circular* 42 (1890).

10 Ibid., 44.

11 Ibid., 45.

12 Ibid., 42.

13 *Abdul Rahiman v. Ussan Umma* (1916), 19 *Ceylon New Law Reports* 175, 184.

14 This finding was in spite of two previous decisions that upheld the maternal grandparents' right to custody against the father: *In re Aysa Natchia* (1861), 1861–1862 *Ramanathan Reports* 88, and *Hadji Marikar v. Ahamado Lebbe* (1862), 1860–1862 *Ramanathan Reports* 144.

15 See *Mohamadu Cassim v. Cassie Lebbe* (1927), 29 *Ceylon New Law Reports* 136. In *Fernando v. Fernando* (1932), 34 *Ceylon New Law Reports* 204, a case where custody was awarded to the father, the Supreme Court mentioned that in the *Sego Meera* case, the father was preferred, but it made no reference to *Sego Meera*'s ruling that custody disputes between Muslims were governed by the common law and not Muslim law.

16 *Hedaya*, vol. 1, 385, as quoted in *In re Nona Sooja* (1930), 32 *Ceylon New Law Reports* 63.

the father, the court has to be satisfied that there is a suitable substitute for the missing mother (see Pearl and Menski 1998: 411).[17]

On the one hand, it appears that the mother's preferential right to custody is a rather rigid rule that could be justified in the context of the overriding power of the father as the guardian of minor children. On the other hand, the general law of Sri Lanka seems to take a more liberal approach. Although the father has a preferential right to custody, the mother may be the preferred custodian in the case of very young children. Moreover, if the child is old enough to choose between the parents, courts would take the child's preference into consideration.

The common law gives an almost untrammeled discretion to deviate from the idea of preferential right by recourse to the overriding consideration of the child's best interest. In cases in which Muslim law was applied in derogation of the general law, courts frequently referred to the importance of the welfare of the child, not as an excuse to deviate from Muslim law, but in an effort to arrive at a decision that was at once equitable and in line with Muslim legal precepts.

Many reported custody disputes have arisen because the mother of the child died or disqualified herself, yet the child was in the care of a maternal relative.

In a divided family, the mother has the custody of minor children, and when this right has been upheld, the father has the right to visit the child. However, the courts are unwilling to grant him extensive visiting rights, such as the right to take the child away for long periods, if doing so would be a serious encroachment of the mother's legal right to the physical custody of the child.[18]

Three judicial decisions have been reported in which the mother was deprived of custody of a minor child in favor of the father. In all the three cases, there were justifications that, according to Muslim law, would award custody to the father. In *Fernando v. Fernando*,[19] it was the misconduct of the mother. In *Hameen v. Maliha Baby*,[20] the mother had remarried a stranger. In the third case, *Faiz Mohamed v. Elsie Fathumma*,[21] the son had reached the age of seven years, when the mother's custody right terminates. In all three cases, the Supreme Court followed the Muslim law and awarded custody to the father, but it did not do so in a mechanical fashion. The court reasoned that it would be in the interests of the child, taking all the relevant considerations into account, to be reunited with the father.

In the first case, *Fernando v. Fernando*,[22] the mother took the child with her on the dissolution of her marriage and did not remarry. According to Muslim law, a mother is entitled to custody of her minor children unless the father can establish factors that would disqualify her, such as misconduct or marrying a stranger. The Supreme Court found that although the mother was a Muslim, she came from a Christian family and was living a carefree life unworthy of a Muslim woman. In contrast, the father was a respectable medical practitioner who cared for his children. The court, having considered all the circumstances of the case, especially the possible influence that her less than exemplary lifestyle would have on the children, decided that it would be in the best interests of the children—including their "moral and religious welfare"—to be with the father. Justice Jayewardene did not regret his decision: "In my view … whether Muhammadan law or the common law applies, the mother by her conduct has disentitled herself from keeping the children."

In the second case, *Hameen v. Maliha Baby*,[23] the mother had married a stranger, which would be grounds to disqualify her from having custody of her child. The judge seemed to approach the question first from the point of view of the common law and then from that of Muslim law. As regards the general law, he observed, "Under any system of law, a paramount and, indeed, a vital consideration … is the interest of the children,

17 In *re Sego Meera Lebbe Ahamado Lebbe Marikar* (1890), 9 *Supreme Court Circular* 42, in which the court refused to apply Muslim law that favored the maternal grandmother, there was evidence that the maternal grandfather and aunt would help look after the child. In *Hameen v. Maliha Baby* (1967), 70 *Ceylon New Law Reports* 405, and *Fernando v. Fernando* (1932), 34 *Ceylon New Law Reports* 204, where the father's right was upheld against that of the mother, there was no claim by any maternal relatives.

18 See *Mohideen v. Kithy Katheeja* (1957), 59 *Ceylon New Law Reports* 570.

19 *Fernando v. Fernando* (1932), 34 *Ceylon New Law Reports* 204.

20 *Hameen v. Maliha Baby* (1967), 70 *Ceylon New Law Reports* 405.

21 *Faiz Mohamed v. Elsie Fathumma* (1942), 44 *Ceylon New Law Reports* 574.

22 *Fernando v. Fernando* (1932), 34 *Ceylon New Law Reports* 204.

23 *Hameen v. Maliha Baby* (1967), 70 *Ceylon New Law Reports* 405.

any other consideration being subordinate to it."[24] The child in this case was nearly seven years old and had expressed a wish to remain with his mother, but the judge shared the concern of the magistrate that the child's consent had been obtained by undue influence. Approaching the question from the point of view of Muslim law, the judge held that the mother disqualified herself when she married a stranger. He expressed the opinion that this disqualification could be overcome only if "it is shown there are special circumstances pertaining to the exclusive interests of the child which require that he should be in mother's custody: evidence does not disclose any such circumstances."[25]

In the third case, *Faiz Mohamed v. Elsie Fathumma*,[26] the father was able to take the child away from his mother, who had remained unmarried, because the child had attained the age of seven years, when the mother's right to custody ends. The court observed that there had to be strong reasons to deny the father his right, and none were found in the case. The father had made financial provision for the son and had him educated in a leading Muslim school. Conversely, the wife (a Christian who had become a Muslim when she married) lived with her parents and sisters, all of whom were Christians and in impecunious circumstances. In these circumstances, the judge had no hesitation in awarding custody to the father.

Subair v. Isthikar[27] may be contrasted with *Faiz Mohamed v. Elsie Fathumma*. Both cases concerned a child who had attained the age of seven years and would ordinarily be given to the father's custody. In *Subair v. Isthikar*, the court held that it was in the best interests of the child to be with the maternal grandparents, with whom the child had lived since the mother and father were divorced. The mother had since then married (presumably) a stranger, but the father made no attempt to seek custody of the child. What prompted the father now to go to court was his impending appeal against a *quazi* court decision ordering him to pay for the child's maintenance. In the court's view, the child had a comfortable life with the grandparents, with whom the child's mother and her husband also lived, whereas the father was not in a position to maintain the child in the way he had become accustomed. Taking all the circumstances of the case into account and giving effect to the best interests of the child, the court decided against the father.

It does not appear that in any of the three cases previously cited, *Fernando v. Fernando*, *Hameen v. Maliha Baby*, and *Faiz Mohamed v. Elsie Fathumma*, custody was claimed by any maternal relative of the child, and that factor explains how the father succeeded in getting back the children. In *Subair v. Isthikar*,[28] in which the maternal relatives of the disqualified mother sought custody, the father's claim failed because he was unable to rely solely on the mother's fault; worthy maternal relatives had succeeded to the disqualified mother's right.

When a mother is disqualified, the right to custody devolves on the maternal relatives, which they can assert even against the mother. In *re Nona Sooja*,[29] the custody dispute was between the child's mother and her parents. The child's mother separated from her husband, and apparently the child was taken into the care of her parents. The mother entered into a second marriage, and when that husband died, she remarried and claimed custody of the child from her parents. Because her husband was a stranger, she was disqualified unless there were special circumstances that justified a dislodgment of that principle. The court could find none and considered that the child was better off with the maternal grandparents.

When a dispute occurs between the father and maternal grandparents, the courts take as the starting point the preferential right of the grandparents (a default right when the mother herself is disqualified) and consider whether there are strong justifications to deprive the maternal grandparents of custody.

There are seven reported cases in which the maternal grandparents or a maternal aunt cared for minor children after the death of their mother.[30] In all these cases—except the aforementioned *Sego Meera* case,

24 Ibid., 406.

25 Ibid., 407.

26 *Faiz Mohamed v. Elsie Fathumma* (1942), 44 *Ceylon New Law Reports* 574.

27 *Subair v. Isthikar* (1974), 77 *Ceylon New Law Reports* 397.

28 Ibid.

29 *Re Nona Sooja* (1930), 32 *Ceylon New Law Reports* 63.

30 The cases are *Hadji Marihar v. Ahamadu Lebe* (1862), 1860–1861 *Ramanathan Reports* 144; *In re Aysa Ntchia* (1861) 1880–1881, *Ramanathan Reports* 88; *In re Sego Meera Lebbe Ahamado Lebbe Marikar* (1890), 9 *Supreme Court Circular* 42; *In re Wappu Marikkar* (1911), 14 *Ceylon New Law Reports* 225; *Mohamadu Cassim v. Cassie Lebbe* (1927), 29 *Ceylon New Law Reports* 136; *Junaid v. Mohideen* (1932), 34 *Ceylon New Law Reports* 141; and *Hassan v. Marikkar* (1953), 55 *Ceylon New Law Reports* 190.

which is considered to have been wrongly decided on the point of reception of Muslim law of custody in Sri Lanka—the father's claim against maternal relatives failed. In all these cases, judges did not rigidly uphold the maternal relatives' right to custody but inquired whether restoration to the father would be in the interests of the child. For instance, in the 1927 case *Mohamadu Cassim v. Cassie Lebbe*,[31] the Supreme Court observed that a court would not remove a child from the custody of the maternal grandmother if awarding custody to the father would be detrimental to the welfare of the child. Similar sentiments were expressed in *Junaid v. Mohideen*, in which the court yet again upheld the custodial right of a maternal grandmother.[32]

Apparently these courts relied on the principle of the welfare of the child, which enabled them to consider all the circumstances of the case. Hence, what appeared to be a rigid principle of the Muslim law of custody of minor children did not cause injustice. Both in India and in Sri Lanka, the reliance on the overriding welfare and interest of the child in Muslim custody disputes was due to the influence of the English law. In this context, what Justice Mahmud said in the Indian case of *Atia Waris v. Sultan Ahmad Kahn*[33] is quite instructive:

> In considering the welfare the court must presume initially that the minor's welfare lies in giving custody according to the dictates of the rules of personal law, but if circumstances clearly point that his or her welfare dominantly lies elsewhere or that it would be against his or her interest, the Court must act according to the demand of welfare of the minor, keeping in mind any positive prohibitions of personal law.

Contracting Out of Muslim Law?

Personal laws operate in derogation of the general law. In other words, persons governed by a personal law are subject to that law only if there is a clear and valid provision. If their personal law is silent, they are governed by the common law. For instance, it is the Muslim law and not the Roman-Dutch law that applies to the custody of minor children. General law, by virtue of its being the residual law of the country, applies to a Muslim wherever the Muslim law is silent. Sri Lankan courts have gone beyond that principle and recognized that it is open to Muslims to adopt legal transactions known to the general law of the land that might be unknown to or inconsistent with general principles of Muslim law. The question is what role the courts have played in facilitating an expansion of the Muslim law in Sri Lanka by incorporating elements of the general law into the customary law of Muslims.

Abdul Rahiman v. Ussan Umma,[34] decided in 1916, concerned the validity of a prenuptial agreement whereby the husband and wife had regulated the destination of property they brought into marriage as well as any future properties belonging to the two of them. Muslim law requires possession of a gifted property to be passed on to the donee at the time the gift is made. It does not recognize the possibility of a gift whose vesting of possession is postponed to a future date. If the prenuptial agreement were construed according to Muslim law, the result would have been to declare it invalid. But the Supreme Court relied on the following reasoning to uphold the validity of the agreement:

> Where the [1806 code of Muslim law] is silent, and there is no special custom on any point, it has been held that the Roman-Dutch law should be resorted to, as being the law generally applicable in the absence of any special law, which takes the matter out of the operation of that general law.[35]

The Supreme Court went on to say that there was evidence that the Muslims of Sri Lanka had adopted principles of Muslim law as found in treatises to fill gaps in the 1806 code in relation to pure donations—namely, donations whose possession passed at the time of the donation—in the construction of wills, deeds,

31 *Mohamadu Cassim v. Cassie Lebbe* (1927), 29 *Ceylon New Law Reports* 136.
32 *Junaid v. Mohideen* (1932), 34 *Ceylon New Law Reports* 141.
33 *Atia Waris v. Sultan Ahmad Kahn*, PLD 1959 (WP) Lah, 205, 214.
34 *Abdul Rahiman v. Ussan Umma* (1916), 19 *Ceylon New Law Reports* 175.
35 Ibid., 184.

and *fidei commissa.* The court also said that in ordinary matters of contract, the principles of general law—and not those of Muslim law—had always been applied, and that courts must recognize the validity of a legal transaction between Muslims that is foreign to Muslim law, unless there is "unequivocal evidence of inveterate custom" that Muslims have refused to recognize the validity of such transactions.

The court was saying that unless the Muslim population of Sri Lanka disapproved a practice whereby a minority of Muslims entered into transactions that were inconsistent with their faith and law, such practices should receive the imprimatur of law. The widespread practice among Muslims of entering into legal transactions that were valid under the general law but not recognized by Muslim law convinced the Supreme Court that the prenuptial agreement was a valid legal transaction.

In the 1932 case *Weerasekera v. Peiris,*[36] the Privy Council had the opportunity to consider whether Muslims were able to enter into legal transactions that were inconsistent with Muslim law, in this case a *fidei commissum.* Like a trust, a *fidei commissum* does not pass into the immediate possession of the donee and is therefore foreign to the Muslim idea of a gift. In *Weerasekera v. Peiris*, the donor gifted certain properties to his son, reserving a life interest for himself and declaring that after the death of the son the property would devolve on the son's children. For the protection of the property right of the second class of beneficiaries, the son's right to dispose of the property during his lifetime was limited to granting any of such property to any of his daughters.

The Supreme Court held that the deed of gift was invalid because it was inconsistent with Muslim law. The Supreme Court came to this conclusion because the deed began by stating that the father intended to make a gift *inter vivos*—absolute and irrevocable—to the son. For that reason, the Supreme Court reasoned that the father intended an absolute gift, or a "pure donation," evincing an intention that he make a gift under the Muslim law. If such was his intention, the rest of the deed was "non-Muslim" because it placed restrictions on the disposability of the property. In addition, the reservation of a life interest was inconsistent with such a pure gift.

The Privy Council considered that the deed had to be read in its entirety. And when so read, the donor could not be said to have intended an absolute gift at all. What he intended was a gift subject to several conditions, including a life interest and restriction of the power of disposal. He did not intend a gift as known to Muslim law: he intended to make a conditional gift, in this case a fidei commissum known to Roman-Dutch law. Therefore, in the opinion of the Privy Council, the question of the validity of the deed depended solely on whether Muslims could enter into transactions not only under Muslim law but also under the general law.

The legislature had seen the undesirability of the Supreme Court decision and had enacted a law to recognize that Muslims could enter into non-Muslim transactions and that such transactions should be governed by the common law. Clause 3 of Muslim Intestate Succession Ordinance 10 of 1931 clarified the position as follows:

> For the purposes of avoiding and removing all doubts, it is hereby declared that the law applicable to donations not involving fidei commissa, usufructs, and trusts, and made by Muslims domiciled in the Island or owning immovable property in the Island, shall be the Muslim law governing the sect to which the donor belongs.

The Privy Council referred to this provision, which had been enacted before it deliberated on the case before it, but the Council did not consider itself bound by the provision, which had only prospective effect and would not be applicable retrospectively to the case. This statutory provision is a good example of a situation where the legislature stepped in to recognize adoption by Muslims of non-Muslim legal institutions.

Despite the clear opinion of the Privy Council and the equally clear legislative intention of drawing a distinction between pure donations, which are governed by Muslim law, and conditional gifts, which are governed by the general law, the question of the validity of conditional gifts came before court for many more years.

---

36 *Weerasekera v. Peiris* (1932), 34 *Ceylon New Law Reports* 281.

One such case came before the Privy Council in 1953 in *Noorul Muheetha v. Sittie Leyaudeen*.[37] In that case, there was no question that a Muslim could grant a conditional gift. The question was whether the mother had legal capacity to accept the conditional gift on behalf of her minor child. If the general laws governed the capacity to accept a gift for minors, the gift would have failed because the general law recognized that a mother could accept a gift on behalf of the minor only if she was the donor. The customary Muslim law was more liberal and recognized that a mother could accept a gift for her minor children regardless of who the donor was.

To uphold the validity of the gift, the Privy Council held that although Muslims were free to enter into legal transactions unknown to Muslim law, the capacity to enter into transactions and—as in this case—the capacity to accept a gift must be determined by customary Muslim law. Why must they be determined by customary Muslim law? According to the general principles of Muslim law, a mother was not a person who had inherent authority as a guardian of property of her children. If that principle was applicable in Sri Lanka, a mother was not a competent party to accept a gift on behalf of a child. To overcome this difficulty, the Supreme Court had decided that there was no evidence that this general principle had been received in Sri Lanka. The Supreme Court found that a custom had grown among Muslims of Sri Lanka recognizing the mother as a proper person to accept a gift to her children. Thus, the Privy Council was able to uphold the validity of the gift to minor children by applying the customary law of the Muslims instead of either the common law or the general principles of Muslim law.

The Privy Council facilitated the adoption of non-Muslim legal institutions into the lives of Muslims by drawing a distinction between (a) the legal elements of such legal transactions, which are governed by the common law, and (b) other aspects of the law, such as the capacity to enter into the legal transaction, which are governed by Muslim law.

When entering into legal transactions foreign to Muslim law, do Muslims opt out of Muslim law? It is incorrect to say that when a Muslim grants a conditional gift unknown to Muslim law, he or she momentarily ceases to be a Muslim or opts out of Muslim law, because—as the Privy Council observed in *Noorul Muheetha v. Sittie Leyaudeen*[38]—Muslim law remains applicable to the making of the transaction (such as the capacity to enter into a contract), although common law governs the essential features of the non-Muslim legal transaction and its legal effect.

Could it be said that what the Muslims have done is to absorb non-Muslim transactions into their law and that consequently the scope of Muslim law has expanded to include such non-Muslim elements? As a full bench of the Supreme Court observed in 1942 in *Aliya Marikar Abuthahir v. Aliya Marikar Mohammed Sally*,[39] the true position appears to be that it is not at all a case of Muslims' absorbing any other kind of gift into their system of law and so evolving a new form of gift. It is simply that Muslims may make gifts—some that are in conformity with their law, and others that are in conformity with the general law of the land. Effect is given to such non-Muslim gifts,

> not because a Muslim donor has manifested a sufficiently clear intention to contract himself out of Muslim law, nor merely because he had made manifest that his intention is to address himself to making such a gift as is known to the general law, but because he has, in fact, made a gift that can be given effect under that law.[40]

Conclusion

Two contrasting examples were used in this chapter to illustrate how Islamic law has interacted in Sri Lanka. The first was the judicial application of Muslim law, without deviating from its essentials. The judiciary did not to replace Muslim law with the common law, but instead interpreted Muslim law with a view to ensuring

37 *Noorul Muheetha v. Sittie Leyaudeen* (1953), 54 *Ceylon New Law Reports* 270.

38 Ibid.

39 *Aliya Marikar Abuthahir v. Aliya Marikar Mohammed Sally* (1942), 43 *Ceylon New Law Reports* 193.

40 Ibid., 202.

the well-being of the child. Thus, the effect on the Muslim was indirect and not inimical to the general well-being of the Muslim community.

The second example was the adoption of non-Muslim legal institutions not by the courts or legislature but by the Muslim community itself. After some judicial uncertainty, the law was settled that there was nothing to prevent a Muslim from benefiting from the common law. If Muslims were bound by customary practices that they had adopted in Sri Lanka and that were inconsistent with general principles of Muslim law,[41] why should Muslims not be permitted to embrace legal ideas unknown to Muslim law? By adopting such reasoning, the judiciary lent its support to efforts to integrate Muslims into the Sri Lankan community, thus enabling transactions not only between Muslims but also between Muslims and non-Muslims according to the common law, which applies to all residents of Sri Lanka regardless of their race or religion.

These two areas illustrate the harmonious way in which Muslim law has operated in the context of the mixed jurisdiction of Sri Lanka. The Sri Lankan experience, as illustrated in this chapter, shows very forcefully that a religious law can be effectively and successfully implemented in a secular state.

References

Cooray, A. 1996. Sri Lanka: Oriental and occidental laws in harmony, in *Studies in Legal Systems: Mixed and Mixing*, edited by E. Örücü, E. Attwooll, and S. Coyle. London: Kluwer, 71–88.

Cooray, A. 2012. Access to nonjudicial justice through Islamic courts in Sri Lanka: Palm tree justice or accessible justice? *Asia Pacific Law Review,* 20(1), 113–33.

Malte-Brun, M. 1834. *A System of Universal Geography or a Description of All the Parts of the World on a New Plan.* Vol. 1. Boston: Samuel Walker.

Pearl, D., and Menski, W. 1998. *Muslim Family Law*. 3rd ed. Andover, UK: Sweet & Maxwell.

Tambiah, H.W. 1968. *Sinhala Laws and Customs*. Colombo: Lake House Investments.

41 See *Sule Amma v. Mohamadu Lebbe Padily* (1907), 10 *Ceylon New Law Reports* 109.

Chapter 16
The Contribution of the Courts in the Integration of Muslim Law into the Mixed Fabric of South African Law

Christa Rautenbach

Contemporary South African law is the product of its historical development.[1] Two main factors played a role in shaping South Africa's legal system. First, the settlement of the white population more than 500 years ago introduced Western legal systems into South Africa.[2] To start with, the Dutch East India Company established itself in the Cape of Good Hope in 1652, bringing with it the law of the rulers of the province of Holland, which was Roman-Dutch law.[3] The replacement of Dutch rule by British rule in the 1800s saw the seepage of English principles into the legal system, though Roman-Dutch law remained the general law of the land to a large extent.[4]

The second factor that affected the development of law was the presence of indigenous communities on South African soil. At first, little attention was paid to the laws of the indigenous communities,[5] and the black population was left to rule itself to a certain degree during Dutch rule (du Bois 2004: 10). After the second British occupation, especially from the 1830s onward, the presence of black people on occupied or conquered land became problematic.[6] Initially, black communities became subject to indirect rule, but eventually a parallel system of law developed, one for the white population and one for the black population.[7] In addition, the legal position of the black population differed in the various territories.[8] In 1927, the various

---

1 South Africa was under Dutch rule from 1652 to 1795 and then again from 1803 to 1806, and Britain occupied the Cape of Good Hope first from 1795 to 1803 and then again from 1806 onward. In 1910, South Africa became a union pursuant to the South Africa Act 1909, enacted by the British parliament. Section 4 of the act proclaimed that "the Colonies of the Cape of Good Hope, Natal, the Transvaal, and the Orange River Colony, hereinafter called the Colonies, shall be united in a legislative union under one Government under the name of the Union of South Africa," with national executive, legislative, and judicial powers subject to supervision by the British Crown. The former colonies became four provinces: Cape, Transvaal, Natal, and the Orange Free State. In 1961, South Africa obtained independence by becoming a republic under the Republic of South Africa Constitution Act 110 of 1983. In 1994, it finally became a democratic state with nine provinces through the enactment of the Constitution of the Republic of South Africa, Act 200 of 1993 (the interim constitution), followed by the Constitution of the Republic of South Africa, 1996 (the final constitution). For the historical development before 1961, see Hahlo and Kahn (1960: 1–291).

2 The term *Western* in this context refers to the legal systems belonging to the Romano-Germanic and Common Law families. See Edwards (1996) for the historical development of South African law.

3 Roman-Dutch law was the law of one of the provinces of the Netherlands, namely Holland (du Bois 2004: 9–13; Hutchison et al. 1991: 27).

4 British rule did not factually replace Roman-Dutch law, because the Articles of Capitulation specified that the law of the captured South African territories would remain in force until altered by the conqueror. See also du Bois (2007: 33–34; 2004: 13–16).

5 These laws are referred to as customary law or indigenous law.

6 Hahlo and Kahn (1960: 1) refer to this problem as "South Africa's colour problem." According to them, the conflicts and reconciliations between the two main population groups of South Africa, the white group and the black group, "make up much of South Africa's history and have left their permanent stamp on her laws and institutions." See also Rautenbach (2009: 223–24).

7 British policy initially favored assimilation of the indigenous population into the colonial structures, but it soon changed to one of indirect rule: "This was a policy whereby indigenous institutions and laws were kept in place (and adapted) as a buffer between the Colonial State and the colonised population" (du Bois 2004: 14).

8 The term *territories* refers to the four main colonies in the former South Africa: the Cape, Natal, Transvaal, and Orange Free State. Each territory had its own legislative bodies and could make laws

territories were unified, and in line with the unification policies of the newly formed Union of South Africa, the Union parliament enacted the notorious Black Administration Act,[9] which was "[t]o provide for the better control and management of Black affairs" in the whole of South Africa.[10] The act remained in force when the Republic of South Africa was formed in 1961, and even after large parts of it were repealed in 2005, certain parts remain in force.[11]

The two factors referred to provided the setting for South African law as it is today. Over a period of more than 340 years, the official law evolved into a distinct mixed legal system comprising transplanted colonial laws (the core being Roman-Dutch law, subsequently influenced by English common law),[12] known as the common law of South Africa,[13] as well as indigenous laws, referred to as African customary law.[14] Over the years, the coexistence of these two legal systems, one based on Western legal principles and the other on African legal principles, has provided a wonderful playground to lawyers and legal scholars alike.[15]

A few other kids on the block also want to play, however, especially in the area of family law. Adherents of Islam, for example, have been immigrating to South Africa since the late 1600s.[16] Although Dutch colonials prohibited the practice of Islam in public places or the conversion of heathens or Christians to Islam, British

---

applicable within the particular territory. The laws of the former colonies remained in force after unification in 1919 until repealed by the Union government. When South Africa became an independent republic in 1961, the legislative power vested in the republic government. The provinces could make subordinate legislation known as *ordinances* (Hutchison et al. 1991: 28–29). Since 1994, South Africa has had not only a national government with original legislative power but also nine provinces with original legislative power in certain areas described in section 104 and schedules 4 and 5 of its constitution. See also the discussion of du Plessis (2002: 45).

9 The legislation was Act 38 of 1927, formerly named the Native Administration Act. Despite severe criticisms voiced against the act, it stood its ground and remained in force into the twenty-first century. The act has been partly repealed by Act 28 of 2005, the Repeal of the Black Administration Act and Amendment of Certain Laws Act. For example, sections 12 and 20 dealing with customary courts are still in operation, though they stand to be repealed in future.

10 See the preamble to the act.

11 Sections 12 and 20 regulating customary courts are still in operation, for example.

12 English common law should be distinguished from the South African common law, though South African common law bears its influences.

13 The English influence is most apparent in procedural aspects of the legal system and methods of adjudication (such as procedural law, company law, and the law of evidence), and the Roman-Dutch influence is most visible in its substantive private law (such as the law of contract, law of delict, law of persons, property law, and family law).

14 For many years, South African common law was the dominant legal system in South Africa. Customary law often had to take a back seat if its rules were deemed to be against common law values. Since 1994, however, customary law has been regarded as a separate but equal legal system available to African people choosing it. The main catalyst for this development is the two South African constitutions, which placed the customary law on an equal footing with the common law. First, section 181 and Constitutional Principle XIII of schedule 4 of the interim constitution recognized the institution of traditional leadership and customary law. Constitutional Principle XIII provided as follows: "Indigenous law [customary law], like common law, shall be recognised and applied by the courts, subject to the fundamental rights contained in the Constitution and to legislation dealing specifically therewith." A new constitution was enacted in 1996, and that constitution replaced the interim constitution on February 4, 1997. Section 211 of this final constitution continued with the trend of giving formal recognition to customary law, and today there is no doubt that it forms part of the South African legal mix.

15 See, in general, chapters 1–9 in Rautenbach, Bekker, and Goolam (2010: 3–186). Elsewhere Rautenbach refers to this mix as *potjiekos*, a uniquely South African pot food consisting of layers of food slowly cooking on an open fire. See Rautenbach (2009).

16 The majority of Muslims came from the former Dutch colonies in the East Indies (now Indonesia), the coastal regions of southern India, and Malaysia as slaves, convicts, and political exiles. Later they were also imported from India to work on the sugar plantations in KwaZulu-Natal (the former Natal colony), and some came on their own account as businessmen (Mandivenga 2000: 347, Moosa 2001: 123). Members of the Muslim community have been quite active in their attempts to have Muslim personal law recognized in South Africa, and although other religious communities (Jews and Hindus) have been less active publicly, their lack of public activism does not mean that they do not feel the same (Rautenbach, Goolam, and Moosa 2010: 189–91).

colonials gave Muslims religious freedom in the 1800s.[17] The latest available statistics reveal that 654,064 of a total of about 44 million people in South Africa adhere to Islam—about 1.5 percent of the total population.[18] This number might appear to some as trivial, but although they are a very small minority, Muslims generally feel that they have the right to regulate their lives in terms of their own legal system—namely, Muslim personal law.[19] To date, Muslim personal law and, more specifically, Muslim marriages, fall outside the legal mainstream (so-called state law or official law), and Muslims receive almost no legal recognition from the state (Roodt 1995: 50). In general, Muslim communities observe their legal rules in the private sphere, and observances thereof are overseen by religious institutions such as the Jamiat-ul-Alama. The institutions' pronouncements are binding only *inter partes*, and dissatisfied parties cannot approach the South African courts to enforce or appeal their findings (Rautenbach 2010: 119).

The Muslim community, in particular, has made numerous attempts to have aspects of Muslim personal law, at the very least Muslim marriages, recognized (Amien 2010: 363, 365). As early as 1860, the South African courts refused to recognize the validity of Muslim marriages because of their potentially polygynous nature. Chief Justice William Hodges, who delivered the majority judgment in *Bronn v. Frits Bronn's Executors*,[20] was highly critical of Muslim marriages, which he felt had not yet "embraced the greater blessings which they would obtain by Christian marriage, by which I mean of course marriage to one wife, which, among the heathen ought to be sanctioned and encouraged by law."[21] In a typical paternalistic fashion, the chief justice expressed the opinion that

> [b]y embracing marriage [according to the law of the Cape colony at that time], polygamy and incest among them [the Muslims] will be checked and discontinued; their wives will be placed under the protection of the law, and a step will thus be taken in the right direction to prepare them for the legitimate blessings accompanying Christian marriage.[22]

This judgment was delivered in the former Cape colony, but the aversion for Muslim marriages continued in the South African courts after unification. The *locus classicus* dates back more than 80 years—namely, *Seedat's Executors v. The Master (Natal)*.[23] Again the Appellate Division's main reason for disliking Muslim marriage had to do with its adherence to Christian values, which disallowed polygyny:

---

17 For a brief summary of the history of Muslims in South Africa, see Arkin, Magyar, and Pillay (1989: 145–53) and Oosthuizen (1979: 529–35).

18 Broken down according to racial groups, the largest group of Islamic followers is classified as *coloured* (people of a mixed race)—namely, 296,021 people. The second-largest group is classified as *Indian* or *Asian*—namely 274,932 people. The other two groups consist of black people (74,701 people) and white people (8,410 people). See Statistics South Africa (2004: 24, 27).

19 Muslim personal law consists of the personal laws (for example, marriage and succession) that apply to everyone who professes Islam. See Markby (1906: 3).

20 *Bronn v. Frits Bronn's Executors*, 1857–1860, 3 Searle 313. The case was heard in the Supreme Court of the Cape of Good Hope when South Africa was still under British rule. The question was whether a marriage celebrated in accordance with Muslim rites was valid and whether the children born from such a marriage were illegitimate. The majority of the court held that the marriage was invalid and that the children born from such an invalid marriage were illegitimate.

21 Ibid., 321.

22 Ibid.

23 *Seedat's Executors v. The Master (Natal)*, 1917 AD 302. In this case, the testator lived in India, where he married his first wife according to Muslim rites. After he obtained domicile in South Africa he revisited India and married his second wife also according to Muslim rites. After his death in South Africa, the testator was found to have executed a will in South Africa bequeathing his estate to executors in trust to realize and to distribute between his two wives and his children according to the Muslim law of succession. The validity of the second marriage did not come into question (probably because the litigants knew that they had a lost case). Rather, the argument was that the first marriage was valid because it was valid in India. The court based its nonrecognition of the first marriage on the principle that "no country is under an obligation on grounds of international comity to recognize a legal relation which is repugnant to the moral principles of its people" (307).

> Polygamy [polygyny] vitally affects the nature of the most important relationship into which human beings can enter. *It is reprobated by the majority of civilized peoples, on grounds of morality and religion*, and the Courts of a country which forbid it are not justified in recognizing a polygamous union as a valid marriage.[24]

The viewpoint in the *Seedat's* case represented the stance of the courts for many years to come. In 1983, the Appellate Division confirmed once more in *Ismail v. Ismail*[25] that a Muslim marriage is *contra bonos mores* and invalid on the following grounds:[26]

- There was no justification to deviate from the long line of decisions in which the courts refused to give recognition to Muslim marriages.
- The concept of polygyny would undermine the monogamous status of civil marriages.
- The marriage laws of South Africa were designed for monogamous marriages, and the recognition of polygynous marriages would create practical problems.
- The recognition of Muslim marriages would be in conflict with the principle of equality between marriage partners.
- Muslims have the right to convert their de facto monogamous marriages into de jure monogamous marriages in terms of the provisions of the Marriage Act[27] and there is thus no excuse for them not doing so.
- The fact that a Muslim marriage is regarded as *contra bonos mores* also renders the consequences of such a marriage *contra bonos mores*, making validation of the marriage contract concluded between the two spouses impossible.

In the past few years, however, these grounds seem to have disappeared behind a line of decisions, the first being *Ryland v. Edros*,[28] that gradually recognized certain aspects of Muslim law, thus contributing to the integration of Muslim law into the mixed fabric of South African law. This chapter discusses some of the pioneering cases that have been instrumental in the integration of Muslim personal law into the mixed legal system of South Africa. In doing so, the chapter highlights the factors leading up to the courts' inability to integrate aspects of Muslim law into South African law or to give recognition thereto, the factors contributing to the liberal approach taken by the courts after 1994, the methodology followed by the courts in giving recognition to certain aspects of Muslim law after 1994, and finally, the prospects of future legislative recognition of Muslim law.

---

24 Ibid., 307–308 (emphasis added). *Polygyny* refers to polygamous relationships in which the husband is allowed to marry more than one wife. *Polyandry*, which allows a wife to marry more than one husband, is not allowed by Muslim law (Heaton 2010: 15n2).

25 In *Ismail v. Ismail*, 1983 1 SA 1006, the parties underwent a ceremony of marriage in accordance with Muslim customs in 1976. At all material times, the marriage was monogamous. In 1980, the respondent terminated the marriage by means of three irrevocable *talaaqi*, and the appellant claimed, among other things, payment of arrear maintenance, delivery of a deferred dowry, and payment of maintenance for a specified period after the termination of the marriage. The appellant's action was based on Muslim customs that, according to her, were uniformly observed by the Muslim community, had been in existence for a long time, and were reasonable and certain. The respondent averred that the customs were *contra bonos mores*, and because they were was contrary to South African law, they could not be altered by means of agreement. The appellant's claim failed in the court *a quo*, and she appealed to the Appellate Division, where the court pointed out that "[t]he central issue in this appeal is whether the proprietary consequences of such a marriage and its termination, according to Muslim custom, are enforceable at law." In a nutshell, the court concluded that the marriage was invalid for want of compliance with the Marriage Act (Act 25 of 1961) and that there was no justification to deviate from the long line of decisions before it that found a Muslim marriage to be invalid.

26 Ibid., 1024–25.

27 Act 25 of 1961.

28 *Ryland v. Edros*, 1997 2 SA 690 (C). The *Ryland* case is discussed later in this chapter.

Why the Change of Heart?

South African judges are the products of their social or cultural background, their legal education, and the formal structures in which they operate. In other words, the judicial functions of a judge will undoubtedly be influenced by the context in which he or she operates. Moreover, important developments in the political dispensation of South Africa since 1994 play an important role in the administration of justice. Before democratic changes were brought about, principles such as parliamentary sovereignty and the limitation of judicial powers regarding the testing of legislation prevented the courts from developing the law, even when fairness dictated otherwise.

Former Boundaries Preventing Judicial Innovation

Although an investigation of all the factors shaping the judiciaries' mindset before 1994 falls outside the scope of this discussion, some of these factors must be briefly discussed. First, it is no secret that judges were mostly white males of the Christian faith, thereby making it "highly improbable that the interests and needs of the non-élite and non-white citizens of the country would have been foremost in the judge's minds" (Corder 1984: 15). The *Seedat's* and *Ismail* cases illustrate this point. In both cases, the judges obviously considered the facts before them in light of the values of their own social groups. As pointed out by Forsyth (1985: 13): "Judges, like all human beings, are, to a greater or lesser extent, the product of their past lives. They remain unique."

A second factor, particularly in the case of judges who held office before 1994, concerned their legal training and tradition. Under the influence of the English legal tradition, South African judges then adhered to principles such as legal positivism[29] and *iudicis est ius dicere sed non dare*.[30] In addition, many judges had been educated academically and professionally in England (Corder 1984: 15), and English law was seen as one of the historical sources of South African law (du Plessis 2002: 273).

The third factor contributing to the conservative stance taken by some of the former judges has to do with the doctrine of *stare decisis* (that is, the doctrine of judicial precedent)[31] followed by the South African courts. According to this doctrine, courts must abide by or adhere to principles established by decisions in earlier cases, especially those higher in the hierarchy. Thus, a court would be highly unlikely to deviate from former decisions, such as *Seedat's* and *Ismail*, without good reason.[32]

A fourth factor that affected the functions of the judiciary was the constitutional framework of the former government, which was based on the British Westminster model and the doctrine of parliamentary sovereignty.[33] During the 1970s, Chief Justice Ogilvie Thompson encapsulated the function of the court as follows: "In South Africa a judge must interpret the enactments of legislatures and administer the law, not as he would like it to be, but as it is set out in the relevant statutory provisions" (Thompson 1972: 32–34). Corder (1984: 18) aptly summarized the predicament the judges were in during those years as follows:

> [T]here can … be no doubt that most of the forces of tradition, training, and structure, backed by the judges' sense of social and political reality, indicated the path of caution, formalism and reserve

29 As pointed out by Corder (1984: 15), "This doctrine would have discouraged overt judicial forays into 'law-making' activity, especially in sensitive areas of policy, and would have stressed the subordination of judges to the legislature. In turn, this approach to law and its administration would not have inspired any judge to great feats of innovation in his constitutional role."

30 This maxim means that the function of the court is to apply the law and not to make the law. This concept was confirmed in *Bloem v. State President of the RSA*, 1986 4 SA 1064 (OPD) at 1075I-J, where the court said, "The judicial task is always to establish what the law is and then to judge in accordance with the law so found." See also the discussion by du Plessis (2002: 255–57).

31 The name of this doctrine comes from the Latin expression *stare decisis et non quieta movere*, literally meaning to stand by previous decisions and not to disturb settled points.

32 The "good reason" for the judgments of the cases that deviated from these two decisions can generally be attributed to the new constitutional dispensation of South Africa. See the discussion later in this chapter.

33 In *Surtee's Silk Store (Pty) Ltd v. Community Development Board*, 1977 4 SA 269 (W) at 273, the court declared: "I am bound by my oath of office to administer the law as Parliament has enacted it."

prescribed for the judiciary by British constitutional history and practice. It was obviously of little concern to the authorities at that time that the Union Parliament was governing an entirely different and heterogeneous population, compared with that in Britain. With the benefit of hindsight and as a result of tragic historical developments, it can be seen that they were misguided not to have allowed for the peculiar nature of Southern Africa's complexities.

A last factor worth mentioning is the judiciary's inability to test or review the validity of legislation, an incidence of section 34(3) of the former Republic of South Africa Constitution Act,[34] which stipulated that "no court of law shall be competent to inquire into or pronounce upon the validity of an Act of Parliament."[35]

The *Seedat's* and *Ismail* cases previously discussed emanated from a time when the sovereignty of the South African parliament was not debatable, long before the commencement of a new constitutional order under a supreme[36] and justiciable constitution, and during a time when segregation policies deepened the divide between cultural and racial groups. The *Ismail* case was the last judgment from the Appellate Division on the issue of a Muslim union before the 1993 constitution came into operation, followed by the current, or final, constitution.[37] These two constitutions changed the nature of the playing field considerably,[38] as this chapter will show.

Constitutional Unchaining: The Liberation of the Judiciary

A new constitutional dispensation came into effect in 1994 and, for the first time, not only could all South Africans participate in the lawmaking process through democratic elections but the courts were also afforded new powers to ensure that they would administer justice without fear or prejudice. Section 165 of the final constitution is perhaps the most important provision regarding the judiciary's newly found authority. It stipulates:

> (1) The judicial authority of the Republic is vested in the courts.
>
> (2) The courts are independent and subject only to the Constitution and the law, which they must apply impartially and without fear, favour or prejudice.
>
> (3) No person or organ of state may interfere with the functioning of the courts.
>
> (4) Organs of state, through legislative and other measures, must assist and protect the courts to ensure the independence, impartiality, dignity, accessibility and effectiveness of the courts.

34 Act 110 of 1983. The act was repealed on April 27, 1994, by the 1993 constitution.

35 See *Savvas v. Government of the Republic of South Africa*, 1988 2 SA 327 (T), 333–34, where the court confirmed: "In my view, as a general rule, the Court has no jurisdiction to test the validity of an Act of Parliament by an assessment of its subject-matter and the possible effect it may have."

36 The supremacy of the South African constitution is confirmed in section 3 of the final constitution, which reads, "This Constitution is the supreme law of the Republic; law or conduct inconsistent with it is invalid, and the obligations imposed by it must be fulfilled."

37 The last case reported on the issue of Muslim marriages before the 1993 constitution came into operation was *Kalla v. The Master*, 1995 1 SA 261 (T). The parties married each other in India under Muslim law. After her husband's death, the surviving wife tried to claim maintenance from his estate under the Maintenance of Surviving Spouses Act (Act 27 of 1990), but the court followed the well-established approach of the Appellate Division in the *Ismail* case—namely, that a potentially polygamous marriage is *contra bonos mores* and invalid, even if concluded outside the borders of South Africa. Ten years later, the Constitutional Court took a different viewpoint in *Daniels v. Campbell*, 2004 7 BCLR 735 (CC). See the discussion later in this chapter.

38 One has to agree with the words of Judge Cameron in *Holomisa v. Argus Newspapers Ltd*, 1996 (2) SA 588 (W), 618C-D: "The Constitution has changed the 'context' of all legal thought and decision-making in South Africa."

> (5) An order or decision issued by a court binds all persons to whom and organs of state to which it applies.

In addition, parliamentary sovereignty has been replaced by the rule of law, which is listed as one of the founding values of the constitution.[39] In *Pharmaceutical Manufacturers Association of SA; In Re: Ex Parte Application of President of the RSA*,[40] the Constitutional Court emphasized the importance of the rule of law and declared as follows:

> It is a requirement of the rule of law that the exercise of public power by the executive and other functionaries should not be arbitrary. Decisions must be rationally related to the purpose for which the power was given, otherwise they are in effect arbitrary and inconsistent with this requirement. It follows that in order to pass constitutional scrutiny the exercise of public power by the executive and other functionaries must, at least, comply with this requirement.[41]

To avoid the mistakes of the past, where the courts had no testing powers if legislation was concerned, the constitution now expressly states that a court may inquire into or rule on the constitutionality of any legislation or any conduct of the president.[42] It is imperative, however, that the declaration of unconstitutionality be referred to the Constitutional Court to be confirmed; otherwise it will not have any force.[43] As alluded to by du Plessis (2002: 84), courts have to refrain from abusing their testing powers because this "right" interferes (albeit in an authorized manner) with the legislative powers of the democratically elected legislature. They should thus use judicial constraint when striking down a legislative provision.[44]

Linking up with the newly established testing powers of the courts is their so-called developmental function, a function that has also been instrumental in their transformation from law interpreters to lawmakers. A fair number of constitutional provisions refer to this function of the courts. Section 8(3)(b) commands a court to develop the common law if necessary to give effect to a right in the Bill of Rights.[45] Section 39(2) instructs the courts to promote the values of the Bill of Rights when interpreting any legislation and when developing the common law. Last but not least, section 173 confirms that the courts[46] "have the inherent power to develop the common law, taking into account the interests of justice."

---

39 Section 1(c) of the constitution reads, "The Republic of South Africa is one, sovereign, democratic state founded on the following values: ... Supremacy of the Constitution and the rule of law." The rule of law doctrine has been debated quite extensively in South Africa, and the judiciary refers to it quite extensively without giving it much content. For a general discussion of the issues, see Devenish (2004) and Dyzenhaus (2007). Lourens du Plessis (2009), albeit in a somewhat different context, discusses other examples of case law in which the courts have contributed significantly to the jurisprudence of difference in the context of religion.

40 *Pharmaceutical Manufacturers Association of SA; In Re: Ex Parte Application of President of the RSA*, 2000 3 BCLR 241 (CC).

41 Ibid., para. 85.

42 Constitution of 1996, section 172. A court lower in status than a high court—for example, a magistrate's court—may not inquire into the validity of any legislation. Ibid., section 170.

43 Ibid., section 172(2)(a).

44 Du Plessis (2002: 84) argues that the judiciary should strike down legislation only in accordance with the exigencies of adjudicative subsidiarity. Du Plessis (2002: 29) explains the meaning of subsidiarity as follows: "Generally speaking subsidiarity obliges a more encompassing, superordinate body (or community) to refrain from taking for its account matters which a more particular, subordinate body or community can appropriately dispose of, irrespective of whether the latter is an organ of state or of civil society."

45 The Bill of Rights is contained in chapter 2 of the constitution of 1996.

46 The term *courts* refers to the Constitutional Court, the Supreme Court of Appeal, and the High Courts.

Although the view has been taken that sections 39 and 173 of the 1996 constitution exclude the operation of the doctrine of judicial precedent,[47] *Shabalala v. Attorney-General, Transvaal; Gumede v. Attorney-General, Transvaal*[48] confirmed that the 1993 constitution does not

> mean that the established principles of *stare decisis* no longer apply. Such an approach would justify a single Judge departing from a decision of a Full Bench in the same Division because he considered the interpretation given to the Constitution by the Full Bench to be in conflict with the Constitution, with resultant lack of uniformity and certainty, until the Constitutional Court … had pronounced upon the question.[49]

A similar stance with regard to the final constitution was taken in 1999 in *Bookworks (Pty) Ltd v. Greater Johannesburg Transitional Metropolitan Council*,[50] where the court had the opportunity to revisit the question of the applicability of the doctrine of judicial precedent under the final constitution. It came to the conclusion that the changes in the final constitution did not free a lower court from the duty to adhere to superior precedent and "[t]o hold otherwise would be to invite chaos."[51] In 2001, in *Ex Parte Minister of Safety and Security in Re: S v. Walters*,[52] the Constitutional Court confirmed this decision and held:

> According to the hierarchy of courts in Chapter 8 of the Constitution, the SCA [Supreme Court of Appeal] clearly ranks above the High Courts. It is "the highest court of appeal except in constitutional matters." Neither the fact that under the interim Constitution the SCA had no constitutional jurisdiction nor that under the (final) Constitution it does not enjoy ultimate jurisdiction in constitutional matters, warrants a finding that its decisions on constitutional matters are not binding on High Courts. It does not matter … that the Constitution enjoins all courts to interpret legislation and to develop the common law in accordance with the spirit, purport and objects of the Bill of Rights. In doing so, courts are bound to accept the authority and the binding force of applicable decisions of higher tribunals.[53]

Not surprisingly, exceptions exist to the doctrine of judicial precedent. Most notably, a court will deviate from previous decisions where it is satisfied that the previous decision was wrong or "where the point was not argued or where the issue is in some legitimate manner distinguishable."[54]

Additionally, the interpretive function of the courts has evolved from one that gives effect to clear and unambiguous legal texts irrespective of the unjust effects of their application (the positivistic approach)[55] to one that involves "making constitutional choices by balancing competing fundamental rights and freedoms," which can only "be done by reference to a system of values extraneous to the constitutional text itself, where

---

47 In *S v. Walters*, 2001 10 BCLR 1088 (Tk), the court incorrectly refused to follow a judgment of the Supreme Court of Appeal.

48 *Shabalala v. Attorney-General, Transvaal; Gumede v. Attorney-General, Transvaal*, 1995 1 SA 608 (T).

49 *Shabalala v. Attorney-General, Transvaal; Gumede v. Attorney-General, Transvaal*, 1995 1 SA 608 (T) at 618 F-H. The comparable provisions in the 1993 Constitution were sections 35 and 98(5), but only the Constitutional Court had the power to test the constitutionality of legislation under the 1993 Constitution.

50 *Bookworks (Pty) Ltd v. Greater Johannesburg Transitional Metropolitan Council*, 1999 4 SA 799 (W).

51 Ibid., 811B-D.

52 *Ex Parte Minister of Safety and Security in Re: S v. Walters*, 2002 7 BCLR 663 (CC).

53 Ibid., para. 60 (footnotes omitted).

54 *Daniels v. Campbell*, 2004 7 BCLR 735 (CC), para. 95, as per the dissenting judgment of Justice Moseneke. The facts of the case are discussed later in this chapter.

55 This approach of the courts is contrary to the one followed before. For example, in *Bongopi v. Council of the State, Ciskei*, [1992] 3 S Afr LR 250 (CK), 265 H-I, the court held as follows: "This court has always stated openly that it is not the maker of laws. It will enforce the law as it finds it. To attempt to promote policies that are not to be found in the law itself or to prescribe what it believes to be the current public attitudes or standards in regard to these policies is not its function." See also the discussion of positivism later in this chapter.

these principles constitute the historical context in which the text was adopted and which help to explain the meaning of the text."[56]

As a final point and in response to what was said initially regarding the social background and legal education of the judges, I must reiterate that although the demographic composition of the judiciary has changed remarkably since 1994,[57] their legal training, especially on a tertiary level, has remained fairly similar.

Judicial Integration of Aspects of Muslim Law into South African Law

Attempts by aggrieved Muslim parties to have certain aspects of their personal law recognized by the South African courts failed miserably in the previous constitutional dispensation. However, since 1994, the courts have had the power to develop the common law if justice requires it. By virtue of section 8(3) of the constitution, a court must (in its application of a provision of the Bill of Rights) develop the common law if necessary to give effect to or to limit a right. In addition, section 39(2) of the constitution compels a court to "promote the spirit, purport, and objects of the Bill of Rights" when developing the common law. Finally, section 173 of the constitution confirms that a court has the inherent power "to develop the common law, taking into account the interests of justice."

In the context of Muslim family law, the first decision willing to develop the common law to give recognition to the contractual consequences of a Muslim marriage was the *Ryland* case.[58] In this case, the two parties concluded a de facto monogamous Muslim marriage in 1976. Their marriage did not comply with the provisions of the Marriage Act[59] and was therefore regarded as invalid. In 1992, the husband (the plaintiff) divorced his wife (the defendant) by serving the *talaaqi* on her. Thereafter, he instituted an action in court to evict her from the house that they shared as husband and wife. The defendant defended the action and instituted a counterclaim[60] based on the "contractual agreement" constituted by their Muslim marriage. During the pretrial proceedings, both the defendant and the plaintiff agreed that the defendant would vacate the house and that the husband would pay half her costs with regard to her counterclaim. The remaining issue, which the court had to decide, was the defendant's counterclaim and, more specifically, the validity of the marriage contract. Before the court could decide this issue, it had to decide if the *Ismail* case,[61] which previously held that a Muslim marriage was *contra bonos mores*, prevented the parties from relying on the marriage contract that formed the basis of their Muslim marriage. The court held that public policy is a question of fact,[62] which can change if the facts on which it is based change. If the 1993 constitution brought about a change in the factual position of public policy, the *Ismail* case could be revised. The 1993 constitution required a reappraisal of the basic values on which public policy was based. If the "spirit, purport and objects" of the 1993 constitution and the basic values underlying it were in conflict with the view regarding public policy expressed in the *Ismail* case, then the values underlying the 1993 constitution had to prevail.[63] The court then considered whether the underlying values of the 1993 constitution were in conflict with the views regarding public policy expressed in the *Ismail* case and came to the conclusion that it could not be said that the contract arising from a Muslim marriage was "contrary to the accepted customs and usages which

56 *S v. Makwanyane*, 1995 3 SA 391(CC) at paras. 302–33.

57 For example, only three of the ten permanently appointed judges of the Constitutional Court are white. The others come from various other backgrounds.

58 *Ryland v. Edros*, 1997 2 SA 690 (C). The case was decided when the 1993 constitution was still in force. However, relevant provisions of the 1993 constitution are similar to those of the 1996 constitution, and the decision is still relevant to the interpretation of the 1996 constitution.

59 Act 25 of 1961.

60 The counterclaim was for arrear maintenance, a consolatory gift, and an equitable portion of the growth of the applicant's estate.

61 See earlier discussion.

62 The judge referred to the 1993 constitution, which was the beginning of the new South African constitutional dispensation. According to Ashraf Mahomed (1997: 189), it is clear that the concept of public policy is not a vague and arbitrary concept that is "open to abuse by an executive-minded judiciary. Rather it operates within definite parameters and is guided by the interpretation provision" of the 1993 constitution.

63 *Ryland v. Edros*, 1997 2 SA 690 (C), 705.

are regarded as morally binding upon *all* members of our society" or was "fundamentally opposed to *our* principles and institutions" as expressed in the *Ismail* case.[64] The court based its decision on the fact, among others, that the viewpoints of only one group in a multicultural society had been taken into consideration and found that

> it is quite inimical to all the values of the new South Africa for one group to impose its values on another and that the Courts should only brand a contract as offensive to public policy if it is offensive to those values which are shared by the community at large, by all right-thinking people in the community and not only by one section of it.[65]

Second, the court referred to the principles of equality and of diversity and the recognition that South African society is a multicultural society. These principles were among the values that underlined the 1993 Constitution. In the court's opinion these values "irradiate" the concept of public policy that the courts have to apply and came to the conclusion that the "values underlying the [1993] Constitution is such that neither of these grounds for holding the contractual terms under consideration in this case to be unlawful can be supported."[66] In the end, the court concluded that the marriage contract was not *contra bonos mores*, and the result was that the *Ismail* case no longer operated "to preclude a court from enforcing claims such as those brought by" parties to a Muslim union.[67]

The *Ryland* case was thus the first case that developed the common law to recognize certain matrimonial consequences of a Muslim marriage as reflected in the marriage contract. It provided the first crack in the wall to allow the integration of Muslim law into the already mixed legal system of South Africa. Although *Ryland* was immediately regarded as a landmark case regarding the rights of Muslims in South Africa, its effect was limited. No recognition was given to Muslim marriages; only the marriage contract that constituted a Muslim marriage that was recognized as a valid contract. In addition, the court did not deal with polygynous Muslim marriages, and up to 2004, a great deal of uncertainty existed regarding the legal consequences of a polygynous Muslim marriage.[68] Last, although the fear has since proved to be unfounded, the decision came from the Cape Provincial Division, and the possibility existed that other high courts could follow a different route because of the doctrine of judicial precedent.[69]

In 1999, the Supreme Court of Appeal, in *Amod v. Multilateral Motor Vehicle Accident Fund (Commission for Gender Equality Intervening)*,[70] had the opportunity to discuss the legal consequences of a Muslim marriage again, but only after the case took its course in two other courts.[71] This time the facts revealed that the parties concluded a marriage in accordance with Muslim rites in 1989. Four years later, the husband died in a motor accident and his widow (the appellant) claimed compensation for loss of support from the Multilateral Motor Vehicle Accident Fund. The fund denied liability for payment on the ground that the couple's marriage was invalid under South African law. The appellant contended, however, that her deceased husband had a contractual obligation to support her. The question before the Durban High Court (the court *a quo*) was whether the fund was legally liable to compensate the appellant for her loss of support.[72] In terms of South African common law, such a liability would exist if the deceased was (during his lifetime) under a

64 Ibid., 707E (emphasis added).
65 Ibid., 707G.
66 Ibid., 707H–709C.
67 Ibid., 711B–711C.
68 In 2004, the judgment in *Daniels v. Campbell*, 2004 7 BCLR 735 (CC), was delivered. See the discussion of that case later in this chapter.
69 The Durban High Court indeed followed a different route in *Amod v. Multilateral Motor Vehicle Accident Fund*, 1997 12 BCLR 1716 (D). For a discussion of the case, see Freedman (1998). The decision was, however, reversed by the Appellate Division in *Amod v. Multilateral Motor Vehicle Accident Fund (Commission for Gender Equality Intervening)*, 1999 4 SA 1319 (SCA).
70 1999 4 SA 1319 (SCA).
71 It was heard for the first time in the Durban High Court in *Amod v. Multilateral Motor Vehicle Accident Fund*, 1997 12 BCLR 1716 (D), and the second time in the Constitutional Court in *Amod v. Multilateral Motor Vehicle Accidents Fund*, 1998 4 SA 753 (CC).
72 *Amod v. Multilateral Motor Vehicle Accident Fund*, 1997 12 BCLR 1716 (D).

common law duty to support the appellant. Because of the *Ismail* case, however, such a duty did not exist if the parties had been married under Muslim law. Although the court agreed that the present law of South Africa resulted in the unequal treatment of persons before the law, it could not change the law to allow illegally married persons to claim compensation.[73]

The appellant applied for leave to appeal directly to the Constitutional Court,[74] but that court held that the crucial question was whether the common law should be developed to allow the appellant to claim damages for support. This question, according to the Constitutional Court, is one that falls primarily within the jurisdiction of the Supreme Court of Appeal, and the application for leave to appeal was dismissed.

The appellant then approached the Supreme Court of Appeal, and the facts of the case were again considered in *Amod v. Multilateral Motor Vehicle Accidents Fund (Commission for Gender Equality Intervening)*.[75] On behalf of the appellant and the Commission for Gender Equality, it was argued that the common law rules make provision for a claim for loss of support of a Muslim widow. In the alternative, it was argued that, if the rules of the common law do not make such a provision, the common law should be developed pursuant to section 35(3) of the 1993 constitution.[76] The fund alleged that a Muslim marriage does not enjoy the same status as a civil marriage, that the duty to support was a "contractual consequence of the union between them and not an *ex lege* consequence of the marriage *per se*," and that the action for loss of support should not be extended to include claims for loss of support pursuant to a contractual duty to furnish support. The action for loss of support, it was argued, should be restricted to cases in which the duty of support is one of the common law consequences of a valid marriage.[77] The court found, however, that the appellant had a good cause of action because the deceased had a legally enforceable duty to support the appellant, because the duty arose from a solemn marriage in accordance with the tenets of a recognized and accepted faith, and because it was a duty that deserved protection and recognition for the purposes of the dependent's action.[78] The question was not whether the marriage was lawful at common law but whether the deceased had a duty to support the appellant during the subsistence of the marriage.[79] The court based its findings on an "important shift in the identifiable *boni mores* of the community" that "must also manifest itself in a corresponding evolution in the relevant parameters of application in this area"[80] and held as follows:

> The insistence that the duty of support which such a serious *de facto* monogamous marriage imposes on the husband is not worthy of protection can only be justified on the basis that the only duty of support which the law will protect in such circumstances is a duty flowing from a marriage solemnised and recognised by one faith or philosophy to the exclusion of others. This is an untenable basis for the determination of the *boni mores* of society. It is inconsistent with the new ethos of tolerance, pluralism and religious freedom which had consolidated itself in the community even before the formal adoption of the interim Constitution on 22 December 1993.[81]

The extension of the common law action for loss of support to spouses involved in a monogamous Muslim marriage is a perfect example of how the South African courts are contributing toward the integration of aspects of Muslim law into South African law, but its effect is limited in two ways. First, no legal recognition has been given to Muslim marriages in general; only the claim of a surviving spouse (married in terms of the

---

73 The court *a quo* distinguished the facts from those present in the *Ryland* case and came to the conclusion that the latter did not hold that a Muslim marriage is a valid one or that it generated a legal duty to support a wife. See *Amod v. Multilateral Motor Vehicle Accident Fund*, 1997 12 BCLR 1716 (D), 1726E.

74 *Amod v. Multilateral Motor Vehicle Accidents Fund*, 1 1998 4 SA 753 (CC).

75 *Amod v. Multilateral Motor Vehicle Accidents Fund (Commission for Gender Equality Intervening)*, 1999 4 SA 119 (SCA). For a discussion of the issues raised in the three cases, see Rautenbach and du Plessis (2000).

76 The 1993 constitution was in effect when the action commenced in the Durban High Court.

77 *Amod v. Multilateral Motor Vehicle Accidents Fund (Commission for Gender Equality Intervening)*, 1999 4 SA 119 (SCA), para. 16.

78 Ibid., paras. 26 and 30.

79 Ibid., para. 19.

80 Ibid., para. 23.

81 Ibid., para. 20.

common law) for loss of support has been extended to spouses married in terms of unrecognized Muslim law. Second, the judicial precedent does not apply to polygynous Muslim marriages, and if a situation involving a polygynous marriage comes up in future, the spouses will have to approach a competent court to consider the facts anew.[82]

Judicial Development of Legislation

Similar to its developmental function regarding the common law, the judiciary has the power to make any order with regard to statutes.[83] In imitation of the earlier decisions that developed the common law to afford protection to aggrieved Muslim spouses,[84] more recent decisions illustrate that the courts are developing legislation to provide similar protection.

The first case, *Daniels v. Campbell*,[85] was initially heard in the Cape High Court in 1998.[86] Mrs. and Mr. Daniels married each other in 1977 according to the tenets of Islam. When Mr. Daniels died intestate (without a valid will), Mrs. Daniels approached the High Court for an order declaring that she was entitled to their common house as the surviving spouse of the deceased. The court dismissed the application on various grounds that included, among others, the invalidity of their Muslim marriage. The court was of the opinion that it could not help Mrs. Daniels by recognizing their Muslim marriage as valid and that new legislation had to be promulgated to recognize its validity.[87] Mrs. Daniels approached the High Court for a second time in *Daniels v. Campbell*,[88] and this time she applied for an order declaring, first, that she was a spouse for the purposes of the Intestate Succession Act[89] and that she was thus an heir in her deceased husband's estate. Second, she applied for an order declaring that she was a survivor of the deceased and that she accordingly had a claim for maintenance under the Maintenance of Surviving Spouses Act.[90] The court concluded that the word *spouse*, as used in the Intestate Succession Act, and the word *survivor*, as used in the Maintenance of Surviving Spouses Act, could not be interpreted so as to extend to a husband or wife in a de facto monogamous marriage according to Muslim rites. However, by not including Muslim spouses, the relevant provisions discriminated unfairly against persons in the position of Mrs. Daniels on the grounds of religion, belief, and culture and were thus in breach of the constitutional guarantee of equality. The court found that the limitation (the exclusion of Muslim spouses) could not be justified in terms of the limitation clause.[91]

Pending the statutory recognition and application of the Muslim law of succession in a manner consistent with the fundamental values underpinning the South African constitutional order, the only appropriate way in which Mrs. Daniels and others in a like position could be afforded effective relief was by a suitable reading-in order. Consequently, the court ordered that the Intestate Succession Act had to include a clause that reads, "'spouse' shall include a husband or wife married in accordance with Muslim rites in a *de facto* monogamous union," and the definition of *survivor* in the Maintenance of Surviving Spouses Act is to be read to include

82 Although *Hassam v. Jacobs*, [2008] 4 All SA 350 (C), and *Hassam v. Jacobs*, [2009] 5 SA 572 (CC), were concerned with a polygynous Muslim marriage, the courts dealt with the constitutionality of existing legislation and not with common law rules.

83 Constitution of 1996, sections 172 and 39.

84 See discussion earlier in this chapter.

85 *Daniels v. Campbell*, 2003 9 BCLR (C). For a discussion of the *Daniels* case, see Goolam and Rautenbach (2004).

86 *Juleiga Daniels v. Casiem Daniels and the Master*, CPD, heard on May 10, 1998 (Unreported case 9787/98).

87 Ibid., 5–6.

88 *Daniels v. Campbell*, 2003 9 BCLR 969 (C).

89 Act 81 of 1987. The act lays down the rules for intestate succession. Under section 1 of the act, the surviving "spouse" of a deceased person has the right to inherit from the intestate deceased estate. The term *spouse* is not defined under the act.

90 Act 27 of 1990. This act describes the circumstances under which a surviving spouse has a claim for maintenance against the estate of the deceased spouse. Under section 1, the term *survivor* is defined as "the surviving spouse in a marriage dissolved by death."

91 Constitution of 1996, section 36.

"the surviving husband or wife of a *de facto* monogamous union solemnised in accordance with Muslim rites."[92]

Mrs. Daniels took the matter to the Constitutional Court for confirmation,[93] and, alternatively, she appealed against the order[94] made by the High Court declaring certain provisions of the Intestate Succession Act and the Maintenance of Surviving Spouses Act unconstitutional and invalid for failing to include persons married according to Muslim rites as spouses for the purposes of these two acts. The Constitutional Court, in *Daniels v. Campbell*,[95] ultimately set aside the order made by the High Court by replacing it with an order declaring that the word *spouse* in the Intestate Succession Act included the surviving partner to a monogamous Muslim marriage and the word *survivor* as used in the Maintenance of Surviving Spouses Act included the surviving partner to a monogamous Muslim marriage. The court had no difficulty in finding that both words in their ordinary meaning include the spouses to a Muslim marriage and that a contextual analysis of the manner in which the words are used in the two acts reinforces the justification for this approach. The purpose of the two acts would be frustrated if surviving spouses were to be excluded from the protection that the acts offer merely because the legal form of their marriages happened to accord with Muslim tradition and not the Marriage Act. Again the court did not recognize the validity of Muslim marriages; neither did it express a viewpoint on spouses involved in a polygynous Muslim union. Thus, the term *spouse* was found to be broad enough to include monogamous Muslim spouses.

Whether one can say that the outcome of the case is about the integration of Muslim law into the mixed legal system of South Africa is debatable. In a strict sense, South African law is being applied to Muslim spouses and not to Muslim law. What is actually happening is that Muslim law principles are being fused with the already mixed law of South Africa to become an integral part of South African law. Elsewhere I have already referred to this mix by explaining as follows (Rautenbach 2009: 240):

> By putting all of the different laws into one big pot, letting it simmer and infuse all of the ingredients with all the different flavours, we might eventually have a wonderfully integrated "potjiekos" mix, distinctly South African, to be enjoyed by all.

Another judgment warrants cursory mention in the context of Muslim law and South African legislation. In *Khan v. Khan*,[96] the Transvaal High Court had to decide if a Muslim husband had a legal duty under section 2(1) of the Maintenance Act to support one of the wives whom he had married according to Muslim rites.[97] The court held that a polygynous marriage created a type of family that also needed legal protection and that the purpose of the Maintenance Act would be frustrated rather than furthered if partners in a polygynous union were excluded from the protection of the act. In holding that partners in a polygynous Muslim union are entitled to maintenance in terms of the Maintenance Act, the court declared:

> [T]he argument that it is *contra bonos mores* to grant a Muslim wife, married in accordance with Islamic rites, maintenance where the marriage is not monogamous, can no longer hold water. It will be blatant discrimination to grant, in the one instance, a Muslim wife in a monogamous Muslim marriage a right to maintenance, but to deny a Muslim wife married in terms of the same Islamic rites (which are inherently polygamous [polygynous]) and who has the same faith and beliefs as the one in the monogamous marriage, a right to maintenance.

92 *Daniels v. Campbell*, 2003 9 BCLR 969 (C), 1005.

93 Under Rule 15 of the Rules of the Constitutional Court, read with section 167(5), read with section 172(2) of the constitution.

94 Under Rule 18 of the Rules of the Constitutional Court, read with section 172(2)(d) of the constitution.

95 *Daniels v. Campbell*, 2004 7 BCLR 735 (CC).

96 *Khan v. Khan*, 2005 2 SA 272 (T).

97 Act 99 of 1998. This act regulates the laws regarding maintenance in South Africa.

> In any event, the purpose of the Act would be frustrated rather than furthered if partners to a polygamous marriage were to be excluded from the protection the Act offers, just because the legal form of their relationship is not consistent with the Marriage Act.[98]

Although the court did not declare a polygynous Muslim marriage valid in terms of South African law, one can argue that the inclusion of polygynous Muslim unions within the ambit of the Marriage Act indeed amounts to an integration of Muslim principles into South African law. However, the integration of Muslim principles into the law of South Africa does not mean that Muslim law is being applied; it means only that South African law is being modified or developed to cater for situations where Muslim law is not recognized but should be.

The next pioneering case to be considered deals with a polygynous Muslim marriage. The case, *Hassam v. Jacobs*,[99] was heard in the Western Cape High Court in 2008. It dealt with the meaning of *spouse* and *survivor* in terms of the Intestate Succession Act and the Maintenance of Surviving Spouses Act, respectively, but this time in the context of more than one surviving spouse. In this case, the applicant was married to the deceased in accordance with Muslim rites. The deceased also had a second wife without the knowledge of the applicant. The executor of the deceased's estate refused to recognize the applicant as a spouse of the deceased pursuant to the Intestate Succession Act and the Maintenance of Surviving Spouses Act, thus effectively excluding her from intestate succession and maintenance. The applicant approached the High Court and initially sought an order, among other things, entitling her to be recognized as a surviving spouse of the deceased for the purposes of both acts. The primary issue before the court was whether the surviving spouses of a deceased Muslim are entitled to the benefits set out in the Intestate Succession Act and the Maintenance of Surviving Spouses Act. In referring to past decisions of the South African courts, the court concluded that a clear shift had occurred in legislative and judicial policies regarding polygynous unions.[100] In addition, it found that a restrictive interpretation of the words *spouse* and *survivor* in the two acts has the practical effect that the widows of polygynous unions

> will be discriminated against solely because of the exercise by their deceased husbands of the right accorded them by the tenets of a major faith to marry more than one woman. Such discrimination would not only amount to a violation of their rights to equality on the basis of marital status, religion (it being an aspect of a system of religious personal law) and culture but would also infringe their right to dignity.[101]

Consequently, the court held that both the words *spouse* and *survivor* included the numerous surviving spouses of a polygynous union and ordered that the two acts be declared unconstitutional and be amended to make provision for the multiplicity of wives of the deceased.[102]

In line with the confirmation requirement,[103] the declaration of constitutional invalidity was referred to the Constitutional Court in *Hassam v. Jacobs*.[104] The issue is whether the statutory[105] exclusion of spouses in polygynous Muslim marriages from intestate succession boils down to an unfair discrimination between spouses.[106] If the answer is positive, the next question will be whether the word *spouse* in the Intestate Succession Act can be read to include spouses in polygynous Muslim marriages. And if such an interpretation

98 *Khan v. Khan*, 2005 2 SA 272 (T), paras. 11.11–11.12.
99 *Hassam v Jacobs*, [2008] 4 All SA 350 (C).
100 Ibid., para. 18.
101 Ibid., para. 16.
102 The court declared the offending provisions in the Intestate Succession Act (section 1(4)(f)) inconsistent with the constitution to the extent that the act makes provision for only one spouse in a Muslim marriage to be an intestate heir. In addition, the court read into the existing provision to provide for more than one surviving spouse to be an intestate heir.
103 Constitution of 1996, section 172(2)(a).
104 *Hassam v Jacobs*, 2009 5 SA 572 (CC).
105 Intestate Succession Act (Act 81 of 1987), section 1(4).
106 Constitution of 1996, section 9(3).

is not possible, the next step will be to decide what the appropriate relief must be.[107] In pursuit of the equality analysis applied in *Harksen v. Lane*[108] and the purposive *cum* contextual interpretive approach endorsed by section 39(2) of the constitution, the court came to the conclusion that the assumption made in the *Ismail* case

> displays ignorance and total disregard of the lived realities prevailing in Muslim communities and is consonant with the inimical attitude of one group in our pluralistic society imposing its views on another.[109]

In accordance with earlier decisions of the court, it reiterated that the ethos that informed the *boni mores* before the new constitutional dispensation must now be determined by the founding values underlying the South African constitutional democracy "in contrast to the rigidly exclusive approach that was based on the values and beliefs of a limited sector of society as evidenced by the remarks in *Ismail*."[110] The court came to the conclusion that the exclusion of spouses in polygynous Muslim marriages from the protection of the Intestate Succession Act is constitutionally unacceptable, unjustified, and unconstitutional.[111] Seeing that the term *spouse* in the act could not be interpreted to include more than one spouse, however,[112] the court had to exercise its powers under section 172(1) of the constitution[113] and did so by granting the application for confirmation in essence, but by reading into the act that the word *spouse* included more than one Muslim spouse involved in a polygynous union.[114]

The Constitutional Court added a disclaimer by reiterating that the case is not concerned with the constitutional validity of polygynous Muslim marriages or the incorporation of any aspect of Muslim law into South African law.[115]

Two other decisions, which are not discussed in detail in this chapter, are *Mahomed v. Mahomed*[116] and *Hoosein v. Dangor*.[117] Both cases dealt with the scope and application of maintenance *pendente lite* (or interim maintenance) where the parties concluded a marriage in accordance with Muslim rites.[118] In both cases, the husbands contended that their Muslim marriages were not valid in terms of South African law and that maintenance *pendente lite* was thus not applicable. In *Mahomed v. Mahomed*, the court found that the entitlement to maintenance *pendente lite* arises from a general duty of a husband to support his wife and children.[119] It provided interim relief in matrimonial actions until the court had finally determined all of the issues, which might well include whether the couple concluded a valid marriage. Consequently, the court held that the applicant and her daughter were entitled to maintenance *pendente lite*.

In *Hoosein v. Dangor*, the court referred to the South African courts' attitude toward certain consequences of Muslim marriages since the advent of the new constitutional dispensation.[120] It also referred to section 15(3) of the constitution, which allows for the statutory recognition of other religious law systems, and pointed out that although this section had not been used to date, it shows that the future recognition of these systems

107 *Hassam v. Jacobs*, 2009 5 SA 572 (CC), para. 20.
108 *Harksen v. Lane,* 1997 11 BCLR 1489 (CC).
109 *Hassam v. Jacobs*, 2009 5 SA 572 (CC), para. 25.
110 Ibid., para. 26.
111 Ibid., paras. 39–41.
112 Ibid., paras. 48–53.
113 This section reads, "When deciding a constitutional matter within its power, a court—(a) must declare that any law or conduct that is inconsistent with the Constitution is invalid to the extent of its inconsistency; and (b) may make any order that is just and equitable, including—(i) an order limiting the retrospective effect of the declaration of invalidity; and (ii) an order suspending the declaration of invalidity for any period and on any conditions, to allow the competent authority to correct the defect."
114 *Hassam v. Jacobs*, 2009 5 SA 572 (CC), para. 57.
115 Ibid., para. 17. This disclaimer of the court seems to contradict my thesis as reflected in the title of this chapter, "The Contribution of the Courts in the Integration of Muslim Law into the Mixed Fabric of South African Law." See also the discussion in the conclusion of this chapter.
116 *Mahomed v. Mahomed*, [2009] JOL 23733 (ECP).
117 *Hoosein v. Dangor,* [2010] 2 All SA 55 (WCC).
118 Maintenance *pendente lite* is claimed under Rule 43 of the Uniform Rules of Court.
119 *Mahomed v. Mahomed*, [2009] JOL 23733 (ECP), paras. 7–12.
120 *Hoosein v. Dangor*, [2010] 2 All SA 55 (WCC), paras. 14–18.

had indeed been envisaged. Until statutory recognition is given, it will be up to the courts to give piecemeal recognition to the consequences of Muslim marriages. The court finally held that maintenance *pendente lite* is available to anyone who alleges that he or she is a spouse, even where such a fact is in dispute, and ordered the respondent to pay such maintenance to the applicant.

Legal Reform: Statutory Recognition of Aspects of Muslim Law

To date, the initiative to actually recognize certain aspects of Muslim family law has been taken by the South African judiciary only. The South African Law Commission[121] has also been investigating the possibility to have certain aspects of Muslim law recognized. For reasons not publicly known, it did not make much progress initially, and none of its findings in the early 1990s, if there were any, were published. The investigation revived again in 1996,and this time a few publications saw the light (South African Law Commission 2000, 2001), including a final report that contained a draft bill on Muslim marriages (South African Law Reform Commission 2003). The report and bill were submitted to the minister of justice and constitutional development in July 2003.[122]

In May 2009, the Women's Legal Centre Trust lodged an application for direct access to the Constitutional Court to seek an order declaring that the president and parliament had failed to fulfill their constitutional obligation to enact legislation recognizing the validity of Muslim marriages. Their application, however, failed, and the Constitutional Court held that the obligation to enact legislation to fulfill the rights in the Bill of Rights does not fall on the president and parliament alone.[123] Consequently, it would not be in the interest of justice to allow the Legal Centre direct access. In this particular case, it would be best to have the benefit of other courts' insights and to engage in a multistage process where issues could be isolated and clarified.[124] Until and unless legislation were enacted to recognize aspects of Muslim law, especially Muslim marriages, the courts would be the only forum to approach if aggrieved Muslim parties wanted to seek redress for any hardships caused by the nonrecognition of their marriages.

In January 2011, the minister published the Muslim draft bill for comment. The public had the opportunity to comment on its contents until March 15, 2011. As a result of the many responses received from the public, the date was postponed until May 31, 2011. By way of background, the bill explains that the aim of the legislative proposals it contains "is to provide statutory recognition of Muslim marriages in order to redress inequities and hardships arising from the non-recognition of these marriages." Although it is unclear how it is going to be regulated, the bill will apply only to persons who elect to be bound by it. It sets out a statutory framework for the legal recognition of Muslim marriages and their consequences. Since the publication of the bill, the government has made no other communication in that connection, and all of us are eagerly awaiting the outcome.[125]

Conclusion

The existence of marriages concluded in accordance with Muslim rites is a social fact in South Africa. Adherents of Islam marry, have children, pay maintenance, and dissolve their marriages. All of this happens in the private sphere under supervision of Muslim bodies outside the realm of South African law. But every now and then an aggrieved member of the Muslim community turns to the South African courts for protection of his or her individual rights. Must South African courts turn a blind eye to the signals they are receiving only

121 On January 17, 2003, the commission was renamed the South African Law Reform Commission.

122 Everyone has not seen the bill in a favorable light. See Motala (2004).

123 *Women's Legal Centre Trust v. President of the Republic of South Africa*, 2009 6 SA 94 (CC).

124 Ibid., paras. 21, 27–28.

125 Wesahl Domingo (2011: 378) argues that the fact that the bill has not been transformed into legislation presents an opportunity to reexamine and rethink the implementation of Muslim law in South Africa. She also discusses various models for its integration into South African law that should be considered by the government in general and the Muslim community in particular.

because the issue arises from a religious legal system not recognized by South African law, or do the courts have the responsibility to extend the protection of the law to everybody living in South Africa?

The influence of the courts should not be underestimated. Although the cases that I have discussed give only ad hoc relief to Muslims, mostly at the instance of an individual who is brave and affluent enough to approach the courts for help, they also illustrate that the South African judiciary has not hesitated to follow a new path when innovation is needed.

An atypical mixed legal system such as that of South Africa provides the ideal breeding ground for new laws. The South African common law is flexible, is adaptable, and should always change to meet the new demands that a diverse society brings to the fore. The judiciary is perhaps in the best position to integrate aspects of Muslim law into South African law as the need arises. Nevertheless, to leave the process of integration of Muslim law entirely in the hands of the judiciary would be unfair. Parliament has the final responsibility to ensure that the matter is laid to rest by ensuring that the court's work reaches a logical conclusion and is turned into a statute. At least then the courts will have something to work with rather than having to bend backward repeatedly to create law, which should not be their primary function.

Finally, in accordance with the disclaimer provided in the *Hassam* case, I am not so sure that the cases I discussed are about the integration of Muslim law into the mixed legal system of South Africa. In a strict sense, South African law (common law or legislation) is giving effect to or being applied to Muslim personal law. In other words, by its incorporation into South African law, Muslim law is also being developed, and not just the other way round, because that which is incorporated is no longer true Muslim law but something else. This is another reason the relevant legislation should happen sooner rather than later.

References

Amien, W. 2010. A South African case study for the recognition and regulation of Muslim family law in a minority Muslim secular context. *International Journal of Law, Policy and the Family*, 24(3), 361–96.

Arkin, A.J., Magyar, K.P., and Pillay, G.J. (eds.). 1989. *The Indian South Africans: A Contemporary Profile*. Pinetown, South Africa: Owen Burgess.

Corder, H. 1984. *Judges at Work: The Role and Attitudes of the South African Appellate Judiciary, 1910–1950*. Cape Town: Juta.

Devenish, G. 2004. The rule of law revisited with special reference to South Africa and Zimbabwe. *Tydskrif vir die Suid-Afrikaanse Reg* (*Journal of South African Law*), 2004(4), 675–91.

Domingo, W. 2011. Muslim personal law in South Africa: "Until two legal systems do us part or meet?" *Obiter*, 32(2), 377–92.

du Bois, F. 2004. Introduction: History, System and Sources, in *Introduction to the Law of South Africa*, edited by C.G. van der Merwe and J.E. du Plessis. The Hague: Kluwer, 1–53.

du Bois, F. 2007. Sources of law: Overview and constitution, in *Wille's Principles of South African Law*, 9th ed., edited by F. du Bois. Cape Town: Juta, 33–45.

du Plessis, L. 2002. *Re-interpretation of Statutes*. Durban: Butterworths.

du Plessis, L. 2009. Religious freedom and equality as celebration of difference: A significant development in recent South African constitutional case-law. *Potchefstroom Electronic Law Journal* [Online], 12(4), 9–34. Available at: http://www.nwu.ac.za/p-per/2009volume12no4.html [accessed: December 13, 2013].

Dyzenhaus, D. 2007. The pasts and future of the rule of law in South Africa. *The South African Law Journal*, 124(4), 734–61.

Edwards, A.B. 1996. *The History of South African Law: An Outline*. Durban: Butterworths.

Forsyth, C. 1985. *In Danger of Their Talents: A Study of the Appellate Division of the Supreme Court of South Africa from 1950–80*. Cape Town: Juta.

Freedman, W. 1998. Islamic marriages, the duty to support and the application of the Bill of Rights: *Amod v Multilateral Motor Vehicle Accident Fund* 1997 12 BCLR 1716 (D). *Tydskrif vir Hedendaagse Romeins-Hollandse Reg* (*Journal of Contemporary Roman-Dutch Law*), 61, 532–38.

Goolam, N., and C. Rautenbach. 2004. The legal status of a Muslim wife under the law of succession: Is she still a whore in terms of South African law? *Stellenbosch Law Review*, 15(2), 369–80.

Hahlo, H.R., and E. Kahn. 1960. *The Union of South Africa: The Development of Its Laws and Constitution*. London: Stevens & Sons.

Heaton, J. 2010. *South African Family Law*. Durban: LexisNexis.

Hutchison, D., D. Visser, C. Van der Merwe, and B. Van Heerden. 1991. *Wille's Principles of South African Law*. 8th ed. Cape Town: Juta.

Mandivenga, E.C. 2000. The Cape Muslims and the Indian Muslims of South Africa: A comparative analysis. *Journal of Muslim Minority Affairs*, 20(2), 347–52.

Mahomed, A. 1997. *Ryland v Edros* [1996] 4 All SA 557 (C). *De Rebus* 1997 (March): 189–90.

Markby, W. 1906. *An Introduction to Hindu and Mahommedan Law*. Oxford, UK: Clarendon Press.

Moosa, E. 2001. Shaping Muslim law in South Africa: Future and prospects, in *The Other Law: Non-state Ordering in South Africa*, edited by W. Schärf and D. Nina. Lansdowne, South Africa: Juta, 121–47.

Motala, Z. 2004. The draft bill on the recognition of Muslim marriages: An unwise, improvident and questionable constitutional exercise. *Comparative and International Law Journal of Southern Africa*, 37(3), 327–39.

Oosthuizen, G.C. 1979. Major religions, in *South Africa's Indians: The Evolution of a Minority*, edited by B. Pachai. Washington, DC: University Press of America, 529–35.

Rautenbach, C. 2009. Mixing South African common law and customary law of intestate succession: "Potjiekos" in the making. In *Mixed Legal Systems at New Frontiers*, edited by E. Örücü. London: Wildy, Simmonds & Hill, 222–40.

Rautenbach, C. 2010. Celebration of difference: Judicial accommodation of cultural and religious diversity in South Africa. *International Journal of Diversity in Organizations, Communities and Nations*, 10(2), 117–32.

Rautenbach, C., Bekker, J.C., and Goolam, N.M.I. (eds.). 2010. *Introduction to Legal Pluralism in South Africa*. 3rd ed. Durban: LexisNexis.

Rautenbach, C., and W. Du Plessis. 2000. The extension of the dependant's action for loss of support and the recognition of Muslim marriages: The saga continues: *Amod v Multilateral Motor Vehicle Accidents Fund* (*Commission for Gender Equality Intervening*) 1999 4 SA 119 (SCA), *Tydskrif vir Hedendaagse Romeins-Hollandse Reg* (*Journal of Contemporary Roman Dutch Law*), 63, 302–14.

Rautenbach, C., N.M.I. Goolam, and N. Moosa. 2010. Religious legal systems: Constitutional analysis, in *Introduction to Legal Pluralism in South Africa*, edited by C. Rautenbach, J.C. Bekker, and N.M.I. Goolam. 3rd ed. Durban: LexisNexis, 187–214.

Roodt, C. 1995. Marriages under Islamic law: Patrimonial consequences and financial relief. *Codicillus*, 36(2), 50–58.

South African Law Commission. 2000. Project 59: Islamic marriages and related matters. Issue Paper 15, South African Law Commission, Pretoria. Available at: http://www.justice.gov.za/salrc/ipapers/ip15_prj59_2000.pdf [accessed: December 13, 2013].

South African Law Commission. 2001. Project 59: Islamic marriages and related matters, Discussion Paper 101, South African Law Commission, Pretoria. Available at: http://www.justice.gov.za/salrc/dpapers/dp101.pdf [accessed: December 13, 2013].

South African Law Reform Commission. 2003. *Project 59: Islamic Marriages and Related Matters—Report*. Pretoria: South African Law Reform Commission. Available at: http://www.justice.gov.za/salrc/reports/r_prj59_2003jul.pdf [accessed: December 13, 2013].

Statistics South Africa. 2004. *Census 2001: Primary Tables South Africa Census '96 and 2001 Compared*. Pretoria: Statistics South Africa. Available at: http://www.statssa.gov.za/census01/html/RSAPrimary.pdf [accessed: December 13, 2013].

Thompson, O. 1972. Centenary celebrations of Northern Cape Division of the Supreme Court. *The South African Law Journal*, 89(1), 23–34.

Part V
Patterns of Mixing in Specialized Areas of the Law

Chapter 17
Islamic Law and International Law in the Islamic Republic of Iran's Constitution

Seyed Mostafa Mirmohammadi Azizi

Considering the main concept being explored in this volume, that of mixed legal systems, some initial remarks regarding the relationship between Islamic law, the Iranian constitution, and international law are necessary.

Following the Islamic Revolution of 1979, the new Iranian constitution was prepared by a number of lawyers, Islamic scholars, and experts and then approved by the people in a nationwide referendum in the same year with a majority of 98.2 percent of eligible voters. The lawyers who engaged in preparing the draft of the constitution had a background in Western legal systems, such as common law and civil law. A special assembly named the Assembly for the Final Review of the Constitution was elected by the people to finalize the draft. Therefore, the Iranian constitution was approved by the people twice, both directly and indirectly. The 1979 constitution was amended in 1989.

The relationship between Islamic law and modern international law from the perspective of the Iranian constitution is very complex and may be described as a multilayered system of Islamic law, domestic law, and international law. Indeed, the constitution has established a unique legal system. To better understand this system, one may find it useful to differentiate between the endogenous (inside) and exogenous (outside) factors of the constitution (see Falsafi 2000):

- *Endogenous factors.* Power in the Iranian constitution has been distributed in a special manner. The constitution's foundation is the consideration of God's exclusive sovereignty and right to legislate and the necessity of submission to God's commands. For the achievement of this kind of sovereignty, the constitution has provided for a leadership institution, known as the Guardianship of the Jurist (*Velayat-e faqih*, or *Rahbari*), and two additional branches of power, the Guardian Council (*Shoraye-Negahban*) and the Expediency Council (*Majme Tashkise Maslahat*). These institutions are under obligation to fulfill the sovereignty of truth and Qur'anic justice.
- *Exogenous factors.* The outside elements of the Iranian constitution are the fundamental charter of Islam (Qur'an) and the interpretation of leadership (Imamate) by the Jafari school of Islamic law.[1] In this regard, article 1 of the constitution stipulates that "the form of government of Iran is that of an Islamic republic, endorsed by the people of Iran on the basis of their long-standing belief in the sovereignty of truth and Qur'anic justice." The constitution's stipulation regarding the sovereignty of Islamic criteria is not limited to article 1. Under article 72, the Iranian parliament (*Majlis*) cannot enact laws that are contrary either to the roots and commandments of the official Islamic school of interpretation of the country or to the constitution. To enforce this limitation, article 91 establishes the Guardian Council, which consists of 12 members: 6 *faqhieh* (Islamic jurists), who are appointed by the supreme leader, and 6 jurists, who are elected by parliament from a group of Muslim lawyers from several branches of law that were proposed to the parliament by the head of the judiciary.

According to articles 4, 72, and others,[2] this council is, among other things, competent and obliged to review all draft laws passed by parliament, regarding their compliance with Islamic law. As an additional safeguard to ensure the superiority of Islamic law, the constitution obliges Iranian judges to refrain from applying any executive decrees and regulations that are at variance with Islamic rules.

1 The term *Jafari school* refers to the sixth leader of the Shiite school, Imam Jafar Sadegh (peace be upon him).

2 These other articles include, for example, articles 49 and 96.

The most important article in this regard is article 4, which shows that Islamic law has been integrated into the Iranian legal system. According to this article, all laws and regulations must absolutely and generally be based on Islamic criteria.[3] Hence, national policies and domestic laws and regulations (article 4) and foreign policy (article 3, paragraph 16) must be based on Islamic rules and criteria, and so must any interpretation of the constitution itself.

Leadership (sovereignty of the most qualified Islamic jurist) is another outside element that, according to articles 5 and 57, is bestowed on the supreme leader. According to article 110, the delineation of the general policies of the Islamic Republic of Iran and the supervision over the proper execution of the general policies of the system are among the duties and powers of the supreme leader.

Thus, in the Iranian legal system, there are three determinant factors: Islamic rules and criteria based on the Jafari school system of interpretation, the Iranian constitution, and the system of *Velayat-e faqih*. In light of these particularities, we can now examine the relationship between Islamic law and international law in the Iranian constitution.

International Law in the Constitution

None of the Iranian constitutions, before or after the Islamic Revolution of 1979, took an explicit position toward international law. However, the constitution that is now in effect, in some of its principles and chapters, points to the relationship between international law and the constitution.

The Iranian constitution is divided into 14 chapters and consists of 177 articles. The sections that are relevant to international law are located in several chapters and articles, including chapter 10 (on foreign policy) and articles 3(16) and 11 (on the Islamic community, or *Ummah*), 77 (on treaties), 81 (on concessions agreements), and 125 (on signing treaties).[4]

In general, a distinction must be made between international treaty law and customary law. Like every state, Iran is party to most major international treaties, including human rights and humanitarian law conventions. With regard to international treaties, article 9 of the Iranian Civil Code states, "Treaty Provisions which have been, in accordance with the Constitutional Law, concluded between the Iranian Government and other government, shall have the force of law."

According to article 9, if the respective treaties have been ratified in compliance with the constitutional prerequisites, they share the rank of regular parliamentary laws in the domestic hierarchy of norms. It seems that the Iranian legislator promulgates theories that tend in the direction of strong monism, giving precedence to domestic law and denying any binding force of treaty provisions that are inconsistent with Iranian domestic law or Islamic law (see Moschtaghi 2009: 386–88).

Unlike the situation of international treaties, there are no explicit provisions in the constitution or the Iranian legal system as a whole regarding the place of customary international law. These rules of international law are acceptable when they are not contrary to Islamic rules and criteria. Under articles 4, 72, and 91 of the constitution, regulations that comply with the Jafari school of Islamic law are to be applied.

Thus, the Iranian constitution is unique and *sui generis* not only in terms of its basis in religion in general but also in terms of its adherence to the Jafari school as the official school of interpretation. Although the constitution is unique, its drafters did not neglect to consider the modern achievements of other legal systems in the field of public law (such as separation of powers). Indeed, the writers of the constitution tried to bring religion and state together in a way that would prevent the negative experiences of Western legal systems. The great Western states experienced religion-based legal systems for centuries before those systems were put aside in favor of secular systems. Aware of these two different experiences, the writers of the Iranian constitution appear to have tried to incorporate the positive experiences of both periods. Therefore, the

3 All civil, penal, financial, economic, administrative, cultural, military, political, and other laws and regulations must be based on Islamic criteria. This principle applies absolutely and generally to all articles of the constitution as well as to all other laws and regulations, and the *Foghaha* members of the Guardian Council are judges in this matter.

4 According to article 77, international treaties and agreements must be approved by the parliament. They become binding after approval by the Guardian Council and signing by the president (article 125).

constitution is loyal to Islamic criteria and at the same time aims to secure justice in society. In this latter aspect, it is influenced by the achievements of public law in Western legal systems.

Certainly, neither Islamic law nor the Iranian constitution are foes of international law; rather, they are opposed to hegemony and colonialism under the guise of international treaties and customary law. The constitutional lawmakers were worried about conventions and international regulations that would protect solely the interest of the great powers. Logically, where international law is a law of all members of the international community and all nations, it must be acceptable by Islamic criteria and by the Iranian constitution as well. Perhaps the lawmakers at the time of codification of the constitution doubted whether modern international law was a law of the nations or a law of the great powers, especially in terms of customary international law and important branches of international law such as the law of the sea, the law governing use of force, and diplomatic law. Not enough signs were available to them to ensure that the international legal norms truly constituted a law of nations,[5] yielding doubts that made the lawmakers wait for further developments in international law standards. In this situation, incorporating international legal norms in the new constitution was very difficult, and its writers had the right to choose silence in this regard.

Not long ago, the socialist legal system was one of the important legal systems in the world, and communist judges held positions at the International Court of Justice (ICJ). Nowadays, most of the states that were part of the communist bloc have returned to the civil law system. Without a lengthy consideration of the causes of the rise and fall of the socialist system, one may argue that in the past century international law developed in the midst of the ideological challenges and interests of two great blocs: those adhering to the communism of the East and those embracing the capitalism of the West. Now, in the third millennium, a more diverse, mixed legal system exists around the world.

But some questions still remain. What are the essential legal elements of mixed systems in general? Do they originate only in common law or civil law, in both, or in neither? What about the international legal system? Does the development and extension of this system depend on political power, as it has in the past through legal intervention in colonial territories, or will the system develop and extend by the power of law?

Some jurists believe that the *Seyar* in the Islamic *fiqh* (jurisprudence) is Islamic international law. Although this idea is correct, it does not influence the Iranian constitution, because the *Seyar* was introduced and developed by the great Sunni schools, whereas the Jafari school interpretation of international law, particularly regarding use of force and peace, was formulated differently. The Jafari school deals with aspects of international law in accordance with the book of *Jihad* in Islamic *fiqh* instead of the book of *Seyar*.

Although the relationship between Islamic law and modern international law is very complex, legally—but not politically—the interaction between the two systems is much less difficult. Nowadays all Islamic states perceive themselves as being principally bound by international law. They have decided to join the United Nations and to participate in its various principal and subsidiary organs. They have accepted the principles and goals of the United Nations and have endorsed these goals in the charter of the Organization of the Islamic Cooperation, which was approved in 2008 in Dakar. The principles and goals include the right to self-determination, noninterference in the internal affairs of the state, respect for sovereignty, the independence and territorial integrity of each member state, peaceful settlement, and the promotion and protection of human rights and fundamental freedoms including the rights of women and children.[6]

Surprisingly, the new charter stipulates that "[a]ll Member States commit themselves to the purposes and principles of the United Nations Charter."[7] Also, any member of the United Nations that has Muslim majority can become a member of the organization.[8]

Only in a few instances have Islamic states rejected their commitment to international treaties with the argument that the provisions of such treaties are inconsistent with Islamic law. Islamic law constitutes one of the major legal systems in the sense of article 9 of the Statute of the ICJ, and in some cases, Islamic law and international law might reach different findings. Clearly, in a situation like this, Islamic states can apply

---

5 For example, article 154 of the constitution stipulates the nonintervention principle in international law by this phrase: "refraining from all forms of interference in the internal affairs of other nations." It is notable that the provision refers to "other nations" rather than "other states."

6 Charter of the Organization of Islamic Cooperation, article 1.

7 Ibid., article 2(1).

8 Ibid., article 3(2).

reservations to avoid obligations that are inconsistent with Islamic law. Indeed, they have done so in the case of some human rights conventions.

Nevertheless, the interaction between Islamic law and international law is undeniable. The ICJ, in some of its decisions (as well as some ICJ judges in their separate opinions), has acknowledged the role of Islam in international law and its contribution to that law.

Influence of Islamic Law on Western International Law

For a comparative perspective, one may look at two valuable viewpoints on the influence of Islamic law on Western international law: those of Judge Christopher Weeramantry and Professor Mohammad Tallat Al Ghunaimi.

Weeramantry was a non-Muslim judge of the ICJ who served from 1991 to 2000. He pointed out that any study of Western international law indicated that both the development of international law and that law itself as we know it have been Western creations. But he found such a conclusion is untenable for several reasons.[9] First, a mature body of international law had already been worked out by accomplished Islamic jurists. The prior existence of this law is an incontrovertible fact. Second, the flow of knowledge in all departments of science and philosophy from the Islamic world to the Western world, commencing from the eleventh century, is likewise an indisputable fact. Third, the fundamental rule of Western international law, *pacta sunt servanda*, established by Grotius in the seventeen century, is the fundamental rule of Islamic international law, where it is based upon Qur'anic verses and traditions of the Prophet Mohammed. Fourth, accomplished fifteenth- and sixteenth-century scholars, particularly in Spain and Italy, viewed knowledge of Arabic as essential for literary fluency. Hence, Arabic literature was known in the days when the first seeds of what was to become Western international law were being sown.

Therefore, in accordance with article 38(1)(C) of the Statute of the ICJ, the ICJ requires that the general principle of law recognized by civilized nations be applied. Given the multitude of Islamic states that are now members of the United Nations, Islamic international law is a body of knowledge that the world court cannot afford to ignore. Of course, in recent years, ICJ judges have turned to Islamic law in their separate (concurring or dissenting) opinions (for example, see Lombardi 2007). Judge Weeramantry (1988: 150–58) also presents 19 possible influences on Hugo Grotius, who is considered the father of modern international law, from Islamic texts and Islamic scholars and jurists.

Al Ghunaimi was a distinguished Muslim jurist from Egypt. In his thesis at London University, Al Ghunaimi discussed the influence of Muslim law on the science of international law. In his writings, he reminds us that Latin translations of Arabic books supplied the educational needs of Europe for centuries. He added that Muhammad Al-Shaybani's work in the eighth century on the Muslim conduct of state toward infidels indicated that international law was a subject of Islamic writing almost three centuries before the first codification of the Western law of war. A large number of the fathers of international law, such as Alberico Gentili, came from Spain and Italy, where Islam was dominant for a long time. Therefore, it is no surprise that Édouard Lambert, the founder of modern comparative law, and René David mention that Shari'a should be treated as one of the leading systems of law in the world today (compare Al Ghunaimi 1968: 82–86).

Nevertheless, most writers of the history of international law in the West insist that a period of nearly a thousand years during which international law was being developed was silent. For a comparative study, it is unacceptable to assume that people around the world were asleep for a thousand years. That period belonged to non-Western civilizations, which need to be taken into account.

Conclusion

Iran's constitution is unique and *sui generis*, both because it is based on religion in and because it is based on the Jafari school of Islamic law in particular. Despite its unique character, its writers did not neglect to

9 Weeramantry (1988: 149–50) pointed out seven reasons for his finding, but I select four of them.

consider the modern achievements of other legal systems in the field of public law and civil law, including such concepts as the separation of powers.

According to article 4 of the Iranian constitution, Islamic law is perceived as the basis of all Iranian laws and regulations, and every norm, including the constitution, must be interpreted in that spirit. Therefore, provisions of international treaties, according to the domestic hierarchy of norms, rank below both the constitution and Islamic law. But with respect to customary international law, the Constitution is silent.

Iran, like most Islamic states, has accepted modern international law and to a very large extent has adapted its state practices to conform with international requirements. Constitutional reforms in Muslim communities have required states to conform to both Islamic law and international legal norms. Islamic law is part of domestic law in Iran and some other Islamic states, and the obligation those states have assumed to adjust domestic law to international legal norms is one of the very important functions of comparative law.

In sum, the Islamic legal system is not a foe of modern international law. Indeed, Islamic law and modern international law are compatible on most occasions. An entirely fresh approach is needed today as we consider the relationship between Islamic law and international law.

References

Al-Ghunaimi, M.T. 1968. *The Muslim Conception of International Law and the Western Approach.* The Hague: Martinus Nijhoff.

Falsafi, H. 2000. *Hoghoghe Baynol-Melale Moahedat* [*Law of Treaties*] [in Persian]. Tehran: Nashre Elm.

Lombardi, C.B. 2007. Islamic law in the jurisprudence of the International Court of Justice: An analysis. *Chicago Journal of International Law*, 8(1), 85–118.

Moschtaghi, R. 2009. The relation between international law, Islamic law and constitutional law of the Islamic Republic of Iran: A multilayer system of conflict?, in *Max Planck Yearbook of United Nations Law*, vol.13, edited by A. von Bogdandy, R. Wolfrum, and C.E. Philipp. Leiden, Netherlands: Martinus Nijhoff, 375–420.

Weeramantry, C.G. 1988. *Islamic Jurisprudence: An International Perspective*. Basingstoke, UK: Macmillan.

Chapter 18
A Study of the Consolidation of Islamic Law and Modern Western Law in the Iranian Penal Code

Hossein Mir Mohammad Sadeghi

There is a truism that "there doesn't exist in the modern world a pure judicial system formed without exterior influence" (Arminjon, Nolde, and Wolff 1950: 49, as cited in Palmer 2007). According to this axiom, no nation's laws can claim to be purely indigenous. The Iranian law is no exception. The two main codes—the Civil Code (enacted in 1928 with no major changes following the Islamic Revolution of 1979) and the Penal Code (first enacted in 1925 and then replaced by post-revolution codes)—contained mixed provisions borrowed from various systems.

In the following two sections, I will discuss the simultaneous influence of various legal systems on these two main codes.

The Civil Code

When enacted in 1928, the Iranian Civil Code was derived in part from the civil law tradition (mainly the French Civil Code of 1804, known as the Code Napoléon) and partly from the Islamic law tradition. The former, however, was not imposed by Napoleon's victorious armies (as was the case in Netherlands, Belgium, Italy, and so on) but through voluntary reception (as was the case in Romania in 1864, Portugal in 1867, Spain in 1889, and so on). Thus, the Iranian Civil Code, although generally regarded as based on Islamic law, has some civil law in it.

Because the private law sphere—including family law (marriage, divorce, succession) and, to a lesser extent, the law of obligations—had the outward appearance of a pure Islamic law system, the Civil Code has undergone few changes since the Islamic Revolution in February 1979.

The Penal Code

Although Iran's private law had the outward appearance of an Islamic law system, its criminal law had the outward appearance of a civil law system. When Iran first codified its Penal Code in 1925, the code was mainly derived from codes of Western countries, particularly the French Penal Code, with hardly any influence from the Islamic Shari'a.

In fact, Iran was not the only Muslim country to abandon Shari'a. Throughout Muslim history and in many Muslim countries, Shari'a remained strong in the field of family law and, to a lesser degree, in the field of contracts; however, its influence has been very small in criminal law. In a great number of Muslim countries, criminal law has been one of the first branches of the law to be replaced by other criminal codes, without any real juristic justification given, apart, perhaps, from the observation that because the "ideal society" intended by Shari'a does not exist today, Islamic criminal law should not be enforced until such time as an ideal society comes into existence.

Because the Penal Code of 1925 was regarded as un-Islamic, the Islamic government that took power after the Islamic Revolution of 1979 decided to "Islamize" the code. So, after some of the code's provisions were abrogated at different times, the Penal Code was totally abrogated by the enactment of a new penal code. Parts of the new code, known as the Islamic Penal Code, were enacted at different times, first in 1982, then in 1991 and 1994, in 1996, and finally in 2013.[1]

There were, however, at least three areas of criminal law in which total change was not possible. One area related to the procedural aspect of criminal law. The second related to the general principles of criminal law. The third related to particular crimes not dealt with by traditional Muslim jurists. I will discuss these three areas in three separate subsections.

Procedural Law

Apart from certain general recommendations on "disciplines of litigation" (*ädäb ul qadä*), there hardly exist "detailed" rules of criminal procedure in traditional Islamic law. So, apart from certain abortive attempts to make changes in the criminal procedure code (for example, to limit appeals, to rename the courts, or to abolish the office of the prosecutor), few changes could be made in the pre-1979 criminal procedure code after the revolution.

General Principles of Criminal Law

The division of criminal law into a "general part" and a "special part,"—which is more clear-cut in the civil law system, as opposed to the common law system—was not very well known to traditional Muslim jurists. Medieval books on Islamic jurisprudence mainly put their emphasis on discussing particular crimes, without dedicating a special section to detailed discussion of the general principles of criminal law. In fact, many other ancient systems followed this practice, including the old common law. So, without detailed rules on the general part of criminal law in traditional books of jurisprudence (*fiqh*), the Iranian legislature had to turn to other systems—particularly the pre-1979 Penal Code, which was based on the French Penal Code—for effective legislation in this area.

For example, the first book of the previous Iranian Penal Code, which was enacted in 1991 and comprises 63 articles, deals with such general issues as mitigation and suspension of punishment; conditional discharge of prisoners; law of attempt; plurality of crimes; recidivism; rehabilitation; general defenses (infancy, insanity, intoxication, duress, necessity, self-defense, superior orders, and so on); and general principles of criminal responsibility.

The aforementioned book replaced the first chapter of the 1925 Penal Code with only few changes. For example, it reduced the age of criminal responsibility to 9 lunar years (8 years and 9 months) for girls and 15 lunar years (14 years and 7 months) for boys[2] and gave the right of pardon of convicted offenders to the supreme leader[3] instead of to the shah.[4] Instead of dividing "crimes" into the three categories (petty offenses, misdemeanors, and felonies),[5] it divided "punishments" into four categories (prescribed punishments, or *hudud*; discretionary punishments, or *t'azirat*; retaliation, or *qisäs*; and blood money, or *diya*),[6] the latter two being the punishments for homicide and bodily harms. This classification follows that adopted in traditional books of jurisprudence and has also been followed in the present Penal Code of 2013.

Although the Iranian legislature has adopted the approach of modern law in dividing the code into a general part and a special part, it has occasionally been influenced by methods adopted in the traditional books of jurisprudence. For example, the code discusses general defenses when dealing with particular crimes. Thus, article 198 of the1991 Penal Code, when explaining the conditions for enforcement of the *hadd* punishment against a thief, makes it clear that the thief should be sane, should be of the prescribed age, and should not have been acting under duress or necessity. These provisions are, of course, general conditions for criminal responsibility, as discussed in the first book of the code, so there is no need to repeat them when dealing

1 As I wrote this chapter in July 2012, a new penal code was being enacted in Iran.
2 See the note to article 49 of the Penal Code of 1991.
3 Penal Code of 1991, article 24.
4 Ibid., article 56.
5 Penal Code of 1925, article 7.
6 Penal Code of 1991, article 12.

with particular crimes. The repetition occurs because the Iranian legislature, although influenced by modern law when dealing with general principles of criminal law, was unable to depart completely from traditional thinking. This situation has been rectified in the 2013 Penal Code, which deals with general principles exclusively in the first part of the act, devoting the second part only to the discussion of particular crimes.

Particular Unprescribed Crimes

Traditional Muslim jurists have understandably been concerned with only a handful of offenses. These crimes include homicide (*qatl*) and bodily harms (*jiraha*), for which the punishment is retaliation, or *qisas*, provided that the victim or the victim's family (in the case of homicide) insists on enforcing this private right. The handful of offenses also includes adultery (*zina*), sodomy (*lawat*), false accusation of unchastity (*qadf*), theft (*sirqa*), resorting to arms in order to frighten people (*muharaba* or *hiraba*), armed rebellion (*baghy*), and wine-drinking (*shurb al khamr*), all of which have prescribed punishments in either the *Qur'an* or the precedent (*sunna*) of the Prophet Mohammed.

Most of these crimes are extremely difficult to prove. For example, the offense of adultery can only be proved by either four confessions (which some say should be in four different sessions) or the clear and detailed testimony of four just witnesses, the occurrence of which is very unlikely. Similarly, for theft to be punished by the prescribed severe punishment of *hadd*, not only must there be two confessions or the clear and detailed testimony of two just witnesses, but many other conditions must also be satisfied, not least that the stolen property must have a minimum value, or *nisäb*, and must have been taken away from safe custody, or *hirz* (that is, from a locked place that is reasonably safe from thieves). This example, in fact, shows the importance attached to the concept of situational prevention in Islamic law.

Therefore, hundreds of other crimes (for example, fraud, abuse of trust, embezzlement, and driving offenses) have not been (and some of them, being new offenses, could not possibly have been) discussed by traditional jurists and must therefore be defined in enacted laws. Furthermore, even those offenses that have been discussed as punishable by *hadd* have been narrowly defined and include only the most basic type of wrongdoing, with all other types only punishable by *tazir*, or discretionary punishment, to be determined by the ruling authority or the relevant branch of the government, such as the legislative branch. For example, the number of non-*hadd* thefts in the Iranian Penal Code, like the number of non-*hadd* theft cases in the Iranian courts, far exceeds that of *hadd* thefts.

Thus, because of the lack of considerable Islamic sources, the Iranian legislature had to act in the same way as any other legislature would act and turn to other sources to define hundreds of crimes and their respective punishments. So when one looks at the *t'azirat* section of the Iranian Penal Code, one does not find much difference between its provisions and those of the penal codes in jurisdictions such as France. The situation is completely opposite when one looks at the section dealing with core offenses punishable by prescribed punishments.

This consolidation has not been without its problems. For example, the punishment for aiding and abetting murder has generally been set at 3 to 15 years of imprisonment under article 207 of the 1991 Iranian Penal Code. However, the traditional Muslim jurists have set the punishment for one particular kind of aiding and abetting murder—holding a victim to enable a murderer to kill him or her (the perpetrator of which is called *momsek*)—to be life imprisonment. Thus, disagreement arises among Iranian lawyers in this regard. Some believe that because article 4 of the Iranian constitution dictates that no laws enacted by the parliament should contradict Shari'a law, this particular kind of aider and abettor should be punished by life imprisonment and not the 3 to 15 years of imprisonment prescribed in article 207 of the 1991 Penal Code. Others, myself included, refer to the general wording of article 207 and believe that the more lenient punishment prescribed in that article should be applied in all cases of aiding and abetting murder. The opposite view would undoubtedly cause unjustified discrepancy, but this view now seems to have been endorsed by article 127 of the 2013 Penal Code, which makes the application of the punishment prescribed for aiding and abetting subject to nonexistence of any other punishment in Shari'a or anywhere else in the law.

Conclusion

Despite the influence of Islamic law and French law on the Iranian legal system, it is doubtful that Iran can be described as a mixed jurisdiction in the true sense of the term. An occasional transplant—or even a series of transplants—from one tradition to another does not necessarily create the distinctive bijurality required to describe a system as "mixed." In other words, as Palmer (2007: 7–8) writes, one of the main characteristic features of a mixed jurisdiction is that it is built on a dual foundation of materials from two opposing systems (for example, common law and civil law), which should constitute the basic building blocks of the legal edifice. This observation, of course, does not apply to the Iranian legal system, in which—by virtue of article 4 of the 1979 constitution—"all laws and regulations, whether civil, criminal, financial, economic, administrative, cultural, military, political, or otherwise, shall be based on Islamic principles." The duty to ensure that this requirement is met has been conferred upon the six jurists of the Guardian Council (*shooray-e-negahban*)[7] who are appointed every six years by the supreme leader.[8] It is thus fair to say that although Iran has some aspects of civil law in its legal system, it should still be regarded as an Islamic law state—not a mixed jurisdiction. Although it may have borrowed provisions from two legal systems, the systems have melded together as one. This situation is in contrast with that in, for example, the Republic of South Africa, which is well-recognized as a mixed jurisdiction, and whose legal system reflects elements of both civil law and common law,[9] so that these dual elements are obvious to an ordinary observer.[10]

References

Arminjon, P., B. Nolde, and M. Wolff. 1950. *Traité de Droit Comparé*. Vol. 1. Paris: Librairie Génerale de Droit et de Jurisprudence.

Palmer, V.V. (2nd ed.). 2012. *Mixed Jurisdictions Worldwide*. Cambridge, UK: Cambridge University Press.

Zimmermann, R., and D. Visser (eds.). 1996. *Southern Cross*. Oxford, UK: Oxford University Press.

7 See articles 4 and 91 of the 1979 constitution. Another six lawyers are appointed by the parliament after nomination by the head of the judiciary. Those lawyers, with the six jurists appointed by the supreme leader, have been conferred with the duty of ensuring that no enacted law contradicts the provisions of the constitution.

8 See article 92 of the 1979 Constitution.

9 South Africa's legal system reflects also some aspects of African customary law. Zimmermann and Visser (1996: 12–15, as cited in Palmer 2007: 8) use an attractive phrase ("the three Graces") to refer to the relationship between civil law, common law, and African customary law in South Africa.

10 Vernon Palmer (2007: 8) regards it as a characteristic of mixed jurisdictions that the presence of dual elements should be obvious to an ordinary observer.

Chapter 19
The Ancient Euro-Mediterranean Aversion for Usury

Ignazio Castellucci

One of the most specific characteristics of Islamic law in economic matters is considered to be the prohibition of interest in financial transactions (*riba*), based on Qur'anic precepts.[1] In fact, most organized societies worldwide have displayed in their legal texts some kind of aversion for usury or at least an attitude calling for its careful regulation.[2]

Everybody can see that excessive imposition of interest on loans can lead to disastrous economic consequences for debtors—including sovereign states, which are required in some cases to pay interest every year on their foreign debt in amounts comparable to their gross domestic product, thus severely affecting their chances of economic development.[3]

The use—or abuse—of lending and financial mechanisms may lead not only to a general increase of the abstract figures of an economy, including gross domestic product, but also to a wide divide between those in control of the financial mechanisms and the mass of citizen—debtors—the former becoming richer and richer, controlling lives and misfortunes of a mass getting poorer and poorer—with a number of resulting social and political issues.

The three legal traditions related to the three major monotheist religions are all based on this wisdom and on the prohibition of those mechanisms allowing money to produce money by itself without association with any apparent human activity. Objectively, these three traditions have rules against the enslavement of men to men by economic means. Understanding how philosophers and lawyers had such a clear view of the distortions of the twentieth century so many centuries or millennia before they became evident on a global scale may be difficult (unless it is explained by taking into account, of course, the divine essence of the sources).

Islamic finance has been booming in recent years, with trillions of dollars of resources managed annually; it is producing a panoply of new financial schemes and facilities designed and operated by financial institutions in the East, reproducing Western financial operations through acceptable Islamic legal mechanisms. As has been observed, this approach in current global Islamic finance amounts to paying formal respect to the Shari'a rule while actually making interest-based finance possible in an Islamic context,[4] thus disregarding the authentic spirit of Islamic law and the underlying substantial economic vision—of which the prohibition of *riba* is just a fragment.[5]

---

1 Examples include the following: "Allah has permitted trading and forbidden riba" (Qur'an 2:275); "O you who believe! Do not devour *riba* doubled and multiplied" (Qur'an 3:130).

2 See, for example, the Hindu legal tradition based on Vedic texts in Jha (1930: 133–45), where the relevant classical Vedic sources are analyzed in detail. For a general overview, see Visser and McIntosh (1998). In Chinese dynastic legal codes as well, a general regulatory frame for interest rates on loans is identifiable through the criminal sanctions imposed for charging excessive interest. See, for example, *lü* 149 of the Great Qing Code, establishing a cap on monthly interest rates and providing that the total amount of interest paid may not exceed the principal, irrespective of the time passed.

3 The phenomenon is well known, and the literature on it is vast. Suffice it to mention here the presence of a significant number of documents issued by the United Nations General Assembly on the subject of external debt sustainability and the economic development of indebted countries. Among the more recent, see United Nations General Assembly (2013), which specifically mentions at paragraphs 13–18 of the draft resolution titled "External debt sustainability and development" the need for public and private creditors to consider debt management and debt relief initiatives in favor of overindebted countries to make their debt service sustainable and their economic development possible.

4 This observation is, for example, the main line of El-Gamal (2006).

5 Ibid., especially in the conclusions at 190–91.

Of course, usury has been a controversial and sensitive issue in Western cultures as well, across space and time, and a significant legal issue for most important Euro-Mediterranean societies for a very long time—since the days when society, religion, and law were much more intertwined than they are now in Western societies. Western legal traditions also feature, historically at least, a degree of aversion toward usury in their social and economic visions.

The contraposition between Western economic culture and laws, on one side, and Islamic ones on the other side, as belonging to two different and segregated worlds—the former characterized by the preeminence of financial economy and liberal, individualist thought; the latter by Islamic, communitarian precepts of social justice and "real" economy—is far too simple and certainly unsatisfactory. Moreover, that narrative may contribute to the consolidation of stereotypes, mutual ignorance, distrust, and divides—and ultimately affect East-West cooperation.

The Aversion to Usury: A Euro-Mediterranean Archetype

The present-day word *interest* is a general one, designating at least two different concepts of patrimonial increase on capital related to the passing of time: one is that of an acceptable compensation for the use of such capital; the other is that of *usury*—that is, an unjustified and thus forbidden increase.[6]

In different times and places, however, this distinction has not necessarily been made. Interest transactions were common practice in pre-Islamic Arabia, as can reasonably be inferred from the fact that the Qur'an and several hadiths in the Sunna prohibited it.[7] In the Middle Ages, banking activities in the Arab world were conducted by Christians and Jews, while the Islamic prohibition of the *riba* was observed by Muslims. Islamic law is rigid on this principle, which under the name of *riba* seems to encompass any type of remuneration for the use of capital, not just an excessive one.[8]

On its face, Islamic law would have great difficulty in overcoming such a clear prohibition because of the well-known operational limits of *ijtihad*, which cannot be used to reach a result contradicting rules established in the Qur'an and the Sunna (see, for example, Doi 1984: 78–79).

The prohibition of *riba* is not a specific feature of just the Islamic tradition, however. Similar precepts can be found in the Jewish sacred texts, such as "Thou shall not lend money for interest to your brother,"[9] effectively prohibiting the practice of charging interest on loans among Jews.

Canon law primary sources also display a marked aversion for usury, both in the Holy Books[10] and in specific normative acts of the Roman Catholic Church since its very early days: the limitation on charging interest on loans—initially limited to the clergy and capped at 1 percent per month at the First Council of Nicaea in 325—was later substituted by a total ban for both clerics and laity. The Third Lateran Council decreed in 1179 that persons who accepted interest on loans could not receive the sacraments or a Christian burial; Pope Clement V declared the belief in the right to impose usury as amounting to heresy in 1314 and abolished all secular legislation that allowed it. At the Council of Vienna in 1314, governments enacting laws enforcing usury were excommunicated. Pope Sixtus V condemned the practice of usury as "detestable to God

6 "When money is lent on a contract to receive not only the principal sum again, but also an increase by way of compensation for the use, the increase is called interest by those who think it lawful, and usury by those who do not" (Blackstone 1915: 1, 336).

7 See, for example, the fragments cited in note 1, and the hadiths, all classified as *Sahih*: "Allah curses the one who accepts *riba*, the giver of it, the two witnesses of it, and the one who writes it"; "One dirham of *riba* that a man devours, while knowing it is *riba*, is more severe (in crime) than 36 acts of fornication (or adultery)"; "*Riba* has 73 doors. The least one (in sin) is as that of a man who sleeps with his mother. And the worst form of *riba* is harming the honor of a Muslim man."

8 See note 1. See also El-Gamal (2006: 190–91).

9 Deut. 23:20–21. Several other references to the prohibition of usury are found in the Old Testament: Ex. 22:24; Lev. 25:36 ff.; Deut. 25:6, 28:12, and 28:44; Neh. 5:7; Ps. 15:5 and 55:12; Prov. 28:8; Isa. 29:5; Jer. 9:5; Ezek. 18:8, 18:12–13, 18:17, and 22:12.

10 References to this prohibition are also found in the New Testament: for example, Mt. 5:42; Lk. 6:35 and 19:23.

and man, damned by the sacred canons and contrary to Christian charity" (Moehlman 1934: 6–7; see also Cremona 2001: 41–42; Noonan 1993).

An element of caution against usury was also present in Roman law, to which canon law is heavily indebted, for which the *mutuum* (loan) was, originally and essentially, an interest-free transaction, unless a special additional stipulation, *pactum de usura*, was clearly formalized.[11]

Canon scholars in the Middle Ages—especially St. Thomas Aquinas in the twelfth century and then Spanish and Portuguese Jesuits in the fifteenth and sixteenth centuries—developed legal doctrines from these prohibitions,[12] including elements of *ius naturale* and of philosophical visions derived from the works of Cicero, Cato, and especially Aristotle, according to whom it is against nature to have money produce money by itself.[13]

Those values were widely shared in the culture and society of Europe in the Middle Ages, just as they were in the Islamic Middle East. Dante considered usury as one of the three violent sins against God and nature (with a clear link of continuity with Aristotle and Aquinas), together with blasphemy and sodomy, and consequently located the three groups of sinners against nature in the same part of his *Inferno*.[14]

In Dante's vision, art and craft are the creation of humanity, just as nature and humankind were the creation of God, in a three-level continuum reflecting the essence of the natural universe—including the fruits of humankind's work—protected with spiritual sanctions against violators. Punishing usury was necessary to protect human work, just as punishing sodomy was intended to sanction the laws of nature and just as the sin of blasphemy sanctioned the recognition of the role of God.[15]

Dante is also a bright example of the "global" reach of elite intellectuals in the Euro-Mediterranean cultural medium of the Middle Ages. He was a devout Christian and a man of his times; thus, he was loyal to his religion and opposed Islam fiercely, both politically and religiously. However, he certainly had access to Islamic culture and appreciated it.[16] Important Muslim characters are included with appreciation and respect in the *Divine Comedy*, such as the great twelfth-century ruler of Egypt and Syria, Saladin (Salah al-Din Yusuf Ibn Ayyub),[17] and the philosophers Avicenna (Ibn Sina) and Averroes (Ibn Rashid)—with an express mention of the latter's commentary to Aristotle[18]—both located with Aristotle and other great Greek and Latin philosophers, poets, and scientists in a beautiful castle in Limbo, symbolizing human wisdom, where great non-Christian spirits are supposed to spend eternity.[19]

11 Roman sources establish the need of a specific agreement on payment of interest in addition to the *mutuum*; in *Justinian's Digest*, see D. XLVI, 2.27; D. XLV, 1,126.2; D. XLIV, 4.2.3; D. XII, 1.30. See also Talamanca (1999).

12 For a review of these doctrines, see Cremona (2001).

13 *Nicomachean Ethics* V, c. 5, l.9; *Politics* I, c. 3, l.7.

14 *Inferno*, XI, 46–51.

15 *Inferno*, XI, 94–111. Those three categories of sinners are located in the seventh circle (violent sinners), third ring (violence against God). Their fate is described in Canto XIV for sinners of blasphemy, those directly violent against God; in Cantos XV and XVI for sodomites, sinners against nature, daughter of God; and in Canto XVII for usurers, sinners against human art and craft—human art being the child of humankind and thus nephew of God.

16 Certainly Dante's mentor Brunetto Latini had spent some years at the Spanish court of Alphonse X of Castille, an enlightened king quite familiar with Arabic language and culture. Dante himself seems to have had access to Islamic works, such as the *Kitab al-Mi'raj*, or *Liber scalae Machometi*. This ancient book, the original Arabic version of which has been lost, narrates the ascension of the Prophet Muhammad to heaven and his visit to hell during a night journey from Mecca to Jerusalem. It was first translated into Spanish by order of Alphonse X of Castille and then into Latin and French. The book, to an extent that is still debated today, may have influenced Dante's *Divine Comedy*. See, for example, Asín Palacios (1919); Cerulli (1949; 1971); Wünderli (1965). According to the traditionalist metaphysician René Guénon, Dante's contact with the Islamic world and its culture also included a deep exposure to Sufism. See Guénon (1925); for an English translation, see Guénon (2004).

17 *Inferno*, IV, 129.

18 *Inferno*, IV, 143–44.

19 *Inferno*, IV, 130–51: Dante found there, together with Avicenna and Averroes, Aristotle, Plato, Socrates, Seneca, Cicero, and others.

Since long before the Dark and Middle Ages, around the shores of the Mediterranean, a society more closely interconnected than many would think possible today existed. Mercantile activities; political events; and the circulation of people, religions, art, and ideas had taken place forever in that complex multicultural environment. Cultural cross-fertilization was common; circulating social values and legal elements were shared across the basin and across political, cultural, and religious divides.[20]

The aversion for usury is a deep cultural archetype and a shared social and legal value belonging to all Euro-Mediterranean societies since very ancient times.

Some three centuries after Dante's *Divine Comedy*, another clear literary example of societal aversion for usury came from England. Shakespeare's play *The Merchant of Venice* depicted how the law, invoked to enforce a usurious contract, was negotiated and ultimately circumvented to the benefit of the debtor, with deep scorn, of course, for the usurer.

Operational Solutions

Credit is a necessary tool for economic life and development, and capital owners are very seldom inclined to lend capital for free. In addition, a just, equitable economic development is recognized as being good for the material and spiritual progress of humankind in all three monotheist religions. Islamic scholars have developed solutions for this seeming dilemma over the centuries, based on the idea that lending money could produce a licit profit or compensation whenever the lender participated in the risk of the venture of the debtor or bore some costs in relation to it (for example, salaries for the lender's employees or administrative costs). The well-known Islamic mechanism of *musharakah, murabaha, taqaful, mudarabah*—the last being at the origins of medieval *commenda* (Çizakça 1996),[21] which is still a feature of commercial law in civil law jurisdictions[22]—and others represent Shari'a-compliant forms of equity-based, risk-sharing economic cooperation between the creditor and the debtor.[23] Secular laws in modern Muslim states reflect and enforce those legal principles, sometimes providing for a separate Islamic banking financial sector along with a conventional banking industry[24] and in other cases enforcing Islamic principles in a most general way.[25]

Canon law also developed doctrines substantially similar to Islamic ones. These doctrines are based on the acceptability of compensation for a service actually given or for a cost or risk borne by the lender (Cremona 2001). Eventually, the area of licit compensation was extended to include lost profits for an alternative use of the lent capital that would have been possible in the idea of cost.[26] After an initial allocation of the burden

20 Specifically on the circulation of legal elements, Glenn (2004) reports how this happened, pivoting around the Muslim kingdoms of southern Spain and Sicily of the twelfth century to transfer significant elements of the Islamic legal tradition into the then-newborn English common law. See Glenn (2004: 226, 227, 232, 236, 237, 254, 255) and the literature cited therein.

21 . A reference to the diffusion of *commenda* in Europe, including England, is in Glenn (2004: 254–55).

22 See, for example, the Italian *società in accomandita semplice*, articles 2313–24 of the Civil Code.

23 Details on the basic instruments mentioned in this text may be found in any of the many available books on Islamic law, Islamic economics, and Islamic finance. See, for example, El-Ashker and Wilson (2006); El-Gamal (2006); Saw and Wang (2008); and Taqi Usmani (2002).

24 For example, Egypt in the 1960s, Kuwait and Dubai in the 1970s, for Malaysia and Indonesia in the 1980s had such laws.

25 Within the Shi'a tradition, the Law on Banking of the Islamic Republic of Iran of 1983—named in the English translation appearing on the website of the Central Bank of the Islamic Republic of Iran (http://www.cbi.ir [accessed: February 10, 2014]) "Law for Usury (Interest) Free Banking"—establishes the prohibition of usury. At the same time, it permits forms of remuneration for capital deposited with banks in the form of bonuses for depositors (article 5) and forms of remuneration for capital invested by banks in the various forms of cooperative economic partnership with the economic sector through precalculated ratios of profit within maximum and minimum margins established by the government (article 20). A similar approach, based on the distinction between usurious interests and a moderate, acceptable compensation for the use of capital, is enforced in several recent laws in the Gulf region.

26 The compensation for lost profits should correspond to real lost profits. Thus, for example, it was acceptable to charge interest only if the merchant, in the case of a sale by installments, could have otherwise

of proof on the lender to indicate the actual lost profit, the system evolved toward the acceptability of a reasonably precalculated amount (Cremona 2001: 125–29).

The Catholic Church itself eventually sponsored the *Mons pietatis*, pawn-based credit shops run by the Church—*ad maiora mala vitanda*—allowing them to take fees to permit the institution to work and be viable and later also to have some excess money at the end of the year. This excess money was intended to cover the risk of not having ends met and of eventually perishing as an institution (Cremona 2001: 133–56).

The doctrines and legal techniques in canon law reflected, like the Islamic ones, a particular vision of the economic relations within a given community, characterized by a social dimension and by a quest for social justice in economic matters—to which the practice of charging interest (at least beyond what is a fair compensation for a substantial service given) was considered detrimental. The doctrines tried to find an acceptable and functional operational balance in the tension between the needs of the economy and the need to enforce those moral and social values.

From "Brother versus Other" to "Brothers and Others"

On the scope of application of the prohibition of interest, it is interesting to note how in Jewish law the prohibition was limited to intracommunity transactions rather than being a general rule: "thou shall not lend money for interest to your brother."[27] This rule is clearly a defensive one, meant to reinforce community bonds and implying an "us versus them" idea and the idea that an act that is inherently evil act can be performed against non-Jews.

Islamic law, too, permits the faithful to commit acts that would otherwise be sinful when in a state of extreme necessity or of need.[28] Included in this idea of need is the necessity to avoid the weakening—and thus pursue the expansion—of Islam, thereby also legitimating *haram* transactions when conducted in a non-Muslim context and against non-Muslims:

> According to Shari'a, Muslims are not obliged to establish the civil, financial, and political status of Shari'a in non-Muslim countries, as these lie beyond their capabilities. Allah (swt) does not require people to do things that are beyond their capacity. Prohibiting usury is a matter that concerns the host non-Muslim countries, and which Muslim communities can do nothing about it. It has many things to do with the socioeconomic philosophies of the host countries. However, in these countries, what is required of the Muslim is to establish the Shari'a's rulings in matters that concern him in person, such as the rules that govern acts of worship, food, drinks and clothes, marriage, divorce, inheritance, and so on. If Muslims choose not to deal with these invalid contracts, including contracts involving usury in non-Muslim countries, this would weaken them financially. Islam is, however, supposed to strengthen Muslims not weaken them, increase rather than diminish them, benefit and not harm them. Some Salafi scholars claimed that Muslims could inherit non-Muslims as this goes in line with the hadith which says: "Islam increases and does not decrease," i.e., increases Muslims in power, wealth, etc. Similar in content is the other hadith which says: "Islam is superior and none can excel it." Therefore, if Muslims are not to trade with these invalid contracts and transactions (where extreme necessity and urgent need is involved), then they will end up paying what is required from them (in transactions that involve usury) without receiving any benefit in return. They will be losers as they will be obliged to honor these transactions, and in return they will get nothing. This way Muslims will be financially deprived and suppressed. Islam never punishes Muslims for their Islam nor abandons them in countries other than their own Muslim countries. Islam never means to let unbelievers abuse Muslims financially or otherwise, at

sold the goods to a different purchaser able to pay the full price immediately. In other cases, there was no lost profit; selling by installments could, in fact, be an advantage to the merchant, because in many cases it could make possible a sale that would not have taken place otherwise. See Cremona (2001: 91–130).

27 Deut. 23:20–21

28 "And He has not laid upon you in religion any hardship" (Qur'an 22:78); "Allah does not want to place you in difficulty" (Qur'an 5:6).

> a time where it prohibits them from getting any benefit in return.... It is permissible for Muslims to trade with usury and other invalid contracts in countries other than Islamic countries. This opinion is held by a number of renowned scholars such [as] Abu-Hanifah, his colleague Muhammad As-Shaybani, Sufayn At-Thawri, Ibrahim An-Nakha'i, and according to one opinion of Ahmad Ibn Hanbal, which was declared as true by Ibn Taymiah, according to some Hanbalite sources. It is also the declared opinion of the Hanafi school of jurisprudence.[29]

Jewish law distinguished *brother* from *other*. So does Islamic law. In addition, St. Ambrose (339–397), bishop of Milan, whose works influenced medieval Christian thinking, considered lending to a stranger (that is, to a non-Christian and living under the rule of a law other than civil law) a legitimate hostile act against an enemy (Banterle 1988: 105–106).[30]

Later in the Middle Ages, Christian Catholic universalistic doctrines affirmed the principle that every human being is a *brother*. The initially religious and ethnically based prohibition of *usura* in canon law was expanded to a general principle, applicable for anyone. St. Thomas Aquinas (1225–1274) remarked about the Deuteronomic double standard: "The Jews were forbidden to take usury from their brethren, i.e., from other Jews. By this we are given to understand that to take usury from another man is simply evil, because we ought to treat every man as our neighbor and brother."[31]

Northern European political events and new religious doctrines at the beginning of modern times, after the Lutheran reform and then that of Calvin, supported different ethics of economy and work (Berman 2003; Weber 1905). As individualistic religious doctrines and social philosophies developed in central and northern Europe, everybody became *other*.[32]

The Western Deviation

At the inception of the modern era, national states were emerging in Europe, consolidating their power and projecting it overseas, where new worlds had been discovered to be explored and exploited. Scientific and technological advances were reached; the economy started growing at an unprecedented pace; and new economic models were implemented, including large-scale finance. Liberal economic thought developed on the basis of Locke's philosophy[33] and grew as a consequence of political revolutionary events in England, France, and the United States in the seventeenth and eighteenth centuries.

In the new, modern world, buying capital in the market for a price became acceptable, along with the idea that capital was a commodity—different from the Aristotelian idea of money as just a measuring unit for the value of "real" things.

As centuries- or millennia-old archetypes and prohibitions were challenged by the forces of modern economy, the law followed suit. The distinction between legitimate *interest* and illegal *usury* was legally formalized in 1545, as England's King Henry VIII passed an "Act Against Usurie" (repealed in 1551 and reenacted in 1571), permitting loans with interest up to 10 percent, while a heated debate preceded and followed the enactment.[34]

---

29 Quoted from a recent *fatwa* of the European Council for Fatwa and Research—a private foundation presided over by the influential Islamic scholar Yusuf al-Quaradawi—aiming at disseminating traditional Sunni Islamic values in the West (http://www.e-cfr.org; as of January 20, 2014, the English version of this website seems to be no longer available). The *fatwa* on "Permissibility of conventional mortgage under necessity," dated January 16, 2014, is available at http://www.globalwebpost.com/farooqm/study_res/i_econ_fin/ecfr-fatwa_mortgage.htm [accessed: February 10, 2014].

30 In the same period, St. Jerome, in contrast with Ambrose, was an early theorist of the universal reach of the prohibition (see *Hieronymi stridonienses epistolae selectae*, letter 58).

31 St. Thomas Aquinas, *Summa Theologica*, question 78, article 1, *ad secundum*.

32 This change of approach over the centuries and its rationalization as a paradigm shift, from "tribal brotherhood" to "universal brotherhood" to "universal otherhood," so to speak, has been brilliantly described by Nelson (1949).

33 Locke (1690) is probably the cornerstone of Western liberal philosophy.

34 For details, see Hawkes (2010).

In the following centuries, modern European nation-states centralized and monopolized the issuing of money and made money more abstract: first, by introducing *notes*, paper money that circulated and represented a value rather than having a value, as had gold or silver coins or bullion; then, further favoring the abstraction of money by authorizing banks and financial institutions to multiply it by mere arithmetic—permitting them to keep only fractional backing for deposits held, thereby multiplying the amounts of circulating wealth. Money in the form of these abstract numbers was no longer a yardstick to measure the value of other things; it represented credits and debts that themselves became commodities. As this commodity was exchanged and lent for a price, according to the law of supply and demand in financial markets, it produced even more of those abstract numbers (Macleod 1894).[35]

A significant and increasing share of the real economy thus came to be operationally related to the financial industry, bound to pay for its services, and eventually, in fact, enslaved to it—as is demonstrated by the world economic crisis that originated in 2007 from the explosion of purely financial speculative bubbles. Since the beginning of the modern era, Western economic and legal thought has deviated from an original vision that had been in line with the prior Euro-Mediterranean tradition of aversion to usury, common to both European and Islamic cultures and legal traditions, toward a more individualistic and debt-based vision of the economy.

Other Western Voices

Modern and contemporary history saw the expansion of Western political and economic power worldwide, notably that of the United Kingdom and then of the United States. Their global success was synergetic with the expansive enforcement of liberalist economic policies, of a more or less unrestricted financial economy based on the credit-debt concept of money, and of the supporting concept of the rule of law promoted within the frame of the common law legal tradition.[36]

In several Western countries, contemporary legislation sanctions usury, establishing caps to interest rates and sanctioning them with invalidity and in some cases imposing criminal sanctions.[37] These civil and criminal legal regimes, however, seldom interfere with current practices of banks and financial institutions, which are subject to very little policy and regulatory supervision with respect to the issue of how much they can charge for their services, probably as a result of both liberal ideas on the sanctity of the "invisible hand" and the actual capacity of the banking industry to significantly affect regulators' decisions through a number of official and unofficial channels.[38]

However, more traditional visions of the economy have survived (if in the minority) the waves of new economic ideas sweeping modern and contemporary Western societies. They supported an economic vision more related to the values of the "real" economy, contrasting to some extent with the idea of liberal interest charging and the features of contemporary, mostly financial Western economy. Adam Smith (1776: book 2, chapter 4) himself has advocated the imposition of a legal ceiling on the charging of interest in financial transactions, which he explained would help prevent financial resources from being apprehended by prodigals and hazardous speculators rather than by those willing to invest more solidly in socially beneficial investments.

---

35 See also Graeber (2011) and Mitchell-Innes (1913, 1914). Both of Mitchell-Innes's articles are reprinted in Wray (2004).

36 See Mattei and Nader (2008), who analyze how the synergetic effect of Western financial economy and common law concepts of rule of law eventually led to the economic failure of many developing countries, mostly to the advantage of Western financial circles and institutions.

37 In the Italian Civil Code, article 1815, the sanction for usurious interest rates is the voiding of the relevant agreement, with the consequence that only the principal will be repaid. The applicable interest rate is fixed periodically by the government according to statutory provisions (Law 108 of 1996 and Law 24 of 2001). The Italian law, moreover, sanctions usurious transactions with criminal sanctions in article 644 of the Penal Code.

38 In Italy, for instance, it was considered a very unusual and significant event when the Corte di Cassazione ruled (in sentence 2593 of February 20, 2003) against the practice of applying regularly and frequently compounded interest—previously normally charged by Italian banks despite a specific prohibition in article 1283 of the Civil Code—on loans being repaid with delay and on negative balances in current accounts.

This explanation was criticized in 1787 as being inconclusive by Bentham (1818), who advocated a laissez-faire approach toward the charging of interest in the financial markets.[39] Smith's arguments against usury may perhaps not seem to be the best available; however—or precisely because of that weakness—they reveal the existence of a deep, hidden, nonverbalized cultural norm, or cryptotype (Sacco 1991: 384–85), against usury.

Even in the twentieth century some nonmainstream voices advocated the abandoning of the credit- and debt-based idea of money in favor of an equity-based one, the return to the gold standard and to the yardstick function of money, and the restriction or elimination altogether of the practice of fractional reserve for bank deposits. Among these thinkers were economists such as Milton Friedman (1960), the anarch-libertarian Murray Rothbard (2004), and the economists of the Austrian school.[40]

Beyond the economists, voices such as that of *maudit* poet Ezra Pound (1937) strongly supported the same vision of usury and financial economy.[41] Recent global financial events certainly contributed to an increased aversion of the Western general public toward the purely financial economy, reflected in corresponding stances of politicians[42] and in some cases government action against speculative transactions.[43]

Global Islamic Finance and Its Hybridity

An initial wave of Islamic finance swept Muslim countries in the second half of the twentieth century, when mostly state-sponsored Islamic financial institutions and Islamic legal mechanisms have been at work on a commercial scale in some national markets to conjugate economic development with adherence to Islamic principles.

It is generally acknowledged that the phenomenon has not been very successful for a number of reasons, including the limited, local reach of the institutions involved (Saw and Wang 2008: 1–8); the legal insecurity related to the multitude of Shari'a schools and scholarly approaches (Venardos 2005: 93, 110–11); the aggregate instability of the industry, caused by the volatility of early Islamic banking accounting and supervisory-regulatory standards (Venardos 2005: 101–17); and the higher costs of Islamic financial services when compared to the instruments of Western finance, resulting in a lack of competitiveness in a not entirely Islamicized environment because of the higher complexity and costs of formalities and transfers of equity (including taxation) necessary to assemble equity-based financial transactions compared to the more straightforward Western substance of agreements simply featuring loans in exchange for payment of interest (El-Gamal 2006: 74–80; Venardos 2005: 99–100).

Toward the end of the twentieth century and at the beginning of the twenty-first, a second wave of Shari'a-compliant financial instruments became an important and growing part of global finance. This wave was probably the result of a changed world political-economic situation and a stronger perception of the Islamic identity in many Muslim regions, as well as the very aggressive stances adopted by some financial markets in Muslim countries to develop a global Islamic financial industry and to promote their products, most notably in

39 Later, Mill (1891) also opposed usury laws, which he considered to be government interference with market forces "grounded on erroneous theories," as per the title of chapter 10 of book 5 of his work.

40 A complete synthesis of the positions of the Austrian school is probably best represented by the works of Ludwig von Mises, of whom Rothbard had been a pupil; see, especially, von Mises (1949).

41 See, in particular, cantos 45 (titled "Against Usury,") canto 46, and canto 51 (which contains a reference to Dante) in Pound (1937).

42 Alan Greenspan (2000), former chairman of the US Federal Reserve, stated that "[the founders of] the Austrian School have reached far into the future from when most of them practiced and have had a profound and, in my judgment, probably an irreversible effect on how most mainstream economists think in this country." Other critical voices against the current mainstream economic and financial thought favoring a debt-based conception of money and fractional reserve banking can be found in a wiki page of the Ludwig von Mises Institute at http://wiki.mises.org/wiki/Criticism_of_fractional_reserve_banking [accessed: February 11, 2014].

43 For example, at the height of the world financial crisis, the governments of Belgium, Italy, and Spain repeatedly issued temporary orders suspending short-selling transactions in their respective national stock exchanges in 2011 and 2012.

the Gulf Cooperation Council countries (El-Gamal 2006; Saw and Wang 2008: 1–8) and in the Far East (see, for example, Saw and Wang 2008: 65–78; Venardos 2005: 144–60).

This trend produced an increased sophistication of Islamic financial products, which were more and more inclined toward mimicking Western products in their economic functionality (including bond issues, short-selling transactions, and even hedge funds), through complex financial algorithms featuring combinations of basic financial tools of the Islamic tradition such as the *mudarabah*, the *suquq*, *salam* transactions, *takaful*, *'ina*, and others (of which the current more complex schemes often keep the names to emphasize their being Shari'a based and Shari'a compliant).[44]

Clearly, a large issue exists here—on which I do not take any position—of assessing whether or not the global Islamic industry is actually enforcing substantial Islamic principles of economic cooperation, development, and social justice.

Several quarters in the Islamic world—though probably not in the mainstream—do criticize the current use in global Islamic finance of combinations of traditional names and legal mechanisms to vest conventional, substantially prohibited financial transactions with acceptable Islamic forms. They advocate a change of mentality that could allow an expansion of Islamic financial activities, consistent with the true spirit of Islam, in more socially useful areas (El-Gamal 2006: 190–91; Venardos 2005: 210–20), such as social lending or microcredit.[45]

Concluding Remarks: Two Stories That May Come Full Circle

First, to put the issue of usury as an "East versus West" issue is misleading. The historical and ideological divide is not a simple, vertical, geohistorical one between East and West. It is first and foremost a horizontal one between the two related but different visions of the "real" economy and financial economy. Historically, these two visions are present in both the East and the West, if in very different proportions, times of appearance, and orders of prevalence. The "financialist" vision originated in what I have labeled a Western deviation from an ancient and common Euro-Mediterranean conception of life and the economy.

Second, the different attitudes in Eastern and Western legal traditions, with their historical differences and divergences, may allow areas of possible convergence. Global finance has produced some economic and legal hybridity already, as the Islamic world demonstrated its capacity to absorb and operate global financial tools through Shari'a-compliant legal techniques—including some speculative operations such as *salam* transactions (short selling), which in some cases recently have been restricted by the governments of some Western countries to limit the negative effects of financial speculation.

A related qualitative and quantitative analysis could be carried out on the different apportionment of the two cultural, legal, and economic models present in the different mixtures identified. However, certainly the divergent developments of the past centuries have come full circle to some extent, producing a reencounter of East and West in the area of present-day global Islamic finance.

The resulting economic and legal environment may certainly be labeled as a hybrid, because substantial economic principles of the Western tradition have been mixed with formal schemes originating in the Islamic tradition. Global Islamic finance, which can be considered a very specific environment within the larger dominion of present-day *lex mercatoria*, can be a very fruitful field of investigation for comparative legal

44 See El-Gamal (2006), especially at 190–91. According to El-Gamal, the higher costs of Islamic schemes compared to the Western instruments that the Islamic schemes tend to imitate have progressively decreased because of the larger scale of transactions and the sophistication of the industry. The extant cost spread is often considered an acceptable price for the instruments' Shari'a compliance.

45 Muhammad Yunus, Nobel laureate in 2006 for his social credit activities in Bangladesh and worldwide, was initially opposed by the conservative Islamic establishment in his country, who considered his Grameen Bank microlending activities to be *haram* (Yunus 1999).

research—especially focused in recent years on the dynamics of legal pluralism,[46] legal transplants,[47] legal mixity,[48] and hybridity[49]—being located at a crux where different legal and economic ideas and religious, political, and societal values meet and interact.

Third, the legal discourse on social justice in the economy is suffering a bit more, comparatively, in current Western economy, law, and practice. This is because of the historical prevalence of a liberal, individualistic approach to life and the economy—and to a "commodity" concept of money and fractional backing for banking deposits—whereas in the Islamic world, religious and political factors have kept ultraliberal, ultraindividualist visions at a distance from the main economic and legal arena.

The social and economic vision behind the Islamic precepts and the corresponding vision also present in (a part of) the Western legal tradition still have to come full circle. To some extent, it still has to be acknowledged that they actually may. This lack of recognition may also be caused by a stereotyped narrative, popular in the West and objectively functional to an expansive strategy of the financial economy—purported as *the* Western model—depicting the aversion to interest as an idea belonging only to the Islamic tradition and distant from the Western one.

The lack of awareness about the historic similarities and possible convergence of the two traditions de facto produces a weakness for the principles of social justice in the economy, vis-à-vis the expansive strength of the ideology behind current global finance. The latter may be suffering a bit now because of the current world financial crisis, but it certainly did manage to produce hybrid legal and financial tools palatable to both worlds, thus introducing or consolidating features of Western financial economy in several Islamic jurisdictions. Time will tell whether this consolidation will amount to a cultural and economic invasion, to a controlled borrowing and absorption, or to a balanced mix of some sort.

Fourth, common principles based on the described ancient Euro-Mediterranean archetype and fundamental vision of life and the economy are at the basis both of Islamic and of Western (most notably Roman and civil) laws. These two streams of thought have existed parallel to each other—certainly with different fortunes in the East and the West—without interacting much so far. Beyond historic differences and divergences, a possibility still exists for this second story to come full circle, too.

Islamic law is scholarly based, like Roman and civil law, with which it shares a number of fundamental principles in the law of transactions (most notably, *favor debitoris*, good faith, and *synallagma*). Its developments, instead, are based on *qiyas*, a process resembling the common law process of analogy and distinguishing to develop the law. Dialogue and debate between Western and Islamic legal scholars and economists is possible—and crucial.

Researching and developing knowledge on the fundamental communality of principles may facilitate this other convergence, perhaps making this second story come full circle too, thus producing increased dialogue and legal tools that will lead to a more just and humane economic development in both worlds.

References

Asín Palacios, M. 1919. *La Escatología Musulmana en la Divinia Comedia*. Madrid: Estanislao Maestre.

Banterle, G. (ed.). 1988. *S. Ambrogio, Discorsi e Lettere*. Milan: Biblioteca Ambrosiana.

Bentham, J. 1818. Letter XIII to Dr. Smith, on projects in arts, &c., in *Defence of Usury*, 4th ed. London: Payne and Foss.

46 On legal pluralism, see, for example, Chiba (1989); Griffiths (1986); Guadagni (1998); Merry (1988); Moore (1973); and Tamanaha (2008).

47 On legal transplants, see Watson (1974). Graziadei (2007) emphasized how the very core of comparative law is in the study of legal transplants. Also see Graziadei (2009). Volume 10 of *Theoretical Inquiries in Law*, in which this article is published, consists of 15 articles, all related to legal transplants.

48 On legal mixity, see Örücü (2008) and Palmer (2012).

49 On hybridity, see Castellucci (2008); Chiba (1989: 270–71); and Donlan in Chapter 2 of this book. The term *hybrid* had already been used by Zweigert and Kötz (1984) to indicate both civil law-common law mixes and Western and non-Western ones. The idea of hybridity is known to other social sciences as well. See, for example, Burke (2009); Clements et al. (2007: 50); and Stross (1999).

Berman, H.J. 2003. *Law and Revolution II: The Impact of the Protestant Reformations on the Western Legal Tradition*. Cambridge, MA: Harvard University Press.
Blackstone, W. 1915. *Commentaries on the Laws of England*. Vol. 1. San Francisco, CA: Bancroft-Whitney.
Burke, P. 2009. *Cultural Hybridity*. Cambridge, UK: Polity Press.
Castellucci, I. 2008. How mixed must a mixed system be? *Electronic Journal of Comparative Law* [Online], 12(1), 1–18. Available at: http://www.ejcl.org/121/art121-4.pdf [accessed: February 11, 2014].
Cerulli, E. 1949. *Il "Libro della Scala" e la Questione delle Fonti Arabo-Spagnole della Divina Commedia*. Vatican City: Biblioteca Apostolica Vaticana.
Cerulli, E. 1971. *Nuove Ricerche sul "Libro della Scala" e l'Islam nell'Occidente Medievale*. Vatican City: Biblioteca Apostolica Vaticana.
Chiba, M. 1989. *Legal Pluralism: Toward a General Theory through Japanese Legal Culture*. Tokyo: Tokai University Press.
Chiba, M. 1998. Conclusion, in *Une Introduction aux Cultures Juridiques Non Occidentales: Autour de Masaji Chiba*, edited by W. Capeller and T. Kitamura. Brussels: Bruylant, 233–72.
Çizakça, M. 1996. *A Comparative Evolution of Business Partnerships: The Islamic World and Europe, with Specific Reference to the Ottoman Archives*. Leiden, Netherlands: Brill.
Clements, K.P., Boerge, V., Brown, A., Foley, W., and Nolan, A. 2007. State building reconsidered: The role of hybridity in the formation of political order. *Political Science*, 59(1), 45–56.
Cremona, D. 2001. *Il Divieto Canonico di Usura: Alle Origini del "Moderno."* Padua, Italy: CEDAM.
Doi, A.R.I. 1984. *Shari'ah: The Islamic Law*. London: Ta-Ha.
El-Ashker, A., and Wilson, R. 2006. *Islamic Economy: A Short History*. Leiden, Netherlands: Brill.
El-Gamal, M.A. 2006. *Islamic Finance: Law, Economics, and Practice*. Cambridge, UK, and New York: Cambridge University Press.
Friedman, M. 1960. *A Program for Monetary Stability*. New York: Fordham University Press.
Glenn, P.H. 2004. *Legal Traditions of the World*. 2nd ed. New York: Oxford University Press.
Graeber, D. 2011. *Debt: The First 5000 Years*. New York: Melville House.
Graziadei, M. 2007. Comparative law as the study of transplants and receptions, in *The Oxford Handbook of Comparative Law*, edited by M. Reimann and R. Zimmermann. New York: Oxford University Press, 441–76.
Graziadei, M. 2009. Legal transplants and the frontiers of legal knowledge. *Theoretical Inquiries in Law*, 10(2), 693–713.
Greenspan, A. 2000. Statement of Alan Greenspan, Chairman, Board of Governors of the Federal Reserve System before the Committee on Banking and Financial Services, U.S. House of Representatives, July 25. Available at: http://democrats.financialservices.house.gov/banking/72500grn.shtml [accessed: February 11, 2014].
Griffiths, J. 1986. What is legal pluralism? *Journal of Legal Pluralism*, 24, 1–55.
Guadagni, M. 1998. Legal pluralism, in *The New Palgrave Dictionary of Economics and the Law*, edited by P. Newman. London: Palgrave Macmillan, 542.
Guénon, R. 1925. *L'Ésotérisme de Dante*. Paris: Gallimard.
Guénon, R. 2004. *The Esoterism of Dante*, in *Collected Works of René Guénon*, edited by S.D. Fohr. Hillsdale, NY: Sophia Perennis.
Hawkes, D. 2010. *The Culture of Usury in Renaissance England*. New York: Palgrave Macmillan.
Jha, G. 1930. *Hindu Law in Its Sources*. Allahabad, India: Indian Press.
Locke, J. 1690. *Two Treatises of Government*. London: Black Swan.
Macleod, H.D. 1894. *The Theory of Credit*. London: Longmans, Green & Co.
Mattei, U., and Nader, L. 2008. *Plunder: When the Rule of Law Is Illegal*. Malden, MA: Blackwell.
Merry, S.E. 1988. Legal pluralism. *Law and Society Review*, 22(5), 869–96.
Mill, J.S. 1891. *Principles of Political Economy*. London: Longmans, Green & Co.
Mitchell-Innes, A. 1913. What is money? *Banking Law Journal*, 30(5), 377–408.
Mitchell-Innes, A. 1914. The credit theory of money. *Banking Law Journal*, 31(1), 151–68.
Moehlman, C.H. 1934. The Christianization of interest. *Church History*, 3(1), 3–15.

Moore, S.F. 1973. Law and social change: The semi-autonomous social field as an appropriate subject of study. *Law and Society Review*, 7(4), 719–46.

Nelson, B.N. 1949. *The Idea of Usury: From Tribal Brotherhood to Universal Otherhood*. Princeton, NJ: Princeton University Press.

Noonan, J.T. Jr. 1993. Development in moral doctrine. *Theological Studies*, 54(4), 662–77.

Örücü, E. 2008. What is a mixed legal system: Exclusion or expansion? *Electronic Journal of Comparative Law* [Online], 12(1), 1–18. Available at: http://www.ejcl.org/121/art121-15.pdf [accessed: February 11, 2014].

Palmer, V.V. 2012. *Mixed Jurisdictions Worldwide: The Third Family*. 2nd ed. Cambridge, UK: Cambridge University Press.

Pound, E. 1937. *The Fifth Decad of the Cantos XLII–LI*. London: Faber & Faber

Rothbard, M.N. 2004. *Man, Economy, and State with Power and Market*. Auburn, AL: Ludwig von Mises Institute.

Sacco, R. 1991. Legal formants: A dynamic approach to comparative law (installment 2 of 2). *American Journal of Comparative Law*, 39(2), 343–401.

Saw, S.-H., and Wang, K. 2008. *Introduction to Islamic Finance*. Singapore: Saw Centre for Financial Studies.

Smith, A. 1776. *An Inquiry into the Nature and Causes of the Wealth of Nations*. London: Strahan and Cadell.

Stross, B. 1999. The hybrid metaphor: From biology to culture. *Journal of American Folklore*, 112(445), 254–67.

Talamanca, M. 1999. "Una verborum obligation" e "obligatio re et verbis contracta." *Iura*, 50, 7–112.

Tamanaha, B.Z. 2008. Understanding legal pluralism: Past to present, local to global. *Sydney Law Review*, 30(3), 375–411.

Taqi Usmani, M. 2002. *An Introduction to Islamic Finance*. The Hague: Kluwer.

United Nations General Assembly. 2013. Macroeconomic policy questions: External debt sustainability and development. Report of the Second Committee, Sixty-Eighth Session, December 13, 2013. Available at: http://www.un.org/ga/search/view_doc.asp?symbol=A/68/436 [accessed: February 10, 2014].

Venardos, A.M. 2005. *Islamic Banking and Finance in South-East Asia: Its Development and Future*. Singapore: World Scientific.

Visser, W.A.M., and McIntosh, A. 1998. A short review of the historical critique of usury. *Accounting, Business and Financial History*, 8(2), 175–90.

von Mises, L. 1949. *Human Action: A Treatise on Economics*. New Haven, CT: Yale University Press.

Watson, A. 1974. *Legal Transplants: An Approach to Comparative Law*. Edinburgh: Scottish Academic Press.

Weber, M. 1905. *Die protestantische Ethik und der "Geist" des Kapitalismus*. Tübingen, Germany: Mohr.

Wray, L.R. (ed.). 2004. *Credit and State Theories of Money: The Contributions of A. Mitchell Innes*. Cheltenham, UK: Edward Elgar.

Wünderli, P. 1965. *Études sur "Le Livre de l'Eschiele Mahomet.*" Winterthur, Switzerland: P.G. Keller.

Yunus, M. 1999. *Banker to the Poor: Micro-lending and the Battle against Poverty*. New York: Public Affairs.

Zweigert, K., and Kötz, H. 1984. *Einführung in die Rechtsvergleichung*. 2nd ed. Tübingen, Germany: Mohr.

Chapter 20
Settling Islamic Finance Disputes: The Case of Malaysia and Saudi Arabia

Mohd Zakhiri Md Nor

The Islamic banking and finance industry gained popularity during the late 1970s in Middle East countries. Following the public acceptance and robust development of the industry, several other players appeared, including Hong Kong, Malaysia, Pakistan, and Sudan. The industry developed quickly, attracting investors who were Muslim and non-Muslim, local and foreign, but disputes and misunderstandings were inevitable. The disputing parties had the option to resort to court litigation or out-of-court settlement.

Drawn from ongoing research, this chapter seeks to analyze the judicial system in two jurisdictions—Malaysia and Saudi Arabia—within the context of Islamic banking and finance disputes. The first section describes the background and constitutional frameworks of both countries, and the second section looks at the judicial structure entailing the hearing and settlement of Islamic finance disputes. The third part examines the independence of the courts, and the fourth part elaborates on selected cases of Islamic finance disputes. The chapter concludes by describing the similarities and differences of judicial systems in the two countries and by suggesting new directions for research in the area.

Background and the Constitutional Frameworks

Located in Southeast Asia, Malaysia had a population of 28.3 million in 2010, 60 percent of whom were Muslim (Jabatan Perangkaan Malaysia 2011). It currently stands out as a developing nation with robust development and growth of international Islamic banking and financial markets. A number of studies have suggested that the growth rate of Islamic finance in Malaysia is impressive by any standards. Hence, Malaysia has the capacity to retain its leadership in global Islamic finance despite the emergence of competition from centers such as Hong Kong and Dubai (Yong 2007). Malaysia has a large number of diverse players and institutions in the Islamic financial system, which includes retail and commercial Islamic banking and finance, general and life *takaful* (the Islamic insurance concept), and Islamic capital markets. A growing range of products and services are being offered, as Malaysia's banking and finance industry becomes competitive in product structure and pricing (Razak and Karim 2008). All these developments have increased the attractiveness of the Islamic financial instruments as an asset class for investments, drawing both Malaysian and foreign investors.

The federal constitution of Malaysia was adopted on August 31, 1957, the day Malaysia gained its independence from the British colonials. Article 3(1) of the constitution declares Islam as the official religion of the federation and guarantees religious freedom. The ninth schedule outlines the legislative lists, specifying federal, state, and common jurisdictional lists. Specifically for the Islamic finance industry, the government of Malaysia passed written legislation to accommodate the finance system's growth in the country. For the banking and financial market, the relevant laws are the Central Bank of Malaysia Act 2009, the Islamic Banking Act 1983, and the Banking and Financial Institutions Act 1989.

The principal regulator of the Malaysian Islamic financial system, the Central Bank of Malaysia, has introduced a comprehensive legal framework for Islamic financial institutions. The Central Bank undertook several initiatives, including a 10-year master plan, an interbank Islamic money market, coverage by the Malaysian Deposit Insurance Corporation, a friendly tax regime, and incentives under the Malaysia International Financial Centre. These initiatives were designed to further enhance and develop the Islamic financial institutions in Malaysia and to allow the country to become an international hub for Islamic banking and insurance. The *takaful* market is also regulated by the Central Bank of Malaysia, and the primary legislation governing the market is the Takaful Act 1984.

The Kingdom of Saudi Arabia is the Middle East's largest state by land area, constituting the bulk of the Arabian Peninsula, and is the second-largest state in the Arab world after Algeria. As of July 2013, Saudi Arabia had an estimated population of 26.9 million, of which 5.6 million were noncitizens. The country encompasses approximately 2.15 million square kilometers (830,000 square miles).[1] Saudi Arabia is an absolute monarchy, although according to the Basic Law of Saudi Arabia, which was adopted by royal decree in 1992, the king must comply with the Shari'a and the Holy Qur'an. The Qur'an and the Sunnah are declared to be the country's constitution; no modern constitution has ever been written for Saudi Arabia (Cavendish 2007: 78).

The legal framework organizing the financial sector of Saudi Arabia could be classified into three groups of laws. The first group comprises the legal fundamentals for the political, social, and economic aspects of the nation; the monetary policies; the original laws of the Arab region; the money and currency control laws; and various commercial laws (Sabri 2009). The second group of laws concerns the organizing activities of financial institutions and includes commercial, specialized, and Islamic bank laws; central banks laws; insurance laws; insurance control laws; leasing financing laws; and social securities agencies and public provident fund laws. The third group of laws comprises the financial markets and includes corporate share laws, securities laws and trading regulations, government securities commission laws, stock exchange laws and bylaws, disclosure and reporting requirements, broker and membership requirements, insider trading laws, and regulations on price limits and margins.

Notably, Saudi Arabia has no formal codified constitution. In March 1992, King Fahd bin Adulaziz al Saud issued the governing law, or Basic Law, which articulates the government's rights and responsibilities. It includes provisions declaring Islam as the official state religion and the Qur'an and Sunnah as the state constitution. The Basic Law provides that the state must protect the rights of the people in line with Shari'a, acknowledges the independence of the judiciary, and bases the administration of justice on the Shari'a rules according to the teachings of the Qur'an, the Sunnah, and the regulations set by the ruler, provided that they do not contradict the provisions of the Qur'an and the Sunnah. On the same notion, article 9 of the Basic Law states that "the family is the kernel of the Saudi society, and its members shall be brought up on the basis of the Islamic faith." Furthermore, article 26 generally provides that the state protects human rights "in accordance with the Islamic Shari'a."

The Dispute Resolution Structure

The dispute resolution system in Malaysia has two parts: the court litigation system and the alternative processes. The court system also has two parts: the Shari'a and the civil judicial systems. Under the Shari'a judicial system, even though Shari'a law provides regulations in all aspects, Shari'a law as it applies in Malaysia is confined to personal matters. The Shari'a courts' jurisdiction covers only matters involving Muslims and deals only with specific personal civil matters. For instance, such matters may include matrimonial matters, matters concerning the administration of Islamic law in the state, land, *waqf* (donation of land, buildings, or money for religious or charitable purposes), *zakat* (a charitable tax payable by Muslims), and *hibah* (a form of voluntary interest payment), and state holidays.[2] In criminal cases, the court can pass sentences of no more than three years' imprisonment, fines of up to RM 5,000, and punishments of up to six strokes of the cane.[3]

The administration of the Shari'a courts falls within the ambit of each state's jurisdiction. Hence, there could be some differences in the civil and criminal jurisdictions of the courts from one state to another. Primarily, Shari'a courts are classified into three levels: the Shari'a Subordinate Court, which is the court of

---

1 Statistics are from the US Central Intelligence Agency's online *World FactBook*, available at: https://www.cia.gov/library/publications/the-world-factbook/geos/sa.html [accessed: December 16, 2013].

2 Federal constitution of Malaysia, ninth schedule, list 2.

3 The Shari'a Criminal Procedure (Federal Territories) Act.

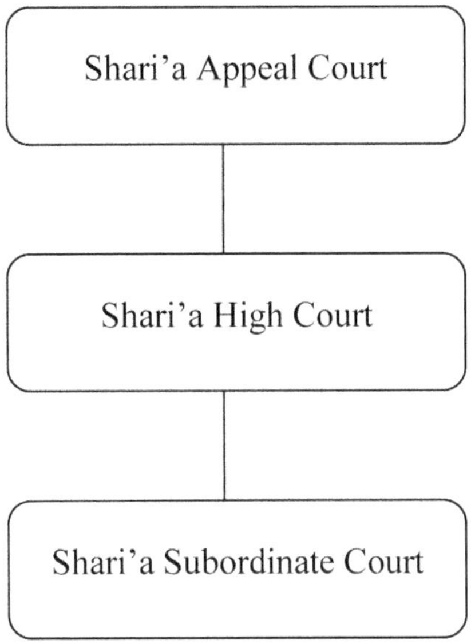

Fig. 20.1 Structure of the Malaysian Shari'a courts

first instance, followed by the Shari'a High Court and the Shari'a Appeal Court. The latter court is the highest authority in Malaysia's Shari'a judicial system in Malaysia (Figure 20.1).

In contrast, the Malaysian civil court system has two levels. The superior level comprises the Federal Court[4] and the Special Court division,[5] the Court of Appeal,[6] and two High Courts of coordinate jurisdiction,[7] one in Malaya and one in Sabah and Sarawak. The second level is the subordinate court, consisting of the Sessions Court,[8] the Magistrates Court,[9] and the Court for Children (Figure 20.2).

According to the Malaysian laws, the proper forum to hear and decide on banking and finance matters, both conventional and Islamic, is the civil courts.[10] Essentially, the first court to hear such matters is the High Court. For the Islamic commercial division of the High Court of Kuala Lumpur in Jalan Duta alone, more than 3,500 Islamic finance cases had been registered for determination by the court from 1983 through January 2010.[11]

Notably, the rule of law is an important concept in any dispute brought before a judge. Within the context of Shari'a, the rule of law is embodied in the source of Shari'a itself. Therefore, the judge must base decisions on the rule of law and not on the rule of authorities. In other words, the judge must follow the guidance prescribed by the Shari'a and must not deviate from it. Nevertheless, judges are bound to uphold the federal constitution of Malaysia as the supreme law of the land, as expressly provided by article 4 of the constitution: "This Constitution is the supreme law of the Federation … ." Thus, judges are under the obligation to uphold the rule of law, but this source of the law is the federal constitution and the written rules, as opposed to the Shari'a.

4 Federal constitution of Malaysia, article 122(1).
5 Ibid., article 182.
6 Ibid., article 121(1B).
7 Ibid., article 121(1).
8 Subordinate Courts Act 1948, section 59.
9 Ibid., section 78.
10 Federal constitution of Malaysia, ninth schedule, list 1.
11 This figure is based on research done by the International Shari'a Research Academy for Islamic Finance in January 2010.

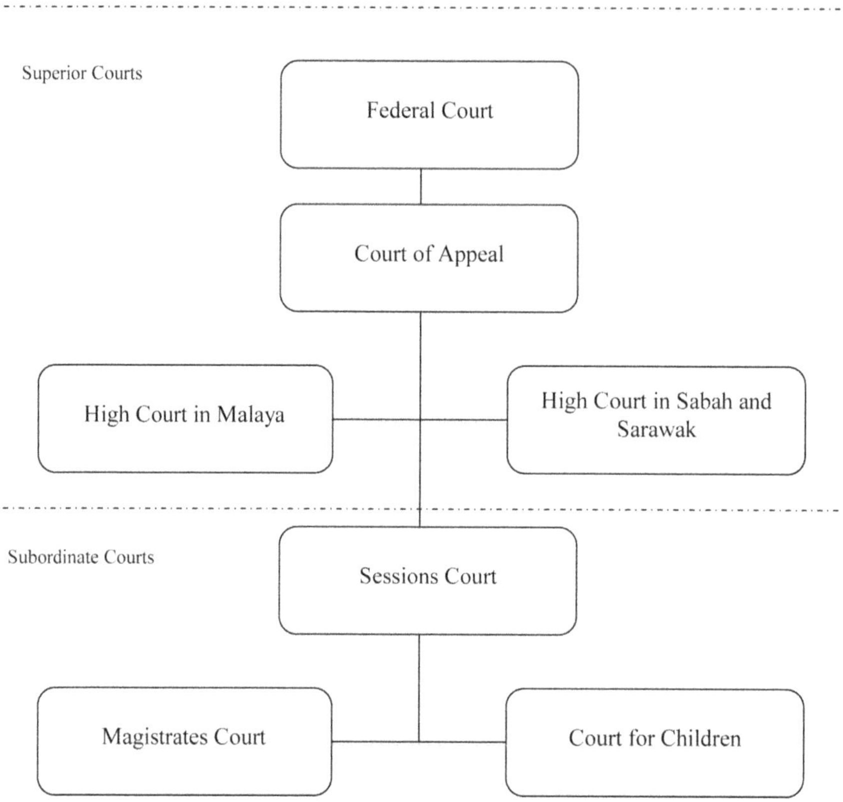

Fig. 20.2 Structure of the Malaysian civil courts

Apart from the obligation of judges to the rule of law, the Malaysian community is receptive to the idea of alternative dispute resolution mechanisms that range from negotiation and conciliation to mediation and arbitration. With respect to mediation, the Central Bank of Malaysia formed the Financial Mediation Bureau (FMB) to resolve complaints by and against financial institutions.

Negotiation is a consensual bargaining process in which the parties attempt to reach an agreement on a dispute or a potentially disputed matter. The essence of negotiating here is to achieve an advantage that is not possible by unilateral action. Meanwhile, in mediation a neutral person—the mediator—examines the claims of the parties and assists them in reaching a negotiated settlement for the dispute.

Mediation is used either before a dispute gets to court or any time the matter remains pending in court before judgment is delivered. In Malaysia, section 14 of the Legal Aid (Amendment) Act 2003 provides exclusively for mediation. The FMB, launched January 20, 2005, under the purview of the Central Bank of Malaysia, handles mediation for Malaysia's banking and finance industry. The FMB covers disputes against commercial banks, Islamic banks, takaful operators, and development financial institutions, as well as selected payment system operators and nonbank issuers of credit and charge cards.

Arbitration is also an option that the parties may use to resolve their dispute. They must submit the dispute for consideration at the Regional Center for Arbitration in Kuala Lumpur or at other arbitration centers elsewhere in the world. This method settles commercial disputes through a binding decision. The Malaysia Arbitration Act 2005 relates to the conduct of arbitrations. It substantially follows the English Arbitration Act 1950, which covers (a) matters of arbitration; (b) arbitrators and umpires; (c) conduct of proceedings and witnesses; (d) provision for awards, costs, fees and interest, special cases, remission, and setting-aside awards; (e) enforcement of awards; and (f) additional provisions related to arbitration. The Kuala Lumpur Regional Centre for Arbitration (KLRCA) issued the 2007 KLRCA Rules for Islamic Banking and Financial Services Arbitration specifically for adoption into Islamic finance matters. Independent of the Malaysian

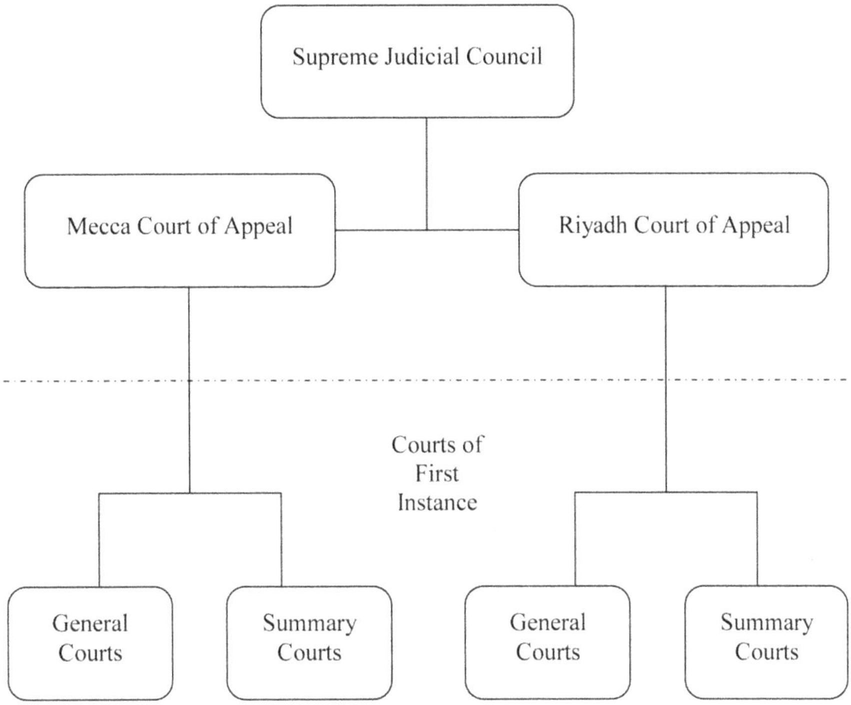

Fig. 20.3 Current structure of the Saudi Arabian courts

government, the KLRCA administers arbitration under the auspices of the Asian-African Legal Consultative Organization, which comprises 48 member states. The KLRCA regulations of 1996 provide for the privileges and immunities of certain organizations, including the KLRCA.

Saudi Arabia has three judicial bodies: (a) the Ministry of Justice, with courts of first instance, courts of appeal, and the high courts; (b) the independent judicial authorities known as the Boards of Grievances, or Diwan al-Mazalim; and (c) the semijudicial committees that work under the supervision of a ministry, such as the Committee for the Settlement of Banking Disputes of Saudi Authority Monetary Agency (SAMA) and the Committee for the Settlement of Customs Disputes, which belong to the Ministry of Finance (Baamir 2010).

The first judicial body in the Shari'a court system constitutes the basic judiciary of Saudi Arabia, and its judges and lawyers form part of the *ulama,* the country's religious leadership. However, there are also extra-Shari'a government tribunals that handle disputes related to specific royal decrees (Esposito 1998: 110–12). The final appeal from both Shari'a courts and government tribunals is to the king; all courts and tribunals follow the Shari'a rules of evidence and procedure (Campbell 2007: 268–69). The Saudi system of justice has been criticized for being slow, arcane (*Economist* 2009), lacking in some of the safeguards of justice, and unable to deal with the modern world (Saleh 2007). The capabilities and reactionary nature of the judges have been criticized, and in 2009, the king made a number of significant changes to the judiciary's personnel at the most senior level by bringing in a younger generation (*Economist* 2001; 2009).

The current Saudi court system comprises the Supreme Judicial Council, the Courts of Appeal, and first-instance courts such as general courts and summary courts.[12] Figure 20.3 shows the current court structure of Saudi Arabia.

The Supreme Judicial Council is the highest authority of the judicial system.[13] It carries out numerous administrative, legislative, consultative, and judicial functions. It holds both civil and criminal jurisdictions and primarily reviews judgments involving death sentences and certain major crimes. The council also

12 Law of the Judiciary 1975.
13 Law of the Judiciary1975, article 30.

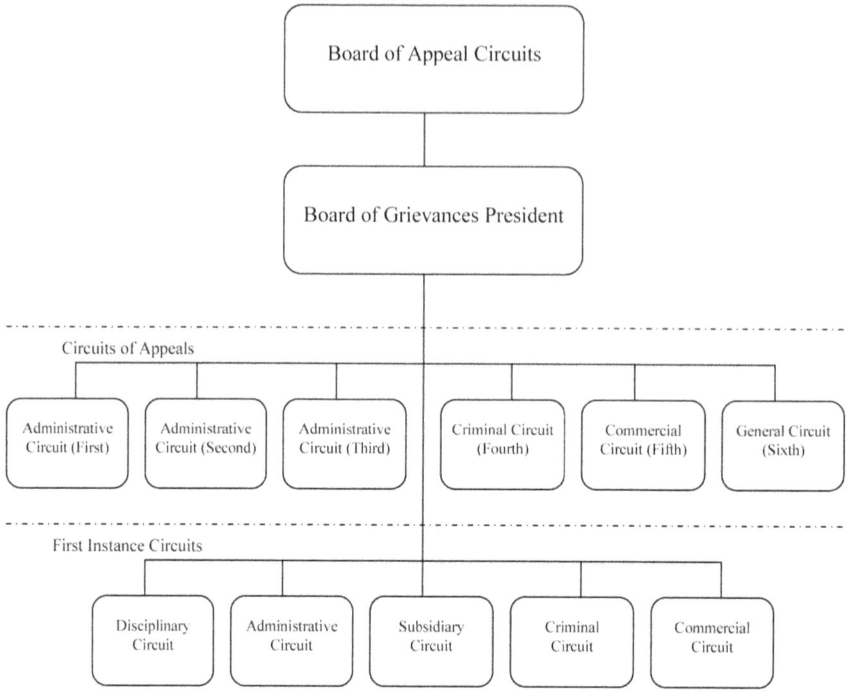

Fig. 20.4 Current structure of the Saudi Arabian Board of Grievances

establishes principles and judicial precedents that the lower courts are bound to follow. The second tier is the Court of Appeal, which hears criminal cases, personal status cases, and other cases that do not fall into the first two categories (Ansary 2008). The Court of Appeal does not reverse the decisions made by the lower courts. It affirms and finalizes the judgments or returns them to the lower court trial judges for modification with its comments. If the judges of the lower court maintain their opinion and do not accept the Court of Appeal's modifications, the Court of Appeal may overrule the original decision and have another judge or panel of the lower court review the case.[14]

The summary courts and the general courts are first-instance courts. Summary courts have jurisdiction over certain *hudud* cases, *ta'zir* cases (excluding those prescribed by a statutory law), and decisions about monetary damages or compensation for crimes that do not exceed one-third of the *diyah* (blood money), which equals approximately SRI 20,000 (US$6,000).[15] Summary courts also have jurisdiction over civil claims for a sum less than SRI 8,000 (US$2,133).[16] Conversely, the general courts have jurisdiction over cases in which the sentence is death or *qisas* (retaliatory punishment).[17] They also have jurisdiction over civil claims for sums totaling more than SRI 20,000 (US$6,000).

Saudi Arabia also has an administrative judicial body known as the Board of Grievances (Diwan al-Mazalim), which stands parallel to the Shari'a courts system and is affiliated directly with the king. The 1982 Law of the Board of Grievances and the 1989 Procedural Rules before the Board of Grievances identify three types of circuits in the Board of Grievances: the Board of Appeal circuits, the circuits of appeal, and the first-instance circuits, as illustrated in Figure 20.4.[18] The Board of Appeal circuits constitute the highest authority in

14 Law of Procedure before Shari'a Courts 2000, Royal Decree M/21, articles 187–91.
15 Ordinance 2514 enacted by the minister of justice, October 12, 1996.
16 Law of Procedure before Shari'a Courts 2000, article 31.
17 Law of Criminal Procedure 2001, article 129.
18 Law of the Board of Grievances 1982, article 6, and Procedural Rules before the Board of Grievances 1989, Council of Ministers Resolution 19, articles 18, 35, and 40.

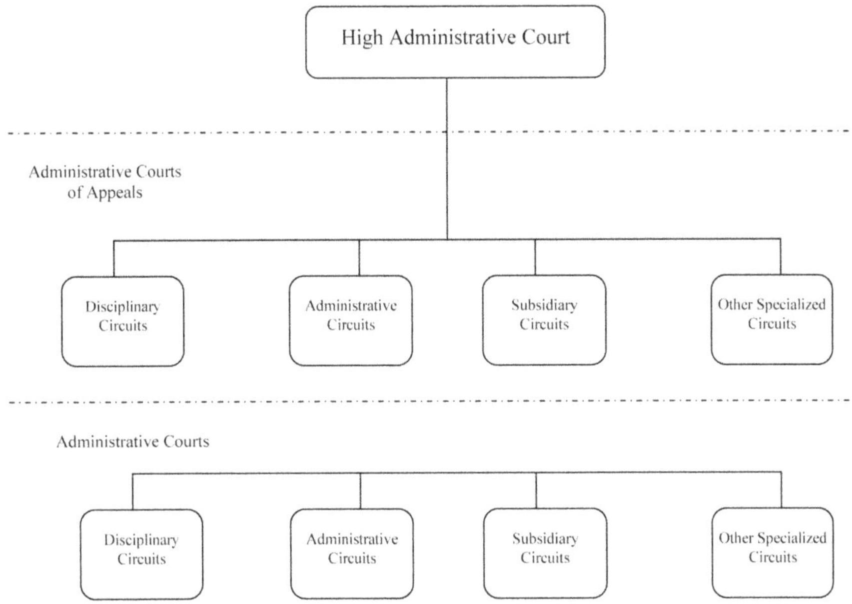

Fig. 20.5 Proposed new structure of the Saudi Arabian courts

the Board of Grievances circuits system and decide only on the abandonment of interpretations or principles. The scrutinizing circuits of appeal function as appeal courts and have the final authority in grievances, thus functioning as administrative circuits. They decide on matters pertaining to administrative disputes, criminal offenses, commercial cases, and general matters. Meanwhile, at the bottom of the Board of Grievances hierarchy stand the first-instance circuits. They hear first-instance disputes concerning administrative, criminal, disciplinary, commercial, and subsidiary matters. These circuits are reformed regularly, and currently one-third of the circuits are devoted to adjudicating commercial disputes and criminal cases.[19]

In this respect, article 48 of the Basic Law of Saudi Arabia upholds the rule of law in the form of the sources of Shari'a, by providing that "[t]he courts will apply the rules of the Islamic Shari'a in the cases that are brought before them, in accordance with what is indicated in the Book and the Sunnah, and statutes decreed by the Ruler which do not contradict the Book or the Sunnah."

Yet the current court system received numerous criticisms from the Saudi people as well as people outside the Arab world. Accordingly, in 2007, King Abdullah bin Abdulaziz al Saud issued royal decrees reforming the judiciary and creating a new court system, although the reforms have yet to be implemented (Otto 2010: 161–62). The intention of the new laws is to shape the Saudi judicial system so that it can meet a higher judicial standard set by the ongoing reforms of the Saudi court system. The new laws represent a major step toward meeting the requirements of a modern and thriving economy, while also improving the business environment (Ansary 2008). Figure 20.5 shows the proposed new court structure of Saudi Arabia.

Under the new structure, the High Court will replace the Supreme Judicial Council as the highest judicial authority in Saudi Arabia. The High Court will exercise its jurisdictions through specialized circuits that are established as and when necessary. The Courts of Appeals will consist of the following circuits: labor circuits, commercial circuits, criminal circuits, personal status circuits, and civil circuits.[20] The new first-degree courts will be formed in the country's provinces, counties, and districts, depending on the needs of the system. The courts will consist of general courts, criminal courts, commercial courts, labor courts, and personal status courts.

19 Procedural Rules before the Board of Grievances, Council of Ministers Resolution 19, articles 14 and 39.

20 Law of the Judiciary, Royal Decree No. M/78, article 16.

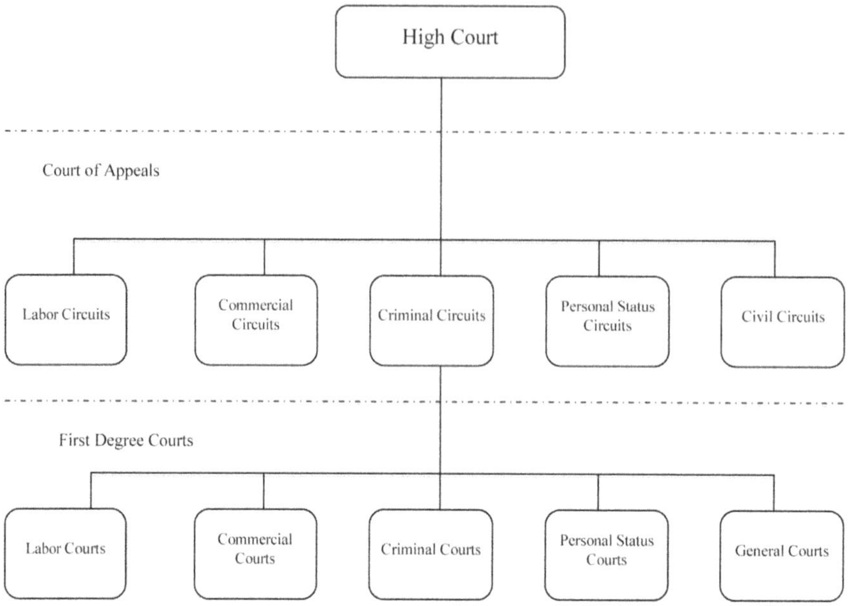

Fig. 20.6 New structure of the Saudi Arabian Board of Grievances

The king also approved a reform to the Board of Grievances, which will continue to stand alongside the Shari'a courts system. The board consists of the High Administrative Court, administrative courts of appeal, and administrative courts. Figure 20.6 shows the new structure of the Board of Grievances of Saudi Arabia. The High Administrative Court will exercise its jurisdictions through specialized circuits that will be formed depending on the needs of the society. The administrative courts of appeal will also function through specialized circuits, as will the administrative courts, whose specialized circuits will include the administrative circuits, employment and disciplinary circuits, and subsidiary circuits.

The third group of the judicial authority is semijudicial and includes the Committee for the Settlement of Negotiable Instrument Disputes (CSNID) and the Committee for the Settlement of Banking Disputes of SAMA (CSBDS). CSNID falls under the jurisdiction of the Ministry of Commerce and Industry and has the power to hear claims on bills of exchange, promissory notes, and checks. The competence to settle negotiable instruments disputes was expected to move to the commercial courts by the end of 2011, resulting in the cessation of the office of CSNID. Meanwhile, CSBDS was established under the purview of SAMA to settle disputes between banks and their clients arising from contracts and transactions that are not concerned with commercial papers. The CSBDS is based in Riyadh.[21]

Recently, arbitration has been significantly improved in Saudi Arabia. The Arbitration Act of Saudi Arabia was adopted by Royal Decree M/46, issued in 1983. The act constitutes a codification of the Hanbali law of arbitration (Saleh 2006). It provides a framework for flexible commercial arbitration with a view to establishing it as a real and effective alternative dispute resolution mechanism in Saudi Arabia. Accordingly, with respect to enforcement and recognition of foreign arbitral awards in Saudi Arabia, the kingdom is a member of two multilateral conventions: the Riyadh Convention for Judicial Cooperation of 1983 and the New York Convention for the Enforcement and Recognition of Foreign Arbitral Awards of 1958. Each convention has been adopted by the Saudi government to enforce and recognize arbitral awards issued in foreign jurisdictions in Saudi territory.

21 Law of Commercial Papers 1963, Nizam Al-Awraq Al-Tijariyah, issued by Royal Decree 37 of 11/10/1383H.

Despite the different structures of the judicial authorities in Malaysia and Saudi Arabia, the judiciary places specific importance upon cases involving Islamic finance disputes. One example is in Kuala Lumpur, where the High Court (*Mu'amalat*) specializes in hearing and deciding Islamic finance cases. In Saudi Arabia, the avenues settling for Islamic finance disputes are threefold: parties can opt for the Shari'a courts, the Board of Grievances, or the semijudicial bodies.

Independence of the Courts

Notably, independence of the courts is one of the vital assurances required in any jurisdiction. In Malaysia, the doctrine of separation of powers (indicating independence of the judiciary and other bodies) is not expressly provided in the constitution, but it could be inferred from the provisions themselves. The third part of the constitution provides for three bodies: the legislature, the executive, and the judiciary. This division prevents abuse of powers by rulers in the executive function, by the legislature, and by judicial authorities. The judiciary is regarded as one of the government offices, and the government controls the appointment of the judges—including their promotions and daily operations. In addition, judges' salaries are paid from the government funds. Although the doctrine of separation of powers denotes the judiciary's independence, the government controls the judiciary's working operations. According to the concept of independence under the Shari'a, this government control means that the judiciary is not independent.

In Saudi Arabia, article 1 of the Law of Judiciary 1975 expressly states, "Judges are independent and, in the administration of justice, they shall be subject to no authority other than the provisions of Shari'ah and laws in force. No one may interfere with the Judiciary." In addition, article 58 of the same law supports the independence requirement by providing as follows:

> A person may not hold the position of a judge and simultaneously engage in commerce or in any position or work which is not consistent with the independence and dignity of the judiciary. The Supreme Judicial Council may enjoin a judge from engaging in any work which, in its opinion, conflicts with the duties of the position and the proper performance of such duties.

Moreover, article 46 of the Basic Law of Saudi Arabia states, "The judiciary is an independent authority. There is no control over judges in the dispensation of their judgments except in the case of the Islamic Sharī `ah." Hence, one can see that Saudi Arabia places importance on the independence of the court officers, who are expected to follow the injunctions of Shari'a in dispensing their judicial obligations.

Selected Cases on Islamic Finance

Most cases of Islamic finance disputes in Malaysia relate to enforcement by the Islamic bank or financial institution after the customer defaults under the Islamic financial contract. Nonetheless, a number of landmark cases are worthy of discussion, especially the dispute over the legality of the Islamic financial contract of *bay' bithaman ajil*, or BBA. Notably, BBA (in Malaysia, *bay' al-'inah*) consists of two contracts of sale and purchase between the bank and the customer, and the legality of the contract is often challenged. Nevertheless, the Shari'a advisers in Malaysia have recognized BBA, and it forms more than 80 percent of the total asset financing in Malaysia. The operational mechanism of BBA is summarized in the Figure 20.7.

Numerous BBA cases have been discussed at the High Court level. Some, like *Arab-Malaysian Finance Bhd v. Taman Ihsan Jaya Sdn Bhd and Others* held that BBA is illegal.[22] Others, like *Bank Islam Malaysia Berhad v. Adnan Bin Omar*[23] and *Dato' Hj Nik Mahmud Daud v. Bank Islam Malaysia Bhd*,[24] found BBA

22 *Arab-Malaysian Finance Bhd v. Taman Ihsan Jaya Sdn Bhd and Others, Koperasi Seri Kota Bukit Cheraka Bhd (Third Party) and Other Cases* [2009] 1 CLJ 419 / [2008] 5 MLJ 631.

23 *Bank Islam Malaysia Berhad v. Adnan Bin Omar* [1994] 3 CLJ 735 / [1994] MLJU 221.

24 *Dato' Hj Nik Mahmud Daud v. Bank Islam Malaysia Bhd* [1998] 3 CLJ 605.

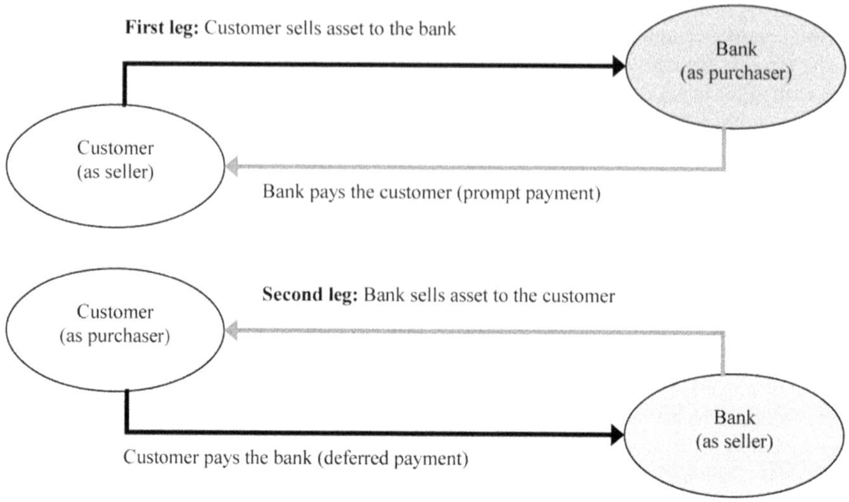

Fig. 20.7 Operational mechanism of BBA in Malaysia

to be legal and in compliance with Shari'a. To date, the highest judicial authority to have decided on the matter is the Court of Appeal in 2010, which found in *Bank Islam Malaysia Berhad v. Lim Kok Hoe & Anor*[25] that BBA is purely legal, complies with the requirements of Shari'a, and should never be equated with a conventional loan given its distinct Shari'a nature. In this particular case, the High Court judge questioned the validity and enforceability of the BBA contracts on two grounds: (a) the judge found BBA contracts to be more onerous than conventional loans with *riba*, or interest, which are prohibited in Islam, and (b) BBA contracts practiced in Malaysia were not acceptable by the four *madhhabs*, or schools of law, in Islam. The judge thereby concluded that BBA contracts were contrary to the basic principles of Islam.

On the basis of this conclusion, the High Court held that an Islamic bank could recover only the balance of the facility plus profit on the balance principal calculated at a daily rate until payment. On appeal, the Court of Appeal held in favor of the Islamic bank and stated that the trial judge's comparison between a BBA contract and a conventional loan agreement was not appropriate. The court found that the BBA contract was a sale agreement, whereas a conventional loan agreement would be a money-lending transaction. Hence, the profit in a BBA contract is different from the interest arising in a conventional loan transaction.

Thus, the trial judge was plainly wrong in equating the profit earned by Bank Islam Malaysia Berhad as being similar to riba when the two transactions could not be similar and when the BBA contract was, in fact, a trade transaction. Furthermore, the comparison between a BBA contract and a conventional loan agreement was of no relevance and served no purpose; the law applicable in a BBA contract was no different from the law that was applicable in a conventional loan agreement. The law is the law of contract, and if the contract is not vitiated by any factor, such as fraud, coercion, or undue influence, the court has a duty to protect the sanctity of the contract entered into by the parties.

On finding that BBA was legal, the litigants further disputed the quantum of claim. One case, *Affin Bank Bhd v. Zulkifli Abdullah*,[26] caused havoc in the Malaysian banking and finance industry and further affected other overseas players and investors in Malaysia. The presiding judge equated the quantum of claim for an Islamic contract with a conventional loan. The issue was finally settled in 2010 by the Court of Appeal in *Bank Islam Malaysia Berhad v. Azmi Bin Salleh*.[27] The court found that the intention of the parties that transpired

25 *Bank Islam Malaysia Berhad v. Lim Kok Hoe & Anor and other Appeals* [2009] 6 CLJ 22 / [2009] 6 MLJ 839.

26 *Affin Bank Bhd v. Zulkifli Abdullah* [2006] 1 CLJ 438.

27 *Bank Islam Malaysia Berhad v. Azmi Bin Salleh & 3 other Appeals* [Civil Appeal No. W-02-609-2010]—Court of Appeal, Putrajaya.

in the legal documentation should be upheld at all times. Given the distinct nature of the Islamic contract, the terms of the legal documentation should be considered in deciding the quantum of dispute. Essentially, the appeal judges decided that the bank is under no obligation to award rebate, or *ibra'*, to the customer in default cases.

However, there is another side to this decision that will affect the practices of Islamic finance in Malaysia. The public will be drawn to think that Islamic finance is burdensome and costs more than the conventional banking system (Yasin 2012). This perception poses a challenge for Islamic banks in Malaysia as they try to attract customers for their financial products and to fulfill their obligations under the Malaysian laws and Shari'a.

In Saudi Arabia, the courts and the Board of Grievances have decided a number of cases relating to Islamic finance disputes. Some of the cases relate to the legality of hire-purchase contracts, as in *Council of Senior Ulama of Saudi Arabia, Decision 52*;[28] the integration and implementation of arbitration agreements in Islamic finance transactions, as in *Diwan Al-Mazalim Decisions* 184/T/4 of 1412H,[29] 61/T/4 of 1415H,[30] and 99/T/4 of 1414H;[31] and the application of *sulh*, or peace, in considering disputes over commercial contracts as in *Diwan Al-Mazalim Decision* 651/1/Q of 1423H.[32]

On this note, although Shari'a prohibits the practice of riba, the Committee for the Settlement of Banking Disputes recognizes charging interest as a valid practice. Therefore, disputes involving interest payments are heard by the committee and honored accordingly on the basis of the legal documentation between the parties. Not similarly, the CSNID applies strict Shari'a injunctions and does not recognize the obligation to pay interest as a valid contract. Therefore, the committee does not have the competence to hear claims for damages in such a case.[33] Since riba is prohibited, negotiable instruments related to usurious transactions are considered void and of no value because the underlying contract is considered void by the committee.[34]

Conclusion

Islamic law is positioned within a constitutional setting in both Malaysia and Saudi Arabia. Similarly, the sources of Shari'a play a significant role in shaping the development of the Islamic banking and finance industry in each jurisdiction. This chapter attempts to highlight the comparative aspect of dispute resolution framework in these two countries by discussing the judicial structure as well as the analysis on selected decided cases of Islamic finance disputes in each country. This chapter could serve as a catalyst for future cross-country research of judicial legal issues and challenges of Islamic banking and finance.

References

Ansary, A.F. 2008. A brief overview of the Saudi Arabian legal system. *GlobaLex* [Online], July. Available at: http://www.nyulawglobal.org/globalex/Saudi_Arabia.htm [accessed: December 16, 2013].

Baamir, A.Y. 2010. *Shari'a Law in Commercial and Banking Arbitration: Law and Practice in Saudi Arabia.* Farnham, UK: Ashgate.

Campbell, C. (ed.). 2007. *Legal Aspects of Doing Business in the Middle East.* Salzburg, Austria: Yorkhill Law.

Cavendish, M. 2007. *World and Its Peoples: The Arabian Peninsula.* White Plains, NY: Marshall Cavendish.

28 Council of Senior Ulamā' of Saudi Arabia, Decision 52 of 20/10/1420 (2000), Riyadh.

29 Diwan Al-Mazalim Decision 184/T/4 of 1412H (1992).

30 Diwan Al-Mazalim Decision 61/T/4 of 1415H (1995).

31 Diwan Al-Mazalim Decision 99/T/4 of 1414H (1994).

32 Diwan Al-Mazalim Decision 651/1/Q of 1423H (2003).

33 Decision of the Committee for the Settlement of Negotiable Instruments Disputes 82/1405 of 08/05/1405H (1985).

34 Decision of the Committee for the Settlement of Negotiable Instruments Disputes 67/1404 of 11/04/1404H (1984).

Economist. 2001. Saudi Arabian justice: Cruel, or just unusual? *Economist*, June 14. Available at: http://www.economist.com/node/656147 [accessed: December 16, 2013].

Economist. 2009. Tentative steps in Saudi Arabia: The king of Saudi Arabia shows some reformist credentials. *Economist,* February 17. Available at: http://www.economist.com/node/13134598 [accessed: December 16, 2013].

Esposito, J.L. 1998. *Islam and Politics*. Syracuse, NY: Syracuse University Press.

Jabatan Perangkaan Malaysia (Department of Statistics, Malaysia). 2011. *Taburan Penduduk dan Ciri-ciri Asas Demografi: Population Distribution and Basic Demographic Characteristics 2010*. Selangor, Malaysia: Department of Statistics, 15. Available at: http://www.statistics.gov.my/portal/download_Population/files/census2010/Taburan_Penduduk_dan_Ciri-ciri_Asas_Demografi.pdf [accessed: November 19, 2013].

Otto, J.M. 2010. *Sharia Incorporated: A Comparative Overview of the Legal Systems of Twelve Muslim Countries in Past and Present*. Amsterdam: Amsterdam University Law Press.

Razak, D.A., and Karim, M.A.A. 2008. Development of Islamic finance in Malaysia: A conceptual paper. Presented at the Eighth Global Conference on Business and Economics, Florence, Italy, October 18–19.

Sabri, N.R. 2009. *Arab Financial Institutions*. New York: Nova Science.

Saleh, S. 2006. *Commercial Arbitration in the Arab Middle East: Shari'a, Lebanon, Syria, and Egypt*. Oxford, UK: Hart.

Saleh, H. 2007. Support for shake-up of Saudi justice system. *Financial Times*, October 4. Available at: http://www.ft.com/cms/s/0/ec3ad182-72a2-11dc-b7ff-0000779fd2ac.html#axzz1RgyCPauT [accessed: December 16, 2013].

Yasin, N.M. 2012. Ibra' and its practice by the Islamic banks: With reference to Malaysia, in *Islamic Banking and Finance: Principles, Instruments and Operations*, edited by A. Trakic and H.H.A. Tajuddin. Selangor, Malaysia: CLJ Publications, 643–72.

Yong, Y.N. 2007. Malaysia way ahead in Islamic finance. *Edge*, December 21. Available at http://www.malaysianbar.org.my/business_news/malaysia_way_ahead_in_islamic_finance.html [accessed: December 16, 2013].

Chapter 21
Mixed Legal Jurisdictions and Clinical Legal Education: Latest Trends

David McQuoid-Mason

There seems to be no consensus on what is meant by *mixed legal systems* or *mixed jurisdictions* (Palmer 2008). The classic approach is to limit mixed jurisdictions to private law systems based on a mixture of common law and civil law (Palmer 2008: 7). The modern, broader approach is to take a legal pluralistic approach that regards mixed jurisdictions as involving two or more different legal systems or traditions within a country's legal system (Palmer 2008: 13). Given the trend toward the globalization of legal practice and legal education, particularly clinical legal education (see generally Bloch 2011: xxv), I intend to adopt the broader pluralistic approach for the purposes of this chapter.

According to the broader approach, the following mixed systems can be identified: (a) mixed systems of civil and common law;[1] (b) mixed systems of civil and customary law;[2] (c) mixed systems of civil, common, and customary law;[3] (d) mixed systems of civil and Islamic law;[4] (e) mixed systems of common and customary law;[5] (f) mixed systems of common and Islamic law;[6] (g) mixed systems of civil, Islamic, and customary law;[7] (h) mixed systems of common, Islamic, and customary law;[8] (i) mixed systems of common, Hindu, Islamic, and customary law;[9] (j) mixed systems of civil, common, Indian, and Islamic law;[10] (k) mixed systems of civil, common, Jewish, and Islamic law;[11] (l) mixed systems of civil, common, Greek Orthodox, and Islamic law;[12]

---

1 Mixed systems of civil and common law include Botswana, Cyprus, Guyana, Louisiana (United States), Malta, Mauritius, Namibia, the Philippines, Puerto Rico (associated with the United States), Quebec (Canada), St. Lucia, Scotland (United Kingdom), Seychelles, and South Africa (JuriGlobe 2013).

2 Mixed systems of civil and customary law include Burkino Faso, Burundi, Chad, China (excluding Hong Kong and Macau), Republic of Congo, Democratic Republic of Congo, Côte d'Ivoire, Ethiopia, Equatorial Guinea, Gabon, Guinea, Guinea-Bissau, Japan, South Korea, North Korea, Madagascar, Mali, Mongolia, Mozambique, Niger, Rwanda, São Tomé and Príncipe, Senegal, Swaziland, Taiwan, and Togo (JuriGlobe 2013).

3 Mixed systems of civil, common, and customary law include Vanuatu. See http://en.wikipedia.org/wiki/List_of_national_legal_systems [accessed: December 17, 2013].

4 Mixed systems of civil and Islamic law include Algeria, the Comoros Islands, Egypt, Iran, Iraq, Lebanon, Libya, Mauritania, Morocco, Palestine, Syria, and Tunisia (JuriGlobe 2013).

5 Mixed systems of common and customary law include Bhutan, Ghana, Hong Kong (China), Liberia, Malawi, Micronesia, Myanmar, Nepal, Papua New Guinea, Samoa, Sierra Leone, the Solomon Islands, Tanzania, Uganda, and Zambia (JuriGlobe 2013).

6 Mixed systems of common and Islamic law include Afghanistan, Bangladesh, Pakistan, Singapore, and Sudan (JuriGlobe 2013). For Afghanistan, see http://en.wikipedia.org/wiki/List_of_national_legal_systems [accessed: December 17, 2013].

7 Mixed systems of civil, Islamic, and customary law include Djibouti, Eritrea, Indonesia, Jordan, Kuwait, Oman, and Timor Leste (JuriGlobe 2013).

8 Mixed systems of common, Islamic, and customary law include Brunei, the Gambia, Kenya, Malaysia, and Nigeria (JuriGlobe 2013).

9 Mixed systems of common, Hindu, Islamic, and customary law include India (JuriGlobe 2013).

10 Mixed systems of civil, common, Indian, and Islamic law include Thailand. See http://en.wikipedia.org/wiki/List_of_national_legal_systems [accessed: December 17, 2013].

11 Mixed systems of civil, common, Jewish, and Islamic law include Israel (JuriGlobe 2013).

12 Mixed systems of civil, common, Greek Orthodox, and Islamic law include Cyprus. See http://en.wikipedia.org/wiki/List_of_national_legal_systems [accessed: December 17, 2013].

and (m) mixed systems of Islamic law and customary law.[13] However, the list is not closed, and other the types of mixed legal systems may exist.

Given the broad definition of mixed jurisdictions, this chapter deals with the following issues:

- What is clinical legal education?
- What types of clinical legal education programs exist?
- What types of skills are taught in clinical legal education programs?
- Why are interactive teaching methods used in clinical legal education programs?
- Which mixed jurisdiction countries have adopted clinical legal education?
- How are clinical legal education teaching methods affected if they are used in mixed jurisdiction law schools?
- How does the service component of clinical legal education work in mixed jurisdictions?

What Is Clinical Legal Education?

Clinical legal education is an interactive, reflective method of teaching practical legal skills to law students in a social justice context. During the process, students are confronted with real-life situations and play the role of lawyers to solve legal problems. They do so by interacting with clients or each other to identify and resolve legal issues, and they are subjected to critical review by their teachers or peers. Clinical legal education enables law students to play an active role in the learning process and to see how the law operates in real-life situations (Brayne, Duncan, and Grimes 1998: 1).

Clinical legal education provides law students with the tools that lay the foundations for their future careers as lawyers. Whereas traditional legal education tends to focus on the theoretical content of the law and to be knowledge based, clinical legal education goes further and provides law students with the necessary skills for legal practice. It also inculcates values such as the duty of lawyers to become involved in social justice issues in society and to display professional responsibility while practicing law (McQuoid-Mason and Palmer 2007: 10).

In most countries, the mission of clinical legal education is to teach law students practical legal skills in a social justice setting (compare with McQuoid-Mason 2000; see also McQuoid-Mason 2002). *Social justice* refers to the fair distribution of health, housing, welfare, education, and legal resources in society (compare with Bhagwati 1987; Honoré 1968: 68). Social justice is concerned with satisfying what poor people need rather than providing what they want. Clinical legal education programs play a valuable role in this respect.

What Types of Clinical Legal Education Programs Exist?

Clinical legal education programs vary greatly, depending on their educational objectives, the client target group, and the method of service delivery used. Examples of different service delivery components of clinical legal education programs include the following: (a) campus clinics,[14] (b) off-campus clinics,[15] (c) mobile

13 Mixed systems of Islamic law and customary law include the United Arab Emirates (JuriGlobe 2013).

14 Campus law clinics usually operate on university campuses in premises closely linked to a law school or elsewhere on the campus. See generally McQuoid-Mason and Palmer (2007: 37–43).

15 Off-campus law clinics operate away from the university campus and the law school. See generally McQuoid-Mason and Palmer (2007: 44–45).

clinics,[16] (d) farm-out clinics or externships,[17] (e) community clinics,[18] (f) street law-type clinics (discussed later), (g) alternative dispute resolution clinics,[19] (h) legislative drafting clinics,[20] (i) clinics teaching legal study skills,[21] (j) mixed clinics,[22] and (k) simulated clinics.[23] Again, the list is not closed.

The two most common types of law clinics used in clinical legal education programs are live client clinics and legal literacy or street law-type clinics.

Live Client Law Clinics

Clinical legal education programs involving live client law clinics include both academic and service components. The former require classroom attendance, and the latter require work in a law clinic.

In clinical legal education programs that are fully integrated into the law curriculum, law students are given academic credit for their work and assessments as in any other law course. The academic part of these programs involves students attending lectures or seminars and taking practical classes on the types of topics that are handled by the clinic during the service component in the law clinic. The emphasis is placed on skills training, and the students are evaluated according to the academic rules of the faculty.

In programs that are not fully integrated into the law curriculum, the faculty may require students to participate in the program on a "duly performed" basis. In such a program, academic credit is not given, but participating students have to complete the program satisfactorily to fulfill the graduation requirements of the faculty. These programs also usually include mandatory classroom work on skills training so that the students are able effectively to deal with the service component of the clinic.

Some programs are entirely voluntary and place much less emphasis on academic work. These programs tend to provide some training in the skills required in a law clinic but may not have a mandatory classroom component (see generally McQuoid-Mason and Palmer 2007: 10–11).

Traditional clinical legal education programs, particularly in developing countries, require students to service live clients under supervision in a law clinic. Very often these programs are held in general practice clinics that take walk-in clients.[24] The students usually give advice to clients and act as clearinghouses for other agencies (compare with McQuoid-Mason 1985: 64).

In the more advanced clinics, law students may assist qualified lawyers to litigate. In some common law countries, such as the United States, and mixed legal systems, such as the Philippines, certain students may even be allowed to appear in court under "student practice rules" (compare with Walker 1980: 1101).[25] In

16 Mobile law clinics are clinics that are based at, but move away from, campus or off-campus law clinics and visit the communities they serve. See generally McQuoid-Mason and Palmer (2007: 46–47).

17 Farm-out law clinics or externships are based on cooperation or partnership agreements between law schools and outside bodies such as nongovernmental organizations, other private bodies, or government departments. In such clinics, law students spend time working with such clients away from the campus or law school. See generally McQuoid-Mason and Palmer (2007: 47–49).

18 Community law clinics involve law students living in a particular community (usually during a university vacation period) to identify and record the types of legal problems that community is encountering. The students then seek to solve such problems by working in the law clinic. See generally McQuoid-Mason and Palmer (2007: 50–52).

19 Alternative dispute resolution clinics train law students in how to use nonlegal methods to resolve disputes. See generally McQuoid-Mason and Palmer (2007: 55–57).

20 Legislative drafting law clinics train law students in how to draft legislation in important areas of the law. See generally McQuoid-Mason and Palmer (2007: 57–59).

21 Clinics teaching legal study skills train senior law students how to teach first-year law students about the law using interactive teaching methods. See generally McQuoid-Mason and Palmer (2007: 59–61).

22 Mixed law clinics may operate on or off campus or as mobile clinics and may combine the activities of all three. See generally McQuoid-Mason and Palmer (2007: 61–62).

23 Simulated clinics do not deal with live clients but are useful for developing legal skills in the classroom in a closed environment. See generally McQuoid-Mason and Palmer (2007: 62).

24 Generally for the types of cases handled by legal aid clinics, see McQuoid-Mason (1982: 139–61).

25 See Philippines Law Student Practice Rule, Rules of Court, rule 168A (1997).

countries with civil law procedural rules that allow people other than lawyers to appear on behalf of litigants in civil cases, law students may also be able to represent clients in court.[26]

The challenge for live client clinical legal education programs is to balance the academic work required of students during their law degree with their duty to provide legal services to poor and marginalized clients in the law clinic (see generally McQuoid-Mason and Palmer 2007: 10–12).

Street Law-Type Clinics

Street law-type clinics are legal literacy programs conducted by law students, usually aimed at high school children, prisoners, and others (see generally McQuoid-Mason 1994). In street law programs, students are taught to teach the law using interactive learning methods. During the process, students are often asked to give advice about practical aspects of the law.

As in the case of live client clinics, street law students are subjected to critical review by their teachers and peers. Street law-type clinical programs also have academic and service components (compare with McQuoid-Mason 2000; see also McQuoid-Mason 2002).

Street law-type programs that are fully integrated into the law curriculum give law students academic credit for their work as in any other law course. The academic component of street law programs involves classroom work. In street law, students are trained to use different types of interactive learning methods to teach schoolchildren, prisoners, or other people about law, human rights, and democracy. Although the emphasis is placed on how to teach interactively, students are also taught lawyering skills such as preparing a mock trial and thinking on their feet. Where street law is a credit course, the students are given grades for their work.

Where street law programs are not fully integrated into the law curriculum, some faculties require students to participate in the program on a "duly performed" basis as part of community service projects. Although no academic credit is given for such courses, participating students are required to complete the program satisfactorily in order to graduate. Even though street law is not a credit course, students have to learn how to use interactive teaching methods.

Street law programs that are entirely voluntary place much less emphasis on academic work. These programs, however, still require the students to be trained in street law teaching skills (for example, in a one-off workshop) but may not have a mandatory regular classroom component (see generally McQuoid-Mason and Palmer 2007: 12–13).

The service component in street law programs requires students to go into high schools, prisons, or other organizations and to teach the target audiences about the law. To do so successfully, students have to be taught how to use interactive teaching methods (see generally McQuoid-Mason 1994).

In street law programs, students give limited legal advice. They usually refer more complicated inquiries to a traditional live client law clinic or recommend that the person seek legal advice from the state legal aid scheme or a private lawyer.

The challenge for students participating in street law-type clinics, as for those participating in live client clinics, is to balance their service work with their other academic work.

What Types of Skills Are Taught in Clinical Legal Education Programs?

Skills Taught in Programs with Live Client Clinics

The clinical legal education curriculum at law schools with live client clinics usually includes the following lawyering skills: (a) client interviewing, (b) client counseling, (c) trial advocacy, (d) negotiation, (e) critical thinking, (f) problem solving, (g) drafting, and (h) oral and written communication skills (McQuoid-Mason and Palmer 2007: 85–86). The majority of these skills are required irrespective of whether law students are

---

26 Student representation was common in Eastern and Central Europe and in Indonesia before the bar associations initiated legislation that gave a monopoly to legally qualified practitioners.

studying in common law, civil law, religious law, or traditional customary law mixed legal systems. Even in jurisdictions that do not allow litigants to be represented by lawyers, law students can still be trained in ways to advise lay clients to represent themselves using lawyering skills.

Client Interviewing

Client interviewing and the taking of instructions are very important because they occur at the first point of contact between lawyers and clients. Students have to be taught how to put their clients at ease and how to build trust between themselves and their clients. They must learn how to make their clients feel free to tell them everything that is relevant. Client-centered interviewing techniques must be used to ensure that the lawyer has a clear understanding of the client's needs and requirements (Alexander 1997: 12; Twist 1992: 20).

Client Counseling

Client counseling involves the lawyer advising the client once he or she has helped the client identify what the issues are. Students need to be trained to take a client-centered approach to counseling. Clients should be given choices regarding the alternative procedures that could be followed and encouraged to make an informed decision on the course of conduct they would like to follow (Chapman 1993: 25). This approach applies whether or not clients will be represented by lawyers or are being advised by lawyers on how to represent themselves in a religious or customary law court.

Trial Advocacy

Trial advocacy skills require law students to be trained in case analysis, trial preparation, and case presentation and questioning (for example, in common law systems, including opening statements, leading evidence in chief, cross-examination, reexamination, closing arguments, and so on). The skills taught will vary according to whether common law adversarial or civil law inquisitorial court procedures apply. Students need to practice the oral and written skills necessary to prepare for, and conduct, a case in court (see generally Palmer and McQuoid-Mason 2000: 32).

Negotiation

Negotiation is a skill that all lawyers require because most of the cases they deal with will involve attempting to reach an agreement about something. Students need to know that litigation is not the only way to settle disputes. They also need to understand the importance of principled negotiation (see generally Fisher and Ury 1981). Law students in clinic situations spend a great deal of time negotiating and need to understand the dynamics involved (see, for example, Lee and Fox 1994: 150–51). In specialist alternative dispute resolution clinics, students may also need to be trained in mediation techniques, including how to listen, what steps are involved in the mediation process, and how to draw up a mediation agreement.

Critical Thinking

Critical thinking requires students not simply to accept what the law is or what the courts or textbooks say the law is. Students should be encouraged to question legal principles and solutions offered and to think creatively about how they can help clients to solve problems using both legal and other remedies.

Problem Solving

Problem solving is the essence of legal practice. When problem solving, students should be able to identify the issues, generate alternative solutions to the issues raised, and develop a plan of action. They should learn to be open to new information and ideas and to be flexible in their approach while dealing with problems (Iya 2000: 62, 67).

Drafting

Students in law clinics may be required to write letters and draft documents, such as pleadings, contracts, wills, leases, and other legal documents. They need to be taught these skills before they attempt to undertake writing and drafting tasks on behalf of clients. The clinics need to imbue law students with a commitment to accurate and good drafting techniques (Barnhizer 1990).

Oral and Written Communication Skills
Communication is the lifeblood of legal practice. Law students need to be trained in both oral and written communication skills. These skills include use of words, thinking skills and logical reasoning, speaking skills, reading skills, and writing skills (Palmer, Crocker, and Kidd 2003: 3–84).

Skills Taught in Programs with Street Law-Type Clinics

Students in street law-type clinical legal education programs acquire the following necessary skills for lawyers: (a) writing skills, (b) communication skills, (c) ability to think on their feet, (d) trial advocacy skills, (d) critical thinking skills, (e) problem-solving skills, and (f) oral skills (McQuoid-Mason 2008: 36).

Writing Skills
Street law students learn to develop their writing skills preparing lesson plans, writing reflective essays, and developing mock trial packages.

Communication Skills
Street law students develop the important lawyering skill of being able to communicate the law and legal principles to laypeople in simple language.

Ability to Think on One's Feet
Street law students have to learn to think on their feet when responding to questions from learners. This skill is crucial for lawyers, particularly those involved in court work, because they may have to answer questions from the bench.

Trial Advocacy Skills
Street law students learn trial advocacy skills when training their target audiences to prepare for mock trials by teaching them about court procedures, the rules of evidence, ways to question the accused and witnesses, and ways to make closing arguments. Teaching others is one of the best methods of learning.

Critical Thinking Skills
Street law students learn about social justice and the public's perceptions of the law and the legal system. Doing so enables the students to think critically about the legal system and how it operates in practice.

Problem-Solving Skills
Street law students are continually faced with the types of practical problems experienced by their target audiences. This challenge gives students an opportunity to develop their analytical skills to identify and solve legal problems.

Oral Skills
While using interactive teaching methods to conduct community legal education programs, street law students develop confidence in public speaking and the ability to interact with school learners and the community in general.

Why Are Interactive Teaching Methods Used in Clinical Legal Education Programs?

Unlike traditional methods of teaching the law, clinical legal education is student-centered rather than lecturer-centered. To achieve a student-centered experience, clinics use a number of interactive methods to train students in legal skills and to sensitize them to social justice issues.

Law teachers using clinical legal education techniques do not rely on the traditional lecture approach. Psychological studies show that lectures are the least effective way of imparting knowledge. They show that what students remember depends on the teaching methods used. The rate of memory retention increases as more student-centered interactive teaching methods are used. The following memory retention rates have been measured according to the teaching methods used: 5 percent if lectures are used, 10 percent if students read for themselves, 20 percent if audiovisual aids are used, 30 percent if students see a demonstration, 50 percent if students discuss issues in small groups, 75 percent if students see a demonstration and then practice doing it themselves, and 90 percent if students teach others.[27]

Some of the interactive teaching methods used in clinical legal education programs are (a) brainstorming, (b) ranking exercises, (c) small group discussions, (d) case studies, (e) role-playing, (f) question-and-answer sessions, (g) simulations, (h) debates, (i) games, (j) hypothetical problems, (k) moots, (l) mock trials, (m) open-ended stimulus, (n) opinion polls, (o) participant presentations, (p) taking a stand, (q) thinking on one's feet (PRES formula),[28] (r) problem solving (FIRAC formula),[29] (s) values clarification, (t) fishbowl, (u) jigsaw, (v) each one teach one, (w) visual aids, (x) use of experts, (y) theater forum, and (z) field trips (McQuoid-Mason and Palmer 2007: 98–118). These techniques are examples of what can be done to ensure that students and other participants are involved in an active learning process. Many other methods can be used. Law teachers should be as creative as possible in their attempts to actively involve students in the learning process rather than using the passive ineffectual lecture method. Ironically, in most law schools throughout the world, the least effective method of teaching law—lectures—is also the most common method.

Which Mixed Jurisdiction Countries Have Adopted Clinical Legal Education?

Clinical legal education has become a global movement (Bloch 2011: xxv), and a wide variety of countries broadly defined as mixed jurisdictions have adopted aspects of clinical legal education in their law schools. Some mixed jurisdiction countries, such as South Africa, Tanzania, Zimbabwe, and Malaysia, have clinical legal education programs that date to the 1970s. In the 1980s, clinical programs developed in countries such as India and Botswana. By the 1990s, clinics were being established in Mongolia and Thailand, and by the first few years of the twenty-first century, a host of clinical programs had emerged in mixed jurisdiction countries in Africa, South Asia, and Southeast Asia. Most recently, Scotland and a number of Middle Eastern mixed jurisdiction countries have established clinical law programs.

Several mixed jurisdictions have embraced clinical legal education. For example, Botswana,[30] the US state of Louisiana,[31] Namibia,[32] the Philippines,[33] the US territory of Puerto Rico,[34] the Canadian province of Quebec,[35] Scotland,[36]and South Africa,[37] with mixed systems of civil and common law, have adopted clinical legal education programs at some of their law schools. Likewise, countries with mixed systems of civil and

27 See National Training Laboratories, Bethel, Maine, Learning Pyramid. The origins of the Learning Pyramid are somewhat controversial, and confusion exists about who the original author was. For an example of the Learning Pyramid, see http://thepeakperformancecenter.com/educational-learning/learning/principles-of-learning/learning-pyramid/ [accessed December 23, 2013].

28 The PRES formula requires students to present their arguments by expressing the following (Palmer, Crocker, and Kidd 2003: 21–23; Palmer and McQuoid-Mason 2000: 47): their Point of view, the Reason for their point of view, an Example or Evidence to support their point of view, and a Summary of their point of view.

29 The FIRAC formula refers to the following: *F* = Facts, *I* = Issues, *R* = Rule of law, *A* = Application of rule of law to facts, and *C* = Conclusion.

30 The University of Botswana has a law clinic (Bloch 2011: 26).

31 For instance, Tulane University has a law clinic.

32 The University of Namibia has a law clinic (Bloch 2011: 26).

33 For instance, the University of the Philippines and Ateneo de Manila Law School have law clinics (Bloch 2011: 38–39).

34 The University of Puerto Rico has a law clinic.

35 For instance, McGill University, Canada, has a law clinic.

36 Strathclyde University, Glasgow, has a law clinic and street law program.

37 Nearly all law schools in South Africa have law clinics (Bloch 2011: 25), and nine of them have street law programs.

customary law, such as Burkina Faso,[38] China,[39] Ethiopia,[40] Japan,[41] Mongolia,[42] Mozambique,[43] Rwanda,[44] and Senegal,[45] have adopted clinical legal education programs. Egypt,[46] Iran,[47] Iraq,[48] Lebanon,[49] Morocco,[50] and Palestine,[51] with mixed systems of civil and Islamic law, also have clinical legal education programs, as have countries with mixed systems of common and customary law, such as Lesotho,[52] Papua New Guinea,[53] Sierra Leone,[54] Swaziland,[55] Tanzania,[56] Uganda,[57] Zambia,[58] and Zimbabwe.[59] A country with a mixed system of civil, common, and customary law such as Vanuatu also has a clinical law program.[60]

Afghanistan,[61] Bangladesh,[62] Pakistan,[63] and Singapore,[64] with mixed systems of common and Islamic law, and Indonesia,[65] Oman,[66] and Jordan,[67] with mixed systems of civil, Islamic, and customary law, have all introduced clinical legal education programs. Similarly, Kenya,[68] Malaysia,[69] and Nigeria,[70] with mixed

38 For instance, the National University of Burkino Faso has a clinical externship program that places students with nongovernmental organizations (Bloch 2011: 32–33).

39 By 2010, China had nearly 80 university law clinics (Bloch 2011: 93).

40 For instance, the Universities of Addis Ababa and Mekelle have law clinics (Bloch 2011: 30), and Mekelle has a street law program.

41 A large number of the 68 new law schools in Japan that opened in 2004 have adopted clinical teaching methods based on the US model (Bloch 2011: 105).

42 For instance, the Pedagogical University of Mongolia has a law clinic and street law program.

43 For instance, the Eduardo Mondlane University, Maputo, has a law clinic (Bloch 2011: 26–27).

44 For instance, the National University of Rwanda has a law clinic (Bloch 2011: 30).

45 For instance, the Université Gaston Berger, St.-Louis, has a clinical externship program, whereby students are placed with nongovernmental organizations (Bloch 2011: 32–33).

46 For instance, Alexandria University, Helwan University, Tanta University, and Assiut University all have law clinics.

47 For instance, Mofid University, Qum, and Teheran University have law clinics.

48 For instance, Baghdad University and Salahaddin University have law clinics.

49 For instance, the Beirut Arab University has a law clinic.

50 For instance, the University of Hassan II has a law clinic (Bloch 2011: 33).

51 For instance, the Islamic University of Gaza has a law clinic.

52 For instance, the University of Lesotho has a law clinic (Bloch 2011: 26).

53 For instance, the University of the South Pacific, Papua New Guinea, has a law clinic.

54 For instance, Fourah Bay College, University of Sierra Leone, has a law clinic (Bloch 2011: 32) and street law program.

55 For instance, the University of Swaziland has an externship clinical program (Bloch 2011: 26).

56 For instance, the University of Dar-es-Salaam has a law clinic (Bloch 2011: 30).

57 For instance, the Law Development Centre and Makerere University have law clinics (Bloch 2011: 29–30).

58 For instance, the University of Zambia has a law clinic (Bloch 2011: 26).

59 For instance, the University of Zimbabwe has a law clinic (Bloch 2011: 26).

60 For instance, the University of the South Pacific, Vanuatu, has a law clinic.

61 For instance, the law faculties of the Universities of Herat, Jalalabad, Mazar-e-Sharif, and Kabul have clinical law programs, and Herat University also has a street law program.

62 For instance, the Universities of Dakar and Chittagong have law clinics, and the University of Dakar also has a street law program.

63 For instance, the Universities of Lahore, Peshawar, Hazara, and Baluchistan have established law clinics, and Hamdard University has a street law program.

64 For instance, the National Management School and University of Singapore have clinical law programs.

65 For instance, the Islamic University of Indonesia, Yogyakarta State University, and Pasundan University have law clinics, and Pasundan University also has a street law program.

66 For instance, Sultan Qaboos University has a law clinic.

67 For instance, the University of Jordan has a law clinic.

68 For instance, Nairobi and Moi Universities have law clinics (Bloch 2011: 29).

69 For instance, the Universiti Teknologi MARA and University Malaya have clinical law programs (Bloch 2011: 38, 41).

70 Eight universities and some of the seven postgraduate law schools that are members of the Network of University Legal Aid Institutions have clinical law programs (Bloch 2011: 32).

systems of common, Islamic, and customary law, have introduced clinical law programs. India,[71] with a mixture of common, Hindu, Islamic, and customary law, and Thailand,[72] with a mixture of civil, common, Indian, and Islamic law, both have clinical law programs. Clinical legal education programs have also been established in Qatar[73] and Yemen,[74] which have mixed systems of common, civil, Islamic, and customary law. Israel,[75] with a mixed system of civil, common, Jewish, and Islamic law, also has several clinical legal education programs. The United Arab Emirates,[76] with a mixed system of Islamic and customary law, has at least one clinical law program.

How Are Clinical Legal Education Teaching Methods Affected If They Are Used in Mixed Jurisdiction Law Schools?

As has been pointed out, clinical legal education is a method of teaching law, and whether it is used in common law, civil law, religious law, customary law, or mixed jurisdictions does not matter. The skills that need to be taught are much the same. What is important, however, is that the instructors using the clinical legal education method are sensitive to local norms and customs. Clinical legal education involves experiential learning, and clinical teachers should always be aware of the environment in which they are teaching. They can do so by drawing directly on the experience of the learners whenever teachers present a clinical legal education program. For instance, when beginning any program, the clinician should always try to assess the experience of the learners by initially eliciting from them their knowledge and experience concerning the topic to be taught.

A brief discussion follows of how certain skills taught in clinical legal education programs that deal with live clients relate to the different jurisdictions. These skills are (a) client interviewing, (b) client counseling, (c) trial advocacy, (d) negotiation, (e) critical thinking, (f) problem solving, (g) drafting, and (h) oral and written communication skills.

Client Interviewing

Client interviewing is important for all jurisdictions where lawyers may represent clients. Even if traditional customary law systems do not allow representation by lawyers, lawyers may still be able to advise clients on how they should conduct their cases. In such circumstances lawyers need to conduct proper interviews so they can correctly advise clients on self-representation.

Client Counseling

Client counseling is important for all jurisdictions where lawyers are required to give clients advice. In all instances, clients must make informed choices regarding the course of action they would like to follow. Informed decisions are necessary regardless of whether clients will be represented by lawyers or are being advised by lawyers on how to represent themselves in courts where lawyers may not appear.

Trial Advocacy

How trial advocacy is taught will depend on the nature of the court proceedings in the jurisdiction concerned. In countries with common law procedural rules, an adversarial approach will be adopted, whereas in countries with civil law procedural rules, the approach will be inquisitorial. Methods of asking questions and making

---

71 All law faculties in India were directed to establish clinical law courses by the Bar Council of India in 1997 (Bloch 2011: 46).

72 For instance, Thammasat University and Chiang Mai University have law clinics (Bloch 2011: 38).

73 For instance, Qatar University has a law clinic.

74 For instance, Sana'a University has a law clinic.

75 For instance, Al-Quds University, Haifa University, and the Hebrew University of Jerusalem all have law clinics.

76 For instance, the United Arab Emirates University, Al Ain, has a law clinic.

arguments will vary according to the different procedures. The same is true (with the necessary changes being made) of clients who are obliged to represent themselves in traditional customary law courts that do not allow representation by lawyers.

Negotiation

Negotiations are used in all jurisdictions to resolve disputes—common law, civil law, religious law, and customary law. Laypeople seeking to use traditional dispute resolution mechanisms need to understand how to conduct meaningful negotiations to protect their interests.

Critical Thinking

Critical thinking is particularly important for lawyers in all jurisdictions. For example, it can be used in common law jurisdictions where lawyers want to persuade the court to distinguish the case before it from a previous precedent-setting case. It can also be used in civil law jurisdictions where lawyers want to persuade the court how to interpret an article in a code or in religious tribunals where a different interpretation may be given to a religious text. Similarly, lawyers can assist laypeople who are representing themselves in traditional customary law courts in thinking creatively about how they will present their cases.

Problem Solving

Problem solving lies at the heart of legal practice in all jurisdictions—both secular and religious. Lawyers advising laypeople faced with self-representation before traditional customary law courts should counsel them on how to represent themselves in a manner that will solve their problems.

Drafting

The drafting of documents is common to all jurisdictions—whether secular or religious—and it is an essential skill required of lawyers. Drafting is even important for lawyers who assist laypeople using traditional customary law processes that do not allow for legal representation.

Oral and Written Communication Skills

Oral and written communication skills are essential for lawyers in all jurisdictions—whether secular or religious. They can also be used by lawyers who help clients draft documents for traditional customary law processes that do not involve lawyers.

The lawyering skills acquired by students in street law-type programs can be applied to all forms of mixed legal systems because they are generic skills that can be adapted to the type of mixed legal jurisdiction in question. For example, the following lawyering skills can be designed to cater for the particular mixes of legal systems: (a) writing skills, (b) communication skills, (c) ability to think on one's feet, (d) trial advocacy skills, (e) critical thinking skills, (f) problem-solving skills, and (g) oral skills.

How Does the Service Component of Clinical Legal Education Work in Mixed Jurisdictions?

How the service component of clinical legal education will work in a mixed jurisdiction depends upon the type of service provided (for example, live client clinics or street law-type clinics) and the nature of the legal rules governing such service.

Live Client Clinics

In most cases, whatever the nature of the mixed jurisdiction, the generic skills required to assist in live client clinics are likely to be the same. The main differences are likely to be the nature of the trial advocacy training undertaken and the extent to which law students working in live client clinics are able to represent their clients in court.

Trial advocacy training for mixed jurisdictions with civil law procedural rules will require students to be taught how to conduct themselves during an inquisitorial trial. Trial advocacy training for students operating in a mixed jurisdiction with common law procedural rules will have to be based on adversarial trial practice.

In mixed jurisdictions with common law procedural rules, very few countries allow clinical law students to represent clients in court. The Philippines is one of the few mixed systems with common law procedural rules that does allow such representation.[77]

Law students may find it easier to represent clients in mixed jurisdictions that use civilian rules of procedure than in those jurisdictions that have common law rules of procedure. This was certainly the case before credible bar associations were established in many transitional societies that had moved from autocracy to democracy. An example is Afghanistan, where the Interim Criminal Code for Courts[78] stated that until Afghanistan has a sufficient number of defense counsel, a suspect or accused person may have the assistance of an educated person having some knowledge of legal issues and that the president of each court should institute a list of such persons. This rule would allow the appointment of senior law students attached to law clinics and nongovernmental organizations as student advocates.

In the past, even in civil jurisdictions that required legal representation by lawyers in criminal cases, it was often possible for anyone to appear in civil cases. Hence, law students could appear just like anyone else. With the rise of established bar associations, licensed lawyers have increasingly obtained a monopoly over legal representation in both criminal and civil cases.

Street Law-Type Clinics

The generic skills that law students learn in street law-type clinics are likely to be the same for all categories of mixed jurisdictions. The main difference is likely to occur in the teaching of trial advocacy and procedural rules relevant to mock trials conducted by the law students.

In mixed jurisdictions where common law rules of procedure are applied, law students will have to be trained in teaching their participating learners how to conduct an adversarial mock trial. Mock trials are an experiential way of learning that teaches students to understand court procedures. In legal literacy and street law programs, large numbers of students can be used in mock trials. For example, adversarial mock trials using five witnesses and an accused can involve up to 28 participants: eight lawyers for the plaintiff or prosecution team and eight for the defense team, three judges (or one1 judge and two assessors), five witnesses, an accused, a registrar, a court orderly, and a timekeeper.[79] One lawyer on each side can make an opening statement, each lawyer can question one witness or the accused, and one lawyer on each side can make a closing statement. The chief judge can control the proceedings, each judge can question one witness or the accused, and one judge can be responsible for giving the judgment. The registrar calls the case, the court orderly keeps order in court, and the timekeeper keeps time. Students are taught the different steps in a trial. They are also taught basic skills, such as how to make an opening statement, how to lead evidence, how to ask questions, how to make a closing statement, and how to give judgments. Students play the roles of witnesses, court officials, judges, and lawyers (McQuoid-Mason 2004: 121–22).

In mixed jurisdictions with civil law procedural rules, 32 participants can be involved in the different processes in a case involving five witnesses and an accused. An inquisitorial trial can involve a team of nine judges: a presiding judge to control the procedure, check the attendances, send the witnesses out of court, and open the case; a judge to ask the prosecutor to read the charge and to explain to the accused his or her rights; a judge to ask questions of the accused; five judges each to ask questions of one of the five witnesses; and a judge to give the judgment and sentence at the end of the case. In addition, such cases can involve a registrar, a court orderly, and a timekeeper (compare with McQuoid-Mason 1999: 30–32). Once again students are taught the different steps in an inquisitorial trial and experience how to ask questions, how to make closing

77 Philippines Supreme Court Rules of Court, rule 138A (1986).
78 Afghanistan Interim Criminal Code for Courts of 2004, article 96.
79 If the procedure allows for jury trials, even more participants can be added.

arguments, and how to give judgments. As in the adversarial mock trial, students play the roles of witnesses, court officials, judges, and lawyers.

Mock trials involving religious and customary law courts can also be designed using the appropriate procedural rules.

Conclusion

In light of the preceding, the following conclusions may be drawn:

- In the broad sense of mixed jurisdictions involving two or more different legal systems or traditions, mixed jurisdictions and clinical legal education are global phenomena.
- Use of interactive and reflective clinical legal education methods in a social justice context can enrich the teaching of law and practical legal skills in all jurisdictions, including those that are mixed.
- Increasing numbers of mixed jurisdiction countries are embracing clinical legal education programs as part of their legal education.
- Types of clinical legal education vary greatly, but in general the two most popular forms of clinical service delivery are live client clinics and legal literacy street law-type clinics.
- Types of legal skills taught in live client clinical law programs usually include (a) client interviewing, (b) client counseling, (c) trial advocacy, (d) negotiation, (e) critical thinking, (f) problem solving, (g) drafting, and (h) oral and written communication skills.
- Types of legal skills taught in street law-type clinical law programs usually include (a) writing skills, (b) communication skills, (c) ability to think on one's feet, (d) trial advocacy skills, (e) critical thinking skills, (f) problem-solving skills, and (g) oral skills.
- Interactive teaching methods are used in clinical law programs because learning through doing is the most effective way of learning.
- Clinical legal education and service delivery methods can be used across all jurisdictions and may be adjusted to meet the requirements of the particular mixed jurisdiction concerned.

References

Alexander, J. 1997. *Client Care*. Durban, South Africa: Butterworths.

Barnhizer, D. 1990. The university ideal and clinical legal education. *New York Law School Law Review*, 35(1), 87–130.

Bhagwati, P.N. 1987. Human rights as evolved by the jurisprudence of the Supreme Court of India. *Commonwealth Law Bulletin*, 13(1), 236–45.

Bloch, F. (ed.). 2011. *The Global Clinical Movement: Educating Lawyers for Social Justice*. New York: Oxford University Press.

Brayne, H., Duncan, N., and Grimes, R. (eds.). 1998. *Clinical Legal Education: Active Learning in the Law School*. London: Blackstone Press.

Chapman, J. 1993. *Interviewing and Counselling*. 1st ed. London: Cavendish.

Fisher, R., and Ury, W. 1981. *Getting to Yes: Negotiating Agreement without Giving In*. 1st ed. New York: Penguin Group.

Honoré, A.M. 1968. Social justice, in *Essays in Legal Philosophy*, edited by R. Summers. Berkeley: University of California Press, 61–94.

Iya, P.F. 2000. Strategies for skills development: The Fort Hare experience in curriculum design for the new LLB, in *Transforming South African Universities: Capacity Building for Historically Black Universities*, edited by P.F. Iya, N.S. Rembe, and J. Baloro. Pretoria: Africa Institute of South Africa and Fort Hare University.

JuriGlobe. 2013. Mixed legal systems. University of Ottawa, Ottawa. Available at: http://www.juriglobe.ca/eng/sys-juri/class-poli/sys-mixtes.php [accessed: December 17, 2013].

Lee, S., and Fox, M. 1994. *Learning Legal Skills*. 2nd ed. London: Blackstone Press.

McQuoid-Mason, D. 1982. *An Outline of Legal Aid in South Africa*. Durban, South Africa: Butterworths.

McQuoid-Mason, D. 1985. Legal aid clinics as a social service, in *Legal Aid and Law Clinics in South Africa: Proceedings of a conference held at the Howard College School of Law, University of Natal, Durban, from 11–13 July 1983*, edited by D.J. McQuoid-Mason. Durban, South Africa: University of Natal, 64–69.

McQuoid-Mason, D. 1994. Reducing violence in South Africa through street law education of citizens, in *International Debates of Victimology*, edited by G.F. Kirchhoff, E. Kosovksi, and H.J. Schneider. Mönchengladbach, Germany: WSV Publishing, 347–53.

McQuoid-Mason, D. 1999. *The Street Law Mock Trial Manual for Eastern and Central Europe, Russia and Former Soviet European and Central Asian Republics*. Washington, DC: Street Law.

McQuoid-Mason, D. 2000. Teaching social justice to law students through community service: The South African experience, in *Transforming South African Universities: Capacity Building for Historically Black Universities*, edited by P.F. Iya, N.S. Rembe, and J. Baloro. Pretoria: Africa Institute of South Africa and Fort Hare University, 89–203.

McQuoid-Mason, D. 2002. Incorporating justice and ethical issues into first year undergraduate law courses: A South African experience. *Journal of Commonwealth Law and Legal Education*, 1(2), 107–25.

McQuoid-Mason, D. (ed.). 2004. *Street Law: Practical Law for South Africans—Educator's Manual*. 2nd ed. Lansdowne, South Africa: Juta Law.

McQuoid-Mason, D. 2008. Street law as a clinical law programme: The South African experience with particular reference to the University of KwaZulu-Natal. *Griffith Law Review*, 17(1), 27–51.

McQuoid-Mason, D., and Palmer, R. 2007. *Draft African Law Clinicians Manual*. Durban, South Africa: Institute for Professional Legal Training.

Palmer, R., Crocker, A., and Kidd, M. 2003. *Becoming a Lawyer: Fundamental Skills for Law Students*. Durban, South Africa: LexisNexis.

Palmer, R., and McQuoid-Mason, D.J. 2000. *Basic Trial Advocacy Skills*. Durban, South Africa: Butterworths.

Palmer, V.V. 2008. Two rival theories of mixed legal systems. *Electronic Journal of Comparative Law*, 12(1), 1–28. Available at: http://www.ejcl.org/121/art121-16.pdf [accessed December 19, 2013].

Twist, H. 1992. *Effective Interviewing*. London: Blackstone Press.

Walker, G.K. 1980. A model rule for student practice in the United States courts. *Washington and Lee Law Review*, 37(4), 1101–58. Available at: http://scholarlycommons.law.wlu.edu/cgi/viewcontent.cgi?article=2538&context=wlulr [accessed December 29, 2013].

Index

www.ingramcontent.com/pod-product-compliance
Ingram Content Group UK Ltd.
Pitfield, Milton Keynes, MK11 3LW, UK
UKHW050753180926
475701UK00007B/1019
* 9 7 8 1 1 3 8 6 3 9 0 3 4 *